"A Hidden Light" by Netanel Miles-Yepez, 2010

This book was generously supported by

The Reb Zalman Legacy Project of the Yesod Foundation:

>Ron Claman
>David Friedman
>Tirzah Firestone
>Thomas D. Hast
>Bobbie Zelkind.

A Hidden Light

Stories and Teachings of Early ḤaBaD and Bratzlav Hasidism

Translated and Retold with Commentary by

Zalman Schachter-Shalomi
and **Netanel Miles-Yepez**

Foreword by **Susannah Heschel**

Gaon Books
www.gaonbooks.com

A Hidden Light : stories and teachings of early ḤaBaD and Bratzlav Hasidism.
Copyright © 2011 Zalman Schachter-Shalomi and Netanel Miles-Yepez. All rights reserved. This publication is in copyright. Subject to statutory exception and to the provisions of relevant collective licensing agreements, no reproduction of any part may be made without the written permission of Gaon Books, except for brief quotations included in analytical articles, chapters, and reviews.

For permissions, group pricing, and other information contact Gaon Books, P.O. Box 23924, Santa Fe, NM 87505 or write (editor@gaonbooks.com).

Manufactured in the United States of America.
The paper used in this publication is acid free and meets all ANSI (American National Standards for Information Sciences) standards for archival quality paper. All wood product components used in this book are Sustainable Forest Initiative (SFI) certified.

First edition
Frontispiece and cover illustration by Netanel Miles-Yepez

Library of Congress Cataloging-in-Publication Data
Schachter-Shalomi, Zalman, 1924-
  A Hidden Light : stories and teachings of early ḤaBaD and Bratzlav Hasidism / translated and retold with commentary by Zalman Schachter-Shalomi and Netanel Miles-Yepez; foreword by Susannah Heschel.
     p. cm.
  Includes bibliographical references and index.
  ISBN 978-1-935604-20-4 (cloth : alk. paper)
  ISBN 978-1-935604-31-0 (Paper: alk.paper)
  1. Ḥabad--Legends. 2. Bratslav Hasidim--Legends. 3. Rabbis--Legends. 4. Jewish legends. 5. Hasidism--History. I. Miles-Yepez, Netanel. II. Title.
  BM532.S332 2011
  296.8'332--dc23
                                      2011019597

A day may come when the hidden light of the East European period may be revealed.
—Abraham Joshua Heschel, *The Earth is the Lord's*

In remembrance of the Rebbe, Reb Menachem Mendel Schneerson and Reb Gedaliah Ahron Kenig.
—Zalman Meshullam HaKohen Schachter-Shalomi

For my mother and first teacher, Rose Marie Miles y Yepez, of whom I am so proud, and from whom I continue to learn the ways of sincerity and courage.
—Netanel David Miles-Yepez

Contents

Acknowledgements 7
Foreword by Susannah Heschel 9
Introduction 13

Part I. The Alter Rebbe and ḤaBaD Hasidism

1. The Making of a Rebbe:
   The Apprenticeship of the Liozhna Prodigy 23
2. The Making of ḤaBaD Hasidism:
   The Liozhna Maggid's Wisdom, Understanding,
   and Knowledge 57
3. The Wars of the Lord:
   Conflict and Consolation in the Later Years of the Alter Rebbe 103
4. The Two Who Are Inseparable:
   The Heirs of the Alter Rebbe, the Son and Disciple 143
5. Seeking Unity: The Teachings
   of Dov Baer of Lubavitch and Ahron HaLevi of Staroshelye 175

Part II. Rebbe Nahman and Bratzlav Hasidism

6. The Ḥiddush: The Hidden Struggles of Young Nahman	213
7. The Mystical Journey: The Descent for the Sake of Ascent	243
8. It's Fire on Paper: The Teachings of Rebbe Nahman of Bratzlav	279
9. Beggar's Wisdom: The Redemptive Imagination and Sacrifice of Rebbe Nahman	325
10. The Empty Chair: Nosson of Nemirov and the Bratzlav Ideal	359
Appendix: Moshe Shneuri, Defender of the Faith	393
Notes	397
Glossary	453
Bibliography	461
About the Authors	473
Index	475

Acknowledgements

We wish to give a heartfelt thank you to those who have helped us with this book: to the newly arrived Vikram Aharon Jesurum Jay, who made me smile when I was feeling overwhelmed, and who may enjoy the parallels we have drawn here when he is older; to Dr. Susannah Heschel who generously agreed to write the Foreword; to Leigh Ann Dillinger who proofread the entire manuscript and prepared the index; to Rabbi Gavriel Goldfeder and Shlomo Barya Nadiv Schachter for identifying Bratzlav sources; to Rabbi Elliot Ginsburg and Rabbi Miles Krassen for helping us to locate important ḤaBaD sources; to Ozer Bergman for all of his help; to Pir Zia Inayat-Khan who graciously entertained us at the Shambhala Mountain Center and gave us permission to use a portion of his writing; to Rabbi Ayla Grafstein who read portions of the manuscript and offered us her photos from Haditch and Bratzlav; to Zachary Yitzhak Malone who lent me his books and looked for sources; to Helena Foster who reminded me of the quote used in the dedication; to Kathleen Cassaday and the reference staff at the Boulder Public Library for helping us to obtain some of the rarer editions; to the University of Colorado Archives for use of the Zalman M. Schachter-Shalomi Collection; to the wonderful *menschen* of the Yesod Foundation—Ron Claman, Tirzah Firestone, David Friedman, Thomas Hast, and Bobbie Zelkind—for their generosity and support for this book; to Mary Fulton for all her help; and finally, to our wives Eve

Ilsen and Jennifer Phares Miles, who have been patient and supporting of our work together.

—N.M-Y. & Z.M.S-S.

I just want to say how much I owe Reb Netanel, whose painstaking work and unique perspectives are represented throughout this book. In some ways, as Rebbe Nahman said of Reb Nosson, "This book is really his." Because of the close relationship we have developed over the years, we are now able to work together in a way that is almost seamless, and which is very helpful to me at this stage of my life. I cannot tell you what a pleasure it is to see how he understands what I have to say, and how he develops and adapts it for the page—and also to see how his own ideas complement and provide a counterpoint to mine. Nothing is more gratifying to a teacher. Therefore, I really want the reader to understand the importance of his contribution. Though he is my student, in this book, he is my colleague and my collaborator, my own Reb Nosson.

—Z.M.S-S.

Foreword

JUDAISM WAS BORN IN MOBILITY—what Heine call a "portable fatherland." Indeed, central to Jewish history is mobility. Jews began with our journey from Egypt to the land of Israel, from Israel to Babylonia, to the Mediterranean basin, Europe, China, even Africa and India, and the Americas, and back again to Israel. From each journey and from each foreign location, we enriched our culture—our languages, Torah interpretations, foods, and even our *halakhah*.

Our journeys were not only outward, but also inward. And Hasidism has a central concern with that inward journey of each Jew. Commenting on God's command to Abraham, *"Lekh lekha,"* Levi Yitzhak of Berditchev, author of the wonderful commentary, *Kedushat Levi,* notes that the repetition in the phrase indicates that God wanted Abraham not simply to go forward on the physical plane, but to go forward on the inward plane—indeed, to move inward more deeply. Hasidism, as Reb Zalman and Netanel write, "involves an astounding heavenly journey with the inner teacher."[1]

Hasidism, too, was on a journey from the outset, moving from special centers, such as Mezhbizh and Sadegora, to villages and cities throughout Eastern Europe. Rebbes would study with one *tzaddik,* then move to learn from another, and then settle in a place where they were most needed. Reb Zalman and Netanel note that Reb Nahman of Bratzlav settled in Uman because it was "a city of lost souls."[2] At times, massive, dangerous journeys were undertaken, such as Nahman's travels to Ottoman-controlled *Eretz Yisra'el* (1798-1799). Hasidic Rebbes recognized this: going to Israel was for Nahman a spiritual ascent of his soul, an expedition of his religious

---

1 Chapter 9, in the section, "The Dream of the Heavenly Master."
2 Chapter 9, in the section, "Uman—The City of Lost Souls."

life. Nahman himself said, "I saw that I would have to die in Istanbul, but the humiliation and insults I suffered saved me. One must overcome many barriers to approach the Holy Land."[3] And Hasidim would often travel great distances to be at the *tish* of their Rebbe, or to have the privilege of a private meeting with the Rebbe—a meeting that was also a journey, elevating their souls to a higher plane.

Hasidism calls our attention to the mobility that takes place throughout the life of an individual Jew: an inner journey. Hasidic teachings, texts, and stories come as guides to that journey. In this beautiful book, Reb Zalman Schachter-Shalomi and Netanel Miles-Yepez recreate the world of early Hasidism, and through their retelling of the journeys of the Rebbes, they bring us to the spiritual landscape of Ukraine, letting us travel from the court of one Rebbe to another, tasting the different traditions and personalities.

For decades, Reb Zalman, too, has been on a journey. One of the central tasks of a Hasidic Rebbe is to practice *yeridah*, 'descent,' for the sake of lifting up lost souls, and that has been one of the great missions of Reb Zalman. For the post-war generations asking, who is there to give us back our souls, Reb Zalman came to us. Bringing with him his own extraordinary journeys through Hasidism, Lubavitch, Sufism, Native American traditions, and much more, he has taught us, inspired us, and lifted up our souls to a higher level. Such work can only be accomplished through a profound empathy with others and a recognition that suffering, whether physical or the depression of spirit, has significance and profound value in the journey of the inner life. Cultivating such empathy and understanding is the great task of the Rebbe. Someone once asked the Apter Rav, Abraham Joshua Heschel of Apt, known as the "Ohev Yisra'el," the lover of the Jewish people, how he could remember the names and the troubles of each of the dozens of people who came to him daily, pouring out their troubles and asking him to pray for them. He explained, "When someone pours out their troubles to me, their pain enters my heart and makes a scar. And when I come to pray, I open my heart to God and I say, look at all these scars." Imagine what it is to be such a person; imagine, too, what a gift it is to have a Rebbe who will listen in this way.

But listening with such empathy requires that a Rebbe experience first-hand what other people are suffering. Reb Nahum of Chernobyl, author of the *Meor Enayim*, was famous for *pidyon shevuyim*, redemption of Jews who

---

3   Chapter 7, in the section, "The Great Pilgrimage to *Eretz Yisra'el*."

had been taken captive by Gentiles. Russian authorities grew suspicious of him at one point and put him in prison in Zhitomir, Ukraine. One day an elderly woman appeared at the door of his prison cell and spoke to him: "*Ha-shem* told Avraham *Avinu, lekh lekha,* go and set out on the road. Since Avraham *Avinu* excelled in the *mitzvah* of *hakhnasat orḥim*, hospitality toward guests, *ha-Shem* wanted him to be able to fulfill this great *mitzvah b'shleimut,* on the highest possible level of perfection. Therefore *ha-Shem* told Avraham *Avinu* to travel, in order to know what it is like to be a guest himself." From this, Reb Nahum explained, "I understood that the reason I was imprisoned was because I am active in the *mitzvah* of *pidyon shevuyim*. Without knowing what it is like to sit in prison myself, it would not be possible for me to do this *mitzvah* on the highest level. Now that I know the reason for my being here, I am confident that I will be released shortly." To redeem others from prison not as a business transaction but as a true *mitzvah* meant that Reb Nahum had to personally come to experience the horrors of sitting in a jail cell. Only then was his redemption of others undertaken with a full heart.

Reb Zalman came to us in America, to a post-war world that found itself suddenly bereft of the richness and vitality of the East European Hasidic life that had been destroyed, and he, too, engaged in a *yeridah*. He left the self-enclosed world of Lubavitcher Hasidism and joined us in our secular, bewildered, alienated Jewish communities that had lost a connection to the roots of its soul in Europe. Immersing himself as an act of *yeridah*, Reb Zalman also empathized with what it is like to live a life of alienation, and he sought our redemption from an intellectual captivity and helped restore to us the Jewish heritage of our souls.

This is a book to be read not only with the mind and the heart, but also with the imagination. Think as you read: what would you say if you had the great opportunity to meet with Nahman of Bratzlav, or with the Alter Rebbe? What problem of your soul would you reveal, what spiritual nourishment would you hope to receive? How would you, too, be lifted up and redeemed?

We may not be living the lives of Hasidim in nineteenth-century Ukraine, but our lives have been inspired and transformed by Reb Zalman. For his work as Rebbe, teacher, and writer, we are deeply grateful.

Susannah Heschel
Eli Black Professor of Jewish Studies
Dartmouth College

Introduction

IN OUR PREVIOUS BOOK, *A Heart Afire: Stories and Teachings of the Early Hasidic Masters*, we introduced you to the holy Ba'al Shem Tov (1698-1760), the founder of Hasidism, and his successor, the Maggid of Mezritch (1704-1772)—along with a few of their major disciples. Now we would like to continue the journey we began there, exploring two of the most important developments of the next generation: the HaBaD and Bratzlav schools of Hasidism.

For while many Hasidic masters established influential courts and dynasties, emphasizing different aspects of the teaching, even taking Hasidism into new regions, only a few of them established anything like a Hasidic 'school.' However, both Rabbi Shneur Zalman of Liadi (1745-1812) and Rabbi Nahman of Bratzlav (1772-1810), the founders of HaBaD and Bratzlav Hasidism, developed coherent systems of thought, distinct spiritual practices, and core texts which have been studied by their Hasidim for over two hundred years.

Interestingly enough, both of these schools continue to be among the most vital and visible expressions of Hasidism in the modern world. After relocating to the United States in 1940, my Rebbe, Rabbi Yosef Yitzhak Schneersohn (1880-1950) began the slow process of rebuilding the foundations of HaBaD Hasidism; and within a relatively short time, he had begun to send out young rabbis like myself and my friend, Rabbi

Shlomo Carlebach, as his emissaries *(shliḥim)* to the younger generation in colleges and universities around the country. This outreach work continued under his successor, Rabbi Menachem Mendel Schneerson (1902–1994), until nearly every major city in North America, Europe, and Israel had a ḤaBaD-Lubavitch emissary.

Today, the organization known as "ChaBaD-Lubavitch" controls a multi-media empire devoted to the dissemination of Hasidic teachings and the promotion of the highest levels of Jewish observance. Former emissaries like Rabbi Shmuley Boteach have now become celebrated authors and public figures, and its *ba'alei teshuvah yeshiva*, Hadar Hatorah (founded by my mentor, Rabbi Yisra'el Jacobson), is known to have been a haven for many 'returnees,' including the musician, Matisyahu, whose Hasidic-inspired, reggae-hip-hop fusion has even penetrated the secular music scene.

In a similar way, Rabbi Avraham Sternhartz (1862–1955), the acknowledged leader of Bratzlav Hasidism in his day, began to reorient the activities of Bratzlav Hasidim after travel to Rebbe Nahman's grave in the Ukraine became impossible during World War II. In 1940, he established the first Rosh Hashanah gathering of Bratzlavers in Palestine and began to dream of the rebuilding of the mystical S'fat community in Israel, which was later made a reality by his holy disciple, Rabbi Gedaliah Kenig (1921–1980). Another disciple, Rabbi Zvi Aryeh Rosenfeld (1922–1978) was responsible for the revitalization of Bratzlav Hasidism among the youth of the United States. This work had significant consequences, leading one of his disciples, Rabbi Gedaliah Fleer, to re-establish the pilgrimage to the Rebbe's grave in Uman (within the Soviet Block) at great personal risk, and another, Rabbi Chaim Kramer, to found the Breslov Research Institute, which is largely responsible for the spread of Rebbe Nahman's teachings the world over, and for publishing exceptional translations of all the Rebbe's works.

In recent years, Bratzlav Hasidism has also reached the motion picture industry. In 2005, the Israeli movie, *Uzhpizin*, starring Shuli Rand, a Bratzlaver Hasid, was quickly hailed a critical success, and was popular among religious and secular Jews alike for its sympathetic portrait of a Bratzlaver couple in Jerusalem. Likewise, Bratzlav-inspired music has become popular in the mainstream, and dancing bands of "Na Nach" Bratzlavers (inspired by Rabbi Yisra'el Baer Odesser, 1888–1994) can now be seen all over Israel. Today, Bratzlav Hasidism appears to be more popular than ever.

Strange Attractors

But, apart from their similar vitality and reach, HaBaD and Bratzlav Hasidism could hardly be more different. And this is part of what has inspired us to bring them together in the same book; for despite their differences, each is like a 'strange attractor' for the other. If we look at the works of many of the most creative and radical thinkers coming out of the traditional Jewish world in the last one hundred years, we see a fascination with the teachings of both HaBaD and Bratzlav: everyone from Rabbi Hillel Zeitlin in the early twentieth-century, to Rabbi Aryeh Kaplan and Rabbi Adin Steinsaltz in its later years, to Rabbi Yitzhak Meir Morgenstern more recently. It is an attraction of opposites, to which I have not been immune either.

When I became a HaBaD Hasid as a teenager, I was amazed at the contemplative depth of my mentors, and absolutely enamored with the marvelous edifice of HaBaD thought, its remarkably precise descriptions of kabbalistic structures, and its contemplative practices. It was by far the best 'tool-kit' in town as far as I was concerned. But as I began my work as a HaBaD *shaliah*, I was constantly being exposed to different religious perspectives, different philosophies, and so I also allowed myself to explore different forms of Hasidism. One of the most fascinating to me was Bratzlav Hasidism. Rebbe Nahman was like nobody else I had ever encountered, and his approach was so different from Reb Shneur Zalman's that I continually found myself caught off guard by his unusual thinking.

Before long, I was translating large portions of Rebbe Nahman's works and teaching them to my students alongside the many HaBaD translations I had made. Back in the late 1950s, I had written a little manual called *The First Step: A Primer of a Jew's Spiritual Life*, basically a guide to HaBaD meditation I would send out to people who contacted me at talks, wanting to learn more about Hasidism. But along with it, I would also send another booklet—my own translation of Rebbe Nahman's *Meshivat Nefesh*—to help them deal with the highs and lows of spiritual life.

Then, in the late 1960s and early 70s, in the midst of the psychedelic revolution, Rebbe Nahman's stories seemed more relevant than ever. So I made a record album of my own translation of the "Tale of the Seven Beggars," a dramatic reading with musical accompaniment that people could listen to as if it were being told at the Rebbe's *tish*.

In this way, HaBaD and Bratzlav gradually became the twin beacons of my teaching, and Rebbe Nahman became as integral to my own

Intuition and Feeling, Thinking and Doing

In some ways, the holy Ba'al Shem Tov was like the 'fertilized ovum' of Ḥasidut, and the Maggid of Mezritch was like its 'stem-cell.' By the time we get to Reb Shneur Zalman, the organism is already evolving very specific manifestations. Thus, he becomes a 'brain-cell,' while his friend and fellow disciple, Reb Levi Yizhak of Berditchev, becomes a 'heart-cell.' This 'brain-cell' of Hasidism, oriented toward the upper triad on the 'Tree of Life,' representing the Divine intellect, is called HaBaD (ḥokhmah, binah, da'at, 'wisdom,' 'understanding,' and 'knowledge'). While the 'heart-cell,' oriented toward the middle triad on the 'Tree of Life,' representing the heart qualities of Divinity, is called ḤaGaT (ḥesed, gevurah, tiferet, 'loving-kindness,' 'strength,' and 'beauty').

Now, the question is, where does Rebbe Naḥman fit? I think many people would want to say that he is also ḤaGaT, like Reb Levi Yitzhak. But while I can understand this view, I want to suggest a third possibility. I believe Rebbe Naḥman was actually KaḤaB, representing keter, ḥokhmah, binah, 'crown,' 'wisdom,' and 'understanding.' That is to say, there was something primordial in his approach that partook of the quality of keter, which is connected to intuition and feeling.

Once I went to see my friend, Reb Gedaliah Kenig, a Bratzlaver *manhig* (leader), who was also known to be a great kabbalist, and I asked him the following question: According to the *Sefer Yetzirah*, there are ten *sefirot*, ten divine qualities, "ten and not nine, ten and not eleven." Nevertheless, the *kabbalah* has two different formulations of these ten qualities. One formulation makes *keter* the first divine quality, followed by *ḥokhmah* and *binah*. Another makes *ḥokhmah* the first divine quality, followed by *binah* and *da'at*. So my question was, "How do you know when to count *keter*, and when to count *da'at*?"

He said, "It depends on which world it is in."

So I asked, "In which world do you count *keter*, and in which world do you count *da'at*?"

He responded, "You can figure this out for yourself."

I said, "In the worlds of *atzilut* and *yetzirah*, intuition and feeling, you count *keter*; in the worlds of *beri'ah* and *assiyah*, thinking and doing, you count *da'at*."

He said, "You are right."

Now this is my point. The ḤaBaD system is mostly operative in the worlds of thinking and doing, and counts *da'at*, while the Bratzlav system is mostly operative in the worlds of intuition and feeling, and counts *keter*. Each has its emphasis, but using elements of both systems, you can cover all four worlds in an extraordinary way.

Tikkun and Tohu

I also tend to think of ḤaBaD and Bratzlav as representing *tikkun* and *tohu*, 'order' and 'chaos.' For, according to ḤaBaD, with the coming of Hasidism, we are now in *olam ha-tikkun*, the 'world of restoration.' What was lost has been rediscovered, the missing element has been found, and the world can now be put right. The architectural plans have been drawn up, and all we have to do is see to the construction of God's heavenly edifice on Earth. But Bratzlav doesn't look at things in this way; according to Rebbe Nahman, we are still in *olam ha-tohu*, the 'world of chaos.' The world is like a spinning dreidel, moving in cycles, constantly bringing about a reversal of fortunes—what is above goes below, what is below goes above, the angel becomes a human being, the human being becomes an angel! Rising and falling is an ever-present possibility. In *olam ha-tikkun* there are clearly defined structures *(kelim)* in the universe and an order to creation *(seder histalshelut)*; there is a ladder that we can climb, and all we need to do is scale it rung by rung. The ladder is static; only the climbing is dynamic. In *olam ha-tohu*, even the ladder is dynamic, like the spinning rope-ladders you find at Renaissance festivals. The principle of indeterminacy is dominant; it is like Purim, when God allows everything to go random.

In ḤaBaD, there is a certain uniform appearance; the Hasidim look like soldiers in the army of God. After Reb Menachem Mendel became Rebbe, the Lubavitcher Hasidim proudly began to wear double-breasted black suits and black fedoras, just as he did. But when I first met Reb Zvi Aryeh Rosenfeld in the late 1950s, I was surprised to find a young man without a beard in a simple suit, sitting and teaching Rebbe Nahman to the Hasidim. In Bratzlav, there seemed to be more room for individual differences. In ḤaBaD, the study of Maimonides' *Guide to the Perplexed* and other philosophical texts was encouraged, but in Bratzlav, *ḥakirah*, or the philosophy of religion is looked upon as a slippery slope. In ḤaBaD, stories and parables are clever and clearly illustrative, having a definite beginning, middle, and end. In Bratzlav, they open out into an unknown world of magic and possibility, having various levels of meaning and more beginnings than endings. Reb Shneur Zalman's discourses unfold in a very linear, logical progression, while Rebbe Nahman's spiral, expanding and contracting, like Yeats' magnificent gyre. Reb Shneur Zalman is like a motor boat, while Rebbe Nahman sails, tacking into the wind.

A Hidden Light

A Hidden Light, while complete in itself, should also be seen as a continuation of what was begun in our previous book, *A Heart Afire.* Thus, what was written in the introduction to that work concerning the "Fourth Turning of Hasidism" and our approach to Hasidic spirituality, applies equally to this book as well. As *A Hidden Light* assumes a certain familiarity with Judaism, Hasidism, and Kabbalah, we would again like to recommend several books to readers who may find this material challenging or unfamiliar. The first are *Jewish with Feeling: A Guide to Meaningful Jewish Practice* (with Joel Segel) and *God Is a Verb: Kabbalah and the Practice of Mystical Judaism* by David Cooper, both of which will provide readers with an understanding of Judaism and Jewish spiritual practice in the light of Jewish mysticism.[1] For those who would like to become more familiar with HaBaD and Bratzlav Hasidism and their founders, we recommend Noson Gurary's *Chasidism: Its Development, Theology, and Practice* and Chaim Kramer's *Crossing the Narrow Bridge* as guides to HaBaD and Bratzlav thought, as well as Nissan Mindel's biography, *Rabbi Schneur Zalman,* and Aryeh Kaplan's *Until the Mashiach: The Life of Rabbi Nachman.*[2]

Part I

The Alter Rebbe
and ḤaBaD Hasidism

Traditional portrait
of Rabbi Shneur Zalman of Liadi

1

The Making of a Rebbe:
The Apprenticeship of the Liozhna Prodigy

IN MY REBBE'S WONDERFUL COLLECTION of pre-Hasidic stories *(Sefer ha-Zikhronot)*, he reveals the mysterious world of the 'hidden righteous ones' who helped to lay the foundations of Hasidism.[3] These were seemingly ordinary people—beggars, blacksmiths, and beadles—whose foremost concern was to serve their neighbors and fellow Jews, helping them both materially and spiritually as best they could.[4] Some of those whose stories the Rebbe told were simply pious individuals who shied away from any acclaim or attention, while others were deeply learned mystics, seeking a life of divine service outside of the official seminaries and synagogues. The latter intentionally hid their great abilities in order to bring hope and inspiration to those who might otherwise fall into despair and distance from Judaism. In this way, they fulfilled the words of the prophet Micah, "Do justice, love goodness, and hide your walk with God." (6:8)[5]

Among them was Yisra'el ben Eliezer, an orphan who had been raised by the hidden righteous ones, the *tzaddikim nistarim*.[6] As a young man, he had travelled from town to town like his mentors—finding work as a teacher of children, a kosher slaughterer, and even as a household servant—bringing help and a little inspiration to everyone he met. During his various travels, he learned first-hand about the miseries faced by the ordinary Jews of the *shtetl* and determined to do whatever he could to make a positive difference in their lives.

In time, he settled down and married and began to receive teachings from the ascended master, Ahiyah ha-Shiloni. Nevertheless, he continued in the ways of the hidden *tzaddikim*, disguising himself as an ordinary innkeeper, even as his father had done before him. Then, shortly before his thirty-sixth birthday, it was revealed to him from 'on high' that the time had finally come for him to make himself known to the world. Hearing this, he was troubled and reluctant to give up his anonymity, not wanting to cease his holy work in secret.[7] But the tradition tells us that he soon received a message that changed his mind. The message was from the leader of the hidden *tzaddikim*, the holy Adam Ba'al Shem, and it spoke of Yisra'el's previous incarnation as a hidden *tzaddik*, and told him why he must reveal himself now:

> "Being that the world was not worthy to sense the fragrance of the spirit of his Torah, this holy soul shall once again descend into the material world, and Heaven shall move this soul to reveal herself.[8] A renewing way shall be revealed through this soul until the world will be filled with knowledge, bringing the nearness of completion."
>
> Now, in the name of our holy teacher and master,[9] I must reveal that *you*, my holy brother, are this same blessed soul who has come to this world again to scent it with the fragrance of purity and to purify it with the spirit of holiness. Thus, very soon, you must reveal yourself and illuminate the hearts of everyone with a renewing light. May the name of Heaven be sanctified through your hand, and the redemption brought near in our day.[10]

With such testimony before him, he finally surrendered to his destiny, and shortly afterward, with the passing of Adam Ba'al Shem, was named the new leader of the *tzaddikim nistarim*. He would now be known as the Ba'al Shem Tov, the 'master of the good Name.'

At first, it might seem that there is a contradiction in his being 'revealed' and yet becoming the leader of a secret society; but this had actually been the tradition for several generations, as we have already described in *A Heart Afire: Stories and Teachings of the Early Hasidic Masters*. For under the title of 'Ba'al Shem,' the leaders of the hidden *tzaddikim* were indeed 'known,' but only as especially potent folk-healers, shamanic adepts, and kabbalists who who were sometimes known to guide a mysterious circle of disciples. Their true identity was safely concealed under this popular cover. So it was that the Ba'al Shem Tov began to be 'known' as a great healer and popular teacher throughout the towns and villages of the Ukraine, while at the same time administering the secret activities and spiritual development of the hidden *tzaddikim*.

Unlike the other *ba'alei shem*, it was the special destiny of the Ba'al Shem Tov to transform the landscape of Judaism in Eastern Europe in ways his predecessors could hardly have imagined. In the past, Eliyahu Ba'al Shem had sought to cultivate kabbalist-saints, Yoel Ba'al Shem to teach shamanic methods, and Adam Ba'al Shem to improve the lot of the degraded Jewish populace,[11] but the Ba'al Shem Tov now sought nothing less than a "sea-change" in the life of Jews everywhere, fusing all of these intentions into one. Using the network of the hidden *tzaddikim*, he began a subversive revolution, undermining and seeking to replace the morally deficient Jewish leadership of Eastern Europe under whom the common people suffered.[12]

For not only were ordinary Jews emotionally and spiritually desolate after the Chmielnicki Massacres and the great Messianic disappointment of Shabbatai Tzvi, but they were also economically depressed and feeling abandoned by their leaders, most of whom had retreated to an ivory tower of learning, often associated with the learned rabbis and great seminaries of Lithuania. The Ba'al Shem Tov was disturbed by the pervasive lack of compassion shown for the common people, and horrified to see how many rabbis tended to 'lord it over' and 'look down upon' the simple and pious Jews of their communities, keeping them in a vice-grip of despair.

Thus, he determined to cultivate a new learned elite who would serve this population both humbly and simply, giving them strength, rather than draining them of self-esteem. This would require a new kind of Jewish leader; one who was not driven by a desire for power or influence, or even for learning or personal enlightenment alone; but one whose desire was to grow in relationship to God through serving others, using their abilities and authority to uplift hearts and to anchor Jewish practice among ordinary Jews. This new kind of leader, connecting both head and heart—who would displace the learned tyrants of the time—would be called a *Rebbe*. And the Rebbe to whom fell the "task of capturing the strongest 'fortress' of the opposition—Lithuania," was Rabbi Shneur Zalman of Liadi, the Alter Rebbe, founder of the great lineage of ḤaBaD Hasidism.[13]

The Secret Service of Barukh of Liozhna

To prepare the ground for this quiet revolution, the Ba'al Shem Tov now sent the hidden *tzaddikim* out to towns and villages across the Ukraine and Russia as recruiters of talent and surveyors of the spiritual landscape.[14] Among the most loyal of his spies and scouts during this period was Reb Barukh Weiskvaliker of Liozhna,[15] whose father had been a teacher of Talmud in Vitebsk and a direct descendant of the great rabbi and kabbalist, Yehudah Loew of Prague.[16] His learned mother, Rahel, on the other hand, was the daughter of Barukh Portugaler, called "the Batlan," a secret disciple of Reb Yoel, the Ba'al Shem of Zamoshtch.[17]

Though a gifted student of Torah and Talmud like his father, young Barukh also took after his maternal grandfather and namesake, showing a marked inclination for solitude. Often, these characteristics came together as Barukh carried his books out of the stuffy *beit midrash* (house of study) and into the woods where he would lie on his back and study in joyful serenity for hours at a time. But sadly, the Eden of his childhood was not to last; for, at only fourteen years old, he lost both of his parents to illness. In the painful desolation that followed their deaths, he became more and more withdrawn, and his natural desire for solitude grew into a strong need to get away from Vitebsk, to get lost in his studies somewhere where no one knew him. Thus, he began to travel from town to town, supporting himself by the work of his own hands, and using his savings to study undisturbed for long stretches.[18]

This itinerant lifestyle of traveling, working, and studying, went on for several years and brought Barukh into contact with many holy souls, some of whom seemed to be more than their outward appearance or circumstances might suggest. Once, while visiting his friend, the holy blacksmith of Dobromyzl, he encountered a young disciple of the Ba'al Shem Tov, Reb Yitzhak Shaul who, despite his various rabbinic honors, had also chosen the life of a simple blacksmith.[19] In Reb Yitzhak Shaul, young Barukh saw a living example of the type of Jew that the Ba'al Shem Tov was hoping to evolve: one who loved both Torah and his fellow human beings equally.[20] Seeing this, he began to long for something more than just learning in solitude and the perfection of his own character—a life of deep and holy service to God.[21]

Through Reb Yitzhak Shaul, Barukh learned of the Ba'al Shem Tov's main doctrines and teachings: of specific personal providence for every aspect of creation; how God is constantly creating the Universe, keeping the world in existence in every moment; how we must adhere and cling to God in every moment, investing intention and consciousness in all our actions, especially during prayer; the importance of continual repentance and serving God with joy at all times; and finally, the equality of the scholar and the common people.

Barukh was overwhelmed by these profound teachings, and soon determined to meet the Ba'al Shem Tov for himself. And so it was that he became one of the Ba'al Shem Tov's secret missionaries in the service of God.[22]

The New Soul

After a while, Reb Barukh was engaged to Rivkah, the daughter of the pious and learned Avraham of Liozhna, the owner of an orchard in which he had worked for a time. Having recognized Reb Barukh's unusual integrity and deep learning, the latter had sought him out as a good match for his daughter, even pursuing him from town to town as he traveled. When he finally caught up with him again, Reb Barukh made no objection to the match, for he already loved and respected Reb Avraham. Nevertheless, he made one stipulation: in lieu of a dowry, Reb Avraham was to build them a house which he and Rivkah—if she did not object—would use as a "guest house" for the hidden *tzaddikim* who passed through Liozhna. Reb Avraham readily agreed and assured him that his daughter Rivkah never turned away a stranger in need.

So, after another short period of study and travel, Barukh and Rivkah married and settled down on an *ahuza*, an 'estate' with an orchard just outside of Liozhna in the house Reb Avraham had built for them. It was good land, and on it Barukh and Rivkah kept a garden, making a living from the orchard, just as her father did on his own estate.[23]

AFTER THEY HAD BEEN MARRIED FOR A YEAR, *Reb Barukh and his wife Rivkah went to see the Ba'al Shem Tov, hoping that he might give them a blessing for children. As fate would have it, the day on which they arrived was the 18th of Elul, the Ba'al Shem Tov's birthday, which was always celebrated joyfully in Mezhbizh. Thus, they found the master in high spirits, and he blessed them whole-heartedly, saying, "Exactly one year from today, you will give birth to a son."*

Barukh and Rivkah were overjoyed, and Rivkah made a solemn promise to consecrate him to the dissemination of Torah and Hasidism (Ḥasidut).

A few months later, Rivkah conceived, and she immediately set about keeping her promise. The daughter of the learned Reb Avraham of Liozhna, Rivkah was herself well-versed in Jewish teaching and had even been raised to study Torah everyday. But now that she was pregnant, she intensified her daily studies and began to seek guidance for deepening her prayer practices during the months of her pregnancy.

Thus, Reb Barukh set out for Mezhbizh in the month of second Adar to personally inform the Ba'al Shem Tov of the pregnancy, and to receive the master's instructions for the baby's prenatal care. On his arrival, the master received Reb Barukh with a heartfelt mazel tov! and soon sent him back to Liozhna with personal instructions for Rivkah. These she carried out faithfully until, on the 18th of Elul, 1745 (5505), she gave birth to a son, just as the Ba'al Shem Tov had said she would. They named him 'Shneur Zalman' after Reb Barukh's father, whom he had lost at when he was still a teenager.

On that same day, far off in Mezhbizh, the disciples of the Ba'al Shem Tov noticed that the master seemed even more joyful than usual on his birthday, and led the services almost as if it were a holy day. Later, while at the table with his disciples, the Ba'al Shem Tov told them ...

"On the fourth day of creation, the two great luminaries were set in the sky.[24] And today—the fourth day of the third week of Elul, the day corresponding to the portion in the Haftorah (reading of the prophets), "Arise, shine forth"[25]—a new soul has come to earth,[26] one which will illuminate the world with two kinds of light (shnei or = Shneur)—the light of nigleh, the manifest Torah, and the light of nistar, the hidden Torah—and who will succeed in establishing Ḥasidut through selfless dedication, thus preparing the way for the Mashiaḥ."[27]

The disciples were understandably awed by this announcement and dutifully recorded it in their memories. Then they listened as the master gave a teaching on the verse, "This one will console us."[28]

On the following Shabbat (Parshat Ki Tavo'), the Ba'al Shem Tov again gave a teaching at his tish (table) on the verse, "Arise, shine forth, your light has arrived, and God's glory shines upon you."

Then, on the 25th of Elul, the day the Midrash says the world was created,[29] the Ba'al Shem Tov held a farbrengen and gave a teaching on the verse, "On the eighth day the flesh of his foreskin shall be circumcised,"[30] and on the Shabbat following (Parshat Nitzavim), he taught on the verse from the Haftorah, "I will rejoice greatly in God"[31] and was unusually joyous, which the disciples marked as a profound mystery.

Years later, when the Maggid of Mezritch—who would succeed the Ba'al Shem Tov—came to Mezhbizh, he heard the tales of these strange events from the other disciples and did not understand them either. Then, a day came when the master took him aside and explained: "Those events of which you have heard were actually a celebration of the birth, the entry into the covenant, and the crucial third day of a child of great destiny. His name is Shneur Zalman, and this is of importance because . . . he belongs to you."[32]

Why is the third day after the circumcision so important? Because it says in Torah, "On the third day, when they were in pain" (Gen. 34:25), Simeon and Levi slew the men of Shekhem in revenge for the rape of their sister, Dinah. It was the third day after all the men of Shekhem had been circumcised. The implication is that they were most vulnerable on the third day. Thus, the circumcised boy must be especially protected on the "crucial third day" after his circumcision when he is most vulnerable to infection and the influence of other negative forces.[33]

AFTER THE BIRTH OF HIS SON, *Reb Barukh came to Mezhbizh to be with the Ba'al Shem Tov for Yom Kippur, but said nothing of the birth of his child to the other disciples; for the master had already warned him on his previous visit not to speak of it, nor to tell the child's name to anyone in Mezhbizh. Nevertheless, he had come to tell the Ba'al Shem Tov of his boy's safe delivery, of his circumcision, and to ask his blessings and guidance for the raising of the child.*

The Ba'al Shem Tov was pleased and gave him precise instructions for protecting the boy from negative influences, telling Reb Barukh to guard him carefully at all times, and to keep him away from envious eyes and loose tongues: "Shelter him, and be careful not to repeat any of his clever acts or words, as many parents are so fond of doing."[34]

In the traditional *siddur*, it says, "Save us today from an evil eye *(m'ayin ra)*." These last instructions of the Ba'al Shem Tov have to do with the same 'evil eye' so often spoken about in the literature of this period. The belief is that people who are dissatisfied with their own lives and envious of others can rob you of your energy. Worse still, some may even try to harm you intentionally because of it. Thus, with such a treasure as this child, his parents needed to be even more stringent in protecting him from the evil eye of envy. This is also what is behind the Ba'al Shem Tov's directive in the next passage, "Cover him with the *tallit* right away."[35]

Thus, the boy was raised in a protected atmosphere of the utmost sanctity, carefully cultivated under the guidance of the Ba'al Shem Tov. Nor was it long before his parents began to notice marks of unusual ability in him; from one month to the next—sometimes even from one day to another—his vocabulary would double or triple, and before long he was speaking full sentences. His parents were amazed. Even more amazing, they began to notice that whatever he saw, he remembered perfectly! Thus, before he was yet three years old, he could already recite numerous psalms by heart.[36]

SHORTLY BEFORE HIS THIRD BIRTHDAY, Reb Barukh asked the Ba'al Shem Tov's permission to bring the child to Mezhbizh for Obsherenish, the traditional haircutting ceremony. The master responded that he should bring him after Shaḥarit (morning prayers) on the 18th of Elul, their mutual birthday, and that the child should be accompanied by his pious mother and his aunt Devorah Leah, Barukh's elder sister.

So, on the 18th of Elul, in the presence of Rivkah and Devorah Leah, the Ba'al Shem Tov himself cut the fine locks of Shneur Zalman's hair, leaving peyot on both sides. He then blessed the boy with the traditional priestly blessing: "May God bless you and keep you! May God shine favor upon you! May God countenance you and grant you peace!"[37] He then told them to "Cover him with the tallit right away" and they departed.

As they drove home, the inquisitive boy kept asking his mother and aunt, "Who was that man?" But the Ba'al Shem Tov had forbidden them to speak his name to the child. So finally, Rivkah responded—"A zeide."[38]

In later years, Reb Shneur Zalman always spoke of the Ba'al Shem Tov as his *zeide*, his grandfather.

Halakhah and a Little Hasidism

Over the next few years, young Shneur Zalman's intellectual gifts seemed to grow almost exponentially. Indeed, so great were they that by the time he was just five years old, he was made an honorary member of the ḥevra kaddisha, the 'society of the holy' who cared for the bodies of the dead in Liozhna. Of course, he was nowhere near old enough to participate at that time; but realizing his tremendous learning and unusual maturity, the society made him a promise that he would be made a full-fledged member when he was thirteen years old.

At first, Shneur Zalman was schooled by local teachers; but when he had surpassed them, his father sent him to Lubavitch to study with Rabbi Yissakhar Dov Kabilniker, a great scholar of the region. By the time he was eleven, Rabbi Yissakhar Dov brought him home, telling his father: "This boy is fit to be my friend and companion, not my disciple; he can make his own way through the sea of Talmud," and he outlined a course of self-study for him.[39] Occasionally he studied with his father, Barukh, who was also a profound scholar, and his maternal grandfather, Avraham, who both took special time out for him; but mostly he studied alone in the orchard, outdoors, much as his father had in his youth.[40] Once, when his great-grandfather was visiting and went to inquire after his study regimen, he asked the boy: "What do you like best?" The boy responded, "I like the pure, unpolluted air best."[41]

During these years, he also began to study mathematics, astronomy, and philosophy. It wasn't considered necessary that he should study these subjects, but he insisted, not wanting to depend on others for explanations of these things.

At thirteen, he became *bar mitzvah* and delivered his first public discourse, after which he was publically acknowledged a Torah scholar of great distinction. He now went to live in Vitebsk with his uncle, Rabbi Yosef Yitzhak, a talmudist of extraordinary ability, who even managed to impress his gifted nephew. Indeed, the young man found he had much to learn from his uncle, including new methods of study and interpretation that he had never encountered before. What he didn't know was that these 'new ways' were actually innovations of the Ba'al Shem Tov, from whom he had been carefully guarded until now. Thus, he underwent a subtle indoctrination; for Yosef Yitzhak, like his father Barukh, was a secret disciple of the Ba'al Shem Tov, and had been given the task of introducing the young genius to Ḥasidut.

Each year, Reb Yosef Yitzhak would travel to Mezhbizh for Shavuot to report on his pupil's progress to the Ba'al Shem Tov, but he was never allowed to disclose the latter's name to his young disciple, or even to speak openly of the movement. The same went for Reb Barukh. For the Ba'al Shem Tov wanted young Shneur Zalman to be kept in complete ignorance of his existence until the time was right, saying always, "He is not destined for me; he belongs to my successor." However, in 1760, during his last visit to the Ba'al Shem Tov, the master said to the Maggid of Mezritch in Reb Yosef Yitzhak's presence:

> "FROM THE DAY THIS SOUL DESCENDED TO EARTH *from the highest worlds to be clothed in the body of Barukh and Rivkah's son, I staked my life for him. Nevertheless, he belongs to you. Still, he must come to you of his own accord, without any outside pressure. Eventually, he will come, and then you'll see what kind of a vessel he really is! Even so, be careful in guiding him so that he may accomplish his true destiny.*"[42]

In all things, it seemed that young Shneur Zalman progressed at a speed that astounded everyone around him. Though they had seen prodigies in their time, no one could remember encountering a genius of his caliber before. Years later, he would confide to his grandson, Menachem Mendel: "All through my youth, I found my Torah studies very easy, requiring little real effort. This was very disconcerting, for I was unable to fulfill the *mitzvah* of 'toiling for the Torah.' It was only when I reached the age of fifteen that I learned who I really was, and what the purpose of my soul's descent to earth really was."[43]

Now, two things happened when he was fifteen that might begin to account for this statement: first, he married Shterna, the daughter of the wealthy and influential Yehudah Leib Segal of Vitebsk;[44] and second, the Ba'al Shem Tov passed on in Mezhbizh.

With regard to the former event, it is said in Hasidism that there is a second descent of the soul at the time of one's marriage. Thus, I can imagine, while standing under the *ḥuppah*, the sensitive young Shneur Zalman may have gotten a true revelation of what his soul's destiny was really about. But also, while living with his new father-in-law in Vitebsk, he was able to continue his studies with his uncle, Reb Yosef Yitzhak, who now began to teach him openly about the Ba'al Shem Tov who had recently passed on.

So for two years, they learned the teachings of Ḥasidut together; and it was likely during this time that Reb Yosef Yitzhak taught him the following teaching of the holy Ba'al Shem:

> THE RABBI OF THE CELESTIAL ACADEMY *began his discourse in the following way:* "Those who consider themselves insignificant are really great; and those who consider themselves great are really insignificant." *For in the world of chaos (tohu), one begins by being great and proceeds to becoming smaller and smaller. Thus we see greatness in the young, but as they stray from the path of divine service, they gradually become smaller—even as they grow older. However, in the world of rectification (tikkun),* "those who consider themselves insignificant are really great," *and the small grow and grow, always being aware and sensitive to how childlike and insignificant their divine service really is!*[45]

One can only imagine what impact such teachings made on the sensitive young man; but we do begin to see that even as he continued to master the entire body of talmudic literature, with all its commentaries and codes, he more and more turned his attention to Kabbalah and the service of prayer. Around this time, he also began to make a major study of the *Sh'nei Luḥot ha-B'rit* of Rabbi Yeshaya Horowitz, the SheLoH ha-Kodesh (ca. 1570–1626) who had integrated German *kabbalah* with the teaching of Rabbi Yitzhak Luria, the Ari ha-Kodesh (ca. 1534–1572).[46] Likewise, he began to lead a small group of young men in the study of Talmud and the ways of Kabbalah, worshiping in a *minyan* together (for a period of three years) according to the teachings outlined by the SheLoH ha-Kodesh.[47]

Vilna and Mezritch

Then, at twenty years old, Shneur Zalman came to a decision: he needed to find a master. Of course, this was no simple task; he was no ordinary student, and to find someone of greater learning or piety would be difficult. But this was precisely the spiritual block he had to overcome, to find someone before whom he could truly humble himself, who might create awe in him, so that he could finally "toil" in the service of God and the Torah.

As he saw it, there were only two choices—Vilna or Mezritch. The road to Vilna led to Rabbi Eliyahu ben Shlomo Zalman, the Ga'on of Vilna (1720–1797), reputed to be the greatest living Torah scholar in the world, and with whom he might find another layer of learning he had not yet discovered for himself. The road to Mezritch, on the other hand, led to Rabbi Dov Baer, the Maggid of Mezritch (1704–1772), the successor of the Ba'al Shem Tov, of whom he had heard from his uncle, Reb Yosef Yitzhak. One promised the possibility of greater learning, the other the possibility of greater service. By the values of the time, the deepening in Torah was to be preferred, but the years of study with his uncle had not been without effect, and he had begun to long for something else, something greater, just as his father had done years before.

Later, he told his son, Dov Baer, the reasons for his choice . . .

IN THE END, it was the teaching of our Sages—"Whoever says, 'I have nothing but Torah,' does not even have that"—that caused me to take the road to Mezritch.[48]

It was true that I yearned deeply to attain greater understanding of Torah; it seemed to me that nothing I had learned up to that point compared with my desire to learn more. By the time I was thirteen, I was already learning almost eighteen *hours a day! And for three years, I divided my weekdays into thirds: first, studying the Gemara (Talmud); second, the poskim (those who have made rulings); and third, TANAKH, aggadah (the non-legal parts of the Talmud), Zohar, and ḥakirah (philosophy of religion). And on Shabbat, I divided my time thus: first, studying the Gemara and the poskim; second, TANAKH, aggadah (the non-legal parts of the Talmud), and ḥakirah; and third, Midrash, Zohar, and kabbalah.*

But one day, I found myself bothered by a question, and asked myself: "How could I possibly remain without a teacher and master? What would this lead to?" Thus, I decided that I must find a master. But where would I find him? At the time, I knew that there were two great lights in the world: one was in Mezritch, the successor of the Ba'al Shem Tov, and the other was in Vilna, surrounded by great scholars of Torah. In Vilna, they teach you how to study, and in Mezritch, they teach you how to pray.

At first, my desire to learn Torah took me in the direction of Vilna; but after a few days walking, I thought: "Well, about study, I know something already; what I don't know is how to serve God in prayer!" So I decided to travel to Mezritch first, and afterward, I would continue on to Vilna.[49]

I have sometimes wondered what would have happened had he gone to Vilna first? Would it have made a difference in later relations between the Hasidim and the Ga'on of Vilna? I don't know. After all, other talented disciples of the Maggid had been there first—Reb Avraham of Kalisk, Hayyim Heikel of Amdur, and Reb Azrael and Reb Yisra'el of Polotzk—and it didn't make a difference. In fact, I think it's likely that the Ga'on would have seen his moving on to Mezritch later as a 'defection' and a 'betrayal'—all the more so for being acquainted with Shneur Zalman's great gifts, which were so like his own. I am also certain that *he would have* moved on; after all, he had already been subtly 'infected' as it were by Ḥasidut through his father and uncle, and it wasn't going to leave him alone until he had explored it for himself.

A Little Higher Than the Angels

At the mere mention of Mezritch, Shneur Zalman's father-in-law flew into a rage and threatened to cut the couple off, but his daughter, Shterna, supported her husband's decision and raised funds for his trip, asking only that he not be gone longer than eighteen months. So, sometime after Passover in 1765 (5525), Shneur Zalman set out on the road with his younger brother, Yehudah Leib. But after the horse pulling their cart collapsed, Shneur Zalman asked his brother whether he had the permission of his wife to come on this journey. He didn't. So he sent his brother home while he continued on foot.⁵⁰ Later, he described his initial experiences in Mezritch to Yehudah Leib . . .

WHEN I ARRIVED IN MEZRITCH and entered the Maggid's beit midrash, I found the ḥevraya kaddisha, the 'holy fellowship,' seated 'round a table discussing the ḥayyot ha-kodesh of the Merkavah, the angelic creatures of the Divine Chariot.⁵¹ One was saying that the angels are entities whose very life is the word of God, while another spoke of how they are continually "running and returning"⁵² between ahavah and yirah, between 'love' and 'awe' of God. As the discussion ascended to higher and higher levels, the disciples of the Maggid rose and became more and more ecstatic. Some began to tremble and weep with the awesome presence of the serafim, whispering silent prayers. Some stood as if paralyzed with their faces ablaze, while others—who were naturally more demonstrative—began making noises and turning cartwheels, as if embodying the ofanim, the 'wheels' of the Chariot. Some seemed almost to be embodiments of the ḥayyot ha-kodesh themselves, making the sounds of the ox, the lion, and the eagle, and almost taking on their appearances!⁵³

Then I heard the Maggid's crutches as he entered the room from his private chamber. He stopped in the doorway and said: "And when the angels drop their wings, they stand just like this," and he let his arms drop to his sides, palms outward, as if to say—like a human being.⁵⁴ The disciples were awed and came out of their ecstatic state.⁵⁵ Then the Maggid continued: Anokhi asiti eretz v'adam aleha barati, " 'I made the Earth, and a human being I created on it.'⁵⁶ Not angels. It is the human being that God wants. And the word, barati, 'I created,' has a numerical value of 613 (the number of the mitzvot), for this is what God wants of us." Then the Maggid retired to his private chamber, and the room was again still and peaceful.

I had witnessed both the great and holy ecstasy of the ḥevraya kaddisha, and the grounded and majestic composure of the Maggid; but it was the sight of the latter that made me a Hasid of the Maggid of Mezritch.⁵⁷

This is such an amazing story, for even though they are not named, you can see a number of the Maggid's leading disciples in this description—Reb Avraham Kalisker, Reb Ahron Karliner, Reb Shlomo Karliner, and Reb Yisra'el Polotzker—all carried away in the ecstasy of the angelic forms! But even though Reb Shneur Zalman was deeply moved by this scene—telling his brother that it "clarified for him the words of Rabbi Shimon bar Yohai, 'I bound myself with a single bond, I became one with him; I was aflame with Him' "⁵⁸—it is nevertheless the "grounded and majestic composure of the Maggid" that seals the deal for him.

Why is this? As my Rebbe put it, "he was—and is—a fiery heart ruled by his brain."[59] Thus, it is likely that if the young genius had only witnessed the ecstasy of Mezritch, he would soon have moved on to Vilna. If Mezritch had only represented another polarity—ecstasy vs. learning—he would have been forced to go on to Vilna to find his own balance again. But when he saw that the Maggid already represented this balance, there was no longer any need for him to seek Vilna at all.[60]

Learning Nigleh and Nistar

It is said that the Maggid once came into the *beit midrash* in the middle of the night with a candle in his hand and looked down at Reb Shneur Zalman asleep on a bench. Peacefully curled up on that quiet night, he looked very young and small to the Maggid, who shook his head and said, "Such a great God in such a small person."[61] In my imagination, I can also see the Maggid leading his son into that dark *beit midrash*, showing him his new disciple, then, as the tradition tells us, taking him aside to confide in him what the Ba'al Shem Tov had told him regarding this special soul—about the day of his birth, his circumcision, and his prophesy that he would one day come to Mezritch.[62]

IT IS WAS NOT LONG AFTERWARD *that the Maggid arranged a* shiddukh *(match) between his brilliant 24-year-old son, Reb Avraham, called the 'Malakh' for his angelic presence and holy ways, and the 20-year-old genius from Liozhna.*[63] *Seeing that Reb Shneur Zalman already had an almost unparalleled knowledge and comprehension of halakhah and codes, while his son, Reb Avraham had a similar knowledge and experiential grasp of kabbalah and mussar, he decided that it would be very beneficial for them both if they were to become friends and learning partners. Thus, he brought the two of them together and addressed them intimately: "I would like the two of you to have a special* ḥevruta *(study partnership): for one hour Zalmina, you will instruct Avramenyu in Gemara, and for one hour Avramenyu, you will instruct Zalmina in kabbalah."*[64]

Later, the Maggid took Reb Shneur Zalman aside and said to him: "Let my son go his own way. Explain the Torah to him as you understand it, and he will interpret it according to his own conception. Show him the Talmud according to the letter, and he will explain its meaning to you according to the spirit." Thus, for six hours a day, they studied halakhah *and* kabbalah *together, spending three hours on each subject.*[65]

The ḤaBaD tradition says that Reb Shneur Zalman got the better of the deal, taking advantage of Reb Avraham's ecstasy; for when Reb Avraham became enraptured with the subject he was discussing, Reb Shneur Zalman would immediately get up and move the clock back to give himself a little more time![66]

A Bagel in Atzilut

In this way, a deep love and friendship developed between the two young men—a friendship that even prolonged the Malakh's life. You see, Avraham the Malakh was a Hasidic anachronism, deeply holy, but only tenuously connected to this world. It seems that he did not embrace the Ba'al Shem Tov's concept of *avodah begashmiut*, serving God through the physical body. So it was the particular challenge of his father and friends to keep him in this world, as this story shows us . . .

ONCE, WHEN REB AVRAHAM AND REB SHNEUR ZALMAN were davenen *(praying) together, they both got very deeply involved in their meditation, eventually reaching the place of* atzilut, *the realm of 'nearness' to God. Suddenly, an awareness arose in Reb Shneur Zalman's heart that his friend, the Malakh, did not wish to come back. So he shook himself out his own meditation and ran into the kitchen, coming back in seconds with a bagel and some beer. Quickly, he tore a piece off the bagel and put it into the Malakh's mouth, forcing him to chew it. Then he poured some of the beer down his throat, successfully bringing him back to consciousness!*

The next morning, the Maggid called Reb Shneur Zalman into his private chamber and said: "Zalmina, I want to thank you; in the place where I was in my own davenen, *I was powerless to do anything about Avraham's situation. I am so glad that you were there with him at that time and able to save my son's life—yasher koaḥ! But one thing I don't understand—Where did you find a bagel in* atzilut?"[67]

Theirs' was one of the great friendships of Hasidism and one of the most mutually beneficial. For Reb Shneur Zalman would in time become one of the greatest kabbalists of the age, seen as the contemplative par excellence, and this had its true beginnings in his *ḥevruta* with the Malakh.[68] From Reb Shneur Zalman, Reb Avraham gained a deep grounding in *halakhah* that no doubt added dimension to his Torah and probably even kept the Malakh in the world longer than he would have been otherwise.

Of Horses and Men

Before we leave our discussion of Reb Shneur Zalman's friendship with the Malakh, it is perhaps worth mentioning one of two teachings the latter gave to his friend, Reb Shneur Zalman, still repeated by Hasidim to this day.

Once, when Reb Shneur Zalman was preparing to leave Mezritch, his friend Avraham the Malakh walked him to the wagon and said to the driver, "Discipline the horses so that they know they are horses." Reb Shneur Zalman stopped and was thoughtful for a moment—then he took his bags from off of the wagon and stayed in Mezritch a while longer.[69]

There was once an Emperor Ludwig in Prague who was friends with the famous rabbi, Yonatan Eibeshutz (ca.1680–1764), and who liked to test the great rabbi's wisdom.

One day, Emperor Ludwig asked to see Rabbi Yonatan Eibeshutz. When he arrived, the Emperor introduced him to a marvelous troupe of trained cats who walked on their hind legs, and which were dressed in miniature versions of the royal livery! Then the Emperor said: "You see, there isn't much difference between an animal and a human being; why should they be treated so differently? Do you have an answer to that? You see how well behaved they are, after all?"

The rabbi says, "By your leave, I'll be back with an answer tomorrow."

He returns the next day and the Emperor introduces the cats again and it is just as before, but then the rabbi opens a box and lets a mouse out . . . and the cats were cats again!

The point of this story is that a human being has a different potential for discipline than animals, but the *etzah* (counsel) of the Malakh already assumes as much, and wants to make another point: if the human being does not exercise that discipline over the body, then one is no different than these cats who are merely dressed up like humans! Thus, when the body knows its place in life and does not arrogate itself to the place of the soul, then all is in its proper order. One has to discipline the body in order for it to know that it is a body, which is to say, a vehicle for the soul.

Hearing this, Reb Shneur Zalman must have felt that he had not yet sufficiently disciplined his body, at least not enough to go home, where he would not have the support of the *ḥevraya kaddisha*.

Davenen Fast, and Davenen Slow

In addition to Reb Avraham the Malakh, Reb Shneur Zalman also formed a number of other close relationships in Mezritch that would last a lifetime. One of the most intimate of these was with Reb Levi Yitzhak of Berditchev (1740–1809), another young genius—just five years his senior—who had come early to the Maggid through one of his chief scouts, Reb Shmelke of Nikolsburg (1726–1778).[70] Though most of their more significant exchanges would happen much later, this little story from their early days in Mezritch is one of my favorites . . .[71]

ONE DAY AFTER DAVENEN *together in the* beit midrash, *Reb Levi Yitzhak approached Reb Shneur Zalman and asked, "My friend, can I ask you why you are davenen so slowly?"*

Reb Shneur Zalman responds, "Only if you'll tell me why you daven so fast?"

So Reb Levi Yitzhak answers: "If you're a wagon driver passing through the forest, sometimes you have to drive fast so that the thieves don't have time to jump on your wagon. Thus, I daven fast so the yetzer ha-ra, the 'evil impulse' doesn't get a chance to jump on me!

So why do you daven so slowly?"

Reb Shneur Zalman responds: "You're lucky the yetzer ha-ra hasn't gotten a hold of you yet! But what do you do when he's already jumped on the wagon? If I'm gonna' throw him off, I can't afford too drive fast!"[72]

Both Reb Shneur Zalman and Reb Levi Yitzhak were known for taking a great deal of time in their *davenen*, so it is likely that this story is referring to the relative intensity and flow of words in the other's *davenen*.

The Tzaddik of the Generation

When the Hasidim in Mezritch weren't *davenen* together or studying Torah, they would often gather around a table and tell stories of the Ba'al Shem Tov, the Maggid, and the other *tzaddikim* of the time, sometimes speculating about their significance in the world. On one of these occasions, the following discussion took place . . .

ONE EVENING, *some of the younger talmidim of the Maggid of Mezritch were sitting around and speculating about who might be the tzaddik ha-dor, the 'tzaddik of the generation.' Various names were mentioned, but curiously, no one mentioned the Rebbe. Most agreed that it was the Aliker Rebbe. Then, Reb Shneur Zalman,* who came into the conversation late, asked the question that no one else had dared to utter—"Why don't you nominate the Rebbe?"

One of the Hasidim answered, lowering his voice to a whisper as if embarrassed: "You know the Rebbe is lame, and you yourself have heard him teach about 'a small defect in the body'[73] . . . He can't be the tzaddik ha-dor. It must be the Aliker Rebbe."

When we speak about the *tzaddik ha-dor*, we are really talking about a person who is, for a time, the 'axis of events' for a community, a nation, or perhaps even the world. Thus, the *tzaddik ha-dor* is the pole-center of the generation, around whom great events take shape. This is very similar to the concept of the *qutub* (axis, pivot) in Sufism, who is the "invisible head of all the Sufis,"[74] around which events turn, the one "whose attention and prayers decide the course of events in a particular society of people."[75]

BUT REB SHNEUR ZALMAN REPLIED to his fellow disciples: "The Rebbe is a tzinor, a 'channel' through which Divinity comes down to us. When he moves his head to the right, it is ḥokhmah (wisdom), to the left it is binah (understanding); when he moves his right hand, it is ḥesed (loving-kindness), his left, it is gevurah (severity). But it is through the legs that Divinity descends into our world: the right leg is netzaḥ (victory), and it delivers the ḥesed; the left leg is hod (glory), and it delivers the gevurah. Now, our Rebbe, in his kindness, wishes to limit the amount of severity that comes down to us, thus he is lame in his left leg! Therefore, he is the tzaddik ha-dor."[76]

Whether he had considered this beforehand, or whether it came from the moment, the illustrations of Reb Shneur Zalman are never merely clever explanations to serve a particular moment, but always address deeper truths; for the way of the Maggid—and the Ba'al Shem Tov before him—was never to put a stumbling block before those who would serve God in truth, but to create openings for people, restricting severity in favor of loving-kindness.

The Mediator

Not only was young Reb Shneur Zalman the greatest defender of the Maggid within the circle of the Hasidim, but also among the *rebbeim*. In this latter role, he showed particular diplomatic skill, at once defending the Maggid without slighting the Maggid's peers among the disciples of the Ba'al Shem Tov.

Once, Reb Pinhas of Koretz (1726-1791)—who disagreed somewhat with the Maggid's approach to public teaching, and generally kept himself aloof from the Maggid's court—arrived in Mezritch to discuss a matter of mutual concern.[77]

YEARS AFTER THE MAGGID *had ascended to the leadership of the Hasidic movement, Reb Pinhas of Koretz paid a visit to Mezritch. However, on entering the beit midrash of the Maggid, he nearly stepped on a piece of holy writing—notes from one of the Maggid's teachings lying on the floor! Likely it had simply been blown off the table by the wind, but Reb Pinhas took this as a sign of carelessness. He picked it up, quickly scanned it and turned angrily to a young Hasid standing nearby, "You see what happens when one is not careful with words?" Meaning, when one is not conservative in speech, teaching things too freely.*

The young Hasid replied:

"Once there was a king who had a son who was very sick. There was only one thing that could help the prince—the central jewel from the crown of the king! If that jewel were to be ground into powder, mixed with water, and given to the prince, it might save his life. But the prince was so ill at this point, it was not even certain that he would be able to swallow the mixture, and the jewel would be wasted for nothing! Hearing this, the king said, 'What good is this jewel to me if my son, the prince, should die to preserve it?'"

The Koretzer listened to the young Hasid's mashal (parable) with careful attention—calm returning to his body—and nodded his approval. Then he smiled at the young man and said, "A good argument for teaching Ḥasidut." He handed the scrap of paper to the young man and entered the Maggid's private chamber.

The young man was Reb Shneur Zalman.

Later, the Maggid took him aside and said, "When the holy master, Reb Pinhas Koretzer became angry in that moment, there arose a storm in Heaven against me and my teaching; your words calmed that storm."[78]

The Maggid was a natural teacher and manifested a lot of teaching, but Reb Pinhas was far more epigrammatic and worried about broadcasting the teachings of Hasidism. This argument, however, seemed to calm his fears, and probably smoothed relations between he and the Maggid. Even though they had strong differences of style and emphasis, both recognized the great qualities of the other and did not hesitate to work together for holy purposes.[79] Later, Reb Shneur Zalman would himself learn with the Koretzer Rebbe and served as the Maggid's emissary to him whenever necessary.[80]

The Opponents

Whatever minor internal strife may have existed among the early Hasidim, a far greater threat was posed to the young movement by the 'religious right' of the time who came to be called *mitnagdim*, or 'opponents' of Hasidism. The *mitnagdim* were precisely those leaders whom the Ba'al Shem Tov's subversive 'revolution' meant to displace. But in no way was this an attempt to harm or defame these leaders, only to cultivate a different kind of leadership and deeper service to God. Nevertheless, in 1770, an unfortunate event took place which gave the already combative *mitnagdim* 'cause' to attack the Hasidim with the full force of the establishment.

Up to this point, the antagonism had been entirely one-sided. As early as 1757, three years before the passing of the Ba'al Shem Tov, the opponents of Hasidism had gathered together in the city of Shklov to denounce the "band of Hasidim and their leader, Yisra'el of Mezhbizh." Nevertheless, the Ba'al Shem Tov forbade his disciples to react in any manner that might provoke further strife.[81] This became the policy of the Maggid of Mezritch as well. If at all possible, peaceful relations were to be maintained; and, even if it were not possible, there were to be no reprisals.[82] But in 1770, an immature and overzealous young disciple of Reb Avraham of Kalisk (1741–1810) went out of his way to antagonize the *mitnagdim* in Shklov, creating a blot on the name of Hasidim everywhere, and provoking a response that would plague them for the next fifty years.

Reb Avraham of Kalisk had himself been a brilliant talmudic scholar and a disciple of the Ga'on of Vilna; but after coming to Mezritch, he quickly became intoxicated with the teachings of the Ba'al Shem Tov, especially his emphasis on 'simple faith' over learned speculation. Then, with the passion of a convert, he went back to his native Kalisk to spread the 'new teachings' of Hasidism and began to train a group of brilliant young disciples in the ways of Hasidism. But the 'Hasidism' of Reb Avraham was thought by some to be too very narrowly focused on ecstatic prayer and an emotionalism that sometimes pushed the bounds of propriety; for he and his Hasidim were known for the kind of ecstatic outbursts and flamboyant behavior—turning cartwheels in the streets and praying in a frenzied manner—that was later to characterize Hasidism in the popular imagination. But there was more of caricature to this depiction than a legitimate characterization of Hasidism generally. Nevertheless, in Kalisk, these ways became the norm for a cadre of more than thirty disciples who took on their master's anti-rationalist tendencies, wild prayer practices, and tendency toward dramatic public behavior, often dressing as peasants and dancing in the streets.[83]

In 1770, one of these exuberant young disciples from Kalisk made his way to Shklov—one of the major outposts of the opposition—and presented himself as an itinerant *maggid*, desiring to preach to the community. Satisfied with his credentials, the community leaders arranged for him to speak to the congregation. For an entire hour, he held his audience enthralled; seldom had they heard a *maggid* as learned and as eloquent as this young man. But once he was assured that the congregation was hanging on his every word, he changed his tone entirely, saying:

> I see that I have found favor in your eyes and that you have enjoyed my lecture. I must confess, though, that I did not come here as a preacher or speaker in order to receive some remuneration. I came to open your eyes so that you may see the truth and to enthuse your hearts to the service of the blessed Creator.[84]

Far from enthusing their "hearts to the service of the blessed Creator," he began to attack and vilify the leaders of *mitnagdim* in Shklov, Minsk, and Vilna, causing shock and horrified reactions among his previously delighted audience. In the furor that followed, he managed to escape and was never seen again. But the matter did not end there. When word of this brazen attack on Torah scholars of spotless reputation reached the other great centers of learning in Minsk and Vilna, the outrage of the Torah establishment was immense and quickly mounted to fury.

But the *mitnagdim* were not the only ones shocked and angered by the behavior of this self-appointed 'representative' of Hasidism. When word reached the ears of the Maggid, he called an emergency meeting of his senior Hasidim, who agreed that Reb Avraham of Kalisk—whether he had given his consent to this act or not—must be severely censured for his irresponsible leadership. Nevertheless, the compassionate Reb Levi Yitzhak and Reb Zushya wished to give the Kalisker every benefit of the doubt, and even asked the Maggid's senior disciple, Reb Menachem Mendel of Vitebsk to intercede on his behalf. He was successful, and Reb Avraham of Kalisk was only given a strong rebuke, though it was agreed that the wild public displays of the Kalisker Hasidim were to be discontinued entirely.[85]

In order to assess the damage that had been caused by the Kalisker Hasid, the Maggid of Mezritch sent Reb Shneur Zalman out on a secret mission to Shklov and other cities that might have been affected by this indiscretion. He was to gather as much information as possible and to bring about any healing of the breach he could without revealing his own identity. Thus he was given the opportunity to walk in his father's shoes, taking on the role of a hidden *tzaddik* for a short time, only now in the service of the Maggid.[86]

On a cold and windy Winter evening, a young man carrying a sack over one shoulder arrived in Shklov and quietly entered the shul of the perushim. This was the synagogue of the scholars who followed the ways of the Ga'on of Vilna, who kept a vigil of learning both day and night. Nearly frozen and exhausted from his journey, he spoke to no one and, shivering with cold, went to warm himself by the stove while a group of men listened to the great lamdan, Rabbi Yosef of Shklov, as he studied a talmudic passage aloud. He had been discussing the passage with himself for several hours without a break, while nearby, another scholar, the humble Rabbi Yeruham Baer the fish-monger waited to ask him a question.

For days, Rabbi Yeruham Baer had been struggling with a particularly thorny problem, and had yet to get a satisfactory answer from any of the scholars with whom he had spoken. Thus, he waited to speak to Rabbi Yosef of Shklov, known as Yosef Kol-Bo, the 'encyclopedia,' who was celebrated for his learning throughout Lithuania, and who had even been heard of in Germany. But there was no interrupting Yosef Kol-Bo while he was studying. Even if he weren't engaged in study, he was still an intimidating man who demanded the respect his status afforded him. Thus, Yeruham Baer waited patiently—and nervously—to ask his question.

While he was waiting, he noticed the young stranger who had entered the shul, and being a kind and hospitable man, he went over to offer his hand and to see if he needed a meal. He also questioned him, albeit obliquely, to see if he was a person of learning—for he kept a spare room in his house for traveling scholars. Seeing that the stranger was obviously a scholar, he casually began to discuss his difficulty with him, thinking he might help him phrase his question to Rabbi Yosef Kol-Bo. But before he had even finished explaining the problem, the stranger began to recite the mishnah, as well as all the related texts, from memory in a sweet and gentle voice, translating them all into Yiddish as he went along! By the time that he was done, Rabbi Yeruham Baer hadn't any questions left; the difficulty had been made utterly clear, being resolved simply by the young man's skillful paraphrasing in Yiddish!

Before long, word had spread that a young stranger had resolved Rabbi Yeruham Baer's difficulty without opening a book or even sitting down to consider it. Everyone was amazed, and soon a crowd gathered around the stranger.

Looking up from his book, Rabbi Yosef Kol-Bo saw the crowd and overheard a few tantalizing bits of their discussion. Amazingly, he left off the question he was pursuing and went to see what was going on. Soon, he too was engaged with the rest of them in a fascinating dialogue with the young stranger, whose profound learning and explanations held them all enthralled.

This dialogue was still going strong when the next shift of learners, called the "early risers," came in at 3 o'clock in the morning. The men had been talking for hours and hours, but no one dared leave the table for fear of missing something.

Now, one of the "early risers" was a brilliant young man named Pinhas Reizes, who was astonished to find a debate going on at this hour, and involving all of the finest scholars of Shklov. Even more surprising was the fact that they were all seated around, and hanging on the word of a young man he had never seen before. Of course, he was curious and came over to listen in. To his astonishment, the stranger was outlining a new method of study for these great scholars, and went on to give an example of its use in a three-hour discourse!

When the stranger had finished, even Rabbi Yosef Kol-Bo, whom everyone present called "our master and teacher," was overwhelmed, and declared the young man's direct and logical approach far superior to the pilpul *method which tended to tie one up in knots.*

By the time he left town the next day, everyone was clamoring to know his name, where he came from, and what his position was; but all he would say was that he was only a student and not a rav. Later, it was learned that the young stranger was none other than the Liozhna illui, *the 'prodigy' who had become a disciple of the Maggid of Mezritch!*

Soon after, the brilliant Pinhas Reizes and none other than Yosef Kol-Bo—though fifteen years Reb Shneur Zalman's senior—set out for Liozhna to become disciples of the young stranger they had met in Shklov. In the coming years, through their influence, more and more of the learned Torah scholars of Shklov became Hasidim of Reb Shneur Zalman. But even those scholars in Shklov who kept their distance because of his Hasidism were respectful of him, holding him in high esteem as a peerless genius of Torah.[87]

Interactions of this sort went a long way to accomplishing the kind of quiet revolution the Ba'al Shem Tov and the Maggid wanted; for wherever Reb Shneur Zalman went, brilliant students—formerly destined for the camp of the *mitnagdim*—were sure to follow. What the Ba'al Shem Tov did for the common people, gathering crowds with his spellbinding tales, Reb Shneur Zalman did for the learned elite, drawing them in with his amazing insights and innovative methods of study. For unlike his contemporaries, he had a way of learning that didn't create difficulties where there were none. He saw things directly and cut to the heart of the matter without getting distracted by tangential side-trips that led nowhere. This ability, coupled with his amazing spiritual insight and gifts of memory and intellect, made him perhaps the most brilliant halakhic mind of his era.

The Rav's New *Shulḥan Arukh*

In every *rebbishe* household, there is a 'house *rav*,' an authority on *halakhah*, chosen from among the inner circle of disciples to decide on legal matters for the Rebbe's family, and often for the circle of Hasidim as well. In Lubavitch, when I was a *yeshiva bokher*, it was Rav Simpson, the Rebbe's *majordomo*, who was called upon to act in this capacity. This was a great testimony to his knowledge and experience, for the Rebbe himself accepted his rulings. So just imagine how great an honor it must have been for the youthful Reb Shneur Zalman to be called "our *ga'on*" by the Maggid, and "the Rav" by his peers, among whom were many luminous Torah sages, such as Menachem Mendel of Vitebsk (1730–1788) and Pinhas of Frankfurt (1730–1805).

Once, the Maggid of Mezritch said to Reb Zushya of Anipol, "Write to our ga'on, Reb Zalmanyu Litvak and tell him to come here." Hearing from Reb Zushya that the Maggid had spoken of Reb Shneur Zalman as "our ga'on," the Hasidim quickly began to call him "the Rav." Soon after, Reb Avraham the Malakh reported this to his father, the Maggid, who responded: "The ḥevraya kaddisha (holy fellowship) are merely giving testimony to the truth; names are significant, for in the halakhah, the law is decided by the one who is called 'rav.' I tell you, his Shulḥan Arukh will be accepted throughout the scattered house of Yisra'el."[88]

To this day, Reb Shneur Zalman is known simply as "the Rav" among most Hasidim,[89] and his great halakhic work as the *Shulḥan Arukh ha-Rav*.

When the Hasidim heard that the Maggid had spoken of Reb Shneur Zalman as "our *ga'on*"—literally 'genius,' but having the connotation of a supreme Torah authority—it was only a confirmation of what they already knew.[90] For when there was a question of *kashrut* (kosher) in Mezritch, this was usually turned over to Reb Shneur Zalman for a decision.[91] And once, when the Maggid had convened a *beit din*, a rabbinical court to appeal to the heavenly court in the case of "desperately ill individual," one of the two judges chosen to preside with him was none other than Reb Shneur Zalman.[92] But if any other confirmation of the Maggid's confidence in him were needed, it would be clear from the fact that he had requested that Reb Shneur Zalman prepare a new *Shulḥan Arukh* in which all of the laws and their applications would be clearly spelled-out, along with their reasoning.[93]

The traditional *Shulḥan Arukh*, literally the 'prepared table,' of Rabbi Yosef Karo (1488–1575) was the definitive code of Jewish law for most Jews at that time. For, using the decisions of accepted authorities, Karo had compiled the laws of prayer, daily living, and the holidays into one book, presenting them concisely (and without scholarly minutiae) for the ordinary Jew. However, finding that Karo had used mostly Sefardic authorities—ruling according to Sefardic custom—Rabbi Moshe Isserles (1520–1572) compiled the *Mappah*, or 'tablecloth,' which used later Ashkenazic authorities and gave varying decisions when Sefardic and Ashkenazic customs differed. Thus, the later work was usually appended to the former in most editions.

So why was a new *Shulḥan Arukh* needed? The answer to this question is discussed in the preface to the first published edition of the *Shulḥan Arukh ha-Rav* (1814) written by the holy sons of Reb Shneur Zalman . . .[94]

EVEN TALMUDIC SCHOLARS *of great distinction find it difficult to decide between the differing views of various halakhic authorities, to draw conclusions from a text with the intent of arriving at a ruling that will be acceptable to the Ahronim, the later authorities, whose waters we drink, and in whose paths we walk; for opinions vary, and one scholar builds an argument that another seems to tear down, one raises questions that another counters; so how can an ordinary person choose a straight path through these views by themselves?*

It was for this reason that the holy teacher, the Maggid of Mezritch, searched among his disciples for someone in whom the spirit of God dwelt, who could sift and clarify these opinions, discerning authoritative halakhic decisions in them . . . setting out the rulings as they appear in the Shulḥan Arukh *(of Yosef Karo), and in the works of the later authorities, in a clear and simple way, along with the reasoning behind the respective rulings.*

For this task, the Maggid chose our revered father and Rebbe who, even at that time, was already overflowing in his knowledge of Talmud and the work of later authorities. He implored him to undertake this work, and to use his wisdom and understanding to penetrate to the depths of the law ... Thus, "he began to explain the Torah"[95] *while staying with the Maggid, beginning with the laws of* tzitzit *and those of* Pesaḥ. *Both of these sections were finished before the luminous and renowned* ge'onim, *Rabbi Shmelke, and his brother, Rabbi Pinhas, arrived there,*[96] *seeking the master's blessing before setting out for Germany, where they would take up their respective posts in Nikolsburg and Frankfurt.*[97] *It was at this time that they perused these sections of our father and Rebbe's work and praised them greatly. They urged him to persevere in the writing of it until it was finished, saying: "This work has been waiting for you; may its merit benefit you and your descendants, as well as all of Yisra'el!"*[98]

It appears that Reb Shneur Zalman began his *Shulḥan Arukh* late in 1770 when he was but twenty-five years old, and completed the first part—*Oraḥ Ḥayyim*, on the laws of prayer, the synagogue, *Shabbat*, and the holy days—late in 1772, around the time of the Maggid's passing. Through the years, he continued to work on his *Shulḥan Arukh*, revising it and adding to it, until it was finally completed. However, only one section was published in his lifetime, and tragically, the completed manuscript was later burned in a fire in 1810.[99] Fortunately, private copies of various sections still existed. These were gathered together by the sons of Reb Shneur Zalman—collated, checked, supplemented—and published in 1814.[100]

The text as we have it today is still incomplete and its sections are labeled according to whether they were from the earlier strata of writing, *Mahadura Kama* (in which the rulings are more conservative), or the later revision, *Mahadura Batra* (whose rulings are bolder and generally according to the Kabbalah).[101] Nevertheless, it is still considered among the great works of *halakhah*, and the Maggid's words—"his *Shulḥan Arukh* will be accepted throughout the scattered house of Yisra'el"—have come true. Today, all Hasidim (not only ḤaBaD Hasidim) look to the Rav's *Shulḥan Arukh* to guide them in spiritual practice; and while the *mitnagdim* now generally study the *Mishnah Berurah* of the *Hofetz Hayyim*, Rabbi Yisra'el Meir Kagan (1838–1933), no serious student of the law can afford to neglect the study of Rav's *Shulḥan Arukh*.[102]

When I was in *yeshiva* in Lubavitch, our *mashpiyyim* often counseled us to consult the Alter Rebbe's *Shulḥan Arukh* before every *yontif* (holiday), reviewing all of the relevant laws and opinions. At the time, some thought this was redundant because we already knew the laws from last year. But they argued that it sharpens your vigilance to do so, saying, "You'll be a lot more careful if you read it."

You Have Lost Your Head

When Reb Shneur Zalman arrived in Rovno—where the Maggid had relocated between 1769 and 1771—coming in answer to the Maggid's summons, Reb Zushya told him that the Maggid had called him "our *ga'on*." Hearing this, he fainted! When he finally came to, he was very ill and confined to his bed. Knowing that the Maggid thought of him as a son,[103] the disciples feared to tell him what had happened to Reb Shneur Zalman. Nevertheless, Reb Levi Yitzhak convinced them that they must.[104] When the Maggid heard the news, he said cryptically: "And God hid it from me! He has the sensitivity of a son. I was like a son to my Rebbe, the Ba'al Shem Tov, and he is like a son to me." No one understood these words at the time, but later, just before he died, the Maggid said to them, "What you sense now, Zalmanyu had sensed last Summer."[105]

This strange illness—apparently brought on by a premonition of the Maggid's death—occurred during another great council held in Rovno in the Summer of 1772.[106] Though the Hasidim had hoped that the uproar over the actions of the rogue *Kalisker Hasidim* would have died down by now, the anger over their behavior only seemed to be increasing. Hoping to stem the tide, Reb Menachem Mendel of Vitebsk attempted to gain an audience with the Ga'on of Vilna late in 1771, but the Ga'on would not see him.[107] Then, early in 1772, the Maggid appointed Reb Shneur Zalman and Reb Avraham of Kalisk as his representatives at a public debate with the *mitnagdim* in Shklov, the city in which the original offence had taken place. They were to explain the situation and to answer all questions put to them. Although they were able to answer most of these questions with ease—refuting all charges against them except one—they could offer no excuse for the outlandish public behavior of the *Kalisker Hasidim*.

Failing to answer this one question, the *mitnagdim* declared their other responses void and condemned the Hasidim as "a menace to the established order and norms of Jewish life."[108] Then a report—repeating the false accusations that had already been refuted—was sent to the Ga'on in Vilna and, just after Pesaḥ, an official ban was issued against the Hasidim bearing the Ga'on's own signature.[109]

The following is Reb Shneur Zalman's own account of what happened next, taken from a letter written to Reb Avraham of Kalisk many years later...

IN THE SUMMER OF 1772 (5532), *I traveled with you to the holy community of Rovno, the seat of our great teacher, whose soul is now in Eden. But you were afraid to* enter without our teacher's permission and remained on the outskirts of town. You then asked me to approach Rabbi Menachem Mendel who was already in Rovno to intervene on your behalf with our holy Rebbe so that you would be permitted to come to him. I did so, and he obtained the Rebbe's consent. I then came to fetch you at the edge of town and together we entered our Rebbe's room. There I witnessed how sternly he rebuked you for the foolish way in which you had guided the Hasidim of Russia—allowing them to indulge in frivolous talk, mocking and insulting the scholars of Torah, turning somersaults and engaging in foolish play in the streets of Kalisk, profaning the name of Heaven in the presence of gentiles.

Early in 1772, at the end of the debate in Shklov, you were unable to defend this behavior, and the rabbis of the holy community of Shklov then wrote to the Ga'on of Vilna, who found the Hasidim guilty and deserving of being cast out, Heaven forbid, like the unbeliever (epikores) who mocks Torah scholars. The somersaulting he likened to the idolatry of pe'or.[110] Then this ban spread from Vilna to Brod, and in the Summer, the pamphlet Zemer Aritzim was published, causing the tzaddikim of Volhynia great distress. Thus, they were forced to flee to Rovno to take counsel with our Rebbe.[111]

This is why you were afraid to enter the town, fearing you might incur the wrath of our Rebbe. But the Maggid (Yehiel Mikeleh) of Zlotchov was also there at that time and intervened on your behalf with the Rebbe.[112]

It's anybody's guess what would have happened if Reb Mikeleh of Zlotchov had not intervened for Reb Avraham. Regardless, there were bigger issues to deal with at the council. The ban of the mitnagdim had unleashed a firestorm of reprisals and anti-Hasidic vitriol. Hasidim across the land were being abused and attacked and the movement seemed threatened. The situation had gotten so bad for the Hasidim in Volhynia that many were on the point of demanding a counter-ban on the mitnagdim. The Maggid, however, counseled his disciples to show restraint and to weather the attack. Then a messenger arrived for Reb Levi Yitzhak, telling him that his family had become the target of new reprisals in his absence!

THOUGH THE MAGGID wished his disciples to show forbearance, the unjust persecution from the mitnagdim was wearing on them, and many wanted to issue a counter-ban on them. Reb Shneur Zalman was one of those who objected to this course, feeling that it was too strong a measure. He said, "Listen, if you put someone in ḥerem, you are endangering their soul; they may even be cut off from God, and it is possible that they will turn to another religion. Do you understand? This may lead to a desecration of the holy name!"

It was then that a messenger came bearing news to Reb Levi Yitzhak: the mitnagdim had taken his family from their home by force and thrown them on a garbage cart, driving them out of town only a few hours before Shabbat! Such behavior was unthinkable; the Hasidim had to fight back! So they put the mitnagdim in ḥerem that very night.

The next morning, the Maggid entered the beit midrash on his crutches and said to the assembled talmidim (disciples): "You have now lost your head; this will be the year of my passing. Nevertheless, you have achieved something—from now on, whenever there will be an argument between Hasidim and mitnagdim, the Hasidim will certainly triumph."[113]

The Maggid passed away several months later on the 19th of Kislev, 1772. Present were his son, Reb Avraham the Malakh, and most of his senior Hasidim, including Reb Menachem Mendel of Vitebsk, and Reb Shneur Zalman of Liozhna.

AFTER THE PASSING OF THE MAGGID, there was a question about who was going to wash and prepare his body for burial. The ḥevra kaddisha (burial society) of Anipol—where the Maggid had moved shortly before his passing—demanded to prepare the body themselves; for everyone who passes on within the precincts of Anipol was their charge as they saw it, and they wanted the honor of taking care of the Maggid as well. But the disciples of the Maggid said: "You don't know who the Rebbe was; how could you do it properly? We have to do it!" So they came to an agreement: only those members of the Anipol ḥevra kaddisha who were also disciples of the Maggid, and those disciples who were members of the ḥevra kaddisha in their own towns, could assist in the washing and preparation of the body.

In those days, they didn't just wash the body over a board, they also submerged it in the mikveh, a ritual bath. So they all entered the water with the body, having drawn lots beforehand to see who would wash the different parts of the Maggid's body. Reb Shneur Zalman had gotten the head. But just as he was about to dunk the Maggid's head in the water, the head seemed to dunk itself![114]

Of course, Hasidim believe that there was significance in the fact that Reb Shneur Zalman drew the honor of preparing the Maggid's head; for not only was he the great intellect of the Maggid's disciples, but his own system of the thought focused on the upper three *sefirot*, or divine attributes of God—*ḥokhmah, binah,* and *da'at*—which are liked to the divine mind. ḤaBaD Hasidim also see in this another significance, that Reb Shneur Zalman would one day become the 'head' of the Maggid's disciples in White Russia and Lithuania. As to the curious dunking of the Maggid's head on its own, it seemed to the other disciples as if there was still life in the master near the hands of his beloved Zalmina.

Let the Horses Run

Now that the Maggid was gone, Reb Shneur Zalman was prepared to return home; and just as he had many years before, his friend Reb Avraham the Malakh accompanied him to the wagon and offered him a bit of advice.

WHEN THE TWO FRIENDS REACHED THE WAGON, the Malakh said to the driver, "Urge the horses on and let them run until they are no longer horses." Reb Shneur Zalman looked his friend in the eyes, shook his head in comprehension and departed for home.[115]

This time, the Malakh's counsel was no longer about disciplining the body, but rather about transcending it; for when you already have a disciplined body, and you know the true nature of the soul, then you can really let the body "run" until it is no longer bound by its physical limitations. This was an exhortation to Reb Shneur Zalman, as if to say, "The Maggid is gone and you are ready for your task in the world; now let the horses run!"

In the Court of the Vitebsker

Before the Maggid passed on, he asked that Reb Shneur Zalman try to put his son, the Malakh in his place, but added, "if he should refuse, let it be Mendel the Litvak," meaning Menachem Mendel of Vitebsk.[116] So when the Malakh refused—as expected—many of the Maggid's younger Hasidim like Reb Shneur Zalman, Reb Avraham of Kalisk, and Reb Yisra'el of Polotzk turned to Reb Menachem Mendel for leadership. Others, like Reb Ya'akov Yitzhak, the "Seer" of Lublin, Reb Yisra'el, the Maggid of Kozhnitz, and Reb Shlomo of Lutzk looked to Reb Elimelekh of Lizhensk for leadership. Much of this had to do with temperament, but also with what region they were from and the shared bond that came with it.[117]

Both Reb Shneur Zalman and Reb Menachem Mendel were Litvaks (Lithuanians) known for their exceptional learning, and they actually lived fairly near to one another. So it was natural that they should spend a great deal of time together in either Minsk or Horodok—the places where Reb Menachem Mendel lived during these years—when they were not with the Maggid.[118] For as great as Reb Shneur Zalman was—even at twenty-seven years old—he was humble enough to know that Reb Menachem Mendel was still his senior in service and maturity.[119] And, although he had been assured by the Malakh that he was ready to go his own way, he was not yet ready to separate from his elder mentor, especially so near to the Maggid's passing.[120]

Reb Menachem Mendel had actually been with the Maggid since he was 11 years old, having been one of the children the Maggid tutored in the early days. Thus, in time, he also became his Hasid and was even taken to meet the Ba'al Shem Tov, his master's master. From his youth onward, the Vitebsker was often chided for his pride, but it was only in his youth that this charge had any truth. For the Maggid often caught him admiring himself in a mirror and combing his hair very carefully. Although these fastidious personal habits remained with him for the rest of his life—always being well-groomed and dressing in fine clothes—later, they were simply a way of concealing his own humility.[121] Reb Shneur Zalman was once supposed to have said of him: "Once, a king was forced to hide a jewel so that it shouldn't be stolen. So, in order to protect it from thieves, he hid it in the outhouse. Likewise, Reb Menachem Mendel hides his humility in the outhouse of pride."[122]

So, before and after the passing of the Maggid, Reb Shneur Zalman often visited the court of the Vitebsker, which was a place where the Hasidim of the Maggid who lived in Lithiuania could gather together for fellowship and occasionally to take counsel together about their problems with the *mitnagdim*.[123] The following story of Reb Shneur Zalman comes from one of these gatherings at the court of the Vitebsker.

ONCE, IT HAPPENED *that Reb Menachem Mendel was called away from a gathering of the Maggid's Hasidim at his court. But the Hasidim, knowing that he would only be gone a short time, decided to stay until he returned. So they sat around the table telling stories and talking about holy matters, when in comes a man with great a* geshray *(cry), yelling: "Rebbes! Rebbes! Please, my son is very sick, and they say that Rebbe Menachem Mendel isn't here—You have to help me! Please give me a blessing for my son in his stead!"*

Then, one of the Hasidim answers him, saying, "Oy! My friend, how can we hope to bless your son in the holy Vitebsker's stead?"

But Reb Shneur Zalman, who was also there at that time, said: "No, we cannot say this to him ... Once there was a king who had many children, and those children were always fighting. And this squabbling between his children displeased the king more than anything else. Always, it was 'Yankele hit me!' or 'Moishe took something from me!' So, finally, he appointed his majordomo to take care of the kids; and if anything was needed for the children, he would appear before the king, and he would make the request himself. Then, one day, it happened that the majordomo was away from the court, and young Yankele fell and hurt his arm badly. Quickly, all the other children ran over to Yankele and tried to help him, but they didn't know what to do. So one of them said, 'We better go and get papa!'

"But another spoke up and said, 'We can't go to papa—the majordomo isn't here.'

Then Moishe spoke up and said, "We only need the majordomo because we're always fighting; but if we all agree that Yankele needs help, we can go to papa ourselves!"

So, Reb Shneur Zalman concluded, "The Rebbe is away; we must give the blessing ourselves."[124]

The Vitebsker Goes to the Holy Land

In 1775, Reb Shneur Zalman accompanied Reb Menachem Mendel of Vitebsk to Vilna to seek an audience with the Ga'on of Vilna. Once again, it was hoped that together they might be able to convince the Ga'on that the Hasidim were being misrepresented.[125]

WE SET OUT FOR THE HOME OF THE PIOUS GA'ON, *may he live long, to discuss the issues with him and to remove any misunderstandings between us.*[126] *This mission was undertaken by myself and the Rav and Hasid, Menachem Mendel of Horodok, of blessed memory. However, twice we found the door locked against us. Even the leaders of the community approached the Ga'on saying—"Rabbeinu, the famous rav (Menachem Mendel of Horodok) of the Hasidim has come to speak with your eminence, and surely when they are convinced of the error of their ways, then peace will certainly prevail in Yisra'el once again." But the Ga'on would not see us. Then, when others of his followers began to plead with him, the Ga'on ended all debate by leaving the city and staying away until we had departed.*[127]

Disappointed, but undeterred, Reb Shneur Zalman and Reb Menachem Mendel went on to Shklov to speak with representatives of the *mitnagdim* there, but again, it was to no avail; their efforts at reconciliation were again rebuffed.[128]

IN 1776, ON THE YAHRZEIT *(death anniversary) of the Maggid (18 Kislev), a number of disciples of the Maggid gathered together in Horodok at the court of Reb Menachem Mendel. Reb Shneur Zalman had come with his brother, Reb Yehudah Leib.*[129] *Other Hasidim of the Maggid in attendance included Reb Yissakhar Dov of Lubavitch, Reb Avraham of Kalisk, Reb Yisra'el of Polotzk, and a number of others.*

After going to the mikveh, *Reb Shneur Zalman and his colleagues—the senior Hasidim of the Maggid—gathered together in their Shabbat garb in the study of Reb Menachem Mendel, who seated Reb Yissakhar Dov of Lubavitch and Reb Avraham of Kalisk to his left, and Reb Shneur Zalman and Reb Yisra'el of Polotzk to his right, while the others, including Reb Yehudah Leib, remained standing. Since all five of the seated masters had been present at the passing of the Maggid, Reb Menachem Mendel invited each of them to speak of something they remembered from that time. Reb Menachem Mendel went first, followed by Reb Yissakhar Dov, Reb Avraham, Reb Yisra'el, and then Reb Shneur Zalman, who spoke until it was time to daven Minḥah, which they all did in the courtyard of the* beit midrash.

After Minḥah, Reb Menachem Mendel repeated a teaching the Maggid had taught shortly before his passing. Then the leading of the Shabbat prayers was divided in the following way: Reb Menachem Mendel would lead kabbalat shabbat, *Reb Avraham would lead Ma'ariv, Reb Yissakhar Dov would lead the following* Shaḥarit, *Reb Shneur Zalman the reading of the Torah, Reb Yisra'el* mussaf, *and Reb Shneur Zalman would lead Minḥah.*

Throughout the various services of Shabbat, Reb Yehudah Leib basked in the beautiful melodies and was in awe of the different styles of davenen *displayed by each of the disciples of the Maggid. It was clear that they were all in deep* deveikut *(intimacy) with their Rebbe, the Maggid, throughout the* davenen. *Then Reb Avraham began to teach in a passionate voice, aflame with his devotion, and afterward, Reb Menachem Mendel invited Reb Shneur Zalman to repeat a teaching of the Maggid, and the colleagues remained together at the table until very late.*

After the Shabbat was over, the five great disciples of the Maggid spent three days together discussing matters of great import. It was decided at that time that Reb Menachem Mendel would emigrate to Eretz Yisra'el, and Reb Avraham and Reb Yisra'el would accompany him. Then they spoke of who should guide the Hasidim in their absence and preserve them through their struggles with the mitnagdim. It was agreed that Reb Shneur Zalman should become the leader of Hasidism in White Russia and Lithuania for this purpose. However, Reb Shneur Zalman demurred, unwilling to accept any such designation while Reb Menachem Mendel lived. He then attempted to delay their departure, but they were determined to depart the following Spring.[130]

This decision threw Reb Shneur Zalman into great turmoil, and by the time Reb Menachem Mendel was ready to depart in 1777—with Reb Avraham of Kalisk, Yisra'el of Polotzk, and 300 followers—Reb Shneur Zalman was debating whether he should go as well. For three months he agonized over this decision, until the intermediate days of Pesaḥ, when he decided. He informed his family and the community leaders of Liozhna that he too intended to emigrate to *Eretz Yisra'el*.

A little while later, he arrived in Mohilev, where he joined the party of Reb Menachem Mendel, who was not pleased to see him there. He urged Reb Shneur Zalman to return, and reminded him of the Maggid and the Ba'al Shem Tov's hopes for him, of how he would establish the eventual success of Hasidism. For three weeks, he dwelt in Mohilev with the party, spending time in private dialogue with Reb Menachem Mendel each day. In the end, the party left without him, and he informed his brothers that he would be returning to Lithuania.[131]

2

The Making of ḤaBaD Hasidism: The Liozhna Maggid's Wisdom, Understanding and Knowledge

WHEN THE SOULS OF THE BA'AL SHEM TOV, the Maggid of Mezritch, and Reb Shneur Zalman were told that they were to descend to Earth, the tradition tells us that each of them asked for a cadre of sixty warriors (*shishim gibborim*) to accompany them. For it is said that around the bed of King Solomon were sixty swordsmen to protect him from the terrors of the night. And if we look at the extraordinary companions and disciples of these three Rebbes, we have to believe that this wish was granted to each of them; but perhaps none did more to consciously cultivate and train that army of spiritual warriors than Reb Shneur Zalman, the Liozhna Maggid.

The first of these 'warriors' were his gifted brothers—the rabbis, Yehudah Leib, Mordecai, and Moshe—who all moved to Liozhna shortly after he had been named *maggid* there in 1767.[132] To them and a few select others, Reb Shneur Zalman gave personal attention and intense instruction in Torah three times a week over the course of several years.[133] Then, after returning from the meeting of the Maggid's disciples in Horodok in 1776, he specifically chose "young men of exceptional intellectual power and broad scholarship"—drawn to him in the course of his travels—and began to teach them the ways of Torah and *Hasidut*.[134] This was the beginning of *Ḥeder Alef*, the first of his three famous *ḥadarim*, or study circles, through which he personally trained some of the finest minds of Lithuania and White Russia.[135]

According to my Rebbe, Reb Yosef Yitzhak Schneersohn (1880-1950), the original Ḥeder Alef consisted of "fifteen students, whose entrance requirements included a thorough knowledge of the Talmud, Midrash, the *Ikkarim* and the *Kuzari*, and a familiarity with the *Zohar*." For the next five years, he taught these gifted students "as if he were locked in the room with them." Then, in 1780 and 1782, he founded Ḥeder Beit and Ḥeder Gimmel,[136] and from these three ḥadarim—over the next twenty years—emerged numerous giants of Torah, as well as Hasidim of great distinction like: Reb Ahron of Staroshelye, Reb Eisik of Homil, Reb Pinhas Reizes, Reb Moshe Meisels, Reb Moshe Vilenker, Reb Yekusiel of Lieple, Reb Shmuel Munkes, and Reb Binyomin of Kletzk. Like the sixty mighty warriors of King Solomon, these loyal Hasidim of Reb Shneur Zalman were both his personal guard and his trusted emissaries ...

ONCE, REB SHNEUR ZALMAN *was visited by his colleague, Reb Shlomo of Karlin, to whom he wished to show the greatest courtesy. Thus, he assigned his distinguished Hasid, Reb Binyomin Kletzker (a student in Ḥeder Beit) to him as a personal attendant. Reb Shlomo was immediately impressed by the qualities he saw in Reb Binyomin and was reluctant to be parted with such a pious and learned Hasid. So, when it came time for him to leave, he was delighted to find that Reb Shneur Zalman had asked Reb Binyomin to escort him as far as Vitebsk.*

Along the way, they discussed Torah, halakhah, philosophy, and Ḥasidut, and Reb Shlomo Karliner was more and more impressed with Reb Binyomin. So, when they reached Vitebsk, and it was time for them to part, Reb Shlomo asked Reb Binyomin if he would mind escorting him a little farther to Beyeshenkovitch. Reb Binyomin agreed and they traveled on.

In the coming days, Reb Binyomin witnessed wonders and basked in the glow of Reb Shlomo's Torah. But even more impressive than his Torah was his awesome davenen *(prayer), which left Reb Binyomin almost in a daze. Then, Reb Shlomo saw his moment and made his pitch to Reb Binyomin, entreating him to come back with him to Karlin. There, he promised him that he would learn things still more wondrous—things that would even deepen his appreciation of Reb Shneur Zalman's teachings—and in time he would gather his own Hasidim!*

*Quickly, the fog in Reb Binyomin's head lifted, and he finally saw what was happening. He remained quiet for a few moments (as if considering Reb Shlomo's offer) and then answered him in colloquial Ukrainian—*Pan-to-pan no nye moy, khlopyetz to khlopyetz no nye tvoy—*"The lord is a lord, but not mine; the servant is a servant, but not thine."*[137]

This became the classic statement of Hasidic loyalty, repeated by Hasidim of different masters across the region for generations to come.

Clearly, it was part of Reb Shneur Zalman's intention from the very beginning to cultivate such loyal and deeply learned Hasidim. Undoubtedly, he hoped that they would help him discharge the enormous task the Maggid had laid upon him—to spread and establish the teachings of the Ba'al Shem Tov throughout the region—for surely he was not supposed to do this by himself.[138] Thus, his *Ḥeder* became a training facility for outreach workers who, after several years, were sent out as emissaries, and often strategically placed in different Jewish communities to spread the teachings of an authentic, Torah-grounded Hasidism, and to recruit new talent.[139]

At first, as he sequestered himself with this elite group of scholars, it seemed to some that he was abandoning the Ba'al Shem Tov's love of simple faith and simple Jews.[140] But this was no more true of him than it had been of the Maggid or the Ba'al Shem Tov as they assembled their own inner circle of Hasidim.[141] For all of them understood that the foundations for Hasidism—and the uplifting of Jews everywhere—must begin with the creation of a new leadership. Only now, the very organic process of the Ba'al Shem Tov had become orderly and methodical in the school of Reb Shneur Zalman.[142]

Thus, before creating the *ḥadarim*, he first set about training its 'professors,' his talented brothers, who in turn could focus their attention on those students who were already grounded in learning from other teachers and institutions. On these individuals, Reb Shneur Zalman also spent personal time, refining their knowledge and introducing them to the deepest levels of Hasidism. When they were sufficiently mature in their understanding, he sent them out as recruiters, to bring in and help train the next group of students who would occupy *Ḥeder Beit*. These students, it was understood, might have less grounding in traditional learning, but would help to prepare the ground for *Ḥeder Gimmel*, which would serve a still broader base of Jews from all backgrounds. For if he was going to create an environment for study in which everyone might have a place and find some benefit, he first had to change the ethic of its teachers and its most gifted scholars. Only then could there be 'rooms' (*ḥadarim*) and the right kind of mentors for the students of *Ḥeder Beit* and *Ḥeder Gimmel*.

So it is clear that Reb Shneur Zalman planned from the beginning to provide the *pashute Yidden*, or simple Jews—as my Rebbe, Reb Yosef Yitzhak of Lubavitch once said—"with spiritual food, just as he did for the celebrated scholars." Hasidism was meant to make a place for people from all walks of life, from the "*ge'onim* and *maskilim* who plumb the profoundest depths of its teachings, to the utterly naïve craftsmen working hard all week just to come home and enjoy a simple *Shabbat*.[143] As far as souls were concerned, Reb Shneur Zalman believed that all Jews were equal, meaning that the simplest worshiper—through sincere, heart-felt *davenen*, fulfillment of *mitzvot*, and love of Yisra'el—could "attain the loftiest levels in divine service, just like the most prominent of scholars."[144]

By the time *Ḥeder Gimmel* was established, it was no longer required that the students be brilliant, only that they apply their whole hearts to the service of God (*avodat ha-Shem*), so that the Rebbe's teachings could take root in them and eventually bear fruit in their lives.[145] In this simple truth, they were supremely confident. It was clear to them that the Rebbe was forging and hammering-out 'Hasidim' in his *ḥadarim*, and that their lives were different because of it, as the following story shows . . .

One day, as Reb Shneur Zalman was returning to Liozhna from a journey, his carriage pulled up and all the Hasidim gathered to welcome him home. However, one Hasid—Reb Shmuel Munkes—left the crowd and went to wait for the Rebbe in front of the beit midrash, *the 'house of study.' I say, "wait," but what he actually did was wrap his gartel, his woven prayer sash around his chest and under his arms, and suspend himself from the second floor window! Not long after, the Rebbe approached the building and looked up at Reb Shmuel—a known prankster—and raised his eyebrows, giving him a bemused smile. Then Reb Shmuel says to the Rebbe: "If you were a cobbler, there'd be a pair of shoes hanging outside your workshop; if you were watchmaker, there'd be a watch; but you are a Rebbe, and what should be hanging from a Rebbe's workshop?—A Hasid!"*[146]

For Reb Shmuel, this wasn't just a joke, but a genuine expression of what had become absolutely clear to him—the Rebbe was a maker of Hasidim! At that time, when fewer people could read, it was common to see cobblers advertising their services with a pair of shoes, or a tailor with a pair of scissors; so Reb Shmuel Munkes asked himself: "How should a Rebbe advertise? What are the proofs of his work? If the Rebbe is a Hasid-maker and a Hasid-fixer—taking coarse young men and turning them into servants of God—then we, his Hasidim, must be the proof and advertise it!"[147]

The Great Debate

In 1783, twenty-three years after the passing of the Ba'al Shem Tov, and eleven years after that of his successor, the Maggid of Mezritch, a great debate was held in the city of Minsk between Reb Shneur Zalman, the Maggid of Liozhna, representing Hasidism, and several leading rabbinic authorities of the *mitnagdim*, the 'opponents' of Hasidism.

THOUGH THE DEBATE *was to be about Hasidism, the* mitnagdim *demanded that Reb Shneur Zalman first allow himself to be tested, for they would not lower themselves to debate with anyone who was not sufficiently knowledgeable in Talmud. However, this was just a ruse. The Liozhna Maggid's extraordinary abilities were already legend in the region. So, as soon as the debate was arranged, the* mitnagdim *set about devising intricate arguments and thinking of various elaborate halakhic problems that might cause him to stumble. Nevertheless, he agreed to this unusual preliminary on the condition that the* mitnagdim *would also agree to be tested afterward. Confident in their own abilities, they too agreed.*

Thus, Reb Shneur Zalman stood on the bimah *in the local* beit midrash *answering their questions for hours on end, day after day, for an entire week. Though this was undoubtedly exhausting, he somehow managed to solve all of their most difficult problems with ease, impressing everyone with the novelty of his answers and the concise way in which he framed them. The spectators were also amazed that he needed no books, quoting sources verbatim from memory—Gemara, Rashi, Tosafot, RaMBaM, Rosh—even little known works as if they were open before him!*[148]

When they had finished with him, he began his own interrogation of the mitnagdim, *among whom were famous scholars like Rabbi Ahron Ya'akov, the head of the* yeshiva *of Slutzk, and Rabbi Zelmele of Slutzk.*[149] *But his interrogation did not last a week, or even a day; for none of the* mitnaged *scholars could answer a single question he asked. Embarrassed and somewhat defensive, they asked him to solve his own questions, which he did, with the exception of two which were obviously paradoxes he had discovered. Then he said, "I want you to know, these questions I have answered can also be answered by all of the senior students in my* ḥadarim.*"*

With this last statement, he was making his point absolutely clear; his own learning was not an exception; the Hasidim of Liozhna were scholars of distinction *as well as* pious in their service to God.

HIS CREDENTIALS HAVING BEEN ESTABLISHED, the mitnagdim then asked Reb Shneur Zalman to defend two particular Hasidic doctrines of the Ba'al Shem Tov that they found objectionable. The first had to do with the inordinate praise he accorded to the prayer of simple Jews, who had only the slightest notion of what they were saying. This, the mitnagdim argued, made them undeservedly proud, puffing them up with self-importance, while diminishing the wholly deserved prestige of the Torah scholars. Their second objection centered around the Ba'al Shem Tov's teaching that even the tzaddikim, the righteous, must serve God by teshuvah, or 'repentance,' as common sinners do. This was simply untenable, that the saint and scholar should be classed with the lowly sinner in need of repentance! In their eyes, this undermined the whole of the Torah and damaged the dignity of the righteous scholars of Torah.

Reb Shneur Zalman listened carefully to their objections, then, when it was time for him to speak, he told them that the foundations of these Hasidic doctrines—to which they took so much exception—were actually to be found in the first revelation of Moshe rabbeinu. He then gave over a teaching of the Ba'al Shem Tov that he had heard from the mouth of his own teacher, the Maggid of Mezritch . . .

IT IS WRITTEN, "And the messenger of God showed itself to him in the heart of the fire, in the midst of the thorn-bush. And he saw to his amazement that, although the thorn-bush was burning, it was not consumed! Then Moshe said, 'Let me turn from here to see this great sight'" (Exod. 3:2-3).[150]

RASHI RENDERS THE PHRASE B'LABAT EISH, "in the midst of the fire" as b'shalhevet shel eish, libo shel eish, "in the flame of fire, the heart of fire." So where does the messenger of the God become known? In the heart afire, which is the sincere and simple inner intention of the heart. And where is this "heart of fire" to be found? "In the midst of the thorn bush."

Now it is also written, "The human being is like a tree of the field."[151] There are fruit trees, which Rabbi Yohanan compares to the wise scholars (talmidei hakhamim), and there is the humble bush (sneh) that bears no fruit, representing the people of the earth (am ha-aretz).[152] And yet, the heart afire is in the thorn bush. To be sure, the scholars engaged in Torah study are filled with fire, for Torah is called "fire";[153] but they cannot claim, "yet it is not consumed," for they can quench their thirst with the insights they gain in study. Not so the humble thorn bushes, the humble and unlearned Jews who are the very heart of fire. With their simple and sincere prayer, in their holy ignorance, they are the flame that is not quenched; their thirst can never be satisfied.

Thus it is written, "And Moshe said, 'Let me turn aside from here to see this great sight.'" Rashi suggests that he meant, "Let me turn aside from here to approach there." Which is to say, Moshe understood the holy message revealing the superiority of the 'ignorance' of the humble ones over the 'knowledge' of the scholars—that the heart afire is only in the thorn bush—and thus he made teshuvah, a turning in repentance. Even though Moshe was himself a tzaddik, a 'righteous person,' he experienced a repentant heart, saying, "Let me turn aside from where I am to come close to that place." So the teaching is, one must never be satisfied with one's humility before God, from the higher to the lower and the lower to the higher, there is always room for repentance.[154]

This teaching of the 'heart afire,' which is the "sincere and simple inner intention of the heart" found in simple Jews, is perhaps the most enduring and important message of Hasidism. It tells us that the genuinely humble offerings and heartfelt intentions of simple people is at the heart of divine service; and the lesson to Moses, the archetypal leader of the Jewish people, and thus to all future leaders in Yisra'el, is that "one must never be satisfied with one's humility before God; from the higher to the lower and the lower to the higher, there is always room for repentance."

WITH THIS, THE DEBATE WAS CONCLUDED; the opponents of Hasidism found no answer that could undermine this teaching, nor did they have the stomach to try. For it was clear that Reb Shneur Zalman had won over the entire audience of spectators, many of whom had initially come to witness the defeat of Hasidism. Between the greatness of his talmudic scholarship and the inspiring power of his Hasidic teaching, everyone was left speechless. Thus it was as the Maggid had predicted, "from now on, whenever there will be an argument between Hasidim and mitnagdim, the Hasidim will certainly triumph."[155]

It is said that four hundred scholars—young and old alike—were converted to the ways of Hasidism that day, and that sixty of them followed Reb Shneur Zalman back to Liozhna. One of the younger ones was Rabbi Ahron HaLevi Horowitz, who would later become Reb Shneur Zalman's most distinguished disciple, Reb Ahron of Staroshelye.[156]

Now, this account always puts me in mind of a similar story that is told of Shankara, the great exponent of Advaita Vedanta, the non-dual school of Hindu philosophy. For Shankara was a child prodigy like Reb Shneur Zalman, who likewise became the chief spokesman of a new way of understanding the Vedas, embarking on what is described as a "victory tour" *(dig-vijaya)* throughout India, debating the heads of the other great schools of Hindu philosophical thought, much as Reb Shneur Zalman debated the *mitnagdim* in various cities throughout Lithuania and White Russia. Of these Hindu philosophical schools, the most influential was the Purva-Mimamsa school, which declared that the true meaning and end of the Vedas (the oldest scriptures of Hinduism) was found *exclusively* in the performance of the Vedic sacrifices and the traditional duties of that stratified society. So the learning of the Mimamsakas was bent entirely toward the study of the Vedas and expressed solely in duties and rituals carried out with mechanical precision. The Advaitins, on the other hand, focused on the inner dimension of the Vedas, seeking an experiential liberation in this life. Thus, the two approaches finally came into conflict and were debated by their greatest exponents, Shankara and Mandana Mishra...

As Shankara approached the village of Mandana Mishra, the great teacher of Purva-Mimamsa, he stopped to ask directions of two women taking water from the river. To his surprise, the simple village women answered his question in rhymed verse, as scholars of the Veda would! Then, as he reached the porch of the house, Shankara encountered two parrots discussing the scriptures! Again, he was amazed, and quickly understood that in the vicinity of the scholar, Mandana Mishra, even simple villagers and household pets knew the scriptures.

Upon entering the house, Shankara found Mandana Mishra, who was of the priestly caste, engaged in the most elaborate ritual ceremony with his disciples. From the quantities and quality of the materials being used in the ritual, Shankara could see that Mandana Mishra was not only a scholar and member of the highest caste, but he was also rich and lived like a *raja* (king) among the people of his village. Now Shankara was also of the priestly caste, but had abandoned wealth and other material pursuits in favor of the life of a wandering mendicant. However, Mandana Mishra thought of Shankara as a heretic who had abandoned his duties and become a traitor to the Vedas. So, on seeing him enter his house, he was incensed, and said, "What do you want here with that shaven-head of yours?"

Shankara answered simply, "I have come to discern the truth with you," that is to say, to debate. So Mandana Mishra's wife was appointed to umpire the debate, but not wanting to decide between her husband and another eminent scholar, she lay a garland of flowers around the neck of each, saying, "The one whose garland withers first will have lost the debate." It was understood that the loser would then become the disciple of the other.

So the debate began and continued for twenty-one days, ranging over all aspects of the Veda, each man quoting endless texts from memory in support of their claim. Mandana Mishra's view was that the Vedic texts are not intended to lead us to a discovery of the supreme Self; their truth is exclusively in the performance of duties and actions—let the ends take care of themselves. But, on the twenty-second day—using the criteria of the Mimasakas against them—Shankara demonstrated that if any word that is uttered in the Vedas must be useful in accomplishing an action, then the many scriptures that do not enjoin any physical action upon us (but only give descriptions of Divinity), must be enjoining us to *know* Divinity through them!

As he uttered these words, a petal wilted and fell from the garland of Mandana Mishra and the debate was concluded. Mandana Mishra became Sureshvara, the chief disciple of Shankara, and the Purva-Mimamsa school and most the other schools—left leaderless after numerous debates with Shankara—largely died-out as their students all defected to the way of Advaita Vedanta.[157]

Aside from the many obvious parallels to the elitism and learning of the *mitnagdim*, and even the prodigious abilities and similar non-dual philosophies of both Reb Shneur Zalman and Shankara, there is another more important similarity in both debates. It is a question: "What is the purpose of Torah and Veda?" For the Mimamsakas, the duties enjoined by the Veda had become an end unto themselves and God all but irrelevant. And while we would not like to say that God had become irrelevant for the *mitnagdim*, we can say that Torah had almost become an end unto itself. As Abraham Joshua Heschel has so aptly pointed out with regard to the modern counterparts of the *mitnagdim*—by stressing "the supremacy of Torah, equating Torah with *Shulḥan Arukh*, in disregard of God and Israel," many of the today's ultra-Orthodox have become involved in something that amounts to "religious behaviorism."[158]

This was so clear in the example of professor Yeshayahu Leibowitz (1903-1994), the Orthodox Israeli philosopher and scientist who wanted to divorce the observance of *mitzvot* from any kind of emotional investment in them, calling this a kind of "idolatry." Thus, he would say of prayer, "Just say the words—never mind about talking to God."[159] This was the disease that Hasidism had come to remedy, to restore the coordinates of God and Yisra'el, i.e., to use the Torah to foster the awakening of God's love in one's heart, and the love of one's fellow Jews equally, whether they be unlearned peasants or scholars of the highest distinction.

The Great Sacrifice

After the great success in Minsk, the numbers of Hasidim who came to Liozhna only continued to grow, and it soon became apparent to the *mitnagdim* that the Hasidim were "growing into a body to be reckoned with," especially those who had been trained by Reb Shneur Zalman; for these were mighty men of tremendous learning and profound piety, as we have already seen. And now that these 'graduates' of the Liozhna *ḥadarim* were spreading out to different towns and villages, and winning more hearts to the Hasidic cause, the *mitnagdim* were growing more desperate and becoming even more conniving in their mission to destroy the Hasidim.[160]

At the same time, Reb Shneur Zalman was beginning to encounter trouble from within the Hasidic movement as well. The new assault of the *mitnagdim* was driving some Hasidic leaders to consider another ban on the *mitnagdim* to punish them for this abuse. As Reb Shneur Zalman was seen as the leader of Hasidism throughout the region, he was asked to join in this ban, or at least to endorse the right of others to do so. So it was that two of his former colleagues from Mezritch, Reb Shlomo of Karlin and Reb Wolf of Zhitomir, came to Liozhna seeking just such an endorsement. However, Reb Shneur Zalman believed that it was forbidden to put the *mitnagdim* in *ḥerem*, for, just as he had argued in Mezritch many years before, he feared that this would cut them off from God. Reb Shlomo Karliner became so frustrated with this position that he actually swore during their heated conversation and left immediately afterward.[161]

This discord with his former brothers caused Reb Shneur Zalman more than a little anguish; but worse still, he felt that it signaled problems to come. These came in the form of an unfortunate dispute with Reb Avraham of Kalisk, whom we have already mentioned.[162] Thus, it seemed to him that the forces of negativity were stirring up trouble within the Hasidic movement, and that a great sacrifice might be required to save it.

AT THIS TIME, *the lights of Yisra'el were dimmed and an evil eye was cast on the Hasidic movement; for strife from both within and without threatened to destroy all for which the Ba'al Shem Tov, the Maggid, and Reb Shneur Zalman had worked so hard. A harsh decree had been handed down from the heavenly tribunal, and the holy Alter Rebbe felt that it might be "time for his sun to set."*

> *Early in the month of Elul 1791 (5552), Reb Shneur Zalman sent his Hasid, Reb Ya'akov of Smilian, to his friend and fellow disciple of the Maggid, Reb Nahum of Chernobyl with a* pidyon nefesh *for himself, and for the entire Hasidic movement—for both were in danger.*

Either Reb Shneur Zalman felt that his life was bound up with this harsh decree, or that it might be necessary to offer his own life as a substitute for the 'life' of the movement. Whatever the case may have been, he evidently hoped that the decree might still be avoided, for he sends a *pidyon nefesh* to Reb Nahum of Chernobyl (1730-1798), whom he admired greatly. Reb Nahum was one of the younger disciples of the Ba'al Shem Tov and one of the elder disciples of the Maggid of Mezritch, known for his great piety, and for traveling from town to town on behalf of Jews who had been imprisoned because of debt. This service was called *pidyon shevuyim*, the 'ransoming of captives.'[163] However, this is not to be confused with a *pidyon nefesh*, which means, 'soul ransom.'

A *pidyon nefesh* is usually a sum of money, a cash donation given for the maintenance of a Rebbe's household or for his charities, accompanied by a *kvittel*, literally a 'billet' or 'slip' of paper on which the Hasid requests the intercession of the Rebbe in some matter. But this was no ordinary *pidyon nefesh*; it required the intercession of a great master of prayer who might be able to 'sweeten' the judgment against the whole Hasidic movement, and possibly preserve Reb Shneur Zalman's life. To whom does a *Rebbe* send such a *pidyon nefesh*? The Maggid of Mezritch had been gone almost 20 years by then, and his elder mentor, Reb Menachem Mendel of Vitebsk had died a few years earlier; so Reb Shneur Zalman chose to send the *pidyon nefesh* to another elder disciple of the Maggid whom he respected, and whose work he sought to support.[164] Moreover, he sends it in the month of Elul, hoping that the decree might be changed before it is sealed in the new year.

> SHORTLY BEFORE ROSH HASHANAH, *he asked to see his beloved daughter, Devorah Leah, and began to tell her the history of the women in the family after whom she was named and what he had intended by giving her this name.*

You may remember, it was Reb Shneur Zalman's aunt, Devorah Leah, who took him to meet the Ba'al Shem Tov when he was but three years old. She was the elder sister of his father, Barukh, and was likewise devoted to the Ba'al Shem Tov. In fact, it was her husband, Reb Yosef Yitzhak of Vitebsk who tutored Reb Shneur Zalman in his late teens, and who was his first teacher of Ḥasidut. But Devorah Leah is not at all in her husband's shadow in the family history, for she was a woman of unusual accomplishment in her time.

According to my Rebbe's *Sefer ha-Zikhronot,* Devorah Leah was a beautiful soul and pious from childhood: "Even as a child she excelled in refinement, modesty, and exceptional goodness of heart. When she was only eight years old, she used to run to help their poor neighbors with their housework or looking after their babies. And, of course, she helped her own mother all she could."[165] But in addition to these traditional virtues, she also had a great longing to learn Torah, and in time became an accomplished scholar.

> From a very early age, Devorah Leah knew that she wanted to learn Torah, but her father was a very traditional man, and didn't think it was necessary to educate girls. Nevertheless, she was not to be put off so easily. Though her father's teaching might be too advanced for her to understand, she could still eavesdrop on their neighbor, Rabbi Noaḥ, who was teaching his young pupils how to read *Ḥumash* (the Torah as bound in a book). So, whenever she had a little time to herself in the Summer, she would go sit on the balcony and listen to Rabbi Noaḥ teach as she did her sewing or mending. In this way, she memorized all the prayers and even learned the translations of the major ones. Soon, she found that she could even read some of the prayers herself in the *siddur* and a little *Ḥumash* too.
>
> But this taste of learning only made her want to learn more; and it bothered her that her father would not have her educated, especially as her mother, Rahel, was a learned woman. For whenever her father left the house, she would see her mother take out a volume of *Gemara* and begin to study. Why didn't anyone ask her if she wanted to learn too?
>
> One day, the sight of her own mother studying was too much for her, and she went off to cry in her bed. Hearing her sobs, her mother came and found her face down on the bed in tears. She asked, "Why are you crying, daughter?"
>
> "Because *your* father taught you Torah . . . to understand everything that is in those big books, and *mine* doesn't believe we should study at all!"
>
> Then her mother then told her that her own father, Reb Barukh the Batlan had been a disciple of the Ba'al Shem of Zamostch, and the disciples of *ba'alei shem* held different beliefs about the education of women; for they thought it was just as important to educate their daughters as their sons.
>
> "So," she told her, "I began to study Torah at five, and I continued for the next thirteen years, learning *Gemara* by the time I was fifteen. Then I married your father, who is from a great family too, but the men of his family do not believe in the education of women. Of course, he knows of my learning—and

has even come to appreciate it—but I do not wave it in his face. Now that I have seen that you are interested in such things, I will teach you myself, but you are not to let your father know or make a great show of it before him."

So her mother began to teach her, and she did so both regularly and systematically until Devorah Leah also became a good scholar. When she felt the time was right, Rahel told her husband who, to her surprise, raised no objections.

Later, after both her parents had passed on, Devorah Leah was introduced to a young genius named Yosef Yitzhak. She liked him and he was respectful of her beliefs, and hearing that her grandfather had served the Ba'al Shem of Zamostch, he told her of his own relationship with the Ba'al Shem Tov. So she agreed to marry him on the condition that he would give her lessons two to three times a week, and that they would share equally in things relating to Torah and *mitzvot*. Most importantly, if they had a daughter, she too would be taught Torah. He agreed to all of these conditions and they were married.

He was later appointed *rosh yeshiva* in Minsk, and they both served the Ba'al Shem Tov in secret.[166]

Now, it is easy to see why Reb Shneur Zalman named his daughter after his aunt (with whom he lived in Vitebsk while studying with his uncle Yosef Yitzhak). But it turned out to be a providential naming as well, for his daughter Devorah Leah was a gifted child, and probably even surpassed her namesake in learning, and was likely the equal of her brothers in piety.[167]

According to one of her father's most distinguished Hasidim, Reb Eisik of Homil, Devorah Leah was "a woman of profound understanding and awe of God," whose devotion to her father equaled that of his greatest Hasidim and excelled that of most. Then, he adds, "She was held in particularly high esteem because we all knew that the Alter Rebbe lived on from the year 5553 (1792) thanks to her actual self-sacrifice on his behalf."[168]

> THIS WAS A SPECIAL MOMENT between father and daughter, but it was also clear to Devorah Leah that her father's heart was heavy over something. So when he began to speak openly to her of his fears for the Hasidic movement, she finally understood what it was: the voices of the 'accusing angels' (kitrug), he told her, were working overtime. Hasidism had achieved great successes, but these had only put "an arrow in the eye of Satan," inflaming an even greater response from the forces of opposition.[169] And now they faced a harsh decree from Heaven.

All at once, Devorah Leah understood that her father's life hung in the balance! Her mouth was so dry and her chest so full that she could hardly speak. Finally, she recovered and almost shouted, "Abba, you cannot agree to this!"

But he said nothing in return.

Over the next several days, Devorah Leah suffered through a terrible turmoil until she came to a private resolution. Without telling her father, she called together three of his senior Hasidim—Reb Moshe Meisels, Reb Pinhas Reizes, and Reb Moshe Vilenker—men of deep wisdom and discernment, whom she knew she could trust to be discreet and to keep their word. But before she would speak to them of her wishes, she asked them to agree to her conditions, and to obligate themselves—under oath—to keep her secret until the entire situation was resolved.

Understandably, the seriousness of her tone and her unusual conditions worried them (though each was known to be a lion in the cause of Hasidism) and they told her that they would need a day to decide. Over the next twenty-four hours, they met several times to talk the matter over. They all knew something was going on with the Rebbe, for he had secluded himself in his study, and even the closest of his Hasidim were denied admittance. It was as if a dark cloud had settled over Liozhna and the senior Hasidim all believed that something was wrong, though no one knew what it was. In the end, the three men felt that they had no choice but to agree to the conditions, for they believed that Devorah Leah's secret had something to do with the Rebbe, and it might tell them how they could help.

The next day, at the appointed hour, Devorah Leah received them cordially, and solemnly began . . . "We are all Hasidim of our father, the Rebbe, and are willing to sacrifice ourselves for his sake, for the sake of his teachings, which are those of the holy Ba'al Shem Tov." But even as she pronounced these words, she began to sob uncontrollably.

Reb Moshe Meisels stood up in alarm and spoke for the others, begging her to tell them why she was crying! But she could not speak. This only increased their fears, and Reb Moshe passionately declared: "I will be the first to sacrifice myself for the Rebbe! Just tell us what to do! We are ready—we assure you!"

Feeling their anxiety, and assured by their love for her father, she recovered herself and said: "First, you must swear by an unbreakable oath that you will do as I ask. Don't be afraid; the oath will apply only to me, but it involves the saving of a life, so it is most sacred!"

So terrifying was her resolve that even Reb Moshe Vilenker, who was known for his steadiness and balance, began to get nervous and to have second thoughts, suggesting that they take more time to think about her conditions. But Reb Moshe Meisels and Reb Pinhas objected, "What more can we say, Moshe? We've all agreed that it is necessary to hear her out."

So all three took the unbreakable oath and 'Rebbetzin' Devorah Leah spoke.

When my Rebbe told this story—based on the account of Reb Eisik of Homil—he began to call her "Rebbetzin" at this point. Now, there was nothing accidental in my Rebbe's storytelling, for he was extremely careful about reporting details accurately. So it seems likely to me that Reb Eisik himself had begun to call her "Rebbetzin Devorah Leah" at just this point in the story when the three men take the "unbreakable oath."

Rebbetzin, of course, is a Yiddish word—basically, Rebbe, with an obscure feminine suffix attached—usually referring to the wife, and sometimes the daughter of a Rebbe. Though it is a title of great respect among Hasidim, as Reb Shneur Zalman's daughter, there is nothing particularly unusual in Devorah Leah being called Rebbetzin here except that it seems to have been done with a particular purpose at a particular moment. Given that it comes at the point at which there was no going back on her resolve, and at which she begins to direct these three venerable Hasidim, I suspect that Reb Eisik is suggesting that she was somehow elevated in status at this moment, or at least, to be highly honored for what she is about to do.

"I APPOINT THE THREE OF YOU to act as a beit din, as court of law to give a binding verdict according to the sacred Torah. For, the trouble which the gossips and slanderers have stirred-up between the rebbeim of Volhynia and the Holy Land against our Rebbe is very serious; indeed, according to my father, the consequences of this situation may even, God forbid, put his life in jeopardy. He himself has told me:

"A healthy tree requires thirty years of careful cultivation to yield its best fruit.[170] The teachings of the holy Ba'al Shem Tov and the Maggid of Mezritch have sprouted into a good sapling. But even now, as it is becoming a 'Tree of Life,' it is in danger of being utterly uprooted by the accusations that are ascending to the heavenly tribunal.... I tell you, I do want to live—as the Torah requires of us—but even more than that, I want this tree to bear fruit, even unto the coming of the Mashiaḥ!

"My Rebbe, the Maggid warned me that such times would come—and even assured me of help—but I have seen my Rebbe (i.e., the Maggid of Mezritch) and his Rebbe (i.e., the Ba'al Shem Tov), and their faces were dark; I believe this means that their teachings are in jeopardy. I also believe..."

At this point, she broke into tears again, saying, "My father! Never!" Then the three men began to cry as well, for they all knew what the Alter Rebbe had said next.

From this account, it seems that Reb Shneur Zalman was making a choice to give his life 'for the cause,' to save the young 'tree' of Hasidism, which was just over thirty years old (counting from the death of the Ba'al Shem Tov). Why was it in danger? Rebbetzin Devorah Leah speaks of "gossips and slanderers" stirring up trouble between her father and the Rebbes of Volhynia (i.e. Reb Shlomo of Karlin) and the Holy Land (i.e., Reb Avraham of Kalisk). That is to say, there were individuals—possibly *mitnagdim,* and some less than pious 'Hasidim'—who were trying for various reasons to drive a wedge between Reb Shneur Zalman and these Rebbes. While this would appear to be true, there is also evidence that jealousy and idealistic differences may also have played a part, as we will see later.

Nevertheless, Reb Shneur Zalman himself speaks of the "the voices of the accusing angels," and "accusations that are ascending to the heavenly tribunal" which have brought about the harsh decree. How are we to understand this? If we think in terms of Rupert Sheldrake's morphogenic field and Carl Jung's collective unconscious, we can see how individual shifts in consciousness may have an impact on the greater field of consciousness. Such a field might even be seen as a kind of 'feedback mechanism.' Thus, as major shifts occur in the thoughts and feelings of individuals or groups of individuals, a ripple-effect is sent through the entire field, causing tiny adjustments and adaptations throughout. Now, if enough of those thoughts and feelings are negative and reach a kind of critical-mass, they can manifest in the world as very real dangers and in destructive acts—disputes and violence. It is on this level that Reb Shneur Zalman is dealing with the issue.

Now how might his sacrifice change this 'heavenly decree'? This is something we will come back to in the life of Rebbe Nahman of Bratzlav; but for now, let us say that a selfless act 'sweetens' a harsh judgment; true sacrifice is a kind of equalizer which restores health and balance to a system.

THEN 'REBBETZIN' DEVORAH LEAH *wiped her eyes and said: "For this reason, I have resolved to sacrifice myself in his place; I will serve as an 'atonement' for my father and give my remaining years to him. I will die, and he will live a long life, carrying out the mission of my grandfather and my great-grandfather (i.e., the Maggid of Mezritch and the Ba'al Shem Tov), preserving the tree of Ḥasidut. In this way, I will share in the merit of all his future teachings.*[171]

THE FIRST NIGHT OF ROSH HASHANAH, the Alter Rebbe came out of his study and asked, "Where is Devorah Leah?" This was surprising because it was known that he did not usually speak on the first night of Rosh Hashanah. Then he caught sight of her and began to say, L'shanah . . . But she quickly stepped forward and cut him off, saying, "No father"—l'shanah tovah tikateiv v'teihateim—"may you be inscribed and sealed for a good year!"

On the second day of Rosh Hashanah, the Alter Rebbe gave a ma'amar (discourse) that lasted until *havdalah*, after which, he asked Devorah Leah and her husband, Shalom Shakhna to come into his study. Later, Reb Shalom Shakhna was heard sobbing, saying: "But what will happen to our child? . . . Just two years old! . . . And such a child!"

The next day—the Fast of Gedaliah—Devorah Leah passed away, though from what cause no one could say. And so passed the threat to the Hasidic movement.[172]

On the second day of Rosh Hashanah, it is clear that she told both her father and her husband what she had done and asked her father to take care of her two year old son, Menachem Mendel, who would become the third Lubavitcher Rebbe.

When Reb Eisk of Homil finished his account, he said: "To this day, Hasidim mention her name with reverent awe, just as it was mentioned at the time by the three venerable Hasidim (Moshe Meisels, Pinhas Reizes, and Moshe Vilenker)" . . . "for everyone is aware that it was her self-sacrifice and noble spirit that saved the Tree of Life."[173] Reb Shneur Zalman lived over twenty more years, becoming old enough to be called forever after, the *Alter Rebbe*, or 'elder' Rebbe.

For this sacrifice, Devorah Leah truly deserves to be called *Rebbetzin*, in the same sense as various other wives and daughters of Hasidic Rebbes—like Rebbetzin Perele of Koznitz, Rebbetzin Rahel of Apt, Rebbetzin Malkha of Belz, and Rebbetzin Malkha of Trisk—who *earned* the devotion of Hasidim (some even taking *kvittlakh*) with their own piety and wisdom, becoming the earliest models of women Rebbes in Hasidism.[174]

The Book of the Beinoni

After the loss of his beloved daughter, what could the Alter Rebbe do but honor her sacrifice? He began to work even harder to establish Hasidism for future generations, and soon his unique blend of scholarship and deep spirituality was drawing thousands of would-be-Hasidim to Liozhna. But as their numbers swelled, it soon became impossible for him to give the new Hasidim the kind of personal attention he had once given the seminarians of Ḥeder Alef. Worse still, he was getting overwhelmed. Thus, he wrote the first set of Liozhna *takkanot*, or 'ordinances,' governing the conduct of his Hasidim and determining how often they could visit him in Liozhna.[175] This gave him a little space, and more importantly, a little time to take thought for how he was going to continue to provide spiritual guidance to this growing community. The solution, as he saw it, was to compose a book of Ḥasidut that the Hasidim could study, and that would address all the major questions of Hasidic spiritual practice.

As early as 1792, handwritten copies of the book, *Likkutei Amarim*, were already circulating among the Alter Rebbe's Hasidim. But far from being a simple 'collection of sayings,' as the title suggests, *Likkutei Amarim or Tanya*, as it is usually called, was a book that was composed with the utmost care and precision. As my Rebbe has written: "not only has each sentence been carefully and concisely composed, but also each letter has been carefully chosen. The work is punctilious in every detail, so that each word and each letter is meaningful." For twenty years, he labored to produce a work of lasting value, serving a variety of needs. In that time, he added many layers and new sections, so that the final book was composed of five parts; the first and largest of these being, *Sefer Shel Beinonim*, literally, the 'Book of the In-betweeners.'[176]

By calling the work *Sefer Shel Beinonim*, Reb Shneur Zalman was sending a clear message to his Hasidim—he had written a book for *them*, and not for the perfectly righteous *tzaddikim*. As he says on the title page of the work, "For it is very near to you; it is in your mouth and in your heart to do it."[177] That is to say, you are not so far from the holy level of the *beinoni*; and it is within you to achieve. But what is the level of the *beinoni*? And how does one achieve it? This is what Reb Shneur Zalman begins to explain in the opening of the *Tanya*:

IT IS TAUGHT (TANYA)—"An oath is administered to us before birth—'Be righteous, and be not wicked; but even if the whole world tells you that you are righteous, regard yourself as if you were wicked.'"[178]

This requires an explanation, for in the Mishnah it says, "Be not wicked in your own estimation."[179] Furthermore, people who consider themselves wicked are often heart-sick and depressed, consequently they aren't able to serve God as they should, with a joyful and contented heart; on the other hand, if they are not bothered by this thought, they may be led into irreverent behavior by it, God forbid. So obviously this matter needs to be discussed further.

In the Gemara, we find that there are five distinct types: the righteous who prosper, the righteous who suffer, the wicked who prosper, the wicked who suffer, and those in-between—beinonim.[180] It is explained, "the righteous who prosper" are the complete tzaddikim, and "the righteous who suffer" are the incomplete tzaddikim. In the Zohar, it is explained that "the righteous who suffer" are those whose evil nature is subservient to their good nature.[181] According to the Gemara, the righteous are ruled by their good nature, the wicked by their evil nature, and those in-between by both their good and their evil nature.[182] Rabbah said, "I, for example, am in-between"—a beinoni. But Abbaye objected, "Master, you make it impossible for anyone else to live."

In the Talmud, we are told that there are five distinct types of people in the world, each defined by the aggregate of their known behavior. That is to say, a person who behaves 'righteously' more often than not is considered 'righteous,' and one who behaves 'wickedly' more often than not is considered 'wicked.' It is basically a tally system for good and bad deeds, qualified by whether one is prospering or not. On the highest end of the scale are the righteous who prosper, or who have it good in the material sense because of the number of righteous actions they have to their credit. Likewise, on the bottom of the scale are the wicked who suffer and who have it bad materially because of the number of their sins. In the middle of the scale is the person in-between—the *beinoni*—being neither very righteous, nor very wicked; that is to say, their good and bad deeds are fairly evenly divided.

Obviously, this system has a number of problems if left unqualified. So Reb Shneur Zalman brings up an example that forces us to rethink this explanation. He quotes the famous saying of Rabbah bar Nahmani (ca. 270-330), "I, for example, am a *beinoni*," and the objection of his nephew, Abbaye (ca. 280-340), "Master, you make it impossible for anyone else to live." By which he meant, "If you, with all your holiness, are only a *beinoni*—having a roughly equal number of sins and good deeds—then the rest of us must be so wicked that we are liable for the death penalty!" Reb Shneur Zalman agrees; someone as holy as Rabbah could *not* be a *beinoni* under this definition:

> WE MUST UNDERSTAND *the essence of the one in-between, for surely the* beinoni *is not one whose deeds are equally divided between good and evil; if this were the case, how could Rabbah make the mistake of classifying himself as a* beinoni? *Especially as it is known that his lips never ceased reciting Torah, so that even the Angel of Death had no dominion over him.*[183] *God forbid that half of his deeds should have been sinful!*[184]

> AS FOR THE WELL-KNOWN SAYING *that the* beinonim *are those whose deeds and misdeeds are equally balanced, while the* tzaddikim *are those whose virtues outweigh their sins, this is only a generalization used to make a point with regard to reward and punishment, because we are judged according to the majority of our deeds, and one who is acquitted in a trial is called 'righteous.' But if we truly seek to define the distinctive qualities of the* tzaddikim *and the* beinonim, *we must look to our Sages who have remarked that the righteous are ruled by their good nature, as it is written, "And my heart is slain within me,"*[185] *meaning that David had overcome his evil nature through fasting. But whoever has not achieved this mastery—even if their virtues outnumber their sins—is not at the level of a* tzaddik.[186]

Now Reb Shneur Zalman begins to evolve a new interpretation of these five categories in terms of clear spiritual identities, each defined by an engagement with intentional energies, as well as by the behaviors that result from them. The strength of his model is that it emphasizes *kavanah*, the 'intention' and motivation behind our righteous and wicked deeds. But to the surprise of many—both then and now—it also prices 'righteousness' out of the market for most of us. For, according to Reb Shneur Zalman, the *tzaddik gamur*, or 'completely righteous person,' like David, has "entirely overcome his evil nature." He or she has so subdued and transformed his or her own demons that there is not even so much as an unconscious inclination to invest energy in a negative behavior; all fascination with sin and wickedness has been completely eliminated— the *tzaddik gamur* can't even conceive of a sin any more!

On the other hand, the *tzaddik sh'eino gamur*, or 'conditionally righteous person,' might have a negative thought, or an unconscious inclination to invest in negative behavior, but wouldn't even come close to acting on it; the fascination with wickedness in them is just a murmur in the deep unconscious. But because these residual negative impulses still exist, the conditionally righteous are subject to *karma* and the reciprocal effects of that negativity, whereas the completely righteous are not.

Now, keeping this in mind, let's see what he has to say about the *beinoni* ...

THE BEINONI IS THE ONE *in whom evil never attains enough power to capture the "little city," to clothe itself in the body and make it sin. That is to say, the three garments of the animal soul (nefesh ha-behamit)—thought, word, and deed— originating in the shell of materiality (kelippah) do not prevail over the divine soul (nefesh ha-elohit) within one to the extent of clothing themselves in the body—in the mind, the mouth, and the other 248 organs—thereby causing them to sin and defile themselves, God forbid.*

The "little city" is the body, which, like a medieval city, needs to be fortified and defended against forces that would overrun it and bring it to ruin. It is disputed territory in a 'holy war' being waged between two opposing forces: the *nefesh ha-behamit*, the 'animal soul,' which would bring it to ruin, and the *nefesh ha-elohit*, the 'divine soul,' which would elevate it to holiness. For Reb Shneur Zalman teaches us that there is a basic duality, almost a schism within in us, caused by these two magnetic poles.[187]

Nevertheless, there is hope, for he also tells us that there is a kind of fulcrum between these poles—like the lever railroad switchmen pull to shift the tracks and change the course of a train—called the *nefesh ha-sikhlit*, or the 'rational soul,' which can shift the balance one way or the other. The rational soul in human beings can 'give reason' to the impulses coming from either the animal or the divine soul. Unfortunately, though impulses come from both, we usually give-in to the wishes of the animal soul more readily than we do to those of the divine soul. Often, we do this by default, moving from impulse to action almost without a thought. At other times, we do it by an interesting 'rationalization' process; for instance, justifying another piece of apple pie as if it were just as healthy for us as an apple.

But the rational soul can also weigh the potential and probable consequences of our actions, making good decisions based on this process of reasoning. In the war between competing impulses—animal and divine—

it might reason: "Really, I could have that piece of pie; after all it is kosher and certainly not forbidden. But I also know that I'm pretty full already, and have to wonder if it is 'good for me'—either physically or spiritually—to give into the wishes of the animal soul. Will I lose the weight I am trying to lose? Will I have taken a step toward releasing myself from the hold of my animal impulses? *Surely not.* If I can be self-disciplined now, I'll find greater freedom afterward. Therefore, I'll abstain."

This is the process of the *nefesh ha-sikhlit* through which we make decisions about our "thoughts, words, and deeds," the "three garments" in which we 'clothe ourselves' in any given moment. Now, we can wear the 'clean clothes' of the divine soul or the 'dirty clothes' of the animal soul; it is up to us. So the rational soul should always be asking, "How should I 'dress' for this moment?" i.e. what is the etiquette appropriate for this moment: if I allow myself to lose my temper or drift into some prurient thought, what will be the outcome?

> ONLY THE THREE GARMENTS *of the divine soul are governing the body of the* beinoni, *that is to say, the thoughts, words, and deeds related to the 613 mitzvot of the Torah. The* beinoni *has not committed, nor will commit a transgression; the name* rasha, *'wicked,' cannot be applied to the* beinoni, *even momentarily.*

Now, here is where things get really interesting; for while the Talmud seems to suggest that the *beinoni* is just 'average'—neither very good, nor very wicked—we see that Reb Shneur Zalman's *beinoni* is something far more than average. Indeed, who among us would not call the *beinoni* extraordinary? For Reb Shneur Zalman tells us explicitly that, while the *beinoni* still struggles with negativity and the urge toward it, the *beinoni* is *never* guilty of succumbing to the temptation in behavior. This is a long way from our understanding of 'average' or 'intermediate.' When this is considered 'intermediate'—between righteous and wicked—most of us, like Abbaye, have to come to terms with the reality of being classified as 'conditionally wicked,' at best! For even one negative act brings one into the category of the *rasha sh'eino gamur,* or the 'conditionally wicked.' Thus it appears that most of humankind—from those who 'sin' only rarely to those who 'sin' fairly often—can be classed under the category of the conditionally wicked.

The 'completely wicked,' or *rasha gamur,* is just that, totally under the governance of negative emotions and the habits of the body. These people are described as completely malevolent and devoid of goodness. They are the opposite of the completely righteous, just as rare, and we might even say, just as unrealistic a category.

You see, the major problem with this and the earlier talmudic paradigm is the sense of a 'locked,' or 'static' identity: in the former, it is a *quantitative* identity, the aggregate of deeds at any given point in one's lifetime defining whether a person is righteous or wicked; in the latter model, it appears to be a *qualitative* identity in a rigid hierarchy which, while theoretically scalable, seems unrealistic with regard to human frailty and becoming. However, I would not say that these categories are altogether wrong, just that they are inaccurate when projected as rigid identities on the human being who is always in transition. Nevertheless, I do not believe that Reb Shneur Zalman was truly suggesting such a static model as is sometimes supposed.

With regard to the statement, "The *beinoni* has not committed, nor will commit a transgression," my Rebbe, Reb Menachem Mendel Schneerson II (1902-1994) has said that this does not mean that the *person* has not committed a transgression and will not, but that the *beinoni* has not and will not.[188] What does this mean? A person is a *beinoni* only as long a he or she is *being* a *beinoni*; while one is in that 'mode,' as it were, one is so distant from one's past sins—and potential future sins—that it is as if they don't exist!

So let's go back and re-examine these five categories again from a new perspective. Let's try to think of our participation in the world at any given moment as being characterized by one of five different states of consciousness, with the aggregate of these momentary-modes—during any given period of time—determining the relative wholeness or health of the individual for that period, *not one's identity*.

Now, each of these five states of consciousness expresses a particular quality of being in a specific moment of decision, and might be re-cast in terms of how much of the divine soul can penetrate them in that moment. Thus, we might think of them in the following terms: 'luminous transparency,' 'relative transparency,' 'translucence,' 'relative opacity,' and 'absolute opacity.' Again, these are not rigid *identities,* but temporary *states of consciousness* in the moment of decision. So, for instance, luminous transparency would be a state of consciousness in which there is not the slightest inclination to invest energy in negativity or a negative act. It is a pure, momentary expression of Divinity in the human being, the ego having become transparent to a *hierophany*, a divine manifestation, free of personal agenda.

Relative transparency then is a state of consciousness in which there may yet be a mild inclination to invest energy in ego-driven agendas, but one succeeds fairly easily in making the ego transparent to the need of the moment, and behaves according to that need. In both of these states, the 'luminous' and the 'relative,' it is still the divine soul (sharing a common ontology with God) that is dominant. Thus, in these states of 'transparency,' one cannot act against the desire of the divine soul or the pure will of the moment, for it would be tantamount to acting against one's own nature.

Just below relative transparency on this scale is the state of 'translucence,' corresponding to the *beinoni*. Now, translucence refers to the diffusion of light as it passes through an object, making objects on the other side appear less distinct; this refers to the state in which one consciously *struggles* with negative, ego-based impulses, but does not succumb to them in actual behavior. Again, it is the fulcrum of the five states, the place of conscious 'turning,' and thus is the state most advantageous to the spiritual practitioner.

In terms of behavior, translucence is the same as transparency, because in action at least, one has succeeded in overcoming the negative impulse. Choice is critical for the person in the state of translucence and this is what makes this state most human. Translucence is a conscious choice not to draw energy from negativity, but rather from the pure well of the divine will; and this decision makes an impression on general consciousness that may, in time, create a positive pattern, opening one to deeper levels of transparency. It is this mode, says Reb Shneur Zalman, that is available to *all of us, all the time.*

Nevertheless, if our relative wholeness, or spiritual health is poor, we may suspect that the balance of our decisions has shifted into the realm of 'relative opacity.' In this state of consciousness, the inclination toward negativity dominates the moment of decision and the battle for transparency-in-action is lost. There is still a little light shining 'through a glass darkly'—the divine will whispering the need of the moment—but it is dimmed by the opacity of one's egoic desires. In behavior, it is either fully opaque, or more likely an admixture, minutely 'warped' for the good by the opposing pull of the divine soul.

'Absolute opacity,' of course, is just that, a momentary eclipse of the light of the divine soul by a negative impulse. The critical difference here between relative opacity and absolute opacity is the absence of conscience. It is a momentary malevolence—whatever the particular act—absent of goodness. Again, this does not speak to identity, but to one's health and wholeness, or the lack thereof. Absolute opacity is utter separation from God in consciousness.[189]

In this way, we can see that these five states represent a spectrum of human consciousness and potential integration, as Reb Shneur Zalman describes:

However, the essence and being of *the divine soul, which is to say, its ten faculties (i.e., the ten sefirot), do not hold a constant and undisputed sway over the "little city," except at very specific times, such as during the recitation of the Shema or the Amidah. At these times—when the celestial mind is in a sublime state—here below, it is a propitious time for the* beinoni *to bind their* HaBaD *(hokhmah, binah, da'at, i.e., higher spiritual faculties) to God, contemplating the greatness of the blessed* Ain Sof, *the 'infinite One,' arousing a burning love in the right chamber of the heart, and adhering to God through the fulfillment of the Torah and its mitzvot as acts of love.... At such times, the evil contained in the left chamber of the heart is subdued and nullified by the goodness that suffuses the right chamber from the* HaBaD *(higher spiritual faculties) of the mind, which are bound to the greatness of the blessed* Ain Sof.

Nevertheless, after prayer, when this sublime state of the blessed Ain Sof *recedes, the evil in the left chamber reawakens, and the* beinoni *begins to feel desire for the world and its delights once again.*[190]

So here we see that some situations have a greater potential for introducing the light of the divine soul into our consciousness than others. At these times, we are best able to touch the place of the *tzaddik*, opening to the infinite dimension of God as *Ain Sof*. But, as the Alter Rebbe says, this situation cannot last, and the pull of the animal soul begins to reassert itself fairly quickly. Nevertheless, this description of a period in which a particular consciousness—in this case, that of the *tzaddik*—holds sway, brings up the issue of identity again.

The Sufi tradition has particularly good language for dealing with these issues, speaking of the difference between a *hal* and a *maqam*. A *hal* is understood to be a temporary 'state,' such as ecstasy, while a *maqam* is a 'station,' or a 'level' of sustained spiritual integration. Thus, it is understood in Sufism that while a person may have an ecstatic or illuminating experience in prayer, it doesn't necessarily indicate any change in their spiritual identity. It is an experience, not a promotion to the rank of enlightened being.

The *maqam*, however, is more difficult to describe; for it is both solid and fluid at the same time. That is to say, it is a general state. For instance, a person might conceivably reach a certain level of maturity on the spiritual path—let us say—acting mostly as a *beinoni*, but is still capable of falling into foolishness, and occasionally of reaching higher. But neither the 'reaching higher,' nor 'falling lower' really has much effect on their station in general. It is as if they are standing on a large platform: from that platform, they may leap up and feel assured of landing solidly on the platform again; and if they happen to fall down, they are only falling on the platform itself. That is to say, people who have reached a certain level of sustained spiritual integration do fall, but they don't often fall off the platform entirely and tend to get up without too much difficulty. It is the tendency to get up, or the consistency of their getting up, that keeps them at that level.[191]

Now, THE LEVEL OF THE BEINONI *is one that is possible for everyone to attain; and let everyone aspire to it. For anyone can become a* beinoni *at any time. The* beinoni *does not abhor evil altogether, for a battle rages in the heart, and does not go the same at all times; but to "turn away from evil and do good"*[192] *in actual behavior— in thought, word, and deed—is something we may choose for ourselves. For even when one's heart craves and desires a physical pleasure—whether permitted or forbidden—one can prevail over this craving with a counter-desire, saying to the heart: "I don't want to be wicked, even for one moment! Under no circumstances do I wish to be severed and separated from God, Heaven forbid! As it says, 'Your iniquities separate you from God.'"*[193]

It was probably in such a moment that the young Hasid, Reb Yekusiel of Lieple, first 'introduced' himself to Reb Shneur Zalman. . . .

Overcome with zeal on his first visit to Liozhna, Reb Yekusiel of Lieple climbed up on the roof of Reb Shneur Zalman's house and pressed himself against the window of the attic where the Rebbe had his study. When he was sure the Rebbe had seen him, he called aloud with great anguish in his voice, "Rebbe, cut off my left side!" Feeling compassion for him, Reb Shneur Zalman motioned for him to come in and he blessed him.[194]

You see, with this he was saying, "Rebbe, please relieve me of the impulses coming from the left side of my heart," from whence come the disturbing urges of the animal soul. At that moment, he wanted nothing more than to be all 'right side,' completely in the service of the divine soul. This is what Reb Shneur Zalman is talking about here.

RATHER, I DESIRE TO UNITE *my* **nefesh, ruaḥ,** *and* **neshamah** *(animative, emotive, and intellectual manifestations of the divine soul) with God, investing them in the three blessed garments of God—thought, word, and deed—as I dedicate myself to Torah and the performance of* **mitzvot** *out of love for God, which is planted deep within my heart, and the heart of all of Yisra'el, who are called 'lovers of Your name.'*[195] *Why, even the most unworthy vessel can offer their soul for the sanctification of Your Name; am I inferior to such a person?"*[196]

So this is the way that Reb Shneur Zalman recommends for his Hasidim, setting the bar high enough to deflate the ego, but not so high as to discourage them from making the effort to attain it. Now you might ask, "What happened to the original statement that he set out to clarify in the beginning?" *"Be righteous, and be not wicked; but even if the whole world tells you that you are righteous, regard yourself as if you were wicked."* This paradox—as Reb Shneur Zalman presents it—is left open. Nevertheless, the explanation is there for the careful reader to discover. It is the same answer that was given to the *mitnagdim* in the teaching of the Ba'al Shem Tov, quoted earlier and implied by Rabbah's comment, "I, for example, am in-between" (righteousness and wickedness); for, according to Hasidism, there is no righteousness without sincere humility and heartfelt *teshuvah*.[197] So why didn't he make this explicit from the beginning instead of seeming to price the level of the *tzaddik* out of the market?

I think the simple answer is that he wasn't writing a book for himself, but for a group of Hasidim with particular needs. Remember, he was a Rebbe for the heady Lithuanians—recently defected from the camp of the *mitnagdim*—many of whom already considered themselves *tzaddikim*, as we saw earlier from the great debate in Minsk. Indeed, one famous ḤaBaD Hasid, Reb Hillel of Paritch once said, "Before I studied the *Tanya*, I thought I was a *tzaddik*; but afterword, I thought, 'Would that I were a *beinoni!*'"[198] So whether the Alter Rebbe was hoping to bring his more brilliant students to humility or to give the less talented a more attainable goal, his approach worked.[199]

According to one ḤaBaD tradition, Reb Shneur Zalman had actually composed a book called *Sefer Shel Tzaddikim*, 'Book of the Righteous,' but this book, along with his *Shulḥan Arukh* burned in a great fire, whose origin we will discuss later ...

AFTER A GREAT FIRE CONSUMED HIS HOME, Reb Shneur Zalman approached his son, Reb Dov Baer, and asked if he had happened to read from the book called Sefer Shel Tzaddikim *in his study—"If you could mention even a single item from it, it might help me to reconstruct the whole!"*

But Reb Dov Baer said, "I'm sorry father—the book was marked, 'Under the ban of Rabbeinu Gershom in this world and the next'—so I dared not read from it!"[200]

Reb Shneur Zalman sighed heavily and said, "For Ḥasidut, you should have dared."[201]

The book in Hasidism that is addressed directly to the *tzaddikim* is the *No'am Elimelekh* of Reb Elimelekh of Lizhensk (1717-1786). In it, Reb Elimelekh deals only with the *tzaddik* and *rasha*; there is no *beinoni* in his teaching.[202] Perhaps Reb Shneur Zalman's *Sefer Shel Tzaddikim* was never *about* the *tzaddik*, but *for* the *tzaddik*, a manual such as Reb Elimelekh's in which he says: "The great realization of the *tzaddikim* is that they cannot reach perfection. This is what distinguishes them as *tzaddikim*. The longer they are in service to God, the more they become aware of the fact that they cannot attain to the level of perfect service, for theirs' is a path without limits, and this awareness is itself service."[203] Nevertheless, the *No'am Elimelekh* already existed, whereas there was nothing like the *Sefer Shel Beinonim of the Tanya* anywhere else in all of Hasidic or Kabbalistic literature. It is a unique treasure and a guide to all ḤaBaD Hasidim.[204]

When I was in *yeshiva*, you would still hear talk of the legendary Hasid, Reb Itche *der Masmid*. His real name was Rabbi Yitzhak HaLevi Horowitz (ca. 1885-1941), and I suppose when he was traveling as the Rebbe's special envoy, he was actually called by that name and treated as a kind of foreign dignitary; but in Lubavitch, he was held in even higher esteem and called, 'Reb Itche,' after the familiar fashion of Hasidim, and '*der Masmid*,' which was to say, he studied Torah and Ḥasidut with *hatmada*, 'diligence.' So great was his diligence in the life of Ḥasidut that my Rebbe, Reb Yosef Yitzhak of Lubavitch, called him a "*beinoni shel ha-Tanya*," meaning that he was a ḤaBaD Hasid who lived up to the holy ideal set by the Alter Rebbe. As you have seen, this was no idle compliment in Lubavitch. To call someone a "*beinoni shel ha-Tanya*" was the highest praise for any ḤaBaD Hasid, and very few Hasidim in the history of the lineage would have been worthy of such a compliment—Reb Eisik of Homil, Reb Hillel of Paritch, and a few others.

Likewise, the Rebbe empowered Reb Itche to take prayer requests *(kvittlakh)* from Hasidim, which was extraordinary trust.

Reb Itche was famous in his day as a great *ShaDaR (shluḥa d'rabbanan),* 'emissary of the Rebbes,' in Russia, Europe and America, establishing *yeshivot* and collecting money for the Rebbe's projects. But he was still more famous for his *Ḥasidut*. The older Hasidim who knew him would speak of how Reb Itche would "*daven* all day, and *farbreng* all night," and we used to talk about Reb Itche's daily routine with a look of awe, and celebrate it as a kind of model for all ḤaBaD Hasidim to strive after. You see, the Rebbe's actions were behind a veil most of the time, so Hasidim like Reb Itche *der Masmid* were providing the example of what we could do in our own lives; and because of him, we knew it was actually possible for a Hasid to be a *beinoni shel ha-Tanya*.[205]

ḤaBaD Psychology and Meditation

Now, once the Hasid begins to understand *who* the players are in the drama of the soul, and even more importantly, *where* the fulcrum of decision is, then the issue is *how* to unseat the habits of the animal soul and replace them with those of the divine soul. It is this question that brings us to ḤaBaD, the central concept of Reb Shneur Zalman's teaching, whose emphasis has marked all of his heirs up to the present day.

So let's take a look at what Reb Shneur Zalman means by ḤaBaD, and then turn to how it is used by his Hasidim. In the third chapter of the *Tanya, Sefer Shel Beinonim,* he gives the following description of ḤaBaD:

> THE TEN SEFIROT, or 'divine attributes,' are divided into two categories, called the three "mothers" and the seven "multiples."[206] The first are *ḥokhmah (wisdom), binah (understanding)* and *da'at (knowing),* and the second correspond to the "seven days of creation"—*ḥesed (loving-kindness), gevurah (severity), tiferet (beauty),* and so on [the others being, *netzaḥ (victory), hod (glory), yesod (foundation),* and *malkhut (sovereignty)*].[207]

These ten *sefirot* are the divine qualities or agencies through which creation was accomplished; thus everything in creation has its origin in one of these *sefirot*, or some combination of them. They are perhaps best understood in terms of their own evolutionary dynamics, flowing down from the top to the bottom of the *etz ḥayyim*, or 'Tree of Life,' like an idea slowly evolving into an action: *hokhmah*, the seed-idea containing the whole sequence; *binah*, the detailed taxonomy of the qualities inherent in the idea; *da'at*, forecasting the possible life of the idea; *hesed*, an open and overflowing expression of it; *gevurah*, the naming of its constraints, boundaries, and limitations; *tiferet*, finding the balance between the ideal and the constraints; *netzah*, raw efficacy, moving boldly toward the accomplishment of an end; *hod*, shaping that bold movement into something more polite and elegant; *yesod*, finding an efficient balance between efficacy and elegance; and *malkhut*, the accomplishment or manifestation of the idea.

The upper three *sefirot*—*hokhmah*, *binah*, *da'at*—are the three "mothers," which give birth to the seven "multiples," their children—*hesed*, *gevurah*, *tiferet*, *netzah*, *hod*, *yesod*, and *malkhut*.[208] When he says that these latter seven correspond to the "seven days of creation," he is saying that each of those seven days was dominated by one of these seven qualities, but he leaves it to us to work out the correspondences for ourselves.

This is one of the notions that led me to design the popular rainbow colored prayer-shawl called the "B'nai Or Tallit." Sometime in the 1950s, I was meditating on the *midrash*, "How did God create the world? He wrapped in a robe of light and it began to shine"[209] and I suddenly imagined a prayer-shawl that was like a rainbow of light with each color representing one of the *sefirot* and its corresponding day of creation:

> The first day of creation *(hesed)* is represented by a two-toned purple or violet stripe, for on that day God said, "Let there be light" (Gen 1:3), and the visible spectrum of light begins with violet which emerges from the invisible 'darkness' of ultra-violet light.
>
> The second day of creation *(gevurah)* is represented by a broad blue stripe, for on that day God said, "Let there be an expanse in the midst of the water, that it may separate water from water" (Gen 1:6), creating the sky and the oceans, which are both blue.
>
> The third day of creation *(tiferet)* is represented by a two green stripes, for on that day God said, "Let the water below the sky be gathered in one area, that the dry land may appear" (Gen 1:9), and "Let the earth sprout vegetation" (Gen 1:11); so it is green for the earth's vegetation, and there are two stripes because God twice saw that "it was good" on that day.
>
> The fourth day of creation *(netzah)* is represented by a single yellow stripe, for on that day God said, "Let there be lights in the

expanse of the sky" (Gen 1:14), meaning the Sun, the Moon, and the stars.

The fifth day of creation *(hod)* is represented by a single orange stripe, for on that day God said, "Let the waters bring forth swarms of living creatures, and birds that fly above the earth across the expanse of the sky" (Gen 1:20); these are the egg-laying creatures whose yolks are orange.

The sixth day of creation *(yesod)* is represented by two red stripes, for on that day God said, "Let the earth bring forth every kind of living creature" (Gen. 1:24) and "Let us make the human being in our image" (Gen 1:26);[210] so these two stripes are red for blood of human beings—"For the life of the flesh is in the blood" (Lev. 17:11)—and the other placental mammals.

The seventh day of creation *(malkhut)* is represented by a broad alternating black and red stripe representing infrared, for on that day, "God ceased from the work of creation" (Gen 2:3) and did not need to do anything but be sovereign over the earth. In the Kabbalah, the attribute of *malkhut*, or 'sovereignty' is receptive just as infrared is receptive in absorbing the radiation of other colors.[211]

The first of these was a heavy reindeer wool *tallit* made by a weaver in New Haven, Connecticut, but it was more a blanket than a *tallit*. So I eventually contacted a weaver named Karen Bulow in Montreal who made *Vetements Religieux*, and she made the first five B'nai Or *tallitot*.[212] Among my ḤaBaD-Lubavitcher friends, only one person truly appreciated this *tallit*, and that was Reb Hendel Lieberman (1900-1976), the father of Hasidic art and the first of the Lubavitch painters whose art is on so many walls and calendars now.[213]

Now, let's return to Reb Shneur Zalman and his presentation of ḤaBaD, as he goes on to talk about how this cosmic process of 'conception' is reflected in the human being, likening it to our own mental and emotional processes, as follows:

LIKEWISE, THE HUMAN SOUL *is also divided into two categories:* sekhel, *the 'intellect,' and* middot, *'emotions.' The intellect in us is made up of* wisdom, understanding, and knowing—ḥokhmah, binah, da'at (ḤaBaD)—*while the* emotions (having to do with the divine) *are love, awe, and wonder at God's beauty*—ḥesed, gevurah, tiferet (HaGaT)—*and so on. The* ḤaBaD *faculties of the intellect are the "mothers" which give birth to the emotions.*

How can this be? Within the nefesh ha-sikhlit, or 'rational soul,' the first conception of something is called ḥokhmah, which is also koaḥ mah, the 'potentiality of what-is.'[214] *Then one can move this idea from its infinite potential to a definite end by using the binah of our intellect to understand the seed-concept, delving into its very depths, and evolving it to another stage. In this way, ḥokhmah and binah are the 'father' and 'mother' which give birth to love (ahavah) and awe (yirah) . . . before God.*

So it should be clear from this that ḤaBaD—an acrostic meaning, 'wisdom,' 'understanding,' and 'knowing'—in Reb Shneur Zalman's thought, refers to a mental process of 'apprehension.' Elsewhere, he calls these three critical attributes, the moḥin, or 'brains,' which parallels what we know of our own triune brains: ḥokhmah, the right hemisphere, capable of concept formation, looking at something holistically in its totality, a flash of insight; binah, the left hemisphere, capable of understanding something thoroughly, analyzing the insight into its component parts; and da'at, which might be compared to the pons in the brain, the seat of the reticular formation system, the 'switchboard' which tells us what to pay attention to and what to ignore. Together, these three aspects of mind constitute a process of mentation that leads to emotion, which in turn becomes the basis for an action.[215]

Now, this tripartite process happens in a blink of an eye thousands of times a day without our ever knowing it. Occasionally, we make more important decisions, going through the process a little more slowly, weighing the decision, and considering its consequences. But even then we are not usually aware of the *process*—we are simply doing it. The innovation of the Alter Rebbe is to suggest that we make this natural process *conscious*, that we make *deliberate* what is automatic, and still more important, that we put what is essentially neutral in the service of the *good*. For when the mind grasps and surrounds an idea, at that same moment, that idea also has the mind in its grasp. If it's an idea of sin or hatred, it is as if one is in the grasp of sin or hatred, in a Hell of one's own making. But if it's an idea of holiness, one is in the grasp of holiness and filled with the wonder of Heaven, as it were. The emotions fostered by these ideas—the 'pain of Hell' and the 'joys of Heaven'—then lead to actions which end up perpetuating these same emotional states, whether they be negative or positive. So, the Alter Rebbe suggests: if negative habits (stemming from the animal soul) are established and reinforced in this way, then why shouldn't we establish better habits in their place through a more deliberate engagement of (the divine soul in) *ḥokhmah, binah,* and *da'at*?

WHEN THE INTELLECT *of the* nefesh ha-sikhlit, *the 'rational soul' contemplates and immerses itself deeply in the greatness of God—understanding how Divinity is both* m'malleh kol almin, *'filling-all-worlds,' and* sovev kol almin, *'surrounding-all-worlds,' and how everything is considered as nothing before it—the mind gives birth to awe and a real awareness of God's majesty, achieving a true humility before the greatness of the blessed One, who is* Ain Sof, *'without limits.' Thus, the heart will be full of an overwhelming awe, and will glow like a burning ember with an intense and passionate love of God, and the soul will yearn and long for the expansive greatness of the blessed* Ain Sof, *the origin and ultimate destination of the soul's passion.*

For the moment, set aside the three kabbalistic concepts mentioned here—*m'malleh kol almin*, *sovev kol almin*, and *Ain Sof*—and focus instead on the activity the Alter Rebbe recommends and the outcome he predicts. He says, "the 'rational soul' contemplates and immerses itself deeply in the greatness of God," and this causes the heart to be "full of an overwhelming awe," and to "glow like a burning ember with an intense and passionate love of God." In short, he is speaking about ḤaBaD meditation, or more precisely, ḤaBaD contemplation, whose goal is to beget love and awe for God.

According to Reb Shneur Zalman, if you want to make a strong shift in your reality, you have to engage the rational soul in a deep form of contemplation that he calls *hitbonenut*. Literally, this is 'self-construction' and is related to the *sefirah* of *binah* in particular. For *binah* asks the question, "How is it put together?" Likewise, the word *boneh* means, 'to build.' So *hitbonenut* is the process through which one 'constructs' a picture of reality. But not just any picture. Reb Shneur Zalman wants his disciples to use this practice to anchor themselves in particular concepts—the love of God, the immanence and transcendence of God, etc.—to the point where these concepts become realities for them. For when these are so anchored, he believes, one is no longer capable of falling into the same level of sin. It would simply run against the grain of the newly conceived picture of reality. Today, we might call this a form of 'cognitive restructuring,' wherein unhealthy and unhelpful thoughts are undermined and replaced with more healthy and helpful thoughts, which in turn, might beget healthy emotions and beneficial actions.

DA'AT, 'KNOWING,' *is to be understood in the sense of the verse, "And Adam knew (yada'a) Hava,"*[216] *which implies a bond of deep intimacy and union. Thus, one can bind one's knowing to the blessed and unlimited greatness of* Ain Sof *with a deep, intimate bond, refusing to let go or to be diverted. Even one who grasps the unlimited greatness of* Ain Sof *with the wisdom and understanding of* ḥokhmah *and* binah *must still bind this to the knowing of* da'at, *fixing the idea with firmness and tenacity; for, unless one does so, it will never produce love and awe in the soul, only vain fantasies. Therefore,* da'at *is the source of the emotions, providing them with their substance, including* ḥesed *and* gevurah, *and all their derivatives.*[217]

Even though *hitbonenut*, as a contemplative process, depends upon the 'building' capacity of *binah*, it is *da'at* that actually makes it transformative for the meditator; for *da'at* is the "spiritual-sense perception of a concept," which almost allows us to speak of an *eros* of knowledge.[218] This is still more obvious in a later description, when he says, *da'at* represents "the bond through which the soul is united with and infused into an apprehension . . . the term *da'at* is applied to sexual intercourse, for it signifies a bond that results in issue, just as *da'at* gives birth to emotions."[219] And, we might add, just as certain thoughts produce sexual arousal in your body, so too, certain thoughts arouse your heart with love and awe.

This is the way of ḤaBaD contemplation, using the head to awaken the heart. Reb Avraham Yehoshuah Heschel, the Apter Rav, says in his book, *Ohev Yisra'el*, "Awaken your heart and put your mind to it," but Reb Shneur Zalman asks, "How are you going to do that? What do you do to rouse your heart when it is asleep?" Then he answers, "You take your thoughts in a direction that will awaken the heart with feelings of love and awe."

Two Kinds of Contemplation

Unfortunately, Reb Shneur Zalman wrote very little about the actual practice of *hitbonenut* to which he so often refers in his writings. Nevertheless, we have found one short *ma'amar* (discourse) in which he differentiates between two types of contemplation, and thus gives us a little clearer picture of what *hitbonenut* is all about:[220]

CONCERNING HITBONENUT, *'contemplation'*—its qualities and how it is done—there are two approaches:

The first is hitbonenut klalit, *'general contemplation,'* deepening one's awareness of a subject in a broad and general way, simply noticing what is coming-up around a particular subject; for example, attaching one's mind to what it means to be in a state of bittul, making the ego 'transparent' to God. But while one may think that one is expanding the mind in this process, in truth, it is actually being contracted. For, even considering a subject like yesh mi'ayin—asking what it means to go from divine 'nothingness' (ayin) to 'being' (yesh)—requires a half an hour of general contemplation to arrive at the most basic image and notion of the concept. This is because one is tiring oneself out on superficial things, trying to abstract the idea from its materiality until it is truly 'spiritual.'

The insights one gains from this kind of contemplation are as light as the wind, and are just as easily scattered by the wind; you get a glimpse of something, you blink, and then it's gone. Many have erred and wasted a lot of time pursuing such vague notions and illusions; for general contemplation spends a lot of time on just a couple of ideas, and does not go into details, if you understand my meaning. Nevertheless, it does cause certain physical effects: the body may be moved to trembling, and there may be a swelling and a feeling of excitement in the heart. But without serious mental effort and exhaustion of thought, you will not achieve the state of bittul before God, and your insights will be lost, leaving you with just a little bit of feeling about the subject.

So the Alter Rebbe begins by pointing-out what his contemplation is not: first, it is not a vague musing of the mind, not simply "noticing what is coming-up around a particular subject." A general sweep of the mind, he tells us, may be able to give you a momentary lift, but it doesn't create any transformation inside of you; transformation only happens when you have installed in your reality map that which you have seen in a more detailed contemplation.

HITBONENUT PRATIT, or *'detailed contemplation,'* on the other hand, creates a true deepening of awareness and a real expansion of the mind—not a contraction. This deepening is akin to the deepening acquired through rigorous study of the literal (p'shat) dimensions of revealed (nigleh) subjects. That is to say, by exhausting a subject in the mind, you are creating expansion in it, as one does in rigorous study, bringing in a variety perspectives, issues, and details, expanding it with all the relevant references, and not simply sticking to one subject in your contemplation.

This parallel between "rigorous study" and "detailed contemplation" is something that all of his Hasidim would have understood immediately, but which is far less clear to us today. You have to understand, these Hasidim were already doing something akin to *hitbonenut* in their study of the Talmud ...

> Imagine a young man sitting on a bench at a wooden table studying a *blatt Gemara*, a page of Talmud by candlelight: he reads the *mishnah* out loud; then he goes over the *gemara* around it, asking all the questions of the Sages as if they were his own, and addressing them as if they were present; then he takes a look at what Rashi and the *Tosefot* have to say; and when he has done all this, he goes beyond the Talmud, looking to see what later authorities have to say about the matter, examining the different decisions that have been made about how one has to behave with regard to this matter — the MaHaRSh"A, the MaHaRaM Shif, and the Rosh.[221] And all this time, he is totally absorbed in this dialogue with the sources, sitting in front of this volume of Talmud for hours, a finger resting on his lower lip as he thinks through all of the arguments!

So this kind of total absorption in an intellectual problem was something that they were already used to; fixing the mind on a target and refusing to deviate from it until it was fully resolved wasn't a problem for them. This would be far more difficult for most of us today. On the other hand, these students of Talmud were not yet 'attuned' to the kind of love and awe he desired. So the Alter Rebbe sought to use their already highly developed study skills to bring them to love and awe through contemplation of more refined subjects. For instance, my Rebbe tells of a conversation between Reb Shneur Zalman and his son, Reb Dov Baer on the subjects of their own *hitbonenut* ...

> On the second night of Sukkot in 1799 (5560), Reb Shneur Zalman asked his son about the theme of his contemplation during the prayers of Rosh Hashanah. Reb Dov Baer replied that he had contemplated the phrase from the morning prayers, "The proud shall bow down before you."
>
> Then Reb Dov Baer asked his father, "And you, what theme did you contemplate as you prayed?"
>
> Reb Shneur Zalman answered: "I prayed with the *shtender*" — the wooden prayer-stand on which the prayer-book is laid upon — "while contemplating how material things and physical matter all derive their existence from God's essence."[222]

CONTRARY TO THE EXPERIENCE in *general contemplation*, which is characterized by physical manifestations in the body, the experience in *detailed contemplation* is often characterized by a movement of the more subtle (nefesh) powers in the mind. Indeed, you are so involved in contemplative effort at this time that you may have little or no thought of 'self' at all.

The quality of this contemplation is far removed from the vague notions and illusions associated with general contemplation, but rather, presents itself in the compelling garb of various analogues, allowing one to see it with the mind's eye. From this process will also come new inspiration and a passionate flow of profound insights; each and every word of this contemplative prayer will be infused with special meaning, and a unique intentionality (kavanah)!

You see, the 'HaBaD Method' of contemplation, like the Ignatian and Salesian Methods of Christianity, isn't trying to throw a 'wrench' into the natural workings of the mind, but rather, wishes to engage and direct the process toward spiritual ends. So, whereas many forms of tranquil meditation want to 'tame the tiger' of the mind, calming it into submission, Reb Shneur Zalman actually wants to put it to use and give it a mission; he doesn't take away its objects, he increases them! For how does the mind create understanding? Through information, references, analogues, parallels, and comparisons. By allowing the mind to fill itself up with these things, bringing to bear all of its natural abilities, allowing it to think creatively, "a passionate flow of profound insights" will start to emerge, and "each and every word of this contemplative prayer will be infused with special meaning." Thus, the reality-map of the meditator shifts.

Now, WHEN ONE IS PROFOUNDLY INVOLVED in the subject of contemplation, one has little or no self-awareness, because the heart is completely under the sway of the mind. But, in *general contemplation*, the hitpa'alut or 'affect' one feels is palpably exciting, because one is straining to deal with the subject in its essence without filling the mind (with all the possible associated references and implications for the subject). This palpable excitement is formed through the confluence of two things: the divine content, and an awareness of the self 'cleaving' in deveikut with it. However, this only ends up creating more awareness of the self (yesh), and moving one further away from the nothingness (ayin) of Divinity. This is close to the old way.[223]

Okay, so here is where a number of concepts introduced in this discourse begin to come together. In the beginning, he gives us an example of a typical subject of contemplation: "attaching one's mind to what it means to be in a state of *bittul*, making the ego 'transparent' to God." Now he says, the reason one cannot *achieve* this state of transparency in general contemplation is because the mind is not fully preoccupied; there is just too much room for awareness of the self. But when the mind is fully absorbed in a rigorous contemplation—not to be confused with daydreaming or mental meandering—bringing to bear all of its powers of insight, analysis, and imagination, there is no thought of self! There is only the holy subject of contemplation, meaning that one is actually *in* a state of 'transparency,' or *bittul,* before God during the contemplation of *bittul!*

This, he explains—as we continue the discourse, is also the reason for the different experiences of *hitpa'alut* in general and detailed contemplation. Now, *hitpa'alut* is the affective outcome, experience, or felt-sense of prayer or contemplation. In general contemplation, he tells us, the *hitpa'alut* is often experienced physically, through "a swelling and a feeling of excitement in the heart." And some, because of their attachment to material forms and manifestations, may think this a more elevated *hitpa'alut* (because it is palpable); but, according to Reb Shneur Zalman, the truth is just the opposite. The awareness of physical manifestations only indicates a lack of absorption in the subject of contemplation. Therefore, the *hitpa'alut* of detailed contemplation and true absorption is necessarily more subtle, and is therefore experienced in the internal 'senses' as the "majestic glory of God" washing over one's being.

IN DETAILED CONTEMPLATION, *the* hitpa'alut, *or 'affect' one feels comes from God alone; for one is not making any external effort to come closer to God; one is simply and completely absorbed in the process of contemplation. Therefore, the affective excitement is in the mind, in the simple awareness, but not because one feels 'close to God' and is enjoying that closeness; the self—being absorbed in the majestic glory of God—has no part in it at all.*

From this description, it really seems as if the Alter Rebbe is making an 'Apollonian and Dionysian' contrast, wherein detailed contemplation partakes of Apollon, the divine quality of the Sun and light (i.e., introversion, thinking, and profound absorption) in Greek mythology, and general contemplation partakes of Dionysius, the divine quality of ecstasy and intoxication (i.e., extroversion, feeling, and excitement).

THE EXTERNALS (Ḥitzonim) *flee from this awareness. As it is said, "The fool does not desire understanding,"*[224] *only getting excited when there is a palpable manifestation in the heart; but this is only because he or she is separated from Divinity!*

That is to say, the 'fool' clings to the physical excitement of the body and its animal tendencies; he or she doesn't long for profound understanding, but is only satisfied with more manifest, emotional/physical effects. And these are only experienced because one is still aware of oneself and one's own body, and thus "separated from Divinity!"

THESE ARE THE MARKS *distinguishing the two kinds of* hitpa'alut: *the affect which is based on vague notions and illusions is tainted by vain desires and coarseness; but the affect derived from detailed contemplation is expressed in true humility, because it leads to a state in which one does not feel oneself as a separately existing being. Being distanced from any identification with external feeling and corporeality, one is also distanced from negative attributes, such as anger, vain desires, and pride. There is no sense of personal accomplishment in this contemplation, as one becomes fully transparent to the existence of God.*[225]

Now, this is only a general overview of the rich process of *hitbonenut* as it was originally taught by Reb Shneur Zalman, but it is the most detailed description he seems to have given in public. It is not until we come to the writings of Reb Dov Baer, his son, that we get a fully elaborated description of the practice. So we will wait until we come to him before going into the actual practice any further. Nevertheless, I think it is worthwhile to give a little context to this particular *ma'amar*, for otherwise, it might give some the wrong impression.

You see, there were other Hasidim doing *hitbonenut* in those days, and Reb Shneur Zalman felt that the way in which they were doing it was open to error. So it is possible that this *ma'amar* is at least in part a polemic against their practices. These were likely the senior Hasidim of Reb Shlomo of Karlin and Reb Avraham of Kalisk, with whom he had many disagreements, as we have seen. Thus, he makes an extreme contrast in the presentation of general and detailed contemplation to make a point about their contemplative practices to his own Hasidim. The point is this: general contemplation, with its Dionysian tendencies, is vulnerable to the co-opting powers of the ego, so it is better to engage in the Apollonian process of detailed contemplation, which circumvents the co-opting process of the ego.

Strong contrasts like this one are good for making points, but are less helpful when it comes to discussing the subtleties of actual practice. Clearly, Reb Shneur Zalman is attempting to 'make a fence' around the practice of *hitbonenut,* setting up a strong contrast that will keep his Hasidim on the side of the 'fence' he feels is safest for them; but it also raises certain practical questions which he likely had to deal with in person. For in setting his ideal of divine absorption at such a height, he is asking his Hasidim to 'aim high.' But the truth is, this level of absorption in the subject is difficult to achieve, and is more often the exception than the rule. So one who is still aware of oneself and one's body in the course of their contemplation is bound to feel that they are 'failing' somehow in their contemplation. This is a mistake. Excellent insights and positive shifts can also come from this zone of contemplation, only—accepting the Alter Rebbe's warning—one must be vigilant to guard against the co-opting tendency of the ego in it, which is always trying to build a more prominent presentation of the self out of our experiences. In this, as with all things, we must throw ourselves on God's mercy, hoping to escape the pitfall of pride.

It is true that there are times when you are so absorbed in your contemplation that you don't hear, you don't see, you don't know anything else, you don't even feel yourself. This also happens to us occasionally when we are engrossed in a good book or a piece of music, and it is a wonderful experience. But even when this is not the case, don't give up on your contemplation. I have had very deep and wonderful experiences doing *hitbonenut* when 'I wasn't there,' lost in *Nishmat Kol Ḥai,* seeing it in all of its details, but I have also had very deep and wonderful experiences when 'I was there,' aware of my own ecstatic love for God, and *'feeling* the intense longing for *deveikut.'* We need the enjoyable *limbic* experience of God just as much as we need the more subtle awakening to Divinity in the cortex; so take the Alter Rebbe's warning and ideal as guideposts to keep you on course as you experiment with *hitbonenut,* using it to deepen your love of God and to broaden your experience of Divinity.

Faith and Knowledge

As we have seen, the purpose of *hitbonenut* is to refine a Hasid's spiritual sensibilities, distancing them "from negative attributes, such as anger, lust, and pride," and creating "true humility." But there is another byproduct of *hitbonenut* that deserves our attention, one which is briefly alluded to in the previous discourse—namely, a "new inspiration and a passionate flow of profound insights" in one's contemplation, infusing "each and every word . . . with special meaning."

Studying the many great *ma'amarim*, or 'discourses' of the Alter Rebbe—collected in the *Likkutei Torah* and *Torah Or*—I am left with the distinct impression that what one is learning in them is likely the direct result of the Alter Rebbe's own contemplative exercises. It is as if we have been given transcripts of his own contemplations and been allowed to peek inside his personal process. Thus, I want give over part of one such *ma'amar* here, both as an example of what a "detailed contemplation" in *hitbonenut* might have looked like for the Alter Rebbe, but also as an important teaching advocating the use of *hitbonenut* in relation to the immanent 'knowledge' of God filling all existence.

Now, how does a Hasidic *ma'amar* begin? An old ḤaBaDnick once said, "The ears open the mouth . . . and the ears can close the mouth."[226] That is to say, it begins with the Hasidim, with their attitude, their ability to listen, and their own willing attunement to the Rebbe. So if the Hasidim desire to hear something from the Rebbe, they have to change the atmosphere and make it a place of listening. So, from some place in the room, a *niggun*, a 'melody' is begun, sometimes by an elder Hasid, sometimes by the Rebbe, and sometimes by a Hasid at the Rebbe's direction. But, however it starts, the *niggun* is the means by which the Hasidim prepare themselves to receive, creating an opening for a teaching to come through the Rebbe and into the hearts of the Hasidim. In the silence, just after the melody fades, the Rebbe begins to speak in sing-song voice, uttering a single *passuk*, or 'verse' from scripture . . .[227]

"AND YOU SHALL KNOW today, and take it to heart, that Yah is God—in Heaven above and Earth below—there is nothing else." (Deut. 4:39)[228]

Let's begin with the introductory *passuk*, "And you shall know today, and take it to heart . . ." If we look at these introductory words in the literal Hebrew, they would come out as, "And you shall know today, *and put it back into your heart . . .*" The implication is that this knowledge—"that *Yah* is God, in heaven above and earth below—there is nothing else," originated in the heart, but has somehow become distanced from it over time. So we are now being told to 'know it' with our mind, and to 'bring it back' into our heart! In this, we can already see the emphasis of ḤaBaD Hasidism, to use the mind to awaken the heart to the love of God.

It is necessary to fully understand the meaning of the word da'at, *'knowledge,' and the content of the word* emunah, *'faith'; for they are two distinct* mitzvot.[229] *It is written, "Know the God of your parents,"[230] which refers to a fully conscious apprehension and intelligent understanding. It is also written, "And they believed, having faith in Yah."[231] Now, what the world usually calls 'faith'—believing that the blessed and holy One is giving life to everything, creating all the worlds* (olamot), *and bringing them forth from nothingness* (ayin) *into being* (yesh)—*does not deserve to be called 'faith.'*

Right away, the Alter Rebbe wants to distinguish 'knowledge' and 'faith' as two separate *mitzvot*, or 'commandments,' and to make two major points: the first has to do with the *necessary* criteria for faith, and the second with what concepts *require* faith. For Reb Shneur Zalman says, you don't need faith for that which *reason* can handle. Often, people say, "I have reason to believe . . ." What do they mean by that? If they mean that their reason has stretched as far as it can, and their faith has been placed on top of that, that is better than applying faith to things you can actually know by reason alone. That is to say, your faith is weak if you haven't filled up the extra space with all that reason can know by itself.

This makes a lot of sense to most of us, but then he makes an amazing statement: "believing that the blessed and holy One is giving life to everything, creating all the worlds, and bringing them forth from nothingness into being" doesn't require faith! According to him, this knowledge of divine immanence is actually something that we can get from reason. What requires faith—he says in another part of the *ma'amar*—is the statement, "For I, Y-H-V-H, have not changed" (Mal. 3:6),[232] which has to do with the immutable nature and the utter transcendence of God.

It is an error to suppose that one needs faith for this, for this can be fully sensed under the category of 'sight.' For even though one does not 'see' this with the eyes, it can become so clear in the 'mind's eye,' that it is as if one actually saw it. As it is says, "From my flesh I envision God."[233] For, "from my flesh" refers to the way in which I can 'see' how the life of my body is dependant on the soul residing in it. Were it not for the soul giving life to the body—quickening it with its presence—there would be no life in the body.

What does he mean here with regard to the body? How is it 'reasonable' to assume the existence of the soul? When he says, "it is *as if* one actually saw it," he means that it is self-evident. As anyone who has ever seen a dead body knows—especially the body of someone close to them—it is immediately clear that there is 'something' missing. The body is literally, 'life-less.' I remember seeing the body of my uncle when I was a child and thinking to myself, "That's not him."[234] It was so obvious at that moment that the body was not the person. Whatever that spark of life is—as yet undetermined by science—it is so noticeably absent in a dead body, that the existence of that 'spark' seems self-evident to us. It is not a matter of faith; it is so clear that "it is *as if* one actually saw it."[235]

SIMILARLY, I CAN SENSIBLY ENVISAGE GOD; *for just as the soul inhabits the human body, I can see how all the worlds—derived from the blessed and infinite One, who brings them into being, enlivening them and giving them existence—are like an immense 'body,' occupying vast reaches of space—including the spiritual beings contained in them, such as angels and individual souls—in which the divine life resides like a soul.*

This is a good example of how the Alter Rebbe uses the analogues he recommends in 'detailed contemplation.' Just as there is a spark of life in the body, he can see how there might also be an analogous spark of life quickening all the worlds. Of course, he is speaking in principle, and not scientifically. But it is important to remember that reasoning is not to be equated with scientific facts. Everyday we make 'reasonable assumptions' about things that we can't immediately verify, but which are nevertheless important 'hand-holds' in our daily climb through life. Someone who feels that they have seen a vision of an angel or a departed friend, who by various other means determines that they are not hallucinating or insane, thinks it reasonable to assume that 'angels' or 'echoes' of their friends might yet exist somewhere. In the same way, Reb Shneur Zalman, and most of the Hasidic masters, were thoroughly convinced of God's quickening all the worlds and 'saw' other spiritual realities as if they were established facts.

CONCERNING THIS, *it is written, "Lift high your eyes and see who created these,"*[236] *for this knowledge is sensibly felt, as if one saw it. Thus, this is not to be defined as* emunah, *'faith,' in the holy tongue, but with the word* da'at, *'knowledge.' Now, the word* da'at *refers to a recognition and a feeling, for it is the profound feeling in the heart of one whose attention does not waver.*[237] *Such knowledge becomes a memorial before the mind's eye; it is unforgettable and does not pass from the heart. However, the word* hirhur, *'a fleeting thought,' a rehearsal*

> *of an action, does not cause anything, for it is not even on the same level as speech. Thus, when we are advised, "Know the God of your parents," the word* da'at *is used. We mean to attain by this that immanent category of divinity called* m'malleh kol almin, *'fills-all-worlds.'*[238]

So how do we go about fulfilling the commandment, "Know the God of your parents," the God of history who creates all things? We use the analogue the Alter Rebbe has just given us: just as the body cannot live without the soul quickening it, neither could the worlds if God were not supporting and infusing them with life. That is to say, if God were not saying, "Be! Live!" they would cease to exist. Without God *believing* in them, they would have no existence at all. This is an important concept to understand, especially as we are drawing fine distinctions between the words 'knowledge' and 'faith.' In the same way, the German Christian theologian, Paul Tillich (1886-1965) draws a strong distinction between 'faith' and 'belief,' saying:

> The most ordinary interpretation of faith is to consider it an act of knowledge that has a low degree of evidence. Something more or less probable or improbable is affirmed in spite of the insufficiency of its theoretical substantiation. This situation is very usual in daily life. If this is meant, one is speaking of *belief* rather than faith.[239]

But Reb Shneur Zalman has already told us that 'faith' should only be applied at the very edge of reason, after reason has been fully exhausted. Everything else, according to him, is available as 'knowledge' proper, or at the very least, as a species of knowledge through analogical reasoning. 'Belief,' as Tillich defined it according to the most common understanding, has little place in the Alter Rebbe's teaching. For that willingness to accept and affirm something "in spite of the insufficiency of its theoretical substantiation" was precisely that of which he wished to wean his Hasidim. It was critical that his Hasidim understand the various degrees of knowledge and push the limits of reason if they were to develop the highest levels of spiritual discernment and be free of religious fanaticism.

There is an interesting interview with the psychologist, Carl Jung, in which he differentiates between the common understanding of 'belief' and the 'knowledge' of Reb Shneur Zalman. After being asked, "Do you now believe in God?" Jung responded, "Difficult to answer . . . *I know*. I don't need to believe . . . *I know*." Then, after another such question, he added:

The word 'belief' is a difficult thing for me. You see, I don't 'believe'—I must have a reason for a certain hypothesis. If I know a thing, I don't need to believe it. I don't allow myself to believe a thing just for the sake of believing it. I *can't* believe it. But when there are sufficient reasons for a certain hypothesis, I shall accept these reasons, naturally.[240]

So what does Reb Shneur Zalman mean when he quotes, "And they believed, having faith in *Yah*," and what do we mean when we say that God said, "Be! Live!" showing a divine *'belief'* in creation? Obviously we are not talking about "an act of knowledge that has a low degree of evidence." We want to redefine this pedestrian sense of belief and make of it a conscious act. For example, if somebody asks me, "What do you believe?" I often don't know what to answer—at one time I believed this, and later I believed that, and now I don't believe either. So I have doubts about my beliefs. But if you were to ask me, "What do you *be-live*?" That is to say, "What are you investing in? What are you acting on? What are you doing?" That is quite different. This is the thing for which I say, "I have reason to believe the situation is like this, and thus I will act accordingly." As we said before, this is a practical reasoning doing its best to react and adapt to life as it is *being lived*.

So, when it is clear to us that 'something' *be-lives* the body, and without it, the body would be 'life-less,' it's not hard—reasoning analogically—to 'see' that 'something' must *be-living* the rest of creation too. In this way, God is truly immanent in creation, its one benefactor, the only one who believes in it.

Now, where does this word 'immanent' come from? It is from the Latin, *immanens*, 'near to hand'—so close you could touch it. In Kabbalah, the divine immanence is discussed with the Aramaic phrase, *m'malleh kol almin*, 'fills-all-worlds,' for in the Talmud, it says, *Mah ha-n'shamah m'mal'ah et ha-guf, ka'kh ha-kadosh baruk hu m'malleh et ha-olam*, "As the soul fills the body, so does the blessed and holy One fill the universe." That is to say, nothing could live and function without God.[241] This in turn is based on the verse, *Ve'ata mehayyeh et kulam*, "And you invigorate them all." (Neh. 9:6)[242] In colloquial Yiddish, the Hebrew word *mehayyeh*, 'invigorating,' means 'a pleasure,' like a lovely breeze. Thus, we say, "Ah! *mehayyeh!* What a pleasure, how wonderful, how refreshing!" And when I pick up a glass of wine and say, *L'hayyim!* "To life!" it is as if I am addressing that power which grants life, saying, "I honor You, God, the life-giving power in the universe, and I drink to You." So, *mehayyeh* is 'refreshing,' 'invigorating,' even 'resuscitating,' as in "I was almost dead, and then you gave me water—Ah! *mehayyeh!*" And this is how we conceive of God as immanent in creation! "Ah! *mehayyeh*, You give life to everything!"

This *meḥayyeh* awakening and realization is the key to Reb Shneur Zalman's thought, for he advises us to get our *da'at*, our 'knowing,' so clear that—as we said earlier—we might speak of the *eros* of 'knowledge,' which arouses the heart with love and gratefulness. For instance, in the morning, if we took seriously the words of the *Modeh Ani* prayer, saying, "Thank You, living God, for mercifully returning my soul to me; great is Your faith in me," can you imagine how it would change the start of our day? Before we go to sleep, we commend our souls to God, so that when we awake it is like a promise fulfilled, and we are grateful. "God took care of my soul in the night and returned it to me in the morning!" And where did my soul go? *Home*—to its own rest in utter fullness! So not only does the body rest, but the soul does as well! These are the kinds of considerations that create the proper affect in us.

Now, how do we put all of these insights into practice? How do we turn these mental concepts into practical tools of transformation? Rebbe Nahman of Bratzlav says, "Every teaching I offer you, you have to turn it into prayer." So his disciple, Reb Nosson, made an entire book of prayers corresponding to each of Rebbe Nahman's teachings in his *Likkutei MaHaRaN!* In the same way, we must take this teaching of the Alter Rebbe and pray with it:

"Dear God—You commanded us that we should '*know today, and put it back into our hearts,* that You are God—in Heaven above and Earth below—there is nothing else,' and I'm asking You to help me, to keep my mind really clear, that I might see Your workings in the universe, to *feel* that You are the life that is invigorating me in this very moment."

Do you see? This is the beginning of a meditation, and by starting with a prayer, you have already moved the material away from the head, which is "*know* today," and you have "put it back into the heart." By praying this sincerely, you are already saying, "This is really important to me; it is important to me that I should *feel* what I *know*." This is what we would do in Lubavitch; we would pick up a teaching of the Alter Rebbe like this one, review it a few times, and then take it into prayer, extending it into detailed *hitbonenut* contemplation until it awakened feeling in us.

So why not give it a try yourself?

3

The Wars of the Lord: Conflict and Consolation in the Later Years of the Alter Rebbe

SHORTLY BEFORE HE PASSED ON, the Maggid of Mezritch said to Reb Shneur Zalman: "Zalmina, Zalmina—*You will stand alone*. However, in the midst of your troubles, I will pull you out, for my soul is bound to yours."[243]

In the old days, ḤaBaD Hasidim used to enumerate the ten troubles the Alter Rebbe endured for practicing Hasidim: the opposition of his father-in-law, brought on by his decision to go to Mezritch; the objections of his former colleagues among the *mitnagdim*; two negative reactions to his teachings by one of his colleagues in Mezritch;[244] the labor of deciding *halakhah* for his *Shulḥan Arukh*; the objections to ḤaBaD teaching by other Hasidic *rebbeim*, especially Reb Avraham of Kalisk; the opposition of the *mitnagdim* and disputations with them over Hasidism; the complaints of his colleagues in Volhynia, especially Reb Shlomo of Karlin, over his refusal to join in excommunicating the *mitnagdim*; the difficulties with his colleagues and his arrests over his support of the settlers in the Holy Land; and his arguments with colleagues over his opposition to Napoleon.[245]

The First Arrest and Liberation—*Yud-Tet-Kislev*

Among the most personally difficult of these troubles were his arrests by the Russian government over his collecting and sending of funds to the Hasidim in *Eretz Yisra'el*. You see, when Reb Menachem Mendel of Vitebsk emigrated to the Holy Land with 3,000 of his Hasidim, the regions of Lithuania and White Russia were basically left in the hands of Reb Shneur Zalman, who considered himself a 'steward of the king' *in absentia*. Thus, he took it upon himself to collect funds for the maintenance of Reb Menachem Mendel and his Hasidim. And this was absolutely necessary, for as the Jewish pioneers (ḥalutzim) of the modern state of Israel found later on, life in the Holy Land was extremely difficult and full of privation. Reb Avraham of Kalisk, who had traveled with Reb Menachem Mendel, himself wrote:

> One who arrives in the Holy Land must accustom oneself to the new way of living. One must often be content with a humble cottage. If we try, however, to live in the style to which we were previously accustomed, we may become distraught and blame the land for our misfortunes.[246]

So it was a hard life, and it is likely—especially in the early years—that Reb Menachem Mendel and his Hasidim would not have survived if not for the fundraising efforts of Reb Shneur Zalman. Nevertheless, this was accomplished at great personal loss to the latter. For these charitable efforts became the focus of one the last and most desperate attempts of the *mitnagdim* to undermine the Hasidic movement by bringing down its most prominent leader.

In 1798, Reb Shneur Zalman was formally denounced to the Russian government for 'suspicious activities' contrary to the interests of the Russian Czar, of secretly undermining the Czar's authority in his teachings, and most seriously, of sending large sums of money to the Turkish Sultan, with whom the Russian government had so recently been at war. This last accusation was the one that really got their attention, for Reb Shneur Zalman was indeed sending funds to Palestine, which at that time was under Turkish rule. Though his accusers knew that this was perfectly innocent, they also knew that the mere appearance of impropriety would make serious trouble for Reb Shneur Zalman and Hasidism generally.[247]

Unfortunately for Reb Shneur Zalman, the accusation came at a time when treasonous activities were already being investigated throughout the region; thus, an immediate order went out to arrest "Rabbi Zalman Barukhovitch of Liozhna" and to bring him to St. Petersburg under armed guard.

As soon as the Russian soldiers arrived *in Liozhna, Reb Shneur Zalman knew they would be coming for him. Fearing that they might take him out to be shot, he decided to slip out the rear window of his study and run away.*

Moments later, as he was making his way to the woods, he heard someone running up behind him. He turned and was amazed to see his Hasid, Reb Shmuel Munkes, trying to catch up with him. Stopping to see what he wanted, he heard Reb Shmuel say: "Why are you running away? I'm not gonna' let you go!"

The Rebbe answered, "You don't want them to shoot me—do you?".

Reb Shmuel replied: "If you are really the Rebbe, then no bullet will harm you; and if you are not, then maybe you deserve to be shot."

The Rebbe looked at him in wonder and said, "Why should I be shot?"

"Because," *says Reb Shmuel,* "on account of you, so many people have lost their taste for the things of this world."

Hearing this, the Rebbe turned back with Reb Shmuel and climbed back in the window to face his arrest.[248]

For me, this is one of the great stories of ḤaBaD Hasidism; for it shows the Rebbe in a truly vulnerable moment, fearing for his life. And he had good reason to fear, being wanted for treason by a government that had no love for Jews. But what is even more interesting is the fact that it is his Hasid, Reb Shmuel Munkes that saves the day with the kind of *ḥutzpah* of which only he was capable. And, in this instance, he turned out to be right.

Now, you could argue that Reb Shmuel's challenge was unfair. After all, the Rebbe really was in danger, and had a right to save his life, and even to be vulnerable in his humanity. So we might rather have had Reb Shmuel say, "I know it's dangerous for you, but you are our Rebbe, and we need you to stand up for us!" But this would not be doing Reb Shmuel Munkes a favor; nor Reb Shneur Zalman. You see, for all the funny stories about him, Reb Shmuel was an extraordinary Hasid who could say these kinds of things in the moment without being guilty of pride or self-aggrandizing. He did it for *Ḥasidut,* and on the Rebbe's behalf, from a place of deep intuition:

> **Once, the Alter Rebbe's Hasidim were having a *farbrengen,* and someone brings in a warm pot full of meat, lungs, and *kishkes,* and sets it down for the Hasidim to eat.**
>
> **Well, the wonderful aroma of this warm food on a cold night after a long day of study and *davenen* causes everyone's mouth to water. So they say, "Come on, let's eat!"**

> But before they can even get the lid off the pot, Reb Shmuel Munkes sits on top of the pot-lid and doesn't let anybody get at it! At first, everyone laughs. But after a few minutes, they're gettin' really hungry and pretty annoyed with him. Finally, they try to take him off the pot by force, but he fights them off. Then, just as they are about to try again, a Hasid comes rushing into the room, yelling: "Don't eat anything from that pot! We just heard from the *rav* that the lung isn't kosher."
>
> Now everyone looks at Reb Shmuel, and someone says: "What's this Shmuel—you're already into *ruaḥ ha-kodesh?* You think you can show off with prophecy already!" So now they want to get at him for pretensions to 'Rebbehood!'
>
> But Reb Shmuel doesn't have any such pretensions, and says: "No, no, no . . . You don't understand; it's not *ruaḥ ha-kodesh*. I heard from the Rebbe that 'Something your body is craving powerfully, even more than usual, should not be indulged.' So when they brought that pot in here, and it smelled so good, and I saw how much I wanted it, I just knew I couldn't eat it!"[249]

You see, a more 'reasonable' and tamer kind of challenge diminishes the moment; Reb Shmuel was acting from the place of genuine insight and thus says just the right thing to turn the Rebbe around: "If you are a real Rebbe, then the miraculous is available to you; and if it is not, then you are no better than we are, and you deserve to face the consequences; for you have deprived us of the pleasures of this world!"

Later, when the soldiers come to arrest Reb Shneur Zalman the next day (for he was not at home when they came the night before), we see that Reb Shmuel was right . . .

> WHEN THE SOLDIERS FINALLY ARRIVED *to take him, Reb Shneur Zalman was just finishing his davenen and approached the soldiers while still wearing his tefillin. But, to everyone's surprise, the soldiers fell back in awe, and dared not come near him. Later, his Hasidim asked him why the soldiers had been afraid, and he answered: "It is written, 'And the nations will see that the name of God is upon you, and they will be afraid of you.'*[250] *Our Sages tell us that this is because of 'the tefillin in the head.'"*
>
> *But the Hasidim said, "We too were wearing our tefillin, and they weren't afraid of us!?"*
>
> *Then the Rebbe said, "The Sages were not referring to the* tefillin *on the head* (tefillin al ha-rosh), *but the* tefillin *in the head* (tefillin she'ba rosh).*"*[251]

Nevertheless, Reb Shneur Zalman was arrested and placed in the infamous black wagon— "covered on all sides with heavy black panels of iron, and with mere slits for air"—reserved for dangerous enemies of the state.[252] Though this was meant to intimidate him (and everyone else who saw it), the Alter Rebbe now kept his composure and went with them as a servant of God, undaunted by the armed guard or the black wagon.

Once in St. Petersburg, he was imprisoned in the Peter and Paul Fortress while his case was officially investigated. Looking around at the thick walls of the infamous "Russian Bastille," he began to wonder if anyone ever left the fortress and struck up conversations with friendly guards to find out all that he could about his situation. Eventually, the superintendent of the fortress came to see the unusual prisoner for himself...

Now THE SUPERINTENDANT *of the Peter and Paul Fortress was an educated man and had a private interest in religion; so hearing that he had a great Jewish religious leader in his prison, he came to greet him, to see if he might be able to address some of his own questions.*

After he had introduced himself, the superintendant said to the Alter Rebbe: "Tell me, why does God say to Adam, 'Where are you?'[253] What kind of question is that? Doesn't God know where he is?"

So the Alter Rebbe replied: "The biblical commentator Rashi asked the very same question and suggested that God didn't want to surprise Adam, who would already be frightened, knowing that he had eaten of the fruit that was forbidden to him. So first he let him hear, 'Where are you?' "

Then the superintendant said, "I have heard a similar answer before, but it must be deeper than that."

"Ah-h-h!" said the Alter Rebbe, "Tell me, do you believe that the Scriptures are eternal, and that every generation and every individual may find themselves in them?"

"I do," answered the superintendant.

"Well, you will understand then that God speaks to everyone in the world, at all times and all places, whispering: 'Where are you in the world? Where are you in your life?' Every one of us is allotted a certain number of years, and God says to us (for instance), 'You are now 46 years old—what have you done with your life? How far along are you in the journey that was meant for you?' "

The superintendant was deeply moved by this answer, but also shocked to hear his exact age given! He laid his hand on the Alter Rebbe's shoulder in a gesture of gratitude, but trembled in the knowledge of what he had heard. He stayed and talked with the Rebbe awhile longer, finally exclaiming, "This is truly divine!"[254]

I love this moment in which the Alter Rebbe is engaged in a sincere, heart-felt dialogue with a Christian of the Russian-Orthodox Church. When I first began to dialogue with the Trappist monks at St. Norbert's in Manitoba, and later with others like Fr. Thomas Merton and Fr. Thomas Keating, it was immediately apparent that it was not the dialogue of theology we were really interested in; it was the dialogue of 'devoutness' that we were seeking. That is to say, a dialogue of the heart, allowing us to meet in the place of our most sincere devotion and love of God. So imagine how pleased I was when I saw what my friend, Fr. Thomas Keating had said of this same passage in his little book, *The Human Condition*:

> This marvelous story of creation is not just about Adam and Eve. It is really about us. It is a revelation of where *we* are. The same question is addressed to every generation, time, and person. At every moment of our lives, God is asking us, "*Where* are you? Why are you hiding?"
>
> All the questions that are fundamental to human happiness arise when we ask ourselves this excruciating question: *Where* am I? Where am I in relation to God, to myself, and to others? These are the basic questions of human life.[255]

Interestingly, I recently came across a postscript to this famous story, which takes place many years later after the Alter Rebbe had already passed on...

Once, Reb Nahum Schneersohn of Niezhin, *the grandson of Reb Shneur Zalman came to Riga to buy one of the state forests being sold at auction. Following the custom of the time, he registered as an official bidder in the auction. When the auctioneer, who was a very old man, started to read the list of bidders, he asked, "Which one of you is Schneersohn?"*

Reb Nahum said, "I am."

The auctioneer asked, "Are you by chance a descendent of Rabbi Barukhovitch of Liozhna?"

He answered, "Yes."

Then the auctioneer turned to the other officials who sat with him and said: "Behold gentleman, the grandfather of this man was a great rabbi, and well-known among the Jews. In the year 1798, I got to know him while he was imprisoned at the Peter and Paul Fortress in St. Petersburg. At that time, I was the superintendant of the prison and he had been falsely accused of something.

The rabbi made a deep impression on me; he was of such a noble and dignified countenance, and his customs and behavior impressed me greatly.

My heart turned to him with a great love in those first days of his imprisonment and I honored him as best I could. I tried to fulfill all his wishes, and took great pains to procure kosher food for him, because he was so very careful about eating, and did not want to partake of things that are forbidden to Jews according to their law. I also encouraged him, and tried to assure him that he would be freed for his righteousness' sake, and his enemies would be shamed. Nevertheless, he didn't seem to need my assurances, feeling that his salvation was coming very soon.[256] *When he was finally liberated, he blessed me with length of days as he was leaving the prison and, as you can see with your own eyes, his blessing was fulfilled!"*[257]

In time, the Alter Rebbe was called before the investigating committee and asked to answer the accusations made against him. However, it soon became clear from their questions that Hasidism was also on trial, and that he had only been arrested as the 'leader' of what was thought to be a subversive movement, seeking to undermine the Czarist government of Russia. Thus, he was asked if he was a follower of the Ba'al Shem Tov and to explain various Hasidic 'innovations' in the daily prayers and *halakhah*. These were obviously complaints fed to the government by a *mitnaged* informer, hoping to support the case of subversive activity. For making trouble in religion was also considered a threatening activity by the government of the time. However, the most serious charges related to his charitable activities and the kabbalistic doctrines he taught.

First among these was the charge that he was sending large sums of money to the Turkish Empire whose lands bordered Russia. As we mentioned before, this was technically true; for he had indeed been collecting and sending funds to support the community of Hasidim in *Eretz Yisra'el* (then under Turkish rule) ever since the emigration of Reb Menachem Mendel of Vitebsk in 1777. But this was fairly easily explained once the circumstances were understood. He told them that the *"Ba'al ha-Neis* Charity Fund" was only an attempt to support the community of Hasidim who had returned to the land of their parents in the Holy Land, and that their Sages had established this custom of supporting the poor of Yisra'el over a thousand years ago.[258] Therefore, it had nothing to do with the current political situation.

The last accusation that his kabbalistic teachings around the concept of the *sefirah malkhut* (sovereignty) were "denigrating to royalty" was harder to explain. This was a cheap ploy of the *mitnagdim*; for they suggested to the royalist government of Russia that because 'sovereignty' was at the bottom of the Tree of Life, and not at the top, that this was a mystically veiled insult to royalty! Nevertheless, it was not easy to explain the doctrines of the Kabbalah to the uninitiated, especially to non-Jews. Thus he asked if he might submit his answer in writing, not wanting to be misunderstood.

After this answer had been translated for the committee, they retired to consider all the evidence. On the 15th of Kislev, the investigation was concluded. Then, on Tuesday the 19th of Kislev (November 27th, 1798), fifty-three days after his arrest, he was declared innocent of all charges and released from prison. Moreover, as nothing in Hasidism was found to be contrary to the interests of the government, the Hasidic movement was now officially sanctioned (much to the chagrin of the *mitnagdim*) and permitted to carry on as before!

News of his release spread like wildfire and the Alter Rebbe soon became a celebrity in the Hasidic world. After all, no one else had ever been so singled-out for persecution, or had so successfully defended it against both *mitnagdim* and the government authorities, winning official sanction for the movement![259]

Upon his release, Reb Shneur Zalman wrote to his old friend and fellow disciple of the Maggid, Reb Levi Yitzhak of Berditchev . . .

I CANNOT TELL YOU ALL THE WONDERS God has wrought for us in this situation, which have magnified and sanctified God's great name among the nations, especially in the court of the Czar. . . . for the day on which God has dealt so wondrously with us is none other than the 19th of Kislev (Yud-Tet-Kislev),[260] the hillula (wedding) and yahrzeit (death anniversary) of our holy master (the Maggid of Mezritch).[261]

This date was even more significant to him because just before the Maggid died, he had taken Reb Shneur Zalman's hands and said to him, "*Yud-Tet-Kislev* is our *hillula*, our day of rejoicing!"[262] Ever since, this has been the great Hasidic holiday of ḤaBaD Hasidim, celebrated with great joy as the "Festival of Liberation," and the Rosh Hashanah of the Hasidic movement.

The *Yeḥidut*—Spiritual Intimacy

For all the great events in which Reb Shneur Zalman was bound up, his real occupation was still working with Hasidim, asking the very question we have already mentioned—"Where are you in relation to God?" This was the work that was done in *yeḥidut*, or 'one-ing,' the private encounter between a Rebbe and a Hasid.[263]

> The great among the Alter Rebbe's Hasidim used to say that *yeḥidut* means: 'clear,' 'defined,' and 'united.'[264] That is to say that the intent of *yeḥidut* is to *clarify* one's position, to *define* a way of service—both in "forsaking evil" deeds and "acquiring good" virtues[265]—and to *unite* oneself to the Rebbe in complete *union*, dedicating oneself to the Rebbe with all one's desires.[266]

Yeḥidut is the term for this encounter in ḤaBaD Hasidism. Among other Hasidic lineages, different terms were used, such as *derlangen a kvittel*, 'to enter to give a *kvittel*,' *poyelen bam rebben*, 'to exact from the Rebbe,' or *birkhat ha-pridah*, 'receiving the parting blessing.' All of these terms refer to different phases of the interview with the Rebbe: the giving of a *kvittel*, a 'slip of paper' with a request for intercession or naming a topic for discussion; the *pidyon nefesh*, or 'soul ransom' which, as we have already mentioned, was a donation for the maintenance of the Rebbe's household; the *etzah*, or 'counsel' which the Rebbe gives to the Hasid; and the *berakhah*, or 'blessing' given by the Rebbe to put a seal, as it were, on the interview.[267]

In Liozhna, a serious Hasid would be expected to go through a good deal of preparation before finally being admitted to *yeḥidut* with the Alter Rebbe. According to my own Rebbe, Reb Moshe Vilenker sat and learned with the Hasidim for five months on his first visit to Liozhna before he felt he was ready to enter the Rebbe's study for *yeḥidut*![268] Sometimes visiting scholars who wished to ask the Alter Rebbe a question would first be interviewed by Reb Yehuda Leib, the Rebbe's brother. If he approved, the postulant would then be put through an intensive course of study in Talmud and *Ḥasidut* for two to three weeks, ending with a thorough examination by the other brothers, Reb Mordecai and Reb Moshe. Only then would he be admitted to *yeḥidut* with the Alter Rebbe.[269]

Once inside, one might expect to see the Rebbe seated behind his desk with two lighted candles, a *Ḥumash*, and a volume of *Zohar* before him. One postulant who reported his experiences in *yeḥidut* wrote afterward: "As I entered the Rebbe's room, I was overcome with an overpowering sense of awe. His impressive face, penetrating eyes, and strong voice as he said to me, 'What is your wish?' left me speechless for a moment."[270] And another said, "For years afterward, the impressions of his awe-inspiring countenance and his profound wisdom remained vivid in my mind."[271]

ONE DAY, *a man who bred and trained horses came to see Reb Shneur Zalman. The man's whole life was horses; he adored them as a breeder, as a trainer, and as a rider. So he told Reb Shneur Zalman all about his passion for horses. Then the Alter Rebbe said, "A horse is truly a wonderful animal; the swifter the horse, the faster you can get where you are going. But then again, if you don't know where you are going, a swift horse you can cause you to stray very far."*

Snap! These words went straight to the man's heart, and he turned away and began to sob. Finally, he said to the Alter Rebbe, "Oh Rebbe, I have strayed so far from the path! How shall I ever make it back?"

Then the Alter Rebbe answered, "Yes, you have strayed from the path, but you also have a swift horse, and with a swift horse you can return just as quickly!"[272]

As so often happens when someone comes to the Rebbe, they find themselves talking about everything but what is needful. Nevertheless, the Rebbe is aware that he isn't being visited for nothing and keeps his antenna tuned to divine guidance; in this way, these kinds of breakthrough moments are allowed to happen, despite the Hasid's subterfuge.[273]

To my mind, one of the most telling stories of how Reb Shneur Zalman worked with people, and what kind of problems he worked with is not a story of Reb Shneur Zalman at all, but one of his friend, Reb Levi Yitzhak of Berditchev, who had the following encounter with a Hasid...

Once, a misguided Hasid came to Reb Levi Yitzhak of Berditchev seeking a *teshuvah* (penance). With complete aplomb, he confessed to having recently committed an act of fornication with an unmarried woman—"But," he added, "I swear Rebbe, we made certain to follow the laws of *niddah* (separation), waiting the required seven days after her menstruation, and until she had been to *mikvah* (ritual bath). Still, I'm sure we need a *teshuvah* for this."

Reb Levi Yitzhak's eyes went wide with disbelief. Finally, disgusted he shook his head and said, "I can't help you."

"Why not?" the Hasid asked.

Reb Levi Yitzhak answered, "If you would have come to me and said that you were so overwhelmed by passion that you didn't care whether she had been to the *mikvah* or not, I would have been able to help you. But if you can find someone who is unmarried and wait seven days after her menstruation for her to go to *mikvah*, firmly committing your will and your mind to this act that whole time—forget it! Go to Reb Shneur Zalman, I can't help you!"[274]

Of course, this is not to say that Reb Shneur Zalman's Hasidim were licentious opportunists—quite the contrary—but that Reb Shneur Zalman seems to have been as adept at dealing with *'mental* natures' as Reb Levi Yitzhak was at dealing with *'passionate* natures.' After all, he was a 'Litvak,' serving the intellectuals of Lithuania, who prized knowledge above all else, but who sometimes became disconnected from their hearts. He seems to have had the Ariadnean thread that could help these types of people to find the way back into their own hearts.

Reb Shneur Zalman also insisted that Hasidim only come to see him for spiritual counsel, and even then, only after they had exhausted the obvious. He only wanted to help in cases of doubt concerning the course of service a Hasid should take. In this way, he reserved for himself the function of a spiritual counselor. Here he was willing to take a definite stand, bringing his own reading of the Hasid's reincarnational record to bear on the Hasid's particular predicament.

ONE DAY, a Hasid came to Reb Shneur Zalman because his wife was giving him a hard time, and he was considering a divorce. So he asked the Rebbe, "Should I divorce her?"

The Alter Rebbe looked thoughtfully at him for a moment and said, "Let's talk it over while we have some kugel." He offered the man a kugel that the Rebbetzin Shterna had baked, the Hasid sat down, made the berakhah, and began to eat the kugel.

They talked things over, and afterward, he went back home and divorced his wife. Later, he married another woman and found that she was worse than the first wife. So they also had a difficult time, until finally, he divorced her as well. Then he decided to marry again, and if the first two had been bad, the third wife was by far the worst! In the end, she threw him out of the house in the middle of Winter! So now he was in a terrible state, and without a single thing to his name. So he decided to go back to Liozhna to complain to Reb Shneur Zalman.

The Rebbe invited him to sit down and have some kugel while they talked it over.

The Hasid took a bite of kugel, and suddenly, he realized that it was the first piece of kugel! The whole long story of which he had come to complain had all happened in his mind in the space of single moment! Recovering from the shock, he asked, "What should I do then?"

Reb Shneur Zalman answered, "You should be happy. Some souls in earlier incarnations have committed capital sins of idolatry that require the death

> penalty, but have not gotten it. Instead, they are subjected to situations that will cleanse them of the sin. So each time she bugs you, you have to understand, you are being given an opportunity to clean it up!"
>
> From that time on, the Hasid began to smile when his wife got after him, and after a while, it all stopped.[275]

This should not be taken as some kind of apologetic for traditional values—a white-wash over unhappy marriages—or as condoning unhealthy and unhelpful behaviors in marriage; for an *etzah*, or 'counsel' given in *yeḥidut* applies to a specific person in a specific situation, though it is often anecdotally applicable to some other situation afterward. Moreover, an *etzah* is a means to an end, creating the desired effect in the Hasid.

In this case, it seems that the Hasid has the means within his grasp of fixing the problems in his marriage, but is either unaware of them, or unwilling to use them. From his perspective, he is merely the victim of a nagging wife, and his only question is whether he should divorce her or not. He doesn't ask what he might do to improve the situation—that is, not until he is shown the outcome of the divorce and his subsequent remarriages. Reading between the lines, one wonders if the Hasid's wives might not have had legitimate complaints to which he may have been insensitive. The wives whom he perceives as irredeemable 'nags' may actually have been women just trying to be heard. But when he begins to smile and see his wife's complaints as an opportunity, something happens which seems to resolve their problems. Perhaps he started listening at that point? At least I hope that's what happened.

While this story may not be very helpful to psychotherapists—depending as it does on the miraculous and otherworldly information—it is nevertheless helpful in showing us how effective Reb Shneur Zalman could be in dealing with deeply stubborn personalities, slowly moving them in the direction of greater consciousness and awareness of God, and ultimately changing their lives.

The Second Arrest and Liberation

Unfortunately for Reb Shneur Zalman, the return to his real work and this respite from his troubles was all too brief. For on the 24th of Tishrei, 5561 (October 13th, 1800), he was again summoned to St. Petersburg and arrested. In some ways, this had been anticipated by his grandson, Reb Menachem Mendel, even before his first arrest:

Until I was nine years old, my grandfather used to take me under his *tallit* for the blowing of the *shofar,* and until my marriage (at the age of fourteen) for the blessing of the *kohanim.* At the time of the blowing of the *shofar* in 1798, I sensed a grave danger threatening my grandfather, and I could not see his escape from it. Maybe this was because his salvation in 1798 was not a complete one (for two years later he faced a similar situation).[276]

The accusations of 1800 were substantially the same as those of 1798, but whereas before, there were only accusations and no actual accuser, now the accusations had a face—Rabbi Avigdor ben Hayyim. Back in 1772, he had purchased Reb Levi Yitzhak's old position as the rabbi of Pinsk, and for years was a leading voice in trying to suppress Hasidism, even influencing the decision to burn Reb Ya'akov Yosef of Polonoye's book *Toldot Ya'akov Yosef* in 1781. But as the popularity of Hasidism continued to grow, Rabbi Avigdor was eventually pushed out of his post in Pinsk after more than 20 years; and being disgruntled, some believe that he may have been behind the first denunciation of Reb Shneur Zalman in 1798. Now he refined the old accusations and brought a host of new ones (based on deliberate misrepresentations) to St. Petersburg, demanding that the Alter Rebbe be brought there to answer them.[277]

After the Alter Rebbe arrived in St. Petersburg, he was placed under arrest again, only this time he was housed in the Secret Department of the Senate. It is here that one of the most interesting stories of his second arrest takes place—his meeting with Czar Paul I of Russia (1754-1801):

HAVING HEARD SO MUCH *about the famous Jew, Rabbi Zalman Barukhovitch of Liozhna, who had now been accused of subversive activities against him twice, Czar Paul wished to see for himself whether this accusation was true or not. Thus, he dressed in the clothing of a political prisoner sentenced to death and ordered the guards to put him in the same room with Reb Shneur Zalman. Once there, he planned to speak ill of 'the Czar' and 'his injustices,' to see if the rabbi would speak his true feelings in the presence of a fellow subversive.*

So the guards did as they were told and put the disguised Czar in the same room with the rabbi, treating him like a prisoner. But that is as far as the Czar's clever plan got, for Reb Shneur Zalman immediately rose to greet him, saying: "Your majesty, allow me to say the blessing one says upon seeing the sovereign of a country, "Blessed are You, Yah our God, who has given of Your glory to flesh and blood!"

Surprised and utterly at a loss, the Czar asked him, "How do you know that I am the Czar? Did someone tell you?"

Then Reb Shneur Zalman answered, "No, your majesty—When you entered the room, a peculiar awe came over me that I recognized as a reflection of God's own sovereignty (malkhut), and from this I knew that you must be the Czar."[278]

Even though such a blessing is mandated in the prayer-book, some might wonder how Reb Shneur Zalman could show such deference for a political leader whose government was less than friendly to Jews. It reminds me of something I once learned from a Native American elder back in the early 1970s. Around that time, I participated in several peyote rituals with Little Joe Gomez, the head of the Taos branch of the North American Peyote Church; and during one of those early meetings, I remember him saying a prayer for president Nixon! At the time, I thought, "Come on, what are you doing?" I didn't much care for Nixon. But then I got it; he was saying, "This man, Nixon, who has power over so many lives—please make him feel good, enlighten him so that he should know what he is doing!" Ever since then, that very sincere prayer has become a model for me when thinking of political leaders.

Sometime after his meeting with the Czar, Reb Shneur Zalman faced his accuser before a secret council of the Senate. As before, he was easily able to refute the spurious accusations and deliberate misrepresentations of Rabbi Avigdor, vindicating himself in the eyes of the Senate council (designated to act as judges in the case). However, Rabbi Avigdor continued to press his claims, submitting supplementary 'evidence' which no doubt delayed the proceedings to a great extent. The effect was that Reb Shneur Zalman had been found 'not guilty' by the council, but was not yet free to leave the capital until everything was resolved. Thus, the case dragged on for many months until larger events brought it to a close. On March 11th, 1801, Czar Paul was assassinated by conspirators close to him, and on March 29th, 1801, his son and successor, Czar Alexander ordered the release of Reb Shneur Zalman as one of his first official acts as ruler of all Russia.

After spending many months in the Russian capital, Reb Shneur Zalman decided not to return to Liozhna, but to accept the invitation of Prince Lubomirski—whom he had met in St. Petersburg—to take up residence in Liadi, a town under the prince's protection, where he would spend the next twelve years.[279]

The Davenen of the Rebbes

Somewhere between 1801 and 1803, a wedding took place in the city of Zhlobin, uniting the families of Reb Shneur Zalman of Liadi and his old friend, Reb Levi Yitzhak of Berditchev. Reb Shneur Zalman's granddaughter, Beila (the daughter of Reb Dov Baer) was to marry Reb Levi Yitzhak's grandson, Yekusiel Zalman (the son of Reb Levi Yitzhak's daughter). So it was a great occasion, bringing together two great Hasidic houses.

As we mentioned before, Reb Levi Yitzhak was the first person to whom Reb Shneur Zalman wrote after being released from prison in 1798, and I can imagine, after the passing of so many years, seeing conflict come between him and so many of his peers, it must have been reassuring and deeply moving to still have the friendship of Reb Levi Yitzhak, one of the Maggid's greatest disciples.

Among the many stories of that great occasion—called simply, "the Wedding in Zhlobin" by ḤaBaD Hasidim—is the following story, once again involving the inimitable Reb Shmuel Munkes . . .

The great wedding in Zhlobin, uniting the families of Reb Shneur Zalman of Liadi and his old friend, Reb Levi Yitzhak of Berditchev, was also attended by many of the senior Hasidim of both Liadi and Berditchev. Among the senior disciples of Reb Shneur Zalman, was Reb Shmuel Munkes, who had been appointed the badkhan, or court jester for the wedding. For Reb Shmuel, this was a delight and an honor, giving him the opportunity to see the unique prayer styles of the different disciples of the Maggid who were present, especially that of Reb Levi Yitzhak of Berditchev, the Rebbe's dearest friend.

After a day or two, Reb Shmuel noticed a difference in the length of time the Alter Rebbe and the Berditchever Rav spent preparing for davenen. So, one morning after the Alter Rebbe had already finished his davenen, Reb Shmuel approached him—pretending to be astonished at finding him finished with his prayers—and said: "Oy! Gevalt! Rebbe, are you finished with your davenen already? Are you sure you shouldn't daven a little longer? Don't you know that the Berditchever Rav, the great tzaddik, Reb Levi Yitzhak isn't even finished with his preparation yet; even now he is meditating on the deepest kavvanot?! What will the other Hasidim say when they hear you are done already?"

So the Alter Rebbe says: "What!? Are you comparing me to my meḥutan, to my holy in-law? Reb Shmuelik, I tell you, he is on such a level that whenever he knocks on the heavenly gates, they open for him. I, on the other hand, must take advantage of God's grace and enter the gates at the appointed times, when they are open to everyone."

Then Reb Shmuel went to find Reb Levi Yitzhak on a similar mission, feigning astonishment at finding the Berditchever Rav still smoking a pipe and meditating before commencing with his prayer. In a quiet voice, he says, "Excuse me, Rebbe—Perhaps you are unaware that the holy rav, the tzaddik of Liadi, the ba'al ha-Tanya, and author of the Shulḥan Arukh, who is so meticulous in every detail of halakhah, is already finished with his prayers, as is prescribed by the Sages? Do you not think that perhaps you should begin already?"

So the Berditchever Rav says: "Oy! Oy! Reb Shmuel—Do you really think you can compare me to my meḥutan, to my holy in-law? He is on such a holy level that he doesn't even need to prepare himself before davenen; he is prepared from the day before! So when he gets up, he can simply begin his prayers. I, on the other hand, must work to prepare myself and build the momentum to reach the same heights that he achieves! And this takes me a long time."[280]

In his *Kedushat Levi*, Reb Levi Yitzhak writes, "because he felt unworthy before the Lord . . . it was necessary for him to pray in order that he should be able to pray." And his student, Reb Ahron of Zhitomir likewise says: "all things require preparation. And surely if we are to appear before a king, we must consider beforehand what we would say, how we would say it and by what means. Indeed one needs more time to prepare for prayer than to recite the prayers themselves."[281]

What do we know of the Alter Rebbe's *davenen* besides this story? The best description of his awesome prayer (and style of teaching) is given in the ḤaBaD chronicle, *Beit Rebbe*:

THE WAY IN WHICH THE ALTER REBBE TAUGHT Ḥasidut was so awe-inspiring that everyone who heard him quickly became rapturous with the thought of deepening his or her own divine service. The Hasidim who heard him would come to a great trembling before God where they stood, becoming enflamed to the service of God in an awesome way, and thus they became good masters of prayer. This is because the Rebbe talked about a subject while actually holding on to its essence; if he was speaking about the great love (ahavah rabbah), he was actually involved in the great love!

Likewise, in his prayer he was tumultuous! As his grandson, (Reb Menachem Mendel) the Tzemaḥ Tzedek said: "So great was his thirst to be absorbed in the divine essence that he would say in the middle of prayer: 'I don't want Your

Garden of Eden! I don't want Your World-to-Come! I want only You, You, You alone!" And this was written in the Tzemaḥ Tzedek's teaching about the root of prayer: "When he prayed alone, he prayed quietly; but when he was davenen with others, he shouted for all the world to hear (mar'ish olamot), praying for hours, sometimes 'till 2 o'clock in the afternoon. On Rosh Hashanah and Yom Kippur at night, he spent a very long time in prayer. And so tumultuous was his prayer that they had to fix padding on the walls, for he sometimes battered his hands against the wall until they bled—and yet he felt nothing at all!"[282]

I always like to point to this description when someone comments on how 'intellectual' Reb Shneur Zalman was; for as sophisticated as his thinking and writings are, he was nevertheless just as my Rebbe described him, "a fiery heart ruled by his brain."[283]

Joy and Broken-Heartedness in Prayer

Having heard this example about his own prayers, one wonders what he might have to say on the subject for others, and what he might recommend to us. The following letter on prayer may give us some idea. It was apparently written to an in-law around 1790, answering an inquiry that seems to have concerned fasting and prayer.

To my beloved meḥutan (in-law), the exalted Rabbi Yitzhak—

I hope that you are well and will not hold it against me for not answering sooner; Heaven is my witness that there was no one traveling in your direction with whom I could send a letter until now.

However, permit me to express my opinion concerning 'fasts' and 'exiles.'[284] God does not desire these! Nor was this the way of my holy teachers, who counseled that one should pray with a joy so great that sinful thoughts simply abandon you, flying like straw before the wind when the angel of God advances.

This was one of the major innovations of the Ba'al Shem Tov, moving the emphasis of divine service away from asceticism and mortification of the flesh into a service of love and joy. Once, his Hasidim asked him, "Now that you have done away with fasting and mortification of the flesh, tell us—What is the essence of service?" The Ba'al Shem Tov answered, "Love—the love of God, the love of Torah, the love of Yisra'el!"[285] Elsewhere, he says, "Just as a child is conceived in joy and pleasure, if one wishes one's prayers to bear fruit, one must likewise offer them with joy and pleasure!"[286]

> Now, the content of joy is God, as it is written, "Let Yisra'el rejoice in its maker,"[287] delighting in the bliss of God's greatness through the praises one finds in the siddur (prayerbook).
>
> Picture before your mind's eye a great and beloved king of flesh and blood, appearing in all his majestic splendor, reigning justly over a vast kingdom, with throngs of joyful celebrants coming to greet him; for it is as if it had actually been proclaimed: "Go out and see Shlomo ha-Melekh."[288] For the time of prayer is one of divine generosity, a time when we may behold our beloved and holy Sovereign, becoming filled with the delightful bliss of God's glorious splendor.

When I was a young man in the *yeshiva*, I was once studying chapter 46 in the *Tanya*—which was one of the few chapters I could understand without anyone having to explain it to me—and was moved to tears by what I read there. For there, the Alter Rebbe tells a parable about a despised man lying on a dunghill who is seen by the king. The king leaves his retinue, the glory of his palace and his station to come to the man, kissing and hugging him, and taking him home to his palace, where he spends time with him until his heart is healed. That image was so powerful to me at that time, and still is, because the distance between the two was so great—as between God and us—and yet it was overcome.[289]

> Nevertheless, one must also invest this prayer with a trembling awe, for this is the secret of "infusing the despised with vigor."
>
> One must also remove all one's sighs and worry before prayer which, paradoxically, is done by breaking one's heart over the sins of the past, weeping with deep regret over them, begging for a complete pardon from God, reciting Psalm 51 in a tearful voice. These tears will remove the anxiety from your heart, and you will find a renewed joy and trust in God, for there is no doubt your sins are forgiven in that very moment!

Why does he advocate "breaking one's heart over the sins of the past, weeping with deep regret over them" here when earlier he speaks of replacing asceticism with joy in prayer? Because it is one thing to 'whip the flesh,' punishing it for its sins, and it is another thing entirely to 'relieve it' by means of weeping, making a way for joy to enter in.

Tears are such an amazing thing, bringing us so much relief in such an unexpected way. Often, we try so hard not to cry, not to let others see us in our most vulnerable moments; nevertheless, it is our tears that express our deepest and most inexpressible thoughts and feelings. And it is only after we have finally released them that we find relief from the feelings that were dammed-up inside, almost choking us. If you have ever had a serious conversation with a friend, a family member, or a lover that began in a heated way and ended in tears and an embrace, you know exactly what Reb Shneur Zalman is talking about. For the tears usually come at the point of breaking through the frustration. Have you ever noticed that we don't often cry when we are afraid, but only when our anxiety has been removed? Sometimes you have to feel safe enough to cry. And sometimes they are also born of the frustration and allow for the breakthrough! Tears express what no words can possibly say, and do what no actions can accomplish—"remove the anxiety from your heart."

Most of your study ought to be taken from the *Zohar* and the *Midrash*, but before prayer, study the "Gate of Repentance" in the *Reshit Ḥokhmah*, the end of the "Gate of Awe," and the end of the "Gate of Holiness." These will help to bring you to a state of broken-heartedness over your sins, leading to the prayerful tears that wash away all anxiety from your heart, allowing it to be filled again with joy and bliss, as you contemplate in prayer, the greatness of your Creator.

When you come to the blessing, "cause us to repent," "forgive us," implore God in all sincerity. Your heart must trust completely in God. If you continue to do this for a while, you will become a totally different person and your soul will begin to live—May God help you in this!

The sickness of melancholia you feel you are experiencing is only the evil one's clever scheme; for just watch how easily you rejoice over material pleasures. When you set out to serve and worship God, then the evil one is quick to undermine your good intentions, entangling you in a net so that you are unable to serve God wholeheartedly in joy.

Interceding for you, and sending you my best—

Shneur Zalman, the son of my father, master, and teacher, Barukh, of blessed memory.[290]

When he says, the "sickness of melancholia you feel you are experiencing is only the evil one's clever scheme," he is not talking about clinical depression, for the next sentence—"just watch how easily you rejoice over material pleasures"—indicates that the person he is addressing can still find delight in such things. What he is really talking about here is the difference between 'sadness' (*atzvut*) and 'bitterness' (*m'rirut*). In 'sadness,' you can get to feeling like such a victim, saying, "I can't help it; I can't do anything about," that you often end-up consoling yourself with something that gets you into a regression (e.g., food, sex, sleep, alcohol). Whereas with 'bitterness,' you get pissed off and say: "I won't stand for it! This has got to change!" and you do something about it. For Reb Shneur Zalman, the service of prayer has a lot to do with the transformation of character.

Conflict and Division

Once, his grandson, Reb Menachem Mendel, asked the Alter Rebbe, "What is the ultimate point of *Ḥasidut*?" To which the Alter Rebbe answered, "The entire point of *Ḥasidut* is to refine and transform one's *middot* (attributes)?"[291] That is to say, to refine one's character. It is in this emphasis on inner-refinement and personal transformation that Reb Shneur Zalman differs from so many other Hasidic masters, many of whom believed that this was *specialized* work that should be left to the Rebbes and their most advanced students. They would interpret the verse, "The *tzaddik* lives by faith" (Hab. 2:4)[292] as "The *tzaddik* enlivens *them* with faith," meaning, the Rebbe is doing the work of inner-refinement, and the Hasidim need only attune to the Rebbe's great *kavanah*—which is supposed to be enough to pull the Hasidim into the proper station. Thus, after the *Tanya* was published in 1796, Reb Avraham of Kalisk—who was of the latter opinion—wrote a letter complaining about this emphasis to his former colleague:

> I HAVE SEEN YOUR SEFER SHEL BEINONIM, *but do not consider it very helpful in the work of saving souls, for they already have an abundance of counsel available to them, and the old means are stronger than the new. For most, it is sufficient to have one 'spark' which will serve many purposes—this is the way of Torah. Too much 'oil in the lamp' may cause the 'flame' to be extinguished, and people will certainly say, "Let's investigate this new thing which speaks of wisdom, understanding, and knowledge" (i.e.,* HaBaD).
>
> *It was the custom of our teachers to be careful concerning their words so that they were not heard by all of the Hasidim, giving only as much as would bring them into the covenant of faith in their leaders. The words of Torah should be few and pure, the "little that contains alot" (mu'at maḥzik et ha-merubah).*[293] *Indeed, my master, the holy rabbi, Reb Menachem Mendel of Vitebsk was greatly distressed over this publicizing of the teaching before his death, and actually tore his hair out over it!*

The Alter Rebbe and ḤaBaD Hasidism

I will not conceal from you, my beloved brother, what is in my heart: I fear, God forbid, that this is the strategy of the Sitra Aḥra (Other Side) to bury the grain amidst the straw for the masses of Hasidim . . . For most Hasidim, it is enough to have faith in the Sages, and that they should be aware of their own faults.[294]

Again, those Rebbes who were proponents of 'tzaddikism,' complete and utter dependence on the Rebbe—Reb Avraham of Kalisk, Reb Shlomo of Karlin, and Reb Barukh of Mezhbizh—felt that Hasidim didn't need to work on these higher levels, believing that it was the Rebbe's task to 'raise them up' through his own effort. But Reb Shneur Zalman couldn't have disagreed more; he believed in the Hasid's potential to make positive changes on their own (much as Rebbe Nahman of Bratzlav did), and was intent on giving them a knowledge-base and tool-kit with which to do it.[295] Thus, he worked to render his personal instructions into a system for the non-*tzaddik*, the *beinoni*, leading his Hasidim to more exalted spheres of love and awe. He did not teach that a person could raise himself any higher than his soul's origin permitted, but he still demanded tremendous exertion of his Hasidim in order that they attain levels higher than they themselves thought possible.

After making his opposition clear to Reb Shneur Zalman, Reb Avraham then wrote a pastoral letter to the Hasidim of Eastern Europe and Russia, saying:

I AM VERY CONCERNED FOR YOU . . . lest your hearts be deceived and turn away from the essence of truth and faith. . . . Therefore, I do not approve of the publication of the heavenly secrets, the writings of the holy ones, whose words are like fiery coals, describing the loftiest secrets of the universe; for not every mind can absorb these things. They are meant for those who possess very holy and saintly souls . . . Were it up to me, I would gather all of these sacred books that are scattered among the novices and return them to the custody of those who are pure in spirit.[296]

Reb Avraham had also written to Reb Levi Yitzhak of Berditchev about this matter, outlining his complaints against Reb Shneur Zalman and defending his opinions, but got back an uncharacteristically strong rebuke from the usually gentle Reb Levi Yitzhak:[297]

IT IS ASTONISHING to me that anyone would even think of complaining about the behavior of our master and teacher (Reb Shneur Zalman), since it is the very essence of our saintly master and teacher, the Maggid's own way, whose major concern was always to teach the people Torah and mitzvot, which, as he taught us, is the essence of divine service. Would that everyone were righteous enough to conduct themselves as he does! Indeed, whoever does not, isn't following the footsteps of our teacher; and whoever complains about it, God forbid, is complaining against our revered master and teacher of blessed memory, whose entire life and service followed this pattern. I am surprised that you are not aware of this, since you were there with us, among the faithful followers of our saintly master and teacher, whose soul rests in Eden.

As for what you wrote to me concerning the late Rabbi Menachem Mendel, whose memory is a blessing, and who was beloved of our master, I have not heard before. But I bear witness to the fact that my meḥutan, the rav and ga'on (Reb Shneur Zalman), was also beloved in the eyes of our master (the Maggid of Mezritch) and esteemed by him, and continually praised by him without limits. And I am surprised that if, as you have written, this (opposition to Reb Shneur Zalman's teaching by Reb Menachem Mendel) goes back twenty-five years, that you have never mentioned it to me before. If it is indeed true, you should have explained why you are only bringing this up to me now. For, in my opinion, this approach (the one taken by Reb Shneur Zalman) is also that of our master, the Maggid, peace be upon him, and the means by which the light of God is given.[298]

These are especially strong words, coming as they do from a known arbiter of disputes who ordinarily took the most compassionate view of events. Thus, they show that Reb Levi Yitzhak was deeply offended that Reb Avraham was attacking Reb Shneur Zalman, whose ways he knew to be pure, and who had suffered so much for Hasidism. Indeed, it must have seemed the height of ingratitude that Reb Avraham was now criticizing him and attempting to set-up his own fundraising network for the Hasidic community of the Holy Land. For this implied a distrust of Reb Shneur Zalman's motives, who had twice been imprisoned for sending these funds!

All of this occurred after a certain Rabbi Elazar of Disna, pretending to be an emissary of Reb Shneur Zalman, settled in *Eretz Yisra'el* and began to vilify Reb Avraham among the Hasidim there. Why? Possibly for dislike of Reb Avraham, as Elazar of Disna was known to be a contentious man (later slandering the Alter Rebbe's son, Reb Dov Baer as well). Or possibly because he hoped to supplant him, using Reb Shneur Zalman's name as authority for his own opinions. Whatever his real reasons, Reb Avraham seems to have accepted that he was indeed sent by Reb Shneur Zalman (probably because Elazar of Disna was a man of tremendous learning) and believed that Reb Shneur Zalman now wished to undermine his position as leader of the Hasidim in *Eretz Yisra'el*.

As we shall see later, this was a position in which Reb Avraham already felt insecure, and thus may have been a little too ready to see conspiracies around him.[299] Whatever the case may have been, he took the words of Rabbi Elazar of Disna as Reb Shneur Zalman's own, and used them to justify the setting-up of his own fundraising network, sending two emissaries to Reb Shneur Zalman in 1803 to abolish the old network. When Reb Shneur Zalman refused to acknowledge this kind of factionalism, the emissaries began a slanderous campaign to undermine confidence in him. It was this that occasioned Reb Avraham's original letter to Reb Levi Yitzhak, who had complained to him about the behavior of his emissaries. Now, having heard Reb Avraham's unsatisfactory explanations of their conduct, Reb Levi Yitzhak continues his reprimand of his former colleague:

THESE WICKED AND UNSCRUPULOUS MEN *have obviously carried evil slander to your ears for their own reasons, as the end attests to the beginning. Having met them, I know that their heads are empty and devoid of learning in Torah.*

The lavish praise you heap on them, calling them "men of scholarship, piety and truth," is unjustified and wholly unearned, for I can see none of it. How can you call them "men of truth," when Tzvi, the bitter one, has spoken so many lies in my presence; if he's a scholar, then I don't know what an ignoramous is!

As for the money matters of which you complained, I am amazed that you should mention it, seeing as you yourself sent emissaries to disrupt the system, increasing discord among Hasidim by allowing them to speak against such a tzaddik as he (Reb Shneur Zalman), saying in your name that you wished none of our money. How could he have acted otherwise? Surely he did the right thing.

With regard to your attendant Hayyim, I am at a loss, for it is surely a lie; Hayyim said nothing to me. As for the wish which you expressed in your own words, namely that "the mouth of liars should be stopped"[300] *it is a curse which your eminence has invoked upon yourself.*[301]

There is nothing that need be said about this last passage. It does not say who was right or wrong in this whole controversy, only that Reb Levi Yitzhak supported Reb Shneur Zalman (his friend and *meḥutan*) in the conflict with Reb Avraham of Kalisk. We have included these fragments of letters because an explanation of this conflict can hardly be avoided in any serious discussion the significant events of Reb Shneur Zalman's life.[302]

It is an unfortunate chapter in the history of Hasidism, but we may also see it as an opportunity to show another side of the Hasidic story—the very human side. Despite the many remarkable stories of these masters, we should not forget that they were also human beings with the same limitations and 'blind-spots' to which all of us are prone at one time or another.

How many gifted teachers—of all traditions—have we seen in our lifetime failing to live up to the high standards we set for them? Was it that they were not the 'real thing'? Was it that their 'insights' and 'realizations' were false? Perhaps in some cases; but there are also those whom God has blessed with genuine insight and realization who have 'fallen short' and made many serious mistakes in their lives. And this situation causes us even more difficulty than the outright frauds and hucksters, for the good and helpful work they have done with people gets tainted by association with their personal flaws and transgressions. (Mind you, we are speaking of serious breaches of trust now, and mistakes that caused serious harm to others, not simple human foibles which should be allowed for in our teachers as much as we allow for them in ourselves.) So what are we to do in these cases?

We must remember that it is the *teaching* and not the *teacher* that should be the true focus of our spiritual lives (though Reb Avraham of Kalisk might disagree), and we can be grateful for the teaching that is helpful, even as we acknowledge that the teacher is not perfect. Just as Rabbi Meir said when asked how he could still associate with his own teacher, Rabbi Elisha ben Abuya, who had become a heretic—"I eat the fruit and throw away the rind."[303]

The important thing for all spiritual practitioners to remember—whether Rebbes or Hasidim—is that the journey is never completed; there is no one realization that finishes all spiritual work for us; there is no accomplishment that grants us a 'free pass' or a status that we do not have to live up to. We cannot afford to leave any stone unturned in our spiritual lives; we must continually look for the 'blind-spot' and uproot pride everywhere we find it, as the Maggid of Mezritch says:

> Pride belongs to our blessed Creator, as it is written, "Y-H-V-H is sovereign and robed in grandeur (*gey'ut,* which may also mean 'pride')" (Ps. 93:1)[304] Thus there is no permanent way to uproot pride within us and we must struggle with it all of our lives, even until the last handful of earth is cast upon the grave![305]

Keeping all of this in mind, I will tell a final story that is both disconcerting and remarkably important. In 1810, Reb Shneur Zalman set out from Liadi in order to raise funds for Jewish families who had been displaced from rural areas by the Russian government's ironically named, "Commission on the Welfare of the Jews." Though these families had been poor in the rural areas, at least they could make a living and put food on their tables. Now, forced into the already overcrowded cities, they had nowhere to live, and being torn away from their livelihoods, were threatened with starvation.

ONCE, WHILE COLLECTING MONEY FOR JEWISH FAMILIES who had been displaced by the Russian government, Reb Shneur Zalman entered the province of Podolia and approached the home of Reb Barukh of Mezhbizh, the grandson of the Ba'al Shem Tov.[306] As he came near the house, Reb Barukh came out onto the balcony and looked down on Reb Shneur Zalman, saying, "Shalom aleikhem—Come up!"

Reb Shneur Zalman, seeing him there said with great courtesy and deference: "Who may ascend to the mountain of God? Who may stand in God's holy place?"[307] Meaning, How shall I ascend to so high a place as that which you currently occupy?

And Reb Barukh answered him by completing the next sentence of the quote, "He who has clean hands and a pure heart,"[308] which is the appropriate response. But then he said, "By what right do you come into my territory?"

Reb Shneur Zalman responded: "I have not come to teach, but to collect tzedakah (charity) for the displaced families of which you have heard; and for that I do not need permission. Moreover, it is written, "The earth belongs to God and the fullness thereof."[309]

Obviously, Reb Barukh was jealous of what he considered *his* territory, and even challenged his own nephew, Rebbe Nahman, on this score when he moved into the same 'neighborhood' in 1802. Thus, Rebbe Nahman, who Reb Shneur Zalman visited in Bratzlav prior to coming to Mezhbizh, was in a unique position to warn the Alter Rebbe about what he might expect of his waspish uncle in Mezhbizh . . .

When the Alter Rebbe visited his young friend, Rebbe Nahman in Bratzlav, he was overjoyed to see the young Rebbe again, and was very pleased with the welcome he received;[310] **for Rebbe Nahman had said to his Hasidim, "Come pay**

tribute to the lord of thousands!"³¹¹ And thus the entire town came out to greet and honor Reb Shneur Zalman, who had suffered so much for Hasidism, and who had successfully defended it against both the *mitnagdim* and the Russian government.

Then the two great Rebbes closed the door on the crowds and spent many hours together sharing spiritual insights and discussing deep matters. While they were talking, a wealthy Hasid of Rebbe Nahman's named Reb Moshe Khinkes knocked on the door and entered. Knowing that Reb Shneur Zalman had come to collect money for the displaced Jewish families, Rebbe Nahman said to Reb Moshe, "Moshe, give *tzedakah* to a true *talmid ḥakham*, to a scholar who is truly wise."

So Reb Moshe reached into his pocket and took out a large gold coin and laid it on the table.

"Is that what you give to a true *talmid ḥakham*?" asked Rebbe Nahman.

Again, Reb Moshe put his hand in his pocket and took out another gold coin.

Now, Rebbe Nahman was more stern, and asked again, "Is this what you give to a true *talmid ḥakham*?"

This sequence was repeated over and over until finally, there were ten gold coins upon the table! Only then was Rebbe Nahman satisfied that Reb Moshe had given the proper amount, and he pushed the pile of coins over to the Alter Rebbe—"A donation for the poor of your region."

Rebbe Nahman then inquired about where he intended to travel next to collect funds, and the Alter Rebbe said, "Mezhbizh."

Rebbe Nahman replied, "Ah! You may have managed *Feterburgh* (Petersburg) well enough, but *Feter Barukh* (uncle Barukh) won't be so easy!"³¹²

"WHAT DO YOU MEAN you don't need my permission?" said Reb Barukh, "I am the grandson of the holy Ba'al Shem Tov!"

"Yes," answered Reb Shneur Zalman, "you are a grandson according to the flesh, and I am a grandson according to the spirit. And it is well that I am, for when they asked me in Petersburg to answer for the Hasidic movement, I might have said: 'Is not the grandson of the Ba'al Shem Tov yet living? Let him come and answer the charges in my stead?'"

Even though HaBaD eventually became a dynastic Hasidic lineage, in this moment, Reb Shneur Zalman makes what is perhaps the most compelling and important statement about merit-based leadership in early Hasidism. Of course, dynastic leadership was still the exception at this time, but Reb Barukh of Mezhbizh was already laying the foundations for what would later become the norm, and what he obviously considered a natural right. And within a generation, this 'right' was almost unquestioned. So this statement becomes more important over time, preserving the original dynamism of Hasidism in this archetypal conflict.[313]

Reb Shneur Zalman was also reminding Reb Barukh that he might easily have disavowed the Ba'al Shem Tov early in his confinement in St. Petersburg, referring all questions to the Ba'al Shem Tov's biological heir; but by choosing to acknowledge himself as a follower of Hasidism's founder and suffering the consequences, he not only prevented Reb Barukh's own arrest, but also earned the right to be called a leader in the movement, subject to no one else's authority.[314]

REB BARUKH WAS INCENSED *and said,* "*How dare you speak to me in this way; I am wearing the* tefillin *of the Ba'al Shem Tov himself?!*"

"*Yes, but a* yud *(the letter yud) on the scrolls within your tefillin has fallen off (making them unfit for use).*"

Then Reb Barukh answered him in anger, "*If you're going to spoil my yud, I will spoil yours!*"—*And at that moment, a fire broke out in Reb Shneur Zalman's home in Liadi, burning many of his most valuable manuscripts, including his* Shulḥan Arukh, *and his* Sefer Shel Tzaddikim!*[315]

There are some people who think of this story in terms of two Rebbes doing combat on the subtle plane—firing magic bullets at one another! But I don't believe Reb Shneur Zalman's remark about the *yud* should be read in this way. He had far too high a regard for his "grandfather," the holy Ba'al Shem Tov to intentionally damage his *tefillin*. Thus, I believe his remark should be taken as a simple statement of fact, and not as some kind of shamanic 'spoiler.' On the other hand, Reb Barukh never would have imagined that the *tefillin* of the Ba'al Shem Tov would be subject to such a flaw, just as he did not consider that *he* might have such a flaw. So when Reb Shneur Zalman says that a *yud* has "fallen off," Reb Barukh immediately assumes that he has used his powers to render the tefillin unfit, and retaliates against the Alter Rebbe's *yud*!

Now what is meant by this reference to the *yud* of Reb Shneur Zalman? A *yud* is a 'point,' and it has the sense of being the point of faith, or the deep essence. So, just as Reb Barukh feels that Reb Shneur Zalman has attacked the symbolic essence of his authority (the Ba'al Shem Tov's *tefillin*), he attacks the holy 'essence' that Reb Shneur Zalman had put into his writings, into the *Shulḥan Arukh* and the *Sefer Shel Tzaddikim*, about which we have already spoken. Fortunately for us, the *Tanya* had already been published, and his briliant *ma'amarim* (discouses) were recorded in his disciples' memories.

A Hidden Light

In our discussion of *hitbonenut* in Chapter 2, we set aside the kabbalistic concepts Reb Shneur Zalman mentions as proper subjects of contemplation—i.e., how God 'fills' and 'surrounds-all-worlds'—because these ideas are based upon a mystical cosmology that we have not yet discussed. Nevertheless, this cosmology is so central to his life and thought that his teaching can hardly be understood without greater familiarity with it. Therefore, let's take a little time to explore the related notions of *Ain Sof, Or Ain Sof,* and *tzimtzum,* as presented in a short teaching from Reb Shneur Zalman's *Torah Or*:

> THE KABBALISTS speak of *Or* Ain Sof, the 'infinite light of Divinity,' which is a lesser reflection of Ain Sof, the 'infinite nothing,' a reflection of its sovereignty.

In kabbalistic literature, God is often called *Ain Sof*, 'infinite nothing,' meaning that God is 'without limits,' beyond our perceptions and transcendent of all our concepts.[316] In short, it refers to God as the one absolute, unlimited by any attributes, parts, or spatial concepts. This is the axiom around which all kabbalistic ideas of God must conform; they must preserve God's sovereignty and transcendence, as it says in scripture, "For I, Y-H-V-H, have not changed." (Mal. 3:6)[317] But transcendence doesn't leave us much to talk about, so the Kabbalah also speaks of *Or Ain Sof*, the 'infinite light of Divinity.'

Now, the Hebrew word *or*—'light'—calls to mind the ability to see and perceive.[318] So we speak of the *Or Ain Sof* as the highest conceptualization of what may be perceived in *Ain Sof*. It is a penultimate category for understanding what is beyond understanding, containing "every possible concept of perfection."[319] It is *the* divine metaphor, as the Alter Rebbe says, "a reflection" of God's "sovereignty."

> IT WAS WITHIN THIS INFINITE LIGHT of Divinity that the tzimtzum, the 'contraction' mentioned in the Etz Ḥayyim occurred. This contraction formed a ḥalal ha-panui, a 'hollow space' or 'void' in the midst of the infinite light—in the infinite light of Divinity—not in Divinity itself, not in the infinite One, God forbid.[320]

In the twelfth and thirteenth centuries, when the philosopher Maimonides (ca. 1138-1204) and the early Spanish kabbalists began to speak of God as 'transcendent' and 'infinite,' a number of questions arose as to how an infinite God could be related to a finite world. After all, infinity isn't a matter of numbers; you cannot say, "Infinity minus one equals a zillion." Even if you subtracted a billion, it wouldn't matter; it is infinity regardless of what you take out of it. So, the kabbalists, having established God as infinite—filling and encompassing all being—were at a loss as to how to reconcile this notion with the existence of a finite universe.

As a solution, some proposed a theory of intermediate steps between the infinite God and finite creation.[321] The thinking was that by putting sufficient distance between 'infinity' and 'finity,' as it were, a subtle shift could be shown to have occurred between the infinite Creator and finite creation. But this solution doesn't actually solve the problem; for the question of just *when* the infinite becomes finite still remains. No matter how many steps are added between infinity and the finite, there is still going to have to be a point at which infinity becomes finite. It's just not possible—the infinite is infinite and the finite is finite, and never the twain shall meet.

It is at this point that the Ari ha-Kodesh, Rabbi Yitzhak Luria introduces the concept of *tzimtzum*, 'contraction' in the *Etz Ḥayyim*:

> *Know this . . .* Before all emanations and creations, a simple light filled all of existence. Everything was filled with this *Or Ain Sof*, 'infinite light'; there was no beginning and no end to it; all was one uniform light. Then the will to create worlds and emanations emerged, and the Infinite contracted itself in the very center of its light, withdrawing from that center to the sides surrounding it, leaving a *ḥalal ha-panui*, an 'empty space,' a 'void.'[322]

That is to say, the infinite light of Divinity (*Or Ain Sof*) 'contracts' itself, making a space in which creation might have a limited autonomy in the midst of God's overwhelming presence.

What is interesting about the Ari's imagery is that the infinite light of Divinity is not contracted inward, from the outer 'edges,' as it were, but *away* from a point in the 'center,' creating a space that is womb-like; this leads us to believe that God is 'pregnant' with creation, and thus, 'surrounds-all-worlds,' *sovev kol almin*.

Now, why is *tzimtzum* so important? Because it represents a 'gap' between the Creator and creation. Before creation, there was only God's infinite Oneness. But when it arose in the divine will to create the finite universe, the infinite light of Divinity contracted itself, yielding a spherical void in which the finite could have a place to exist in the presence of God. Of course, the vital question is, how do we interpret this gap? Are we to understand this as a *literal* or a *metaphorical* contraction? The literal interpreters—led by the Rabbi Eliyahu ben Shlomo, the Ga'on of Vilna—were on the front-line in the defense of the theistic idea of God, whereas the metaphorical interpreters—led by Reb Shneur Zalman—were the forerunners of a new, pantheistic, reality-map.[323]

The literalists believed that God *actually* removed the divine essence from the *ḥalal ha-panui*, leaving a God-less vacuum for creation. Thus, it is from 'outside' the Void that a theistic God in Heaven 'oversees' the creation, directing the world as if from above. As a proof for this literal view, they argued that if we were to understand *tzimtzum* metaphorically, we would be forced to conclude that God's essence is found in 'unworthy places' and 'lowly things,' which would be totally unacceptable. To put it another way, a metaphorical interpretation of *tzimtzum* would mean that God's essence would still be here in this space, *even in such things as excrement and garbage;* for a metaphorical *tzimtzum* is really only the divine 'wool pulled over our eyes.'

Now, even though the theists could not accept this view, they still had to wrestle with the statement in the Zohar that says, "No place is devoid of God."[324] So they interpreted this statement to mean that it is only God's *hashgaḥah*, or 'providence' that pervades the Void, and which is still there. God *actually* rules from a distance, like a king 'overseeing' his domain from a castle—an ivory tower, if you will—where he remains unsullied by the day-to-day affairs of the kingdom.[325] This was the hold-out position of the theists.

But Reb Shneur Zalman proposed another interpretation. He said, if God were to withdraw from a 'place,' this would imply a limitation on God's power and suggests that God changes or is changeable. But the scriptures say, "I, Y-H-V-H, have not changed." So this is not only philosophically unacceptable, it is also unacceptable according to the scriptural tradition. Thus, he points-out the inconsistencies in the literal interpreter's reasoning, saying it is impossible to apply literal concepts belonging to the material world to God who is immaterial and incorporeal. Also, to distinguish between God and God's *hashgaḥah* is to carry the simile of the king overseeing a kingdom too far. That may apply in this world, but with God, it is impossible to say God's knowledge is something separate from God's essence, for Divinity "is one in all respects."³²⁶

Of course, some literalists countered that it is also a limitation on God's power to say that God *cannot* have withdrawn the divine essence from a space. But Reb Shneur Zalman doesn't deny this, he only says that it didn't happen that way. He points to the proof-text, "Do I not fill the heavens and earth, says God?" (Jer. 23:24).³²⁷ And because there is an exegetical rule in Judaism that no verse may be *excluded* from a literal interpretation, it becomes necessary to accept this verse as literal, forcing one to read *tzimtzum, the withdrawal of God from a place* as metaphorical. Otherwise, the two ideas would be in contradiction.³²⁸ So *tzimtzum* should actually be understood as a metaphor for the *hiding* or *concealing* of God.³²⁹ Moreover, it does not take place in "Divinity itself, not in the infinite One, God forbid," but within the divine 'metaphor' of the infinite light.³³⁰

THIS TZIMTZUM *(contraction) was for the sake of bringing the physical world into existence, thus allowing human beings to bring about a revelation of God's infinite sovereignty in this world, just as it was before creation; for prior to creation, the infinite light of Divinity filled all of existence, and this will ultimately be revealed again in the physical world, unrestrained by the contraction of light. Thus it is written, "I am first and I am the last, and there is no god but Me."*³³¹

When Reb Shneur Zalman says, "the infinite light of Divinity filled all of existence" before creation, he is suggesting that just as infinity cannot be made finite, neither can the *Or Ain Sof* allow for the existence of anything separate and distinct from it because it already fills *all* existence. For even though it is a penultimate category of absolute Divinity, by its very nature, it must also partake of the infinity of *Ain Sof*. So without this *tzimtzum* in the *Or Ain Sof*, nothing else could have independent existence.³³²

Thus, *tzimtzum* is a necessary prerequisite for creation, so that what is created should not be overwhelmed by the homogenous perfections of *Or Ain Sof*. The purpose of the Void, or the negative light created by the *tzimtzum* is to act as a barrier against the *Or Ain Sof*, 'screening' us from God so that creation is not overwhelmed.³³³ This is what the *Zohar* calls a *botzina de kardenuta*, or 'lamp of darkness,' an energy source that radiates darkness.³³⁴ Thus, it is said, "God wrapped in a garment of light"—i.e., the *Or Ain Sof*—and "hid in the darkness"—i.e., the *botzina de kardenuta*.³³⁵

Now, this *botzina de kardenuta* or *ḥalal ha-panui* is analogous to what is called *maya* in Hinduism. *Maya* is the cosmic drama, the universe of God's dream in which we have a limited kind of existence. In *maya*, what we call 'existence' and 'reality' are neither in comparison to the absolute existence and reality of God, the divine dreamer; we are but figments of God's imagination. Nevertheless, existence in God's 'head,' as it were, is not the airy nothing of our limited imaginings, but a force powerful enough to construct a world so complete and absorbing that we can even forget the existence of God! As one of my own teachers of Vedanta said to me, *maya* is "the force which conceals our Divinity."[336]

Those who seek to comprehend the truth of God's *maya*, according to the Hindu tradition, are engaged in a fool's errand. Nevertheless, countless spiritual aspirants have gone on this futile journey. Among the greatest was the holy sage, Narada, of whom the following story speaks . . .

Once, a great ascetic who had fulfilled many vows was granted a boon from God.

He said, "O Sovereign of the Universe, "If you are truly pleased with me, allow me to comprehend your *maya!*"

But God responded, "No one can comprehend my *maya;* no one ever has, and no one ever shall. Long ago, there lived a holy sage and seer called Narada, whose devotion was even greater than yours, and who, like you, I granted a boon. He too wished to comprehend my *maya,* to know its secret; but I told him that this was impossible. Nevertheless, he insisted, so I said, 'Go dip in that body of water and you shall experience the essence of my *maya.*'

"Narada waded out into the water until he came to a depth where he might dip. Closing his eyes, he dipped under the waves. When he emerged again, he was no longer Narada, but a lovely young woman—Sushila, the virtuous daughter of the king of Benares. Now Sushila was soon wedded to the son of the neighboring king of Vidarbha. It was a good match and Sushila loved her husband, and their delight in love brought them happiness and many children.

"After a while, the old king of Vidarbha died, and the kingdom passed to his son, Sushila's husband. A territorial dispute broke out between the new king of Vidarbha and Sushila's father, the king of Benares, which eventually degenerated into open war. This war soon built to a crescendo of violence, a great battle in which both Sushila's father and husband were killed, as were all her brothers and sons. So great was her grief that she commanded her servants to build a great funeral pyre upon which she might throw herself. Then, calling out the names of her loved ones, she leapt into the fire!

"Then there was a splash, and suddenly, coughing smoke and ash, Narada

emerged to find himself chest deep in water. Even more amazing, he felt grief stricken and was pouring tears for the loved ones he never knew!
God said to him, 'Who are these people for whom you weep?'"³³⁷

As Narada comes out of the water, he is ashamed of his hubris and prays that he should be granted perfect faith, because while the essence of God's *maya* may be realized, it may not be comrehended.³³⁸ This could also be said of the *halal ha-panui,* which we may realize, but which is not to be comprehended by us. It is the screen and filter that protects our individual consciousness; and on the other side of that screen, there is no 'I' to understand anything... only pure consciousness. Therefore, it is only the *maya* of God's dream that 'appears' to us, and on whose stage we are but players.

Nevertheless, Reb Shneur Zalman tells us, the *Or Ain Sof,* 'the infinite light of Divinity' "will ultimately be revealed again in the physical world, unrestrained by the contraction of light," and he quotes the verse, "I am first and I am the last, and there is no god but Me." Thus, he goes on to explain . . .

> "I AM FIRST," refers to the state of existence prior to the tzimtzum. "Last," refers to the end of things, beyond creation, when "God alone will prevail."³³⁹ "There is no god but Me," refers to the time between, in the midst of the contraction, when we say, "we have no sovereign other than You," despite the concealment. This is the revelation that overcomes the concealment and hiding of the light.

Now, Reb Shneur Zalman is challenging his disciples to really wrap their heads around the paradox implied by God's absolute transcendence. For it's not enough to say that God is transcendent; you have to really understand what that means, as much as this is possible for us.

In this passage, he is reminding us—just as God was alone before the creation of the world, so God is alone after its creation. In chapter 36 of the *Tanya,* he writes: "It cannot be said that before God there is either 'up' or 'down,' for God fills all these worlds equally. Before the world was created, God and God's name were one, filling all 'space,' and 'since' God created the worlds, there has been no change in God."³⁴⁰

There has been no change either in God's essence or in God's knowledge, for God's knowledge is Self-knowledge. God knows all creatures introspectively, for all is from God, and nullified within God. As Maimonides expressed it: "God is the *knower*, the thing *known*, and *knowledge* itself. This is a thing which is in the power of no mouth to utter, or in the power of no ear to hear, nor is it possible for the heart of any human to grasp its full significance."[341]

This is difficult for our minds to imagine. Therefore, the prophet says: "For My thoughts are not your thoughts, and your ways are not My ways, says the Lord. For as high as the heavens are above the earth, so are My ways above your ways, and My thoughts above your thoughts." (Isa. 55:8-9)[342] Concerning this it is said: "Can you find out the experience of God? Or can you find (the way) unto the utmost limits of the Almighty?" (Job 11:7)[343] And this was Job's question: "Have You eyes of flesh, or will You see as a mortal sees?" (10:4)[344] For we see and know all things with a knowledge which is external to our self, but the blessed and holy One knows all from a knowledge of God's own Self.[345] All of which is to say, God is the one authentic 'I' of existence, which Reb Shneur Zalman tells us "is the revelation that overcomes the concealment and hiding of the light."

Now, in the next passage, Reb Shneur Zalman brings the whole message together, talking about how the infinite light of Divinity "overcomes the concealment."

THIS LIGHT *comes through Torah, as it says, "The Torah is light,"*[346] *so that even now, in the midst of the* tzimtzum, *Torah channels and brings about a revealing of the infinite light of Divinity, just as before the* tzimtzum.[347]

Now there is just one problem with all of this talk of God's infinite sovereignty and the qualified reality of our own existence. Having undermined all of material existence, including our own, how do we continue to affirm the importance of Torah and *mitzvot*, the commandments given to us by God, which are all related to this 'fictional' world?

Reb Shneur Zalman actually suggests the answer to this problem throughout this teaching. In the beginning, he tells us that the *tzimtzum* only occurred "for the sake of bringing the physical world into existence, thus allowing human beings to bring about a revelation of God's infinite sovereignty in this world." In the *Zohar*, it says that God created the world so that we would be able to know God, so that we, as finite beings, would come to a realization of the infinite, and a recognition of our own Divinity. To put it another way—God wished to discover God's own Divinity through us! Why? Because, as we have said elsewhere, God is an atheist; God does not have a God, and is thus deprived of the joy of discovering Divinity—except through us. With the *tzimtzum*, Divinity pulled the wool over its own eyes and decided to have a human experience, creating the potential for a realization of itself.³⁴⁸ In this way, and as this happens in more and more people, "God's infinite sovereignty" is revealed in the world.

This is what he means when he says, "we have no sovereign other than You"—acknowledging God's greatness in the midst of the *tzimtzum*—"despite the concealment. This is the revelation that overcomes the concealment and hiding of the light." Or, we might say, this is the realization that overcomes the ignorance that causes all our fears and doubts in this world.

Now, what does this have to do with Torah and *mitzvot*? In this last passage, he tells us that the Torah is the 'clue' and the 'life-line' for discovering our true identity and revealing the hidden light of Divinity.³⁴⁹ As he says, "The Torah is light." It is through the Torah that we learn, "For I, Y-H-V-H, have not changed," and "Do I not fill the heavens and earth, says God?" "And you shall know today, and take it to heart, that *Yah* is God—in Heaven above and Earth below—*there is nothing else.*"³⁵⁰

Torah is one of the pillars on which the world stands. The 'world,' *ha'olam*, was interpreted by Reb Shneur Zalman as denoting that which is 'hidden,' *he'elem*.³⁵¹ Thus, one of the pillars on which God's hiddenness stands is also Torah. And the purpose of creation—God's hiding in order that God may be found—is also realized in Torah. God who gave Divinity to human beings in the Torah can also be found in it.³⁵² Thus, the whole purpose of life revolves around the study of Torah and the finding of God in Torah.

There is a Hasidic teaching that says: What was the first word uttered on Mount Sinai? *Anokhi*, 'I am.' According to the Talmud, this is an acronym for *Ana Nafshi Ketavit Yehavit*, "I Myself gave it to you in writing" (i.e., the Torah), which is interpreted in Hasidism as, "I gave Myself to you in writing."³⁵³ Thus, Torah contains God's essence. And what does the Torah teach us but how to deal with the world and matter, to take physical objects and to use them to perform *mitzvot*, sanctifying them through such use, releasing the sparks of holiness in them, creating more and more consciousness of God.³⁵⁴

Elsewhere, the Alter Rebbe says, "The Torah and *mitzvot* are the 248 channels through which the category of the transcendent is drawn down to us."³⁵⁵ That is to say, the *mitzvot* are the means by which we connect with God through matter, and also through which we bring consciousness to matter. They are the God-connections bringing about the divinization of the planet, ultimately "revealing of the infinite light of Divinity, just as before the *tzimtzum*."³⁵⁶

Beyond the Wall—The Passing of the Alter Rebbe

Though this teaching on *tzimtzum* is somewhat weighty, we have included it because it has a bearing on a beautiful moment during the Alter Rebbe's passing, which we are now fast approaching. Nevertheless, the Alter Rebbe had one last trial to overcome yet—Napoleon's invasion of Russia.

Napoleon Bonaparte's (1769-1821) war with the other European powers was the subject of much debate among the Rebbes. Some saw him as a great liberator, while others saw him as a slippery slope. Rebbes like Reb Menachem Mendel of Rymonov (1745-1815) supported him, hoping that he would bring freedom and equality to the Jews of Europe. And this seemed like a distinct possibility, as Napoleon had invited the Jews of North Africa and the Levant to unite under his flag to re-establish Jerusalem. He had also summoned a "Sanhedrin" in Paris to speak to Jewish issues.[357] Of course, these measures certainly had political ends, but even so, it represented a major shift in the state of affairs for many Jews. Nevertheless, other Rebbes like Reb Yisra'el, the Maggid of Kozhnitz (1733-1815) were bitterly opposed to him, and carried out a battle against him in the upper worlds.[358] Reb Shneur Zalman was in this latter camp, writing to his disciple, Reb Moshe Meisels:

> It was revealed to me . . . that if Bonaparte is victorious, there will be great material prosperity in Yisra'el, but the Jews will become estranged from God. But should *adoneinu* (our Lord) Alexander (the Czar of Russia) be victorious, even though they would suffer great poverty, the children of Yisra'el would draw closer to God in Heaven.[359]

You see, it was not that Reb Shneur Zalman did not believe Napoleon's promises of societal reform with regard to the Jews, it was that he feared what that would mean in the context of the secular world's lax morality and unbridled opportunities. So, as Napoleon's army advanced into Russia in 1812, Reb Shneur Zalman, not wanting to reside under the conqueror's dominion for even for a single day, took flight for inner Russia with a personal escort of Russian soldiers.

Shortly before Napoleon's army reached Liadi, the Alter Rebbe and all his household, and numerous Hasidim—sixty wagons and many men and women on foot—made their way into the Russian interior. But after they had gone just over a mile,[360] the Alter Rebbe suddenly stopped. He summoned the soldiers who had been assigned to escort him, and asked them to supply him with a light carriage. They did as he asked, and he sped off with two of his Hasidim, proceeding as fast as the horses would take them back to Liadi!

Returning to his home, he told the Hasidim to search the house thoroughly for anything that he might have left behind. They looked everywhere. In the attic they discovered an old pair of the Rebbe's slippers, rolling pins, and a sieve. They brought these to the carriage, and the Alter Rebbe commanded them to set the house on fire!

Just after they departed, Napoleon, his adjutants, and his personal gaurd arrived in Liadi and quickly made their way to the Alter Rebbe's home. Finding it ablaze, he ordered that the fire be put out and offered a reward to anyone in Liadi who might bring him an object that had belonged to the Alter Rebbe . . . even a coin that had been given them by the Rebbe. But no one came forward, and his troops were unable to recover anything from the ruined house.[361]

A HaBaD tradition says that Napoleon had been heard to say, "Whenever I ride, that blonde Jew rides before me."[362] This was thought to be a reference to Reb Shneur Zalman who was supposed to have had blue-eyes and blonde hair. And, in this story at least, it appears that Napoleon was somehow aware that a famous Jewish mystical leader was living in Liadi; and he wished either to speak with him or to have some object that he possessed as a kind of talisman. Realizing this, the Alter Rebbe quickly returned to take the last objects from his home and to burn the house to the ground, rather than have anything of his used for such purposes.

Though there seems to be no proof, there are persistant rumors that Napoleon had been initiated as a freemason during his campaigns in the Mid-East in 1798. Whether this is true or not, it seems that he at least held unconventional religious views throughout most of his life, sometimes even identifying himself as an adherent of different religions. What is most certain is that Napoleon used religious sympathies to gain the support of the diverse populations in his empire, making strong overtures to the Jews of the empire and portraying himself as a friend to French Catholics. One of the most interesting instances of this tendency was seen during his Egyptian campaign, during which he showed great respect for Muslim holy sites, pardoning the imams of the Al-Ahzar Mosque who had been caught up in the uprising against him. In the Spring of 1799, Napoleon actually had it proclaimed to Egyptian Muslims that he "loved the Muslims, cherished the Prophet, instructed himself by reading the [Qur'an] every day, and desired to build a mosque unrivalled in splendour and to embrace the Muslim faith."[363] It may be that he hoped to make similar gestures in Russia by appealing to the Alter Rebbe, the most famous Jewish leader of the region.

The caravan of the Alter Rebbe continued on its way, fleeing the forces of Napoleon, traveling many weary miles over many days until they arrived in a town called Piena, where he took sick with a severe cold in his weakness. For five days he lay ill, gradually becoming worse and worse. After *Shabbat*, he recited his evening prayers and *havdalah*, then asked for a pen and paper and wrote a mysterious letter:

How truly humble is the being of the soul. At the root of her operation, she is engrossed in the physical Torah, both for herself and for others. What is the work of charity but an approaching of mind to mind, and a counseling from far away, dealing with family matters, although most of these are just a pack of lies? Yet it is impossible to do it differently and still to do a kindness; for truth is only in the Torah, and Truth said of human beings, "Create them not."[364] But Grace said: "Create them for they are full of graces." Thus Truth is cast to the ground, and a world is built on a Grace that is not true; for nowadays it is all done not with the Truth of Torah, but by (the Rebbe's) approximating the mind of the one (the Hasid) who must do the work, in order to gain cooperation. Though it be far from the Truth, there is no other way, and this way is a very humble one; so all we can do is accept the facts as they are and do so in love and generosity."[365]

At the end of his life, it seems, the Alter Rebbe was still concerned with what it means to work with a Hasid in spiritual intimacy. He appears resigned to the fact that there could be no other way but to enter into the ignorant "lies" of interpersonal relationships—and the false way in which we experience the world—giving counsel out of a love far greater in its redemptive value than the Truth, which devastates us and says "Create them not." He knew that a Rebbe must enter into the Hasid's labyrinth to help them find their way out, an idea which we will see again in Rebbe Nahman of Bratzlav.[366] For the Rebbe realizes that the labyrinth of confusion, caught up in God's *maya* serves the Hasid as a temporary defense against the problems of the world. This is precisely why the principle of grace is invoked and not that of truth.

―――――――――――――

THEN, AS HE LAY UPON HIS BED, *looking at the wall, the Alter Rebbe asked his grandson, Reb Menachem Mendel, "Mendele, do you see the wall?*
Reb Menachem Mendel answered him, "Yes, zeide, I see the wall."
Then the Alter Rebbe said, "I don't see it anymore—I only see the word of God holding it all together." Soon after, he died.[367]

―――――――――――――

I can only imagine what he saw in that moment—a vision of the letters of creation in infinite combinations, like glowing source code standing in place of the wall.[368] It was as if at the moment of his passing, the veil between the worlds began to lift, revealing just a fraction of what was concealed in the *tzimtzum* of God's *Or Ain Sof,* in the infinite light of Divinity, which he must have longed to see all of his days.

Thus passed the Alter Rebbe on the 24th of Tevet, 5573 (December 27th, 1812) Reb Shneur Zalman ben Barukh of Liadi who, as the Ba'al Shem Tov prophesied, had come to earth to "illuminate the world with two kinds of light—the light of *nigleh*, the manifest Torah, and the light of *nistar*, the hidden Torah," and to "succeed in establishing Ḥasidut through selfless dedication, thus preparing the way for the *Mashiaḥ*."[369]

4

The Two Who Are Inseparable:
The Heirs of the Alter Rebbe, the Son and Disciple

EVEN BEFORE THE UNEXPECTED PASSING OF THE ALTER REBBE in the Russian interior, the Hasidim of Liadi had already been speculating about who might succeed him. Most separated themselves into one of two camps: the more conservative base supporting Reb Dov Baer Shneuri (1773-1827), the Rebbe's eldest son and most trusted companion; and a smaller, more radical contingent supporting Reb Ahron HaLevi Horowitz (1766-1828), the Rebbe's most beloved and distinguished disciple.[370]

As young men, the two had been close friends, spending nearly all their time together in study and prayer. They were each of them 'sons and disciples' of the Alter Rebbe—one a 'disciple' of the flesh, and the other a 'son' of the spirit—both sharing a deep love and devotion for him. But sadly, as time passed, an ideological and political wedge was driven between them as they cultivated subtly different models of HaBaD Hasidism. Thus, after the passing of the Alter Rebbe, the HaBaD community, which had so long been unified under one teacher, split into two separate lineages: HaBaD-Lubavitch and HaBaD-Staroshelye, each named after the town in which the two heirs of the Alter Rebbe eventually settled.

From the perspective of Hasidism's first two generations, this shouldn't have been a problem, as both the Ba'al Shem Tov and the Maggid of Mezritch had numerous legitimate heirs doing their work in different towns and villages.

But the Alter Rebbe had created such a homogenous community in his lifetime, holding sway over such a large territory, that his community could hardly conceive of the possibility of there being more than one legitimate heir.

Thus, even as I sat in the Lubavitcher *yeshiva* over 130 years later, I occasionally heard Reb Ahron HaLevi—who was much beloved in the Alter Rebbe's lifetime—characterized in a somewhat negative light, as if he had done something wrong in becoming a Rebbe. Now I understand that I was learning the 'history of the victors'—for the ḤaBaD-Lubavitcher lineage stemming from Reb Dov Baer eventually absorbed Reb Ahron's own ḤaBaD lineage in the next generation, and quietly dismissed it as an aberration. Thus, it seems only right that we should remedy this situation today and restore Reb Ahron to his rightful place in the history of ḤaBaD Hasidism, creating a more unified and holistic picture of ḤaBaD teaching as it evolved from its source in the Alter Rebbe.

Of the two, we know the least about Reb Ahron HaLevi, for comparatively few stories from his court in Staroshelye seem to have survived to the present day. Nevertheless, most of his extraordinary writings are still extant, and we have done our best to piece together a picture of him from the few remaining ḤaBaD sources that speak of him.[371] Of Reb Dov Baer, who inherited the largest part of his father's community, and whose voluminous teachings are also still available, we know far more. Nevertheless, his legacy also seems to have been diminished by the conflict with Staroshelye, for his role in the history of ḤaBaD-Lubavitch is often treated in a cursory manner before moving on to Reb Menachem Mendel I of Lubavitch (1789-1866), who once again unified the lineage in the next generation. Thus, I think we can best honor both of these extraordinary Rebbes by bringing them together in the same chapter, telling their respective stories side by side, as they once stood in love and friendship.[372]

The Maggid's Prediction

Reb Dov Baer's story actually begins a little less than a year before he was born. Indeed, it is just before the passing of his namesake, Reb Dov Baer, the holy Maggid of Mezritch (1704-1772) that he is first mentioned in ḤaBaD lore...

On the 17ᵀᴴ of Kislev, three days before his passing, the Maggid of Mezritch spoke to his disciple, Reb Shneur Zalman, saying: "The last three days of one's life, it is possible to perceive God's creative word in everything—the essence of its reality." Then he told him that he would soon be blessed with a son whom he should call "Dov Baer" after him. He then gave Reb Shneur Zalman precise instructions for the newborn's first eight days leading up to the brit, the 'covenant' of circumcision.³⁷³

In the light of the Alter Rebbe's own last words about the wall—"I don't see it anymore; I only see the word of God holding it together"—this first remark of the Maggid takes on a new meaning, and I wonder if he too was also seeing the 'source code' of creation at this moment?

Nevertheless, the more important part of this anecdote for our story is the prediction of Reb Dov Baer's birth by the Maggid, which happened a little less than a year later on the 9ᵗʰ of Kislev, 1773. It is perhaps worth noting that Dov Baer would become the only major successor to a disciple of the Maggid to be named after the Maggid himself; and even more interesting, that the child should be so different from his father, and so curiously like his namesake in mind, body, and spiritual disposition!

A Born Rebbe

Not surprisingly, Reb Dov Baer turned out to be a tremendously gifted child who often reviewed the lessons of the older children along with his own to fulfill his tremendous thirst for learning. While still very small, he had learned to translate Torah, and before long had memorized the entire TANAKH and was soon deriving deeper teaching from it, as the following story shows.³⁷⁴

> ONE EVENING, LITTLE "BEREL," as he was then known, came into the room called the "Lower Garden of Eden" where three Hasidim were waiting to be called for yeḥidut (the encounter) in the Rebbe's study, called the "Upper Garden of Eden." One of them was Reb Shmuel Munkes, who Berel loved like an uncle; the others were Reb Shlomo Rafaels and Reb Yosef Kol-Bo, who in addition to being great scholars, were also businessmen in their respective cities.
>
> So Berel came running over to see Reb Shmuel and overheard him asking Reb Yosef—"Why do you look so glum?"
>
> Both he and Reb Shlomo answered solemnly, "The economy isn't so good" ... "Business is bad."
>
> Then Berel spoke up, saying to Reb Shmuel: "Why do you need to ask the reason for their 'sadness' (atzvut)? It says in the Tehillim, 'Their 'sadness' (punning on the word, eitzev, 'idol') comes from thinking that silver and gold are the work of human hands.'"

> *Then speaking like a miniature version of his namesake, he said: "People are sad because they think that they can make silver and gold for themselves. They think that the more work they do, the more money they can make. So they rush off to buy more stuff from the fair in Leipzig (which was where Reb Yosef bought his merchandise), or race over to Koenigsburg (which was where Reb Shlomo bought the liqueurs he sold) always trying to make more silver and gold."*

In the Psalms it says, "The idols of the nations are silver and gold, the work of men's hands" (Ps. 135:15), which little Dov Baer—taking advantage of the similarities between *atzvut* and *eitzev*—has turned into, "Their *sadness* comes from thinking that silver and gold are the work of human hands." He is reminding these men that they cannot *make* "silver and gold" any more than they can control the economy. As the Stoic philosophers might say, unhappiness and discontentedness comes from acting against *nature*, i.e., ignoring *reality-as-it-is* in favor of *reality-as-we-would-have-it*.[375] Thus, the "sadness" of these businessmen comes from wanting to control what they cannot, rushing to and fro in their anxiety from Leipzig to Koenigsburg, working longer and longer hours trying to manufacture destiny—all the while—forgetting God's providence.

> Now the little prodigy continued: *"People become so 'blind' in their work that even though 'they have a mouth' and sometimes use it to speak about Hasidism in their studies, they don't allow it to rule over their lives—so it is useless to them. 'They have eyes, but cannot see; they have ears, but cannot hear.' They see and hear only the externals of things and miss the work of God's compassion and providence all around us! They are cut-off from all of their spiritual senses, and thus become 'like a stone idol' which cannot see or hear!"*[376]

With this he finishes his interpretation of the rest of the passage (Ps. 135:16-18). In effect, he is saying that we become 'sad' about such things because we allow ourselves to forget what we have learned in *Hasidut*, i.e., that God's providence is at work at all times and in all places. Forgetting this, we fail to see the hidden 'opportunities' in our apparent misfortunes. Worse, in so doing, we have also forgotten God, setting ourselves up as idols, thinking we *can* and *must* control circumstances that we cannot. Thus we fall into sadness and melancholy over our own idol-like impotence, just like a clay statue.

One wonders whether Reb Shlomo Rafaels and Reb Yosef *Kol-Bo* had come to speak with the Alter Rebbe about just this subject in *yehidut* and perhaps found their relief while still in the "Lower Garden of Eden?"

The Commander of God's Armies

And what do we know of Reb Ahron HaLevi's early life? Unfortunately—very little. Nevertheless, the classic HaBaD chronicle, *Beit Rebbe*, does record some of the important details of his family's background and tells us a little about his disposition in childhood.

THE MOST UNIQUE STUDENT *of the Alter Rebbe was our master, the holy teacher, whose soul is in Eden, Reb Ahron HaLevi, better known to the world as the Rebbe of Staroshelye. He was the son of the Hasid, Reb Moshe HaLevi Horowitz, who was descended from a great and holy family. It is said that the divine image that existed in the father was not effaced in the son.*

The root of their family was the master, Rabbi Yeshaya Horowitz, the SheLoH ha-Kodesh, 'the two tablets of the law,' of whom Reb Ahron was an eighth generation descendant. From his youth onward, he utterly rejected the attractions of the world, putting all of his attention on the Torah of God, for which his yearning and delight was awesome. While he was still young, he became close to our master, the Alter Rebbe.[377]

So we see that Reb Ahron HaLevi was a direct descendent of Rabbi Yeshaya Horowitz, the author of the *Sh'nei Luhot ha-B'rit*, 'the two tablets of the law,' which the Alter Rebbe so admired.[378] Thus, he was probably raised in the traditions of his famous forbear, learning both Talmud and Kabbalah at the highest levels available in the non-Hasidic world.[379] The only glimpse we get of Ahron's personality in this passage is the comment: "From his youth onward, he utterly rejected the attractions of the world, putting all of his attention on the Torah of God, for which his yearning and delight was awesome." This is as much as we know of him until his seventeenth year, when he makes the journey to Minsk to hear the great debate between the 38-year-old Lithuanian genius, Reb Shneur Zalman of Liozhna, and the scholars of the *mitnagdim* (see "The Great Debate" in Chapter 2). Fortunately, an account of this first encounter with the Alter Rebbe has been preserved in the HaBaD tradition by a young Hasid who was privileged to hear it from Reb Ahron HaLevi's own lips.

ONCE, A YOUNG HASID named Reb Abba of Tchashnik was taken to the court of Reb Ahron of Staroshelye for a bar mitzvah blessing. Though his father was himself a Hasid of Reb Dov Baer of Lubavitch, his father-in-law was an important Hasid of Reb Ahron HaLevi. Thus, he was privileged to be able to hear the Rebbe deliver a ma'amar (discourse) to his Hasidim in Staroshelye and to be given a special yeḥidut blessing.

Though he was too young to understand the Rebbe's ma'amar, he was awestruck by the Rebbe's words, which seemed to him like fire from Heaven, and he noticed that whenever the Rebbe would mention the name of his holy teacher, the Alter Rebbe, he would rise in silence and stand motionless for sometime, as if lost in holy *deveikut (absorption)!*

Later, when he entered the Rebbe's study with his father-in-law for yeḥidut, the Rebbe told them the story of the first time he ever saw the Alter Rebbe, just before the great debate in Minsk with the mitnagdim . . .

"At the time, I was just seventeen years old, and had come to Minsk with others to witness the debate between the leader of the Hasidim and the great scholars of the mitnagdim.[380] We had heard that he would be speaking at the *shul (synagogue)* before the debate, so we went there to get a look at him. Fortunately, we arrived well ahead of time, for the shul was soon full and the courtyard teeming with people. Then he entered, looking like the 'great commander of God's armies!'"[381]

At this point, Reb Ahron HaLevi became ecstatic and paced back and forth for some time, saying, "Oy! Oy! Oy! The holiness of his face!" When he recovered himself, he began to deliver the teaching the Alter Rebbe gave that day, as if the words came directly from the holy of holies! "The Alter Rebbe went up to the podium and began to speak in an awesome voice, and everyone fell silent as if commanded to listen . . ."

"SHEMA YISRA'EL—Hear (hehren) and understand (derhehren) that Y-H-V-H is our God! This phrase tells us that our very life-force is derived from the letters of God's name, Y-H-V-H . . . The letter yud stands for ḥokhmah, 'wisdom,' the heh for binah, 'understanding,' the vav for the six middot, or 'emotional attributes,' and the last heh for malkhut, divine 'sovereignty,' all of which are within us. And when we say, Y-H-V-H is one, we mean that God's unity transcends all distinctions and differences!

"Thus, it is clear that each of us carries Divinity within us, and it is our responsibility to reveal this Divinity in the world around us, transforming the planet into a vessel of holiness. And how do we accomplish this?

Through studying Torah, fulfilling the mitzvot, and praying with great love (ahavah) and awe (yirah). As it is written, 'The soul of the human being is the candle of God.'[382] Just as a candle may illuminate a house, so may the soul—as it is expressed in these three things—bring light to the darkness of the world!

"Concerning this, it is written, 'On that day, Yisra'el shall be ... a blessing on the earth,'[383] meaning that Yisra'el will draw 'Y-H-V-H ... from eternity'[384]— from the hidden world into the manifest world. This is accomplished when we stir the innermost 'heart' within us and tease the divine soul out of the shell of materiality, unifying our being in Y-H-V-H is one!

"When one takes these ideas into a deep contemplation (hitbonenut), the soul begins to break its bonds and bursts into flame with a passionate love of God. As it says, "To You, Y-H-V-H, I lift up my soul!"[385]

"FROM THAT MOMENT ON, I and the others who had come with me, were bound to the Alter Rebbe as if by an eternal knot!"

Later on, Reb Abba who told this story became a disciple of Reb Menachem Mendel I of Lubavitch (after the passing of Reb Dov Baer), but he never ceased to be stirred by the words and holy presence of Reb Ahron Starosheyer, whom he considered a great tzaddik.[386]

I can remember the first time I was introduced to the idea of God as *Ain Sof* (without limits) in Lubavitch. I was so overwhelmed, all I could say was "Oh, w-o-w!" It was as if in that moment, the *Gottenyu*, the 'little God' of my childhood was expanded to infinite dimensions and blew my mind in the most wonderful way.

So you can imagine how these ideas must have set Reb Ahron's passionate nature ablaze and catalyzed his electric intelligence. This is what he had been looking for all along. Here he had a mysticism that was expansive, and yet completely and cohesively wedded to Torah and *mitzvot*.[387] And from this point forward, it seems as if Reb Ahron was utterly absorbed with these two ideas: the non-dual understanding of God's absolute oneness, and the work of contemplation that reveals it. These are the two hallmarks of all his further teaching, and this seems to have its roots in the first teaching he heard from the Alter Rebbe!

The Curse

When next we hear of Reb Dov Baer and Reb Ahron HaLevi, they are sitting opposite one another in the "Lower Garden of Eden." Reb Dov Baer is now twelve years old, and Reb Ahron is nineteen. Having witnessed the power of Reb Shneur Zalman's intellect and hearing the profound teachings he repeated, young Ahron was utterly overcome and followed the Hasidic leader back to Liozhna, where it is likely that he was accepted into Ḥeder Gimmel. However, it was not long before Reb Shneur Zalman noticed his exceptional character and abilities—so like his own—and made him the study partner of his precious elder son, Dov Baer.

It is also hard not to notice a parallel in this act to the Maggid's pairing of the learned and charismatic Reb Shneur Zalman with his own introverted and deeply holy son, Reb Avraham "the Angel," exactly twenty years earlier. Whether there is a deeper significance to this, I don't know, but this is what happened, and this is where we find both Reb Dov Baer and Reb Ahron at the beginning of this fascinating account.

ONE HOT DAY IN THE SUMMER OF 1785, *Reb Pinhas Reizes, a senior disciple of the Alter Rebbe, was studying outside with a number of other disciples when a simple wagon pulled into the Rebbe's courtyard.*

Sitting atop the wagon were two men—one shorter and older, and the other taller and younger. The elder man was the venerable Reb Shlomo of Karlin, and the younger was Reb Wolf of Zhitomir, both disciples of the Maggid of Mezritch. When the wagon came to a stop, the two men descended and spoke to Reb Pinhas and the other disciples. Unfortunately, their accents were so strange that no one knew what they had said. Thankfully, Reb Shmuel Munkes, who was familiar with the region from which they had come, translated for them: "They asked—'Where is the home of Reb Zalmina Litvak.'" Hearing the name by which his Rebbe had been known in Mezritch, he laughed and pointed in the direction of the Rebbe's house.

Then Reb Pinhas and Reb Zalman Henyes, showed them the way to the Alter Rebbe's house, and took them into the room which the Hasidim called, "Lower Garden of Eden," where two young men were seated at a table, studying. The elder of the two was Reb Ahron HaLevi, and the younger Hasid was Reb Shneur Zalman's oldest son, Reb Dov Baer.[388]

Seeing Reb Pinhas escorting two obviously important guests, Reb Dov Baer rose and greeted them with a Shalom aleikhem. They responded in kind and asked Reb Dov Baer what he and Reb Ahron were studying. To Reb Pinhas' surprise, Reb Dov Baer understood their accents and told them the subject of their study. Then the two men asked again where they might find "Reb Zalmina Litvak." Reb Dov Baer recognized the name and smiled. He was about to speak when the Alter Rebbe suddenly opened his door and the two men smiled with delight. The Alter Rebbe gave them his Shalom, and they entered his study to speak with him in private.

A few hours later, little "Moishe," the Rebbe's youngest son came running into the courtyard where the disciples were gathered, yelling—"They're arguing with abba, and abba says, 'It's forbidden!'" No one knew what he was talking about until Reb Ahron came running out of the beit midrash, crying—"Berel! The Rebbe's son Berel has fainted!"

The Hasidim raced to the little beit midrash—the "Lower Garden of Eden"—where they found Reb Dov Baer lying unconscious near the door of the Rebbe's study. Two of them, Reb Hayyim Eliya and Reb Avraham Zalman, cried out—"Oy! Rebbe! Oy! Rebbe!"

The Rebbe quickly came out of his study and the Hasidim carried Reb Dov Baer to a sofa, where he lay with his eyes closed and his head resting in his father's hands. The Rebbe asked for some cold water, and when it arrived, he sprinkled some of it on Reb Dov Baer's face until he opened his eyes and sighed deeply. Then the Rebbe asked everyone to leave the room except for Reb Pinhas Reizes, Reb Zalman Barukh Ratchover, and Reb Ahron Orshayer, who were to stay and watch over Reb Dov Baer while the Rebbe returned to his guests.

When Reb Dov Baer finally came to, he was feverish and shook as if he were chilled. So Reb Pinhas and Reb Zalman Barukh carried him into the other half of the Rebbe's house where the Rebbetzin and the other children were, and laid him in his own bed. He quickly fell asleep, and Reb Zalman Barukh stayed at his bedside to watch him.

Then Reb Pinhas went back to the little beit midrash to question Reb Ahron about what had happened. But no matter how much he implored him, Reb Ahron would say nothing. Finally, he broke down in tears and Reb Pinhas understood that he had heard something that had disturbed him greatly. So he decided to change tactics. Being one of the Rebbe's most senior and intimate disciples, Reb Pinhas offered him something the younger Reb Ahron could not refuse—some of the personal teachings the Rebbe had given him in yehidut!

There is nothing more tantalizing to a young Hasid than those personal stories and insights given directly to another Hasid in counsel, or which another Hasid has been witness to; for by such intimate knowledge, the Hasid hopes to elevate his or her soul. Here we see that Reb Ahron HaLevi was so passionate for such information that he is able to overcome his fear of what he had heard and begins to tell the story to Reb Pinhas Reizes . . .

So Reb Ahron began to tell Reb Pinhas what had happened after he and Reb Zalman Henyes left the little beit midrash:

"After the Rebbe's guests had been in his study for a while, we began to hear raised voices coming from within. At first, we tried to ignore them and carry on with our studies. But as they began to get more heated, and carried on for more than an hour, we finally decided to see if we could hear what they were saying. So we went and stood near the door, being as quiet as possible. To my ears, it sounded like a debate over some aspect of Torah; but then it became clear that the Rebbe's guests had come to get his endorsement for the excommunication (ḥerem) of the mitnagdim, *God forbid!*

"Apparently, a minyan of the ḥevraya kaddisha, *the 'holy fellowship' of the Maggid's disciples, had already come to this decision. And now they wanted the Rebbe to endorse it. But he replied that such an act was* assur, *'forbidden'; for an individual who is excommunicated may become cut-off from the root of his soul and may fall into unbelief, God forbid! And this, he said, would cause a great* ḥillul ha-Shem, *a 'desecration of the divine name.'*

"The elder of the two men (Shlomo of Karlin) said that the ḥevraya kaddisha *had weighed all the possibilities, and had decided to go ahead with the excommunication anyway; for the* mitnagdim *were jeopardizing the life of the entire movement!*

"But the Rebbe held firm in his position and would not be a party to anything that might put another's soul in jeopardy. It was at this point that the elder of the two men uttered a curse, and hearing it, Berel fainted, as you saw."

As you may have noted already, this is the full story of Reb Shlomo of Karlin's (1738-1792) famous visit to Liozhna which was mentioned twice in Chapter 2.[389] Reb Shlomo was one of the senior disciples of the Maggid, and the successor to another mentor, Reb Ahron of Karlin after his early death. By all accounts, Reb Shlomo "could move mountains with the power of his prayers," and even put special emphasis on mental exertion (i.e., contemplation) in prayer, though Reb Shneur Zalman seems to have had reservations about his method.³⁹⁰ In this and so many other things—as our story shows—these two Rebbes found themselves on opposite sides of the divide. But in Reb Shlomo's defense, the persecution he personally suffered was immense. You see, at that time, many of the *mitnagdim* thought of the Hasidim as the "Karlinist sect," owing to the early influence of Reb Ahron of Karlin. So Reb Shlomo, having become the Karliner Rebbe after Reb Ahron, appeared to many to be the leader of Hasidism, and he suffered much abuse because of it. Thus, it is perhaps understandable that his passion over this issue got the better of him in this moment, and he uttered what he should not have uttered—"a curse."

Now, this may have simply meant that he 'swore' out of frustration in this moment, but in the Hasidic context, 'swearing,' 'cursing,' and 'imprecating,' all carried the older meaning of 'invoking evil' or 'divine retribution upon someone,' and was considered a very serious act. So you can imagine when Reb Ahron and Reb Dov Baer overheard this, they were extremely frightened; and Reb Dov Baer, being much younger and of a much more sensitive nature, fainted and became fevered.³⁹¹

Reb Pinhas then decided to tip-toe over to the door of the study and himself heard elements of the same conversation being rehashed. Only now they discussed the three levels of excommunication. Then, little Moishe came running into the room with a shout and proceeded to run around the pulpit used for the Torah Reading in the little beit midrash.

Soon after, the door to the Rebbe's study opened and the Alter Rebbe came out with his guests, still talking about the issue of excommunication—only now in a much more subdued tone. Then, Moishe ran over and hugged the Rebbe around the waist, and the Rebbe put his right hand affectionately on his head.

Reb Shlomo of Karlin made one last attempt—"Zalmina, think it over carefully, and consider joining us."

The Alter Rebbe replied, "As I have said, the Torah does not allow me to endorse such a ḥillul ha-Shem, and I don't intend to."

Reb Shlomo of Karlin repeated his curse and stormed out. Nevertheless, the Rebbe courteously saw them both to their wagon. Reb Wolf of Zhitomir decided to stay on for a while in Liozhna, but Reb Shlomo wanted to leave immediately. Thus, the Alter Rebbe sent Reb Binyomin Kletzker with him as a traveling companion.³⁹²

For several weeks after this, Reb Dov Baer lay in bed with a high fever, physically and spiritually disturbed by the curse he had heard at the door of his father's study. It was only after the Rebbe had discussed the entire matter with him that he began to recover.³⁹³

Sadly, Reb Shlomo Karliner was forced to leave Karlin because of the attacks of the *mitnagdim* and take up residence in Ludmir, where he was later shot and killed by a Cossack in 1792.³⁹⁴ It was not that the Alter Rebbe did not sympathize with him, or that the Alter Rebbe was not himself persecuted (as we have seen), but that he was unwilling to endanger another person's soul for the sake of protecting his own material existence. To him, this would be a "desecration of the divine name," and he refused to have any part in such an act. Reb Ze'ev Wolf of Zhitomir (d. 1798), Reb Shlomo's younger companion may have been swayed by the Alter Rebbe, for he stayed on in Liozhna for almost three months. He was not of the same fiery temperament as Reb Shlomo. In fact, he was known to pray in deep stillness and disapproved of uncontrolled anger. He once wrote: "Angry people fill their mouth with live coals, with needles, sharp and hard.... Each of us must be a master of his mouth."³⁹⁵

The Training of Rebbes

In 1788, when he was just fifteen years old, Reb Dov Baer married Sheina, the daughter of a pious teacher. It is at this point that we begin to see him going through the struggle to mature from a gifted young man into someone with the potential to be a Rebbe. I say, "struggle," because the maturing process usually involves some very painful mistakes. This is as it should be, for how else do gifted Hasidim like Reb Dov Baer and Reb Ahron HaLevi learn to have compassion for those who are less gifted than themselves? Therefore, I am grateful that the HaBaD oral tradition had the wisdom to preserve a few of these classic stories of the mistakes the Rebbes made before coming into their own.

ONCE, WHEN HE WAS STILL A TEENAGER, *Reb Dov Baer was sent on an errand to a small town by his father. After he had completed his errand, he went to the local* shul *to say his prayers; but just as he was getting ready to pray, he noticed a man* davenen *(praying) in a wild and noisy manner, waving his arms about and screaming every word! Well, this was completely foreign to Dov Baer, who was extremely quiet in his own prayer. He shook his head in disapproval and said derisively:* Oikh mir a davenen, *"That's what he calls* davenen?"

Just then, the man turned around and grabbed Reb Dov Baer by his lapels, and said to him: Berel! Vos ha dein tatteh in zin gehat ven ehr hot dikh gemakht? Vos hot mein tatteh in zin gehat ven ehr hot mikh gemakht. *"*Berel!*"—he called him by his first name, not showing him any respect—"What did your father have in mind when he made you? And what did my father have in mind when he made me? I must* daven *how I must* daven!"

What did he mean by that? In a basic way, he is saying: "How dare you judge me? You have had all the advantages, and I have had none! This is how I have to pray in order to overcome my animal soul!" Likewise, the Ba'al Shem Tov taught: "Do not laugh at one who moves his body, even violently, during prayer. A person drowning in a river makes all kinds of motions to try to save himself. This is not a time for others to laugh."[396]

But on another level, this interesting exchange is explained by what is written in the second chapter of the *Tanya*:

As for what is written in the *Zohar*[397] about behaving in a sacred manner during sexual union—which is not the case with the children of the ignorant—it should be understood that there is not a *nefesh, ruaḥ,* or *neshamah* which is not a 'garment' inherited from the *nefesh*-essence of one's father and mother, affecting the way in which we must accomplish each *mitzvah*. Even the loving-kindness that flows to one from Heaven is given through that garment, and thus, through self-sanctification (in the sexual act), one can cause the descending of the *neshamah*, the sacred garment of one's child. But however great a soul it may be, it will still need the father's sanctification.[398]

THIS REBUKE so shocked Reb Dov Baer that he immediately begged the man's forgiveness.

Later, when he returned home to his father, he began to cry and said to him—"Abba, I haven't even begun to serve God. I've been given such a wonderful, transparent garment, and others have not had the same advantages. My own service has been nothing in comparison with this man whom I have affronted! He has put such effort into his prayers, and I have done nothing in comparison!"

After a while, this same Hasid came to Liozhna for yeḥidut with the Alter Rebbe; but as soon as the Rebbe saw him, he called his gabbai (attendant) and asked him bring some schnapps and lekakh-cake, saying: "I want to thank you; you have made a Hasid out of my son! If you hadn't challenged him in this way, he would have continued to think of those who didn't measure up to his level as nothing; he wouldn't have recognized how much work it takes to serve God in truth! So I owe you for having made a Hasid of my Berel."[399]

So you can see how this kind of *bitush*, or verbal 'barb,' can be an important means of sharpening true vocation when it is used in the right way. Sometimes the Rebbe would also intentionally expose a disciple to situations of this sort in order to test his vocation, as we see in this little anecdote about Reb Ahron HaLevi.

> ONCE, THE ALTER REBBE tested Reb Ahron HaLevi in his use of power, and Reb Ahron failed because he was too strict with the younger Hasidim. Later, when he came to complain about a lack of feeling in his prayer to the Rebbe, the Alter Rebbe told him that this was due to his strictness with the other Hasidim—"One who is harsh with God's children, finds God being harsh with him."[400]

In many ways, this lesson is much like the former learned by Reb Dov Baer; for the tendency of the gifted is to measure everyone else against the standards of the gifted. But a Rebbe must have compassion for everyone and teach them according to their own abilities, always judging them on the side of merit, adjusting for their individual needs.

Another interesting anecdote concerns Reb Dov Baer's tendency to get so lost in his prayers that he could not come out of them when circumstances required it, drawing a strong rebuke from his father.

> ONCE, WHEN THE ALTER REBBE and Reb Dov Baer were davenen *together, both having entered deeply into their own contemplation, the Alter Rebbe suddenly heard a thud on the floor above and then a baby's cry! He immediately shook himself out of his meditation and rushed upstairs to his grandchild's crib. There was little Nohum, Reb Dov Baer's son on the floor! The Alter Rebbe picked him up, kissed him, and carried the child back to where his father was* davenen. *When Reb Dov Baer had finished his prayers, the Alter Rebbe rebuked him, saying, "You may enter deeply into your* davenen, *and you may get lost in your* hitbonenut—*but you should still be able to hear it when your baby cries!"*[401]

Again, I see a parallel in this story to the moment in Chapter 1 ("A Bagel in Atzilut") when Reb Shneur Zalman saves his friend, Reb Avraham the Malakh, from getting permanently 'lost' in his own contemplation. And this was likely a motivating factor in his strong rebuke of Reb Dov Baer in this instance; he doesn't want his son to die an early death like Reb Avraham, with whom Dov Baer obviously shared so many spiritual tendencies. So he stresses the importance of being able to hear the baby cry—to find a bagel in *atzilut*—even in the midst of the most absorbing meditation!

Some meditation traditions try to produce a state in which one is so absorbed in the object of meditation that one is completely unaware of *everything* else. However, more recently, people like the Sufi teachers, Pir Puran Bair and Susanna Bair have emphasized a heart-rhythm meditation technique in which one may produce the delta and theta waves characteristic of deep meditation while still being aware of one's surroundings.[402] In some ways, this is a kind of 'corrective' which addresses the sad story of Khwaja Qutb ad-Din, a master in their lineage who bears some similarity to Reb Dov Baer and Reb Avraham the Malakh.

As Pir Zia Inayat-Khan tells the story, Khwaja Qutb ad-Din was an ecstatic with an extremely otherworldly temperament, keeping a vigil every night, his meditation taking the place of sleep for him. So extreme was his "otherworldliness," he says, that he even neglected his family . . .

> **It came to pass that Khwaja Qutb ad-Din's son became gravely ill, and all the while, he sat in meditation. Finally, he was woken from his ecstasy by the cries of his wife. He called his *khalifa* (deputy) and asked, "What has happened?" "Oh *huzur,* your son has passed away." Khwaja Qutb ad-Din was deeply moved, shaken to the core of his being, and he repented his negligence. He told himself, "If only I had prayed to God for the well-being of my son, God would have answered my petition, but I was lost in the divine unity."**

As Pir Zia points-out, Khwaja Qutb ad-Din's story is a paradoxical one; for as a result of his absorption in the divine unity he had "privileged access to God's 'ear,'" and could have gotten a favorable response from God had he prayed for his son, but his very absorption prevented him from availing himself of the "benefits of this exalted position." Thus, it was useless to him, and not long after, he died while absorbed in an ecstatic state.[403] Thank God, Reb Dov Baer avoided this same fate and, as a result of his father's timely rebuke, went on to serve the community as a more deeply grounded Rebbe.[404]

The Two Who Are Inseparable

By the time Reb Dov Baer was seventeen years old, the Alter Rebbe had appointed him to guide the studies of the younger married men of the court, thus grooming him for leadership.[405] This became a customary practice among the Rebbes of the HaBaD-Lubavitch lineage. Even my own Rebbe, Reb Yosef Yitzhak (at around the same age) was entrusted with the task of guiding the students and overseeing the operations of the Tomkhei Temimim Yeshiva founded by his father in Lubavitch.

Interestingly enough, we actually have an eyewitness account of Reb Dov Baer in this role; for in 1795, an adherent of the *Haskalah*, the Jewish Enlightenment Movement, came to Liozhna in disguise and later described a number of scenes he witnessed there, including Reb Dov Baer in his early twenties teaching the younger Hasidim:

> IN ANOTHER ROOM, *I saw a large group of young men studying the [Tanya]. Leading them was a young man who read from the text and explained it at great length. The subject of his commentary was the eighth chapter of the book, which concerns the eating of forbidden foods and the consequent defilement of one's body and soul. He discussed the differences between the defilements caused by arrogance, foolishness and idle behavior, which have a dulling effect on the heart and senses, and that caused by studying secular philosophy. He then explained that Maimonides and Nahmanides had avoided this defilement because they had studied secular philosophies in the service of God. I had to admit, his arguments were sound and compelling. Later I learned that this was none other than the Rebbe's elder son, Dov Baer, who taught two groups of students twice a week, each group having about twenty-five students.*[406]

As they continued to mature, both Reb Dov Baer and Reb Ahron HaLevi were each given more and more responsibility in Liozhna's communal affairs. By 1796, when the last set of Liozhna *takkanot*—'ordinances' governing the behavior of HaBaD Hasidim—were published, both were personally assisting the Rebbe in teaching and spiritual guidance; for in the *takkanot*, new visitors to Liozhna are ordered to report to Reb Dov Baer and Reb Ahron, who were to gauge the Hasid's character and conduct, verifying their admissibility to hear the Rebbe's teachings. But they were also themselves allowed to give Hasidic discourses, explaining the Rebbe's teachings to other Hasidim, which was the highest possible mark of the Rebbe's confidence.[407]

Reb Ahron HaLevi's status in the court of the Alter Rebbe is confirmed by the fact that he was authorized to write letters to the Hasidim on the Rebbe's behalf. In one such letter, he appeals to the Hasidim to send funds to support the Rebbe's growing activities, which included the maintenance of his *yeshiva* students, the Hasidim in the Holy Land, and the underprivileged who came to him for help.[408] Moreover, when the Rebbe was arrested in 1798, it was Reb Ahron who set out on the road, showing "great self-sacrifice" while traveling to various ḤaBaD communities to collect funds for the release of the Alter Rebbe.[409]

> ONE PERSON WAS DESIGNATED to travel for the purpose of collecting money for the maintenance of the Rebbe's family. Others who understood the law traveled to Petersburg to determine why the Rebbe had been arrested. And the holy master, Reb Ahron HaLevi of Staroshelye, who was a very special student of our master, traveled throughout the country, into all the regions where our Hasidim dwelt, and they opened their hands to him with great generosity to help the Rebbe.[410]

In fact, it is said that the reason ḤaBaD prayer shawls (tallitot) don't have an embroidered 'crown' (attarah) at the top edge is because Reb Ahron collected all these as a means of raising funds for the Rebbe's release![411]

Likewise, Reb Dov Baer was given similar responsibilities, for instance, writing letters on the Rebbe's behalf, asking for financial support after the fire in 1810 consumed the Rebbe's home. However, he was also authorized to write pastoral letters to the Hasidim, including one which began, "I have been ordered by my father the Rav to write in his name a reproof from hidden love to the fraternity in general . . ." concerning the need for contemplation before prayer.[412]

But none of this says anything of the special friendship that existed between Reb Ahron and Reb Dov Baer, which seems to have been both sweet and intense for a very long time. The *Beit Rebbe* has most to say about this in its section on Reb Ahron HaLevi:

> INDEED, OUR MASTER loved him greatly, and brought him very close, putting him on the bench with his own son, the Mittler Rebbe,[413] Reb Dov Baer, so that they might study together. And there was a great love between these two as well; they were like brothers, always studying the revealed Torah (nigleh) and Ḥasidut together. Words cannot express their relationship. And Hasidim came to both of them to hear the repetition of the Alter Rebbe's teachings with their additional explanations. Reb Ahron was one of the few people who could enter into the Alter Rebbe's presence without permission, just as if he were one of the Rebbe's sons.[414]

In the early years, the older Reb Ahron appears to have been an important mentor to Reb Dov Baer, sometimes writing him letters of encouragement and advice; but later they obviously met as equals, studying Talmud and Hasidut together, as only the most profoundly gifted of the Alter Rebbe's disciples could. *Oy!* How I would want to eavesdrop on one of those study sessions![415] However, the real sweetness of their early relationship is most clearly seen in the following anecdote I once heard...

ONCE, AN ELDER HASID *saw Reb Dov Baer and Reb Ahron HaLevi holding hands while walking down the street together and said aloud,* Trein rai'in d'lo mitparshin, *"The two friends who are inseparable." Hearing this, the Alter Rebbe added with some gravity,* Ha-levai, lo mitparshin, *"May they never be separated."*[416]

This beautiful moment says so much about the importance of friendships on the spiritual path. For as much as we can get from a Rebbe, *who* we share it with, and *how* they help us to work it out, is every bit as important. Indeed, this is almost the first teaching Reb Dov Baer gives to the younger Hasidim after his father placed them in his care...

AFTER THE ALTER REBBE *placed his son over the younger Hasidim, Reb Dov Baer immediately encouraged them to cultivate friendships, for he said:* "Hasidim are seldom in the same place at the same time. Thus, when you are struggling with a problem, your friend will likely be in a position to help you. And as the two of you discuss it, it will be as if there are two yetzer ha-tovs (good inclinations) fighting against one yetzer ha-ra (evil inclination), and the yetzer ha-ra will be overcome!"[417]

Was this the voice of his own experience with Reb Ahron coming through? I tend to think it must have been. I wonder if any *yetzer ha-ra* ever faced two such formidable *yetzer ha-tovs*?

Ecstasy—Manifest and Hidden

Nevertheless, there were significant differences between them in personal style and expression. As others have pointed-out, Reb Ahron HaLevi seems to have "stood for open, tumultuous expression of emotion," while Reb Dov Baer's example was that of "silence and stillness."[418] Why is this important? Well, it tells us a great deal about their personalities, but it is also probable that these contrasting public personas had a lot to do with the choice Hasidim made between Lubavitch and Staroshelye later on.

So let's begin by looking at Reb Dov Baer's prayer of deep stillness . . .

HIS PRAYER WAS UTTERLY SILENT, *without the slightest movement or stirring of his limbs; but within, it was as if he was consumed with burning flames that no one else could see. One Yom Kippur, Reb Dov Baer prayed for hours on end, but was absolutely still, moving not a single muscle; nevertheless, so great was the inner intensity of his davenen that his attendant had to change his shirt several times, for it was completely drenched with sweat and tears!*[419]

Again, I am reminded of Reb Avraham the Malakh who once sat in prayer the whole night of Tisha b'Av unmoving, remaining in that silent meditation until Tisha b'Av was over.[420] Even more interesting, Reb Dov Baer's prayer actually parallels a description of contemplative prayer that his namesake, the Maggid of Mezritch gives in *Likkutei Yekarim*:

It is possible to pray in such a way that no other person can know of your devotion. Though you make no movement of your body, your soul is all aflame within you, and when you cry out in the ecstasy of that moment—your cry will be a whisper.[421]

To me, this seems like a perfect description of Reb Dov Baer's prayer, and might also serve as a good description of his other more public practices. For this 'inner service' comes up again in another anecdote involving Reb Levi Yitzhak of Berditchev:

Wishing to taste Reb Dov Baer's holy ecstasy and deveikut (divine absorption), Reb Levi Yitzhak of Berditchev asked the son of his dear friend to say the grace after meals. Obliging, Reb Dov Baer recited the blessing simply, like someone who only understood the literal meaning of the words, without any apparent emotion. Reb Levi Yitzhak expressed some surprise at this to Reb Shneur Zalman, who replied: "Don't be surprised or, God forbid, alarmed at this apparent simplicity my friend; he knows the great kavvanot (intentions) from the highest to the lowest levels, and is filled with an inner love and awe so great that even I am jealous! Nevertheless, it does not show on the surface."[422]

Obviously, this anecdote strengthens the point about Reb Dov Baer's inner service, but it also shows us that his appearance of calm and simplicity could give some people the wrong impression. Indeed, if a master as discerning as Reb Levi Yitzhak of Berditchev could be fooled—even temporarily—into thinking Reb Dov Baer might not be up to par in the 'Rebbe department,' so might others of less discernment, as we will see later on.

So what was Reb Levi Yitzhak looking for? Probably something like Reb Ahron HaLevi's prayer, which has been characterized as being "of a frightening intensity, an outpouring of religious fervor and enthusiasm expressing itself in a mighty roar as the prayers were pronounced."[423] Though I know of no real anecdotes or stories about his prayer, the following description from *Beit Rebbe* seems to have been witnessed and affirmed by all who knew him...

> THE MANNER OF HIS PRAYER AND SERVICE *was awe-inspiring, full of great energy and tremendous ecstasy, so much so that anyone who saw or heard him in prayer was stirred and enflamed by that fervor. Moreover, all those who were close to him also prayed with great emotion and fervor.*[424]

This is likely what Reb Levi Yitzhak was expecting from Reb Dov Baer; for he and most of the Hasidim of the Maggid tended to pray with great intensity, causing a holy fear and trembling to fall upon all who witnessed it. Indeed, so intense was the Ba'al Shem Tov's prayer that it sometimes overwhelmed his disciples, including the Maggid. It is said, even the grain in the barrels on the other side of the house trembled because of it![425] However, in his *Tzava'at ha-RiBaSh*, there is support for both Reb Dov Baer's and Reb Ahron's styles of prayer:

> ... when you first begin to pray, rouse yourself through your body—use all your physical strength—to allow the power of your soul to shine through. Thus it is written in the *Zohar* (III:166b, 168a), "Logs that will not burn should be splintered; then they will light." After this, you will be able to worship with just your mind, without any need for bodily movement.[426]

Likewise, when a wood-fire first begins to burn hot, the wood and its sap crackles and pops, sometimes with explosive intensity. But later, when the wood has all burned down, the embers remain red-hot, though they no longer make any noise. These examples would seem to be good descriptions of the respective prayer-styles of Reb Dov Baer and Reb Ahron HaLevi; but while both suggest that the sound and the fury of the one is merely a preparation for the quiet after, the personal example of the Alter Rebbe actually legitimized both as wholly legitimate for the entire period of prayer, as his grandson, Reb Menachem Mendel I of Lubavitch says: "When he prayed alone, he prayed quietly; but when he was *davenen* with others, he shouted for all the world to hear."[427]

However, for those who did not see the Alter Rebbe in his private prayer, Reb Ahron's prayer must have seemed like the most obvious continuation of the way of the master. And indeed, it is not a criticism of Reb Dov Baer to admit that Reb Ahron's style of prayer and personal expression more closely resembled those of the Alter Rebbe. For compare what you have read about Reb Ahron above with what it says of the Alter Rebbe in the *Beit Rebbe* (also quoted in Chapter 3):

> The Hasidim who heard him would come to a great trembling before God where they stood, becoming enflamed to the service of God in an awesome way, and thus they became good masters of prayer. . . . Likewise, in his prayer he was tumultuous! As his grandson, the Tzemah Tzedek said: "So great was his thirst to be absorbed in the divine essence that he would say in the middle of prayer: 'I don't want Your Garden of Eden! I don't want Your World-to-Come! I want only *You, You, You alone!*'" . . . "And so tumultuous was his prayer that they had to fix padding on the walls, for he sometimes battered his hands against the wall until they bled—and yet he felt nothing at all!"[428]

If the emphasis in the sources on Reb Ahron's ecstasy is to be believed, this picture of the Alter Rebbe's prayer could easily be a description of Reb Ahron's own. But that doesn't mean his style of expression was any more legitimate than Reb Dov Baer's, as some people surely thought at the time. For the master-disciple relationship of Reb Shneur Zalman and Reb Ahron seems to have been an obvious attraction of two 'similars.' That is to say, both men were similarly gifted in heart, mind, and temperament, so that they must have had a very natural affinity for one another. Indeed, Reb Ahron even seems to be a more extreme version of Reb Shneur Zalman at times, or at least a definite continuation of the master.

But this is also what makes the father-son relationship between Reb Shneur Zalman and Reb Dov Baer even more extraordinary; for Reb Shneur Zalman overcomes the patriarchal urge to make his son in his own image and allows him to develop along his own trajectory. Indeed, the mirroring of the Alter Rebbe that Reb Ahron did probably wasn't even possible for Reb Dov Baer. For the resemblance between father and son might be compared to a plaster cast taken of someone's face. That is to say, what is 'convex' in the father becomes 'concave' in the son who is, as it were, the 'cast' taken from the father. Thus, his expression was necessarily different. At the very least, this would seem to be the case with Reb Dov Baer, and his father respected it in him. Once he is reported to have said to him: "For both of us the intellect is in control of the heart but for me it controls only the external heart; but for you it controls even the inner heart."[429] In this way, he nullified the usual Oedipal conflict between father and son.

Nevertheless, it is usually the older disciples that have a more difficult time with these differences, as my favorite anecdote of the Lekhovitcher Rebbe shows...

> **After the passing of Reb Mordecai of Lekhovitch, his son was made Rebbe in his place. But the son, Reb Noaḥ of Lekhovitch had an altogether different style than his father, and some of the elder Hasidim complained to him, "You don't do it like your father did it." To which he answered, "I do it exactly like my father did it; my father didn't copy anyone, and neither do I!"**[430]

The Ordination of the Rebbes

Was it these differences in personal expression that eventually drove them apart? I don't think so; these are things that friends learn to accept and appreciate in one another early in their relationship. It is more likely that ideological differences played a larger part in separating them. Nevertheless, in discussing Reb Ahron HaLevi's departure from Liadi, the author of the *Beit Rebbe* doesn't point to either of these possibilities, but suggests another more insidious cause—*gossip*.

> WHEN OUR MASTER RETURNED FROM PETERSBURG *and settled in Liadi, Reb Ahron also bought a house there, and settled his own family in Liadi for the next eight years. However, a few years before the passing of our master, the Alter Rebbe, a number of people began to speak against Reb Ahron, bringing gossip about him to the Rebbe, and causing him to suffer a great deal because of this. Thus, he sold his house and moved his 'tent' to the city of his birth in Orsha, where he continued in the ways Torah and divine service, coming to visit our master, the Alter Rebbe, from time to time.*[431]

What was this gossip about? And why would people begin to "speak against" the person who was considered to be the Rebbe's "leading disciple"?[432] We should remember that by the year 1808, the year in which Reb Ahron leaves Liadi, both he and Reb Dov Baer are mature men—35 and 42 years old respectively. At this point, they had both come into the fullness of their abilities and had developed very definite ideas about how Ḥasidut was to be taught and experienced. And naturally, as they continued to lead the community as 'officials of the court'—each representing the ideal of ḤaBaD Hasidism in his own way—younger Hasidim must have begun to attach themselves to one or the other with sincere devotion. But as this was also a time when the Alter Rebbe's health appeared to be failing, many Hasidim had probably begun to wonder: "Who will lead them when Reb Shneur Zalman is gone? Will it be the quiet but deep Reb Dov Baer, his son, or the brilliant and charismatic Reb Ahron HaLevi, his favorite disciple?"

As we have already mentioned, the Alter Rebbe had created such a homogenous community in his lifetime, holding sway over such a large territory, that the community could hardly conceive of the possibility of there being more than one legitimate heir. To them, the extended community of ḤaBaD Hasidim seemed to parallel the secular kingdoms and empires with which they were so familiar. And that being the case, they asked—How could you have more than one king? Or more than one capital for that matter? You see, even though the Ba'al Shem Tov and the Maggid of Mezritch had managed to maintain an efficient *meritocracy* in their own day, it was still a radical notion in the environment in which they lived. So it was only a matter of time before the forces of normalization attempted to adapt the model into something more familiar and 'acceptable'—the dynastic model of succession.

Thus, I think it likely that an influential element within Liadi—one who believed that the Rebbe's son should succeed him—probably began a subtle campaign to limit Reb Ahron's powerful influence among the younger Hasidim. This would almost certainly involve carefully worded suggestions that his service was 'not quite up to the standard' of Reb Dov Baer's, and whispers about his 'ambitions.'[433] As the author of the *Beit Rebbe* tells us, these whispers eventually became open gossip that reached the ears of the Rebbe, causing Reb Ahron "to suffer a great deal," and to move his family from Liadi. But as much we can guess from the *Beit Rebbe*'s pithy account, there is one question that remains unanswered—What did the Rebbe think of all this?[434]

Fortunately, there still exists a description of their final *yehidut* before Reb Ahron left Liadi. It is found in a little known biography of Reb Shneur Zalman called *Shivhei ha-Rav* by Mikhael Levi Rodkinson (1845-1904), a grandson of Reb Ahron, who was primarily known as a collector of Hasidic folktales and as the first translator of the Talmud into English.[435] Thus, it appears to be a family tradition that would not likely have found its way into other ḤaBaD-Lubavitch books. In this account, it appears that Alter Rebbe has called his beloved disciple, Reb Ahron HaLevi into his study for a private discussion of these very matters . . .

FOR 30 YEARS, THE HOLY REB AHRON *served his master in great intimacy—like the levi'im (temple attendants of the tribe of Levi) of old who poured water over the hands of the kohanim (temple priests who were the descendants of Ahron) before they blessed the people—and never ceased to love him. To him was revealed all the hidden parts of his master's wisdom, and no secret escaped him. All that which was hidden was made manifest and clear to him. However, three years before his master's passing, the Rav placed his hands upon him and blessed him, and bestowed three changes of white robes upon him.*[436] *He then sent him home to Orsha, the place of his birth, where he began to give evidence of his own strength, and to write his own sacred books.*[437]

Though Rodkinson is not explicit about why the Alter Rebbe is sending Reb Ahron away, I think we can assume that he is responding to the situation mentioned in *Beit Rebbe*. Does that mean that the Rebbe accepted the rumors as true? I can't imagine that this kind of gossip would have had any real effect on the Alter Rebbe. It is much more likely that he was concerned over what the gossip represented—unrest in Liadi and the destabilization of the community.

Whatever the motive, this small anecdote is far more important for the dimension it gives to what must have been a tremendously difficult moment for both the Alter Rebbe and Reb Ahron HaLevi; the one having to send his most beloved disciple away for the sake of keeping peace in Liadi, and the other being pushed out of the nest amidst vicious rumors. But it is also important for another reason—it gives us a rare glimpse into what amounts to a *rebbishe* ordination. For in the language of Hasidism, the gift of white robes coupled with a blessing would seem to indicate an authorization to act as a Rebbe.

In Hasidism's first three or four generations, Rebbes and their senior Hasidim were known to wear white robes on *Shabbat* and other holidays as a mark of purity. Whether anyone other than the Rebbe wore white robes in Liadi at that time is unknown to me. Nevertheless, Reb Ahron HaLevi is being given three of the Rebbe's *own* white robes as he is being sent away. This is an unmistakable gesture, not only in Hasidim, but also in other mystical traditions, such as Sufism ...

> When the great Sufi master, Khwaja Mu'in ad-Din Chishti of Ajmer felt it was time for his disciple, Khwaja Qutb ad-Din to lead disciples of his own, he drew him near and placed a turban upon his head, gave him the staff of his own master, and wrapped him in one of his own tattered cloaks. "This is a trust," he said, "which has been handed down to me from my own master, and which I now hand to you. Go forth, I entrust you to God, and pray that you will reach your goal." Then he sent him on to Delhi to represent Chishti Sufism in that region.[438]

Likewise, when the Maggid of Mezritch took over the leadership of the Hasidic movement, he was given the white *bekeshe* (caftan) of the Ba'al Shem Tov, putting it on before the assembled disciples and delivering his first discourse as the leader of Hasidism. This is the ancient and profound notion of 'investiture,' wearing the garments of the previous leader, which carry the powerful *baraka*, or 'blessing' of the former owner. I have no doubt that this is the meaning of the Alter Rebbe's gesture.[439]

However, it appears that Reb Ahron HaLevi was not the only one to receive the Alter Rebbe's personal authorization to act as a Rebbe before his death. According to one of his great disciples, Reb Pinhas Reizes, Reb Dov Baer was likewise given the Rebbe's personal endorsement in 1811, as the following letter makes clear ...

LISTEN TO ME, PEOPLE OF MY HEART; *I have a secret that I must now reveal. Listen carefully to my words, open your ears and apply the sensitivity of your spirit to them and God will hear you (in your time of need).*

Near the end of our Rebbe's life, at the wedding of his granddaughter with the Chernobyler Rebbe's son, the current Rebbe, Reb Dov Baer and I were taken aside by the Rebbe, who closed the door behind us. He then began to speak to us in the beautiful manner for which he was known, and which I could not possibly represent here. However, the gist of it was this: intrinsic to his son's nature is a concern and ability "to cause the well-springs to flow outward,"[440]

> that is to say, to bring the words of the living God to his community. This is his delight, his longing, and his intention, and on nothing else has he put his eye or his heart. Therefore, the Rebbe commanded me, for reasons known only to him, to make certain that the pidyonot should be passed through the Rebbe, Reb Dov Baer's hands alone after the Rebbe has gone on to the 'yeshiva' above.

As we have already discussed *pidyonot* in an earlier chapter, there is no need to go into it again here.[441] Moreover, the function of receiving *pidyonot* is really beside the point. Obviously, this is not an 'ordination' moment as we saw in the case of Reb Ahron HaLevi, but it does show us that there *had* indeed been such a moment with Reb Dov Baer as well. For if the Alter Rebbe is declaring that Reb Dov Baer can accept *pidyonot* after he is gone, he must already have taught him how to read a *kvittel*, and how to counsel and deal with a soul in *yeḥidut*. And Reb Dov Baer confirms this assertion when he later says, "When my father placed this task on my shoulders, he said to me, 'The proper way to look at a person (in *yeḥidut*) is to see them as they stand in the primordial thought of *Adam Kadmon*.'"[442]

So the real question is—Why is the Alter Rebbe externalizing the moment in front of Reb Pinhas Reizes? This is answered as Reb Pinhas continues his letter...

> WHEN WE HEARD THIS, *we began to shiver and could not answer him, as our hearts were like stones. Woe that we should have to hear what God was planning to do so soon, for he told us that he—the crown of our head—would soon be taken from us, as those above were looking to bring him to them. And who would sit on his throne?*
>
> *Thus he made me the witness of his intentions, and his steward concerning the matter of the* pidyonot. *For he understood the humility and the simplicity of his son, as we have heard from him many times. Thank God, his wishes were carried out in a good way, and his son, our lord, is now sitting on his throne, giving life to all, and sustaining us upon the earth. Even during the life of his father, it was he who brought people in and out, and he who drew forth and poured out the Torah of our holy teacher. It was through his holy mouth that we all received the teachings. His only vocation was Torah, and the Rebbe put both his hands upon him, and made him a vessel to contain much until he was overflowing.*[443]

It seems that the Alter Rebbe was concerned that Reb Dov Baer, in his humility, would not assert his right to the 'throne' as he should. But why did this occur to him in the middle of the wedding festivities?

You have to understand that both Reb Dov Baer and Reb Mordecai of Chernobyl were sons of great Rebbes, fellow disciples of the Maggid who respected one another, but they were quite different personalities. You may remember that when Reb Shneur Zalman felt his life was in danger, he sent a *pidyon nefesh* to Reb Nahum of Chernobyl, Reb Mordecai's father. But while the father was a Rebbe who despised all show and splendor, the style of his son Reb Mordecai was altogether different. There is a little story of Reb Barukh of Mezhbizh and Reb Mordecai that may illustrate ...

Once, Reb Barukh of Mezhbizh was on his way to meet with Reb Mordecai of Chernobyl. Reb Barukh traveled in a fancy carriage and behind him was another carriage that had his wardrobe. As the two carriages neared Chernobyl, Reb Barukh told his driver to stop. He got out, went to his wardrobe and changed out of the silken *kapotte* (caftan) and into a blue embroidered *kapotte*, and then traveled on. When he arrived in Chernobyl and Reb Mordecai greeted him, both were wearing blue embroidered *kapottes*![444]

So Reb Barukh had 'seen' the fancy blue robes Reb Mordecai was wearing while still on the road and had decided that he was not to be outdone! Can you imagine Reb Shneur Zalman paying any attention to such considerations? Even in Mezritch he had been known for the simplicity of his dress. But here, in the midst of the wedding feast for Reb Dov Baer's daughter, amidst all the charismatic Hasidic princes in their finery, it probably occurred to him that many would overlook Reb Dov Baer's profoundly simple and holy service in favor of such showy splendor. So, to remedy the situation, he took him aside in the presence of Reb Pinhas Reizes, one of the leaders of the community, and made it known that he should be Rebbe after him.

It is also likely that he knew that there would be division in the community after he was gone, and likewise wanted to shore-up his son's legitimate claim to authority. Now, some might ask—Why should he even be concerned with having a dynastic heir? After all, he was not one himself, and he even made the classic case against this in his dispute with Reb Barukh of Mezhbizh. Well, I'm not so sure that it had anything to do with 'dynasty.' For he almost certainly believed that his son carried the soul of his own Rebbe, the Maggid of Mezritch, and it was clear that Reb Dov Baer, whatever his birth—perhaps even despite it—had become a Rebbe by his own efforts and abilities.

The Succession

Just one year later, in December of 1812, the Alter Rebbe died during his flight into the Russian interior. Sadly, neither Reb Ahron HaLevi nor Reb Dov Baer were present. The *Beit Rebbe* describes the circumstances and what happened next:

> AT THE TIME OF THE WAR, the Mittler Rebbe (Reb Dov Baer) *fled with the Rebbe into the Russian interior. After they found a little quiet, his father sent him to Krementchug to find a place where they could all weather the Winter. But while he was there, news reached him that the Rebbe had died. After they brought the Rebbe to his resting place in Haditch, he stayed in Krementchug until after Pesah, when the Hasidim sent emissaries to him, inviting him to become Rebbe. At first, he wished to return to Liadi, but much of the city had been burned. Then a Russian noble called Tchekhovsky came forward and offered Lubavitch as a place for the newly appointed Rebbe to settle.*[445]

When he learned of his father's passing and burial, it is said that Reb Dov Baer was completely overcome and lay prostrate for a long time. However, when he rose up again, he said: "My father is now teaching in *Gan Eden*, so we shall have to arrange a 'postal system' between here and there!"[446] Shortly thereafter, he accepted the leadership of ḤaBaD Hasidism.

> NEVERTHELESS, THE MITTLER REBBE'S WAY *was not that of Reb Ahron HaLevi, and therefore, after the great master, Reb Shneur Zalman passed on, and before the Mittler Rebbe came to Lubavitch, Reb Ahron wrote to some of the Hasidim inviting them to come to him so that he might teach them the way of ha-Shem, and many accepted his letter, turning away from the Mittler Rebbe.*

Some might consider this invitation strange, but it was simply a way of saying, "I'm open for business; you needn't experience any interruption in service." You see, continuity had become very important to the Hasidim. For over thirty years, they had only one Rebbe and largely uninterrupted teaching from him. Reb Ahron understood that they were bound to be feeling a little lost now. So he wrote letters to the old communities letting them know that the Alter Rebbe's teaching would be continued through him.

BUT THERE WERE OTHER GREAT DISCIPLES of the Alter Rebbe who did not wish to follow the Mittler Rebbe either, and even opposed him. Some of them said, "Just as many of the students of the Ba'al Shem Tov and the Maggid went their own way after the passing of their masters, so might we." Still others said, "There is no one who can fill the Alter Rebbe's shoes! Oy! Oy! Oy! Hasidism is dying!" For his part, our master, the Mittler Rebbe, was peaceable and wrote them letters, encouraging them not to create further strife in Yisra'el. He also traveled extensively in order to bring the Hasidim close to him. He also wished to visit Reb Ahron Staroshelye in Orsha.

This last sentence touches me. I don't know what Reb Dov Baer wished to accomplish with this visit, but it seems to suggest that he wished to extend a hand to Reb Ahron at this difficult moment for both of them. Nevertheless, it is doubtful whether that visit ever happened, probably because of the encounter he had next in Vitebsk.

IN VITEBSK, one of the disciples of the Alter Rebbe told the Mittler Rebbe that he should go to southern Russia and to the Ukraine, because there they would be more apt to accept his words, and may like his repeating his father's teachings; but in Vitebsk they would not care for that, nor would they accept him.

Our master, the Mittler Rebbe, asked him, "So what will happen in this region?"

He responded that the disciples would take turns traveling into the city.

Then our master said: "No! I'll be the one who comes to teach here, and I'll teach you so much it'll come out of your noses!"

After that, he took a different attitude toward these disciples and acted with more self-assurance.[447]

Basically, this unidentified disciple of the Alter Rebbe was suggesting that perhaps Reb Dov Baer should relocate and teach in a small city where people were less familiar with his father's teachings—suggesting that such people might be more impressed by his more ordinary abilities than in Vitebsk, having so many giants of Torah and Ḥasidut. Clearly he had misjudged Reb Dov Baer in both ability and originality.

By the end of this conversation, Reb Dov Baer had had enough of this foolishness from his father's disciples. He recognized that the very Hasidim who were criticizing him needed his guidance as much as those who had come to him willingly, and he declared that he would give it to them until it came out of their noses! Seeing this change in his persona, many more of the senior Hasidim gave him their allegiance, and those who did not he cut loose.

According to one source, among the fifty-seven great disciples of the Alter Rebbe still living in 1813, twenty-six are said to have followed Reb Dov Baer, while only five followed Reb Ahron HaLevi. However, this says nothing of how the many lesser disciples were divided among them, for Reb Ahron appears to have had a considerable following of Hasidim in Staroshelye, Slonim, and Vitebsk, despite the small number of supporters among the major disciples of the master.[448]

Interestingly enough, five others are said to have openly opposed Reb Dov Baer (though one of these, Reb Moshe Vilenker later became a supporter), leaving twenty-one of the great disciples unaccounted for. It is likely that many, being contemporaries or even much older than either of the two candidates, simply chose to remain Hasidim of the Alter Rebbe *in absentia,* though many of their sons did become Hasidim of Reb Dov Baer.[449] However, this gap, when coupled with other evidence might also suggest that there may have been a third major candidate even more problematic than Reb Ahron—Reb Moshe Shneuri (b. 1780), the youngest son of the Alter Rebbe, about whom one hears many strangely contrasting stories.

Whatever the case may have been with the other possible successors and the unaccounted for disciples, what is certain is that HaBaD Hasidism would have two centers for the next fifteen years.

From the time of Reb Ahron's departure from Liadi, a separation was made between the two friends, between Reb Ahron and the son of our master, Reb Dov Baer, who were already separated in the way of their spiritual service. But after the passing of the master, the breach widened as the Hasidim separated into two parties: one who went with the Mittler Rebbe, Reb Dov Baer, whose soul is in Eden, and who filled the place of his father; and another who looked to Reb Ahron as their teacher.

Thus, he moved to Staroshelye in the province of Mohilev, and from there began to shine the light of his Torah into the world according to his own unique design, and his disciples traveled there to receive teachings from his holy mouth.[450]

Up to this point, we have talked about the politics that effected the friendship of Reb Ahron HaLevi and Reb Dov Baer, but not about what happened to their friendship. If the *Beit Rebbe* is to be understood as an accurate reflection of events, it seems that the well-meaning supporters on both sides—by placing themselves between the two friends—may have become the actual means of separation. However, I suspect that the deep love was still there, even after they had gone their separate ways. For Reb Menachem Mendel I of Lubavitch, the Alter Rebbe's grandson, once told a tragic story of how Reb Ahron had been abused by Reb Dov Baer's Hasidim, much to their Rebbe's displeasure . . .

ONCE, AFTER THE DEATH OF THE REBBE, *Reb Ahron HaLevi came to visit the grave of the Alter Rebbe in Haditch. But the people of the city were mostly followers of my father-in-law, Reb Dov Baer, and were disrespectful to him and refused to give him the key to the ohel (structure over the grave). Nevertheless, his willingness to sacrifice himself for the Rebbe was great, so he used a ladder to get into the ohel through a high window, dropping to the floor inside with a cry—"Oy! Rebbe!"*

Later, when he wished to leave, he found no ladder on the inside to reach the window again. So he was forced to bang on the door of the ohel for a long time until a Jewish smith came and broke the lock. In return for this service, he blessed the smith that he and his children should be wealthy. But to the people of Haditch who had abused him, he said: 'Because you wished to separate me from my Rebbe, you will find no peace in this city; you will always fight amongst yourselves!"

When my father-in-law, Reb Dov Baer, came to Haditch later on and heard this story, he was very angry with the people for having treated Reb Ahron in this way.[451]

This is the last, and perhaps the most important statement on the controversy between Reb Dov Baer and Reb Ahron. Surely they disagreed, and without a doubt, each believed it was for the sake of Heaven that they did so; but I believe that their love remained, even though the active friendship had ended. I say this from a very personal place, knowing that there are friends whom we love dearly, but with whom we can no longer agree.

5

Seeking Unity:
The Teachings of Dov Baer of Lubavitch and Ahron HaLevi of Staroshelye

MY REBBE USED TO SAY, when Reb Dov Baer would teach Ḥasidut, there was perfect quiet among the Hasidim. Nevertheless, in the middle of his teaching, he would whisper, *"Sha, sha . . ."* This was to quiet the thoughts that were crowding into his head as he spoke.[452]

Both Reb Dov Baer and Reb Ahron HaLevi were natural teachers from whom the words of the living God overflowed like water that had been dammed. Sometimes, it was all that they could do to keep the dam from bursting. Thus, each of them took to writing out their teachings: Reb Dov Baer focusing on lengthy treatises about various aspects of spiritual practice; and Reb Ahron devoting himself to book length explorations of cosmology and prayer.

Reb Dov Baer's empathy for the diverse range of his Hasidim was truly profound. It is a celebrated fact among ḤaBaD Hasidim that he wrote ten works, each for a different personality type: from *Poke'aḥ Ivrim*, a treatise in Yiddish on the ways of penitence, to the most elusive and abstract mysteries of Jewish mysticism in the *Imrei Binah*. However, he is most celebrated for his treatises, *Kuntres ha-Hitbonenut* and *Kuntres ha-Hitpa'alut*, on contemplation and the ecstasy that follows it. In these works, as well as the others, he wished to provide his Hasidim with texts that would allow them to verify—through their own experience—what the Alter Rebbe had written in the *Tanya*.

Reb Ahron HaLevi, on the other hand, was driven by a different desire altogether. From the moment he first heard the holy words of the Alter Rebbe in Minsk—"Thus, it is clear that each of us carries Divinity within us, and it is our responsibility to reveal this Divinity in the world around us, transforming the planet into a vessel of holiness."—this became Reb Ahron's singular focus and unwavering mission. Thus, his *Sha'arei ha-Yiḥud ve-ha-Emunah* is an interpretation and explanation of all the Kabbalah and Ḥasidut in the second part of the *Tanya*, similarly titled, *Sha'ar ha-Yiḥud ve-ha-Emunah*, in which the Alter Rebbe deals with the cosmology of God's universe, and particularly, God's radical immanence and transcendence.[453] But as the Alter Rebbe had also said—"When one takes these ideas into a deep contemplation *(hitbonenut)*, the soul begins to break its bonds and bursts into flame with a passionate love of God."—Reb Ahron also wished to show his Hasidim how they could discover that Divinity within themselves, causing them to burst into flame with the love of God as he had. So he wrote the *Sha'arei ha-Avodah*, which dealt with the first part of the *Tanya*, called the *Sefer Shel Beinonim*. Both of these works he called *sha'arei*, 'gates,' because he saw their teachings as doors through which one might enter more deeply into the Alter Rebbe's own teachings.

About the manner of Reb Ahron's teaching and work with Hasidim, we are blessed to have the testimony of one of his own Hasidim, Reb Tzvi Hirsh of Tchashnik, a disciple of the Alter Rebbe who had decided to follow Reb Ahron to Staroshelye...

THE GREAT VIRTUE OF THAT PIOUS AND HOLY MAN, *our master and teacher, Rabbi Ahron HaLevi Horowitz, whose soul is in Eden, is well-known by those who remember him, and famous is his holy Torah. May his merit protect us! He was a beloved disciple of our holy master, the divine genius, Rabbi Shneur Zalman, from whose holy teachings he watered the thirsty flocks which trembled at God's word, explaining them every Shabbat, every new moon, and every holy day.*

His sole intention in this teaching was to establish love and awe in the heart of each person through the service of God in prayer. He continually warned the seekers who longed for the words of the living God to pray with a mighty effort of both heart and mind, and to bind themselves (hitkashrut) *strongly to God's unity and inherence in the worlds, above and below, at all times, knowing that "in Heaven above and Earth below—there is nothing else." He wanted the experience of bittul, 'transparency' before that "nothing else"* (ain od) *of God in prayer to remain with his Hasidim for the whole day, even as they attended to their bodily needs and went about their work in the world!*

In Antwerp, I knew of a ḤaBaD Hasid who worked in the diamond business, who used to disappear every so often to the safe where he kept a copy of the *Tanya*. He would study it for a few minutes and then return to his work. This is very much like the story of the Alter Rebbe's famous Hasid, Reb Binyomin Kletzker . . .

> Reb Binyomin Kletzker, in addition to being a great scholar and Hasid, was also a businessman, a lumber merchant. But one day, his business partner noticed that as he balanced the company accounts, Reb Binyomin inadvertently wrote—*ain od milvado*, "There is nothing other than God"[454] instead of zero beneath a column of figures!
>
> Well, the business partner thought this was too much, and admonished Reb Binyomin for bringing these things into the workplace: "Everything has a time and a place, Reb Binyomin! This is a time for work, and we serve God through doing this work!"
>
> But Reb Binyomin responded: "You know, we consider it perfectly natural when our minds wander off to the fair in Leipzig during prayer; is it so terrible then if we have a *maḥshavah zarah*, an 'alien thought' about the greatness of God in the middle of work?"[455]

All who were close to him know how great was his attachment (deveikut) to God, which burned like a sacred fire whenever he taught on the foundations of God's unity, teachings which he had received from his own holy master. About him, it was truly said: "The seekers of Your unity, you protect like the pupil of Your eye."[456]

This reminds me of a little anecdote my *mashpiyya*, Reb Shmuel Levitin, once told us in the Lubavitcher *yeshiva* . . .

> When people went to hear *Ḥasidut* from Reb Ahron of Staroshelye, they would say, *M'geit tzu der shavueh*, "We're going to the oath!" For Reb Ahron was known to pound on the table in his ecstasy and proclaim, "I swear—*ain od milvado*—there is nothing other than God!"[457]

I personally witnessed our Rebbe's great piety and detachment from worldly things; the care with which he approached all matters of holiness and purity, and all the details of his holy service were revealed to me. Always he wished to root love and awe in the hearts of his Hasidim, establishing them in the ways of Torah and worship of God's blessed unity. May his holy merit protect us, reflecting the quality of his namesake, Ahron, the lover of all Yisra'el, who drew the people's hearts to their heavenly Parent.[458]

Now, about Reb Dov Baer's style of teaching and ways of dealing with Hasidim, there are many accounts and stories in the ḤaBaD-Lubavitch tradition. So we'll give just a few of them here to give you a sense of his holy presence as it was perceived by his Hasidim and others who knew him. One contemporary wrote after his passing . . .

> He taught Torah in public *in order to show his Hasidim the way of the Lord according to the wisdom of the* kabbalah, *and he composed many kabbalistic works which have spread throughout the communities of Yisra'el. He was like the father and head of the Sanhedrin when he taught Torah in public, and all his Hasidim gathered around him on every side, united with one heart to hear the words of the living God which issued from his mouth like sparks of fire.*[459]

According to the *Beit Rebbe*, Reb Dov Baer was well-known for the depth and sophistication of his Torah, especially with regard to kabbalistic teaching, which he gave over freely to the Hasidim; indeed, even more freely than his father was willing to give it, as the following anecdote makes clear.

> During the life of his father, *the Alter Rebbe, he was the Rebbe's intermediary and delivered teachings to the Hasidim with additional explanations of his own, according to the grace God had given him. Among these were many things his father did not wish to manifest, but which he brought into the open for everybody.*[460] *Regarding this, his holy father said—"What should I do? Each generation has its own teachers, and perhaps this generation needs what my son is offering."*[461]

This is a remarkable statement from the Alter Rebbe, especially as both Reb Dov Baer and Reb Ahron sought to explain his teachings in greater depth, revealing aspects of Ḥasidut that the Alter Rebbe had intentionally left vague. But in this moment, he recognized the potential needs of a different generation and consciously allowed for a paradigm shift in Hasidic teaching. Thus, Reb Pinhas Reizes, one of the Alter Rebbe's senior Hasidim wrote of Reb Dov Baer:

> Greater wisdom has he *(the Alter Rebbe) given over to him to hear, to learn, and to teach the words of the living God with intellectual clarity, like a spring that is overflowing, a source of wisdom and holy Torah. He is like a cistern that is completely full, for he has absorbed the teachings of our Rebbe like a sponge, missing not a single drop. His speech is extremely clear and his words are orderly, everything in its right place with him.*[462]

Perhaps my favorite story concerning Reb Dov Baer's teaching comes from the time of the great wedding in Zhlobin, or shortly thereafter, during Reb Levi Yitzhak of Berditchev's visit to Liadi. At the time, Reb Dov Baer was in his late twenties, and if you remember from our last chapter ("Ecstasy—Manifest and Hidden"), his grace after meals had surprised Reb Levi Yitzhak for its simplicity. Thus, I suspect this incident followed after that and entirely changed the opinion of the Berditchever Rav.

ONCE REB DOV BAER was requested by his father to teach Hasidut for his friend, Reb Levi Yitzhak of Berditchev. Thus, Reb Dov Baer went inside and drew forth holy Torah for the two great masters seated before him. When he was finished teaching, Reb Levi Yitzhak was so impressed by the profound depth, insight, and clarity of the young man's Torah that he immediately rose and placed his own tallit (prayer-shawl) around Reb Dov Baer to protect him from the ayin ha-ra (evil eye), as he suspected that even the angelic hosts might look with envy on him, having heard him describe the mysteries of the holy kabbalah.[463] Then, a short time afterward, the three men got up to leave the room and Reb Levi Yizhak insisted that Reb Dov Baer have the honor of passing through the door first. But Reb Dov Baer protested that he could not go before his father. So Reb Levi Yitzhak suggested that they all pass through the door together . . . Amazingly, the door made way for all three of them, allowing them to pass through side by side![464]

It seems that the three masters had become so attuned to the *divine reality* through Reb Dov Baer's teaching that even the quanta of *physical reality* was ready to yield before them! Just as at the moment when the Alter Rebbe could no longer see the wall but divine code of creation.

Counseling Hasidim

Unfortunately, we don't have a true example of how Reb Ahron HaLevi dealt with his Hasidim in *yehidut*. The nearest we come to it is Reb Abba of Tchashnik's remembrance of his meeting with Reb Ahron after his *bar mitzvah*.[465] So, for examples of *yehidut* we must look to Reb Dov Baer, and leave it to our imaginations to consider how Reb Ahron's counseling might have differed.

By all accounts, Reb Dov Baer treated his Hasidim with the attentiveness and care a devoted parent gives to the education and guidance of an only child. Indeed, his concern with giving them all that they needed was so intense that it even threatened his health. For my Rebbe tells us that from infancy, Reb Dov Baer suffered from heart and lung problems and was often exhausted by his teaching and counseling work.[466] At one *farbrengen*, he spoke with such intensity that the elder Hasidim feared for his life. Later, they asked him why he put himself at risk in this way, and he explained:

WHEN MY FATHER *placed this task on my shoulders, he said to me, "The proper way to look at a person (in yeḥidut) is to see them as they are reflected in the primordial thought of Adam Kadmon."*

I learned three things from these words:

The soul as it is reflected in the primordial thought is on the level of a 'child.' When it descends and becomes invested in a body, it is more like a 'servant.' But since I was charged to see a person as they stand in the primordial thought, I learned that the soul can be a 'child' even in its lowest descent.

What does this mean? *Adam Kadmon*, the 'primordial human' is the archetype of human potential. Thus, when we see a person as reflected in *Adam Kadmon*, we see them as a 'child of God,' full of unmanifest potential and basking in the unconditional love of God. But when the soul enters the body, it is more like a 'servant' charged with carrying out the will of God.

THE SOUL, *as reflected in the primordial thought, has such inherent potential that it is clear how it can effect the task of* birrur, *'threshing out' the good from the bad, and how it is possible to reinforce and actualize these powers to effect a change. That is to say, the potential powers of the 'child' are hidden in the 'servant' and must be brought into manifestation from the hidden potential.*

That is to say, when a Rebbe looks at a person in *yeḥidut* for the purpose of prescribing a *tikkun* (fixing) for their soul, they must look into the archetype of all their potential for the solution to the problem. Within the archetype, all the hidden resources of the person are clear, and the Rebbe then knows, as it were, what pressure-points to manipulate to stimulate and unblock the flow of *chi* that will restore the person to health.

> THE SOUL *as it is reflected in the primordial thought also includes all the manifest and unmanifest souls of the world's duration, up to the coming of the* Mashiaḥ *(anointing), at the completion of all. Although each soul is granted freedom of choice in the manner of its service, the general disposition of this service is nevertheless influenced by one's parents and the garment they give to the child. Thus, a father may give merit to his son, and then it may happen that the son's power supersedes that of his father. On the level where the soul is reflected in the primordial thought, all the details of its work here below are included—whether it is to be active or passive, though in either mode, souls receive passively from those above them, and in turn actively influence those below them.*
>
> *Now the statement, "The proper way to look at a person (in* yeḥidut*) is to see them as they are reflected in the primordial thought of* Adam Kadmon*" applies not only to others, but also to one's own self. And, as I reflect on the task of my soul and the generations to follow me, whose care was entrusted to me—that of the Hasidim of today and the future—how is it possible for me to contain myself?*[467]

That is to say, he saw himself as so interwoven in the fabric of all life, and so critical was his work in creating cohesion within that fabric that he could not cease to do it, even if it cost him his life. This is based on his belief that, "The soul as it is reflected in the primordial thought also includes all the manifest and unmanifest souls of the world's duration." Basically, the individual soul is a hologram containing all other souls.[468]

So this is how Reb Dov Baer looked at his work and how he approached the counseling that occurs in yeḥidut, as is borne out in the following story.

> ONCE, REB DOV BAER *stopped in the town of Smargon for a short visit. As the news of his arrival spread, the Hasidim quickly gathered to see the Rebbe in* yeḥidut, *and his hotel was soon surrounded by crowds of people. For several days, the Rebbe saw one Hasid after another, listening to their troubles and prescribing the proper* tikkun *(remedy). Then, suddenly the Rebbe ordered his door shut, even though crowds of people still awaited an audience.*
>
> *Shortly afterward, Reb Zalman, the Rebbe's* gabbai *(attendant), entered the Rebbe's rooms to see what might be the matter, only to hear Reb Dov Baer sobbing as he chanted* Tehillim *(Psalms)! What could be wrong?! Then the Rebbe lay down to rest for a while, and when he got up again, he entered into a deep contemplation such as he was known to do during the High Holidays*

when all the people were in need of repentance! After this, he delivered a ma'amar (discourse) on the need for sincere teshuvah (repentance) and told Reb Zalman that he was ready to see people for yeḥidut again.

All of this was very mysterious, and the subject of much speculation. So one intrepid Hasid who had come for yeḥidut ventured to ask him the reason for his strange behavior. The Rebbe answered: "When a Hasid comes to me for yeḥidut and tells me of their issues and their sins, I must find a parallel to that issue or sin within myself, even if it is merely the reflection of a reflection. When I have corrected that flaw within myself, I can tell them what they must do. But that day, someone came to me whose terrible sin I could not find within myself, no matter how much I tried. Then it occurred to me that the reason I could not find it was because I was completely blind to it, allowing it to lie hidden like a worm within me. This thought was so disturbing that I immediately turned to God in great teshuvah, seeking to bring this hidden flaw to light!"[469]

Once, I came to see the Rebbe, Reb Menachem Mendel Schneerson, for yeḥidut and was told to come back later. Of course, I wondered what was wrong; had he seen something in me that needed such an admonishment? Had I displeased him somehow? But when I next came to see him, he said: "I'm sorry I could not see you that day; the one whom *you* came to see was not here at that time."

A Longing for Unity

Though we were not encouraged to read his works as ḤaBaD-Lubavitcher Hasidim, it was well known that Reb Ahron HaLevi of Staroshelye was considered one of the five great exponents of the Alter Rebbe's teachings, especially with regard to his more radical teachings on non-dualism.[470] As my old colleague, Louis Jacobs, pointed out in his study of Reb Ahron: "he is both the most systematic and the most consistent representative of the ḤaBaD philosophy, as well as being the one thinker of this school who does not shrink from drawing the most radical conclusions from its premises. . . . More than any other traditional Jewish thinker, he is the great seeker of God's unity."[471]

This was a fact acknowledged by everyone who knew him, for Reb Ahron was by far the most thoroughgoing non-dualist of all Reb Shneur Zalman's disciples, and perhaps in all of Hasidism. This is almost certainly the reason the author of the *Beit Rebbe* tells us . . .

> OUR MASTER AND TEACHER, the Mittler Rebbe (Reb Dov Baer of Lubavitch), whose soul is in Eden, used to say that whenever he recited the words: "The seekers of Your unity, you protect like the pupil of Your eye," he always thought of his friend, the holy Reb Ahron.[472]

Though a non-dual philosophical perspective is inherent in everything the Ba'al Shem Tov and the Maggid of Mezritch teach, and becomes far more explicit in Reb Shneur Zalman—to whom most people look for guidance in this regard—it is really completed in Reb Ahron's incredible works. For, wherever one looks in his *Sha'arei ha-Yihud ve-ha-Emunah*, *Sha'arei ha-Avodah*, or *Avodat ha-Levi*, you find continual references to the unity of God and new explanations of seemingly dualistic statements in Torah. In this, he is even more philosophically minded than Reb Shneur Zalman, and more willing to be explicit in what he reveals of the Torah's 'secrets.' But, as we have already delved into this topic in Chapter 3 ("The Hidden Light"), we will give just a couple of examples from Reb Ahron's works that may add some dimension to the Alter Rebbe's teaching.

One of Reb Ahron's chief contributions to the discourse of non-dualism in Hasidism is his use of *perspectival* language, always clarifying the particular point-of-view in discussions of God's immanence and transcendence, as we can see in the following passage:[473]

> WE ARE OBLIGED TO BELIEVE that the worlds have no existence apart from God, who is blessed, and that Divinity and the worlds are actually one; for there is nothing apart from God, and nothing outside of God. The worlds all function solely by God's power, and in all the worlds there is only God's power.... When it is said that God is incorporeal, this means even from the perspective of the worlds, and that all change is only from our point-of-view (l'gabbei didan), but from God's point-of-view (l'gabbei did'hu) there is no world at all; for before God, who is blessed, there is neither tzimtzum, nor any concealment whatsoever.[474]

The use of these phrases—i.e., 'from our point-of-view' and 'from God's point-of-view'—is extremely helpful is such discussions. For how else are we to explain the contradiction in our language concerning God—sometimes speaking as if God were outside ourselves, in relationship with human beings, and sometimes speaking of God as the transcendent absolute, the reality which utterly nullifies all egos and all material existence, leaving no distance by which to judge relationship? The answer is that this is not a real contradiction, but a matter *perspective*—moving back and forth between the relative and absolute points of view.

Consider the following analogy:

> [From] the sun's perspective, the sun neither rises nor sets; there is neither darkness nor concealment nor varying shades of light. By definition, darkness cannot be where light is. However, from the perspective of an individual upon the Earth, the sun rises and sets; there are both light and darkness and varying shades between, and it is valid to label the sun an enemy of darkness. These are two seemingly contradictory propositions, both equally valid, and true, once their particular perspectives are correctly understood. Nevertheless, note that what is valid from one perspective *is not* valid from another. From the sun's perspective, 'all is light.' From darkness' perspective, there is relative light and relative darkness and every shade in between. The question becomes, 'Who do you identify with?'[475]

Now, it is important to say that there are not "two types of being or two types of truth, but one reality, one truth, as seen from two different perspectives."[476] In the Hindu philosophical tradition of Advaita Vedanta, these two perspectives are very helpfully described as relating to God (Sanskrit, *Brahman*) in one of two aspects:[477]

> *Brahman* the ultimate Reality, as we have seen, is unconditioned, without attributes, without qualifications. But it is the same Reality that is called God when viewed in relation to the empirical world and the empirical souls. *Brahman* is the same, as *nirguna* (attributeless) and as *saguna* (with attributes). There are not two *Brahmans,* as wrongly alleged by some critics. Even when God is referred to as the lower *(apara) Brahman,* what is meant is not that *Brahman* has become lower in status as God, but that God is *Brahman* looked at from the lower level of relative experience. These are two forms *(dvirupa)* of *Brahman* and not two *Brahmans: Brahman* as-it-is-in-itself, and *Brahman* as-it-is-in-relation-to-the-world.[478]

Thus, when we relate this back to the kabbalistic concepts of *m'malleh kol almin*, God 'filling-all-worlds,' and *sovev kol almin*, God 'surrounding-all-worlds,' we see that the latter is the sovereign and transcendent light of Divinity "as-it-is-in-itself," and the former is the immanent light of Divinity "as-it-is-in-relation-to-the-world." There is no contradiction between the two, only a change in perspective.[479] This very helpful language is one of Reb Ahron's greatest contributions to the discourse of non-dualism in Hasidism.

Nevertheless, one of the most original and interesting passages in Reb Ahron's *Sha'arei ha-Yiḥud ve-ha-Emunah* is actually found in an extended note detailing four distinct perspectives on the concept of *tzimtzum*, taking off from a *midrash* that proposes four different perspectives on God.[480] For purposes of clarity, we have taken this teaching out of its difficult homiletical wrappings and given you a condensed summary...

IN THE MIDRASH,[481] *we are told that particular statements made by Yitro, Na'aman, Rahav, and Moshe rabbeinu actually represent four different ideas about God in Torah. For Yitro says—"Now I know that Y-H-V-H is greater than all the gods."*[482] *And from this it appears that Yitro was acknowledging the existence of other gods, even though he believed Y-H-V-H to be greater than any of them. But this is not the case; for when Yitro spoke of other 'gods,' he was actually referring to the 'seventy princes'* (ayin sarim),[483] *the external powers through which God controls the worlds. You see, Yitro believed that the purpose of the* tzimtzum—*the 'withdrawal' of God from the ḥalal ha-panui (void)—was to allow for the creation and existence of real worlds, and thus he believed that these 'princes' were created by God to rule over them. However, he did acknowledge that they were utterly dependant on the life-giving power of Y-H-V-H, whom they serve, creating a kind of 'unification' in God's simple unity.*

In the original *midrash*, Jethro's statement might be taken to represent a position which the Orientalist, Max Muller called, 'henotheism.' That is to say, worshipping one god, but accepting the existence of other gods. Or perhaps more specifically, Julius Wellhausen's 'monolatry,' which recognizes other gods, but believes that only one is worthy of worship. Many have argued that early biblical beliefs about God took one or another of these forms. However, Reb Ahron does not even begin to credit this original midrashic formulation; for he assumes that all four biblical personages actually had some understanding of God's unity. Thus, he interprets the whole discussion as having to do with the concept of *tzimtzum*, God's actual or metaphorical 'withdrawal' from the space of the worlds.

As he sees it, Jethro acknowledges the *tzimtzum* spoken of in the Lurianic Kabbalah, but believes that it was a literal withdrawal of Divinity from the void, leaving an essentially 'god-less' space, whose sole purpose is to provide the worlds with life and an autonomous existence. Thus, at this 'Yitroic' stage of understanding, a person is only capable of conceiving the basic fact that God had to remove the divine essence from a space in order to make a world; and the simple purpose of this act was to give reality to the worlds. Within the worlds are God's 'princes' or angelic forces who are dependant on God who created them, and who are thus, in a sense, 'subsumed' or 'unified' under God's greater power to create them.

> ON THE OTHER HAND, Na'aman said—"Now I know that there is no God in all the earth, except in Yisra'el."[484] Obviously, he too recognized that there are no gods upon the earth. Nor did he think God was present in the *tzimtzum*, but he did believe that it was Yisra'el's duty to make God's glory manifest upon the earth. Thus, God's purpose in the *tzimtzum* was not merely to create worlds and have them enjoy a real existence, but to have God's glory revealed in them. However, this is only from our limited perspective, for God's fuller purpose is hidden in God's infinity, which is beyond our capacity to understand.

The Na'aman of the *midrash* would seem to be making a 'monotheistic' statement—"There is no god but Yisra'el's God." This is much like the *shahada*, the basic creedal statement of Islam—*la illaha illa 'llah*, 'There is no god but God." But Reb Ahron takes another view of it, again assuming that all four of the speakers have already acknowledged God's unity. Thus, he believes that Na'aman also conceived of *tzimtzum* as a literal withdrawal, but with a more sophisticated purpose. For at the 'Na'amanic' stage of understanding, one also conceives of God as having to remove the divine essence from a space in order to make a world, but believes it is Yisra'el's purpose to re-introduce Divinity into the world through the teaching of Torah and the keeping of *mitzvot*.

*Now, Rahav understood better, saying—"for Y-H-V-H, your God, is God in Heaven above and on Earth below."*⁴⁸⁵ *Thus she acknowledged that there is one God over both Heaven and Earth, but the midrash nevertheless states that "she left God out of the space of the world." That is to say, she left God out of the space between them. What does this mean? Rahav acknowledged that from God's perspective, God is the same in both Heaven above and Earth below. But a tzimtzum was necessary to create a 'space' between Heaven and Earth, a 'concealment' of God that would allow for creation, and thus the revelation of God. Rahav still believed that this tzimtzum had created a real space between God and creation, even though from God's perspective, God was still fully sovereign over creation. She felt that the revelation of God in the worlds required a contrast with the 'lowly,' which needed separation from God. Thus she believed that God was separated from the worlds and did not acknowledge the words of Moshe regarding God—"there is nothing else."*

This position is most like that of the Ga'on of Vilna, who seems to have believed in a literal *tzimtzum*, or 'withdrawal' of God from the space of the worlds, but who nevertheless believed that God's *hashgahah*, or 'providence' continued to pervade the worlds. Thus, God was both *in* and *out* of the worlds at the same time. This 'Rahavic' position was thought necessary, lest God be found in 'lowly' things, as was discussed in Chapter 3. Philosophically, this is close, but ultimately fails to deal with all of the logical and traditional considerations in a satisfactory manner. Thus, we come to the final, 'Moshaic' stage of understanding...⁴⁸⁶

*Finally, we come to Moshe rabbeinu who saw more clearly, saying—"And you shall know today, and take it to heart, that Yah is God—in Heaven above and Earth below—there is nothing else."*⁴⁸⁷ *"There is nothing else" means, "even in the space of the world." Moshe understood that there is only God, and nothing else—ain od—nothing separate from God. The worlds only appear to have a real existence from our point-of-view, but have none from the point-of-view of Divinity, even after the tzimtzum; for tzimtzum is only a 'concealment' of Divinity. God's true purpose was for it to be revealed to us that "there is nothing else," and this is brought about through the service of Yisra'el.*

*These are the stages through which a person's passes in their understanding of the nature of God's relationship to the world.*⁴⁸⁸

In this position, all four statements are integrated: a limited autonomy is given to the worlds through the concealment of God in *tzimtzum;* the purpose of Torah and *mitzvot* are reinforced, as it is through them that a consciousness of holiness enters the world and we may come to the understanding that everything is divine; the relative contrasts between the sacred and profane are acknowledged from the point-of-view of this world; and everything is unified under Moshe's statement, "there is nothing else."

I love that Reb Ahron seems to see these as *stages* of understanding, recognizing that it takes time for a person to really absorb the radical implications of *tzimtzum*. More recently, a ḤaBaD rabbi, Noson Gurary, has made a similarly helpful presentation of four traditional views of *tzimtzum:* that of the Ga'on of Vilna, Rabbi Yonatan Eibeshutz, Rabbi Hayyim of Volozhin, and finally, Reb Shneur Zalman.[489]

The Width, Length, and Depth of Contemplation

Though Reb Dov Baer wrote most of his treatises with particular types of Hasidim in mind, his *Kuntres ha-Hitbonenut* is a general work written for all Hasidim. In it he expands upon his father's little known discourse, *Hitbonenut Klalit u'Fratit* (Chapter 2, "Two Kinds of Contemplation") in great detail. But it is no *mere* elaboration. It is nothing less than the definitive guide to contemplation for all ḤaBaD Hasidim, without which, the practice of *hitbonenut* might have been quickly forgotten. For nowhere does his father write anything so clear and descriptive with regard to the practice, though it is everywhere implied in his teachings. Therefore, we must be grateful to Reb Dov Baer for taking what was likely an orally transmitted practice and detailing every aspect of it in his own unique way.

It is worth noting that my Rebbe called this work "the key to the teachings of Ḥasidut," and hopefully, these selections drawn from its first chapter will help you to unlock the long hidden contemplative experience of Hasidism.[490]

Hitbonenut, or 'contemplation' *involves powerful concentration, gazing into the depths of a concept, and keeping one's mind on it for long periods, until it is thoroughly understood in all its particular parts and details.*

This is the inner aspect of binah, *'understanding,' which in the language of Talmud is called* iyyun, *or 'in-depth analysis,' as it says, "There is* girsa, *'superficial study,' and there is* iyyun, *'in-depth analysis.'"[491] In* girsa, *one goes* over the material quickly, gaining only a cursory understanding of the subject; one does not pause to consider it or understand it thoroughly. For example, a person may look at an object without really considering it, without asking: How is it made? What is its function? And because there is no investigation, it leaves no real impression and one can only speak about it in the most general terms. Indeed, they will certainly forget it entirely before long.

So this *girsa* is our usual mode of study, going over the material, familiarizing ourselves with its basic concepts, but not involving ourselves with much concentration and authentic curiosity. It is simply 'what we have to know for the test,' but not something in which we are deeply involved. This is similar to what Reb Shneur Zalman called *hitbonenut klalit*, or 'general contemplation.'

Now, EVERY CONCEPT *has three dimensions: width, length, and depth. The 'width' is the explanation of the concept from every angle, and in all its detail. Such an explanation is analogous to a broad river, while a cursory look at a concept is like a little stream.*

Now, he is beginning to talk about the "inner aspect of *binah*, 'understanding,' which in the language of Talmud is called *iyyun*, or 'in-depth analysis.'" Here we think about the idea or concept in an objective way, attempting to understand it intellectually, down to its very last detail. This is the stage of gathering together and going over all of our information in our minds, like the Ph.D. candidate writing a thesis and researching a subject from every conceivable angle, reviewing all the related literature, and assembling a complete picture of everything we know about the subject.

For Reb Dov Baer, this would be a review of all the relevant sources from Torah, Talmud, Kabbalah, and *Hasidut* that might shed light on a particular subject, laying them out in his head like keys on a piano. When I was in *yeshiva*, we would prepare for a period of *hitbonenut* by 'boning-up' on a subject beforehand, often reviewing a *ma'amar* of the Rebbe several times, memorizing and mastering a particular thought-sequence in all its rich detail before taking it into a contemplation.[492] This, according to Reb Dov Baer, is what makes the river of contemplation "broad." Otherwise, there simply wouldn't be enough information to keep the mind occupied and involved, and very little material with which to make new connections.

> THE 'LENGTH' *refers to the associative dimensions of the concept, how it is drawn out and explained through different analogies, so that even a small child might be able to understand it. This is analogous to a long river, flowing over vast distances.*

If you've ever looked at a river on an aerial map, seeing how it twists and turns its way through a landscape like a great snake, you get a real sense of its *gestalt*, its basic pattern. From that pattern, you immediately begin to make descriptive associations, as I have already done—"like a great snake." Or a river with lots of branching tributaries might look like "a hoary old tree." It doesn't matter what the association is, Reb Dov Baer is simply telling us that this creative leap is a major feature of *hitbonenut*. It is this aspect of the contemplation which looks for interesting analogies and metaphors that will strengthen and reinforce the pattern of our understanding.

> LIKEWISE, THE 'DEPTH' *of a concept is analogous to a river's own depth; this is the strength and essence of the river, the current which directs its flow from the source. The surface of the water, its width, and even its length, are all secondary to its depth; they are only extensions of its strength. So too, the depth of a concept is its essential point. Everything else is an extension of that essence— the 'width' of its various angles and details, the 'length' of its associations and analogies, and even the 'height,' which rises and swells to the higher dimensions of the concept. All of these flow from the essence and depth.*

Have you noticed yet that he is doing the whole process even as he is explaining it? The river and its width, length, and depth! It is likely that he is not even doing this on purpose; for a person who engages in *hitbonenut* begins to think and to present their thoughts according to the pattern of the process.

Now, the "depth" is the essential thrust and flow of an idea, the electric element that makes it important. In some ways, it is simply the pattern of the "length" boiled-down to its very essence. Here he talks about it as the "current" that drives the river through a territory, and which, depending on the circumstances, might rise and flood over the banks, which is like opening to the higher spiritual dimensions of a concept.[493]

> THIS IS ALL A PART OF IYYUN, *'in-depth analysis'—keeping one's mind on the concept, analyzing it all its dimensions, and trying to reach its innermost essence. This*

is analogous to the activity of scrutinizing an object, looking on it with great curiosity and attention until every aspect is known to us, both within and without. This kind of 'analysis' is called hitbonenut, 'contemplation.' The word, hitbonenut, is spelled with two nuns, which tells us that one is to enter deeply into one's contemplation.

Since hitbonenut could legitimately be spelled hitbonut, with only one nun, the second nun is understood to suggest that contemplation of this sort requires a greater level of intensity and effort.

Now, JUST AS THERE IS a width, length, and depth in binah, 'understanding,' there is also a width, length, and depth in ḥokhmah, 'wisdom,' which is like the spring from which the river flows, its source concealed deep within the ground. As it is written, "the well-springs of the abyss burst open,"[494] revealing the hiddenness of the depths. This is why it is said, "wisdom comes from nothing,"[495] which is to say, from the hidden depths of ḥokhmah.

Most of what we talk about with regard to hitbonenut has to do with the "in-depth analysis" of binah, but Reb Dov Baer wants to remind us that this process is actually happening on a number of different levels and dimensions. So he points out that ḥokhmah also has a width, length, and depth that must be explored.

You see, most of the time when we talk about the right hemisphere of the brain (ḥokhmah), we talk about it from the left hemisphere (binah). If you want to know what the right hemisphere is really all about, you should read what Catherine Shainberg has to say about "right brain language" in *Kabbalah and the Power of Dreaming*, or the neuroscientist, Jill Bolte Taylor's account of living in the right hemisphere after having a stroke.[496] There are really no words there, and yet, there is an undeniable knowing. There is awareness, but it is not an awareness with limits. That's why people who are in that place feel at one with everything, because that's how the right brain operates. Between the right brain and the left brain is the *universe*—the *uni* is in the right brain, and the *verse* of distinctions is in the left brain.

Now, because ḥokhmah, "wisdom" on the Tree of Life flows from keter, which is sometimes called "the nothing," he associates it with the spring that comes from the hidden recesses of the earth, fed by a secret source. Ḥokhmah-insight emerges, as it were, from the ground of nothingness, which is most holy, and which must be remembered throughout our contemplation.

> Now, ḥokhmah is a flash of insight *that illuminates the mind like a bolt of lightning.*[497] *Its source is hidden in the depths of its innermost essence. . . . Nevertheless, it says, "Understand with wisdom and be wise in understanding."*[498] *According to the teachings of* Ḥasidut, *to "be wise in understanding" refers to the ability to understand an insight with* binah, *'understanding,' meaning the* iyyun, *'in-depth analysis' which we have already discussed. . . . Now, "understand with wisdom" refers to the potential explanations which* ḥokhmah *itself might bring (to the initial insight).*

It is important to stay connected to *ḥokhmah* and the insights that continue to illuminate what is happening in *binah*. You see, even though *ḥokhmah* provided the seed which *binah* is incubating, *ḥokhmah* continues to reveal new insights as *binah* opens that seed to do its work. This is seen as the continuous flow of *ḥokhmah* from the source. Where some people run into trouble in this kind of contemplation is when they allow *ḥokhmah* to get threshed-out in *binah*. That is to say, they see *ḥokhmah*, *binah*, and *da'at* as sequentially separate, or perhaps like three beads without a string of connection running through them. This is a mistake. This is why the *Zohar* calls *ḥokhmah* and *binah*, "the two lovers who are not separated."

> Da'at, or 'knowing,' *is the strong connection which is forged between one's feelings and the concept. It is a particular concern one brings to the 'depth' of the concept after one has submitted it to* iyyun, *the 'in-depth analysis' mentioned earlier.*
>
> *Now,* da'at *also has a width, length, and depth; for there are people with broad and narrow interests, long and short attention spans, and people who invest deeply in a concept and some who invest shallowly. . . . Those who are immature are usually attracted to the surfaces of things and often have very shallow feelings about the objects of their desires. Thus, they are easily fooled and led into traps. However, those who are mature look deeper, having concerns and interests that penetrate to the heart of the object of their desire. Possessing this 'depth,' those who are mature automatically invest broadly and at great length in their contemplation, and appear to be wholly absorbed and concentrating very deeply with the mind.*[499]

As we said earlier, *da'at* is the key to the transformative effect of *hitbonenut*. I really want to make this as clear as possible so that you might begin to find your own way into the contemplative practice of *hitbonenut*. So follow me as I describe the function of *da'at* again, and give a contemplative 'dry-run' on how to do such a meditation.

My Rebbe, Reb Yosef Yitzhak Schneersohn, always emphasized the importance of *ada'ata d'nafshei*, or 'soul knowing' in *hitbonenut*, which is the same as what Abraham Joshua Heschel called "situational thinking" in *God in Search of Man*:

> There are two types of thinking; one that deals with concepts, and one that deals with situations. . . . Conceptual thinking is adequate when we are engaged in an effort to enhance our knowledge about the world. Situational thinking is necessary when we are engaged in an effort to understand issues on which we stake our very existence. . . . The attitude of the conceptual thinker is one of detachment: the subject facing an independent object; the attitude of the situational thinker is one of concern: the subject realizing that he is involved in a situation that is in need of understanding.[500]

So, *ada'ata d'nafshei*, or situational thinking is that which fills us with an immediate emotional awareness, and even provokes us to action. For example, if a doctor friend of mine shows me a slide under the microscope, and says, "See this is a healthy cell, and this is a cancerous cell." I say: "Ah-ha, that's so interesting! I see you stained them with a dye so you can see them better." It's all conceptual to me. But when he says, "Do you remember the biopsy I took of you last week?" I respond: "Oh my God! Is that *my* sample?" You see, I immediately switch to a situational mode of thinking. It gets into my *kishkes*, and my heart starts to pound in my chest because I have suddenly placed myself in the middle of that situation. That is what we do in *da'at*.

Now, in *hitbonenut* we are trying to activate and catalyze our deeper feelings about God so that they move us toward a corresponding action and positive habit formation. So the subject of our contemplation is usually some aspect of Divinity, or how Divinity manifests in the world.[501] But we don't want this to be merely conceptual, so we put ourselves 'in the picture.' It is 'participatory epistemology.' For instance, one *Shabbat* in the early 1940s, I meditated 'till five in the afternoon, transfixed in front of an old Maple tree in Boro Park, and didn't go home until late that evening.[502] I was contemplating the mystery of the amazing power of the miraculous and a HaBaD teaching that points to a paradox—If God were totally absent, life would be withdrawn from everything, and nothing could exist; but if God were totally manifest and present, all life would be utterly eclipsed by God's overwhelming presence! Thus, God is concealed from us, and yet continues to give life to everything. And as I meditated in front of that tree, feeling God's living energy flowing through everything, I felt as if I actually saw the tree breathing!

So let me give you an example of how to do such a contemplation yourself: First, you may want to decide on a proper subject for your *hitbonenut* and spend some time studying the relevant sources and getting familiar with your subject from a number of different angles. Then carve-out some time to pursue your subject in a sacred atmosphere, thinking about the idea or concept in an objective way, attempting to understand it intellectually, down to its very last detail. When you have finished filling-out the concept and have mastered the thought-sequence in all its rich detail, you should then move into the dimension of situational thinking. That is to say, re-investing the conceptual material with a real-life-context.

Now imagine you are going to do a traditional contemplation on the divine indwelling in creation through the kabbalistic concept of *m'malleh kol almin*, God's 'filling-all-worlds' with life. In the past, people generally had a notion that God was 'out there,' 'somewhere' in the universe. But the *Tikkunei Zohar* says, *Le'it maḥshava te'fisa bah klal*, "There is no thought that can take hold of You." Thus, in trying to think about God, we find ourselves at a loss. Nevertheless, it continues, *aval nit'fas i'hu be're'uta de'liba*, "but the Infinite God is taken hold of by the longing of the heart." The longing of the heart is not something that is reaching toward an *idea*, but toward a *presence* and a *being*.

You see, when the "longing of the heart" takes over, we are no longer dealing with the God-*idea* in the third person; we are dealing with the second-person *presence* of the living God. Here, I find myself alive in the divine *milieu*. I am not talking *about* God, I am speaking to "You, my life, my beloved, who shaped and created me in love, and by whose love the very words arising in my mouth, and the feelings rising in my heart, are made possible!"

So we contemplate God 'filling our universe' with life, and we do this *ada'ata d'nafshei*. Here and now we are filled with life, and with Divinity. We wonder at our own being, at our own body; this amazing biological factory, converting oxygen and food into consciousness and life. Our hearts beating and our minds full of curiosity, we revel in this field of being, this creation that is not held together by our own volition, but by the grace of God enlivening it!

We are only tiny parts of this great universe, *v'olamot ain mispar*, "worlds without number." There are worlds that are so short-lived, like muons and psions, mere fractions, millionths of a second, and worlds that are so vast that our galaxy itself pales beside them. Thus, we can begin to see the vastnesses of these vibrations in which a whole life can happen in a millionth of a second, or so slowly that one circuit of the Sun around the Milky Way takes 226 million years! Each of these is 'filled' by God. So when I speak of God and think only of the vast and expansive God, I sometimes fail to recognize God in the infinitesimal life of a muon. We must remember that Divinity *fills-all-worlds*, great and small!

When we face this tremendous fact, we feel something in our hearts; but that feeling is not as important as *whom* we feel. When we reach this point in our contemplation, we must hold on to it. In this, we face and behold God. As the emotion subsides, the subtlety of the meditation deepens, and form gives way to formlessness. It is at this stage that we *allow* the divine to dwell in us without reserve, and its power to re-orient our souls.[503]

This is a practice that bears repeating, over and over again. When I was a young man in the *yeshiva*, my *mashpiyya*, Yisra'el Jacobson, would insist, "Repeat, repeat, repeat." As Reb Pinhas of Koretz says, "The soul is an indifferent teacher . . . it doesn't repeat anything twice!"[504] Therefore, we have to help the soul by ruminating on the experience, repeating the sequence over and over again.

Today, there is a great deal of talk about "Jewish meditation," and I am very happy about it. Seeing the restoration of meditation in Judaism has been one of my primary interests for many years.[505] But I have also been a vocal critic of practices that just seemed to be 'Vipassana with *shmaltz* on it,' that is to say, essentially Buddhist *Shamatha-Vipashyana* practices in Jewish clothing.[506] Thus, I have tried to point-out parallel techniques that actually come from the kabbalistic tradition, like Rabbi Yosef ibn Gikatilla's *shivithi* breathing.[507] I hope I have in some small way encouraged my students who were trained in eastern meditation techniques to look more deeply within the Jewish tradition for such practices. However, I have also been concerned to re-awaken interest in the most deeply rooted Jewish meditation practice—*hitbonenut*. For there is emptiness meditation (focusing on an object like the breath in order to empty the mind of its contents) and there is fullness meditation (filling the mind with positive content in a disciplined contemplation). And Judaism, throughout its history, has tended to focus mostly on the latter. Even in Rabbi Avraham Maimonides' (1186-1237) Sufi-Hasidic *Kifayat al-Abidin*, there are clear references to *hitbonenut*:

The third person reflects on the same subject matter (as the second), but becomes absorbed in profound contemplation (*sh'hitbonein*)[508] and is lifted to a state of true holiness, rejoicing in God whose majestic light is illuminating them from within. This occurs as they contemplate the greatness of God as reflected in creation.[509]

Throughout its history, Judaism has been concerned that spiritual aspirants should place themselves in the presence of God—*nokhaḥ p'nai ha-Shem*. So I would say, even if you are not filling the landscape of your mind with thoughts of God in *hitbonenut*-contemplation, but alternatively, are finding mental quiescence in *hashkata*-meditation, at least do it in the presence of God. Invite God to be present as you enter into the silence, which after all, is God's first language.[510]

Ecstasy—Authentic and Inauthentic

Now, Reb Ahron HaLevi does not write anything nearly so detailed about *hitbonenut*, but both he and Reb Dov Baer write a great deal about *hitpa'alut*, the 'ecstasy' or 'emotional arousal' associated with prayer and contemplation. This is mostly because they want to address various mistaken notions about *hitpa'alut* that were then current in the ḤaBaD community. Though most of what they had to say was similar, the subtle differences between them became the subject of some controversy between Lubavitcher and Staroshelyer Hasidim.

As we have said already, *hitpa'alut* refers to a state of 'emotional stirring' or 'ecstasy,' which follows from contemplation and prayer. Back in 1963, when Louis Jacobs first translated Reb Dov Baer's treatise on *hitpa'alut* as a *Tract on Ecstasy*, I was a little troubled by his translation of the word *hitpa'alut*.[511] 'Ecstasy' seemed to be too loaded with libidinous connotations for modern culture, having become somewhat distanced from its original meaning—'standing outside one's everyday self.' The Hebrew word *hitpa'alut* actually means 'deeply stirred,' 'strongly moved,' or 'affected.' Nevertheless, in most cases, I think it is best to leave the original word in the text, allowing the reader to build meaning from the context in which it is used. Ecstasy, or 'standing outside one's ordinary self,' actually corresponds to the Hebrew, *hazazah mi-mekomo*, 'a movement from one's place' or 'an altered state,' which Reb Dov Baer also uses in his treatise.[512]

Now, let's begin to explore the issues having to do with *hitbonenut* and *hitpa'alut* that most concerned Reb Ahron and Reb Dov Baer. The basic problem is perhaps most thoroughly described by Reb Dov Baer in the introduction to his *Kuntres ha-Hitpa'alut*:

> As I have said in my first letter,[513] there are many in our community (anshei sh'lomeinu) who are confused and in error, and guilty of many mistakes, some of them extreme.... This is the result of insufficient training and effort, as well as the self-important teaching of 'expounders' (ha-darshanim) who claim to hold the 'secrets' of true prayer. But they delude both themselves and others in this belief, and thus have fallen into great error. And this makes me very sad, especially as they attribute these 'secrets' to me!

Who were these "expounders" who claimed to hold the "secrets" of true prayer? These were likely loosely affiliated members of the ḤaBaD community who visited the Rebbe and took it upon themselves to repeat his discourses in their various towns and villages—though apparently without proper understanding and maturity. Worse, they were misleading their listeners with self-important talk about "secrets" that they attributed to Reb Dov Baer himself.

In the whole debate on *hitpa'alut* between the Hasidim of Lubavitch and Staroshelye, this last sentence by Reb Dov Baer may be the most important. For how much damage was done by people who claimed in their ignorance and spiritual immaturity to be speaking for the Rebbe? How much trouble was stirred-up between the two groups of ḤaBaD Hasidim? In this case, it's likely that newer Hasidim, basing themselves on the personal example of Reb Dov Baer in prayer—his utter stillness and silence—had begun to proclaim this as a model for everyone. Apparently, they mistook his stillness for an absence of physical intensity and emotion in the heart, which, as we have seen, is complete nonsense.

> There is a confusion in our community regarding *hitbonenut*, or 'contemplation' in prayer. For many, it seems, emphasize the *binah*, 'understanding' aspect of contemplation, but forbid themselves the *hitpa'alut*, or 'stirring' of the heart that follows it, thinking that this interferes with comprehension. But when a person forbids this kind of *hitpa'alut*, they also circumvent any *hitpa'alut* in the mind as well, and eventually fall asleep amidst a host of random thoughts!...

> *They have forbidden* hitpa'alut *in the heart as something unfit for Jews, and take it upon themselves to ridicule those who cry out in the joy or bitterness of their hearts in prayer, embarrassing them until feel they have done something wrong and resolve to suppress their most sincere feelings. Thus, they control themselves and sit still until they simply fall asleep amidst the dullness of their thoughts. Oh, who is truly guilty in this situation? They who have quashed the sincere feelings of a heart awakening to God—whether in repentance, or bitterness of heart—or those who experience a true* hitpa'alut *that comes from the practice of* hitbonenut *according to their capacity?*[514]

Here we see just how well the lesson was learned in Reb Dov Baer's teenage years; for the boy who had once scoffed at the elder Hasid shouting in his *davvenen* with great exertion has now become the defender of sincere prayer in whatever form it must take.[515]

Interestingly, Reb Dov Baer's argument—that forbidding *hitpa'alut* in the heart derails the entire process of *hitbonenut*—also mirrors Reb Ahron HaLevi's own feelings on the subject, which he frames slightly differently in the introduction to his *Sha'arei ha-Avodah*, challenging a more sophisticated version of the "expounders" argument.

> IT WILL BE CLEAR *from this how foolish is the error of those who reject* hitpa'alut, *the 'emotional arousal' in the heart. They argue that where there is stirring and sensation in the heart there is also an awareness of the self* (yesh). *But I say, when the heart is not moved, and not experiencing* hitpa'alut, *the animal soul* (nefesh ha-behamit) *is in complete control of one's awareness, and the divine soul* (nefesh ha-elohit) *cannot be revealed at all!*

For Reb Ahron, this notion was utterly ridiculous. It was a folly comparable to that of the Enlightenment thinkers who believed that reason could dictate everything, that emotion could be stored-away in a great closet with other untidy things one didn't wish to know about. Thus, the "Age of Reason" gives birth to the Marquis de Sade and France's bloody revolution of 1793. For in the Jungian equation, the denial of one's feelings creates a tyrant in the unconscious. So Reb Ahron is pointing-out that one who tries to put the animal soul in 'shadow,' forbidding the *hitpa'alut* of the heart, is actually creating a situation in which both will control everything from behind the scenes.

BUT WHEN THE HEART *is affected with* hitpa'alut *because of the love of God, even though there is still an awareness of self in this love, the faculty of* da'at *(experiential knowing) distinguishes the desire to become transparent to God (and included in the divine unity) from the desires of the self—and refines it.*

The mistake of those who reject hitpa'alut *in the heart comes from having heard that there should be no admixture of self-awareness in our awareness of the divine, and that* da'at *makes the distinction. But the actual intention of my master (Reb Shneur Zalman) was that* hitbonenut, *or 'contemplation' should be practiced in the context of prayer, allowing one to experience* hitpa'alut *in the heart through love and awe. Once this* hitpa'alut *is attained, the rest of prayer should consist of removing as much self-awareness or ulterior motive from the act of loving as possible, attempting to become truly transparent to God. This is the battle we face in prayer, as it is said, "The hour of prayer is an hour of battle."*

Most people are engaged in this battle all their days, and the righteous succeed in removing the admixture of self-awareness according to the level of their prayer. The greater one's attachment to God, and the greater the intensity of one's love, the more one succeeds in making the self transparent to God. But each person has their own battle to fight. As I have written elsewhere—in the name of our holy teacher, whose soul is in Eden—on the verse, "And I will remove sickness from your midst,"[516] *no one can remove the awareness of the self entirely except the blessed and holy One. Only in death is this particular bodily awareness removed. The Torah speaks of these bodily sensations when it says, "For there is not one who is righteous on the earth, who does good alone, and doesn't sin."*[517] *Only Moshe* rabbeinu, *peace be upon him, was able to attain such a state of utter transparency.*[518]

Reb Ahron's basic point in this passage is that the faculty of *da'at*, or 'knowing' distinguishes the between the true *hitpa'alut*-ecstasy of the heart and the little secondary motives the ego tries to 'piggy-back' on it. Thus, *da'at* acts as a filter for these, making the meditator aware of their own hidden motives, even as it allows the purer elements of ecstasy to be accepted as a personal love gift to God.

At the same time, he also wants to say that it is not even possible to achieve a *hitpa'alut* that does not have some admixture of self-awareness. Who would even know about the *hitpa'alut*-experience if awareness were not present in some measure? Thus, he tells us that the first step is to awaken the heart and then to refine the admixture of self-awareness down to the most subtle levels by one's approach and commitment to *hitbonenut*-contemplation.

In the next passage, Reb Ahron tells us that the existence of the body necessitates sensation and self-awareness, and the awareness of the lover who knows that he or she wishes to be united with the Beloved is already a pretty good version of this, and may be further refined in the following way:

> BECAUSE THE DIVINE SOUL *is clothed in the garment of the animal soul, whenever the former awakens in love there is bound to be an admixture of self-awareness in this awakening, the awareness of a lover who desires to be joined to God. But if one would move beyond this self-awareness, one must reflect in* hitbonenut *on the tremendous majesty of God as our sovereign Lord…Our teacher, whose soul is in Eden, used to explain this by means of a parable:*
>
> *When a king chooses to reveal the splendor of his majesty, people come from all around to witness the spectacle…Those who are admitted into the throne room of the king's palace, into the very presence of the king, come in order to enjoy the company of their sovereign, to make petitions for his kindness, and to carry out his commands. But first they must reflect on the greatness of the king's power and the exalted position he holds in relation to themselves; otherwise they might imagine that their association with him implies equality and gives them status as persons worthy of associating with the king. But when they reflect on the king's great power, the truth of their own position is revealed, and they willingly submit to his authority in all humility.*
>
> *So it is with regard to divine worship, which is always seeking greater intimacy with God, holding tightly to God in love, seeking union, and hoping to become transparent to Divinity and its blessed will. But this requires that one contemplate the infinite greatness of God's exalted splendor in relation to the worlds (in* hitbonenut*), considering how they are utterly annihilated in the divine presence, and are actually as 'nothing' (ain) before God…The sole purpose of the worshipper should be to contemplate the greatness of Divinity alone, and to become as nothing before God.*[519]

The parable Reb Ahron uses in this passage—attributed to the Alter Rebbe—is actually very important in HaBaD Hasidism as a kind of 'antidote' to what the Tibetan Buddhist teacher, Chogyam Trungpa Rinpoche used to call, "spiritual materialism."[520] That is to say, the ego doesn't stop at the co-opting of secular experiences and trappings, but is just as willing to build an inflated identity out of spiritual experiences and trappings as well. For so called 'mystical experiences' can all too easily become the jewel in the ego's crown, effectively poisoning the entire spiritual process. Thus, Reb Ahron proposes a contemplative theme that effectively under-cuts one's individual identity.

In all of this, Reb Ahron HaLevi and Reb Dov Baer are basically agreed. It is only when Reb Dov Baer begins to draw a strong distinction between 'authentic' and 'inauthentic' *hitpa'alut* that the two begin to part ways on the subject. So let's take a look at what Reb Dov Baer has to say about 'inauthentic' *hitpa'alut*.

> THERE IS A RUMOR *that has spread throughout our community that* hitpa'alut, *as it is physically sensed in the heart, belongs to the 'old way' of Hasidism, and has no place among us today. But this is a great mistake of the blind who cannot tell the difference between darkness and light!*[521] *Yes, we want to avoid those apparent expressions of ecstatic-*hitpa'alut, *such as shouts that are mere contrivance, issued only for the purpose of being heard by others! About these it is said, "She raised her voice against Me—Therefore I have rejected her."*[522] *For the heart is not connected to these outbursts, as is required by the Torah: "Their heart cried out to Adonai"*[523] *and "Then they cried."*[524] *So even when people cry out for the purpose of expelling invasive and unwanted thoughts* (mahshavot zarot), *stirring the heart to warmth through these cries, this is not unto Adonai.*[525]

Did you notice the reference to the "old way" of Hasidism? It is interesting how ḤaBaD Ḥasidim were already beginning to see themselves as a new creation, and even as a corrective to previous generations. But while Reb Dov Baer will own certain refinements in the process of *hitbonenut*, he feels it is necessary to rein-in the Ḥasidim who have become too absorbed in this distinction, and who have obviously misunderstood the nature of the refinement. He says that it has nothing to do with removing *hitpa'alut* "as it is physically sensed in the heart." Rather, we only want to make a distinction between 'authentic' and 'inauthentic' expressions of *hitpa'alut*. Thus, he gives us two examples of the latter type: a completely spurious outburst born of the ego's desire to be recognized; and an outburst that only wants to overcome the assault of distracting and unwanted thoughts during the time of prayer.

Here is where the disagreement comes in; for even though Reb Ahron would certainly agree that the first example given by Reb Dov Baer is 'inauthentic' and without merit, he is not so willing to dismiss the second as such. In this passage, he explains his reasons . . .

> ALTHOUGH I HAVE WRITTEN IN THE NAME *of our teacher, whose soul is in Eden, that a person's work in prayer should consist of removing as much self-awareness as possible, nevertheless, he always encouraged every heart's unique expression of* hitpa'alut *according to its own capacity. Thus, no one's heart should be troubled because our ideal* hitpa'alut *in prayer seeks to be free of all self-*

awareness and any admixture of ego.[526] God forbid, that someone should begin to view all hitpa'alut in the heart with suspicion because it might contain a measure of self-awareness, condemning that love as 'tainted,' 'illusory,' or 'inauthentic,' cutting themselves off from those contemplations which elicit a love that may be sensed and experienced in the heart!

All of the Tanya is based on the application of the verse: "No, the thing is very close to you, in your mouth and in your heart, to observe it."[527] Thus, the student of his holy work will see that all his words are intended to encourage the unique expression of hitpa'alut in each person, whatever form it takes, and not—God forbid—to reject it.

Moreover, my teacher, whose soul is in Eden, explained the verse, "My dove, undefiled"[528] by interpreting the word yonah, 'dove,' as if it read ona'ah, 'fraud.' He said that no one should be over-concerned that their prayer is 'fraudulent,' containing an admixture of good and evil, for even if it is not entirely 'authentic,' it is still 'undefiled.' Each of us must assess our own capacity for ridding ourselves of this admixture, and work according to our measure. As we have already said, "The hour of prayer is an hour of battle." But in a war, sometimes one side wins the battle, and sometimes the other. Should we cease fighting because the other side occasionally wins a battle? If we did that, the enemy would certainly prevail in the war and we would fall into the hands of the animal soul and the Sitra Aḥra, the 'Other Side.'

We must also remember that there are degrees of victory in accordance with each person's capacity. What might be considered a high degree of self-awareness for one on a higher level might be considered an absence of self-awareness for one on a lower level; for the degrees of authenticity and inauthenticity in this regard are infinite. Thus, the Rabbis have said, "It is not your job to complete the work, but you are not free to walk away from it either."[529] That is to say, we must endeavor to work diligently upon ourselves in prayer, laboring with both body and soul to uncover the hidden love of the heart through knowledge and understanding. Nevertheless, it is not our duty to complete the work, expecting to attain perfection in it, even if we cannot cease from that work.[530]

Clearly, Reb Ahron wants to err on the side of mercy with regard to hitpa'alut. For, he says, even if a person shouts in frustration to dispel 'disturbing thoughts' in their prayer, this is still done for the sake of Heaven, so that one may get past these and into the authentic presence of God. This is just a frustrated stirring of the heart borne of longing. Even though the measure of self-awareness is high, its intentions are still good and it may even help. Thus he refers to a category of 'inauthenticity' that is 'undefiled.' That is to say, it is 'inauthentic' in as much as it is still full of self-awareness, but it is 'undefiled' because its motives are mostly good.

By framing the discourse in terms of 'authentic' and 'inauthentic' *hitpa'alut*, presenting five distinct categories as he does in his *Kuntres ha-Hitpa'alut*, making a stark contrast between them, Reb Ahron feels that Reb Dov Baer has placed the bar too high and unintentionally placed "a stumbling block before the blind" (Lev. 19:14), which we are commanded not to do. This he fears will cause some Hasidim to become unnaturally obsessed with whether their *hitpa'alut* is authentic or not: "God forbid, that someone should begin to view all *hitpa'alut* in the heart with suspicion because it might contain a measure of self-awareness, condemning that love as tainted, illusory, or inauthentic, cutting themselves off from those contemplations which elicit a love which may be sensed and experienced in the heart!"

In all of this, Reb Ahron really just wants to make sure that the Hasidim continue in their spiritual work without becoming discouraged. Thus he says: "We must also remember that there are degrees of victory in accordance with each person's capacity. What might be considered a high degree of self-awareness for one on a higher level might be considered an absence of self-awareness for one on a lower level." In this, he is very respectful of the unique differences in Hasidim, and wants to point-out a flaw in defining the limits of experience too severely. Nevertheless, he ends with Rabbi Tarfon's exhortation from *Pirkei Avot*, which really defines his entire position: "It is not your job to complete the work, but you are not free to walk away from it either." Don't be too hard on yourselves, but continue the process of purifying your awareness.

Accepting all of this, we must still understand that Reb Dov Baer was concerned with the problem of how to verify the authenticity of *hitpa'alut*, and how to measure one's success in it. Thus, he wanted to describe how it was possible to achieve a state in which one is almost entirely unaware of the self. In order to be truly 'authentic,' Reb Dov Baer believed that *hitpa'alut* (derived from the reflexive verb *hitpa'el*) had to be a reflexive situation, motivated solely by an inner *compulsion* of the heart or spirit. It could not be a product of external 'peer pressures' or even conscious effort or direction. For him, all *hitpa'alut* that is authentic, and deserves the reflexive *hitpa'el*, comes after and follows from a deep and authentic *hitbonenut*-contemplation. The more authentic the *hitbonenut*, the greater the *hitpa'alut* resulting from it. Thus, the true *tzaddik*, the one who has experienced illumination, is always completely aligned with the divine process, utterly at one with and inseparable from this process.

How could one be outside oneself and wholly absorbed into a divine object if, at the same time, one is also aware of feelings toward the object? Reb Dov Baer gives us a readily understandable example to illustrate:

> CONSIDER THE NATURE of the hitpa'alut, the 'stirring absorption' produced by a niggun, a 'melody.' It is completely spontaneous and does not require even the slightest act of will. It is 'experienced,' but the one who experiences it is not really aware of it. And because it-is-as-if it were not 'experienced,' being unrealized in the moment, it may be said that there is a lack of self-awareness.[531]
>
> When a person is suddenly moved to an ecstatic-hitpa'alut, perhaps experiencing the joy of receiving some good, the hitpa'alut is experienced in the heart and they may suddenly make an involuntary gesture, perhaps even clapping their hands as people sometimes do. Nevertheless, this is done without any conscious choice; they simply clap their hands involuntarily. This act proves a lack of awareness during the moment of hitpa'alut.[532]

With this example, Reb Dov Baer gets around the problem of self-awareness. Awareness is still present in some form, for the experience is known afterward, but one is so absorbed in the moment that *it-is-as-if* there is no self-awareness. This kind of *hitpa'alut* happens like an invasion. The medieval mystics of Catholic Christianity called this 'infused contemplation,' an 'apophatic' (non-discursive) mystical experience which comes like a 'gift' or 'infusion' from God. This experience is the real answer to those who have thought that Judaism only has a discursive type of meditation, and not that in which the soul loses itself totally, being still and at rest on the level of *yeḥidah*, on the level of the pure will (and beyond it, as *yeḥidah*, the true 'one-ing' implies).

It is doubtful whether Reb Ahron would have disputed the experience Reb Dov Baer describes in this example. It is only that he feared Hasidim would begin to over-analyze their *hitpa'alut*, and thus dilute it. I also tend to think that Reb Ahron might have agreed with Reb Dov Baer's categories of 'inauthenticity,' even though he might rather have pointed it out as something that 'should not be done.'

> IN OPPOSITION TO THIS IS THE EXTERNAL ECSTASY of the heart's flesh, which is merely an enthusiastic inflammation of the heart born of a 'strange fire' and excitement in the blood, which is unrelated to the fire of Divinity. This is nothing more

than a warming of the fleshly heart with the fire of excitement for the purpose of experiencing ecstasy! This is a great error which opens a person up to the worst illusions and self-deceptions of the physical world.*533*

Now, this is a very interesting distinction that requires some explanation, especially as there were some overzealous Lubavitcher Hasidim who believed Reb Ahron to be guilty of this very kind of inauthentic ecstasy. Allow me to illustrate Reb Dov Baer's objection to this ecstasy with a story . . .

Once, a young Reb Ya'akov Yitzhak of Lublin was on his way to see his Rebbe, Reb Elimelekh of Lizhensk, and stopped in a little town for *Shabbat*. While praying in the *beit midrash*, he heard another man praying with deep fervor. So amazing was his prayer that he struck up a conversation with him afterwards and ended up staying with him for *Shabbat*. After observing him for a while, he suggested that the man come with him to Reb Elimelekh who would appreciate his prayer. The man agreed and they traveled on to Lizhensk. But no sooner had they crossed Reb Elimelekh's threshold then the Rebbe turned his back on them. Even though Reb Ya'akov Yitzhak was a beloved disciple, the Rebbe would not so much as take his hand or even look at him.

Soon, he realized that it must have something to do with his companion, and he quickly removed him to a local inn. Then Reb Ya'akov Yitzhak returned to the Rebbe who greeted him warmly, asking—"Why have you brought such a man to me?"

"What is wrong with him, Rebbe?" asked Reb Ya'akov Yitzhak.

"The image of God is distorted in him. Sometimes a person begins to serve God with ulterior motives and pride enters into that service. Though it may appear to be very great and full of fire, it actually comes from the place of *nogah*, where good and evil are mixed indiscriminately. It is an impure fire. Unless that person makes a great effort to change, they become a resident of *nogah* without even being aware of it. Such a person may burn with intensity, but is utterly unaware of the source of that fire."

Later, Reb Ya'akov Yitzhak returned to his traveling companion and told him what the Rebbe had said. He burst into tears and ran to the Rebbe to beg his help. And thus he found his way out of *nogah*.*534*

Now, *kelippat nogah* is an energy system in the world which is basically neutral, neither good nor bad. It is just something that can be used one way or another, like a knife. But because that person davened out of *kelippat nogah*, and not out of pure motives in the service of God he was captured, as it were, in the shell of his own desires without recognizing it.

If I am just worshiping out of the energy of my body, whipping myself into a frenzy and hoping to experience a 'high,' this is *davenen* in *kelippat nogah*, and is considered an 'unholy fire' and an 'inauthentic ecstasy.' This is the same experience that has also disillusioned some Christians I have met who have said that one day they realized that the fervor of the 'revival meeting' was the same fervor they had experienced at a rock concert! This is why Reb Dov Baer wants to make this distinction—to prevent such disillusionment by protecting the sanctity of the more authentic experience.

Now, as I have said, in the campaign to discredit Reb Ahron—who was known for his great ecstasy and the overwhelming intensity of his *davenen*—some people whispered that perhaps his ecstasy was of this type, and therefore 'inauthentic.' And this becomes the set-up for a very important little anecdote in the HaBaD tradition with which I would like to end the discussion. For in it, none other than the Reb Menachem Mendel I of Lubavitch is Reb Ahron's defender...

ONE OF THE GRANDCHILDREN *of our master, the Tzemah Tzedek (Reb Menchem Mendel I), said that he once entered his grandfather's room and found among his papers something that our master, the Alter Rebbe, had written condemning the display of emotion in prayer. Upon it was written a note in the hand of the Tzemah Tzedek, saying that this was not the general opinion of the Alter Rebbe, but pertained to a specific Hasid who was in need of a reprimand regarding his extreme emotion in prayer. The grandson of the Tzemah Tzedek assumed that this Hasid must have been Reb Ahron, the Staroshelyer, and mentioned this to his grandfather.*

The Tzemah Tzedek responded: "God forbid! I was not talking about Reb Ahron of Starosheye; for his was a truly divine ecstasy! And he served our master, the Alter Rebbe, with great exertion, up to the point of offering his own life!"[535]

The Passing of the Rebbes

Though their respective reigns were short in comparison with that of the Alter Rebbe, whose lasted almost forty years, his two heirs accomplished many great things and lived remarkably similar lives. Indeed, not only did the events of their lives parallel one another's, but also that of the Alter Rebbe himself. For both masters continued to support the Hasidim in the Holy Land and were arrested by the government for treason and forced to defend themselves as the Alter Rebbe had done over twenty-five years before.

After settling in Lubavitch in the province of Mohilev, on 18 Elul in 1813,[536] Reb Dov Baer began the task of rebuilding the HaBaD community which had been severely disturbed by the Napoleonic war and the division of the senior Hasidim after the Alter Rebbe's passing. In 1814, he created a special committee of Hasidim to see to the physical reconstruction of various Jewish communities in White Russia that had been destroyed in the war. Then, the next year, he managed to persuade government officials to set aside tracts of land in the province of Herson for Jewish resettlement. He encouraged many of his Hasidim to settle on this land and to take up farming. This was all part of his attempt to alleviate the problem of Jewish poverty in the larger cities. Shortly thereafter, he also established a Jewish colony in Hebron, the burial site of the Matriarchs and Patriarchs, which he personally supported until his death. He also longed to go there himself, for he said that prayers recited in Hebron were particularly effective, as tradition held it to be the gateway to paradise.

In the early 1820s, Reb Dov Baer's already precarious health began fail and he was forced to cut back all of his public activities, especially the giving of public discourses and counseling Hasidim in *yehidut*. Thus, he empowered his most trusted Hasidim—likely Reb Eisik of Homil and Reb Hillel of Paritch—to handle more minor issues in his name. Hasidim with more serious issues were to seek the counsel of his brother, Reb Hayyim Avraham, or his son-in-law and nephew, Reb Menachem Mendel, who would later succeed him. Only in the most serious cases was a Hasid granted access to Reb Dov Baer.[537]

In the summer of 1825, he made his way to the hot springs at Karlsbad for health reasons, and on his return trip met Rabbi Akiva Eiger (1761-1837), an opponent of Hasidism and one of the foremost Talmudists of his time. This meeting would prove to be crucial in the easing of tensions between Hasidim and *mitnagdim;* for Eiger was impressed with Reb Dov Baer's scholarship, and Reb Dov Baer was likewise deeply affected by Rabbi Eiger's piety.

In 1826, a group of wealthy *mitnagdim* used their influence with the Russian government to renew the false accusations they had made against the Alter Rebbe many years before. Only now, both Reb Dov Baer and Reb Ahron HaLevi were arrested for treason and taken to Vitebsk for trial. Both were imprisoned for almost two months in Vitebsk, and through their own effective arguments they were both released on the 10th of Kislev, which is celebrated as a holiday among ḤaBaD Hasidim.[538]

His health no better from imprisonment, Reb Dov Baer made plans to settle in the Holy Land. However, before going, he set out on a pilgrimage to his father's grave in Haditch to pray there concerning the infamous Cantonist Decree, which authorized the conscription of Jewish boys into the Russian military for a period of twenty-five years. On his way back from his father's grave, he fell ill and died in the town of Niezhin, where he was buried. It was the 9th of Kislev, his own fifty-fourth birthday, and just one day shy of the anniversary of his release from prison the year before. His last words were, "For with You is the source of life."

Reb Ahron HaLevi died just one year later. Sadly, all the known details of his later life have already been told, and so we will simply offer these final few paragraphs from his biography in the *Beit Rebbe* . . .

ALL THE DAYS OF HIS MINISTRY *came to about fifteen years, from the year 1813 (5573) to 1828 (5589). He died in Staroshelye on Shemini Atzeret at the age of 63. On his grave was erected a stone edifice, and there are people who still travel to it*[539]—*May his merit protect us!*

Reb Ahron had two sons: the first of which was the great and well-known Hasid, Reb Hayyim Rafael of Staroshelye; and the second was a great Hasid, Reb Mikhael David of Vitebsk. After his passing, many of his Hasidim traveled to Lubavitch to (become Hasidim of) the Tzemah Tzedek.[540] *Many others looked to his son, Reb Hayyim Rafael in Staroshelye; unfortunately, he became ill after a few years and he died while still young in the city of Malatzin. Then, most of his Hasidim went to Lubavitch, while others went to the Rebbes of Lekhovitch, Vilednik, and Kaidenov, and some remained unattached.*

Among the stories that are told of Reb Ahron are many miracle tales, but as we cannot verify these accounts, we have not copied them here. Anyone who is interested can read those stories for themselves.[541]

Earlier we mentioned the Hasid who called Reb Dov Baer and Reb Ahron HaLevi "the two friends who are inseparable," and how the Alter Rebbe, perhaps glimpsing the future, added, "May they never be separated." It occurs to me now that this wish was in a strange way, fulfilled. For even though the two were indeed separated by time and circumstance, and even in opinions, they have nevertheless been joined ever since by nearly everyone who has written about them. Whether by the original ḤaBaD historian, Hayyim Meir Hielman, or later academic scholars like Louis Jacobs, Rachel Elior, and Naftali Loewenthal. Their lives, as we have seen, were so interwoven, that it is difficult to speak in depth about either without mentioning the other.

In my own private musings, I like to think that in the heavenly academy, they are seated at a table together once again, studying Torah in great love—point and counterpoint.

The synagogue at the grave
of Rabbi Shneur Zalman of Liadi in Haditch
Photo by Ayla Grafstein

The *yarmulke* of Rabbi Nahman of Bratzlav
Courtesy of Mochin Studios

Part II
Rebbe Nahman
and Bratzlav Hasidism

6

The Ḥiddush:
The Hidden Struggles of Young Nahman

THE ORAL TRADITION TELLS US that the story of Rebbe Nahman actually begins long before his birth, in the time of his great-grandfather, the holy Ba'al Shem Tov. It is not simply that his great-grandfather's life is important to his story, though this is undoubtedly true, but that the Ba'al Shem Tov actually seemed to be preparing for Rebbe Nahman's coming. Why else would he be so determined to marry his granddaughter to the son of his *majordomo*? And why else would he have controlled the timing of Rebbe Nahman's birth so precisely from beyond the grave? Had he seen something important coming in the future of Hasidism? Bratzlaver Hasidim believe that he had.

What had he seen? A child, of course, but what was that child to become? Another Ba'al Shem Tov? *I don't think so.* The child who would grow up to be Rebbe Nahman of Bratzlav was not the second coming of his illustrious ancestor. The mists of legend were not to rise again in his lifetime, bringing with them endless stories of miracles from a 'new' Ba'al Shem. The holy founder of Hasidism would not return in his great-grandson, as some undoubtedly hoped. But I think this is precisely what the Ba'al Shem Tov may have seen coming—not a resurrection of himself—but a *ḥiddush*, a true 'original.'

Rebbe Nahman would be bold enough to emerge from the shadow of his famous forbear, and radical enough to search out the roots of divine service for himself. Thus, he became a true heir of the holy Ba'al Shem and a renewing force in Hasidism, which—though only two generations old—

was already becoming stale and static in his eyes. Infinitely audacious and humble at the same time, Rebbe Nahman was the paradoxical unwinder of all forms and assumptions, challenging the inexorable forces of calcification in Hasidism. He was an intrepid explorer, searching for a true *fons vitae*, a spiritual well-spring of continual renewal and eternal life. And there are many who would say that he found it.

So let's begin to look at Rebbe Nahman in this way, as a seed planted in the time of the Ba'al Shem Tov as insurance against stagnation in the Hasidic movement, a stirring counter-current, creating a permanent, creative ferment in the river of Hasidic piety.

Nahman of Horodenka and the Ba'al Shem Tov

So how did the Ba'al Shem Tov go about preparing the way for Rebbe Nahman? To answer this question, we first have to get to know Rebbe Nahman's other celebrated grandfather and namesake, Rabbi Nahman of Horodenka (ca. 1680-1766).

Though more attention is usually given to the Ba'al Shem Tov, in many ways, Reb Nahman of Horodenka, his paternal grandfather, was just as significant to his spiritual development. Although far less well known today, Reb Nahman Horodenker was seen in his time as a master almost on par with the Ba'al Shem Tov himself. Being much older than the Ba'al Shem, the elder Nahman had probably established himself as a great scholar and student of Kabbalah while the latter was yet a child.[542] Actually, this is fairly certain, as he was known to be a member of the famous Brod *kloiz* long before meeting the Ba'al Shem Tov.[543]

The Brod *kloiz* was one of the two great kabbalistic conventicles in the region (the other being in Kittov), and was known to be an oasis of Jewish learning and piety. Its members were, almost without exception, profoundly learned in both *halakhah* and *kabbalah*, and usually of distinguished ancestry.[544] And Nahman of Horodenka certainly met both of these qualifications, being a peerless scholar and a descendant of King David himself.

Little else is known about the Horodenker before the Fall of 1740, when at approximately sixty years old, he traveled to *Eretz Yisra'el* with his son, Rabbi Shimshon Hayyim.[545] Being of advanced age for a man of that time, one would expect that he was traveling to the Holy Land with the intention of staying there; but for some unknown reason, he returned to the Ukraine within a single year. Nevertheless, his return at this time became the set-up for an early Hasidic anecdote reported by Reb Mikeleh of Zlotchov . . .

That year, Reb Eliezar Rokeah of Amsterdam traveled to Eretz Yisra'el *in order to meet Reb Nahman of Horodenka, for he believed, "If we are both in* Eretz Yisra'el *at the same time, it may be that we can bring Mashiaḥ." When Reb Eliezar arrived, the people came out of their homes to greet the holy sage. But when he asked Reb Shimshon, the son of Reb Nahman Horodenker, where he could find his father, he learned that Reb Nahman had already returned to the Ukraine!*[546]

This tells us just how highly regarded Reb Nahman Horodenker was among his contemporaries; for it was believed that if two truly great masters of Kabbalah were to meet and work together in the Holy Land, they might bring about the final Redemption. A similar tale is also told of the Ba'al Shem Tov and Rabbi Hayyim ibn Attar, the great Moroccan kabbalist, who were not 'allowed' to meet lest they bring the Messiah too soon. This also appears to be the case with Reb Nahman and Reb Eliezar, as the postscript to this anecdote makes clear:

Now, when Reb Nahman of Horodenka learned that Reb Eliezar had gone to Eretz Yisra'el *in order to find him, he immediately hurried back in 1741. Unfortunately, Reb Eliezar died in S'fat shortly after learning that he had missed Reb Nahman.*[547] *So Reb Nahman stayed on for a while but returned home upon the death of his wife.*[548]

It was probably around this time that Reb Nahman Horodenker first encountered the Ba'al Shem Tov, who had begun his public ministry just a few years before.

It is likely that Reb Nahman, like most of the kabbalists of the Brod *kloiz*, was at first opposed to way of the Ba'al Shem Tov. To them, he seemed too 'popular,' too 'permissive,' and worse still, a dangerous 'innovator.' In contrast, they were elitist, strict in their asceticism, and traditionalists in their approach to *halakhah* and *kabbalah*. Nevertheless, in time, most of the major figures associated with the elite *kloizen* of Brod and Kittov came around to the way of the Ba'al Shem Tov. The tales of how some of these former antagonists were 'converted' are the stuff of Hasidic legend.[549] Unfortunately, we have no such tale of the 'conversion' of Reb Nahman Horodenker. Nevertheless, he was known to have said, "Once, I afflicted my soul and immersed myself in a cold *mikveh* every day, but I could not rid myself of impure thoughts until I attached myself to the Ba'al Shem Tov."[550] This may have been connected with a dream he had in which he saw two types of medicine, one bitter and one sweet. If both medicines work, the sweet one, his dream told him, is to be preferred.[551] This teaching, of course, was one of the 'innovations' of the holy Ba'al Shem.[552]

After the Ba'al Shem, there was no one more respected among the Hasidic leadership than Reb Nahman of Horodenka. Being older and more learned than most of the other Hasidim, he was treated as an honored elder and as the great sage of the movement. His teachings are quoted in the *Degel Mahanei Efraim* of Rabbi Moshe Hayyim Efraim of Sudilkov, the grandson of the Ba'al Shem Tov, and in the writings of Rabbi Ya'akov Yosef of Polonoye, one of the Ba'al Shem Tov's other great disciples, who puts special emphasis on Reb Nahman's learning, calling him "the scholarly and distinguished MaHaRaN."[553] The acrostic, MaHaRaN, means *moreinu ha-rav Nahman*, 'our teacher, the rabbi Nahman.' Interestingly enough, this title was later applied to his grandson, Rebbe Nahman of Bratzlav as well. Considering Reb Ya'akov Yosef's own great learning, this means of address stands out. Moreover, the Ba'al Shem Tov himself was even known to seek Reb Nahman's advice on halakhic matters.

Though already an old man when he met the Ba'al Shem Tov, Reb Nahman of Horodenka became his chief emissary, traveling far and wide to carry-out missions on his behalf.[554] He also traveled with the Ba'al Shem Tov as his most trusted friend and confidant, the person with whom he could share his private thoughts, and as someone whose power in prayer matched his own. Whatever the particulars of their relationship might have been, it seems obvious that theirs was a relationship of deep personal and spiritual intimacy,[555] as the following story makes clear . . .

WHEN REB NAHMAN HORODENKER *was almost seventy years old, he was approached by his friend and Rebbe, the Ba'al Shem Tov, about a possible match to the younger sister of Reb Yitzhak of Drohobitch.*[556]

"What?" Reb Nahman replied: "A marriage at my age? You're not serious. She is yet a young woman and I an old man!"

But the Ba'al Shem Tov was serious. "My friend," he said, "she is meant for you, and I encourage you to give her joy, and to have joy in your elder years, for there is great purpose in this." And he would say no more.

So Reb Nahman Horodenker married the sister of Reb Yitzhak of Drohobitch as the Ba'al Shem Tov had asked him to do.

Of course, this was not Reb Nahman's first marriage. He had been married before to the daughter of Yitzhak of Zholkiev and had two children with her, a daughter and a son.[557] As we mentioned before, he was widowed while on his second trip to *Eretz Yisra'el* before he met the Ba'al Shem Tov.[558] So it appears that approximately ten years had passed by the time the holy Ba'al Shem proposed this match between Reb Nahman and the sister of Reb Yitzhak of Drohobitch.

At the time, it was expected that a widower, even a man of advanced age, would eventually remarry. For, as it says in Torah, "It is not good that man should be alone." (Gen. 2:18) More than this, it was expected that a person should be fully engaged in life until their dying day, and for a Jew, the *mitzvah* of marriage was particularly important.[559] So what objections might there have been for Reb Nahman Horodenker? As the story suggests, there seems to have been a great disparity in age between Reb Nahman and his prospective bride, especially if she was still of child-bearing age—perhaps as much as 40 years! And while it was not considered unusual for an elderly widower to remarry, it was most often to a woman closer in age to him than this.[560] So Reb Nahman's reticence in this case is entirely understandable.[561]

Just after the wedding took place, something strange occurred. Reb Nahman disappeared. No one could find him anywhere. Needless to say, his new bride was concerned and immediately sought the aid of the Ba'al Shem Tov.

Before long, the Ba'al Shem Tov had divined his hiding place, and Reb Nahman was forced to explain the reasons for his strange disappearance. It seems that even as they stood under the ḥuppah (wedding canopy) together, Reb Nahman had a vision in which he saw that his new wife would die in childbirth. Thus, in order to preserve her life, he fled before the marriage could be consummated.

You have to understand, Reb Nahman Horodenker was truly humble, and thus he was loathe to see anyone harmed on his account. Indeed, he would rather see himself harmed or embarrassed before either should happen to another, as we see in the following story . . .

Once, on a cold night, Reb Nahman Horodenker offered his home as shelter to a poor traveler. However, in the morning, when he awoke, he noticed that the poor man had gone off and taken his overcoat. Reb Nahman shrugged his shoulders, and said, Gam zu l'tovah, "This too is for the good," and he went to *shul* to pray.

When he arrived at *shul*, a young man came running up to him and said: "Rabbi, I just saw a man leaving town in your coat! At the time, I wasn't sure, but now that I see you're not wearing it; he must have stolen it from you!"

Reb Nahman calmly asked the young man, "Did it fit him?"

Confused, the young man answered, "Yes . . . I suppose it did."

"Good," said Reb Nahman, "Let him keep it; he is poor and the Winter is cold."[562]

HEARING THIS EXPLANATION *from her new husband, the bride turned white and began to tremble. She knew too much of Reb Nahman Horodenker's reputation to doubt his word. Nevertheless, she begged him to stay and consummate the marriage anyway, saying only: "It will be as God wills . . . but perhaps ha-Shem will give me just a little time with my child."*

Nine months later, the child was born and they named him, Simhah—'joy'— remembering what the Ba'al Shem Tov had said when he had arranged their match. And indeed, his mother was granted a full month with the boy before her body eventually gave way to the omen. At her passing, Reb Nahman was heard to say: "So great was her faith in ha-Shem as she learned her fate that she would have been granted a long life too, if only she would have asked it."[563]

After his second wife's passing, Reb Nahman Horodenker came with his infant son to live in the house of the Ba'al Shem Tov. This was probably a great comfort to them both, for Reb Nahman was often away on journeys for the Ba'al Shem, and in the house of the Rebbe, Reb Nahman could rest assured that his son would be well cared for by Adel, the Ba'al Shem Tov's daughter.[564] Moreover, Adel's own daughter, Feiga, was a child of the same age, and the boy and the girl could be reared together as brother and sister. It probably seemed like a perfect arrangement. Nevertheless, Reb Nahman did not consider that the Ba'al Shem Tov might have his own purposes in bringing them into his house . . .

ALMOST TEN YEARS LATER, *as the holy Ba'al Shem Tov prepared to depart from the world, he called Reb Nahman Horodenker to his side, saying: "I have one last favor to ask of you before I go, my friend . . . I want you to give your beloved son, Simhah, in marriage to my granddaughter, Feiga. For I tell you, these two are meant to be together, both for themselves and for the good of future generations."*

Reb Nahman Horodenker was clearly taken aback by this suggestion, which he had never before considered. You must understand, for Reb Nahman, such a match was almost inconceivable. After all, his was a lineage of unparalleled distinction, being directly descended from none other than David ha-Melekh, and counting such great masters as Rabbi Moshe Isserles *and Rabbi Yehudah Loew of Prague among his recent ancestors. And from whom was the Ba'al Shem Tov descended? It was well known that he was of humble and obscure origins, being unable to point to any ancestor beyond his own father, Reb Eliezer!*

Rest assured, Reb Nahman was not being arrogant in this reaction. The rules of matchmaking in this period were complex and stringent. Marrying *inv'ha-gefen b'inv'ha-gefen*, 'the vines of this good grape to that good grape' was a paramount consideration.[565] Even when my own grandchildren were marrying into established *rabbonishe* families here in America, I somehow felt compelled to remind them that we too have *yihus* (lineage), being descendents of Rabbi Natan Neta Shapira of Krakow (1585-1633) who wrote the *Megaleh Amukot*, and of Rabbi Moshe Yagid who wrote a book on the laws of marriage.[566] In the case of the Ba'al Shem Tov and Reb Nahman of Horodenka, the situation was very clear: it would have been an egregious breach of societal rules if Reb Nahman, a 'prince' in terms of both his family lineage and Torah learning, were to marry his son to the granddaughter of an apparently unlearned magician and inn-keeper's son.[567]

AFTER A LONG PAUSE, *and with a deep sigh, Reb Nahman finally answered him: "You are my master and my dear friend, and though I love little Feiga, I don't know how I can agree to your proposal. I can assure you, it is not me, but my family yihus, my pedigree, that gives me pause and prevents me from agreeing to your proposal at once. As you know, I am a direct descendant of David ha-Melekh, Rabban Gamliel, Rabbi Yohanan ha-Sandlar, and Rashi, and you know what sanctity there is in the preservation of a great lineage. And, my friend... you must forgive me... it is well known that your own family origins are, well...obscure. So how can I justify myself before my ancestors in making such a match? On the other hand, who knows of your great* ahavah *(love) and* yirah *(awe) before* ha-Shem *better than I? And I would not even have my beloved Simhah were it not for your matchmaking...So what can I do? It seems I must deny my yihus and submit to the match."*

The Ba'al Shem Tov smiled gently in the face of Reb Nahman's obvious anguish and put a hand on his shoulder. "My old friend," he began, "I honor your sacrifice, and consider it a great testimony of your love and friendship. And because you have made it, I can tell you what I have not confided to anyone else." As he said this, he leaned-in conspiratorially and continued, "Though it has become covered in the mists of time, I too am descended from David ha-Melekh.[568] You know me too well to doubt my word."

"Nu?" said Reb Nahman, said with great surprise, "Then my ancestors must be satisfied with that, and I can agree without the slightest reservation!"⁵⁶⁹

In the *Shabbat* prayers, we say, "By your holy name you have sworn unto David that his light shall never be extinguished."⁵⁷⁰ Remember, the children of David were to be conduits for the Messiah, and when one considers how this potential conduit could be blocked, who knows what difficulties this might cause in bringing the Messiah later on. For the belief in the coming of the Messiah is very real among Hasidim and prayed for continually. So it was as if Reb Nahman Horodenker was saying, "How can I justify this to my ancestors, if by this action, I may be blocking or diminishing the chances that the Messiah might come through this lineage?"⁵⁷¹

After the passing of the Ba'al Shem Tov, Reb Nahman waited a long time for a sign. For many years, whenever he heard that a party would be traveling to *Eretz Yisra'el*, he would bring up the possibility of his going with them. But the holy Ba'al Shem always discouraged him. He continued these requests until one day the Ba'al Shem Tov convinced him that the "Ark of the Holy Temple" was actually in Mezhbizh.⁵⁷² So even after the master had passed on, he continued to wait for a sign that he might finally go back to *Eretz Yisra'el* . . .

WHEN REB NAHMAN WISHED TO TRAVEL to the Holy Land once again, he went with Reb Yosef of Kaminka to visit the grave of the Ba'al Shem Tov. When they returned from praying there, Reb Yosef noticed that Reb Nahman was in a joyful mood, so he asked him, "What has gotten into you?"

Reb Nahman answered, "The holy Ba'al Shem Tov has finally granted me permission to travel to Eretz Yisra'el! Didn't you hear him?"

Reb Yosef appeared puzzled, and said, "No."

Reb Nahman asked, "Didn't you see him standing next to me and speaking of this?"⁵⁷³

Reb Nahman entrusted his son to Adel's care and prepared to leave Mezhbizh. He was then eighty-four years old. At that time, Russia was threatening to invade Poland, and many Hasidic masters, including Reb Pinhas of Koretz, were worried about the impact this might have on the Jews of Poland. How many innocent Jews would be caught in the crossfire? Reb Pinhas actively began to oppose them in the spiritual worlds. Nevertheless, he felt the 'battle' was too great for his strength, saying, "There was no one in the whole country with shoulders broad enough to prevent the danger except for Reb Nahman Horodenker." But Reb Nahman was already on his way to *Eretz Yisra'el*.

Later, Reb Pinhas said: "As long as Reb Nahman was in Poland, Russia did not cross the Dnieper River. Though they had made many attempts, they had failed to enter Poland; but on the day Reb Nahman crossed the Dniester River on his way to *Eretz Yisra'el*, the Russian troops crossed the Dnieper."[574] It is clear from this anecdote that, in the opinion of Reb Pinhas at least, after the death of the Ba'al Shen Tov, there was no master among the Hasidim greater than Reb Nahman of Horodenka... Even when taking Reb Ya'akov Yosef of Polonoye and the Maggid of Mezritch into consideration.

Leading a group of Hasidim,[575] Reb Nahman passed through Romania and departed from Galatz (Galati), a city with access to the Black Sea. He reached Istanbul on the 27th of Tammuz and waited for a ship until the 18th of Elul, the birthday of the Ba'al Shem Tov. During the voyage, however, a violent storm threatened to capsize the ship, but Reb Nahman Horodenker took up a *sefer Torah* and cried aloud, "Even if it has been decreed that we perish in this storm, may God forbid it, for we will not accept this verdict!" They survived the storm and arrived in Akko on the 12th of Tishrei, 1764.[576]

In one letter written from *Eretz Yisra'el*, Reb Nahman Horodenker, who was then leading the Hasidic community in T'veryah (Tiberias),[577] said: "Tradition tells us that the very air of *Eretz Yisra'el* makes one wise. Before I came here, I hoped that I would learn to utter one prayer properly. Now that I am wise, would that I were able to utter one *word* properly."[578]

Reb Nahman Horodenker died shortly after and was buried in the cemetery of T'veryah.[579] Many years later, his grandson, Rebbe Nahman of Bratzlav would say... "*It is not on account of my grandfather the Ba'al Shem Tov, but on account of my grandfather Reb Nahman that I have attained my present standing.*"[580]

A New Rebbe Nahman

According to Bratzlaver Hasidim, Feiga, the mother of Rebbe Nahman of Bratzlav, like her own mother, was also in touch with the soul of the Ba'al Shem Tov and received messages from him, as we see in the following story...[581]

WHEN SIMHAH AND FEIGA *reached the age of thirteen, they were married in Mezhbizh amid a host of tzaddikim and their blessings. And the match was a success, just as the Ba'al Shem Tov had predicted. But despite their happiness, there were no children, even after several years of marriage.*

As the years passed, the absence of children began to concern Feiga and her mother Adel. As Adel's concern grew, she began to seek a dream from her father, the Ba'al Shem Tov. When the dream finally came, she cried out to him, "Abba, you have done so much for the world; can you not help my Feiga, who is childless?"

The Ba'al Shem Tov consoled her in the dream, saying: "Don't cry, Adeleh; Feiga will soon give birth to a son who should be named 'Yisra'el,' after me. Later she will have another son who will illuminate the whole world."

Soon after this, the Ba'al Shem Tov began to appear in Feiga's dreams as well. He told her that she was pregnant with a son, and that she should name the child after him. These dreams disturbed Feiga greatly, for she knew that her grandfather had asked that no one name their children after him. Even worse, all the children who had been named after him had died in infancy![582]

Needless to say, she had her doubts about these dreams. She was still young, and her experience with dreams and visions was not yet mature. Moreover, she feared the worst for her child. When she gave birth to a boy, as the Ba'al Shem Tov said she would, her fears mounted. Still, she did not know what she would do at the moment of naming. Seven days later, at the circumcision, when the mohel proclaimed, "And his name will be called in Yisra'el . . ." Feiga froze, but her mother quickly called out, "Yisra'el!" and Feiga fainted.

Nothing could be done now, her mother had said it.

The child, Yisra'el, as she feared, was sickly and not fated to live long.[583] *Nevertheless, after a few years, Feiga conceived again and gave birth to another son, and this child was named, Nahman, after his other grandfather, Rabbi Nahman of Horodenka.*[584]

While the tradition among Sefardic Jews is to name their children after the living, Ashkenazim name their children after the dead. The idea is that this gives the deceased an opportunity to continue their soul-development in another incarnation. For instance, I was named after my own grandfather, Meshullam Zalman Yagid, who died an early death in World War I. Because he had not been allowed to live out his full allotment of years, it was assumed that he would be able to do so through me. And, in truth, I have always felt a connection to this grandfather, and even the burden of living out the years that were denied him.⁵⁸⁵ So in the Hasidic context, it is assumed that there is a soul-connection that is brought about through the naming of the child at the *brit*, for the name, it is taught, binds the soul to the body.

It is clear from this story that the unique soul of Rebbe Nahman was not to continue the soul-development of the Ba'al Shem Tov, as we have already mentioned, but that of his other grandfather, Nahman of Horodenka, who was in the shadow of his master in his own lifetime.⁵⁸⁶ Instead, the holy Ba'al Shem is reincarnated in the first child for a brief time for his own purposes, thus 'making room' for the incarnation to come.

Why the delay? It may be that Reb Nahman Horodenker had not yet passed on when Feiga first became pregnant. But after little Yisra'el had died and Feiga became pregnant again, the elder Reb Nahman had also passed on and there was no longer any question after whom the child would be named.⁵⁸⁷ Thus, from the perspective of this story and the one preceding it, it seems that the Ba'al Shem Tov was intentionally shaping events to bring about the birth of Rebbe Nahman.

In another tale, Feiga is visited by the biblical Matriarchs in a dream and given information about the coming child. When the story starts, her husband Simhah, who has been away in solitary meditation, has not arrived home as expected, and thus Feiga is afraid that something has happened to him...

ONE DAY, CONCERNED OVER HER HUSBAND'S LONG ABSENCE, *Feiga lay down to get a little rest. When she fell asleep, her mother Adel appeared to her in a dream accompanied by the Mothers of all Yisra'el—Sarah, Rivkah, Rahel, and Leah. Immediately, they assured her that her husband Simhah would be home for Shabbat. Then they brought Feiga to the Chamber of Souls where she noticed an unusually bright mote of awareness. This, they told her, was the soul of her grandfather, the Ba'al Shem Tov. Then, as they moved on, she saw another bright mote of awareness, which was brighter and more luminous than the first. In surprise, she asked the assembled Mothers, "To whom does this soul belong?"*

*They replied, "This soul is soon to be given to you to bear." With this, Feiga awoke to find that her husband had returned in time for Shabbat. She then went to the mikveh, and that night she conceived the child that would become Rebbe Nahman.*⁵⁸⁸

Once again, special emphasis is put on the fact that it is not the soul of the Ba'al Shem Tov that is in Rebbe Nahman. In this case, however, no mention is made of Reb Nahman Horodenker, but it can be assumed from the larger context of stories that this is his soul. Some may wish to make much of the fact that the second "mote of awareness" was "brighter and more luminous than the first," speculating that Rebbe Nahman's soul was somehow greater than that of the Ba'al Shem Tov, but this doesn't seem to be the point of the story. For in the end, it is the brightness of each mote of awareness that draws Feiga's attention, and it is the brighter of the two that is meant for her. It may be that having already borne the soul of her grandfather in her child, Yisra'el, who passed on early, she was allowed to see his soul once again. But as it was the night of her conception in the story, the soul that shows brightest is the one she is about to receive.

Mitzvot and Berakhot

Even before her second child was born, Feiga knew that he would be special. She thought constantly of how she would raise him in righteousness, in the ways of her holy grandfather, the Ba'al Shem Tov. And having lost her previous son, Yisra'el, after only a short time, she wasn't going to take any chances with this child. Therefore, she decided that she would bring him up in the knowledge of *mitzvot* from his first moments, as a talisman against all harm.

FROM THE MOMENT HE WAS BORN,[589] *Feiga took his tiny hands and laved water over them in the ritual manner, as if he had just awakened from sleep. Then, after he had been bathed and swathed in a blanket, Feiga took out a tiny yarmulke she had knitted and put it on his little head.*

From that day forward, the child's head was always covered; and whenever he would awake to nurse, Feiga would wash his hands again, just as required of an adult. In this way, young Nahman was raised to holiness from the day of his birth.[590]

It's wonderful to see how she wished him to be involved in *mitzvot* from the day he was born. It says in the *Shulḥan Arukh* that a person who sleeps even for twenty minutes is required to wash the hands upon waking. From Feiga's perspective, the child in the womb had been as if asleep, in a kind of dream consciousness, and thus required *netillat yadaim*, a 'raising up of the hands' when he was born.[591]

There is a traditional belief, now little heeded, which says that a newborn should be handled by as few people as possible and protected from all negative influences, being carefully inculcated with good impressions from its first moments. Among the Oglala Sioux of Black Elk's era, when it was time for the baby to enter the world, "parents would go out and select two women, good natured and of good character" who would then assist in the birth and see to the immediate needs of the newborn. It is thought that the intimate care given by these women at this crucial moment in the child's life left an impression that might permanently affect the disposition of the child. If one of the women was grouchy, the child would be grouchy too, but if she was gentle and conscientious, the child might be as well.[592]

The Sufi master, Hazrat Inayat Khan, likewise puts great stress on the education of infants, saying:

> It is never too soon in the life of a child for it to receive education. The soul of an infant is like a photographic plate which has never been exposed before, and whatever impression falls on the photographic plate covers it; no other impressions which come afterwards have the same effect. Therefore when the parents or guardians lose the opportunity of impressing an infant in its early childhood they lose the greatest opportunity.[593]

So it would seem that Feiga is only acting according to an important belief of traditional societies. Nevertheless, she does it in the Hasidic fashion taught by her grandfather, infusing baby Nahman with the deepest impressions and highest standards of holiness among Jews of the time, thus marking him for an exceptional life.

Eight days later, on Shabbat ha-Gadol *(just before Pesah), young Nahman was brought into the covenant in the presence of many holy souls. Among them were disciples of the Ba'al Shem Tov, his parents and grandparents, and most notably, his uncle Barukh, the Rebbe of Tulchin (and later Mezhbizh).*

Now, Barukh of Tulchin had been raised to be a Rebbe from childhood, learning at the feet of his grandfather, the Ba'al Shem Tov, and later with his grandfather's great disciple, Pinhas of Koretz. So his presence at the brit milah was eagerly sought by his sister, Feiga, who watched him intently for any sign of special interest in her child. She, of course, already knew that the child was born to a high destiny—she was not called Feiga ha-Naviah for nothing—nevertheless, she looked to have her brother's blessing for her newborn son as a testimony of this fact, and as further insurance against harm.

After the circumcision, the attendees parted ceremoniously as Reb Barukh came forward to look at the child. He stood over young Nahman and stared at him for several minutes, paying special attention to his eyes. Then, suddenly, he broke off and looked up at his sister and brother-in-law with a look of surprise, saying, "You should know that this child has a high destiny; he is a treasury of virtue!" He then blessed Feiga and Simhah that they would be able to raise him in the ways of the tzaddikim and that they would have much nahas (satisfaction) in him.[594]

But Feiga was not content with her brother's blessing, for she also wished him to bless her son directly, and said, "My brother, I beg you to bless my son as well, that he should not encounter opposition and obstacles on his path."

At this, Reb Barukh sighed, almost as if he had feared she would ask this. He was pensive for several minutes, looking at no one and holding his closed fist almost worriedly to his mouth while everyone waited in absolute silence. Then, quite suddenly, he waved his hand in a gesture of frustration and quickly left the room without saying a word![595]

Why this strange reaction? It may be that Reb Barukh was aware of the *ḥerem* (ban) that had been signed by the Vilna Ga'on that same day against the Hasidim, and thus he may have taken this as an indication of future obstacles that would be placed in the way of his nephew.[596] This explanation is supported by another Bratzlaver tradition involving Reb Barukh . . .

Many years later, when the grandson of Reb Barukh came to visit his grandfather, he would often gather to hear the talk of the visiting Hasidim. Though he was only a child, he took great delight in their talk, and most of all, hearing his grandfather's responses. On one occasion, however, the talk of the visiting Hasidim turned to Rebbe Nahman. Sadly, some of the visitors took to criticizing the Rebbe, saying that his teachings were not consistent with *derekh ha-Ḥasidut*, the 'way of Hasidism.' Worse still, Reb Barukh said nothing to defend his nephew!

Later, the child approached his grandfather and asked him, *"Zeide*, why didn't you say anything when they said what they did about uncle Nahman?"

Reb Barukh sighed and said: "Little one, I want you to listen carefully. Your uncle Nahman is a very great person, and those people who speak negatively about him have no idea who he really is. But there is something you must understand. The criticism and opposition that is raised against him is something that has to be; indeed, this opposition is actually beneficial to him. For your uncle Nahman's soul is extremely holy, in some ways, too holy for this world, and thus it is only by opposition that it is kept in this world."[597]

Whether this story is apocryphal or authentic, the fact remains that Rebbe Nahman would be involved in several serious Hasidic controversies and forced to endure much abuse from other Rebbes and their Hasidim. Some of these controversies were ideological, while others seem to have been territorial disputes, motivated at least in part by jealousy. Whatever their origin, Rebbe Nahman was tormented by them and many of his teachings bear the marks of his pain. And perhaps his pain was all the worse because one of these later disputes was with none other than his own uncle Barukh, who may have seen this conflict coming long before.[598]

Learning with the Tzaddikim

Living in Mezhbizh, amidst the extended family and disciples of the Ba'al Shem Tov, it is perhaps not surprising that young Nahman showed an unusual inclination toward all things spiritual, even in his earliest years...

Once, when Nahman *was only five years old, Rabbi Hayyim of Krasnoye arrived in Mezhbizh with a group of Hasidim on their way to visit the* Ba'al ha-Toldot, *Rabbi Ya'akov Yosef of Polonoye.*[599] *Hearing this, young Nahman was overcome by a desire to see the great old man, the beloved* Yossele *of the Ba'al Shem Tov. He immediately cried out to Reb Hayyim and the Hasidim, begging them,* "Take me with you!"

The Hasidim only smiled and said, "No-o-o, no-o-o, it's a long journey, and too difficult for a yingele (little one), like you."

But young Nahman only pleaded harder, "Please, I want to see the Rav!"

Still, the Hasidim wouldn't hear of it.

Then, as the time came for them to depart, young Nahman repeated his request, but it was no use. Just then, as the driver took up the reins, Nahman thrust his foot between the spokes of the wheel! His mother, Feiga, gasped and cried out for the driver to "Stop!"

Reb Hayyim, recognizing the determination of the boy, called out, "Feigele ... Why don't you let him come with us; I'll take care of him, I promise."

And this is how Rebbe Nahman came to meet the Ba'al ha-Toldot.[600]

You have to imagine how important this visit must have seemed to young Nahman. Today, children venerate superheroes from comic books and movies, but in the circumscribed conclave of *shtetl* life, within living memory of the holy Ba'al Shem Tov, the great disciples of the master must almost have seemed to spring from the pages of a Harry Potter story—the Rav, Ya'akov Yosef of Polonoye like the Headmaster of Hogwarts, Albus Dumbledore, and his own grandmother, Adel, a Professor McGonagall. These were persons out of legend, about whom tales of miracles were told by those who had witnessed them personally. It was a world in which an aspiring 'magician' might hope to apprentice with the greatest 'wizards' of the age.[601]

Consider this story young Nahman might have heard from the lips of his own uncle, Reb Barukh, who was himself introduced to Reb Ya'akov Yosef of Polonoye as a young man . . .

> As a boy, Reb Barukh had been sent to apprentice with Reb Pinhas of Koretz, and continued to visit him after he settled in Ostrog. Now, after the passing of the Ba'al Shem Tov and the emigration of Nahman of Horodenka, Reb Pinhas often sought the company of the Ba'al ha-Toldot, Reb Ya'akov Yosef of Polonoye, whom he respected above all other *tzaddikim* in the Ukraine. So highly did he respect him that he would often make the long journey to Polonoye in order to spend *Shabbat* with him. On one of these occasions, he also brought young Barukh with him to meet the Rav.
>
> After the *Shabbat* had passed, the Ba'al ha-Toldot retired to his private room to meditate. In the meantime, Reb Pinhas received an urgent message bidding him return home at once. This was a problem, for he wouldn't think of departing without taking leave of the master. But neither could he wait for the Rav to emerge from his seclusion, which might last as long as twenty-four hours! Thinking that the youth would be excused for interrupting him, he asked Barukh to go to the master's private room to seek his permission for them to return home on urgent business. But Barukh was likewise terrified to disturb the Rav's solitude. And yet, he couldn't disobey his master either! So, with fear and trembling, he suggested that they both go the Rav's private room together.
>
> Soon after, the Rebbe and his *talmid* (disciple) approached the door of the Rav's private sanctuary. They found the door warped and in disrepair. As they touched the doorknob, it fell to the floor with a heavy thud, and the door opened by itself with a terrifying creak! The two stepped forward to look into the room and were amazed to see the Rav engaged in study with a heavenly *maggid*! Frightened by the sight, they turned to flee. But Barukh lingered just a moment to take in the awesome sight.[602]

Later Reb Barukh said, "It is because of this that I know what an angel is! I had known," he added, "that the Ba'al ha-Toldot studied with a heavenly *maggid* (a familiar spirit)," but he had hardly conceived of what this meant until he had actually seen it. It was said that the Ba'al Shem Tov had known early on that the Rav had a *maggid*, but recognized that it was not one of the true *maggidim*, so he took this *maggid* from him and gave him a true *maggid* in its place. It was this true *maggid* that Reb Pinhas and Reb Barukh had seen.[603]

It is very likely that young Nahman had heard such a story from his uncle in awestruck silence and thus, quite understandably longed to meet the great Ba'al ha-Toldot himself.

Growing up in Mezhbizh, a pilgrimage place of Hasidim, young Nahman must have had the opportunity to meet many disciples of the Ba'al Shem Tov and other great *tzaddikim*. We have already mentioned the Ba'al ha-Toldot, Hayyim of Krasnoye, Barukh of Mezhbizh, not to mention his pious parents, Simhah and Feiga,[604] and his grandmother Adel, but he was probably also influenced by his other uncle, the elder brother of Reb Barukh, Moshe Hayyim Efraim, the rabbi of Sudilkov (1746-1790).

Reb Moshe Hayyim Efraim was a retiring personality, but of the greatest personal piety, continuing in the ways of his grandfather, the Ba'al Shem Tov. Though he shied away from any attention or leadership in the Hasidic movement, he was nevertheless a venerated *tzaddik*, who was known to be a great scholar and preacher as well. He is often called 'the Degel' after his book, *Degel Mahanei Efraim*, a classic of Hasidic wisdom, and one of the most important sources of the Ba'al Shem Tov's teachings.[605] Though there are only a few references to him in Bratzlav literature, the presence and influence of such a *tzaddik* in young Nahman's life should not be underestimated, especially when one considers the following anecdote ...

WHEN REBBE NAHMAN WAS A BOY, *his uncle the Degel would often talk to him about his service to ha-Shem, and about the importance of Torah study. On the day of his bar mitzvah, Rebbe Nahman remembered with gratitude how he was taken aside by the Degel, who blessed him, saying: " 'You are My son, I have fathered you this day.'*[606] *Becoming bar mitzvah is like being born again; it is new start for one's service to God!" He then urged him to devote all of his energy to* avodat ha-Shem *(service of God) all the days of his life.*[607]

It has been suggested that in quoting these words from the Psalms, the Degel was actually giving young Nahman *smikhah*, 'ordination' as a Rebbe,[608] or at least "charging him with the responsibility of carrying on the family name."⁶⁰⁹ However he understood this blessing, Rebbe Nahman was eternally grateful for this small word of wisdom, and always spoke to his Hasidim of his uncle's wisdom and righteousness. His disciple, Reb Nosson later commented on this moment, saying, "These words were as dear to the Rebbe as finding a great treasure."⁶¹⁰

As much as anything, it was likely the living example of his uncle Moshe Hayyim Efraim that made such a profound impression on the young man. For here was a true exemplar of Hasidic modesty, gentleness, and piety who, like his nephew, was critical of the many "false *tzaddikim*" that had arisen since the time of the Ba'al Shem Tov. In this way, he stood in perfect contrast to his younger brother, Barukh, who lived in royal splendor, and who is often described in the sources as angry and arrogant. Certainly, Reb Barukh was not without his gifts, and undoubtedly did great service to *ha-Shem*, but his was not the model upon which the young Nahman wished to base himself.⁶¹¹

The Words Yet Unsaid

That young Nahman venerated the memory of his great-grandfather, the Ba'al Shem Tov, and felt an especially strong connection to him, goes without saying. As a boy, it is said that he would often get up in the middle of the night to go and pray at the grave of the holy Ba'al Shem. In that place, still resonant with holy *kavvanah*, he felt he could really open his heart to *ha-Shem*—and not cold, wind, or snow could convince him to go inside on those long nights.⁶¹² Even then, it was clear to him that the true legacy of the Ba'al Shem Tov was not one of learning, nor of miracles, but of intense and profound prayer. And this is likely what he hoped to find there. But he also looked to the legendary example of the Ba'al Shem Tov who, in his own youth, wandered into the forests and fields in his loneliness and poured out his heart to God. Perhaps young Nahman also felt alone in the world, isolated by the expectations of so many people, and sought the consolation of the One who is truly *alone* . . .

> In his father's house—*which had also been the house of the Ba'al Shem Tov—young Nahman would climb up into the attic when he needed to speak to God in solitude, whispering his prayers amidst the feed and straw that was stored there.*
>
> *In the beginning, he took with him a book of* Tehillim *and poured tears upon the pages as he prayed. But it was not long before he had exhausted the*

words of David ha-Melekh, and still he found that there were parts of himself that had not been uttered. So he found other books of prayers to take into the attic—Sha'arei Tzion[613] and different siddurim of his father's—and he prayed these too with all of his heart, seeking to tell ha-Shem those things yet unsaid. But still, there were thoughts and feelings in the shadowed corners of his heart that had not been uttered when he had exhausted these as well.

Now, having come to the end of the books (even the prayers printed in Yiddish for women), and finding that he had still not uttered his own secret heart to ha-Shem, he broke down in frustration. He began to tremble and cry, saying: Oy! Gevalt, zisser foter in himmel, "Help me, my sweet heavenly parent! What is it that I have not said? What are the secret words that still want to come from my lips? Help me to say them!" Then he sighed and just began to talk, talking to God from the depths of his breaking heart, as if talking to a friend, as if talking to his mother or father—If only he could have told them the secrets he now uttered to his 'sweet heavenly parent!'[614]

This little story introduces us to what would later become the cornerstone of Bratzlav Ḥasidut, the practice of *hitbodedut*, or 'aloneness,' a concentrated, extemporaneous prayer in the vernacular, usually prayed in solitude.

In many ways, this was a breakthrough; for throughout Jewish history, prayer has mostly been based around the Psalms. Indeed, even Rebbe Nahman says: "David ha-Melekh was the paradigm of repentance" and he "composed his Psalms in such a way that everyone can find themselves in them."[615] So the idea of prayer in the Jewish tradition has been to 'coast' on the expression of the biblical David, to find ourselves in his words, in his joy and exultation, as well as in his fears and sadness. This is a very important notion and a true way to pray. But young Nahman's frustration is rooted in a recognition that there is still something lacking—the pure, unmediated prayer of the heart. That is to say, the expression of our own unique feelings, our own longing and pain in the world, and the certainty that there is nothing else quite like it. His breakthrough was to rediscover for Judaism that it is not enough to pray the words of David, we must actually pray as David prayed! As he would later express it: "David ha-Melekh was able to compose the Psalms because he was rooted in *hitbodedut* (aloneness), hiding himself from others while he poured out his heart before God. This is why he said, 'Every night I drench my bed, I melt my couch in tears.' (Ps. 6:7) This practice is the highest of all, and the one who can follow it will be happy."[616]

As we continue to look at Rebbe Nahman's life and teachings, we will come upon a number of different expressions of *hitbodedut*. Hopefully, by the time we are done, this practice will have begun to take on a definite shape for you, and perhaps you will have started to make it a part of your own prayer practice.

The Wedding Gift

So much has been written about this period in Rebbe Nahman's life: how he struggled to overcome his desire for physical comforts, to control his impulses, often going to extremes of asceticism. By his own admission, nothing came easy to him, not even learning. When he could not comprehend a passage in the *Mishnah* as a child, he would plead with God for understanding, often bursting into tears and begging God to have mercy on him. And it was only in this way, he claimed, that he made any progress at all in learning or prayer. But what is most interesting about all this is that he made every effort to hide these spiritual struggles from everyone around him, even those who were closest to him.[617]

Why did he do this? One explanation may be that he wished to continue in the pattern of the Ba'al Shem Tov, who spent many years among the *tzaddikim nistarim* (the hidden righteous ones), who concealed all of their service to *ha-Shem*.[618] But I tend to think that there may have been another equally compelling reason for his discretion.

Growing up in Mezhbizh, the great-grandson of the Ba'al Shem Tov, and the nephew of Reb Barukh, the expectations for young Nahman were particularly high. It is unclear whether his uncle Barukh looked at him as a potential heir, but it is almost certain that others looked on him as the next great *tzaddik* of the family.[619] And this carried with it certain consequences. For young Nahman would not have been unaware of such speculations, and being the sensitive child he was, would almost certainly have felt trapped by them. How could he hope to go his own way and escape from the disease of complacency and showy Hasidism he was beginning to see among the Hasidim if he was forced into the very mold they were making? And to be considered Reb Barukh's 'heir' must have felt like the least tenable option of all; for while he may have respected his uncle, their ideas of what a Rebbe should be were almost diametrically opposed. Indeed, Rebbe Nahman was almost certainly in rebellion against the model being set forth by his uncle and his Hasidim.

But from another perspective, all of this speculation is irrelevant; because the ambition of a truly devout and spiritually inclined boy like Nahman is not to become a *Rebbe*, but to become a *Hasid*. Not in the sense of being the 'Hasid of so and so,' but in the sense of growing in piety, day by day, over the entirety of one's life. That's the real goal, even for those who must serve as Rebbes. So the problem for young Nahman was to figure out how he was ever going to get anywhere on the path of Ḥasidut if he was always being treated like a Rebbe, especially in his formative years. Only one way presented itself to him, to hide his service, and to consciously disappoint expectations whenever possible.

Just how he went about doing this becomes abundantly clear in the next few stories. But the story of his wedding day is particularly important. For here we see him both hiding and 'peeking through' on a special occasion. So let's take a look at this important moment, which was witnessed by his very first disciple, Reb Shimon of Krementchug . . .

As was the custom *in those days, a marriage was arranged for Nahman soon after his bar mitzvah. His young bride-to-be was Sashia,[620] the daughter of Reb Efraim, a wealthy and respected tax-farmer from the village of Usyatin.[621] Thus, the wedding took place in the city of Medvedevka, which was near his father-in-law's home.*

After covering the face of his bride, shortly before the wedding, Nahman called over a number of young men and spent a little time with each of them. He was testing them in subtle ways, trying to find out what they were really like. In this way, he attracted the attention of a young man a few years older than himself.[622] His name was Shimon ben Baer, and soon he started a conversation with him as well. But Shimon, unlike the others, was shocked by young Nahman's talk, for he was pretending to crude opinions that were not his own. Thus, Shimon kept silent until Nahman said to him: "Do you mean to say you're not interested in such things? You're human, aren't you? Come on?"

But Shimon only said, "I'm just a simple person trying to be a Hasid."

Nahman smiled and said, "It looks like we'll be getting to know one another then."

Then he confided to Shimon that he had spoken in this way to the other young men as well and found that they were all easily led into crude and useless talk. Then the two decided to go for a walk together, eventually finding themselves in the fields near the edge of town.

They looked out on the fields in silence for a time before the young groom suddenly turned to Shimon and said: "Today is my wedding day, you know? Do you understand what a great day this is? On the day of one's wedding, all one's sins are forgiven. A person has to know how to make use of such a day. The person who knows how to think the proper thoughts on such a day can make a great change. Do you understand what a great opportunity this is?"

Shimon looked at the thirteen year old in wonder as he continued: "Shimon, what do you think our purpose in this world is? Why were we created with such challenges? Was it not because ha-Shem wants us to struggle with our yetzer ha-ra (negative impulse) to overcome our desires and put all our energy into serving God?"[623]

Shimon had never heard anyone talk in this way before, let alone someone so young, but he knew that these were the words of challenge that he had longed to hear. Perhaps this descendant of the Ba'al Shem Tov was a true inheritor of his forbears, one who could truly help him grow his soul. Finally, Shimon spoke up, and said, "I see that you will be a great tzaddik one day; I only ask that you to allow me to be your gabbai (attendant)."

The young groom looked down for a moment and said, "It is not yet that time, my friend." And they went on talking this way until it was time to return for the wedding ceremony.

Reb Shimon later said, "It was then that I abandoned all thought of other Rebbes and followed this boy instead."[624]

This wedding match was typical for that time, hoping to unite learning and piety with the prosperity that allowed one to pursue it. Moreover, for Reb Efraim, who was of a respected family, it was a match to another family of growing renown.[625]

According to tradition, the wedding day is considered the 'Yom Kippur of life.' This is why I always make sure to call the family together before the wedding so that they forgive one another before the couple is married. It is a powerful moment, and as much good that can be done with it should be done. For as Rebbe Nahman says, on this day, "all one's sins are forgiven."[626]

This is obviously a very important moment in Rebbe Nahman's life, and perhaps for the first time he is socializing the moment of his realization, anchoring it in reality by sharing it with someone else. In doing this, he becomes a Rebbe. Providentially, it is Reb Shimon who is captured by this sharing and who becomes his first disciple. And what does the name 'Shimon' mean? 'One who listens.'

Praying in Nature

Though the young Rebbe had made his first 'public appearance,' as it were, it was really just an audition, and he quickly retreated into his preferred solitude, hiding his service to God as much as possible. As he suggested to Reb Shimon, "It is not yet that time, my friend."

Nevertheless, we do know a great deal about this period in the young Rebbe's life, some of which is reported on by both Reb Shimon and his later disciple, Reb Nosson...

ONCE, MANY YEARS LATER, *when the Rebbe was already well-known, Reb Shimon was traveling with him on a road near Usyatin, where the Rebbe had lived with his father-in-law, and where he had worked so hard in his service to God. As they passed through the land surrounding Usyatin, the Rebbe's voice betrayed deep emotion as he said, "How good it was for me here; with every step I took in this place, I felt the taste of Gan Eden." For it was in these places that the Rebbe had gone off alone to practice* hitbodedut. *As they continued, he said, "It was so very good here; what do I need all of this fame for?"*

On another occasion, I (Reb Nosson) was present when the Rebbe said that often, as a young man, when he would come back from practicing hitbodedut *alone in these woods or fields, he felt that the whole world had been renewed. It was no longer the same world at all; everything was completely different!*[627]

In Usyatin—no longer confined to his father's attic and midnight visits to the Ba'al Shem Tov's grave in Mezhbizh—Rebbe Nahman was free to wander the woods and meadows like his great-grandfather, seeking a tryst with God in nature, sometimes praying there as evening approached. Later, he would say: "The best place for *hitbodedut* is in the meadows, on the outskirts of the city. You should try to do *hitbodedut* in grassy fields, for the grass will awaken your heart." And "How wonderful it would be if we were worthy of hearing the song of the grass; every blade of grass sings a pure song to God, expecting nothing in return. It is wonderful to hear its song and to worship God in its midst."[628] In this ecstatic mood, he almost sounds like Walt Whitman, asking, "What is the grass?" Or singing the song of "The Mystic Trumpeter"...

> Blow trumpeter free and clear, I follow thee,
> While at thy liquid prelude, glad, serene,

> The fretting world, the streets, the noisy hours of day withdraw,
> A holy calm descends like dew upon me,
> I walk in cool refreshing night the walks of Paradise,
> I scent the grass, the moist air and the roses;
> Thy song expands my numb'd imbonded spirit, thou freest, launchest me,
> Floating and basking upon heaven's lake.[629]

Of course, these lines bring to mind another famous tableaux in which we see the young Rebbe setting off at dusk in a boat down the river, letting the current take him as it willed while he stands alone in it, knowing that he will be forced to cry out: "Save me *ha-Shem!* Protect me from the waters that seek to swallow me. I trust in You, please don't forsake me."[630]

WHEN REBBE NAHMAN WAS YOUNG and still lived in Usyatin with his father-in-law, he often walked down to the banks of Tyasman River, a tributary of the Dnieper, to pray among the reeds and rushes. Sometimes, when he wanted more privacy, he would set out on a small boat, rowing to a place beyond the taller rushes where he could be alone with God. Later, the Rebbe said that it was in this place that he attained his great standing.

Though he had little experience with boats, he would sometimes take himself out to the middle of the river, far from the shore, praying as the boat rocked back and forth. Sometimes the river was so violent that the rocking of the boat made him fear for his life, and the Rebbe was forced to cry out to God with uplifted hands, acknowledging his utter powerlessness before God until the waters calmed, or until he was able recover his own calm and row back.[631]

We see in this that young Rebbe Nahman was exploring his relationship with God out in nature, feeling the flow of life, seeing where it might take him, and listening for whispers from God in the wind. But this was still a private exploration, as we have already said. From everyone else, even his family, he tried to keep all of this secret, which in time, also caused him to cry out to God for help.

A Voice Crying in the Wilderness

AFTER HIS WEDDING DAY CONVERSATION with Reb Shimon and the young men of Medvedevka, Rebbe Nahman resumed his secretive ways, covering his service to ha-Shem under a cloak of disinterestedness. Being a teenager, he acted like all the other teenagers of Usyatin. He went to the local yeshiva, participated in

> the games of other young men, and learned to fit in with them in all that they did. As much as possible, he sought to conceal his more serious occupations from everyone ... especially his personal prayer and study. Unfortunately, by hiding himself in this way, he was also seriously harming his relationship with his father-in-law. After all, in marrying his daughter to the scion of a great lineage, Reb Efraim had hoped that Rebbe Nahman might grow into a great tzaddik, or at the very least, a pious Hasid. But now it appeared that he had gotten neither! He was supporting nothing more than an ordinary boy, neither pious nor clever.

For all of Rebbe Nahman's extraordinary pursuits in his childhood, there are numerous references that also say, "Despite this, the Rebbe acted like a normal child his age, playing, jumping and taking walks."[632] This is often characterized as him 'concealing his service,' acting childishly in public to divert the attention of those who might notice his true service, even into his teenage years after his marriage.[633] While this is likely true as well, I want to give Rebbe Nahman more credit than that; for he was someone who truly appreciated the simple pleasures of life, and found that he could serve God even through these activities. This continued into his later years, as we see him playing chess with the local apothecary in Uman. So I don't want to bury the youth of Rebbe Nahman too prematurely, explaining away all of his exuberant behavior as a pious cover. Can't we allow him to be a child, and all that a child is, even as we recognize his extraordinary qualities? After all, Rebbe Nahman was the first to say, "I'm no different from you."

So, even in his play, Rebbe Nahman models something new for us, a life of simple pleasures and joy, even as he struggled with the difficulties of his spiritual life. "New?" you might say. New in that it was a different model than what was seen as the ideal of that time. As Rabbi Arthur Green pointed out in his study of Rebbe Nahman's life: one need only compare the description of Rebbe Nahman's childhood to that of Reb Shneur Zalman of Liadi, which we have already discussed, to see how the cultural ideal of the young genius entirely absorbed in his studies differed from Rebbe Nahman's emotional and spiritual struggles. There are no descriptions of ordinary childhood pursuits or hidden struggles in the early life of Reb Shneur Zalman, though these almost certainly existed. What is reported is only what was most acceptable to the culture of pious learning that dominated that time.[634] And the expectations of this culture are precisely what create the tensions in this story.

ONE DAY, SEEING REBBE NAHMAN *throwing snowballs with the other boys his age, Reb Efraim reached his limit and threw up his hands in utter frustration, crying out to God:* "Ribbono shel Olam! What a mistake I've made! What am I going to do about this boy?" *Then a sudden resolution took hold of him and he stormed home to prepare to have it out with his son-in-law.*

Now, as it happened, a disciple of the Maggid of Mezritch, who was also a family friend, had just arrived in Usyatin by coach, and had stopped at Reb Efraim's door just as he was arriving home. Reb Efraim, who was both a wealthy and a pious man, had a good name among the tzaddikim, and it was well-known that they were welcome to stay with him when they were traveling.[635] *So the disciple of the Maggid came in, and before long, the two men began to talk personally. Reb Efraim immediately started to tell the Rebbe of his troubles with young Nahman, who was showing no signs of seriousness in his studies and was, in his opinion, on the road to becoming an* epikores *(idolator)!*

"What can I say?" Reb Efraim told him, "My son-in-law causes me great heartache! At first, I was so proud to see my daughter marry a great-grandson of the Ba'al Shem Tov, but now I find that he has inherited nothing from him! All my pride has turned to shame, for he is ignorant and neglectful of his studies, and does nothing but daydream and play games with the other boys!"

The Maggid's disciple was evidently shocked by Reb Efraim's story, but was nevertheless reluctant to think ill of any descendant of the holy Ba'al Shem Tov. So he tried to calm Reb Efraim, and said, "My friend, let me have a word with him, and I'll see how his learning is coming along."

When Rebbe Nahman came home after playing outside with the other boys, the Maggid's disciple called him over for a little study. He took a copy of the Gemara—Bava Kama—from Reb Efraim's bookshelf, and opened the volume to the mishnah which begins, "The dog and the goat that jumped from the top of the roof" and asked Nahman to read the passage.[636]

Young Nahman, seeing what was going on, looked at the page as if in confusion and began to read haltingly, as if he could barely comprehend the words: " 'The dog . . . and the goat . . . that jumped . . . ' " but instead of reading "from the top," m'rosh, he mispronounced it, m'rash.

Hearing this careless mistake, the Maggid's disciple began to think the boy might just be as ignorant as Reb Efraim had claimed, but he saw no need to rebuke him for this in front of his father-in-law. Instead, he determined to speak privately with young Nahman a little later. Perhaps it would be possible to inspire him to work harder on his studies. After all, did he want to bring disgrace on his entire family?

The next day, as he was preparing to leave, he happened to see Rebbe Nahman playing rough games with the other boys, just as Reb Efraim had described. Now he was genuinely disturbed and he called aloud for Nahman to come to him, "Immediately!"

"Is it really possible" he said, "that the great-grandson of the holy Ba'al Shem Tov, the grandson of the venerable Nahman Horodenker, could behave in such a way? You are acting like a child, wasting your time on foolish games, while ignoring your obligation to the holy Torah! Aren't you ashamed to bring such disgrace on your family?"

But even as he was speaking to Rebbe Nahman in this way, the boy turned his head distractedly to see what his friends were doing. This apparent affront threw the disciple of the Maggid into a momentary rage, and without thinking, he slapped Rebbe Nahman hard across the face and stormed off! A half-hour later, the Maggid's disciple boarded his coach to continue his journey.

When the coach reached the outskirts of Usyatin, it passed into the woods that lay on the borders of the village. Now, from the moment of his angry encounter with Rebbe Nahman, the Maggid's disciple had been unable to think of anything else. He was ashamed of his own behavior, but didn't know how to make amends. How could he make himself understood to this ignorant boy? But even as he was thinking this very thought, he suddenly became aware of a strange and eerie sound coming from the woods. He leaned his head out the window and found it was the sound of someone sobbing and crying out in pain!

"Do you hear that?" he asked the coachman.

"How could I not? Maybe they are being attacked by wolves?"

"Head in the direction of the voice! We have to help him!" the Maggid's disciple ordered. The coachman turned the horses carefully into the wood, heading in the direction of the cries. But as they drew closer, the Maggid's disciple realized that what they were hearing was not the cries of someone pain and distress, but the grief-stricken prayers of someone crying out to God in bitterness of heart.

He told the coachman to stop, and the Maggid's disciple quickly got out of the coach, heading off in search of the voice on foot. Suddenly, he came upon a sight that shocked him ... the prayers were coming from Reb Efraim's son-in-law, Nahman!

He quickly withdrew behind a tree and listened carefully. Never had he heard such prayers! There was young Nahman, clad in tallit and tefillin, but without a siddur, speaking to God like his dearest friend or a confidante! He sobbed in his loneliness, in being misunderstood, and in the difficulty of his burden and service to ha-Shem!

Once again we see young Rebbe Nahman engaged in *hitbodedut*, this time giving over his burden to God. The Maggid's disciple is amazed at the intensity and uniqueness of these prayers. But what was Rebbe Nahman's burden? That he was persecuted by those who were fooled by his impious cover? Perhaps—for though he considered this cover necessary for his own spiritual development, it was nevertheless hard to maintain. On the other hand, as we have already mentioned, it may also have been the burden of knowing that it was possible to be pious, even a genius, and still be a boy, though the prevailing culture would not accept this fact.

FINALLY, THE MAGGID'S DISCIPLE UNDERSTOOD . . . The young man was a hidden tzaddik! This was no rough and ignorant boy, but a true grandson of the Ba'al Shem Tov and Nahman of Horodenka, even in his hidden service to God!

He stood and watched in shocked silence and deep regret for having caused this young tzaddik so much pain. He waited until he had finished his prayers. Then he approached him slowly, and with head bowed, humbly begging Rebbe Nahman's forgiveness.

Rebbe Nahman was taken aback by the tzaddik's presence there, but quickly recovered his composure, saying: "How could you have known? I was trying so hard to conceal myself from you."

"You forgive me then?" the Maggid's disciple asked.

"On one condition," said Rebbe Nahman. "Promise me that you will not tell anyone of what you have seen."

"Of course," he agreed, "but you must allow me to do one thing for you; let me speak to Reb Efraim on your behalf. I will not tell him what I know, but he is near the breaking-point, and must not be allowed to bring shame on his house by treating you as badly as I have."

To this condition, Rebbe Nahman agreed.[637]

The Rebbe is Revealed

After being reassured by the Maggid's disciple, relations between Rebbe Nahman and his father-in-law seem to have improved somewhat. He now made allowances for what he considered Rebbe Nahman's eccentricities, and I tend to think he must at least of had an inkling that Rebbe Nahman may have been hiding something, even if he didn't fit the mold of what he had expected in the beginning.

In this next story, the truth is finally revealed to Reb Efraim, and to many others besides.

NEAR USYATIN WAS THE CITY OF ALEXANDREVKA, which had a large Jewish community. Usyatin itself was a simple village with comparatively few Jews, so Reb Efraim and Rebbe Nahman were often forced to travel to Alexandrevka to pray with a minyan. Thus, when the yahrzeit (death anniversary) of Reb Efraim's father came around, they set out on the road to Alexandrevka so that Reb Efraim could recite the Kaddish with a minyan and read mishnayot in his father's honor.

As soon as they arrived in Alexandrevka, Reb Efraim and Rebbe Nahman made their way to a local shul where they were greeted by Reb Efraim's acquaintances. Soon a conversation developed and the men of Alexandrevka tried to draw Rebbe Nahman into their discussion. Seeing as he was getting older, the learned men who had heard that Rebbe Nahman was the Ba'al Shem Tov's great-grandson, wanted to see what kind of scholar he was becoming. But no matter what they asked, he only shrugged or pretended not to understand what they were talking about. Finally, after many such questions, he got up and went off to be alone with his thoughts.

Nevertheless, the men of Alexandrevka were still curious. They couldn't believe that he was really as ignorant as he seemed. So they suggested to Reb Efraim that he give his son-in-law the honor of reading of the mishnayot for the yahrzeit.

Reb Efraim, who had ceased to judge his son-in-law after being counseled against this by the Maggid's disciple, had held his peace while the men speculated about Rebbe Nahman. And though he still did not know what to think of his son-in-law, he was now reasonably certain he could read the mishnayot. So he assented and asked Rebbe Nahman to do this for him.

To his surprise, and the surprise of the men of Alexandrevka, Rebbe Nahman simply nodded his head and turned his face to the wall to begin reading aloud. He read without mistakes and everyone sat listening to the reading. But, at the point they might have expected him to finish, he continued. He was reading slowly and with great concentration, as if lost in the text. But the men of Alexandrevka grew impatient for him to finish, and finally, they approached Reb Efraim, asking him to stop his son-in-law's reading.

Seeing that the men were growing impatient, and fearing to make a scene, he walked over to where the Rebbe was facing the wall and reading and touched his son-in-law on the back. Then something incredible happened. The moment Reb Efraim touched Rebbe Nahman's shoulder, Reb Efraim's body began to tremble and quake until he fainted and hit the ground with a thud.

In an instant, all of the men were on their feet and rushing to Reb Efraim. After a few minutes, they were able to revive him, but it was a while before he was able to utter a word.

When he finally recovered, Reb Efraim began to describe what had happened to him, and he trembled again as he told them what he had seen. It seems that the moment he touched Rebbe Nahman's shoulder, he had a vision of his dead father, whose yahrzeit it was that day. His father, he said, appeared angry that young Nahman had been treated with such disrespect through the years, and had been subjected to the probing of these men, saying, "Have you no better way to test a tzaddik than with a mishnayot reading?"

When the men of Alexandrevka heard this, they were fearful and ashamed. Reb Efraim was known to associate with the holy disciples of the Maggid of Mezritch, and was far too pious a man to make up stories. They had all seen him faint in this extraordinary way, and none of them doubted what he had seen. Then the men of Alexandrevka fell back in awe before Rebbe Nahman and treated him with respect, whispering to one another that he was indeed one of the tzaddikim.[638]

After this, Rebbe Nahman began to attract disciples, chief among them, Reb Shimon, whose heart he had already captured several years before.

7

The Mystical Journey:
The Descent for the Sake of Ascent

EVEN THROUGH HIS HIDDEN YEARS in Usyatin, Rebbe Nahman had been courted as a Rebbe. Besides Reb Shimon, there were others who sought him out as 'the heir and great-grandson of the Ba'al Shem Tov.'[639] But these were not the kind of Hasidim Rebbe Nahman was looking for, nor was he quite ready to take on this role. Nevertheless, after the incident in Alexandrevka, he began to see that he could hardly avoid it much longer. Soon, events beyond his control would bring him out into the world.

It seems that during the time Rebbe Nahman lived in the house of his father-in-law, Reb Efraim was widowed; and with the improvement of their relationship, Rebbe Nahman helped to arrange a new marriage for him. So it was that during the wedding feast, Rebbe Nahman was asked to speak; and having had a little wine during the *simḥah* (joyful event), he was not as careful in concealing himself as he might have been. Thus, he spoke movingly and with great erudition, and soon his words were reported in all the towns from which the many guests had come. In Zaslav, they reached the ears of Reb Yissakhar Dov Baer (d. ca. 1795)—a disciple of the Ba'al Shem Tov and a relative by marriage of Reb Pinhas of Koretz—who publicly declared Rebbe Nahman a true *tzaddik*, thus bringing him into the Hasidic spotlight.[640]

But there was another more significant consequence of the wedding—a new member of the household. Even though Rebbe Nahman had arranged the marriage, this did little to endear him to his new mother-in-law. soon, things became untenable between them. Very soon Rebbe Nahman decided it was time that he and his young family found a home of their own. Using the dowry Reb Efraim had pledged before their marriage, they settled in the nearby town of Medvedevka. But when this had run out, he finally accepted a stipend from a group of admirers and allowed himself to be supported as a Rebbe.[641]

It wasn't long before his new Hasidim found that the young Rebbe's court was different from that of other Hasidic masters. For Rebbe Nahman soon made it clear that he wanted to revive the spirit of the 'original Hasidism' of the Ba'al Shem Tov, seeking nothing less than to make *tzaddikim* out of each and every one of them! What was unspoken in this desire, though apparent to most, was a rejection of the popular Hasidism and Hasidic courts that had sprung up all over the Ukraine, which were focused more on charismatic, wonder-working Rebbes than on the deep spiritual practice of their Hasidim.[642] This emphasis on spiritual 'work' almost certainly soured the milk for many would-be disciples, but, at the same time, it drew another more serious and discerning group. Among these new recruits were seasoned Hasidim like Yudel of Dashev, who had been a disciple of Pinhas of Koretz, and Yekusiel the Maggid of Tirhovitza, who had been a disciple of the Maggid of Mezritch. Though many of these disciples were older and had already known great *tzaddikim*, it seems they found something new and equally profound in the young Rebbe.[643]

The Mysterious Journey to Kamenitz

After several years in Medvedevka, the already unconventional Rebbe unexpectedly left home on a mysterious journey, which was the cause of much speculation by his disciples. This journey to an unknown destination opened one of the most fascinating episodes in Rebbe Nahman's life; and if the tradition is to be believed, perhaps the most significant. This is likely the reason it is also the episode about which we have the most detailed information. Indeed, the level of detail and literary skill is so great in this account that it has been praised as having the flavor of an "adventurous novella."[644] The most complete presentation of the story is found in Reb Nosson of Nemirov's *Shivḥei ha-RaN*, and has been translated in full by Aryeh Kaplan in *Rabbi Nachman's Wisdom*. In this chapter, we have only translated and retold the parts of the larger story that we considered most significant for our purposes here. However, those who would have the fullest possible understanding of these events should acquaint themselves with all the details of the story as Reb Nosson, his chief disciple, originally told it.

In the selections that follow, we have tried to bring in details from other sources, such as Reb Nosson's *Ḥayyei MaHaRaN* to supplement the readers' understanding, and to contextualize certain vague features of the account. We have also adapted it into more of a story, leaving out much of the commentary, and adding the names of persons only referred to obliquely. Nevertheless, as Reb Nosson so aptly says in his introduction to *Shivḥei ha-RaN*, "What is recorded here is less than a drop in the ocean of the Rebbe's" great journey.[645]

ONE DAY IN MEDVEDEVKA, *Rebbe Nahman suddenly said to Reb Shimon, "There is a journey before me...I do not know where I am going, but I am going anyway." So Reb Shimon went and called for a carriage and made ready for the journey. Soon after, they left Medvedevka and took the road leading to Mezhbizh. However, shortly before arriving there, Reb Shimon asked if they could stop in the village of Volkhovitz to pick up a second gabbai (attendant), as he was not feeling well and wasn't certain he would be able to serve the Rebbe for the entire journey.*[646]

After this, the three travelers arrived in Mezhbizh and went to the house of the Rebbe's holy parents, who were overjoyed to see him. When they had finished catching up, his mother, Feiga, said to him, "When are you going to visit your great-grandfather, my son?" meaning, when was he going to visit the Ba'al Shem Tov's grave.

The Rebbe answered her, "If my great-grandfather wishes to see me, let him come to me."

Later that night, the Rebbe received a vision of the Ba'al Shem Tov who told him that he must travel to Kamenitz. The next morning, his mother said, "So, now that your great-grandfather has been to see you, perhaps you'll go and pay him a visit?"

To which he replied, "God willing, I'll visit him when I return."[647]

Since Rebbe Nahman was known to visit the grave of the holy Ba'al Shem Tov at every opportunity, his response to his mother on this occasion deserves a closer look. The great neo-Hasidic philosopher, Martin Buber (1878-1965), thought he detected in this response a possible "fear" that his great-grandfather might "oppose his intention" to travel to the Holy Land after this journey; but I think this is unlikely.[648] When we consider that Rebbe Nahman did not actually know where he was going on this journey, it seems almost certain that he came to Mezhbizh looking for guidance from the Ba'al Shem Tov. Why didn't he go to the grave then, as his mother asked? It may be that he was seeking a dream or vision of the master, and therefore wished to 'draw him out' by *not* visiting the grave, as was his custom.

REB SHIMON, WHO HAD FALLEN GRAVELY ILL by the time they had reached Mezhbizh, could not go with the Rebbe to Kamenitz, as he foresaw, and thus the Rebbe traveled on with his other gabbai.

Although he was already famous, Rebbe Nahman traveled simply, hoping to draw as little attention to himself as possible. Thus, everywhere he went, he allowed others to think that he was just an ordinary merchant, and even warned his attendant not to reveal his true identity. After a long journey, he finally came to Kamenitz.

Now Kamenitz, at that time, was a city without Jews. For Jews were not allowed to live in the city, nor even to spend the night within the city limits! So all Jews who had business in Kamenitz could only enter the city for the day. At night, they were forced to leave and find lodgings elsewhere. Thus, Rebbe Nahman entered the city with his gabbai, and remained there until nightfall. As evening approached, the Rebbe told his attendant to leave the city, saying only: "I'll stay here alone tonight. Come back in the morning and meet me at this place." The attendant wanted to protest, but it was no use. Fearing the worst, he left the Rebbe in the city overnight.

The next morning, his attendant returned and was surprised to find the Rebbe unharmed. He never learned what had happened during that awful night. Once they were reunited, the Rebbe led his attendant on a tour of the city, visiting many houses in Kamenitz and finding excuse after excuse to enter each one. The Rebbe used a number of different ploys to do this, sometimes even asking the owner for a drink of schnapps!

When the Rebbe had completed his 'work' in Kamenitz, he and his bewildered attendant returned home. But it was noted soon after that Jews were once again given permission to live in Kamenitz. Later, the Rebbe said, "Whoever knows why Eretz Yisra'el *was first in the hands of the Kena'ani (Canaanites), and only later settled by the Jews, knows why I journeyed to Kamenitz before traveling to the Holy Land."*[649]

What did all this mean? Well, that's the big question. On the one hand, a clear parallel is being drawn between the gentiles of Kamenitz (preventing the Jews from living there) and the Canaanite peoples who once occupied *Eretz Yisra'el*. But what is not so easily explained is the mystery of Rebbe Nahman's personal mission, and how he accomplished what he did.

At one time, of course, Jews had made a relatively peaceful home in Kamenitz, but the relationship had become a troubled one in more recent centuries. In the mid-17th-century, the Jews of Kamenitz had suffered devastating losses in the Cossack raids of Chmielnicki. And prior to Rebbe Nahman's visit, the city had been entirely closed to Jews for almost fifty years. But still more troubling was the fact that, in the mid-18th-century, Kamenitz had been at the center of the Frankist controversy, and the place in which the Talmud had been publicly burned in 1757.[650]

In the Jewish consciousness, the Canaanites have long been connected with idolatry, for it was their idolatry that had polluted the land of Canaan before the Hebrews came to dwell there. Likewise, in the Ukraine, the city of Kamenitz had also become polluted by the heresy of Jacob Frank (1726-1791) and the anti-Jewish agenda of the Bishop Dembowski. For in the late 1750's, the radical Sabbatian Frank aligned himself with Christian authorities hostile to Judaism, claiming that the Talmud was an essentially anti-Christian work. Thus, a farcical debate between the Frankists and a group of rabbis was arranged in Kamenitz and judged by the rabidly anti-Jewish Bishop Nicholas Dembowski. Of course, the Frankists 'won' and the Talmud was denounced. It was then gathered from homes and synagogues throughout the area by soldiers and the police (assisted by the Frankists) and publicly burned in Kamenitz. It is thought that as many as 1,000 volumes of Talmud were burned at that time, leading to great mourning in Yisra'el.[651]

It should be remembered that most of this was happening in the last few years of the Ba'al Shem Tov's life, and that he was himself heavily involved in the struggle against Frank. In one story, the Ba'al Shem Tov even sent a messenger to Bishop Dembowski in Kamenitz warning him of dire consequences from on high if he did not retract the decree to burn the Talmud. The bishop scoffed at the warning, and on the day of the burning, personally threw volumes of the Talmud on the fire as the Ba'al Shem Tov looked on from a distance. But even as he was doing so, he suddenly collapsed in agony and died soon after!

In addition to opposing Frank and the Sabbatian heresy in the spiritual realms, the Ba'al Shem Tov is also said to have participated in the public debates with the Frankists. After the death of Bishop Dembowski, the anti-Jewish agenda was stalled temporarily. But the Frankists continued to lobby for another debate, and in 1759, a second debate was held in Lvov (Lemberg) under the auspices of Bishop Mikolski. However, this time, things didn't go quite as the Frankists planned. The debate lasted four days and included, according to some, the testimony of the Ba'al Shem Tov himself, and his disciples, Rabbi Meir Margoliot (1700-1790) and Rabbi Hayyim Rappaport, both famous scholars. In the end, Bishop Mikolski decided in favor of the rabbis and annulled the decree against the Talmud. Moreover, he condemned the Frankists who, soon after—perhaps fearing further sanction—converted to Christianity.[652]

While some Jews rejoiced in this news, the Ba'al Shem Tov was profoundly saddened by the conversion of the Frankists, hoping to the last that they might return to the body of Yisra'el. But even as he expressed his sadness over this fact, his enemies used his grief against him, claiming that he had secret sympathies for the Frankist agenda.[653] Thus, the last year of his life was spent defending the Hasidic movement against these spurious claims, even though he might rather have wished to continue working for the souls of the converted Frankists. For so much of his work was concerned with making a *tikkun* (repair) for lost souls. So it may be that when the Ba'al Shem Tov appeared to Rebbe Nahman in Mezhbizh and told him his destination, he may also have entrusted the Rebbe with a mission to complete the work he had himself begun so many years earlier: to bring about a *tikkun* for the souls of the Frankists in the place of their greatest heresy, and to clear out the 'subtle residue' of this heresy so that Jews could safely return to Kamenitz.[654]

So what was he doing that long night in Kamenitz? Who can say, but can you imagine Rebbe Nahman sneaking about in secret through the streets of the city, moving from shadow to shadow like a tribal shaman, 'smudging' the city of its impurities with his prayers? When I was a young *yeshiva bokher* in Lubavitch, the Rebbe once sent us out onto the streets of New York to "purify the air" with our recitation of *mishnayot*. Perhaps Rebbe Nahman had something similar in mind. And the next day, entering the houses of the gentiles! This is a great example of Rebbe Nahman's signature boldness. But it would take boldness to bring the Jews back to Kamenitz. Perhaps the drinking of a *l'hayyim* of schnapps with a gentile in his own home was *tikkun* in itself.[655] Still, before we get too carried away with any of these speculations, it would be best to remember what Rebbe Nahman's closest disciple said of the many theories that existed in his own day:

The journey to Kamenitz was a true mystery. Everyone had their own explanation—some praising the Rebbe, and others criticizing him—but they were all wrong. Even those who saw good in his journey didn't even come close to understanding his true purpose. The Rebbe hinted at this purpose to his close disciples, but even though they guessed at fragments of the truth, they still didn't comprehend his larger plan. Some said that the Rebbe went to Kamenitz to find the secret writings that the Ba'al Shem Tov was supposed to have hidden in a great rock there,[656] but the Rebbe thought this was ridiculous, saying: "That was not my reason; if I needed those writings, they would have been brought to my own house! But I have no need of them."[657]

The Great Pilgrimage to Eretz Yisra'el

On the *Shabbat* after Rebbe Nahman's return from Kamenitz, he gave a profound teaching on the verse, "My soul clings to You." (Ps. 63:9)[658] Afterward, he said in exultation, "If this kind of teaching comes as a result of my having been to Kamenitz, how much greater will the teaching be when I return from the Holy Land."[659]

At this point, the tale of Rebbe Nahman's great journey begins in earnest. But before we begin it, we must make a few things clear about *who* is really telling the story. We have already mentioned that it is Reb Nosson who has written this account, but Reb Nosson did not actually become a Hasid of Rebbe Nahman until 1802, some four years after many of these events took place.[660] So from whom did he learn the details of the journey?

In the beginning of *Shivhei ha-RaN*, Reb Nosson says, "I myself heard some of these accounts from the Rebbe's holy lips. Others were gleaned from those who knew him during his lifetime."[661] The latter was certainly true in this case, for it is extremely unlikely that this detailed account was gleaned from Rebbe Nahman alone. So who was the other source? It is obviously Rebbe Nahman's traveling companion who is not identified as anything other than "his attendant" throughout this account. Nevertheless, there is a tradition in Bratzlav that this attendant was none other than Reb Shimon, Rebbe Nahman's first disciple and primary *gabbai*.[662] But Reb Shimon was extremely humble, and it was likely at his own request that the otherwise punctilious Reb Nosson omitted his name.

A little story will illustrate just how humble Reb Shimon really was, and just what kind of traveling companion Rebbe Nahman was taking with him...

> Though Reb Shimon made his living as a businessman, he was also a gifted scholar, and made many notes of his Torah insights as he studied. Nevertheless, he always tried to keep these abilities and insights hidden from view; for he was a humble person, and did not wish for any public acclaim. However, once when he was traveling with Reb Nosson, the two began discussing certain ideas, and it was then that Reb Nosson noticed Reb Shimon's manuscript. He asked if he might look at it, and Reb Shimon assented for fear of offending Reb Nosson by a refusal. After a few minutes, Reb Nosson proclaimed his astonishment: "Reb Shimon, this is wonderful! Such Torah and wisdom deserves to be seen and studied! You should let me publish it."
>
> Reb Shimon was silent, for he did not wish to cause an argument by refusing Reb Nosson, who still had the manuscript in his hands. Later, after they had arrived at the inn, Reb Nosson set down his belongings—including the manuscript—and went to speak with the innkeeper. Reb Shimon, who had been looking for an opportunity to get the manuscript back, finally saw his chance! He picked it up and quickly made his way across the room to the fireplace and threw the entire manuscript in the fire! Reb Nosson was astonished that Reb Shimon would so willingly destroy what he had worked so hard to create, but now knew that his desire to remain hidden was far greater than any desire for personal fame.[663]

Knowing this, we can easily see why Reb Nosson would leave Reb Shimon's name out of the account of Rebbe Nahman's journey. But now we would like to restore his name to this extraordinary story, so that his holy example of humility and service may be fixed in the reader's heart with a name. As the Talmud says, *Sh'yih'yu nikra'im 'al sh'mo*, one who brings a citation in the name of the original speaker causes redemption to be brought into the world.[664]

The day before Pesah, 1798 (5558) the Rebbe emerged from the mikveh and told his gabbai, "This year I will definitely be in the Holy Land." When the Rebbe's family heard this, they all burst into tears. Nevertheless, he could not be moved, and would only say: "It's impossible for me not to go; no matter what happens, I must make this journey... Most of me is already there, and the minority must follow the majority."[665]

Later, he said, "I have set my heart on this journey, and though I know I will find the way blocked by countless obstacles, as long as there is a spark of life within me, I will do everything in my power to forge ahead." After a brief pause, he added cryptically, " 'And God will do what is good in the sight of Heaven.' "[666]

These early statements from Rebbe Nahman about his journey are very important. You see, right from the beginning, he knew there would be extreme obstacles *(meni'ot)*, saying, "Every step I take in the Holy Land will be at the risk of my life."[667] Nevertheless, he feels it is an absolute necessity for him to go, even in the face of these dangers. He also says, "And God will do what is good in the sight of Heaven," which makes one wonder whether a heavenly decree had been set against his going to the Holy Land. Or was he speaking of the dangerous opposition of the 'Other Side' *(Sitra Ahra)* which might test his resolve, even to the point of taking his life?

In the Ba'al Shem Tov's time, there had indeed been a 'decree' against his going to *Eretz Yisra'el*, and it had nearly cost him his life when he had tried. Thank God, his daughter Adel (Rebbe Nahman's grandmother) was there with him. For it was only through her willingness to sacrifice herself for him that his life was spared. But the point is—he had wanted it so badly that he made the journey in spite of the heavenly decree![668] Now, nearly fifty years later, it seemed that Rebbe Nahman was about to attempt the same thing. Only this time, he had been forewarned about the obstacles. Had there been more to that vision in Mezhbizh than the mission to Kamenitz? Had the Ba'al Shem Tov also given him the key to accomplishing what he himself could not?

I can imagine how this event in the Ba'al Shem Tov's life must have intrigued Rebbe Nahman in his youth. The Ba'al Shem Tov failed? How could this be? Might *he* find a way where his great-grandfather could not? Could *he* find some means, some 'strategy' for dealing with the obstacles that would allow him to accomplish the mission of his holy forebear? There is such hutzpah in this notion! But the Hasidic Rebbes were known for their hutzpah, the audacious way in which they dealt with obstacles, even divine decrees.

What does it mean to go against the 'will of Heaven'? Or *is it* the will of Heaven? This is definitely a gray area. But perhaps there is something to be learned about this in the way the Sufi master, Hazrat Inayat Khan deals with the notion of *karma:*

> I have myself heard a person say, "I have been ill for so many years, but I have been resigned to it. I took it easily because it is my *karma* I am paying back." By that he or she may prolong the paying—which was perhaps to last ten years—for the whole life. The Sufi in this case acts not only as patient but, at the same time, as doctor to him or herself. The Sufi says, "Is my condition bad? Is it the effect of the past? I am going to cure it. The past has brought the present, but this, my present, I will make the

future." The Sufi does not allow the past influences to overpower his or her life; the Sufi wants to produce in the present the influence to make his or her life better.⁶⁶⁹

You see, the Sufi is not fatalistic about *karma*, but realistic and practical. We can own that temporal and psychic factors have coalesced into a kind of karmic 'knot,' but what should we do about it? Should we not address it if we are able? Even if it costs us some pain, it may be worth untangling it in the service of God. In much the same way, Hasidism tends to deal with the divine 'decree' *(gezerah)* and the 'obstacle' *(meni'ah)*.

On Lag b'Omer, *Rebbe Nahman set out joyfully from Medvedevka with his gabbai, Reb Shimon, heading toward Nikolayev. There he found a ship transporting grain, which he took as far as Odessa, where he found another ship traveling to Istanbul.*⁶⁷⁰ *They set off on the Black Sea, but on their first day, a great storm arose. The powerful winds hurled waves over the ship's deck, and the Rebbe and Reb Shimon closeted themselves in their cabin to protect themselves from the torrent of water. The howling winds, the thunder and lightning were terrifying, and the roaring noise of waves wracking the ship made it impossible for them to sleep at night. For four days they endured this until they finally arrived in Istanbul.*

Not knowing the Turkish language, and ignorant of where to go, the Rebbe and Reb Shimon simply sat down on the dock, waiting for someone to help them. As they were unable to tell the Jews from the Turks, they were forced to wait for a Turkish Jew who might recognize their predicament. Eventually, someone came along who was able to translate for them, and he also helped them to find lodgings. He then told them that several emissaries from the Holy Land were currently staying in the area, and among them were two of the Rebbe's own countrymen. When the Rebbe heard this, he agreed to meet with them, but warned Reb Shimon, "If they ask about me, do not tell them who I am."

Later, when they were introduced to the Hasidim returning from the Holy Land, one of the men (who turned out to be from the same area in the Ukraine) immediately recognized Reb Shimon and asked, "What are you doing here?"

"I'm traveling to Eretz Yisra'el *with," Reb Shimon paused momentarily, "this . . . young man."*⁶⁷¹

"But who is he?" asked the man.

On the spot, and trying not to reveal the Rebbe's identity, Reb Shimon could only say haltingly, "He has a card to travel from the government of the Kaiser of Oestereich (Austria)."

> Well, this little subterfuge only made things worse, for the Hasidim who had only been curious, now became suspicious of Rebbe Nahman. They believed that Reb Shimon's strange reply meant that the "young man" was really a government agent, hoping to make trouble for Rabbi Avraham of Kalisk in Eretz Yisra'el. They immediately imagined that he was being sent to spy on Reb Avraham; and being convinced of this mistaken idea, began to cause problems for the Rebbe.[672]

This, of course, was not Reb Shimon's fault. After all, what could he say? He had not expected to be recognized by anyone. Moreover, he was not allowed to tell the truth . . . But he was not told to lie either! Caught up on the horns of this dilemma, he said whatever he could think of, and unfortunately, the two Hasidim made the worst of it.

Now, as we have already seen in our look at the Alter Rebbe, Reb Shneur Zalman of Liadi, the political situation in the Holy Land made things difficult for the Hasidim who lived there, as well as for those who raised money for their maintenance.[673] Thus, the suspicion of these two emissaries is entirely understandable. With such a strange reply, it was natural for them to think this mysterious young man might be a *mitnaged* (opponent of Hasidism) acting as a spy for the Austrian government.[674] Unfortunately, things seem to go well beyond suspicion as the two Hasidim begin to interrogate Reb Shimon and Rebbe Nahman.

> ADDRESSING THEMSELVES to Reb Shimon, they asked, "Is he carrying a letter?"
> "No," replied Reb Shimon.
> "Then why is he going to the Holy Land?"
> "I do not know," he replied.
> Thinking that he too was attempting to mislead them, they said to him, "Once, we thought you honorable, but now it is seems that you too may have lost your integrity."[675]

Whatever the Rebbe's purpose in hiding his identity, this was a severe test for Reb Shimon. In order to do what the Rebbe asked, and without the slightest explanation, he is also condemned by the two Hasidim. Nevertheless, he perseveres and proves himself a worthy disciple. Whether this is an intentional test or simply a matter of circumstance, 'tests' are common fare for disciples in many traditions. Once again, one of the Sufi master Hazrat Inayat Khan's teachings may help us to understand this:

There are tests of many kinds that the teacher may give to his pupils to test their faith, their sincerity and their patience. Before a ship puts out to sea the captain goes and makes sure that everything is in order for the voyage. Such is the duty of the teacher. Of course, it is a very interesting duty. Besides, the path of the mystic is a very complex path. What he says may, perhaps, have two meanings: the outer meaning is one, and the inner meaning is another. What he does may also have two meanings, an outer and an inner meaning. A person who only sees things outwardly cannot perceive their inner meaning. Since he only sees their outer aspect, he cannot understand his own teacher's actions, thoughts, speech or movements. It is in this way that the pupil is tested. Thus, to the pupil, the teacher may often appear to be very unreasonable, very odd, very meaningless, very unkind, cold or unjust.[676]

Nevertheless, he says, if the disciple endures through all of this, then not only is a greater trust established between them, but a higher level of spiritual initiation is reached by the disciple as well. So this is the place in which we find Reb Shimon at this moment, being cooked in the crucible of initiation!

COMPLETELY IGNORANT OF THE MYSTERIOUS COMPANION'S IDENTITY, they asked Reb Shimon, "Have you asked your master, Rebbe Nahman of Medvedevka, whether it is appropriate to travel with this young man?"

"Yes," answered Reb Shimon. But they no longer believed anything he said. They were certain that the Rebbe was an agent intending to cause trouble in the Holy Land.

Now they approached the Rebbe directly and began questioning him about his identity, asking him about his home and family. But the Rebbe revealed nothing to them. They used every trick they could think of to discover his true identity, but the Rebbe saw through these ruses and easily answered their questions in such a way that they learned nothing about him. He twisted their questions and turned them back on them, confusing the men until the only thing they could say for certain was that they knew nothing at all!

It seemed that each time the Rebbe spoke to them, he played a different role. For instance, one day, they asked him if he was a kohen (i.e., of the priestly caste), and he answered that he was. The next day, in order to test him, they asked him if he was a Yisra'el (a common Israelite). He said that he was! So they said excitedly, "Yesterday, you said you were a kohen, and now you say you are a Yisra'el! How can this be?"

The Rebbe answered, "Kohen is the attribute of Mercy; Yisra'el is another attribute. Thank God, I have both attributes."[677]

"It's obvious that you are an enemy come to oppress the Hasidim in Eretz Yisra'el, and are only using these tricks to conceal your true intentions!" they shouted.

Then these Hasidim took such a strong dislike to the Rebbe that they began to hurl every possible insult at him, cursing him in every way imaginable until they left Istanbul. One of them was particularly vicious in what he said to the Rebbe. Nevertheless, the Rebbe made every attempt to be friendly and courteous. He tried to explain: "I cannot give you the reason for my journey, for 'my heart has not even revealed it to my mouth.' Still, how good and how pleasant it is when brothers can live together in unity."[678]

Hearing this friendly overture, they said, "If you tell us your reasons, you will surely receive great good for it."

But the Rebbe responded: "I do not need this good from you, and no matter what you do, I will not tell you my reasons. But if you wish, you may obtain much good from me."

"You talk as if you think that you are a famous tzaddik or something, as if you were Barukh of Tulchin, Shalom of Prohobitch, or Nahman of Medvedevka! They're known for speaking in these ways, but you're not on this level and should be ashamed to speak as if you were. We know your business well enough—it is to make trouble for the great tzaddik, Reb Avraham of Kalisk!"

The entire time he was in Istanbul, these two men continued to insult the Rebbe at every opportunity. Nevertheless, he endured it all, never revealing his identity, despite their taunts.

All of this was done intentionally by the Rebbe. He allowed himself to be insulted in every possible manner, explaining to Reb Shimon, "These insults are actually beneficial; they're 'clearing the way' there and back. Before I reach my goal, I must overcome obstacles beyond imagining. If it were not for this degradation now, it would be impossible for me to set foot on the soil of Eretz Yisra'el." On another occasion, he said: "I saw that I would have to die in Istanbul, but the humiliation and insults I suffered saved me. One must overcome many barriers to approach the Holy Land."[679]

At this point, we need to make a major *excursus* to explore a very difficult kabbalistic concept, the idea of the 'descent for the sake of ascent,' in which the *tzaddik* "who seeks to rise to the most sacred of places must first descend and seek to purify the most defiled of human space."[680] In physical terms, this might be compared to the bicyclist who uses the momentum from going down one hill to propel themselves up an opposing hill, which would otherwise require great effort. Nevertheless, the descent is not without its dangers. For the bicyclist, the speed of the descent makes the bicycle unwieldy and difficult to steer; likewise, for the *tzaddik*, there is a danger that the momentum and gravity-pull of the material world will lead them into a degradation that they do not intend. That is to say, it's hard to enter the bar and not to drink! But this is the crucial difference between the Hasidic notion of the 'descent' and the heretical Sabbatian notion, with which it is sometimes confused. For the Sabbatian, the 'descent' includes the transgression of established values, whereas in the Hasidic idea, one only 'courts' danger, experiencing the pull of temptation, which is then transmuted into holiness.[681] That is to say, the temptation is uplifted by the decision not to partake of it. But in courting danger, there is always the possibility of harm. Therefore, this is not a recommended path for most Hasidim. In Hindu and Buddhist tantric terms, it is what might be called a 'left-handed path' of spiritual development, only to be undertaken by the most adept of practitioners.

But Rebbe Nahman was not an ordinary Hasid; he was *tzaddik* of extraordinary discipline with a perilous task before him. If he was going to reach the Holy Land in safety, bringing about the unifications he felt it was necessary to make, he was going to have to find a way of navigating through a minefield of obstacles and opposition. So he chose the path which he felt offered the greatest chance of success. Even if it held its own dangers, he considered these negligible in comparison to the obstacles and dangers set by the *Sitra Aḥra* (Other Side), which may have meant his death.

So what was this 'left-handed path'? Sometimes I like to talk about this as 'over-joining,' leaning-in to a negative situation in order to take the initiative back from it.[682] But in this case, I don't think this would do justice to the difficult paradox in which Rebbe Nahman finds himself. So I would like to try to get at this idea in a couple of different ways. First, I want to look at Rebbe Nahman's whole endeavor in Jungian terms, specifically in relation to the concept of 'shadow.' This is one of the most popular and often most misunderstood of Carl Jung's psychological concepts. Of course, we can only begin to touch upon its true importance here, but perhaps you will get the drift of its significance and its application to this critical episode in Rebbe Nahman's life.

Once, my wife was co-presenting at a mystery school workshop with Jean Houston and, at the last minute, found that she had to take my eleven-year-old son along with her. He had expressed some interest, and she asked

Jean if it would be alright if he sat in on the session. Jean said that it would be fine and he seemed to be following along with interest while she spoke. Then Jean asked the question, "What is 'shadow'?" Well, nobody in this room full of psychologists ventured an answer, so after a minute, one little hand crept up in the corner. Jean smiled and took the microphone over to my son, who said, "I think it is all that we don't know about ourselves, and all the stuff we do know but wish we didn't." Jean looked up and said, "Does anybody have anything to add?" That is shadow in a nutshell.[683]

From this, we can see that 'shadow' is the psychological equivalent of the observable phenomenon in which light hits an object and creates a corresponding darkness. 'Light,' in this case, is what we consciously identify as good or positive, and 'shadow' is what is thrown over other related (though unconscious or consciously suppressed) parts of ourselves that are not entirely in accord with what is being called 'good.'[684] This unconsciousness, or conscious suppression is tantamount to denial. And, as we know, denial doesn't actually do much to check the reality of what is being denied, and more often than not, actually causes it to rebel and act out in one way or another.[685]

How does this apply to Rebbe Nahman's journey to the Holy Land? Well, in psychological terms, if the 'light' in Rebbe Nahman's journey is the Holy Land and the spiritual elevation that contact with it will bring, this is necessarily going to create a 'shadow' of equal proportion. That is to say, if the Holy Land is what is 'good,' then everywhere else is in some sense, 'not-good.' And if spiritual elevation is somehow attained there, and likewise, considered 'good,' those parts of the personality that continue to exist and do not suit the definition of this good, will become in some sense, 'worse.'[686] Both the rest of the world and the unappreciated aspects of the personality are thus thrown into a deeper shadow, if you will. And because what exists does not like to be denied, there tends to be a rebellion of sorts when they are put in this shadow; these elements of the world and one's being tend to 'cooperate' with the forces of the *Sitra Aḥra*, the Other Side, that cause problems for us and put 'obstacles' in our path.[687]

Perhaps more than any other *tzaddik*, Rebbe Nahman anticipates Jung and is aware of what we call 'shadow' today. More importantly, he deals with it in a truly insightful and skillful manner. In *Shivḥei ha-RaN*, he is quoted as saying, "For a long time I have known that when a person wants to do something holy, he must face great barriers."[688] This, of course, is not much different than anything the Ba'al Shem Tov might have said. But when Reb

Nosson tells us that he "allowed himself to be insulted in every possible manner, explaining to Reb Shimon, 'These insults are actually beneficial; they're *clearing the way* there and back,'" he is actually demonstrating a sophisticated spiritual technique for dealing with shadow.[689]

By acknowledging the power of these forces to obstruct him (i.e., bringing them into consciousness) and engaging in a ritualized form of propitiation, he is able to avert disaster.[690] That is to say, by making a symbolic offering of what these forces would take of their own accord, Rebbe Nahman was able to mollify them to such an extent that he could complete his mission. For, as he said to Reb Shimon, "If it were not for this degradation now, it would be impossible for me to set foot on the soil of *Eretz Yisra'el*." And, "I saw that I would have to die in Istanbul, but the humiliation and insults I suffered saved me." Seeing that the forces of the *Sitra Aḥra* were demanding his life, he found a way to give it what it wanted by consciously surrendering his ego, which is the same thing in psychological terms.[691] As Rebbe Nahman himself says, "Shame is considered equal to death."[692] By denying himself the adulation and consequent ego-inflation which his name would have brought him from the two Hasidic emissaries, even enduring their abuses and playing the part of a fool, he knew he was reducing his ego to a size that would allow him to pass into *Eretz Yisra'el* without setting off any alarms. Knowing that he would experience great exultation and spiritual elevation there, he needed to make profound sacrifices of his ego early on in order to ensure a safe return.

The Jungian therapist, Robert Johnson, in his excellent little book on shadow, notes how aware Jung and his early students were of the ego-catastrophes that often follow success, and how they went about making small ego-sacrifices to head them off:

> Dr. Marie-Louise Von Franz and Barbara Hannah, who shared a household in Kusnacht, Switzerland, had the custom of requiring whoever had some especially good fortune to carry out the garbage for the week. This is a simple but powerful act. Symbolically speaking, they were playing out the shadow side of something positive. Dr. Jung often greeted a friend by asking, "Had any terrible successes lately?" because he also was aware of the close proximity of light and darkness.[693]

In this context, perhaps it is somewhat clearer what Rebbe Nahman is trying to accomplish with this strange behavior. For if he can 'pay the shadow cost' of his journey up front, not only will he be allowed to continue, but he can also avoid paying it later in ways *not* of his own choosing.[694]

The idea of 'paying shadow cost' is also akin to G. I. Gurdjieff's greater metaphysical 'Law of Reciprocal Maintenance' and the 'way of sacrifice' through conscious 'abasement.' From his perspective, the planet—indeed, the whole universe—as an ecological system, seeks its own continuance and evolution through the processes of birth and death. When the energies are well-balanced between these two processes, all is well in the greater system. But when they become imbalanced, the intelligence of the greater system often brings them back into balance by terrifying means (from the human perspective)—war, famine, earthquakes, and social upheaval.[695]

As human beings, Gurdjieff argues, we bear a special responsibility in this process.[696] Because we can be conscious and aware of greater processes, we have great potential for aiding evolutionary shifts and averting disasters. But when we choose to be unconscious, avoiding participation in the natural order—avoiding physical, emotional, mental, and spiritual sacrifices—the greater system seeks to correct the balance, often at devastating human cost.[697] Thus, we must be careful to honor the needs of the greater system: to let the land rest when we could be pushing it to produce more; to sacrifice the convenience of some of our machines to save our bodies; to make a little time in our lives for prayer and meditation, instead of burning the candle of our minds at both ends; to make the little sacrifices for our families and friends that make their lives better; and most importantly, to sacrifice our egos continually.[698] These are all real sacrifices, 'little deaths,' that affect the greater system, furthering evolution and ensuring life. Really, reciprocal maintenance is just another way of saying 'recycling,' only it is applied as a principle of the universe, effecting all levels of being.[699]

So we can see Rebbe Nahman engaged here in a similar process of intentional sacrifice, paralleling Gurdjieff's law and anticipating the Jungian idea of shadow. It is a sacrifice that has meaning for him personally, but that is also having effects on a much greater scale. For Rebbe Nahman, at this time, made himself a lightning rod for the planet, and this should be remembered as we continue through the rest of this chapter.[700]

THE TWO HASIDIM THEN TOLD THE REBBE *that they would be sending a letter to the Holy Land ahead of him, warning the community that he was a spy and a troublemaker, and not to be misled by him. They also went to the ship's agent, a Polish Jew married to a Sefardi woman, hoping to plot against the Rebbe. For*

> the father-in-law of the ship's agent was an important official and had access to the Sultan's palace. Soon this agent came to see the Rebbe and Reb Shimon, saying: "Tell me about yourself and your family and I'll help you; but if you don't, I can easily prevent you from continuing on your journey. You will be imprisoned, and no bribe will be able to help you!"
>
> Hearing this, the Rebbe told the agent the truth: he was the "great-grandson of the Ba'al Shem Tov and the grandson of Rebbe Nahman of Horodenka." The agent's attitude quickly changed, and when they next met, he showed great deference to the Rebbe, saying: "May God be with you, Rebbe! If you had not told me who you were, I would have had you imprisoned. Consequently, I would have been punished in this world and the next! But now that you have told me the truth, I will certainly do everything I can for you. Whatever you need, a ship or anything else, I am ready to serve you in any way I can."[701]

At this point, the Rebbe was up against it and could not afford to deceive the man. Nor did he have any need to, for the issue of the 'descent' was more critical with the Hasidim. You have to imagine, wherever he goes, Hasidim are giving him *koved* (honor). Even when he was departing from Odessa, there had been crowds of Hasidim escorting him to the ship, singing and dancing joyously in his honor, and doing it because he was the great-grandson of the Ba'al Shem Tov.[702] Now, this is not the kind of honor he wants to receive, nor is it going to be helpful to him as he attempts to overcome the obstacles. Therefore, in Istanbul, he tries to rid himself of the burden of this identity, to bury it once and for all. For, he knows, if he is able to reach the Holy Land—as the Ba'al Shem Tov could not—and to return from it, he will no longer be 'Nahman, the great-grandson of the Ba'al Shem Tov,' but simply 'Rebbe Nahman' in his own right—both in the eyes of others, and more importantly, in the inner world. So, with these Hasidim he buries all the unearned honor of being born an heir of the Ba'al Shem Tov, and all the self-conceit that would protect his own honor, and his own ego. Having done so, he becomes free, free even to use this identity as he wills now. Once we have overcome the past, we are free to take it up again, as he now does with the ship's agent.

> THE NEXT DAY, THE AGENT CAME to tell them that a ship carrying Jews had arrived from Europe. Among them, he said, was a shohet who could provide them with kosher meat, as well as the renowned tzaddik, Ze'ev Wolf of Charni-Ostrog. The agent introduced Reb Shimon to Reb Ze'ev Wolf, and since he had not been told not to, Reb Shimon told him the truth about the Rebbe's identity. Reb Ze'ev

Wolf immediately invited the Rebbe to stay with him, urging him with great kindness and courtesy, but the Rebbe would not accept. He only answered, "Thank you, but it is good for me where I am."

It turns out that the Rebbe was avoiding Reb Ze'ev Wolf because of the foolish things he felt compelled to do in Istanbul, such as running through the streets barefoot and hatless, wearing only his yarmulke and coat-lining, playing war games with the children he found there. One child he called, "France," another something else, and the children and he engaged in mock warfare, using real battle strategy.[703] But soon an epidemic broke out on the Rebbe's street and forced him to move in with Reb Ze'ev Wolf who made a great feast in the Rebbe's honor.

The Rebbe did many things while staying with Reb Ze'ev Wolf that the latter may have found shocking, but he was so fond of the Rebbe that he ignored all of it. As the saying goes, 'Love breaks down all barriers.'

The first Shabbat the Rebbe stayed with Reb Ze'ev Wolf, the latter led ma'ariv (evening prayers) according to the custom of the great tzaddikim. The Rebbe, however, had prayed earlier and was already eating the Shabbat meal when Reb Ze'ev Wolf began to daven (pray). The same thing happened when it was time for Shaḥarit (morning prayers). And by the time Reb Ze'ev Wolf was ready to begin the Third Meal (shalosh seudot), the Rebbe was already reciting birkat ha-mazon (grace after meals). He told Reb Shimon to let him know as soon as the stars became visible, and as soon as they were, he prayed ma'ariv. Then he recited havdalah (the separation between Shabbat and the week), lit his pipe and entered the house. Reb Ze'ev Wolf was just beginning the Third Meal in the way of the tzaddikim when in walked the Rebbe with his coat wide open, wearing only his yarmulke and smoking his pipe. Nevertheless, Reb Ze'ev Wolf greeted him with the utmost respect, immediately said the birkat ha-mazon, prayed ma'ariv and recited havdalah. He then sat up speaking with the Rebbe all night with the utmost affection.[704]

Here we see another permutation of Rebbe Nahman's 'descent for the sake of ascent.' Whereas before he was dealing with Hasidim and 'paying the shadow cost' of being a Rebbe, now he is relating to a peer he must honor in spiritual intimacy while continuing to efface his own ego. It is a different situation, and in many ways, far more difficult for him. Obviously, he would rather have avoided it altogether, as we see when he turns down the invitation to stay with Reb Ze'ev Wolf. He is embarrassed by the necessities imposed upon him for this journey. But when an epidemic breaks out in his quarter, he is forced to accept the invitation. Now it is not a matter of hiding his identity, but of walking the razor's edge between discourtesy and serving the necessity of his mission.

As we mentioned before, it is not that Rebbe Nahman was acting contrary to the law in these instances, just unconventionally, especially for a Hasid. However, he does go to the point of allowing Reb Ze'ev Wolf to think that he *may* be lax with regard to the law. In doing this, he is taking the path which in Sufism is called, 'the path of blame' *(melamet)*. For the Sufi *melamiyya* (blameworthy) consciously engage in unconventional behavior, exposing themselves to criticism which is considered good for the soul, loosening the hold of the *nafs*, or the false self:

> The goal of the Melami path is to live a moral and sincere life for the sake of God alone and not to be concerned with appearances. . . The Melami even goes so far as to avoid and escape the praise and good opinion of people by making public or even exaggerating his own shortcomings, while keeping his superior qualities hidden, or attributing them to God. . . . One doesn't defend oneself; one doesn't try to explain oneself. If someone thinks in a certain way about you, it may be useful and even healthy for you to be totally nondefensive about yourself.[705] . . . How different this is from the touchiness of our egos when we feel we are slighted in some way, not given our due, or not recognized as we think we ought to be recognized; immediately we are wounded, our egos are wounded. But the Melami learns to embrace blame.[706]

Even within Judaism, in the *mussar* (ethical) schools of Novorodok, a young neophyte of such a school might go to a candy store and ask for coal, courting ridicule, and in this way achieve a kind of equanimity about praise and blame.

Now, it is worth saying a word about Reb Ze'ev Wolf of Charni-Ostrog (d. 1823) and the way of Hasidic *Shabbat* observance. First of all, Reb Ze'ev Wolf was one of the major disciples of the Maggid of Mezritch, and perhaps also of Reb Pinhas of Koretz. He was likewise a friend and in-law of Reb Zushya of Anipol, but his closest friend seems to have been Reb Meshullam Feibush of Zbarazh. Indeed, so close were the two friends that Reb Ze'ev Wolf refused to emigrate to the Holy Land while Reb Meshullam Feibush was still alive. Thus, it was only in 1798 after the latter had died that Reb Ze'ev Wolf finally set out for the Holy Land and met Rebbe Nahman along the way.[707]

Through him, we are able to see the custom of the Hasidim of the Maggid, who spent long periods in *davenen*, and who put a special emphasis on the Third Meal; for this was the time of the holiest *tish* (table), 'the Yom Kippur of the *Shabbat*,' when then they would tell the deepest Torah, sitting in a room that is getting gradually darker and darker, until all the candles were burned out. Although this was ordinarily the custom of Rebbe Nahman, he now acted contrary to this custom to 'court blame,' as it were, rushing ahead in his prayers and eating the *Shabbat* meal as soon as it was permitted. Nevertheless, Reb Ze'ev Wolf is not put-off and provoked to anger as the Hasidic emissaries were. For they let themselves be drawn into behavior that was not suitable for Hasidim, whereas he continued to behave as a *tzaddik*. It is irrelevant that he knew the identity of Rebbe Nahman, for the situation is reversed here. Had the Hasidim known, they would likely have remained in awe of him and explained away his extraordinary behavior. But a peer would be more inclined to be judgmental, standing on the same level, as it were. Nevertheless, he treats Rebbe Nahman very beautifully, with the utmost courtesy, continually adapting and cutting short his own practices to spend time in spiritual intimacy with his guest. For this alone, Reb Ze'ev Wolf deserves the greatest praise.

It is clear from the Rebbe's own testimony that he felt he was in tremendous danger in Istanbul; he was almost certain that he would die there. He said to Reb Shimon, "Neither the Ba'al Shem Tov nor the holy rabbi Naftali Katz were able to reach the Holy Land for all the obstacles that were set in their path." And the truth was, there was sickness everywhere he went in the city, and there was even war in the region; and when the Rebbe returned from Rabbi Naftali Katz' grave in Istanbul, he suddenly fainted and lay unconscious for several hours.[708] He was then placed in a bed where he lay all night on the verge of death. Around noon the next day, however, God miraculously intervened and restored him to health. He believed that his childish and degrading behavior had made the difference.

At this time, France had invaded the Sultan's territory in Egypt and Palestine, and the news had quickly reached Istanbul that war had broken out and the French were patrolling the waters of the Mediterranean. Thus, the Jewish community warned Jewish travelers not to leave the city, and absolutely not to travel by sea. The Rebbe, however, ignored this advice and was prepared to risk everything to come to the Holy Land. Nevertheless, he told Reb Shimon: "I am willing to endanger myself, but not to risk your life. Please, take this money for expenses and return home in peace, if that is your wish. I am content to travel alone, hidden and concealed as I am from the people of Istanbul. I am truly resigned to whatever happens."

But the loyal Reb Shimon refused to leave the Rebbe, saying, " 'Wherever you go—whether unto life or death—there will I go also.' "[709]

Now, it was God's will, at that time, that a great sage from Yerushalayim (Jerusalem), who had been collecting charity for Yerushalayim's poor in Istanbul, got up and spoke to the Istanbul Jewish community. He said: "It has been revealed to me that I must return to Yerushalayim immediately; the day is fast approaching when I will be taken from this world, and it has been decreed that my burial place is in Yerushalayim. So those of you who would travel to Eretz Yisra'el, but are frightened, may travel with me. You need not fear that the French will harm any Jew going to the Holy Land. God will watch over all who travel with me, and we shall arrive in peace." Immediately, a large ship was booked for the many stranded travelers, and the Rebbe was among them.

However, as soon as they were at sea, a great storm began to brew, and the ship was endangered. The waves began to toss the ship—"They mounted to the heavens and plunged to the depths."[710] Everyone on board feared this would be their end, and they cried out to God, weeping, confessing, and begging for forgiveness. It sounded like Yom Kippur aboard the ship! And yet, the Rebbe sat absolutely still. People asked him how he could keep still at a time like this, but the Rebbe said nothing. Then a rabbi's wife who had been crying and screaming all that night began to berate the Rebbe for his silence, almost cursing him.

The Rebbe responded, "If you will only keep calm, everything will be well. Just remain calm and you will see, the sea too shall become calm." He said this with such confidence that the woman and the people who heard him began to quiet down. It was then near daybreak, and quite suddenly, "God turned the storm into calm, so that its waves were still. And they rejoiced."[711]

A short time later, they disembarked at Haifa.[712]

It is clear from many of Rebbe Nahman's comments that, after Istanbul, the sea voyage was the last great danger to him before reaching *Eretz Yisra'el*. For his ancestor, Naftali Katz had died in Istanbul in 1719 on his way to the Holy Land. And now that Rebbe Nahman had survived Istanbul, even if just barely, he still had to face the obstacle that finally overcame his other illustrious ancestor, the Ba'al Shem Tov, whose ship was wrecked after leaving Istanbul for the Holy Land. Fortunately, through the grace of God, Rebbe Nahman made it through this stage of his journey in safety and reached the coast of the Holy Land.[713]

AT THE PORT OF HAIFA, the Rebbe first set foot on the Holy Land. He had finally come to the place of which he had always dreamed. For this, he had risked his life, very nearly casting his soul aside. He set foot on Eretz Yisra'el and his joy at that moment was beyond imagining. If all the seas were ink, and all the lands paper, neither would be sufficient to describe his joy! In that instant, the Rebbe had attained all. He later said, "By the time I had walked just four ells in the Holy Land, I had achieved my goal."

The afternoon he arrived, the Rebbe went to the mikveh before going on to the synagogue, where he remained until after ma'ariv. When he returned to his room, he was overflowing with joy and said to Reb Shimon, "O happy man! You are so fortunate to be here!" Then the Rebbe told Reb Shimon to read all the kvittelakh (prayer requests) his Hasidim had given him to pray for in the Holy Land. His mood was so intoxicating at that time that the entire household shared in his joy all through the Rosh Hashanah meal. This happy mood continued until everyone went to bed.

Rosh Hashanah morning, they went to the synagogue again. But by the time they had returned to their room, the Rebbe's mood had changed drastically. He seemed preoccupied and broken-hearted and would not speak to anyone for the rest of yontif (the holiday).

By the end of Rosh Hashanah, the Rebbe declared that it was time to return home. He hadn't even left Haifa, but he wanted to return at once. He seemed to have no interest in visiting anywhere else, even the holy cities of S'fat (Safed) and T'veryah (Tiberias). But Reb Shimon still wanted to travel, to see all the holy places of Eretz Yisra'el. He told the Rebbe that there was a caravan leaving shortly for T'veryah that they could easily join.

The Rebbe replied, "You want to go to T'veryah? Then go hire the donkeys!"[714]

For the moment, we will merely take note of Rebbe Nahman's elation and sudden depression as it occurs again only a short time later. Likewise, the sudden desire to leave, followed by urging from Reb Shimon to stay is another motif that will be repeated. Suffice it to say for now, they were not immediately able to go to Tiberias because Reb Shimon became ill. This then led to the following episode.

WHILE THE REBBE WAS STILL IN HAIFA, *a strange and mysterious event occurred.*

One day, a young Turk (Ishmaelite) came to see the Rebbe, speaking to him at length in Turkish. But the Rebbe didn't understand a word of Turkish. Still, the Turk was there for every meal, day and night. To all appearances, he seemed very fond of the Rebbe.

Then, one day, the Turk came in to see the Rebbe, apparently enraged and armed to the teeth. He yelled at the Rebbe in Turkish and the Rebbe appeared stunned and confused. When the Turk left, a woman from Wallachia (a region in Romania, near Turkey) who had overheard told the Rebbe: "For God's sake! Flee this house! That Turk has just challenged you to a duel!" Hearing this, the Rebbe left immediately and took refuge with Reb Ze'ev Wolf (of Charni-Ostrog), who concealed him in an inner room.

The Turk soon returned to the house where the Rebbe had been staying and asked: "Where is the man who was staying here? Please tell him I am very fond of him. If he still wishes to go with the caravan to T'veryah, I will give him the donkeys. I'll even give him my own horse! He has nothing to fear from me anymore!"

The Turk was telling the truth. The Rebbe returned to the house and, once again, the Turk came to the house and sat down, smiling and saying nothing to the Rebbe. Then he became very friendly and showed the Rebbe great affection.

This whole episode was very strange, and the Rebbe's comments did little to clear it up. However, he did say, "I suffered more from that Turk's love than his hatred and anger."[715]

This is certainly the most mysterious episode in Rebbe Nahman's entire journey, and the one that has been the most interesting to me through the years. For I have always wondered about the inter-faith possibilities of this encounter—a Hasid and a Sufi perhaps? What a wonderful thought!

Of course, encounters between Jews and Muslims in Muslim countries are nothing remarkable in themselves; but encounters of spiritual significance in that decidedly *un-ecumenical* paradigm is something else entirely.[716] And one between Rebbe Nahman, a Hasidic master from the Ukraine and a Turkish Sufi would be truly extraordinary.

What makes me think he might have been a Sufi? Precisely those seemingly inexplicable behaviors that make this story so mysterious. For anyone who is familiar with Sufism has heard dramatic tales of God-intoxicated *(madjdub)* Sufis acting in extraordinary ways. Moreover, 'wordless dialogues' between spiritual adepts is a wonderful genre of spiritual stories in many traditions, even when there is no language barrier as we have here.

But if we are going to propose such a possibility, the least we can do is offer an alternate explanation and allow the reader to judge between them. Indeed, many years ago, Martin Buber, for just such a purpose, suggested that this Turk might simply have been looking to hire his animals to Rebbe Nahman. Thus, he showed up day after day, showing him kindness while trying to make a deal. But, as he had gotten no response, he finally decided he was being insulted and became enraged. Later, however, he felt bad that he had caused the Rebbe to flee, and decided to give him the necessary donkeys and even his own horse for his trip to Tiberias.[717]

Now, most of this seems like a reasonable explanation. And were it not for the ending of the story, I might be inclined to accept this as an explanation of the external events, at least. But I find it difficult to believe that this Turk would give up such valuable animals of over a misunderstanding! By all means, give him a rate, perhaps even a donkey, but it seems excessive to surrender what is tantamount to his very livelihood. This would be rather extraordinary for a simple businessman. But it would be less so for a Sufi. So perhaps it is worth considering another possibility, as unlikely as it may sound at first.

Now, we must understand that Muslim Sufis in that region enjoyed the luxury of a certain liberal mindedness, and a freedom unknown to Rebbe Nahman. For Rebbe Nahman was a Jew from the Christian dominated Ukraine, relatively untraveled up to that point, and likely unfamiliar with people of other spiritual trajectories and different cultures. Unlike Islam, Christianity had no concept of a 'people of the book,' respecting the rights other 'children of Abraham.' Thus, a Jew from the Ukraine, having suffered endless persecution by Christians, had good reason to be cautious about all overtures from the 'enemy camp,' and was not likely to feel anything but suspicion in encounters with Christians. And should it be any different with Muslims? Nevertheless, Muslim Sufis enjoyed the luxury of belonging to the dominant culture in a meeting place of cultures, where Jews and Christians came and went regularly. And coming from such a place, Sufis were often far more friendly toward their Abrahamic siblings. So indulge us, if you will, in a little speculation . . .

Now one can imagine that a Sufi adept might be 'sensitive' to the presence of such a soul as Rebbe Nahman possessed, recognizing the 'fragrance' *(attar)* of holiness about him. Thus, he wishes to meet with him and share the warmth, just as he would with his Sufi brethren. However, being ignorant of both Hebrew and Yiddish, he shows him affection in every other way possible. But Rebbe Nahman, even if he *too* recognizes the 'fragrance' of holiness about this young man, has no context for accepting such a possibility from a Muslim. For unlike Maimonides, and more importantly, the son of Maimonides, he was not raised in a Muslim country and exposed to the genuine piety of devout Muslims.[718] Thus, the Rebbe is polite, but generally unresponsive to his Muslim companion. Now suppose that after a day or two, this Muslim Sufi realizes the true impediment and decides to resort to a kind of 'display' of dervish

wisdom that will certainly communicate. If the impediment is mistrust, then it should be brought out into the open. Thus, it is as if the young Muslim said to Rebbe Nahman, "So, you don't understand my affection? This you'll certainly understand! And now that what you've expected is out in the open, I can make an apology for it and perhaps we can start again!" After this, they sat in peaceful silence together and the Sufi gave Rebbe Nahman a gift that would allow him to go on his way in peace.

From this perspective, we can easily understand why the Rebbe said afterward, "I suffered more from that Turk's love than his hatred and anger." For the anger was only what was expected from a non-Jew, but the love was troubling and raised disturbing questions for him.

I cannot say that this is what happened, but I want to offer it as a possibility to be considered alongside the others, because there is hope in it.[719] Interestingly enough, this story has a kind of postscript. For, a few years ago, professor Zvi Mark, who has also written on Rebbe Nahman, told me something that seemed to confirm it. Sometime before, he was visiting someone in a hospital in Haifa. It was a two-bed hospital room, and in the other bed was an old Palestinian man who overheard them discussing Rebbe Nahman. After a moment, he begged their pardon, and said, "It was my great-great-grandfather who met with that rabbi."[720]

For whatever reason, he didn't pursue it. But oh the questions I would have had for him! You can choose the scenario you wish to accept, but if it was Rebbe Nahman that his great-great-grandfather had met, then why would a simple donkey merchant's tale have been passed down for five generations?[721]

During the intermediate days of Sukkot, the entire Jewish community went to Eliyahu's Cave to celebrate with singing and dancing. The Rebbe went too, but did not celebrate with the others. He seemed depressed, and just sat there as if broken-hearted. Reb Ze'ev Wolf approached Reb Shimon and asked: "What's this all about? Your master has been depressed since Rosh Hashanah. Can this be good for him? God only knows."

On Simhat Torah, spirits were high, and the Hasidim were making the hakafot in the synagogue, dancing joyfully with the sefer Torah. The Rebbe was there too, but he refused to carry the Torah. He just sat there with his head bowed, looking utterly dejected.[722]

This is the reason Arthur Green called his biography of the Rebbe, *Tormented Master*, for Rebbe Nahman was not concerned to conceal his internal struggles and bouts of depression, probably because he was convinced that they were all of great spiritual value, and that there was always a way through them. And this is the difference between these episodes and clinical depression—the Rebbe *knew* there was meaning in them. Thus, Reb Nosson writes of this episode without concern: "Of course, this was always the Rebbe's way. Each time he wanted to accomplish something important, it was preceded by an extremely broken-hearted mood. This happened very often."[723] That is to say, Reb Nosson interpreted these "broken-hearted moods" as internal 'descents,' parallel to the physical 'descents' that we have already discussed. Moreover, these 'descents' also have a parallel in the Jewish tradition; for before Purim, a joyous holiday, we fast, and before Pesah, in which we receive our freedom, the first-born fast again. Likewise, in Christianity, there is the Lenten fast and the fast of Good Friday before the celebration of Easter. The function of these fasts is preparatory, bringing oneself to humility, so that one can say, "All this I receive by the grace of God." For how can I reach that place unless I release my ego beforehand?[724]

AFTER SIMHAT TORAH, *the Rebbe told Reb Shimon again, "Thank God I have reached my destination and everything has been accomplished. I was going to stay longer—I love this land—but I've changed my mind. Arrange passage as soon as possible for us to return to Istanbul. I'm ready to go home today!"*

Once again, Reb Shimon spoke up and said, "Rebbe, if you don't mind, I'm not quite yet ready to return yet; I still want to see T'veryah and the other holy places."

The Rebbe sighed and said, "I suppose, if you really must see T'veryah, then hire donkeys and let's go." This was the Rebbe's way—he was never stubborn about anything.[725]

This response was characteristic of Rebbe Nahman, who was known to say, "I am very firm—*on not insisting.*" And he didn't. Even while suffering from tuberculosis, he didn't even insist on coughing![726] Thus, when Reb Shimon quite naturally wants to stay a little longer—given that they had just arrived—Rebbe Nahman agrees without much persuasion. Was this also Rebbe Nahman's way of sidling-up to the obstacles, of tacking into the winds of opposition? Perhaps, but it is just as likely that he is simply yielding to Providence.[727]

SO THE REBBE LEFT HAIFA and traveled to T'veryah, arriving there by evening. He was immediately inundated by visitors and well-wishers who came one after another. Many of them even dressed themselves in their Shabbat clothes to honor him. There were so many visitors that he was unable to sleep that night.

At first, the Rebbe stayed with his cousin—the son of Nahman of Horodenka's elder son—Shimshon Hayyim. The Hasidic community of T'veryah, however, felt that a larger house would give him more peace. So it was decided that the Rebbe should stay in the home of the saintly Rabbi Tzvi Harker.[728]

At that time, Rabbi Avraham of Kalisk, the head of the Hasidic community in the Holy Land, lived in T'veryah. And soon after the Rebbe's arrival, Reb Avraham sent a message to the Rebbe, saying that he had not been well and could not come to greet him. The Rebbe answered that he had intended to come to Reb Avraham, and did not expect the latter to visit him. He then went to see Reb Avraham who greeted him affectionately and with respect. Immediately, a true bond of friendship was forged between them.

Reb Avraham then asked the Rebbe to stay with him, but the Rebbe answered that he could not put the master out, but would be delighted to spend Shabbat with him. The next day, Reb Avraham sent a message to the Rebbe inviting him for the next Shabbat (Parshat Noah).

That Friday night, the Rebbe bowed his head before Reb Avraham to receive his blessing. But Reb Avraham pulled back, trembling all over. He spoke so excitedly that it was impossible to understand him. But his last words, at least, were discernable: "We are abashed before a descendent of the holy Ba'al Shem Tov!" And he refused to bestow his blessing on the Rebbe. However, as soon as Reb Shimon bowed his head, Reb Avraham blessed him.

The Shabbat meal was filled with great joy and Reb Avraham asked the Rebbe to deliver a dvar Torah (a word of Torah), but the Rebbe refused to teach when his elder was present. So Reb Avraham delivered the dvar Torah himself with enthusiasm, speaking so energetically that it was almost impossible to understand him. Once again, only his last words could be understood, "This is the root of our devotion to God," but the Rebbe praised the teaching for its greatness.

The next day, the same offer was repeated by Reb Avraham during the afternoon meal and again at the Third Meal, but the Rebbe refused and the teachings were given by Reb Avraham. Later on, the Rebbe said, "Perfect sincerity only exists in the great tzaddik, Reb Avraham," and "I have seen many tzaddikim, but I have seen perfection only in this holy man."

> That Sunday, Reb Avraham visited the Rebbe and the two men conversed for a long time. But a day or two later, the Rebbe fell ill and was forced to send a pidyon (redemption offering) to Reb Avraham, asking for prayer. After this, Reb Avraham visited him everyday until he was well again.[729]

Now, this positive description of Reb Avraham of Kalisk might be a little unexpected after what we saw of him in our chapters on Reb Shneur Zalman.[730] But we must remember that the context is also different.

In his relations with Reb Shneur Zalman, it is fairly difficult to see Reb Avraham in a positive light unless we accept his criticisms of Reb Shneur Zalman's teachings as valid. And it is only because of those criticisms and his different values that he even comes into that story. But Rebbe Nahman's meeting with him happens in a much more congenial context. Here he is on his own ground, welcoming a descendant of the Ba'al Shem Tov with whom he has no conflict whatsoever. Of course, the situation might have been different if he knew more about Rebbe Nahman, and almost certainly if Rebbe Nahman's own radical teachings had been published at that time. But in this moment at least he seems to have felt extremely honored to have Rebbe Nahman with him in Tiberias.

You see, Reb Avraham was also a close friend and co-worker with Reb Barukh of Mezhbizh, Rebbe Nahman's uncle, and had a special respect for the descendants of the Ba'al Shem Tov. For him, the Ba'al Shem Tov was the ideal of everything he held most dear—deeply emotive prayer, simple intentions, sincerity of heart—and he eschewed contact with everything that he felt was in conflict with these. So even though I don't agree with his criticisms of Reb Shneur Zalman, I would not say that Reb Avraham was insincere in them. He believed in the ideal he taught, and within the zone of those teachings, which were appropriate for him and his people, he was capable of great things. Thus Rebbe Nahman could say, "Perfect sincerity only exists in the great *tzaddik*, Reb Avraham," because that was the place in which he met him.

Nevertheless, there is still an underlying tension in this meeting. For, in truth, Hasidism was not exactly thriving in *Eretz Yisra'el* under Reb Avraham. At least not in comparison with the impact it was having in the land of its birth.[731] There had been a strong impetus to establish a community in the Holy Land when Reb Menachem Mendel of Vitebsk originally led masses of Hasidim there, including Reb Avraham, but the energy to maintain it seems to have waned after his passing. They were pioneers, after all, and it was hard to make a go of it. So, when word reached Tiberias that Rebbe Nahman, a descendant of the Ba'al

Shem Tov and the great Nahman of Horodenka, had arrived in the Holy Land, there was surely a great excitement in the Hasidic community. Had he come to take the reins in *Eretz Yisra'el*? What would that mean for the leadership of Reb Avraham Kalisker, his elder, who had already been there for so long? Thus, Rebbe Nahman quickly diffused the situation, showing great deference to the Kalisker, and making it clear that he had no such intention.

WHILE IN T'VERYAH, *the Rebbe went to visit the grave of his grandfather, the great Nahman of Horodenka, who is buried there. He also traveled to Meron to visit the cave where Rabbi Shimon bar Yohai the author of the Zohar is buried. The Rebbe advised all the young men who accompanied him to pray and study the Zohar, which they did enthusiastically. Nevertheless, the Rebbe looked as if he was doing nothing, merely standing around in the cave filled with joy. But every few minutes he went over to Reb Shimon and said, "O happy man! You are so fortunate to be here!"*

That night, the Hasidim went from room to room in the cave of Shimon bar Yohai, and the Rebbe again cautioned the young Hasidim to recite passages from the Zohar. But the Rebbe merely walked around happily, humming contentedly to himself until dawn. He then donned his tallit and tefillin and prayed for several hours.

From there, they went to the cave where the great sage Hillel lies buried, and the Rebbe was again filled with joy, chanting Psalms 33 and 34. Then they went on to the grave of the great sage Shammai. But the Rebbe's mood changed drastically here, and soon he appeared quite depressed. At first, he was surprised at this change in mood, but later he said that he understood it. However, he did not reveal the reason.[732]

The sages, Hillel and Shammai, represent ḥesed (love) and gevurah (restraint) respectively, so perhaps it is not surprising that Rebbe Nahman was not as happy at the grave of Shammai. But of far more significance in this passage is his visit to the grave of Shimon bar Yohai.

One might have expected more to be said here of his visit to his grandfather, Nahman of Horodenka's grave in Tiberias, as this was purported to be one of the primary purposes of his pilgrimage; but strangely, it is little more than a footnote in Reb Nosson's narrative.[733] However, that isn't to say that Rebbe Nahman did not feel strongly about this visit, only that little is mentioned of it in this account. It may be that the visit to the grave of his grandfather was more of a personal matter to him, whereas his visit to the grave of Shimon bar Yohai was more deeply connected with his life's mission. For it is believed among Bratzlav Hasidim that Rebbe Nahman and the great Shimon bar Yohai are actually manifestations of the same soul. Indeed, more than this, they shared a similar destiny; for Rebbe Nahman is thought to be the Shimon bar Yohai of his generation.

What does this mean? Well, first one must understand *who* Shimon bar Yohai is in the tradition. A first century *tanna* (scholar of the *Mishnah*), Rabbi Shimon was one of the great disciples of Rabbi Akiva, renowned for his scholarship, his spiritual discipline, and his courage in standing up to the Romans. But beyond all of this, he is celebrated as the mystic *par excellence* in the kabbalistic tradition, and as the author of the *Zohar*, the book of books in Jewish mystical literature.[734] Thus, Arthur Green, in his biography of Rebbe Nahman, looks closely at the significance of Shimon bar Yohai in the Bratzlav tradition and quotes this passage from the *Zohar* in order to demonstrate just how significant this association is for them:[735]

> Blessed is the generation in which Rabbi Shimon bar Yohai is present. Blessed is its lot both above and below. Of it, our scripture says: "Happy are you, O land whose king is a master."[736] What is the meaning of "master"? He lifts up his head to reveal secret things and is unafraid. What is the meaning of "whose king"? This refers to Rabbi Shimon bar Yohai, the master of Torah and wisdom. When Rabbi Abba and the companions would see Rabbi Shimon, they would run after him, saying, "The LORD will roar like a lion, and they shall march behind Him."[737]

This shows us just how powerful an event this must have been for Rebbe Nahman, to reach the burial place of his former incarnation, and to allow the two manifestations of the one soul to mingle and bask in one another's presence. There is also a sense of his experiencing the nostalgia of visiting his former home, the legendary cave in Peki'in where he had once lived for thirteen years!

WHILE IN THE HOLY LAND, *the Rebbe was continually absorbed with study and prayer. Everyday he spent time writing down his insights, and was heard to say, "The difference between the understanding of Torah in the Holy Land and elsewhere is like the difference between East and West."*

Everyday people approached the Rebbe, offering to serve him in order to hear his holy wisdom and Torah. At times, he was even approached by renowned teachers and leaders. Once, a respected scholar and kabbalist, reputed to know the entire Talmud by heart, visited the Rebbe and asked to be left alone with him. Everyone left except for Reb Shimon, who was allowed to remain.

Then the kabbalist said to the Rebbe, "I know that you have not come here like most travelers, with moḥin d'katnut (constricted consciousness), merely to walk four ells in the Holy Land in order to be worthy of olam ha-ba (the world to come), or for similarly limited reasons. I see that you have come in a state of moḥin d'gadlut (expanded consciousness), to accomplish great deeds of devotion. If you are willing to reveal the holy deeds you wish to do here, I am prepared to serve you with both my body and soul."

The Rebbe replied: "My dear friend, please don't pain me in this way; for to reveal my true reasons and actual devotions is not a simple matter. It may be that I am bound by an oath in this matter..."

But the kabbalist continued, saying: "Then at least teach me one of the precious insights God has granted you here. Please, understand, I don't have an ulterior motive in this, Heaven forbid. I only want to hear some ḥiddushei Torah from you that will help me in my service to God. In this way, if God wills, I may also be worthy of perceiving some hint about your mission here."

As he was speaking, the Rebbe's face began to glow, burning like fire, and his deveikut (adherence to God) was so intense that his hair stood on end and his hat fell to the floor! Then, a question formed on his lips like a tongue of fire, "Do you really understand the secret of the tefillin?"

The kabbalist replied by offering some traditional kabbalistic ideas about the tefillin.

But the Rebbe interrupted, "No! This is not the true meaning of tefillin; you do not know the secret of the four directions in the Holy Land! So I will give you a hint." But as soon as the Rebbe began to explain this, he also began coughing up blood! When he had recovered a little, he said, "Now you see with your own eyes that I am forbidden to reveal any of this to you!"

When the kabbalist saw this, he lowered his head in shame and begged the Rebbe to pardon him. Frightened, he would not move until the Rebbe forgave him for this indiscretion.[738]

The *tefillin* have to be square, not round, right? Thus, the *tefillin* refer to the four directions. Nevertheless, we did not merit to learn more, as there was a seal on his teaching at this time.

All through his journey, it is clear that Rebbe Nahman is experiencing great insights, and especially in *Eretz Yisra'el*. Indeed, it almost seems as if he is filling up on Torah in the Holy Land, perhaps in preparation for the next phase of his life in Bratzlav. Even at an early stage of their trip, the Rebbe tells Reb Shimon to buy a large quantity of paper and ink. And as soon as they board the ship in Odessa, he begins to write down Torah insights. But he warns Reb Shimon that he is not even to look at these writings!⁷³⁹ For it seems that, just as in this situation, most of these teachings are not yet ready to be revealed. Either they are specifically meant for later revelation, or it is that what is written in moḥin d'gadlut (expanded awareness or the manic phase), is not always appropriate for public consumption. Nevertheless, one feels that it has to be written down.

WHEN IT WAS TIME TO DEPART ERETZ YISRA'EL, *the Rebbe obtained passage on a Turkish ship. After they were well on their way, a storm broke out, and for several days and nights, the ship was tossed like driftwood on sea. The storm was so bad that even the captain didn't know how to control the vessel, as it says, "They reeled and staggered like a drunken man, all their skill to no avail."*⁷⁴⁰

They began pumping the compartments day and by night, but still the water kept rising. Soon, water flooded the Rebbe's compartment, making it impossible for he and Reb Shimon to sleep in their beds. Thus, they climbed up to an upper compartment and lay down. Meanwhile, the sailors resorted to trying to remove the water in large barrels with a pulley as the storm raged, raising mountains of water to the heart of the heavens!

The next morning, the Rebbe told Reb Shimon, "I am faint with terror, and deep down, I know that we are in great danger. I don't know what the sailors are doing, but the heart sees . . ." Then Reb Shimon went to see the cargo hold where they were drawing out water, only to find it completely flooded! All of the cargo had been washed away or thrown overboard, the water having taken its place! The ship was riding too low and the sailors were working frantically to pump the water out.

Seeing this, Reb Shimon realized that nothing less than a miracle could save them. When he returned to their compartment, he was trembling so badly with fright that he couldn't manage get a word out. The Rebbe said, "Where is your tongue, Reb Shimon? Why are you so afraid?"

Reb Shimon finally managed to speak, saying: "Rebbe, there is no hope for us without a miracle. The water is rising faster than the men can remove it and they are already weary, having been without food, water, and sleep for almost 24 hours!"

Then it occurred to Reb Shimon that he had not yet prayed shaḥarit and said as much to the Rebbe. But the Rebbe told him: "You needn't recite the whole service right now; but accept the yoke of the Heaven as you say the first verse of the Shema, *and say the first and last three blessings of the* Amidah. *That is enough in these circumstances."*

The Rebbe then told him, "Take every kopek (penny) that we have and divide it in half—you will bind your half to your body and I'll do the same with mine."

Reb Shimon wondered at this, and asked, "Why should we bother, Rebbe?"

The Rebbe replied, "Do as I tell you ... The Jews were in the Reed Sea and did not drown ... At least we are still in a ship!" Then Reb Shimon did as he was told.

Having done this, the Rebbe told him to put his fur coat on and to bind his belt tightly around it. The Rebbe did likewise, as if they were about to disembark the ship. Then Reb Shimon asked: "Rebbe, why don't you pray for us? I may not be able to open my mouth to God at a time like this, but you know how to pray at all times."

The Rebbe replied: "I am in a state of moḥin d'katnut (constricted consciousness) right now, and far from God. But we are in real danger, and I have no choice but to make use of the merit of my ancestors, which I have never done before. I will pray that God will help us for the sake of my great-grandfather, Rabbi Yisra'el Ba'al Shem Tov, of blessed memory, for the sake of my grandfather, Rabbi Nahman of Horodenka, of blessed memory, and for the sake of my grandmother, Adel!"[741]

Suddenly, an ominous dark cloud appeared in the distance and they were both filled with dread. It seemed as if one trouble was being added to the other, like being bitten by a wasp and a scorpion at the same time. Just then, God came to their rescue, and a strong wind began to blow, taking the ship to safety. Then the Rebbe joyously chanted Psalm 107, "Give thanks to God."[742]

Rebbe Nahman had boarded this ship in Acre (Akko) while fleeing the widening conflict between Napoleon, the English, and the Turks in the Holy Land. Unfortunately, in the confusion, he and Reb Shimon hadn't noticed that this wasn't the Turkish merchant vessel on which they had booked passage, but a Turkish warship! Thus, they had placed themselves in the greatest possible danger, and it was not long before the ship was fired upon by the French. Soon their error was discovered, and the captain was none too happy to find two 'stowaways' aboard his ship in the middle of a war. So they tried to make themselves invisible most of the time, hiding out in their small cabin. Fortunately, the cook took pity on them and brought a little coffee to them whenever he could.

After the battle was over, a storm began to wrack the ship, as we have already seen, and Rebbe Nahman and Reb Shimon truly feared for their lives. It is at this point that a miracle takes place in our story, and this is something especially noteworthy, as Rebbe Nahman's chronicler, Reb Nosson, is usually quite reluctant to mention the miracles that occurred around Rebbe Nahman.⁷⁴³ Why should Reb Nosson consciously deemphasize the miracles? Arthur Green makes this clear when he writes:

> Accounts of his master's supernatural powers would defeat the religious purpose of his writings. In contrast to all other Hasidic chroniclers, [Nosson] has no desire to minimize the humanity and the personal struggles of his master and model. If anything, it may be that Nahman's conflicts are disproportionately magnified by the repeated way in which [Nosson] makes reference to them, particularly in *[Shivḥei ha-RaN]*. The reader must be given the full story of Nahman's life and struggles, with no omission of the very human conflicts which many a saint's biographer would prefer to pass over in silence.⁷⁴⁴

But in this case, the miracle does not show Rebbe Nahman as a supremely confident *ba'al mofet* (miracle worker) spreading his hands over the waters. He is completely human in his reaction. Nevertheless, he is able to push through his fear, just enough to gird himself as the ancient Hebrews crossing the Reed Sea, and to call upon the merit of his ancestors, something he had never done before.

AFTER NUMEROUS OTHER ADVENTURES, *Rebbe Nahman and Reb Shimon eventually returned home, whole in body and deep in Torah, for the Rebbe merited to attain great vision and insight in the Holy Land. But all that we have told is less than a drop in the ocean of all the pain and anguish the Rebbe suffered on his pilgrimage. The dangers he faced were beyond description, but God was with him, performing miracles for him every step of the way. Thus, he entered in peace, left in peace, and returned home in peace.*⁷⁴⁵

These last lines remind us that Rebbe Nahman, like Rabbi Akiva, had entered the dangerous places of spiritual elevation, and knowing their secrets, was able to return in peace when others were not.⁷⁴⁶

This is probably a good moment to point-out what some discerning students of Hasidism will already have noticed: the stories of Rebbe Nahman's life are somehow different from the stories of other Hasidic masters. Most Hasidic stories and anecdotes lay a heavy emphasis on the unique powers of the master and often have a characteristic 'Ah-ha!' moment. But the stories of Rebbe Nahman's life are much more modern, introspective, and biographical, giving you the feeling of a 'real life' and its struggles. In this sense, they are much less two-dimensional than the hagiographic portraits of other Hasidic masters. This is because the actual day to day features of Rebbe Nahman's life are of far more importance to his Hasidim than those of other Hasidic masters. Again, Arthur Green points out:

> The life and teachings of Nahman . . . portray inner life and inward struggle to a degree otherwise unknown in Jewish sources. Here it is made utterly clear that the true core of religion is that struggle for faith which goes on within the heart of the individual believer, that the essence of prayer is *hitbodedut*, or lone outpouring of the soul before God, and that the single most important model for the religious life is the tortured young master himself . . .[747]

Rebbe Nahman is the model of one who struggles for faith, and who achieves it through his great longing. Thus, this "mythological autobiography" is of the greatest use to Bratzlaver Hasidim, who are able to use it to navigate the difficult terrain of this life as they attempt to achieve their own intimacy with God. In this way, Rebbe Nahman continues to guide them long after his passing, and nowhere more explicitly than in this long tale of his journey to the Holy Land.

8

It's Fire on Paper:
The Teachings of Rebbe Nahman of Bratzlav

AFTER HIS RETURN FROM *ERETZ YISRA'EL*, Rebbe Nahman visited a number of leading Rebbes, including Rabbi Mordecai of Neshkiz (1752-1800), Rabbi Tzvi Aryeh of Alik (d. 1811), and Rabbi Shneur Zalman in Liozhna.[748] Of particular importance was his visit to the latter, as the Kalisker had specifically requested his help in re-establishing peaceful relations with the Alter Rebbe.[749] While the peace he achieved was only temporary, Rebbe Nahman was nevertheless received with honor in Liozhna and a true friendship was established between the two Rebbes.[750]

IN THE SUMMER OF 1799, even before returning home to Medvedevka, Rebbe Nahman traveled on to meet with Reb Shneur Zalman. When he finally reached Liozhna, the whole town—including Reb Shneur Zalman—came out to greet the Rebbe in their Shabbat clothes. Then the Alter Rebbe invited Rebbe Nahman to stay with him, and personally led the way to his own home.

Later, a reception was held in Rebbe Nahman's honor, and the two Rebbes spent hours discussing Torah and delighting in one another's company. Then Reb Shneur Zalman asked Rebbe Nahman to say Torah for the Hasidim, but Rebbe Nahman refused. The elder Rebbe urged him several times, but Rebbe Nahman would not budge. So Reb Shneur Zalman gave a rousing teaching that lasted for eight hours![751]

It seems that Rebbe Nahman considered it bad form to teach before another Rebbe's Hasidim, and though usually not stubborn about any request, he would not break this rule. At the time of this meeting, Reb Shneur Zalman was about fifty-four years old, and Rebbe Nahman, twenty-seven, just a year older than the Alter Rebbe's son, Reb Dov Baer, whom he likely met as well. Though most HaBaD Hasidim didn't talk about other Rebbes, Reb Menachem Ze'ev Greenglass, one of my Rebbe's Hasidim from Warsaw, once told me that the Alter Rebbe had called Rebbe Nahman, "A nice young man," and that he had supported him through his later troubles.

In 1800, Rebbe Nahman moved his court from Medvedevka to Zlatopol, which was near Shpola, where Rabbi Aryeh Leib, the Shpola Zeide (1725-1811) had his seat. As Zlatopol was considered the 'territory' of the Shploa Zeide, a few disgruntled individuals in that town began to stir up trouble between Rebbe Nahman and the Shpola Zeide, who had been friendly toward the Rebbe while he was in Medvedevka. As with the other conflicts we have discussed, the issues were both temporal and ideological, but I don't think we will learn anything new by looking more closely at this one. It is sufficient to say that Rebbe Nahman suffered greatly under the vicious attacks of the Shpola Zeide, and when the latter sought to bring a *herem* (ban) against him, several prominent Rebbes came to his defense, including his uncle Barukh, Reb Shneur Zalman, and most importantly, the saintly and venerable Reb Levi Yitzhak of Berditchev.

Perhaps to diffuse the situation, Rebbe Nahman moved his court to Bratzlav in 1802, which was near Tulchin, the residence of his uncle Barukh. Nevertheless, the attacks continued, and worse for Rebbe Nahman, only a year later, his uncle also began to oppose him over "his alleged lack of respect for the Ba'al Shem Tov."[752]

This was perhaps the lowest point of Rebbe Nahman's life. His previous depressions and suffering were nothing compared to that which he experienced now, being attacked by both the Shpola Zeide and his own uncle. He was embattled and fighting to keep his head above water, but he was also finding his strength. And it is in response to this situation that the struggle to overcome such external obstacles becomes central to the teachings of Bratzlav Hasidism.

Still, amidst all the furor, there was one great consolation for Rebbe Nahman during these early years in Bratzlav—the arrival of a very special disciple. Within two weeks of making this move, a brilliant young Hasid came to Bratzlav in search of a Rebbe. His name was Rabbi Nosson

Sternhartz, and his meeting with Rebbe Nahman is a pivotal moment in the history of Bratzlav Ḥasidut. For it is through the eyes of Reb Nosson that future generations of Hasidim would look at Rebbe Nahman, and it is thanks to Reb Nosson that we have access to the profound Torah of the Rebbe. Indeed, all of the teachings in this chapter were collected and edited by Reb Nosson, the most important collection being the *Likkutei MaHaRaN*, which is the foundation of Bratzlav Hasidism, first published in 1808.

Surrounding Reb Nosson's literary activity, there is an important anecdote remembered in the Bratzlav tradition . . .

From the first, Reb Nosson listened carefully to everything that the Rebbe said, especially his Torah derashot (interpretations) given on Shabbat. After the Shabbat was over, Reb Nosson would recall the Rebbe's teaching from memory and put it in writing, giving a written form to the Rebbe's living thoughts. When he was finished, he would then show the written teaching to the Rebbe and ask for his approval.

One Shabbat, Parshat Yitro, Reb Yekusiel, the Tirhovitzer Maggid, one of Rebbe Nahman's most respected Hasidim, was greatly inspired by the Rebbe's teaching and wondered to himself: "Is it even possible to put such words of fire down on paper? Could mere ink and paper convey such holiness?" But the next day, when Reb Nosson brought his version to the Rebbe for his approval, Reb Yekusiel was allowed to see it and was amazed at what he saw. "It's fire on paper!" he exclaimed.

Later, on his way home to Tirhovitza, Reb Yekusiel stopped in Herson to visit his son-in-law, Reb Yitzhak, a schoolteacher and a fellow Hasid of Rebbe Nahman. But before Reb Yitzhak could ask him anything, Reb Yekusiel burst out excitedly—"I've just come from Bratzlav where I saw something amazing! I can barely describe it. As you know, I have often seen flames as the Rebbe revealed the secrets of Torah, and have often wondered, 'How could anyone possibly capture that fire in writing?' Well, I saw them again as he spoke this time, but the next day, the question that bothered me for so long was answered! I saw this very teaching written on paper the next day . . . and the flames burned even on the page! It was truly black fire on white fire!"[753]

As Rebbe Nahman himself said of Reb Nosson, "I thank God for sending me this young man who will ensure that not a single word of mine will ever be lost again." But Reb Nosson was far more than an amanuensis or scribe; his genius was such that he could actually follow Rebbe Nahman's thought, making the leaps with him as he moved from idea to idea, and then put it down in way that would make sense in writing, often providing the connective tissue himself. Thus, Rebbe Nahman and Reb Nosson, though Rebbe and Hasid, achieve a 'voice' together that is unlike any other in all Hasidic literature. We can only hope that we have done justice to it in these translations, preserving some measure of that "fire on paper."

Restoring the Soul

The following teachings are taken from a wonderful little book called *Meshivat Nefesh*, 'restoring the soul,' which is a collection of Rebbe Nahman and Reb Nosson's teachings on what to do when one finds oneself in the "dark night of the soul," as Rebbe Nahman so often did in this period. The teachings given below are all by Rebbe Nahman, and only a small sample of what is actually contained in the *Meshivat Nefesh*.

IF YOU WANT TO WALK *the path of teshuvah (return), you must become an expert in* halakhah *(walking the way). Then, nothing in the world can trip you up, whether you are 'rising' or 'falling.' No matter what happens to you, you must remain steadfast and faithful, fulfilling the words, "If I rise up to Heaven, You are there! If I make my bed in Hell, You are there!"*[754] *For God is available even in the unfathomed depths of Hell!*

But you must be proficient in the halakhah *of 'running and returning' (ratzo v'shov). As it says in the Zohar, "Deserving is the one who enters and exits."*[755] *Thus, "If I rise up to Heaven," entering the divine precincts and running to God, or "If I make my bed in Hell," seeing the need of exiting and returning to Heaven—"You are there!" Wanting to return to God, you must gird yourself tightly, and hold on tenaciously to the knowledge that God is there, no matter where you are!*

Whether you have been granted a higher level of awareness or a lower one, you must not be content to remain there—always aspire upward! True proficiency in halakhah *(walking) lies in knowing that it is both possible and necessary for you to go on, to aspire to higher levels! And if you should fall to a lower level, even into the depths of Hell, you must not despair. No matter what happens to you, wherever you may be, to the very best of your ability, seek the blessed One and look for God. For even there, one can be reunited with God. This it what it means to say, "If I make my bed in Hell, You are there!" This is the expertise of 'returning.'*

> *Thus, the consciousness of 'running and returning' consists of proficiency in these two aspects of* halakhah*—'running,' desiring and working always for a higher awareness of God, and 'returning,' holding fast to the blessed and holy One, even if you have fallen to the lowest levels. When you have learned to 'walk in this way,' you will find that the right hand of God is always extended to receive the penitent, whose contrition is causing them to mend their lives.*[756]

Halakhah, of course, refers to Jewish law, which decrees both 'observances' and 'abstentions.' But here, Rebbe Nahman uses the literal meaning of the word, *halakhah*, 'walking the way,' to talk about the ebb and flow of life, going forward and coming back, which he relates to the kabbalistic concept, *ratzo v'shov*, 'running and returning.'[757] Reb Shneur Zalman in his introduction to the *Sha'ar ha-Yihud ve-ha-Emunah*, writes in a similar vein:

Those who are familiar with the esoteric meaning of scripture know the significance of the verse, "For a *tzaddik* falls seven times, and yet rises again."[758] Especially since a person is called "mobile" and not "static," and must ascend from level to level, and not remain forever in one state. Between one level and the next, before one can reach a higher level, one is in a state of decline from the previous level. Yet, it is written, "Though one falls, they shall not be utterly cast down."[759]

When I was a young man, I learned a little anecdote about an old HaBaD Hasid who couldn't pronounce the letter 'r,' and who was known to say: "A *mitnaged* (opponent of Hasidism) is like a po-tait (portrait). Today is like *this*, and tomo-ow (tomorrow) is like *this* also—neve' (never) changing. But a Hasid is alive! Today is like *this*, tomo-ow like *that*—in the mud, out of the mud—but *alive!* Not just a po-tait."[760]

This is the point that Rebbe Nahman so often wants to make. There are no promises that times will always be good—or feel good—but a Hasid has the capacity for living fully, for living truly in the presence of God, and for redeeming each moment in its uniqueness. Above all else, we must know, as it says in Isaiah 43:2, that God is with us whether we are threatened by flames or surrounded by waters.[761] Even in such places, we are never separated from God.

> UNDERSTAND THIS WELL, *before you can be raised from one level to another, first you must fall, for this strengthens you for the service of God. Having fallen, you learn to persist in the greater ascent, to overcome the pitfalls and degradations*

of this world. For latent in every fall is the determination and energy to climb still higher. Eventually, you realize that the purpose of the descent is actually the ascent. But those who have truly fallen into degradation and self-loathing do not think so; they think it's just a steady climb to up to Heaven for God's elect. Nothing could be further from the truth. Everyone falls, and everyone can rise again . . . and rise still higher. For God's compassion extends both upwards and downwards.[762]

People who are struggling often think it is somehow easier for others, imagining that others aren't faced with the same obstacles and temptations. This is especially true of the saints, who we often treat as 'super-human.' But Rebbe Nahman goes out of his way in his teachings to say, *That's just not true! Look at me—nothing has come easy for me!* And Reb Nosson attests to this, telling us that not a single devotion came without effort for Rebbe Nahman.[763] It's only that those who *have* weathered and overcome the obstacles are the stronger for having gone through them. For God needs strong servants to do the 'heavy lifting,' and the *tzaddikim*, the 'righteous' have been 'toughened,' as it were, for this very work.

You see, the pitfalls and obstacles are, in Rebbe Nahman's own words, "God's compassion" which "extends both upwards and downwards." How is this compassion? Because they strengthen one "for the service of God." Consider how the mare who has just foaled doesn't make any effort to help the newborn stand on its wobbly legs. She knows, instinctively, that if the foal cannot muster the determination to stand on its own—thereby strengthening its legs—it is not likely to survive. While some may see this as callus, it is nevertheless, Nature's proven wisdom. We call it 'tough love,' and often it proves to be the best love for the long-term.

EVERYONE WHO BEGINS TO SERVE GOD, *even those on the lowest level, standing in the very center of the Earth, will immediately encounter all kinds of opposition and resistance, both within and without. For the* kelippot *(obstructing husks) will send an entire arsenal of desires, fantasies, and illusions to trip you up, to prevent you from rising higher. There are also many good Hasidim to whom this occurs and who believe they have fallen, but it is not really a 'fall.' It is simply the nature of the* Sitra Aḥra *(Other Side) to obstruct the path of those who are about to ascend to another level. The opposition is necessary for further ascent; the greater the show of force, the greater the potential for growth. Therefore, one has to brace oneself in order not to be downcast or discouraged by this. These obstacles are presented so that one may break through them and ascend even higher.*[764]

Instead of getting mired in a discussion of evil, the *Sitra Aḥra*, and *kelippot*, let's look at this in terms of gravity. For in both physics and the Kabbalah, the center of the Earth has a definite 'pull' on the human being. In Kabbalah, the density of the center of the Earth represents the most dense and solid materiality, and the place that is furthest from spirituality. It is a kind of dead matter whose inherent Divinity is difficult to awaken. Thus, Rebbe Nahman tells us that it is simply its "nature" to "obstruct" us. This is very much like gravity; for gravitational forces basically draw objects toward the center of the Earth,[765] creating a situation in which one must exert an extraordinary counter-force to escape their pull. So whether the challenge is to grab hold of a lifeline, to make a 'slam-dunk,' or to send a rocket to the Moon, we must somehow turn desire into a propellant, an extraordinary upward force that can overcome the pull of gravity, helping us to accomplish our end. Thus, Rebbe Nahman tells us, *Don't get discouraged; get fired up!*

DROWNING IN A SEA OF NEGATIVITY, *locked in a* kelippah *(shell) of ignorance on the lowest level, you might think it impossible to approach the holiness of the One whose name is blessed* (ha-Shem yit'barekh). *However, you must know that you can find Divinity wherever you are, even in the fathomless pit. Even there, under countless layers of disguise, you can still be reunited with the holy One through sincere* teshuvah, *for God "is never far from you."*[766]

THERE ARE PLACES SO LOW *as to seem utterly remote from God, but you must know that the supreme life-force is invested and concealed even in these places. This is a "mystery of the Torah," that even one who has fallen so low, into such an infernal place, can still turn and find the One whose name is blessed concealed there, in the very garments of Hell. In this discovery, many mysteries and secrets of the Torah are revealed.*[767]

As Rebbe Nahman says, when we discover that God is available even in such places, then "many mysteries and secrets of the Torah are revealed." This is the secret of God's non-duality, of God's presence in all things everywhere. For there is no place where God is not, even though it may seem that way to us. As it says in Torah, "And you shall know today, and take it to heart, that Yah is God in Heaven above and Earth below—there is nothing else!" (Deut. 4:39)[768] But the 'secret' is not 'revealed' in any intellectual understanding of this fact, especially today, when the word 'non-duality' is bandied about as if it were some sort of personal triumph of understanding. It is only revealed when we are able to uncover the presence of God "in the very garments of Hell." Only then will we be free to serve God who is truly free.

A NEGATIVE IMPULSE *(yetzer ha-ra) of the subtlest form has an almost diaphanous shell (kelippah) of distorting translucence. This type of negative impulse is sent to challenge those who have already achieved some measure of success on the spiritual path. But even the subtlety of this negative impulse is nothing compared to the negative impulse of the* tzaddikim, *for their negative impulse is nothing less than a holy angel!*[769]

THERE IS ALSO A NEGATIVE IMPULSE *that drives a person close to the One whose name is blessed, sometimes with great intensity and fire. This passionate drive, greater than it ought to be, is of the* Sitra Aḥra *(Other Side), and of the category, "Lest they force their way up to God."*[770] *One must pray hard to arouse God's mercy in order to be also saved from this unholy desire!*[771]

So here we are faced with two interesting paradoxes. In the first, we are told about a *yetzer ha-ra,* or 'negative impulse' that isn't actually negative at all. In the second, Rebbe Nahman speaks of a *yetzer ha-ra* that disguises itself as a *yetzer ha-tov,* or 'positive impulse.'

Of course, we have already discussed the 'negative impulse that isn't actually negative' in our commentary on previous passages. But here the point is made absolutely clear: for the spiritual adept, the *yetzer ha-ra* is treated very much like a professional boxer's sparring-partner. The boxer isn't antagonistic toward the sparring-partner because it is understood that their function is actually to sharpen the boxer's skills, to ready him or her for the *real* fight. Thus, for the *tzaddikim,* both metaphysically and attitudinally, the *yetzer ha-ra* is treated like a "holy angel."

But what of this "unholy desire" for God that disguises itself as a positive impulse? This is a hard one to contextualize in the Jewish tradition. On the one hand, we might look at Rabbi Shimon ben Azzai, who entered the Pardes (mystical orchard) with Rabbi Akiva and died there as an example of a 'love of God' that the tradition does not encourage; for he so wished to be one with God that he gave up his life in the mystical 'orchard.' But what do we really know about the totality of his motivation? Thus, I would be hesitant to call this an "unholy desire." So I tend to think that this passage is referring to the religious mania of an unstable or spiritually immature person. In this case, the mania is born of a kind of passion for God, but is clearly unhealthy for the individual.

Many years ago, I had a student at the University of Manitoba who had gotten into just such a holy mania. At the time, I was in New York, in Lubavitch for *yontif*, and I was outside "770" (Eastern Parkway, Lubavitcher headquarters) speaking to some friends. Back then, there was a phone booth on the sidewalk there, and the phone starts ringing. Well, it kept on ringing, and I thought, "Let me put that person out of his misery." So I answered the phone, and the voice on the other end says, "Zalman?"

I recognize the voice immediately, and say: "Gary? How did you know to reach me here?"[772]

He says, "I have *The Answer!* Tell the Lubavitcher Rebbe the answer is *arbitrarily*, *arbeit-rarely*." It was a pun, by which he meant, 'work very seldom.'[773]

Then he says: "I'm on fire! I have to touch people ... The more people I touch, the more people will become enlightened, and the closer we'll be to *Mashiaḥ* ... Tell the Lubavitcher Rebbe!"

So I said to him: "Gary, you have to do me a favor ... Go back to Winnipeg immediately, and go out to St. Norbert's (the Cistercian monastery where I had friends), and ask father abbot to accommodate you for a few days until I get back."

But he was too heavily involved in his mania and wasn't able to do that. So he went around trying to touch people—to infuse them with his light—and the mounted police picked him up and took him to the mental hospital in Winnipeg, where I came to see him when I got back.

Later, after he had recovered, I asked him, "How did you know where to call me?"

He said, "I wanted to talk to you, and I *saw* that number."

But if the connections he was making were in some ways brilliant, and the visions he was having had substance, what made it unhealthy for him? His 'vessel' wasn't strong enough, he wasn't grounded enough to be able to hold the visions in a way that wouldn't blow out his practical mind. In a similar category, we might also put the passion of religious extremists, whose "intensity and fire" drive them into fanatical views and judgments that eventually end in violence and other acts of hatred. We should all "pray hard to arouse God's mercy" that we may be "saved from this unholy desire!" as Rebbe Nahman says.

WHEN A PERSON EXPERIENCES CALAMITIES and tragedy, they must mobilize all their defenses against the negative impulse (yetzer ha'ra). At such times, the temptation to despair gains great strength, since it derives its life from these terrible difficulties.[774]

Depression and melancholy also strengthen the negative impulse (yetzer ha'ra). It is for this reason that one must arm oneself with good counsel and seek the paths leading to joy. For all strength of the spirit is derived from joy and gladness. As it is written, "The gladness of Y-H-V-H (Yah) is Your strength."[775]

As we have already seen, Rebbe Nahman was no stranger to depression, and yet, he never totally succumbed to it either. Why? Perhaps because he knew the secret of the 'descent for the sake of ascent.' That is to say, Rebbe Nahman had an absolute conviction that even his depression served a holy purpose, and that God was available even in the darkest places. Moreover, though he may have been predisposed to periods of depression, he was also keenly aware of its subtle egotism, or the 'hubris of despair.' For despair is a kind of arrogant presumption, pretending to knowledge it doesn't actually have, i.e., certain knowledge of unhappy endings. But in our tradition, we always say, *gam zeh yavor*, 'this too shall pass,' and *gam zu l'tovah*, 'this too is for the good.' So Rebbe Nahman encourages us to fight back, saying, *Gevalt! Yidden zeit aikh nisht m'ya'esh!* "Don't despair! Never give up hope!" For this is only the descent for the sake of ascent, and in that you must rejoice. So rejoice and put despair to flight!

The subjective experience of rejection and isolation is the beginning of acceptance. When one wants to come close to God and to be accepted, one usually finds obstacles and suffering, as if shunned by Heaven. But understand, this is all for the good, and acceptance is behind it all. If you can conquer these moments of despair, withstanding the temptation to take this 'acceptance' as 'rejection,' you will learn that everything that happens is for the good. These obstacles are given so that the energies of transcendence may be liberated from despair. For through this experience, one approaches Heaven, and it is in this sense that "rejection is the beginning of acceptance."[776]

Following up on the previous passage, Rebbe Nahman says here, *Don't be fooled, the obstacles are not a sign of God's rejection, but rather, are proof of God's desire to elevate you to the level of acceptance! What you see as a stumbling-block, is really a step for going up!* Thus he urges us again and again to embrace God in the obstacles, in the darkest places of apparent rejection, because these are only hurdles on the path to the finish line, tests of stamina and perseverance, ultimately bringing us closer to God. "Rejection,' he says, is only the beginning of "acceptance."

The Soul's Outpouring

If the exhortations of *Meshivat Nefesh* tell us *how to think about* life's difficulties, the teachings collected in *Hishtap'khut ha-Nefesh*, or 'the Soul's Outpouring,' tell us *what to do* in the midst of them. For this small but profound book is entirely concerned with prayer, especially the prayer-meditation practice of *hitbodedut*, 'aloneness,' already touched upon in Chapter 6.[777] In Bratzlav Hasidism, *hitbodedut* is both a daily practice and the answer to the question, 'What do we do when we find ourselves in the difficult places described in the *Meshivat Nefesh?*' We pray to the God hidden in such 'lonely' places, for Rebbe Nahman says, "know that you can find Divinity wherever you are, even in the fathomless pit."

Pour out your thoughts to God *like a child before its parent. For it is written, "You are children unto Y-H-V-H (Yah), your God."*[778] *Therefore, we must express ourselves and tell our troubles to God just as a child pesters and pleads with its parents.*

Toward the end of his life, Rebbe Nahman was visited by his four-year-old grandson Yisra'el, whom he seated on his lap. "Yisrolickel," he said, "Your *zeide* is sick . . . pray to the *Rebboina shel Olam* that he will get well again."

Little *Yisra'el*, who loved to play with his *zeide's* pocket watch, replied, "*Zeide*, give me your watch and I will say a prayer for you."

The Hasidim who were present began to laugh, saying, *A sheiner Rebbe! Er nemt shoin!* "He's already a 'Rebbe'—he knows how to take (*pidyonot*)!"

But Rebbe Nahman gave the child his watch without question, and his grandson said aloud: "God! My *zeide* is sick! You can heal him . . . Please heal him! Amen."

Again, the Hasidim laughed and grinned, thinking the child cute. But Rebbe Nahman looked at them in surprise, and said: "Why should you laugh? What do you think I do when somebody comes to me asking for prayer? I don't walk with my boots into the heavens![779] I pray just as he has done!"[780]

This little anecdote tells us a great deal about Rebbe Nahman's simple and profound approach to prayer, as well as a great deal about himself and his approach to spirituality. For though Rebbe Nahman was truly brilliant, a genius even among Rebbes, he always sought to serve God as a *prostak*, as a 'simpleton.' Indeed, he viewed this as absolutely necessary. For anyone who approaches God must humble themselves and admit their deepest ignorance before the unfathomable depths of Divinity. He says, "I have talked with many great *tzaddikim*, and all of them attained their high stations through absolute simplicity, secluding themselves in simple prayer with God."[781] Thus, he continues . . .

Sometimes it seems that we have done so much wrong that we don't even deserve to be called children of God. Nevertheless, this is not for us to say, for we are taught, "Whether good or evil, we are always called God's children."[782] So even if it feels like God has rejected and disowned you, still you must say to yourself, "Let God's will be done, but as for me, I will behave as a child of God should." Therefore, if you must, plead until the tears pour from your eyes, as a child weeping before its parents.[783]

In the same spirit, the Christian Russian Orthodox mystic and near contemporary of Rebbe Nahman, *staretz* (elder) Theophan the Recluse (1815-1894) says, "God abandons no one; all of us are God's children." Elsewhere, Staretz Theophan, who was instrumental in translating the *Philokalia* (the mystical classic of Greek Orthodoxy) into Russian, speaks in a style that is very reminiscent of Rebbe Nahman, and often of similar subjects. Listen to this passage that could have come from Rebbe Nahman's own mouth:

You cannot tear things out of the hands of God with force, but with tears, you can gain everything. Simply ask the Lord to 'please' give what you need—don't insist! Don't act as if it is your right; everything is grace. It is possible that God creates situations that cannot be overcome. Nevertheless, one must pray and try and do whatever one can. Perhaps the Lord will be compassionate and receive that prayer. Then we will come to the joy of having been saved. But this prayer must be humble and broken-hearted; there is no such thing as getting God's grace by right.[784]

But *hitbodedut* is far more than an outpouring of sorrow and longing, it is an endless conversation with God, a give and take, talking and listening, filling up the corners of one's life with Divinity. In this way, it is utterly simple and immensely profound. Thus, when Rebbe Nahman first introduced Reb Nosson to *hitbodedut*, he put his arm around his shoulder and said, "It's very good to pour your heart out to God just as you would to a true friend," for this implies all the intimacy, the joy and sorrow, warmth and depth one finds in the most profound friendship.

The following passage is perhaps the most explicit presentation of hitbodedut in all of Rebbe Nahman's writings . . .

HITBODEDUT IS A HIGH PATH, *and you should set aside an hour or more for it each day, doing it by yourself in a room, or out alone in a field.*

Hitbodedut is just a good, flowing conversation with God, a pouring-out of complaints, excuses, and other words seeking grace, acceptance, and reconciliation, begging and pleading for God to bring you closer, allowing you to serve in the way of truth.

Your words needn't be fancy—just talk to God in the language of your heart, and of your daily conversation. Hebrew is good for saying the prescribed prayers, but how can you express what you're really feeling in a language that isn't your own? Moreover, if you are not accustomed to speaking Hebrew naturally, the heart doesn't follow in the path of the words! But when you use the language in which you speak everyday, it's so much easier to express yourself. The heart is so much closer to this language. The moment you speak, your heart follows and finds itself at home with your words. Therefore, use your native tongue to express what is in your heart and tell it to God.

As I said, your conversation can be of regret or repentance, pleading to be found worthy of approaching God, or of returning to the path of truth. But always speak to God at your own level, from the place in which you find yourself. Spend an hour in hitbodedut *everyday if you can, and the rest of the day you will find yourself rapt' in joy and ecstasy.*

This is an extremely powerful practice and will certainly bring you closer to God.[785]

At first glance, this may seem immensely simple, even simplistic, but it is nevertheless one of the most important and transformative prayer practices in all of Hasidism. One of the reasons is because Rebbe Nahman makes of it a practice of sustained focus, asking his disciples to do it alone in a room or out in nature (hence the name, *hitbodedut*, 'aloneness') for up to an hour each day. As this becomes more and more natural to the Hasid, the practice begins to open up new dimensions of intimacy with God, creating a relationship of natural ease in which the flow of communication is continually moving back and forth.

Of course, this kind of prayer has never been absent from the Jewish tradition, and is seen throughout the T*anakh*. It is perhaps best known in the prayer of Hannah (1 Samuel 2). Nevertheless, this extemporaneous prayer is usually reserved for occasions of special need, and emerges from a cry of the heart, as in Hannah's case. Prayer in the Jewish tradition since the time of the Great Assembly has mostly been defined by prescribed prayers that became the basis of the *siddur*, the Jewish prayer book. But spontaneous prayer is still considered primary. The innovation of Rebbe Nahman is to turn the cry of the heart into a daily practice, to make it a regular feature of one's prayer-life, and to give it enough attention to allow it open one to genuinely meditative depths.[786]

Christians—especially Protestant Christians—will readily recognize this kind of prayer. For though it is known in Catholic Christianity, especially in the monastic setting, as *oratio*, 'affective prayer,' it is a far more prominent feature of Protestant Christianity. One of my own most significant mentors, an African-American mystic named Reverend Howard Thurman (1899-1981), first introduced me to this prayer of Christianity in a class at Boston University that he called, "Introduction to Spiritual Disciplines and Resources, with Labs." Later, he wrote a book based on those classes in which he refers to this type of prayer in ways that would be familiar to any Bratzlaver Hasid:

> Every person who is concerned about the discipline of prayer must find the ministry of silence in accordance with his particular needs. . . . We must seek a physical place of withdrawal, a place of retreat, if this is possible. It may be achieved merely by closing the door as a signal that one wishes to be alone; it may be by remaining in bed for a spell after everyone else is up and about; it may be by taking a walk or by extending a walk beyond the initial requirement or demand; it may be by withdrawing one's participation in conversation, even though one has to remain in the midst of company.[787]

He then gives an example of a kind of '*hitbodedut*' practiced by a old woman in New England who told him about her prayer over a very difficult issue in her church, and of how precisely she had prayed about it, saying:

> I gave myself plenty of time. I went through a thorough review of the highlights of the sixty years I have been a member of the

church right up to the present situation. I talked it through very carefully. It was so good to talk freely and to know that the feelings and the thoughts behind the words were being understood. When I finished I said, "Now Father, these are the facts as best I can state them. Take them and do the best you can. I have no suggestions to make."

A fresh meaning flooded the words "Thy will be done."[788]

One would be hard pressed to come up with a better description of *hitbodedut* than this short summary of an old Christian woman's prayer over an issue of deep concern to her, especially as she concludes, "A fresh meaning flooded the words 'Thy will be done.'"

But what if the words just won't come? After all, this kind of prayer is a foreign experience for many people. So what do you do then?

ALTHOUGH IT IS IMPORTANT TO DO HITBODEDUT, *expressing your intimate thoughts to God each day, sometimes you find that you simply can't do this, and must be content to say a singe word before God, and this is also very good.*

If you can only say one word, you should say it with concentration, and repeat it over and over again, countless times. You might even make this your prayer for a number of days, which is also a good practice.

If you persist in repeating this word countless times, God will certainly have mercy on you and open your mouth, allowing you to express your thoughts freely![789]

Who can read this without thinking of the practice of *mantra* meditation, or *zikr*, as it is called in Sufism? But Rebbe Nahman's version has a different purpose: to stimulate the flow of words that make up a session of *hitbodedut*.

This reminds me of something else I heard from Howard Thurman. Once, when I was teaching at Camp Ramah, a summer camp set up by the Jewish Theological Seminary, I took a group of kids on a tour of New England synagogues and other houses of worship before bringing them to Boston University, where Howard Thurman agreed to speak to them. He gave a nice, gentle talk to the kids and then asked for questions. One teenager got up and asked, "What do you do if the morning comes and you don't feel like praying?" That is to say, you have a religious obligation to say your prayers, but you just don't feel like it—what should you do?

So Thurman answered, "Everybody has a phrase that feels good to the heart . . . Recite that phrase a few times, and you'll see, it will make a difference."

The boy thanked him, but he said to me afterward, "Yeah, yeah . . . Sure." But a few months later, I received a three-inch tape reel in the mail from the young man. I put it on, and he said: "I want to tell you, this morning, I didn't feel like saying my prayers. And so, there I was in bed, not feeling like getting up, and I remembered what Reverend Thurman had said. So I said, *La'El barukh nemut yiteinu, La'El barukh nemut yiteinu,* 'To the blessed One, give him nice things.' I said that phrase a few times, and pretty soon, I was all fired-up to pray! So I just wanted you to know that 'Yeah, yeah' was really true!"

I would highly recommend that you consider making *hitbodedut* a part of your prayer-life. As Rebbe Nahman promises, it will forever alter your relationship with God. If you want to learn more about the practice, you can obviously look into Reb Alter of Teplik's little collection of Rebbe Nahman's teachings on prayer, *Hishtap'khut ha-Nefesh*, translated by Aryeh Kaplan as *Outpouring of the Soul*. But today there are also other resources, such as Chaim Kramer's chapter on *hitbodedut* in *Crossing the Narrow Bridge*, and most recently, Ozer Bergman's book, *Where Earth and Heaven Kiss*, which is itself a complete guide to the practice. Likewise, the movie *Ushpizin*, which centers around the life of a Bratzlaver husband and wife in Jerusalem, also shows some excellent examples of *hitbodedut* and illustrates numerous other teachings of Rebbe Nahman.

Teaching the Body

There is a little story in the Bratzlav tradition which might connect our previous discussion of *hitbodedut* to one of my favorite teachings of Rebbe Nahman, 'The Teaching of the Body,' which I consider one of the most important for us as spiritual practitioners today.

> When his Hasid, Reb Shmuel Yitzhak of Dashev first came to Rebbe Nahman, he asked the Rebbe how he could begin to overcome the *yetzer ha-ra* (negative inclination) of his body. Thus, the Rebbe began to speak to him about the process of *hitbodedut*. He told Reb Shmuel that when he practiced *hitbodedut*, speaking to ha-Shem as a friend, he should also talk to his body, even to the individual limbs and organs! The Rebbe told him that the body should be made to understand its mortality, how it will eventually molder in the grave.

Moreover, he told him to teach every part of his body the lessons of the spirit, to master the desire for physical comforts and pleasures; for the body must be brought to desire *avodat ha-Shem* (the service of God), even as the soul does.

Reb Shmuel wasted no time in putting Rebbe Nahman's counsel into practice. Day in and day out, he talked to his body, attempting to teach it the lessons the Rebbe had given him. But after a little while, Reb Shmuel came back to see the Rebbe and complained: "Rebbe, I don't think my body is listening; nothing has changed . . . My *yetzer ha-ra* hasn't relented!"

Still, Rebbe Nahman told him not to be discouraged, to keep it up, that this practice would eventually have an effect on the *yetzer ha-ra* of his body. So Reb Shmuel did as he was told and continued the conversation with his body. In time, the *yetzer ha-ra* began to lose its grip on his body, and he became adept at this practice, having the 'ear' of his body, as it were, so that he was able to control even the smallest impulse. Indeed, so sensitive was his body to his every word that once, while questioning the purpose of the body before friends, he suddenly fainted and was revived only with great difficulty. When he came back to consciousness, he realized that this practice had become so powerful that his heart had almost stopped working! He realized that he had better use it carefully from now on, speaking less disparagingly of the body; after all, he didn't need to depart before it was his time![790]

Among those who seek spiritual 'enlightenment' in various traditions, there are basically two attitudes toward the body. One is that the body is a hindrance, an obstacle we must overcome in order to release our spirits. This leads to a denial of the body, to fasting and mortification in an attempt to override the demands of the flesh. Body and spirit are seen as separate and conflicting entities. This is an attitude that predominates among kabbalists before the coming of the Ba'al Shem Tov, and is also strong in the accounts of Rebbe Nahman's youth. But with the Ba'al Shem Tov, a new attitude begins to come into play that sees the body as a natural part of our being, and becomes a fundamental tenet of Hasidism. The distinctions between body and spirit are acknowledged, but the nature of the relationship is seen as cooperative and unifying. The joys of the body enhance the joys of the soul; when the body dances, the soul claps her hands. Thus, Rebbe Nahman teaches . . .

A PERSON SHOULD TAKE PITY *on the body's flesh, enlightening it with all the insights of the soul, so that the body, too, will have this realization. This is the meaning*

> of, *"From your flesh, do not hide,"*[791] *which is usually taken to refer to your family. However, we must also read this in the most literal way, as referring to the flesh of one's own body.*
>
> *This compassion that one has for the body needs to focus on refining and preparing it to receive all the enlightenment and realizations attained by the soul. It is the nature of the soul to see and comprehend the higher realizations to which the body alone would have no access. For this reason, one must—out of compassion for the body—cleanse and purify it to become a vessel for the soul's teachings.*[792]

We can see from this that the "compassion" Rebbe Nahman has in mind still has the flavor of the ascetic about it—a kind of 'tough love'—but this need not be negative. If one truly thinks of the body as 'an instrument upon which God plays,' then it is vital that the body be 'tuned' correctly. If it is not, then the 'music' it makes is liable to be distorted and 'off-key.'

What does this compassionate tuning of the body look like? Obviously, the first "insights of the soul" that must be taught to the body are those *mitzvot*, or divine instructions that have to do with the body, such as dipping in the waters of the *mikveh*, keeping the food-laws of *kashrut*, and those of sexual purity. So, at the first level of inquiry, we might ask—"Is the food we are consuming kosher?" But then we could go on to ask, "Is it eco-kosher?" Meaning, was it produced without genetic manipulation and in an environment in which the animals were treated humanely? Then we can ask ourselves: "Are we over-eating? Are we being gluttonous with what is itself kosher and eco-kosher?" At this point, we might begin to notice (as many spiritual practitioners do) if particular foods tend to produce certain moods and physiological symptoms that are not helpful before prayer and meditation. "Are we purifying ourselves with the appropriate blessings and intentions over the food?" All of this has to do with 'teaching the body,' training it for spiritual practice, and tuning it to receive spiritual benefit. And we could ask similar questions about cleanliness, exercise, and sexual purity. So at the very beginning, Rebbe Nahman wants to get our thinking going in this direction.

But we can also take this one step further. For this teaching need not be limited to conventional spiritual topics. Just as Reb Shmuel teaches his body that the flesh must serve the spirit, it may be that we can also teach the body other insights. Perhaps we can teach the body about our personal insights or about various kabbalistic concepts. For example, our friends, Michael Kagan and Levi Ben-Shmuel have created a wonderful practice that integrates *tai chi* movements and *chi*-flow with the *sefirot* as they are expressed in and through the body!⁷⁹³

> BUT THIS PROCESS *is also of great benefit to the soul. For the soul is liable, from time to time, to fall from its level. But if the body is pure and transparent to the divine light, then the soul can lift herself up and return to her level by means of the body! For when a body experiences pleasure, then the soul can also remember her own bliss, attune to it, and rise again. If the body is fit (kasher) and not a slave to comfort and selfish pleasures, it will not become a prison for the soul, and the soul may rise again to her level through the bliss of the body.*
>
> *You see, the pleasure the soul shares with the body makes an impression on it, which can bring the soul back to remembrance of the pleasures afforded by its own enlightenment and realization. Thus, it is able rise yet again! As it is written, "From my flesh I see God."⁷⁹⁴ Precisely—"from my flesh!" Through my body's very flesh, the soul can say, "I will see God," meaning, I will realize and perceive God! For a body made transparent can perceive the Divinity with which the soul is ever in contact!*
>
> *But if the body is unfit (treif), spoiled and truculent, then the soul cannot even approach it, let alone teach it of her realizations. For a body addicted to its pleasures can become a trap for the soul, degrading it with its ways. Thus, the soul needs its own strength and holy pride to remain above such degradations. Remember, the real 'I am' of a person is the soul, and when it sighs, it can break the aggressiveness and recalcitrance of the body, bringing 'flesh' and 'bone' together.⁷⁹⁵ For it is written, "sighing breaks the body."⁷⁹⁶ And when the will of the body is broken, the soul may safely approach it without fear of being trapped.⁷⁹⁷*

Now Rebbe Nahman is really opening things up. Before he was only talking about how to ready the body for spiritual realization, but now, he tells us that the body can also lift the soul. For sometimes the soul slips and falls from her rung; and if the body is clear and luminous, focused and in harmony within itself, then the soul can use it to raise herself back to her rung. She can ride on the body's delights in its own energy and so remember her own delights and re-connect with them. The body remembers all the light it received from the soul and, in turn, reflects it back to the soul. In these ways, the soul can use the body's ecstasy to recapture her own. That is to say, there is an open connection between body and soul. So much so that the Ba'al Shem Tov once said, "Even if you are free from sin, when your body is not strong, your soul will be too weak to serve God in the proper way."

Nevertheless, it is not enough to simply be aware of this connection; we must also make use of it. By paying attention to what the body is feeling, watching for proprioceptive 'landmarks' during our spiritual practice, we can make them accessible to recall. Before prayer, for instance, or *Shabbat*, it may be useful to spend a little time recalling past ecstatic body-responses to different soul states. Thus, when bathing and dressing for *Shabbat*, if we can hum a *niggun* (Hasidic melody) or recite an appropriate phrase with deep *kavanah* (intentionality), the recalling becomes easier.

Each time we have a holy, ecstatic, celebrative experience and say the blessing *Sheheheyanu*, we can add this experience to a garland of personal holy moments. At any time we are free to return to them, and, in the way of the body memory, we can re-experience them and give thanks for them in a holy mini-vacation.[798]

This teaching is very profound, and the reader should take time to consider it in all of its dimensions. For creating deep and holy connections between the body and the soul is one of the great challenges and unique opportunities of our time. As an aid to you in this process, I want to recommend a wonderful book of Rebbe Nahman's teachings on the body compiled by Chaim Kramer and Avraham Sutton, called *Anatomy of the Soul*, which looks at the body and its organs from a spiritual perspective.

The Torah of the Void

From here to the end of the chapter, we will focus on one long teaching of Rebbe Nahman. In my opinion, it is one of his most profound and important teachings. It is found in *Likkutei MaHaRaN*, and is known as *Bo el Paroh* (Go to Pharaoh), taking its name from the opening line of the biblical passage (Exod. 10:1-4) that served as a jumping-off place for Rebbe Nahman. Nevertheless, I have always called it 'Torah of the Void,' as this is the subject that it treats throughout.

For me, this is the quintessential fusion of Rebbe Nahman and Reb Nosson, and truly "fire on paper." Thus, I took an unusual approach to its translation, as I feared that something special might be lost if I approached it in a conventional way. I determined to translate it in a poetic format to slow the reader down, encouraging them to read every word aloud with feeling, imaging the way in which Rebbe Nahman might have spoken them himself. For as I first read this teaching, I could almost hear the original Yiddish underneath Reb Nosson's excellent Hebrew, and even Rebbe Nahman's pregnant pauses. For this reason, I tried to get away from the usual left-brain language, imaging how it might have sounded in colloquial Yiddish, and then translated that into English. How far I have succeeded in this is up to you to decide.

Before we begin this teaching, I want to explain the form of the commentary and make one suggestion to the reader. It is important to me that this teaching not be disturbed or interrupted by commentary. I really feel it should be read through to the end at least once before you try to understand it. Allow it to seep into your heart and mind slowly and organically. Make your own associations. There is a part of you that understands *without* the intellect, and it is this part of a person that Rebbe Nahman is trying to address most of the time. (I believe the same is true of Rebbe Nahman's stories.) So try to open your 'pores' to this teaching and give it a chance to 'seep' into your affective body before taking it apart intellectually. The commentary we have provided is not meant to explain the teaching as much as it is meant to be helpful in stimulating your own understanding of it. Read whatever part of it seems interesting to you.[799]

I

God, for Mercy's sake,
Created the world
To reveal Mercy;[800]
For if there were no world,
On whom would Mercy take pity?

So, to show God's Mercy,
God created the Worlds—
From the peak of Nearness (atzilut)
To the very center of the Earth!

Now God wished to create,
But there was not a where
In which to do it,
For all was Infinitely God (Ain Sof),
Blessed be that One-ness!

Therefore, God condensed
The Infinite Light (Or Ain Sof)
That filled all of existence
Sideways—and thus was space made,
An empty Void (ḥalal ha-panui).

In that space,
'Days' and 'measures' came into being,
And thus the world was created.

This Void was needed
For the world's sake,
So that it could be put into a place.

Don't strain to under-stand the Void!
It is a Mystery not to be realized
Until the future is the now;
For about the Void,
We must say two opposing things:
It-Is and It-Is-Not.

The Void is the result
Of the contraction (tzimtzum),
In which God withdrew
From that space
For the world's sake;
But the truth of the truth is...
God is still there.
For without God's
Life-giving energy,
Nothing could exist![801]

Thus, there is no way
To grasp the Void
Before the future is the now.

"God, for Mercy's sake..." There is a saying in the Talmud, "More than the calf wants to suck, the cow wants to give milk."[802] In this case, God (whose name, *Y-H-V-H* is connected with the quality of Mercy) has an innate desire to give of the divine essence, which is Mercy, and if there is no one there to give it to, it is like a mother with milk and no child to nurse.

"*So, to show God's Mercy,...*" From the most subtle and ethereal places in the highest worlds, in the world of *atzilut*, meaning 'nearness,' to the most dense and concretized materiality in the molten core of *assiyah*, the lowest world of 'action,' God is ever-present and is continually creating it all. As Rebbe Nahman said in our first passage from the *Meshivat Nefesh:* " 'If I rise up to Heaven,' *entering* the divine precincts and *running* to God, or 'If I make my bed in Hell,' seeing the need of *exiting* and *returning* to Heaven—'You are there!' Wanting to return to God, you must gird yourself tightly, and hold on tenaciously to the knowledge that God is *there*, no matter where you are!"

"*Now God wished to create . . .*" At this point, Rebbe Nahman begins to recapitulate the great cosmogonic myth of the holy Ari, Rabbi Yitzhak Luria, in which he describes the process of *tzimtzum,* which we have already discussed in Chapter 3, "A Hidden Light."[803]

"*Don't strain to under-stand the Void!*" One of the Hebrew words being used for 'understand' here is *l'hasig,* which means, 'to reach.' Thus, it has a sense of straining to grab hold of something. In this, it is much like the Latin, *conceptus,* 'with it I capture,' from which we get the English word, 'concept.' So you see, Rebbe Nahman is telling us not to strain to get underneath, to get to the bottom of the Void. He is saying, don't try too hard to conceptualize it; it's not something that can be known until we will have come into our future inheritance.

"*The Void is the result . . .*" This *tzimtzum* is a necessary prerequisite for creation to take place, so that what is created is not overwhelmed by the homogenous perfections of *Or Ain Sof.* Thus, the purpose of the Void *(ḥalal ha-panui)* created by the *tzimtzum* is to act as a barrier against the *Or Ain Sof,* again, so that creation is not overwhelmed by Divinity.[804]

II

You should know that[805]
There are two kinds of unbelief:
One that originates with
The outer, external sciences . . .
The questions raised by them
Can be answered;
As it is written . . .
"Know what to answer
The unbeliever (epikoros)*"*[806]
For outer knowing is still rooted
In the order of holiness.

*For at the breaking
Of the vessels (shevirat ha-kelim),
The holy light was so
Overwhelmingly powerful,
That it burst the vessels
That were meant to hold it!*

*And when these vessels burst,
The fragments of holiness took form,
Becoming the outer, external sciences.*

*So you see, even from holiness
There is a kind of dross, or slough;
Just as the body sweats and excretes
And must remove hair and nails,
So too, holiness has its slough;
These are the outer sciences
And the knowledge of externals.*

*When this slough is used
For the sake of power,
To twist the world,
You have source-ery,
Which has likewise fallen
From a higher wisdom.*[807]

*One who can,
Should strive to avoid
The trap of the outer sciences;
But even if one should stumble
And fall into this trap,
All is not lost.*

*For one who seeks God,
Can surely find God,
Even there, amidst the shards
And sparks (nitzotzot) of holiness
That give life to these sciences,
Even in the very signs and symbols
By which these sciences express themselves!*

For as long as there is rhyme and reason,
There is holiness in the form of the sparks;
As long as there is life in the world,
God is in the world too;

As long as the sparks are present,
Unbelief allows for a reply,
And for a return to holiness;
Thus, it is written . . .
"Know how to answer
The unbeliever (epikoros)."

But there is another kind of unbelief,
Rooted in un-wisdom,
Though it seems profound
For being un-real-izable,
Yet its 'profundity' is nonsense;
Such nonsense is often thought wise,
And one who is unlearned
Will often be stumped by it;
Being caught in a web of false reason,
How can one unmask it?
If one has no true knowledge,
One thinks the dissembler wise.[808]

Likewise, the sophists
Make objections to true knowledge,
Issuing questions and answers
That are not rooted in wisdom,
But rather in un-wisdom.

Because human sense and reason
Knows not how to settle these issues,
The questions seem profound.

But in truth, there is no settling them,
For they come not from the sparks
Of holy somethingness,
But from the Void
Of unholy nothingness;
This is Void even of God,
So there is no way to find God there,
And no way to reply or repent.

If one could find God there,
There would be no Void,
Only Infinite God (Ain Sof)

Therefore, there is no way
To answer this unbelief, as it is said,
"One who goes there cannot return."[809]

How can the God-wrestler (Yisra'el)
Face the Void and live in it with God?

The God-wrestler believes
And skips over the sciences,
The lore of the Void,
Because with simple faith,
They know that God
"Fills and surrounds all worlds."[810]

And the Void?
It is actually nothing,
And takes up no space at all;
All it does is separate
Between the Divinity which "fills,"
And the Divinity which "surrounds."

Without the Void,
All would have been One,
But then there would not
Have been any creature,
Or any world in existence;
So the Void is a kind of
Divine wisdom of not-being,
Allowing for separation between
One kind of being and another.

This wisdom of not-being,
The wisdom of the Void,
Cannot be realized!
It is not a something, and yet,
It makes all somethings possible;
Each something is infused with God
And surrounded by God,
But in-between is the Void that is not.

This simply cannot be known by knowing,
But it can be faithed by faithing
Through and beyond it.

This is why the God-wrestlers (Yisra'el)
Are called Hebrews (Ivri'im), 'through-passers,'
And why God is known as
"The God of the Hebrews,"[811]
'The ones who have passed beyond.'

The wisdom of the Void is dangerous,
Because where it is strong,
There is no sense and no knowing.
So, be guarded and seek to escape
The snare and trap of the Void,
For "One who goes there cannot return."

"*You should know that . . .*" The first kind of unbelief originates with what we have called the "outer, external sciences," ḥokhmot ḥitzoni'ot, which is more literally, 'outer wisdoms.' These forms of unbelief, Rebbe Nahman tells us, can be "answered" because they are "still rooted in the order of holiness." You see, 'outer knowing' is based on what comes into us through the senses from the physical world. This in turn becomes the focus of scientific investigation, which obeys the laws of logic and determines 'truth' by hypothesis, experimentation, observation, and analysis. This is contrasted with 'inner knowing,' which is based on what comes to us through intuition from the world of the spirit, which obeys *other* laws. While 'outer knowing,' from a spiritual perspective, may not give us the whole picture by itself, it was nevertheless created by God to be of use to us, and has an intelligible language through which the unbeliever can be answered. The "unbeliever," in this case, being the one who does not accept the validity of 'inner knowing.'

Nevertheless, it should be noted that the "external sciences" are not considered equivalent to "unbelief" by Rebbe Nahman; he only says that there is a form of unbelief "that *originates* with the outer, external sciences." What he is opposed to are errant conclusions drawn from the facts of science; for knowledge of physical causes for phenomena does not prove that there is no God. So unbelief in this case would be an outright denial of the inner world and 'inner knowing,' giving precedence to the language of reason and observable evidence. The potential heresy of this situation is that the unbeliever is prone to a reductive point of view, reducing the fullness of human experience to science and logic alone. In this situation, objectivity becomes a false god, leading one into the heresy of objectivising the world and other human beings. One begins to treat everything and everybody according to their utility, which is an attitude that has proven costly in recent centuries, both in terms human life and in damage to our environment.

In Martin Buber's terminology, this attitude is epitomized by an exclusive *I-It* engagement with life. Of course, we cannot avoid falling into an *I-It* mentality; after all, it is the default mode of human experience and serves many practical purposes. But if we are not open to an *I-Thou* experience of life, embracing the totality of the *other* in all of its uniqueness and freedom, we live a half-life that is damaging to both ourselves and others. Thus, Buber says: "The primary word *I-Thou* can only be spoken with the whole being. The primary word *I-It* can never be spoken with the whole being."[812]

Though many people today contrast science and spirituality, it is not necessary for the spiritual seeker to do so, unless their value-system is wedded to a worldview that cannot accommodate emerging science. This is why the mystical traditions of the various religions are so important, and also why they have often been at odds with the normative religious authorities. For mysticism is focused on the 'experience of religion' and not necessarily in defending 'religious dogma.'

Therefore, the Muslim Sufi can say the *shahada*, the primary creedal statement of Islam, in a sense that is wholly different from the way in which literalist Wahabi Muslims might, fully acknowledging a modern scientific perspective. For instance, when a traditional Muslim translates the part of the *shahada* that says, *la illaha illa 'llah*, 'There is no god but God,' they mean that there is only one God, and that they belong to a monotheistic faith. But the Sufi takes this to a still deeper place that is realistic, and yet deeply personal and experiential at the same time. For these words can also be translated, "There is no God . . . *nevertheless, God.*" That is to say, in the world of the senses, and in the world of science, there is no observable or demonstrable God. And we can concede this. Nevertheless, the testimony of my inner experience keeps whispering, *"God,"* in spite of all 'scientific evidence' to the contrary.[813] This is why Buber liked to use this beautiful little phrase for faith—'holy insecurity.'[814] For it is what we believe by 'inner testimony' without necessarily being able to justify it by anything other than the change it has made in our lives. This fact creates humility in us, both because of the grand paradoxical totality of God, and because we have no evidence on which to 'stand.' Thus, Rebbe Nahman says, "Don't strain to *under-stand* the Void!"

"For at the breaking..." At this point, Rebbe Nahman brings in another of the holy Ari's mythic motifs, that of the "breaking of the vessels" (*sh'virat ha-kelim*). According to the Ari's teaching, God originally created ten vessels to contain the Infinite Light *(Or Ain Sof)*, but these vessels were unable to give and interact with one another, and thus they shattered, scattering sparks of light and shards into the lower worlds, where shells (*kelippot*) formed around the sparks *(nitzotzot)*. The shards of the vessels that fell into the lower worlds became the *prima materia*, or 'original matter' of creation, and embedded within this are the sparks of the Infinite Light.

Now, Rebbe Nahman tells us that the "external sciences" are likewise formed of this *prima materia*, which implies that they too contain sparks of Divinity.

"So you see, even from holiness..." This idea that holiness should have "a kind of dross, or slough" is a radical statement. You aren't likely to find anything like it in ḤaBaD Hasidism. But this is part of what makes Rebbe Nahman so special; he is deeply engaged with the kind of root-metaphors that can communicate the most holy ideas in the most impactful ways.

"When this slough is used..." Here Rebbe Nahman mentions 'magic' or 'sorcery.' However, you will have noticed that we have taken advantage of the homophonic relationship between the word 'source' and 'sorcery' to bring out another dimension of this teaching. For as we are talking about the abuse of the "external sciences," it is important to think of the idea of 'source code,' and its misuse and abuse by some scientists. Are we being responsible with genetic manipulation? And while splitting the atom may have been an achievement, Hiroshima and Nagasaki were horrific beyond reckoning. Therefore, we must ask ourselves in all seriousness, Are we mature enough to handle the 'source-code'? Or are we only 'twisting the world' with it?

"For one who seeks God..." Again, Rebbe Nahman tells us that this kind of unbelief can be answered, and because it can be answered, there is a way out of it for those who become trapped in its limits and limitations. "For," he says, "as long as there is rhyme and reason, there is holiness in the *form* of the sparks." That is to say, as long as the language is intelligible and based in sound reasoning, God's own order is still represented there, and you can use this language to begin to return to the Source.

Now I want to take just a moment to look at the word that is being translated as "unbeliever" here. For this word has an interesting history, and I think the reader of this passage may benefit from knowing the original source. The word in the original text is *epikoros*, which is a word used throughout Jewish texts for a heretic. However, this is not actually a Hebrew word, but a term borrowed from Greek philosophy—*epikouros*, an epicure, or Epicurean. In many ways, the *epikoros* to which Rebbe Nahman is referring here has more to do with the Epicurean of Greek philosophy than the out-and-out heretic we usually associate with this concept.

This Epicurean is not the connoisseur of fine food and drink we tend to think of today, nor the hedonist of popular misunderstanding; but a person who follows the teachings of Epicurus (341-270 B.C.E.), who founded this school of philosophy in Athens around 306 B.C.E. Epicurus did indeed propose that pleasure is the path to happiness, but contrary to popular belief, he also urged his students to carefully discriminate between pleasures, rejecting those which were only momentary passions leading to later troubles and pain. He was actually an advocate of moderation in all things, and considered the greatest pleasures to be the delights of the mind, finding the highest good to be an inner calm and freedom from fear. But in his quest to rid people of the continual fears that plagued their lives, he also urged them to reject their superstitious fear of the gods and death; indeed to leave off all thought of the gods and metaphysical speculation.[815] In this, he was very much like the Jewish Enlightenment *(haskalah)* philosophers of Rebbe Nahman's time, who rejected 'superstitious' Judaism in favor of an 'enlightened' rationalism. Given his later dealings with these men, and what looks like a personal mission to save them, this reading regarding science, rationalism, and Epicureanism seems somewhat justified.

So even if we dispense with the caricatured Epicurus *(epikoros)*, we are still left with a philosophy that is difficult to marry with traditional Jewish belief. As a philosopher, Epicurus could quite reasonably say: "I don't know about the afterlife. Maybe when you're dead you're dead." But for the Jew, this idea is contrary to "All Yisra'el has a place in the World to Come."[816]

"But there is another kind of unbelief..." Here, Rebbe Nahman is talking about sophists, hypocrites, and advocates of 'scientism,' who use learning to cover the truth, and who cover their own ignorance with learned subterfuge. These kinds of people are often caught up in their own subterfuge and lead the ignorant astray.

"*Likewise, the sophists . . .*" The weak-minded and spiritually immature cannot usually hold paradox, and often make the paradox into a contradiction. They even turn answers into questions! Rabbi Akiva says, "All is foreseen, and freedom is given."[817] This is an answer, and also a paradox; but a sophist of the Void turns it into a question again, "If all is foreseen, how can we be free?" The paradox twisted into a question is the foolishness of the Void.

"*But in truth, there is no settling them . . .*" The lie and the contradiction come from the place of "unholy nothingness," which is also known as "the concealment of the concealment," where the seeming absence of God is at its nadir, and all is confusion, dogged un-logic, and irrationalism. The epitome of this place is seen in the case of extreme neurosis, where a person cannot escape from the 'loop' of their own illusion.

"*So, there is no way . . .*" This is a bit of holy hyperbole to say, "Just don't go there; don't even approach this place." For, as Rebbe Nahman has already said in this chapter: "There are places so low as to seem utterly remote from God, but you must know that the supreme life-force is invested and concealed even in these places . . . even one who has fallen so low, into such an infernal place, can still *turn* and find the One whose name is blessed concealed there, in the very garments of Hell." However, one cannot come out of this place without help, as Rebbe Nahman will later show.

"*The God-wrestler believes . . .*" Again, this is to say that there is a knowledge beyond the knowledge of the outer sciences, the testimony of the spirit, which shows itself as holy insecurity, or faith, as we have discussed earlier.

"*And the Void?*" The Void, Rebbe Nahman tells us, is merely a concealing screen between us and God. Imagine a glass bottle floating just below the surface of the ocean. It is filled with water from the ocean, and yet also surrounded by the water of the ocean. Now imagine that the glass of this bottle is getting thinner, and thinner, and thinner, until the bottle is just a glass membrane between the water inside and the water outside. Similarly, the Void is the separation "between the Divinity which 'fills' *(m'malleh kol almin)*, and the Divinity which 'surrounds' *(sovev kol almin)*."

"This is why the God-wrestlers (Yisra'el)..." This passage can be understood in two senses, based on the meaning of the word, *Ivri'im*. First, as Rebbe Nahman said earlier, "The God-wrestler believes and skips over the sciences, the lore of the Void, because with simple faith, they know that God 'Fills and surrounds all worlds.'" That is to say, the Hebrews *(Ivri'im)* 'pass-over' the difficulties presented by the external sciences with their pure and simple faith. But they also 'pass-through' the pairs of opposites, transcending them in their faith, holding the paradox in holy insecurity.

"The wisdom of the Void is dangerous . . ." Rebbe Nahman goes back and forth between positive and negative valences of the Void, never really taking the pressure off the paradox. He keeps it in your face all of the time, until finally, you surrender to it. At this point, he is continuing to emphasize the extreme danger of "the concealment of the concealment," where God is so hidden that it is possible to lose oneself in utter confusion. He wants to warn his Hasidim to avoid this place at all costs.

III

Know this . . .
There is one tzaddik,
A 'Moshe,' who must
Study the Void-thoughts,
Although there is
No settling these issues;
By entering the Void,
He raises the lost souls
Who have become
Entangled in the Void's web,
Souls that want to
Voice their objection
Amidst the mass of
The Void's unreason;
But no voice can
Carry in that emptiness,
Where there are no words;
For in the Void,
There is only silence.

> *All creation comes*
> *From the word...*
> *"By the word of God*
> *Heaven was made,*
> *By the breath of the mouth,*
> *All their hosts"*[818] ...
> *For wisdom and sense*
> *Inheres in the words.*
>
> *All speech is bordered*
> *By the five limits of the mouth;*[819]
> *Thus, all creation is limited*
> *Within five dimensions...*[820]
> *"In wisdom have You*
> *Made them all."*[821]
>
> *The Void has no limits,*
> *No echo—burning questions*
> *Are not answered there;*
> *Those who have seen*
> *The martyrs of Torah,*
> *Want to know, "Why?"*
> *And are answered with "Silence—*
> *Thus is the decree of Thought!"*[822]
> *Such thought is not given to words,*
> *Such thought is void of words.*
>
> *But this tzaddik who is like Moshe*
> *Is tongue-tied and used to thought*
> *That cannot be worded,*
> *And must give thought to the Void*
> *In order to save the souls who are lost.*

"Know this . . ." Rebbe Nahman is himself this "Moshe" who is able to "study the Void-thoughts" in safety. Like Moshe, he is able to cross over into the 'Egypt' of the Void and bring the slaves from its midst. He is able to enter the cloud of darkness which others are not allowed to approach and to find God there. This is the solution to the seeming contradiction of Rebbe Nahman's earlier words, when he says: "Therefore, there is no way to answer this unbelief, as it is said, 'One who goes there cannot return.'" That is to say, "One who goes there cannot return" without help from a *tzaddik*. For the *tzaddik* can enter into the confusion of the Void, can enter into its paradox in safety, and bring the one who has become entangled in its web out of the confusion. This teaching is perhaps nowhere better illustrated than in Rebbe Nahman's parable of "The Turkey Prince" (Chapter 9).

"*The Void has no limits...*" This passage takes up the fate of Rabbi Akiva, who was martyred by the Romans. For when Moses was shown the future and saw that this *tzaddik* would die such a horrible death, he asked, "Why?" and was answered with silence.[823] Death is an insoluable in our world. There are reasons, there are explanations, and even meaning, but none of it is ever satisfying. This belongs to the Void.

"*But this* tzaddik *who is like Moshe...*" Moses understood the ineffability of the Absolute and knew that it could not be expressed in words. This was a part of his great humility, knowing the paradox of his own being. This is part of how he could "save the souls who are lost." For Moses was the humblest of men, knowing his full greatness as well as his lowest, most vile self. Others would lose their minds in this knowledge; it is difficult to understand the full debasement and glory of being a human being in the presence of God. One who hides the full truth of *yes* and *no*, of *is* and *is-not* cannot be in the Void without bursting to pieces. When speaking, only one side can be 'worded' while the other side clamors to be heard. But Moses could contain both *yes* and *no*, *noble* and *base*, in one wordless thought.

For Moses, all of the illusions were gone. Most of us, in order to operate and not to be totally depressed, have to have some illusions about ourselves, some veil between our ordinary consciousness and the total depravity that is somewhere a potential within us. On the other hand, if we didn't have the other side of it, to know the total exultation of our souls, we wouldn't make it either. To be able to keep both of these things at the same time is the genius of Moses. Thus, the Hasidim say, 'On the one hand, we must know that we are but dust and ashes; on the other hand, we must also know that for us was the world created.'

This is the secret of Moses' humility, that he knew both the humiliation of his own base desires and the exultation of his own divine inheritance. Rebbe Nahman said, "One has not attained true humility unless he is on such a high level that he himself can say that he is modest." And Reb Nosson added, "This was the level of Moses, who could write about himself (Num.

12:2), 'And the man Moses was very humble, more so than any other man.'"[824] Likewise, he also wrote of Rebbe Nahman: "The Rebbe took pride in his great modesty. This may seem like a contradiction, but he was actually humble to the ultimate degree."[825] A story of the Lubliner to illustrate . . .

> Reb Ya'akov Yitzhak Horowitz, the *Hozeh* of Lublin was often badgered by the *mitnaged* rabbinic authority known as the *Eiserner Kop*, the 'iron head,' who was also a Horowitz. The two of them were like the right and left hemispheres of the brain. The *Hozeh* was a 'seer,' a visionary, while the *Eiserner Kop* was all intellect, which was why he was called the *Eiserner Kop*, for his mind was like a steel trap. So the two always argued.
>
> Once, the *Eiserner Kop* said to the *Hozeh*: "Why don't you tell your Hasidim that you are not a Rebbe? I know that you are not a Rebbe, and you know that you are not a Rebbe; so what are you fooling all these people for?"
>
> So the *Hozeh* says, "You're right; I'll tell them all next *Shabbat*."
>
> The next *Shabbat* he did as he said he would, telling all of his Hasidim: "I want you to know, I'm not really a Rebbe. I'm not worthy of being considered a Rebbe."
>
> But the next week, even more people came to see him. So he says to the *Eiserner Kop*, "You see, I did exactly as you told me to and it didn't help."
>
> On another occasion, the *Eiserner Kop* chided him about his students, asking, "So tell me, do you think that your disciples are humble?"
>
> The *Hozeh* answered, "Yes—would you like to see?"
>
> So he calls Reb Shlomo of Lutzk, his attendant, and says, "Would you please bring Reb Shalom of Belz to see me?"
>
> After a minute, Reb Shalom Belzer comes in and the *Hozeh* asks him, "Tell me, Reb Shalom, is it true that you are as humble as Moshe?"
>
> Reb Shalom answered quietly, "Yes," and walked out of the room.[826]

In the moment of transparency to God, overwhelmed by God's infinity, what else is there to say? So, knowing the true depths of the Void in themselves before the infinity of God, the *tzaddikim*—Moses, Reb Shalom Belzer, and Rebbe Nahman—are capable of bringing souls out of the Void.

While so much of Hasidism wants to elevate the *tzaddikim* above the level of human beings, Bratzlav Hasidism is always in touch with the humanity of the *tzaddik*, as this wonderful statement for Reb Nosson makes clear:

> Before I came close to our master, of blessed memory, I could not picture in my mind how it was that Moses our Teacher was a human being like others. But once I became close to our master and had seen how human he remained despite his greatness, I was able to understand how it was that Moses, too, was still a human being.[827]

IV

How is the Void made?
By strife . . .
One tzaddik says this
And the other that,
And between there is
Strained a void;
Difference serves the purpose
Of making the Void . . . void.

Thus, there is space
For a whole world
To settle between them;
In this sense, the tzaddikim
Help the Creator to create;
Of this, tzaddikim must not
Talk over much;
Words are enlightening,
And too many words
Create too much light;
This causes a 'breaking,'
Leaving more shells and shards,
More evil and dross;
All talk must be limited to
The limit of the Worlds.

Thus it is said,
"All my days
I grew among the wise
And found nothing
Better than silence;
One who multiplies words
Multiplies sin and pollution."[828]
The furies of the world
Are made from too much talk.

"*How is the Void made? By strife...*" This is an unusual statement. So many people want to rush to harmony, but Rebbe Nahman is willing to endure the opposites. He knows that if you get to a premature agreement, it is probably too weak to survive. This is what we have so much of today. With the best of intentions, many people will look at our religious diversity and say, "It's all one!" and they don't know why. Not only don't they know why, but it's not real, because it's just an 'answer.' There is not a deep knowing beneath it. There is not embodied knowledge of the one-ness.

V

A tzaddik is a singer,
And if the tzaddik is a 'Moshe,'
Souls lost in the Void
Can be lifted up
With that Moshe-song!

Every science
Has its own song;
Every science
Issues from a melody;
Even the un-wisdom of the Void
Has a melody of its own.

Thus, the Sages asked—
"What was wrong
With the heretic?"
They answered themselves—
"Greek songs never
Ceased from his lips;
All day he hummed
From the songbook
Of the Greeks."[829]

You see, the song and the heresy
Each depend on the other—
The wisdom and its tune,
The science and its scale.

For heresies fall in book-loads
From the one who sings
The tune of heresy.

Every wisdom draws
From its own melody;
Even the higher ones
Draw from melodies higher up,
Up even to the point
Of the first emanation (atzilut),
Beyond which there is nothing
But the Infinite Light (Or Ain Sof)
Surrounding the Void,
Which contains the something.[830]

In the beyond of the Void,
There, too, is wisdom,
But it is Infinite Wisdom
And only the Infinite One (Ain Sof)
May attain to it;
God's wisdom cannot be
Reached at all:
There is nothing there,
Save faith—
To faith in God,
The blessed and holy One—
That God's Light embraces the All
Endlessly surrounding all worlds!

And faith, she is also a song
With a tune unique to her faithing.

Even those who worship
The stars and constellations,
Mistaking symbols for reality,
Have a special tune for each star,
For each sign of the Zodiac,
To which they sing and by which they
Celebrate in their houses of prayer.

Conversely, in the true
Worship of holiness,
Each faith has a special
Tune and song,
Attuned to the song
Of faith, most high,
The faith transcending
All wisdoms,
That faith in the
Self of the Endless Light (Or Ain Sof),
Bathing all worlds in its radiance,
Which also has a song and a tune,
Beyond any other belonging
To other wisdoms and creeds;
Yet they all derive a note,
A phrase, a pattern and inspiration
From that tune, most high,
Which passes all understanding.[831]

And when the future becomes the now,
All nations will have mouths of purity,
Calling with the Name Y-H-V-H,
All faithing in the One, fulfilling the words—
"Sing from the heart-springs of faith,"
The tune most sublime.

Now, only a tzaddik like Moshe
Merits to know this tune,
The song of silence—"Be still!"[832]
Thus, the thought arose
That was beyond words and expression.

> *And this is why it is said,*
> *"Then will Moshe sing,"*[833]
> *For that song has not yet been sung,*
> *For it is a dead-raising song of silence.*
>
> *And through this tzaddik's niggun—*
> *When that tongue-tied Moshe sings—*
> *All the lost souls will rise from the abyss*
> *To find their way out of the Void;*
> *All tunes are re-absorbed*
> *In the song of silence,*
> *Where all heresies are*
> *Integrated and dissolved,*
> *Both tune and word,*
> *In the great song of thought.*

"*A tzaddik is a singer...*" The *tzaddik* is a singer and a *niggun* (melody) maker, a creator of holy atmosphere, attuning and harmonizing Hasidim. After all, what does a *niggun* do? If you are going to follow me in a melody, you have to attune to my voice. When you attune to my voice, you can also attune to something more than my voice. In the Psalms, it says, "From my depths I call You forth, *Yah*; hear what is *in* my voice!" (Ps. 130:1)[834] If you really listen to what is in my voice, you can attune to its *kavanah*, its intentionality. Thus, when the *tzaddik* sings a *niggun*, it isn't merely for the purpose of making music, but it is for the purpose of 'tuning' the Hasidim to the right 'note,' as it were.

"*Every science has its own song...*" If the *tzaddik* can discern the original melody from which a particular science issues, then it can be used to bring someone back to God who has become lost in that science.

"*Thus, the Sages asked—*" The "heretic" in this passage refers to Elisha ben Abuya, called *Aḥer*, 'the other one,' one the four sages who entered the Pardes, the mystical 'orchard' in the well-known story from the Talmud. Of them it is said:

> Ben Azzai gazed and died. Concerning him, the scriptures say, "Precious in the eyes of God is the death of the faithful."[835] Ben Zoma gazed and was damaged. Concerning him, the scriptures say, "If you find honey, eat only what you need, lest, surfeiting yourself, you throw it up."[836] Aḥer cut his roots. Rabbi Akiva entered and left in peace.[837]

"Aḥer cut his roots," which is to say, he became a heretic. About him it was said, "A Voice came from Heaven, saying, 'Return all you wayward children, *except the Other One.*'"[838]

I once translated a story by Moshe Shamir about the horse Aḥer rode on *Shabbat* while his former disciple, Rabbi Meir walked beside him, continuing to learn from him. Now, sitting on the horse was a breach of *Shabbat*, so people asked Rabbi Meir, "How can you continue to learn from him?" Rabbi Meir replied, "I eat the fruit and throw away the rind."

Now, as they are walking, Aḥer says to Rabbi Meir, "Return Meir, for I calculate by the steps of the horse that we have reached the boundaries of *Shabbat*." But Rabbi Meir turned to him and replied, "You too, Elisha, *return.*"[839]

Of him it is said, "Greek songs never ceased from his lips; all day he hummed from the songbook of the Greeks."[840] So what was wrong with the Greeks? In Torah we learn that Noah had three sons. One was named Shem, the other Ham, and the last, Japheth (Yeffet). Of the latter, it says, *Yaft Elohim le'Yeffet, v'yishkon b'ohalei Shem*, "May God enlarge Japheth, and let him dwell in the tents of Shem." (Gen. 9:27) Now, since Japheth is seen as the progenitor of the Greeks, this sentence is often interpreted to mean, "God made Japheth beautiful," punning on the word *yaft* from *yafeh*. From this we get the idea that the Greeks have beauty and are very concerned with aesthetics, while Jews are less so because of the left leg that Jacob injured in wrestling with the angel, the leg which represents the quality of *hod*, elegance and aesthetics.

Now, Hanukkah—the holiday celebrating the miracle of the oil and the victory over the Greek armies—is the holiday of *hod*. For rabbis in Hanukkah sermons speak of "the beauty of holiness, and the holiness of beauty." The Greeks, they said, celebrated the holiness of beauty, while the Jews celebrated the beauty of holiness. This gives us a clue as to what is wrong here. For by singing from the songbooks of the Greeks, Aḥer got into the holiness of beauty, i.e., philosophy for its own sake, and departed from the beauty of holiness. You see, the trouble is that aesthetics can get us into a radical self-absorption, such as we find when Nero fiddles while Rome is burning.[841]

"*Even those who worship the stars and constellations . . .*" In Jewish and Islamic terms, these people are called, *oved kokhavim u'mazzalot* and *abd al kabkab wa-minzal* respectively, those who serve the stars and constellations thinking that they have a power of their own. So when a Muslim says, *Allah hu akbar*, it means, 'God is greater' than these. In fact, they are all God's servants. One of the reasons the Sun is called *shemesh* in Hebrew is because it is the *shamesh* or 'servant' of God.

And yet, there is still a sense that there is something to astrology, that there are certain tendencies that come around, and which can be helpful in discerning a course of action. Indeed, Rabbi Avraham ibn Ezra, the great poet and Torah commentator wrote an entire treatise on astrology. So what Rebbe Nahman and many others in the tradition are saying is that the stars are servants of God; they do have a power, but it is under the dominion of God.[842]

"Conversely, in the true worship of holiness . . ." In this wonderful passage, Rebbe Nahman hints that there is a place of deep ecumenism where all religions meet in their phenomenological structures, and still deeper in the "Self of the Endless Light." When he says, "Each faith has a tune and song," I can imagine him remembering a melody or song that the young Turk he met in the Holy Land may have shared with him. Certainly in Istanbul he heard the beautiful call to prayer of the *muezzin*, and in the Ukraine, the chanting of the Latin Mass.

"And when the future becomes the now . . ." If you dig a little deeper, you will see that there is purity among all peoples, and that all of them call-out in the name of God. In the Messianic era, there will be reconciliation, and we will see how the faiths are related in the original music of creation, "the tune most sublime."

"And through this tzaddik's niggun—*"* "Where all heresies are integrated and dissolved." This is like saying, heresies are just confusions, mix-ups, but can be unconfused and unmixed, reordered and integrated. Or, another way to think about it is that many heresies are minority truths that people have trouble integrating. Who are the people who have the greatest trouble integrating them? The people who are in power in a given religion. So when a conservative Catholic priest says, *Nula salus extra ecclesiam*, "No salvation outside of the Church," the Dalai Lama is automatically labeled a heretic. But that is much easier to do when you haven't met the Dalai Lama, when you haven't been confronted with his life of utter piety and the great compassion he shows for everyone he meets.

Then there are the people at the edge of things, the people who Gershom Scholem talked about as the 'un-housebroken' mystics. These are the 'heretics' who bear witness to divine truths that are outside of the safe boundaries of ordinary believers, especially as defined by the people in power.

VI

And this is why God
Says to Moshe,
"Come to Pharaoh"—
The obstacle to freedom,
The Void-weaver—
"For I have made his heart
Heavy and hard."[843]
For in the Void,
Only the hard questions,
And the contradictions remain...
Thus, Moshe comes to the Void
Where no one else may come,
For it is void of God, voided by God,
"So that I might set forth
My wonders in its midst."[844]
The wondrous creation
Which needs a Void to hold it,
"In order that you may tell it
In the hearing of every
Child and grandchild."

For, in the creation,
In the some-thing,
You can tell and talk,
For there is a multiplicity
Of names and forms,
Letters and phrases,
Notes and songs,
All for Mercy's sake.

For all Mercy was condensed
So that the world could contain it:
Mercy is the world's possibility.

And the child and grandchild
Are Mercy's special objects,
And can be told some-thing for pity's sake,
"That which I mocked-up in Egypt"[845]—

For it is all a game, a monkey-shine, a circus
Made from the junk of broken vessels,
Still iridescent with the residue of holiness,
So that even there, in that place,
"You may know that I am God."[846]

So that even in the middle of the joke,
In the middle of the shards,
In the middle of the heresy,
The partial and broken truth,
Even there you can know God,
The blessed and holy One!

"Know how to answer the unbeliever"
With that portion of truth most needed
To ply them and mend their partial truth.

"Moshe came to Pharaoh,"[847]
The Void, and said, "Tomorrow
I bring the Arbeh (the swarms)
Of locusts into your midst."[848]
For tomorrow is the time of receiving reward.

What is the reward all about?
To perceive great perception,
To have cosmic insight, today un-attainable.

And then we will know
How the Void was like the locust,
Its cloak and being one,
All veils and garments;
But God outer, inner God,
Word and wordless God,
End and endless God,
Tune and singer God,
Most high and abyssal God,
Void God, Fullness God,
I-God, You-God, God-God!
Be-it-so — Amen.[849]

"And this is why God says to Moshe, 'Come to Pharaoh'—" Here we come back to the quote, *Bo el paroh,* "Come to Pharaoh" which seems to have set this whole teaching in motion. Why does it say, "Come to Pharaoh?" Pharaoh refers to a kind of revelation, an uncovering of things, as if to say, "You can't see the abyss ... but *pssss,* come look at the abyss!" Rebbe Nahman is hinting that the act of concealing is actually a 'revelation' that something lies hidden beneath, and he has been about pulling back the veil.[850]

"Know how to answer to the unbeliever ..." V'da'a mah shetashiv l'epikoros. Da'a, 'know,' has the sense of intimate knowledge, as in "And Adam *knew* eve his wife." (Gen. 4:1)[851] So when you are dealing with someone who is an unbeliever, don't just talk abstractly; speak from experience, from your first-hand knowing.

But Rebbe Nahman also says that sometimes you have to *use* a partial truth to get to the truth of truth. This is akin to what is called in Buddhist *Madhyamika* philosophy, 'using a thorn to remove a thorn.' Therefore, you have to *ply* the unbeliever with their own language to lead them to a new, more spiritual language.

"And then we will know ..." With this reference, Rebbe Nahman is saying that the locust is one with its outer skin, just as God's garment is still one with God. If we look at this in terms of current science, we are beginning to realize that there is an aggregate intelligence to the swarm of locusts and bees, etc. We also see this with heart-tissue that begins to beat together, and when women's cycles synchronize in the same household. There is something more to the totality than an assemblage of individual parts; there is a group-mind that manifests.

9

Beggars' Wisdom:
The Redemptive Imagination
and Sacrifice of Rebbe Nahman

SHORTLY BEFORE ROSH HASHANAH IN 1806, Rebbe Nahman declared to his Hasidim, "Now I'm going to start telling you stories."[852] According to Reb Nosson, he was disappointed that his discourses weren't having the effect he would have hoped. Indeed, he tells us, "All his life, he made great efforts to bring us closer to God, but when this didn't work, he began to tell us stories."[853] While it's not likely that the discourses weren't having *any* effect, it is possible that they were not the best form of teaching for all of his Hasidim. After all, not everyone was as learned as Reb Nosson or Reb Shimon, nor was it even a matter of intellect, but of 'learning styles.' This was one of Rebbe Nahman's great insights—that there were some who were more attuned to learning through stories;[854] for stories are a universal mode of teaching, allowing for one's own insights ('a-ha!' moments) at an intuitive level.

It is also as a storyteller that Rebbe Nahman first became known to the larger world, and was recognized as a creative genius on a world scale. Martin Buber's *The Tales of Rabbi Nachman*, which first appeared in German in 1906, had a lot to do with this. However, there are others in the non-Jewish world who know Rebbe Nahman's name through quite another source—the Greek poet, novelist, and philosopher, Nikos Kazantzakis. It is likely that Kazantzakis' first introduction to Rebbe Nahman came through reading Buber, but it is obvious from his writings that he must have had another source as well. This was likely a Jewish poet named Rachel Mintz (Rahel Minc), whom he had met in Vienna in 1922 on Yom Kippur, and who first introduced him to the Jewish tradition and its literature.[855]

Very quickly, Rebbe Nahman the storyteller became an important mentor to the young novelist, who had not yet written his greatest works. In his memoir, *Report to Greco,* he tells us: "I had been struggling for a lifetime to stretch my mind until it creaked at the breaking point in order to bring forth a great idea able to give a new meaning to life, a new meaning to death, and comfort to men." He then goes on to tell a story of Rabbi Nahman, "a rabbi of ancient times," who had taught him to know the hour when he was to take up his pen and write.[856] The story went something like this . . .

> Once, the disciples of Rabbi Nahman came to him and said, "Why can't you teach us like Rabbi Tzaddik?[857] When Rabbi Tzaddik teaches, he gives you the whole idea. It has a beginning, a middle, and an end; it is all very clear. But you teach us like an old grandmother telling stories."[858]
>
> Rabbi Nahman was silent for a little while. Then he smiled and said, "Maybe I can explain it to you with a story? Once, the thistle came to the rose and said 'You've got thorns, I've got thorns—so how come you make roses and I make thistles?' The rose thought about this for a while and said, 'It's simple: from the moment I emerged from the seed, putting my roots into the earth and pushing my head through its crust, stretching my leaves toward the Sun to receive sustenance, I have only one thought in mind . . . *the Rose, the Rose, the Rose.* No matter what happens to me, no mater what the weather, I have only one thought in mind . . . *the Rose, the Rose, the Rose.*' "
>
> His disciples said, "We don't understand."
>
> Rabbi Nahman laughed: "And do you think I understand? Perhaps what I mean is this: when I get an idea, I think hard about that idea, I walk with that idea, I sleep with that idea, I love that idea. Finally, a time comes when I know I must share that idea, and when I open my mouth to speak, out comes a story!"[859]

Thus, over the last few years of his life, stories become a primary mode of teaching for Rebbe Nahman. He even begins to talk more about their power in his discourses. The following passages drawn from his *Likkutei MaHaRaN* are a good example of this new emphasis on the importance of stories:

WHERE IS THE SHEKHINAH *(Divine Presence) right now? Listen to the talk and tales of women. It says in the* Megillah, *"Mordecai walked past the women's quarters at court to know the peace (shalom) of Esther."*[860] *Now, Esther is the* Shekhinah, *and Mordecai realized that if you want to know where the* Shekhinah's *peace is, you must listen to the talk and tales of women.*[861]

LIKEWISE, KNOW THIS! *The stories of the* tzaddikim *and the tales of what happened to them are very important. For a person's thoughts are purified when these stories are told by one who can distinguish between light and darkness. This is critical, because opposing each tale of a tzaddik are parallel tales of the corrupted. While* tzaddikim *affect their wondrous deeds by prayer, the corrupted do so by manipulation and power from the side of darkness. Therefore, it is crucial to know the difference between light and darkness.*

But what if one cannot discriminate between them? Then let them have faith in the difference between light and darkness. The faith needed to tell a tale rightly has to be wholesome and pure. So much so, that in that faith one experiences the tale as if it was seen with one's very own eyes!

The discerner of light and darkness can tell these tales and bring about the purification of thoughts. Such a one is saved from trouble, and stumbles not into the dark of contracted awareness. For the stories of the tzaddikim *are taken from a palace of expanded awareness, from the grand architectonic of creation, and as such, they run counter to the narrow and contracted mind that is the source of all trouble.*

My Rebbe used to emphasize the need to utilize the *hush ha-tziyur,* the 'imaginative faculty,' which Rebbe Nahman calls the holy *m'dammeh,* the 'comparer.' Rebbe Nahman warns that the *m'dammeh* of the person whose mind has not yet been cleared of the "troubling yeast" is unreliable. The imaginative faculty depends greatly on the images that are stored in the mind. One who has images that have been nurtured by meditation and prayer will find that the *m'dammeh* will create a matrix of holiness and heavenly beauty, whereas one whose images have been polluted by evil and "troubling yeast" will find that the *m'dammeh* will create associations of selfish sensuality, distracting them from being in the presence of God.

ONE MUST ALSO KNOW *how to tell a story; for each story is a crystallization and microcosmic representation of a greater reality. So the teller must take hold of the words of the tale and enter into the thought beyond them. The tzaddik whose story is being told is on a subtler plane, and thus, what is word-told must become vision, seen in the thought of the teller who contacts the mind of the tzaddik. To do this, one rises through the Worlds and enters the Universe of Thought (beri'ah).*

Now, Thought is very subtle. One who wishes to enter the Thought-World must be silent, for even the most worthy thinking spoils the Thought. It is so easy to be distracted by intruding and confusing thinking, so one needs a clear and pure Thought—the stories themselves will help with this.

*Finally, to know the difference between light and darkness, one must free oneself from the slavery of comfort and fear, and enter into the reign of Divine Providence; for this is what all the tales of the tzaddikim are about—living by Providence.*⁸⁶²

In Genesis 1:4, we read, "To separate between light and darkness."⁸⁶³ About this, the *Midrash* says, " 'Light' refers to the *ma'asim* of the *tzaddikim*, while 'darkness' refers to the *ma'asim* of the wicked."⁸⁶⁴ Now, the word *ma'asim* can mean either 'deeds' or 'stories,' for when we are speaking of deeds, we are also reporting about an event and thus telling a story.

So this is where Rebbe Nahman takes off from; but he goes much further, saying, "The stories of the *tzaddikim*, and the tales of what happened to them . . . bring about the purification of thoughts." Thus, they are an important part of Hasidic life and living. They should be listened to, learned, and retold as a spiritual practice, purifying one's thoughts and the thoughts of others. For Bratzlaver Hasidim, this applies both to the stories of Rebbe Nahman's life (such as those of his mysterious journey to Kamenitz and of his pilgrimage to *Eretz Yisra'el*) as well the stories and parables he told himself, the most important of which may be the "Tale of the Seven Beggars."

Beggars' Wisdom

If you look at the *Sippurei Ma'asiot*, which contains all of Rebbe Nahman's stories and parables, you will see that each page has Hebrew on top and Yiddish on the bottom. Because it is on the bottom, some people think the Yiddish is a translation of the Hebrew, but this is not so. For in the second introduction of the *Sippurei Ma'asiot*, we are told that Rebbe Nahman told these tales in the "Yiddish spoken in our land," and only later did Reb Nosson translate them into Hebrew.⁸⁶⁵

Thus, when I originally translated the full "Tale of the Seven Beggars" many years ago, I chose to translate it from the Yiddish, rather than the simplified Hebrew.[866] For the language of the story is far richer and more alive in the Yiddish original, as if it were just out of the Rebbe's mouth. You have to remember that the Hebrew used in the *beit midrash* of the time was a language of comparatively few words, while Yiddish was the language of life, used for every conceivable purpose. If we didn't have any Yiddish for a concept, we simply borrowed words from Russian or Polish to make a quilt of language that covered the topic.

So as I translated these tales into English, I tried to keep as much of the folksy flavor of the Yiddish as I could, sometimes using highly idiomatic English to preserve the spirit of the story when the letter would not serve the same purpose. This is perhaps most true in the introduction to the "Tale of the Seven Beggars," which begins like this . . .

So you think you know about joy? *Oy! Once they really knew how to rejoice! Let me tell you how they used to do joy in days past . . .*

Once, there was a king *who had an only son; and so great was his love for him, that he wished to make his son king, even in the midst of his own life and reign. All because he wanted to be around to enjoy his only son's kingship!*

So the king made a banquet. And let me tell you, when the king wants to be festive and have a good time, everyone enjoys themselves! How much more then was their joy in witnessing the king's own joy as he acknowledged his only son's kingship, giving him the keys to the kingdom! Oy! What a joy this was!

Princes and princesses came, governors and officials—all the 'bigshots' were there; they all came to have a blast. And the rest of the people? They too were glad, both for the king and for themselves; because for the king, it is an honor—an honor that very few kings really appreciate—to make their own child king while they are yet living.

Oy! It was some party! All kinds of bands and music, shows and spectacles, and everyone was getting high in their joy. And when the king was good and high, he said this to his son . . .

"My son, I see in the stars *that someday you'll no longer be king. This is just how it'll have to be. But I want you to promise me that you won't be sad when you're no longer king. Even then, be glad! And if you'll be glad, then so will I; and even more so, because I'll know you have sense. But even if you are sad, I'll still be glad; because if you are sad, then you are not made of the stuff kings are made of, and then I'll be glad that you're no longer king."*

So this is the opening of the story in which Rebbe Nahman introduces two of his most important themes: the divine inheritance we are given by God, *which God wants the pleasure of witnessing*; and the problem of forgetting that divine inheritance, becoming cut off from God in our awareness and falling into sadness and depression.

So the king's son became king in his place. And he ruled well and wisely, prizing reason greatly, making the wise rich, and honoring them according to their own wishes. Soon, they became so immersed in reasoning that they forgot all about warfare; everyone was rational, and no one was cunning at all.

But it turned out that all that reasoning—all the time—wasn't so good. It had made them all so rational that they had abandoned their faith in God, so that now, they only trusted their own minds. And since reason is capable of so much un-reason, those who reasoned best found themselves lost the most. Indeed, even the king and his lords and ladies had lost themselves in doubt and ambivalence. However, the simple folk couldn't match the reason of the intellectuals, so they were able to keep their faith in God.

Now, the king's son was really a good person, and he often asked himself: "Where am I in this world?" Then he sighed, fasted and even prayed; but as soon as he began to use his reason, he was lost again . . . Lost, poor man, in his speculations. Oy! There is no end to speculations! You can say, "What if?" till Doom's Day. And 'What if?' isn't a 'What?' a 'How?' or even a 'Why?' There's no 'Because' with which you can answer a 'What if?' So everyone got lost.

Now, this should sound at least a little familiar after reading the "Torah of the Void" in Chapter 8. In fact, there is a sense in which "The Torah of the Void" might be read as a commentary on the the "Tale of the Seven Beggars," and vice versa. For this teaching was given shortly before Rebbe Nahman announced that he would start telling stories, believing that his Torah was not being understood.

Nevertheless, I would suggest that you wait until you have read the entire "Tale of the Seven Beggars" before going back to look at "Torah of the Void." It's just not the kind of story you want to interrupt with too much commentary. There is something about its mythopoeic form that resists conventional explanation and interpretation. It's as if it wants to be understood from within by intuition, imagined and felt in the body first. So allow it to enter into your consciousness in this way, absorbing it through your skin, as it were, before you turn to any commentary for help in understanding it. Trust your intuition.

It is for this very reason that we will be keeping our comments to a minimum, and—because this is primarily a book of commentary—we will only be giving a few selections of the larger story in this chapter. Nevertheless, we trust that you will still get a strong sense of the whole, and will go on to read the rest of the story in one of the many excellent translations that are available.[867]

ONE DAY, BIG TROUBLE *came to the kingdom, and everyone had to run for their lives. As they ran, a little boy and a little girl of the same age got separated in the forest and were lost. But God be praised, they found each other, and being babes in the wood, they held hands and began to walk together. Nevertheless, they soon became hungry and started to cry. Then, suddenly, along came a beggar who gave them some bread.*

The children were overjoyed, but noticed that the poor man was blind. Now these were smart children, and they wondered, "How can a blind man get along so well?" And we might also wonder how children so small could know about the blind and the miseries of other people? Anyway, the beggar blessed them that they might become as blind and old as he, and he gave them some bread and traveled on. In this way, the children understood that God had sent this man to help them.

The next day, the bread was gone, and again, they were hungry and cried, and along came another beggar! They started to talk to him, but he only pointed to his ears and shook his head, as if saying, "It's no use, I'm deaf." Nevertheless, he gave them bread and blessed them too, saying, "May you become as deaf as I," and he was gone.

So the next day, they were starving again, and again they cried, and another beggar came. This one was a stutterer and a mumbler. The children tried to talk to him as well, and he answered, but it made no sense... They couldn't make out a single word; all they heard was m-m-m-mumble. But he gave them bread and blessed them (in a mumble), and was gone like the others.

The next day, a beggar with a twisted neck treated them the same, and the next a hunchbacked beggar, and the next day one with disfigured hands, and the next day one with clubbed feet... But each one blessed them and left them a little bread.

The day after that, they came out of the woods and found some houses and people. Again they were hungry and cried, and being children, the good people there took pity on them and fed them. This is how the children became beggars. They agreed never to separate and made themselves beggar-pouches.

Wherever there was a simḥah (joyous occasion)—a wedding, a birth, or a brit (circumcision)—they would come, eat, and take some food away in their pouches. With the help of God, they went from town to town in this way, getting to know the markets and fairs and the other beggars. And these beggars got to know the children too; they all liked them very much, and always spoke of them as "the kids who got lost in the woods."

After many years had passed, all the beggars found themselves together at a great fair, and Oy! they noticed that "those kids who got lost in the woods" were now old enough to get married! And who should they marry but each other? So they started to arrange the wedding. One of them suggested that they should go to the king's birthday party, where everyone would be given bread, wine, and meat; and from what they would get there, they could make a great wedding celebration. So they went to the party, begged for food, and took the leftovers away with them. Then they set-up a wide feasting place, big enough to hold hundreds of people, covered it with piney boughs, and there they made the wedding banquet!

Now this is the set-up for the six tales that follow in the full story. Here we will only give you the first three, as these are the most accessible and require the least explanation. Nevertheless, they are every bit as rich in detail and spiritual import as the others, and demonstrate the pattern in which the later tales follow.

The Blind Beggar's Tale

I recommend that you read these three tales aloud, or listen to someone else read them so that the words enter into you through your ears, and not simply through your eyes. Listen with the innocence of a child hearing a bedtime story, or with the liquid mind of the dream-state in which one does not question 'How?' or 'Why?' Simply allow them to work their magic on you, unfolding and gaining complexity in your waking hours.

So with that in mind, let's begin with the blind beggar's tale . . .

Oy! In their happiness, *the 'kids' remembered all the good that God had done for them, how they had found one another, and how the blind beggar had given them bread and blessed them. Then they said, "Wouldn't it be nice if he were here now?"*

But even as they said this, the blind beggar suddenly appeared, saying: "Here I am! And I have a gift for you both . . . To be as old as I am!

"I suppose you think I am blind? Neh! Not at all! It's only that the world's 'long time' is nothing but a flutter of the eyelids to me. So I seem blind in the eyes of the world because I don't look the world in the eye; but the truth is, there is really nothing to look at because it only lasts a wink, and my sight looks both deep and long. Indeed, I am very old, but also very young! You may not believe it, but even the great Eagle, the undying Phoenix, has said as much; and on this hangs a tale . . .

"Once, there were many boats at sea, and many people sailed in those boats. Then there arose a great wind, which broke all the ships to pieces. Thank God, all the people were saved and came to a big tower, which they all ascended. At the top of the tower, they found all manner of food and drink, and all the delights of the world!

"Then, they said, 'Each of us must tell the first thing he or she can recall, as far as his or her memory reaches.' Now, there were old and young people there, and they honored the oldest of them with the first word. And the oldest of them said, 'What can I tell you? I remember when they cut the apple from the tree.'

"Now, even though they were wise people there, no one knew what this meant, so they said, 'That is so strange; it must have been an ancient event!'

"The second speaker was a little younger, and said: 'You call that ancient? I can remember the burning light.' And everyone agreed that this must be even more ancient.

"The third speaker was younger still, and said, 'I can remember when the fruit began to form.' And everyone agreed, this was still more ancient.

"And one younger still said: 'This is nothing! I remember when the seed was brought to be planted on the fruit.'

"And one still younger than that said, 'I recall when the sages conceived and invented the seed.'

"And the sixth speaker said, 'I remember when the taste entered the fruit.'

"And the seventh speaker even remembered the fragrance that preceded the taste.

"And the eighth speaker remembered the form and the color.

" 'And I' " (said the beggar), " 'I remember all of these events, even the nothing that preceded them!'

"Then everyone agreed, 'This is the most ancient tale!' And they were amazed, seeing that I, a mere child, remembered all these things.

"Then the great Eagle came soaring in, saying, 'It's time to return you to your treasures, the oldest first and the youngest last!' And he took me from the tower first, and the oldest man last, since he was really the youngest.

"Then the Phoenix said: 'Let me explain this to you. The one who spoke of the cutting of the fruit was referring to the cutting of the navel cord and remembered the birthing. The one who remembered the burning light, was remembering the womb and the light from the instructing angel's candle. The one who remembered the forming of the fruit was talking about the fetal form. The one who remembered the seed, was remembering the semen's flow at the time of the one-ing. The one who remembered the sages at the planning, was remembering the drop as it bathed the brain. The one who remembered when the taste entered the fruit, spoke of the memory of nefesh, the animating soul. The one who remembered the fragrance, spoke of the memory of ruaḥ, the affective soul, and the one who remembered the 'looks' of the memory, spoke of neshamah, the intelligent soul. Those interior levels of the soul, they remembered. And you, the child who remembered the nothing, remember even the No-thing-ness, which is higher than the soul.'

" 'So, now,' the Phoenix said, 'go back to your ships—the broken vessels are rebuilt.' Then he blessed them, and to me he said: 'You! Come with me! Being like me, you are very old, and yet very young. You haven't even begun to live, and yet you are old as I am old, and still so very young.'

"So you see, even the Phoenix agreed I am very old. So I give to you my long life!"

And when they heard this, they all rejoiced.

There is so much wonder, imagination, and Kabbalah, so neatly packed into this short tale that a person could spend hours on it alone. Can you imagine the looks on the faces of Rebbe Nahman's Hasidim when they first heard it? For my part, I always think of Rebbe Nahman himself, just 38 years old, and already nearing the end of his short life; for he was truly 'the youngest who was really the oldest,'' because he still remembered the *Nothing*, and was preparing to return to it. The remembrance of the *Nothing*—the substrate of existence—is like the fountain of youth, the unknowing which washes us clean of all the limitations knowledge has placed on us, bringing us to the place of 'beginner's mind' and 'conscious innocence.'

Why is the beggar blind? He is blind to time as it seems to be in this world; he is blind to its illusion. How do we get caught up in that illusion, in that powerful *maya*? By taking time too seriously. Thus, he wishes the young couple to be as blind as he to time's illusion. This is his wedding present to them.

The Deaf Beggar's Tale

Just as Rebbe Nahman was both the storyteller and a protagonist in the blind beggar's tale, he shows up again and again throughout the tales, as we will see in the deaf beggar's tale . . .

On the second of the seven days of joy and wedding, the young couple remembered and yearned for the second beggar, the deaf one, who had given them bread when they needed it. "Where is the deaf beggar, the one who restored us to life?"

And just as they spoke in their longing for him, he appeared and said, "I am here!" Then he embraced and kissed them, and said: "Now I can give you your present! To be like me . . . For once I blessed you to live a good life—a life like mine—and now this blessing will be fulfilled. For I give it to you as a wedding gift!

"You think I am deaf? I am not the least bit deaf! But as I do not value the world, it is inaudible to me; its needs cannot rouse me to take notice of them. All the sounds that are made are made because of need, each crying, shouting, and sounding another need. And what do you think the shouting of joy is all about? Need again!—A need that was felt and fulfilled! But I do not hear the needs of the world at all. I live such a good life, one in which there are no needs. You may not take my word for it, but the people of the country of riches, even they have agreed that I truly live the good life. Do you want to know what it consists of? I eat bread and I drink water.

"Oh, so you want to hear about the country of the rich? Well, there is a land whose inhabitants are very rich, owning all kinds of treasures. And once they all got together and started to boast about their riches and good life. Hearing each one boast, I said, 'My life is so much better than yours; for if you truly lived a happy life, you'd be able to help the people of the unhappy land.'

" 'The unhappy land?' they asked.

" 'Yes, the unhappy land. There, they had a garden, an orchard with all kinds of fragrance, all kinds of taste, all kinds of color, and all kinds of shape to please every sense. And the reason the garden was so blessed was because of its gardener.

" 'But the gardener disappeared, and so the people of that place could no longer enjoy the fruit. All was withered except for the weeds and the after-growth. Still they managed to eke a living out of the wild growth in the garden.

" 'Then came a cruel king who ruined even that livelihood. But he didn't destroy the garden completely—he left three platoons of servants there and commanded them to spoil the sense of taste, so that everything tasted like rot and carrion. They spoiled the sense of smell too, so that it was distorted—everything smelled rotten to them. They even spoiled the sense of sight, so that everything looked foggy, cold, and gray. This was a result of what the king had his servants do to the people in the land.

" 'So! You claim to live the good life? You really know how to enjoy life? Well, if this is true, then show me how you would help the people of that unfortunate land. For if you don't help them, the pall of that land will spread among you too, God forbid!'

"So the rich went to the unhappy land, and I went with them. As they traveled, each lived their own good life, having taken along what he or she treasured most. But as soon as they came close to the unhappy land, their tastes were spoiled, and their senses of smell and sight were distorted! So I said to them: 'Even from this distance, already your tastes are spoiled! How are you going to help these people if your senses are distorted too?'

"I took out my own bread and water and gave it to them. Oy! How the taste, the smell, and the sight of that bread and water set their senses right! Indeed, so right were their senses now that their senses from before weren't even 'right' by comparison!

"Still, the people of the unhappy land languished and thought, 'Oy! Who can help us?'

"They just couldn't stand it anymore. All their senses were spoiled, and they wanted to set things right. So they said to themselves, 'There is somewhere a country of the rich who live the good life . . .' And it seemed to them that their garden must be from the very same root of which the people of the rich land grew.

"So they decided to send out messengers to the rich land, to the land of the good life, for surely they would find help there. The messengers went out, and sure enough, encountered the emissaries of the good life along the way.

"The emissaries of the good life asked them, 'Where are you going?'

"They said, 'We are going for help to the land of the good life.'

"So they told them that they were the people of the good life they sought; and indeed, that they were already on the way to help them. But I spoke up and said: 'You good-lifers cannot help them; for you are both in need of what I have. Stay here, and I'll go to help the people of the unhappy land.'

"So I went off with them and entered the first city in the unhappy land. There I saw and heard people huddling together, telling jokes and laughing, guffawing. I paid no attention to the jokes; it was all mouth-filth—one person telling a bawdy tale, and the other topping it more slyly, causing even more laughter. In another town, they quarreled over business deals, going off to a court of 'justice' where one was held right and the other wrong. Still they kept on quarreling, and went to another court that made a different ruling. But this ruling didn't hold either, and they continued their quarrel, going from court to court across the unhappy land. I could see that truth wasn't available in these courts; for they respected bribes and status, and Truth was lost!

"Others, I saw, were full of promiscuity, and to them it seemed alright! Then I knew that the cruel king had truly done his work well, sending his platoons of spoilers throughout the land: some of these spoilers filthied mouths and spoiled the taste; other spoilers bribed, dulling the sight, because it is written, 'The bribe blinds the eye of the wise.' Still others spoiled the sense of smell, the fragrance of life by promiscuity. No one could enjoy the fragrance any longer.

"So I said to the people of the unhappy land, 'Seek to right these wrongs; ferret-out the spoilers and your senses will return, and so too will your gardener—for he is still here among you!'

"And this is what they did. They began to right the wrongs, looking around and questioning people, 'How did you get here?' In this way, they found the servants of the cruel king and cast them out.

"Then they had a startling realization—maybe the 'madman' who has been shouting that he is the gardener all this time really is the gardener! That poor man had been shouting, 'I am the gardener!' all this time, and we—shame on us!—cast stones at him, and chased him away! So they brought him to those who had set about righting the land, and I," said the deaf beggar, "was there also. And I said to everyone, 'This is the true gardener!'

"So you see, I was the one who righted that unhappy land; and the people from the land of the rich also agreed that I truly live the good life. They had to admit, only one who lives the good life as well as I could possibly help the unhappy land. So my children, today is your wedding day. My good life I give to you! L'ḥayyim tovim."

Now the joy was truly great and overflowed. All the beggar-family brought their gifts, and the couple knew the long life of the blind beggar and the good life of the deaf beggar.

Every time I read this, I think this is a story that could have been written yesterday. If it was relevant in Rebbe Nahman's day, it is even more relevant today. What was it that spoiled the taste of their food? It was *nivel peh*, lies, gossip, obscenities, "mouth-filth." So the deaf beggar says, "If you're gonna' listen to that stuff, you'll never know the truth of what's going on." So he blesses them that they should be deaf to these things, never having their taste for life warped by them.

The Mumbling Beggar's Tale

The mumbling beggar's tale is one of my personal favorites, and one that illustrates the point that I was trying to make earlier. In these tales, Rebbe Nahman is truly speaking from the *mashal ha-kadmoni*, the primordial world of imagination and metaphor in which conceptual structures no longer function in the same way. In this mythic world, there are no more one-to-one symbolic equivalences. It's just too fluid for that. If you try to make sense of it with the *sefirot* or *olamot*, you only end up limiting it in awkward ways, and it continues to elude you. It's similar to the attempt to make a rigid system out of the *Zohar*, or like making a concrete bed for a river—the whole riparian interface between the land and the river is spoiled.

ON THE THIRD OF THE SEVEN WEDDING DAYS, *the couple reminisced and remembered the third beggar who mumbled; and praise God, the mumbling beggar appeared, saying, "Behold! Here I am!" They hugged and kissed, and the mumbling beggar said to them, "In the beginning, I blessed you to be like me. Now, I have come to give you this gift at your wedding.*

"You think I'm tongue-tied? I'm not tongue-tied at all! It's just that the words of the world are not aimed at God, who is blessed; they are not words of prayer or praise, not words of Torah or holy law ... They are all so incomplete! So I seem tongue-tied because of the maimed and crippled words of the world. But only let me use whole and unblemished words aimed at God, and I can speak beautifully and clearly. In fact, I compose poems and speak with artful elegance, arranging celebrated sonnets and ballads! All wisdom and knowledge is in my poems, and to prove it to you, I'll tell you what the great one of true grace said about my children, and that too is a whole story ...

*"*ONCE, THE WISE ONES ALL SAT TOGETHER, *each one praising their own wisdom. One was proud of having invented black-smithing. Another copper-smithing.*

Yet another was proud of having invented silver-smithing, which was more valuable. Still another was proud of gold-smithing. Another was proud and claimed precedence for weaponry. Another demanded that alchemy be given the greatest praise, because metals could be made from other substances by it. Yet another was proud of the science by which gunpowder was made. Finally, there was one who said, 'I am still more gifted, for you see, I am as wise as the day!' This, they did not understand, so the wise one explained: 'If all your wisdoms were put together, only an hour would be amassed. For although each science is taken from another day of creation, on each day, another realm of being was made, and all sciences are compounds of wisdom, each one taken partly from one day, and partly from another still. So all the sciences together make up only one hour. But I am as wise as a full day.'

"Then I ... I ... the ... the ... the ... sss ... stu ... stutterer said, 'Like which day are you wise?' And the wise one turned to the rest and said, 'I know this one (meaning me, the sss ... stu ... stutterer) is wiser than I, because of the question, Like what day? But I am as wise as any day you will choose. Still, the stutterer is wiser, because the question tells me that the stutterer can be as wise as any day too, and that is also connected with a tale.'

"So, pointing at me, the wise one said, 'The being of true grace is truly great, and the stutter goes about, all over, garnering acts of kindness, and giving them to the being of true grace.'

"'Now, this you need to know ... Time is not eternity; time is made. But, in order to make time, one needs many acts of true grace, because time itself is a creature, and to keep time flowing, this stutterer helps to make time by giving the acts of true grace collected from all over to the being of true grace.'

> You see,
> There is a hill;
> And on that hill
> There is a stone;
> And from that stone,
> There flows a spring.

> Now, everything has a heart;
> The world as a whole has a heart;
> And the heart of the world
> Is a complete form, a body,
> With a face, hands, and feet;

And even the nail on the toe
Of the heart of the world
Is more heart than any other heart.

And the hill with the spring …
This hill is at one end of the world,
While the heart is at the other;
The heart and the spring
Stand opposite each other.
Now, the heart is always
Longing and yearning
To reach the spring;
And the longing and yearning
Of the heart for it is wild;
So it cries out in its longing;
And the spring, too,
Craves the heart
In the same way.

Now, the heart
Has two afflictions:
One is the Sun that
That pursues and scorches it
Because it cannot bear the heart's
Longing for the spring;
And the other is from
The sheer exhaustion of
Its yearning and longing.
But when the heart
Must find a little rest,
To regain its breath,
A bird flies above it
And spreads its wings,
Hiding it from the Sun;
Then, in that shade,
The heart rests a little;
Yet, even then, it looks
Across to the spring,
And yearns for it.

*So why doesn't the heart
Just go to the spring?
Because, it stands facing the hill,
And looks at the top of the hill
Where the spring
Emerges from the stone;
And as soon as it tries to move
In the direction of the hill,
It no longer sees the top,
And it can no longer
See the spring,
Without which, God forbid!
It might die of longing.
And if the heart died, God forbid!
The whole world
Would be annihilated,
Because the heart is the heart
Of the Life of every living thing;
And how could a world exist
Without a heart to beat in it?
So the heart cannot move.*

*And the spring . . .
The spring has no time;
For it has no day,
No time in the world at all,
For it is above the time of the world;
The spring only has time
When the heart gives it a day
As a gift of love.
And when the day
Is about to end,
They begin to bid
Each other Farewell!
The heart and the spring
Tell each other parables,
And sing songs to each other
With great love and longing.*

" 'And the true being of grace has charge over it all. As the day draws to its end, the true being of grace and good deeds comes and gives the heart a day, and the heart gives the day to the spring, and the spring again has a day. When the day comes, it also comes with parables and songs containing all the wisdoms. And there are differences between days, because there are Sundays and Mondays, New Moons and Festivals, and each comes with its own songs, according to the day.'

"AND NOW, THIS I GIVE TO YOU *as a present, that you may be like me!"*
Oy! did the joy rise high! And that is what joy is all about. So that night—after the joy—the couple rested well.[868]

Like Orpheus, who has to sing everyday for the Sun to rise, the mumbling beggar has to go around collecting the moments that contain good deeds in order to get another day together to give it to the being of true grace. But how does he get the day together if people don't do good things? So we must begin to think of ourselves as contributors in the maintenance of the world, builders of the future, who construct it with our good deeds. This is the gift the mumbling beggar gives to the young couple.

"The Tale of the Seven Beggars" was Rebbe Nahman's final story, told while he was already gravely ill, just a few months before his death in 1810. It is generally regarded as the climax of his storytelling activity. And yet, it is unfinished, having only six of the beggars' tales. We never hear the seventh beggar's story. Reb Nosson, who recorded the tale for us, writes: "The end of the story—of the seventh day and the beggar without feet—we did not merit to hear from him. He would tell no more . . . We will not be worthy of hearing it till the Messiah comes." And this is surely the reason for Rebbe Nahman's silence: the seventh beggar represents the completion of our own tale of Redemption, which is not yet full.

The Turkey Prince

One of the things we haven't really discussed up to this point is Rebbe Nahman's approach to working with Hasidim, that is to say, his means of counseling. We have talked about the kind of advice and practices he would give, but not of how he conceived of his work with Hasidim. Though he speaks about this in numerous places, I think it is perhaps best described in one of his most famous parables, "The Turkey Prince."

ONCE, THERE WAS A PRINCE who lost his mind and believed he was a turkey. Thus, he stripped off his clothes and began to sit naked under the royal table, pecking at scraps of food that fell on the floor. For a while, the royal doctors tried to cure him, but they were unsuccessful and finally gave up, leaving the king utterly bereft.

Then a wise man came along and said, "I think I might be able to cure him."

So the wise man stripped off his clothes, crawled under the table, and sat naked next to the prince, pecking at the crumbs that had fallen from the table.

The prince turned to him and asked, "Who are you, and what are you doing here?"

But the wise man only answered him with another question, "Who are you, and what are you doing here?"

"I'm a turkey!" answered the prince.

"So am I!" said the wise man.

So they went about their pecking under the table together for a long time and became friends. Then a day came when the wise man gave a sign to the king's servants to drop a couple of shirts under the table. Then the wise man put a shirt on as the prince looked at him in disbelief. So he said: "What? A turkey can't wear a shirt? A shirt doesn't make you any less of a turkey." So the prince put a shirt on as well.

Later, the wise man gave the servants another sign, and they dropped a couple pair of pants under the table. Just as before, he said: "What? A turkey can't wear pants? A pair of pants doesn't make you any less of a turkey."

So the wise man continued on in this way until both he and the prince were completely dressed. Then he gave the servants the sign that they were to be given plates of food from the table. Again, the wise man said: "What? A turkey can't eat food from a plate? You'll stop being a turkey if you eat food that hasn't fallen on the floor? You're a turkey and you'll eat what you want!" So they both ate the food from the plates.

Finally, the wise man said, "What makes you think that a turkey has to sit under the table? Even a turkey can sit on a bench." And the wise man continued on in this way until the prince was completely cured.[869]

Clearly Rebbe Nahman believed that it was sometimes necessary for him to enter into the Hasid's problem on such a primary level that he actually embraces for a time the symbol system of the Hasid.[870] I'll give you an example: Once, a long time ago, a rabbi I knew asked me to talk to his son who was a schizophrenic. I took a walk with him and he began to tell me about all the frightening things going on in his head. So I followed him as far as I could and did my best to enter into his world. But after a while, a feeling of anxiety began to build up in me, and I started to worry that I might be caught up in that terrible vision of the world. So I said to him, "Please stop—I'm coming to a point, beyond which, I'm afraid I won't be able to come back." Suddenly, he stopped talking and turned to me with the most genuine look of gratitude. After we came back to the house, he told his father that here was somebody with whom he could talk, and who understood.

You see, I had entered into his mind-space, and he had appreciated that I had experienced the kind of fear that he felt on a daily basis. But in asking him to stop, I had done what he could not do for himself. I had lent him my own 'filter,' that part of our minds which acts a kind of safety net against these kinds of terrifying thoughts. At that point in his life, his own filter wasn't functioning; but mine was, and through it, he was able to stop. Thus, he felt both relief and gratitude.

Of course, this anecdote and Rebbe Nahman's parable are both describing very extreme situations, but they are nevertheless helpful in showing us how he must have approached the more ordinary delusions of the Hasidim as well. I also believe this is what Reb Shneur Zalman was talking about in the mysterious letter he wrote just before his death (see Chapter 3, "Beyond the Wall"), when he suggested that the Rebbe must "approximate the mind" of the Hasidim, following them into their own delusions, "in order to gain their cooperation." This, according to him, is the victory of Grace over Truth. For as he enters into that fantasy world of the Hasid, he knows that it is not a true world. Nevertheless, he must enter it if he is going to bring the Hasid out. Thus, Rebbe Nahman says elsewhere, "I feel their pain even more than they do."[871]

The Dream of the Heavenly Master

As extraordinary as Rebbe Nahman's stories and parables may be, his dreams are just as fascinating. It is so rare to find dreams as intimate and exceptional as those of Rebbe Nahman in the literature of Hasidism.

Occasionally you come across one or two that deal with the process of the Rebbe's self-knowledge, but few are told as candidly as these were to Reb Nosson, who dutifully recorded them for posterity.

The first of these involves an astounding heavenly journey with the inner teacher . . .

IN MY THIRTY-SEVENTH YEAR, *after lighting the first candle of Ḥannukah, I dreamt that a stranger came and asked me, "How do you make your living?"*

So I said to him, "My livelihood is not located in my home; it comes to me from outside."

Then he asked me, "What do you study?"

I told him and we began to speak of Torah. Soon we were talking like old friends with an intimacy that issues from the heart, and I began to muse, "How does one reach any rung in holiness?"

And my guest said, "I will teach you."

Then I started to think, Perhaps he is not a human being. I thought about this for a moment and immediately my faith in him became strengthened. I called him "Rebbe," and said, "Before I begin anything else, I want to know how to honor you properly, for an ordinary human being would not know what to do about this."

Then he said to me, "I have no time now; I will come another time and teach you this."

So I said to him, "Even this I must learn from you; how far must I accompany you?"

And he said to me, "Up to the door."

I thought, I don't even know who he is! So I said, "I am afraid to go with you."

He replied, "Why are you afraid? Do I not sit and teach you? If I wanted to harm you, who would have stopped me?" I began to walk with him to the door. He took hold of me and caused me to fly high and I felt cold. He gave me a garment and said to me: "Take this garment and you will feel fine; you will have food and drink, and all will be good, and you will sit in your home."

Suddenly, I saw that I was at home. I could not believe it! Then I looked around and saw that I was speaking to people. I was eating and drinking like any other human being. Then, suddenly, I saw myself flying in the air as before! Then again, I was sitting at home. Back and forth I went between home and flying in the air.

Then he brought me down into a valley between two mountains, and there I found a book. In that book there were all kinds of connections of letters and illustrations of vessels. And the vessels themselves were letters. Inside the vessels were more letters. With these letters inside the vessels, one could make such vessels. I wanted to study this book, but I began to see that I was again at home, so I returned and found myself once more in the valley. I decided to go up on the mountain path so that I would find some settled place.

Whenever I read this, I can't help thinking of the story of the Ba'al Shem Tov's meeting with his own heavenly teacher, Ahiyah ha-Shiloni, who commands him to meet "between the second and the third hill" in the nearby mountains, where he reports . . .

As we reached the second hill, which was to be the place of meeting, I descended from the sleigh and walked into the vale between the second and the third hill. Suddenly, the venerable one, my teacher and holy master, appeared right in front of me, saying, "Follow me." I followed him until, unexpectedly, a door opened to a cave in the cleft of the rock! I looked and saw that it was full of light, and inside was a table and two chairs. My holy teacher and master sat on the first chair and said to me, "Sit, my child." I sat in the second chair. He then took a book from his pocket and laid it on the table. The name of this book I mustn't yet reveal.

He began from its beginning and said to me, "My son—look!" His face was shining and dazzling like starlight—it was as if a celestial soul had entered me. I began to read aloud from the book, and he lifted his hands above my head in blessing. Though I had never seen this holy book before, I found my understanding was immense. My eyes were illumined, and the paths of Heaven were laid out before me. The gates of understanding were opened to me as they had been at the Revelation at Mount Sinai.[872]

This book which contained "all kinds of connections of letters and illustrations of vessels" is very interesting. For he says: "And the vessels themselves were letters. Inside the vessels were more letters. With these letters inside the vessels, one could make such vessels." I immediately think of fractals, shimmering fractals. At one point the letters are letters, and at another they are vessels. That is to say, the letters are not to be thought of as 'only letters,' because they are meant to contain something. But it can't stop there either, because they have to give something also. There is no end to the fractalization, because as you break it down, it only becomes more fractals. This is what we see in the *sefirot*, each of which contains all the others, e.g., ḥesed containing ḥesed of ḥesed, gevurah of ḥesed, etc. Even ḥesed of ḥesed breaks down to another level!

> As I ascended the mountain, *I saw a golden tree with branches of gold. From the branches hung all sorts of vessels that were like those depicted in the book. Inside of these vessels were other vessels that were made out of these vessels and the letters in them. So I wanted to take the vessels from there, but I couldn't, because the thicket did not permit me to get through.*
>
> *Then I saw myself again in the house, and it was very amazing to me that I was sometimes here and sometimes there! I wanted to tell this amazing thing to people, but how can you tell them such a thing? It's impossible to believe.*
>
> *I looked through the window and I saw my guest. I begged him to enter, and he said to me, "I have no time, for I am going to you."*
>
> *I said to him, "Even this is amazing; for I am here! What does it mean that you are on your way to me?"*
>
> *He said: "The hour when you decided to come with me and accompany me to the door, I took your soul from you and gave her a garment from the lower* Gan Eden *(Garden of Eden). All that remained with you was* nefesh *(the animating soul) and* ruah *(the affective soul), while I had taken up the* neshamah *(the thinking soul). Therefore, when you raise your thought up to that level, you are there and you receive your illumination from it. But when you return your thought to this level, then you are here."*

This is a wonderful illustration of how we occupy manifold worlds at the same time, and how we can experience (or lack) insight based on how we direct our awareness. The Sufi master, Hazrat Inayat Khan speaks to this point in his work, *Spiritual Liberty*:

The soul, during the satisfaction of every bodily desire, descends to Earth from above. That is what the myth of Adam and Eve explains, when they were driven out from the Heavens and sent down to Earth. This tells the seer that Heaven is the plane where the soul dwells freely in its own essence and is self-sufficient, and that the Earth is the plane where the soul experiences the passing joys through the satisfaction of bodily desires depending on external objects.[873]

Thus, when the dream-Rebbe gave Rebbe Nahman the garment from the lower Garden of Eden, saying, "Take this garment and you will feel fine; you will have food and drink, and all will be good, and you will sit in your home," he was referring both to the self-sufficiency of the soul on "the plane where the soul dwells freely in its own essence" as Hazrat Inayat Khan says, and also to the fact that the body would be taking care of itself in the lower realms.

All this I saw, but I did not know from which world he was, but I decided he was truly from the good world. And the story has not yet been completed, nor has it found its end.[874]

Was this a dream-vision of Ahiyah ha-Shiloni, the heavenly teacher of the Ba'al Shem Tov? Various motifs do match those reported by the Ba'al Shem Tov. But perhaps it was Eliyahu ha-Navi, who was known to guide the Ari ha-Kodesh, Rabbi Yitzhak Luria? Perhaps, perhaps . . .

The Dream of the Great Sin

This dream of Rebbe Nahman's is something truly unique, especially in Hasidism, where so much of what is recorded of the Hasidic masters is sanitized hagiography, leaving no room for human imperfections and doubts. Few Rebbes would have had the courage Rebbe Nahman had to reveal his personal fears and insecurities. Most people would be tempted to edit their dreams, so as to show themselves in a more flattering light. But here, Rebbe Nahman reveals a Kafkaesque dream in which he has been abandoned by his followers and is reviled and whispered about wherever he goes. Worse still, he is beginning to lose his gifts . . .

In the winter of his thirty-eighth year, *the year before his death, Rebbe Nahman said:*

In my dream, I sit in my house, and no one enters. This so amazed me that I went into the other two rooms and still there was no one. So I went outside and I saw that people were standing in circles and whispering about me. This one is mocking me, and this other one winks knowingly in my direction, another laughs, and still another is disrespectful to me. Even among my Hasidim there were some who were against me; some of them actually looked at me with scorn and whispered together.

I called one of my men and asked him, "What is this?"

He answered, "How could you have done such a thing; how could you have committed such an awful sin?"

I didn't have any idea what he was talking about or why they made fun of me. So I called this man again that he should go and gather a group of my people. When he came back, I considered what to do, and decided to travel to a different country.

When I arrived, I found that even there, people were standing in circles and whispering about me. Even they had gotten to know of this thing. So I went and sat down in a forest and five of my Hasidim came with me. We sat there together for a while, but as we needed something to eat, we sent one of the men to buy some food. When he returned, I asked him, "Have they stopped making this noise against me?"

He replied that the tumult was just as great as before.

Then an old man came along and said he wanted to speak to me. I went with him, and he said: "How could you do such a thing? Aren't you ashamed before your ancestors, your grandfather Nahman of Horodenka, your great-grandfather the Ba'al Shem Tov? Why aren't you ashamed before the Torah of Moshe and your holy forebears Avraham, Yitzhak, and Ya'akov? What do you think—You will continue to stay here? You can't stay here forever; eventually you'll run out of money, and being a weak man, what will you do? Do you think that you can go to another country? Either they'll know who you are, or they'll have heard of your deed. If they don't know who you are, you'll still not be able to earn your keep."

So I said: "Well, if it is so, then what am I to do? Will I yet have a part in the world to come (olam ha-ba)?"

He said, "Do you think that they will still give you a part in the world to come? Even Hell is not sufficient for you to hide, for you have caused a great desecration of the holy name."

I said to him: "Here I thought that you would console me and speak to my heart, and you only bring me pain . . . Go away!"

The old man went away.

Then I began to fear that since I had been away from home and my study for so long, I might forget all that I had learned. So I looked for the man whom I had sent to buy the food so I could have him get me a book. He went off but came back empty-handed. It was impossible for him to get any book without telling who needed the book. So I was terribly distressed. Not only was I in exile, but I couldn't even have a book to preserve my learning!

Then the old man returned carrying something in his hand, and I asked him, "What have you got in your hand?"

He said, "A book."

So I asked, "Could you please lend me the book?"

He gave it to me, but I couldn't even understand how to hold the book. Finally, I opened it; but I couldn't understand the meaning of the words, for it was like a strange language in a foreign script. I became even more upset, fearing that my people would leave me when they realized I could no longer read a book.

So the old man called me so that he could speak to me. Again, he began to upbraid me for having committed such a grave sin, saying, "Even in Hell, there will be no place for you to hide."

I replied, "If a soul from the Higher World were to tell me such a thing, I would believe it."

He said, "I am from there" and he proved it to me.

Then I remembered the story of the Ba'al Shem Tov, who had also thought at one point that he had lost his part in the world to come, and had said, "I love the One whose name is blessed even without reward in the world to come."

As with the last dream, there seems to be a parallel in Rebbe Nahman's dream-life to events in his great-grandfather's life. In the case of the Ba'al Shem Tov, he had gone against the heavenly decree barring him from traveling to the Holy Land, as we have already mentioned. And thus, while on the Aegean Sea, a storm arose and the ship foundered on the rocks of a tiny island, stranding him with his daughter Adel . . .

. . . to his horror, the Ba'al Shem Tov discovered that he had lost part of his memory; he could not remember any of the Torah that he had ever learned or taught!

He began to walk the shores of the island with Adel at his side, desperately chanting the letters of the alef bet (the Hebrew alphabet), hoping that God would arrange the letters into prayers! Seeing that her father had become impotent in his prayer, Adel decided to say what he could not, praying his teshuvah, making clear his intention to turn from his course, to give up the attempt to reach the Holy Land in his lifetime. "Sovereign of the universe," she said, "please lift this decree and return my father to his proper place in the world; help him to find the footprints you have laid before him once again; he knows he is outside of his destiny and your perfect will . . . please return him to his place, my beloved!" At that moment, the Ba'al Shem Tov's teacher, Ahiyah ha-Shiloni, suddenly appeared before him and announced the lifting of the heavenly decree![875]

But Rebbe Nahman had no one to help him in his dream, no one to speak his *teshuvah* for him, as Adel did for the Ba'al Shem Tov. So he continues . . .

So I CAST MY HEAD BACK in great sorrow, and as I did so, there gathered about me all the great people, and the old man said that I should be ashamed before them, before my grandfathers and all my ancestors. Then they recited the sentence, "The fruit of the earth is for beauty and for pride." They said to me, "We are very proud of you." And they brought to me all my people and children; all of them consoled me greatly. With such sorrow had I cast my head back, even one who had transgressed the entire Torah would have been forgiven. I won't tell you the rest of the story, though it was truly good.[876]

By this time, Rebbe Nahman had experienced many personal trials, being attacked and vilified by former friends among the *rebbeim*, and even by his own uncle. But as difficult as these experiences were, there was somewhere in him a fear that a time would yet come when he would lose nearly all his remaining support; even many of his own Hasidim would leave him, or look askance at him. And why? He could not conceive of what he might do to deserve such a fate, just as he was often bewildered by the attacks he had suffered up to then. Strangely enough, such a time would come when his actions would raise doubts even among his Hasidim, causing the most loyal to question him, and the weak to abandon him. But it was no sin of his that caused this, only a holy boldness that the short-sighted could not understand.

Among other Rebbes, there are few examples of such humble self-disclosure. One of the most honest and touching comes from Reb Kalonymus Kalmish Shapira (1889-1944), the Piasetzno Rebbe, who in his journals, speaks of the deep humility and *teshuvah* of the greatest Rebbes:

A terror came over me yesterday during *Shalosh Seudos* as the thought came to mind: what would happen if my demise were nearby? The Mishnah says to repent one day before one's death (*Avot* 2:15). I wonder how I could do it. Just to refrain from forbidden behavior and thought by simply controlling oneself is possible even at the prime of one's life—just keep in mind your possible imminent demise. But to really change everything that needs change and to heal all the wounds of my soul the way I know I really should and indeed want to—this is not so easy to do.

So when I think about what would be if I were suddenly called before God with all these blemishes on my soul, I become gripped by panic and terror—I am not nearly as afraid of death, even a premature one, as I am afraid of this specter.

But the truth is, why am I afraid to face God just in higher worlds with my blemished soul and not embarrassed to face Him on earth? Who knows? Perhaps God has already rejected my soul and banished it far out of His Presence.

There is nothing left for me to do other than to cry out to Him: "God! Save me because I am drowning!"[877]

The Dream of the Atonement

On Yom Kippur in 1809, Rebbe Nahman had a dream that is one of the most important in the Hasidic canon; not because its contents are so profound—though they are certainly deep—but because they seem to be directly related to events in the external world that occurred shortly after, namely, the deaths of two of the greatest Hasidic masters.

It was Yom Kippur, the Day of Atonement, and I dreamed. It was very clear to me at that time that in Heaven they demand one person's life as a sacrifice every Yom Kippur. Thus I volunteered, but they said to me that I must put it in writing. So I wrote it out and signed it. Then they wanted to offer me up as a sacrifice, but I now had regrets and wanted to hide. I saw a large group of people had gathered around to witness the sacrifice and I could not hide from them. I then sought to go out of the city, but even as I left, I noticed that I had somehow just returned! I entered into the city thinking I might hide among the non-Jews. Nevertheless, I knew if they were to come searching for me, I would be given up to be sacrificed. Then another tzaddik agreed to be sacrificed in my place. Nevertheless, I am still afraid of the future.[878]

In *Ḥayyei MaHaRaN*, where this dream is recorded, Reb Nosson writes that the conclusion of the dream has been omitted. Then he tells us that he recalls hearing that it was in fact, the holy Reb Levi Yitzhak of Berditchev who agreed to take the Rebbe's place!

Now, Reb Levi Yitzhak had a special relationship with Rebbe Nahman. More than any other Rebbe, Reb Levi Yitzhak—Rebbe Nahman's elder by thirty-two years, and perhaps the most universally respected Rebbe of that time—was his staunchest defender during his troubles with the Shpola Zeide and Reb Barukh of Mezhbizh. Indeed, he was once heard to say, "If only I knew that the world would listen to me, I would cry aloud in a voice that could be heard from one end of the Universe to the other, that whosoever wishes to be upright and to serve the Lord in truth should attach himself to Rabbi Nahman."[879] So perhaps it is not surprising that he might offer himself as the Yom Kippur sacrifice in Rebbe Nahman's place. But what evidence is there for this Bratzlav tradition? Amazingly, there is a story from the other side, in Berditchev, which also takes place on Yom Kippur in 1809 . . .

> At the close of Yom Kippur, Reb Levi Yitzhak of Berditchev emerged slowly from the *beit midrash* and said to his disciples gathered around him, "I must tell you, dear ones, today my life-line has finally expired and I should be departing from this world, even within this very hour; for I am the sin offering of Yisra'el. Nevertheless, I was aggrieved upon learning this because I would miss the opportunity of fulfilling the *mitzvot* of dwelling in the *sukkah* and saying the *berakhah* (blessing) over the etrog (citron) one last time. Thus I prayed that my sentence should be commuted until the completion of *Sukkot*, and the creator has granted my request." It was as Reb Levi Yitzhak said—the day after Simḥat Torah, the holy Berditchever Rebbe suddenly fell ill and died a day later.[880]

Reb Levi Yitzhak of Berditchev died on the 25th of Tishrei, 1809 (5570). In Bratzlav, two days later, Reb Nahman began to speak to his disciples about the departure of a *tzaddik*, the Glory of Yisra'el, from this world. He said: "Surely it is possible that there was a pillar of light going before his coffin, for the true leader of Yisra'el has died. He who has eyes in his head knows that the light has gone from the world and darkness has enveloped us all." But it was not until the following week that the news actually reached Bratzlav of Reb Levi Yitzhak's death. Then the disciples knew that Reb Nahman had been speaking of Reb Levi Yitzhak, whom he often referred to as the "Glory of Yisra'el."[881]

Whether Reb Levi Yitzhak was the *tzaddik* who sacrificed himself for Rebbe Nahman or not is for you to decide, but the synchronicity of these two stories touches me, and seems consistent with the stories of both Rebbes. Nevertheless, as Reb Nosson also points out, Rebbe Nahman's words, "I am still afraid of the future," were likewise prophetic, for he would himself pass on shortly after Yom Kippur the very next year.

Uman—The City of Lost Souls

In April of 1810, just six months before his passing, Rebbe Nahman began to speak of moving to Uman, a city he had visited just twice in his life. Not long after, a delegation of Hasidim arrived in Bratzlav inviting the Rebbe to move to Uman. Without the slightest hesitation, he said yes to them and began his preparations for the move.

Less than a month later, a fire broke out in Bratzlav and Rebbe Nahman's house was burned to the ground. Four days after that, he left Bratzlav in the company of Reb Nosson and traveled to Uman.[882]

More than a few people were taken aback by this decision. After all, why should he want to settle in Uman when he already had such a good position in Bratzlav? His enemies speculated that it was because Uman was a wealthy city, saying that the Rebbe was motivated by greed. But nothing could have been further from the truth. Rebbe Nahman was not concerned with the city's material wealth, but with its poverty of spirit. As he saw it, Uman was a city of lost souls.

Just over forty years before, in 1768, Uman had been the site of a bloody massacre. A wealthy and fortified city, Uman was laid siege to by the Haidemak rebels (Ukrainian Cossacks and peasants rebelling against the Polish nobility). After three days, the city fell to the Haidemaks, despite a courageous defense by both Poles and Jews. What followed was one of the bloodiest massacres of the rebellion. It is estimated that as many as 20,000 Jews were put to the sword at that time.[883] According to Rebbe Nahman, the blood of these Jews continued to cry out from the earth for help, for a *tikkun* that would allow them to be made whole again; and this is the real reason he had come to Uman.

While traveling there, Rebbe Nahman hinted at this purpose to Reb Nosson:

As we neared Uman, *the Rebbe began to tell me a story of the Ba'al Shem Tov:*

"Once," he said, "the Ba'al Shem Tov came to a certain town and fell into a very deep depression. The Hasidim who were with him noticed this, but were afraid to ask him about it. This went on for a day and half, until Friday afternoon, when the Ba'al Shem Tov suddenly asked that any visitors in the city should be invited to be his guests for Shabbat. It turned out that there were only two visitors in the city beside himself—two men who had come on foot. Later on, the Ba'al Shem Tov was heard arguing with these men."

> *The Rebbe could not remember all the details of the story, but said that the point was that this city was one in which there were countless souls who had been unable to ascend for 300 years. So when the Ba'al Shem Tov arrived there, they all came to him at once, begging to be released. They had been waiting all this time for someone who could accomplish such a tikkun for them. Thus, he became depressed; for there was only one way to make a tikkun such as this . . . through his own death. Nevertheless, God brought it about that these two men should take his place, and the Ba'al Shem Tov was saved. It would appear that some harm befell these men later on.*[884]

When Rebbe Nahman was still a child, he had learned that he could communicate with the dead. He had wanted so much to be able to work with disembodied souls (just as the Ba'al Shem Tov had) that he begged God to reveal such a soul to him. But when this wish was finally granted, he screamed in terror at the sight. Nevertheless, over time, he learned to control his fear and began to help those souls that came to him for a *tikkun*.[885] Interestingly enough, he told his disciples that this was far easier than helping them . . .[886]

> THE REBBE SAID: *"As I've said in the past, it takes time and a great deal of energy to help the living. Even helping the righteous few of this world—raising them up and bringing them to a higher rung—is hard work. It is much harder than helping the souls of departed sinners, though there be thousands upon thousands! In this world, it is hard to get anywhere with people because of their sense of free will. Indeed, one must overcome this willfulness if one is to lead them to the true path. It is much different with the dead. In death, even the greatest sinner becomes a willing servant, ready to do whatever you tell them. But in life, even the most righteous person is hard to work with because of their inherent willfulness, making it difficult for the Rebbe to bring them to the truth.*[887]

Presumably, the souls of the dead are less encumbered by the desires of the body, and being trapped between worlds, they are ready to do whatever it takes to make the transition to the next world. Thus, he began to turn his attention to these souls, preparing to accomplish something else his great-grandfather had not been able to in his own lifetime. For just as he had successfully managed the dangerous journey to the Holy Land, he would now go to Uman and give up his life on the soil of that great massacre for the purpose of redeeming the myriad souls imprisoned there.

This was not a new idea, nor was it born of his illness, as one might expect. For Rebbe Nahman had actually begun to speak about this in veiled terms as early as 1806 after the death of his infant son, Shlomo Efraim. It was only in the Fall of 1807 that he began to show signs of tuberculosis, which was often called consumption in those days, as it seemed to consume the person from within. From that point forward, the Rebbe's health was precarious, and it was considered a miracle that he survived the next three years.[888] Now, as his conditioned worsened, he sought to make a last *tikkun*, one that he could only accomplish with the giving up of his life.

Near the end, he called Reb Nosson aside to tell him his secret:

The day before he died, the Rebbe said to me: "Do you remember the story I told you?"

"Which story?" I asked.

"The story of the Ba'al Shem Tov I told you on the way to Uman."

"Yes," I said.

"For a long time now they have been trying to bring me here. But there are not just thousands of souls here; there are hundreds of hundreds of thousands."

Then he spoke of the Jewish martyrs that had been executed in Uman, and later he said: "None of you have anything to worry about, seeing as I am going before you. Those who have already passed on might have had some ground for concern, but you, you don't have to worry at all. If the souls which have not known me are awaiting this tikkun *from me, then you can certainly be confident."*[889]

The day of his passing, Rebbe Nahman asked Reb Shimon to dress him in his finest clothes, to make sure that his appearance was neat and tidy, and to see that the blood was washed out of his beard. Then, Reb Noson writes:

The Rebbe lay on his bed looking very relaxed. He rolled a small ball of wax between his fingers as he often did toward the end when he was considering deep matters. Even now, in this last hour, it seemed that his mind moved freely through the worlds, exploring their great expanses. Then they brought him a little soup. So he washed his hands, made the blessing and ate at little. Later, they wished him to eat a little more, but he could no longer eat anything.

As the Rebbe lay there, a great noise erupted in the town—a fire had broken out on the next street! Worse, a violent wind was whipping up the flames. The wind was so strong that it had even blown down the Rebbe's sukkah. Nearly everyone was already running to the fire, but I was unsure what to do: I didn't want to leave the Rebbe on any account, but I felt I needed to see what was happening. I knew that the Rebbe wouldn't die in the short time I would be gone, so I ran to the location of the fire, where I was told that the fire had gone out, despite the wind.

When I got back, it was clear to everyone that the Rebbe was near the end. People were gathering and beginning to say the prayers for tzaddikim. Soon after, it seemed as if he was already gone, and I started to crying, and called out—"Rebbe! Rebbe! To whom are you leaving us?!" He heard this and stirred a little, turning to us as if to say, "I am not leaving you—God forbid!" Not long after, Rebbe Nahman died.[890]

Just one year after Reb Levi Yitzhak had taken his place on the sacrificial alter, Rebbe Nahman offered himself up as the atonement for his people. It was the 18th of Tishrei, 5571 (October 16th, 1810); he was 38 years old.

Bratzlaver Hasidim believe that the power of Rebbe Nahman's 'atonement' continues to this day, and thus they congregate at his grave in Uman throughout the year, but especially on Rosh Hashanah as they did in his lifetime. For he promised that any who would come to his grave, give a *kopeck* (penny) to charity, and recite ten psalms especially chosen by him, he would help, no matter how great their sins. "I will do everything in my power, spanning the length and breadth of creation, to help this person." This is what the Bratzlaver Hasidim call the *Tikkun ha-Klali*, the 'general remedy.'[891] And this is what I think the Rebbe meant when he spoke of the "hundreds of hundreds of thousands" awaiting redemption in Uman. He was pursuing the endless path as he always had and looking into the future at the thousands upon thousands of pilgrims coming to his grave in Uman, year after year. Thus he said, "My fire will burn until the coming of the *Mashiaḥ* (Messiah)!"

10

The Empty Chair:
Nosson of Nemirov and the Bratzlav Ideal

NOW, IT WOULD BE A SHAME if we were to leave anyone with the impression that the rich tradition of Bratzlav Hasidism somehow formed of itself after Rebbe Nahman's passing. For, were it not for the extraordinary efforts of Reb Nosson Sternhartz of Nemirov (1780-1844), it would almost certainly have disappeared from the face of the earth. At best, it would have become an interesting aberration, or a footnote in the history of Hasidism, not the thriving and vital movement it is today. Reb Nosson's role in the creation of the Bratzlav ideal was critical. Not only was he singularly dedicated to the recording and publishing of Rebbe Nahman's teachings after the Rebbe's passing—even amidst tremendous opposition and physical hardship—but he also became the exemplary model for all future Bratzlav leaders *(manhigim)*, and the authoritative source for understanding Rebbe Nahman's radical teachings. Thus, Bratzlaver Hasidim continue to say—"Were it not for Reb Nosson, we'd have stumbled long ago."[892]

Born in Nemirov to a pious and prosperous textile merchant, young Nosson enjoyed a comfortable childhood and was known to be a diligent student. Though gifted beyond most of his peers, he was of a quiet and reflective nature, and not disposed to any dramatic demonstrations of his own intellectual abilities. Indeed, he was hardly aware of them.

Nevertheless, the more discerning among his teachers noticed that he seemed to understand things naturally, and often penetrated to the heart of an argument without resorting to the usual mental gymnastics. When he was chided by some of the other boys for his apparent simplicity, he only responded, "What can I do if I don't have questions?"[893]

It was clear that there were depths in this reserved boy that were not easily appreciated by the casual observer. Nowhere is this youthful depth more apparent than in this simple anecdote from his childhood . . .

As a child, Nosson was especially close to his maternal grandfather, and often sat with him in the front of the shul among the elders of the community. The elders were also fond of Nosson and questioned him about his studies whenever they saw him. Thus, he got to know them all and looked forward to seeing them each day in shul.

Then a day came when one of the elders was not in his usual place, and Nosson asked his grandfather—"Zeide, where is Reb Hayyim today?"[894]

His grandfather answered him, "Nossele leben, Reb Hayyim has 'gone to his fathers.'"

"What does that mean, zeide?"

"It means that Reb Hayyim died . . . His life ran out, and his body is now buried in the earth."

This answer troubled Nosson, and he began to wonder if this life leads only to death; and if it does, "What is its purpose?" From that time forward, this question burned inside him and troubled his sleep.[895]

So, from an early age, the quest for *meaning* and *purpose* took center stage in Reb Nosson's life. It was this quest that would eventually lead him to Rebbe Nahman's doorstep, and which would become the focus of his own ministry. But like so many profound journeys, it begins with an ejection from 'Eden' and the feeling that the world is somehow broken.

When he was just twelve years old, a marriage was arranged for Nosson to Esther Sheindel, the daughter of the saintly and renowned scholar, Rabbi David Tzvi Orbach (d. 1808), the *rav* of Sharogard, Kremenitz, and Mohilev.[896] So for the next two years, Nosson lived in the house of his father-in-law in Sharogard learning Talmud and Codes under the rav's tutelage. It was clear that the *rav* hoped that Nosson might one day take his place in one of his own communities.[897] But Nosson himself wasn't so sure this was what he wanted. For though he was skilled in his studies, they lacked taste for him. Worse still, he had trouble with his prayers. He found it difficult to stay connected to the words, and he received little satisfaction from them. In his heart, he longed to find fulfillment in his studies and to serve God in his prayers—it was just that nothing seemed to work for him. Whenever he thought about this, the old question reared its head and mocked him, "What is the purpose of this life?"

Eventually, Nosson decided to go back to Nemirov and learn the family business, thinking that he might at least find some purpose in the duties of a householder. But his malaise only worsened. On the cusp of developing either into a great halakhic authority, or at the very least, a pious and successful businessman, Nosson could find no desire for either.[898]

Climb! But Keep A-Hold of Yourself!

In the Winter after his return from Sharograd, Nosson began to study in the local *beit midrash*. His study partner was a young man named Lippa, who came from one of the Hasidic families in Nemirov. Up to that time, Nosson's own family had simply kept aloof from the burgeoning Hasidic movement, but his father-in-law—though personally very pious—was a fierce opponent of Hasidism on ideological grounds. So Nosson, who had just spent two years under his father-in-law's roof, was not particularly disposed to hearing about it from his new study partner. Nevertheless, Lippa was persistent, and slowly his descriptions of Hasidic devotion and fervor began to break through Nosson's defenses. For the truth was, what he wanted more than anything else was to be inspired.[899]

> AROUND THIS TIME, *a Hasid from Anipol passed through Nemirov and Nosson invited him for a meal. The man accepted and Nosson watched him carefully as he washed his hands and recited the blessings with deep kavanah. Impressed by this, Nosson asked if he had perhaps met the famous disciple of the Maggid, Reb Zushya of Anipol. The man replied enthusiastically: "Met him? I owe all of my kavanah to Reb Zushya! He is so holy that when it is time for* Tikkun Ḥatzot, *the midnight prayer, he leaps out of bed crying: 'Zushya! Zushya! Get up already! You can sleep when you're dead!" Hearing this, Nosson was immediately infused with a desire to see Reb Zushya for himself.*[900]

For all his father-in-law's learning and saintliness, he did not radiate the feeling and fervor of devotion Nosson was seeking. But now he knew that there were other *tzaddikim* who did, and who actually taught their disciples how to experience these things.⁹⁰¹ Thus, over the next six years, Reb Nosson traveled to the courts of various Hasidic Rebbes looking for the one who would inspire him to the heights of divine service. He saw for himself the extraordinary fervor of the humble Zushya of Anipol (d.1800), and witnessed the courtly splendor of both Barukh of Tulchin (1753-1811) and Shalom of Prohobitch (1771-1803), but it was not until he came to Berditchev and sat at the feet of the great *tzaddik*, Reb Levi Yitzhak (1740-1809), that he found anything close to what his soul needed.⁹⁰²

IN BERDITCHEV, Reb Nosson was inspired by the kind and venerable example of Reb Levi Yitzhak and began to see some improvement in his devotions. But he was still unsettled. Though he was making progress, he was still troubled by doubts, and often felt he was failing far more than he was succeeding.

Then, one night in the Summer of 1801, while sitting in the company of the other Berditchever Hasidim during melavah malkhah *(the meal which follows* Shabbat*), the Hasidim cast lots to see who would go for bagels. Reb Nosson lost. As he went out that night, he asked himself, "Is this all I am good for . . . getting the bagels?"*

It wasn't that he was complaining about this little service—which he was ordinarily happy to do—but that he knew there was greater potential in him which he couldn't seem to access.⁹⁰³ From his childhood to this moment, he was continually hounded by the same sense of waste and futility, and was always falling short of the mark at which he was aiming.

A LITTLE LATER, Reb Nosson went off to a deserted corner of the beit midrash and began to recite tehillim. *As he prayed, his heart suddenly broke open and he collapsed in weeping until he was exhausted and finally fell asleep.*

In his sleep, he dreamt of a great ladder reaching from Earth up to Heaven. He began to climb the ladder, but quickly fell off. He got back up and climbed a little higher, but fell again. Each time he climbed higher, and yet, each time he also fell lower. Finally, he determined to try once more. He climbed nearly to the top of the ladder—but alas!—fell just before reaching it. He was so broken now that he despaired of ever reaching the top. Then, someone appeared at the top of the ladder and called down to him: "Climb! But keep a-hold of yourself!"

*This dream made a profound impression of Reb Nosson, and the face of that man remained in his memory.*⁹⁰⁴

"*Climb! But keep a-hold of yourself!*" Though these words came from a dream, they might just as well have come directly from Rebbe Nahman himself, for no one else teaches this lesson as strongly as he. Yes, a major part of the spiritual work is climbing the ladder, but it is also important not to 'lose your rungs.' Keep a-hold of yourself—don't let your cravings and weaknesses take the victory from you. Once Reb Nosson finally learned this lesson, the rest of his life became a testimony to his ability to hold on.

Now I Am Not Alone

During the next year, Reb Nosson was forced to deal with more conventional problems. He was now twenty-one years old, and both his father and father-in-law were becoming increasingly impatient with him. It seemed that the head on which they had placed so many hopes was slowly being 'ruined by Hasidism.' Rabbi David Tzvi wanted him to follow in his footsteps and assume a rabbinic post; but Reb Nosson had no desire to make Torah his means of earning a living. For this reason, he tended more in the direction of his father's desire that he commit to the family textile business; but this also had its problems, as it interfered with his spiritual practice. In the end, he decided on a compromise. He would move to Berditchev where he could be close to Reb Levi Yitzhak and open a shop to sell his father's textiles. But just as he was about to execute this plan, providence interceded.[905]

On the 10th of Elul, 5562 (September 7th, 1802), Rebbe Nahman—who had been living in Zlatopol, hundreds of miles to the east—arrived in Bratzlav, just nine miles from Nemirov. He told his Hasidim, "Today we have planted ourselves in Bratzlav, and we will be called Bratzlaver Hasidim forever after."[906] Then, he said, almost as if speaking to himself, "I see a great soul in the Ukraine near Bratzlav . . ."[907]

SOON AFTER THE REBBE'S ARRIVAL in the area, Reb Lippa—Reb Nosson's old study-partner—decided to spend Shabbat with Rebbe Nahman in Bratzlav. When he returned to Nemirov on Saturday night, Reb Nosson and his friend Naftali noticed him davenen (praying) the Aveinu prayer near the end of the selihot (penitential prayers) with a new fervor and concentration! Obviously, he had been inspired to do this by Rebbe Nahman, and thus, the two friends decided to visit Bratzlav the very next day.[908]

They had both heard of the unconventional young Rebbe—celebrated by some, and vilified by others—and had long wanted to see him for themselves; but *the Rebbe's court in Zlatopol had been too great a journey for them. Now that he had relocated to Bratzlav, however, there was nothing to prevent their seeing him. So it was that Reb Nosson and Reb Naftali first came to Bratzlav on the 22nd of Elul (Sunday, September 18th) and presented themselves to the Rebbe. Following the custom of the day, they introduced themselves by reciting the names of their distinguished ancestors. The Rebbe responded, "All good Jews!"*

Then Reb Nosson mentioned that he and the Rebbe were actually distantly related through Reb Nahman of Horodenka. At this point, the Rebbe said mysteriously: "Now I am not alone ... We have known each other for a long time, though it's been a while since we've met."[909]

As we mentioned in an earlier chapter, Rebbe Nahman is believed to have carried the soul of Rabbi Shimon bar Yohai, the great 1st-century mystic who inspired the *Zohar*. And Bratzlaver Hasidim likewise believe that Reb Nosson was Rabbi Shimon's own great disciple, Rabbi Abba, as this passage suggests. Thus, it is possible that when Rebbe Nahman said, "it's been a while since we've met," he was referring to this previous incarnation.[910]

However, there is another possibility. For Rabbi Yitzhak Luria (ca. 1534-1572), the Ari ha-Kodesh, who himself brought down another revelation of the Kabbalah, is also said to have carried the soul of Rabbi Shimon bar Yohai in his generation. Thus, Rebbe Nahman may have been referring to a more recent incarnation as the holy Ari and Rabbi Hayyim Vital (1542-1620), just over two hundred years before.[911] The symmetry of this possibility is actually very strong. For just as the brilliant and talented Hayyim Vital was almost exclusively responsible for collecting and interpreting of the radical Kabbalah of the Ari (*Kitvei ha-Ari*), the radical Hasidic teachings of Rebbe Nahman (*Likkutei MaHaRaN*) are likewise known only through the lens of Reb Nosson.

As if he were aware of all this, Reb Nosson was once heard to say: "When people speak of Moshe *rabbeinu*, they also mention his disciple, Yehoshua. When they speak of Rabbi Shimon bar Yohai, they mention his disciple, Rabbi Abba. When they mention the Rabbi Yitzhak Luria, the Ari ha-Kodesh, they mention Rabbi Hayyim Vital ... And when they mention Rebbe Nahman, they will mention me!"[912]

In the *Shivḥei ha-Ari*, Rabbi Hayyim Vital tells the following story:

One day, I accompanied the Ari to the place where Rabbi Shimon bar Yohai had created and held the Greater Assembly. There, on the eastern side of the path was a stone containing two large fissures. The Ari walked to the northern

fissure and seated himself there; so I turned to sit in the southern fissure. Then, the Ari explained that the northern fissure had been the place wherein Rabbi Shimon bar Yohai had seated himself, and the southern had been the seat of Rabbi Abba. Rabbi Elazar had seated himself at the foot of a nearby tree, which faced the two fissures. Some time after, he explained to me the significance of what had taken place, and it was then that I knew what he meant when he told me that I contained a spark of one of the members of the *Idra* (assembly).

The Rebbe then spoke to both Reb Nosson and Reb Naftali for a long time, telling them three Hasidic anecdotes. The first concerned a Hasid of Reb Mordecai of Neshkhiz who listened carefully to the Rebbe's every word and found specific directions for his life in them. The second was about a Hasid of Reb Shneur Zalman of Liadi who for eight years gave original interpretations of a single discourse by the Rebbe.[913] Then, the Rebbe told this final anecdote:

"WHEN REB MIKELEH OF ZLOTCHOV *first came to the holy Ba'al Shem Tov, he was awestruck in the Rebbe's presence. But later, he seemed to feel it less. Then he thought of the talmudic warning that says: 'When the ignorant person see a tzaddik for the first time, they think of the tzaddik as a precious golden vessel; later they think of them as a silver vessel; and later still as a piece of pottery. Finally, they become disillusioned and think of them as broken shards!'*[914] *So Reb Mikeleh began to wonder if he were becoming an ignoramus, when suddenly, the holy Ba'al Shem Tov grabbed his wrist and said, 'Mikeleh—You're an ignoramus!'* "

Now, even before Rebbe Nahman began telling this last anecdote, Reb Nosson had been having the same thoughts as Reb Mikeleh of Zlotchov, and had even thought of the same words from the Talmud. So he was taken aback when Rebbe Nahman began to speak of this, and he wondered if the Rebbe might be reading his mind. Then, just after Rebbe Nahman had finished the anecdote, he grabbed Reb Nosson's wrist, just as the Ba'al Shem Tov had done to Reb Mikeleh, and said, "Mikeleh—You're an ignoramus!"

Reb Nosson was both embarrassed and exhilarated, for at that very moment, he realized that Rebbe Nahman's was the face he had seen at the top of the ladder in his dream! He had found his Rebbe at last![915]

Before he met the Ari ha-Kodesh, Rabbi Hayyim Vital was already accomplished in both the revealed and the hidden Torah. For a time, he had studied under the great kabbalist, Rabbi Moshe Cordovero in S'fat; but when he did not find in him a teacher for his soul, he moved on to Damascus where he continued to pursue his own understanding of the *kabbalah*. There he took on disciples, wrote a commentary of the *Zohar*, and soon began to settle into a fairly high regard of himself.

After a while, Rabbi Hayyim heard that Rabbi Moshe had passed on, and that his students were now learning with Rabbi Yitzhak Luria, called the Ari, who had succeeded him in S'fat. Rabbi Hayyim was curious to see the Ari for himself, but doubted if he had anything to learn from him, as he had learned much since he had studied with Cordovero. So he dismissed the idea out of hand. But his curiosity about the Ari continued. At first, it nudged him in quiet moments when he was away from his studies. Annoyed, he pushed it away. Then it began to disturb him during his studies. Again, he pushed it away. Finally—and much to his discomfort—the Ari began to speak to him in his dreams, urging him to come to S'fat so that he may teach him Torah!

Rabbi Hayyim was shaken by these dreams, but held firm, thinking, "What could I learn from *him*?" So night after night, for three months, the dream came again and again. Then, one day, he was laboring over a portion of the *Zohar*, and try as he might, he could not understand it. Finally, he closed the book in frustration. The next day, he opened the *Zohar* again hoping to go on to the next passage, but found the gates locked against this one as well! It was the same with the following passage on the third day! Never before had such a thing happened to him. He was beside himself, saying: "First the dreams, and now I am blocked in my studies! I'll go to this master in S'fat . . . If he is unable to unlock these passages, then he is no greater than I, and I'll be rid of these dreams and frustrations."

After a short journey, Rabbi Hayyim arrived in S'fat and immediately called on the Ari. To his amazement, the Ari himself received him at the door and treated him with such warmth that his own conscience pricked him for his arrogance. Nevertheless, he was not so easily turned from his purpose. He quickly produced the impenetrable passages and challenged the Ari with them. The Ari only smiled as if Rabbi Hayyim had offered him the most precious gift. This reaction completely bewildered Rabbi Hayyim, for he had made little effort to hide his own contempt, and here again he was met with genuine kindness. Now he melted in his seat as the Ari's eyes penetrated him, seeming to inhale and absorb the zoharic rays of the passages. Then he closed his eyes and began to reveal the meaning of the first passage, clearly and elegantly. Rabbi Hayyim felt as if he were moving down a river, with scenes of tremendous beauty rising up to meet him on either side and passing him by. Then, the Ari continued in the same way, explaining the second passage as well. But the vision faded as the

Ari stopped abruptly, lowering his head and opening his eyes. Then he said: "Through the gates of this third passage, you cannot pass . . . You have reached the limits of your understanding."

A sudden shame overwhelmed Rabbi Hayyim, and a confusion of thoughts arose in him amounting to one question, "What have I done?" Nervously, he thanked the Ari and left as quickly as he could. A whirlwind of thoughts and emotions enveloped him. He found a room nearby and fell upon his bed, sickened with his own pride, crying hot tears until they suddenly stopped. He had come to a decision. He went to the *mikveh* and then returned to the Ari. "Master," he said, "please receive me; I wish to be your disciple."

The Ari replied after a long silence: "I have long desired you, and have called you these many months. But the decision was not mine; it was yours. Your tears have bathed and prepared you to receive fresh garments. Come," he said, "these matters shall not be hidden from you any longer," and he embraced him.

A Fire is Burning in Bratzlav!

Hearing from the other Hasidim that Rebbe Nahman particularly wished his Hasidim to be with him on Rosh Hashanah, Reb Nosson and Reb Naftali, who had only come for a short visit, both hurried home to Nemirov and prepared to return at the end of the week. When they came back to Bratzlav on Friday afternoon, they went to see the Rebbe, who told them the following:

"I WILL LEAD YOU on a path which no one has ever traveled before . . . It is both very old and completely new.

You know I have three circles of Hasidim: one circle who come only for shirayim (the food distributed by the Rebbe at his table); another who comes to learn my Torah; and a third circle who are engraved on my heart."

Then turning to Reb Nosson and Reb Naftali he said, "I want you to be engraved on my heart."[916]

There is a proverb in Judaism, "More than the calf wants to suck, the cow wants to give milk."[917] The *tzaddik* in Rebbe Nahman's 'book' is not concerned with acquiring Hasidim to people his court, as it were, but with accomplishing a transformation in those who are willing to do the work for themselves. This is connected with a teaching that he once gave concerning a person's ability to comprehend the *tzaddik*. He said that a *tzaddik* is like a seal that is impossible to read until it has been stamped on the soft wax of the Hasid. The seal is not to be comprehended in itself because its letters and design are in a reversed-relief. Therefore, it is only through its effect upon the wax that you can read the message of the seal! Thus, the *tzaddikim* are known through the impressions that they make upon their disciples.[918]

Interestingly enough, Rebbe Nahman once said, "Only Nosson understands me, and Naftali a little." This is an amazing statement, as Reb Nosson and Reb Naftali were among the youngest and most recent additions to Rebbe Nahman's inner circle. And the praise is all the higher when one considers the caliber of the other close disciples: Reb Shimon of Krementchug, a truly humble soul who had "broken all his evil traits"; Reb Shmuel Yitzhak of Dashev, a great master of prayer who had the power to make a *tikkun* for souls; Reb Yudel of Dashev, a learned kabbalist whom the Rebbe allowed to accept *pidyonot*; Ahron the Rav, who Rebbe Nahman had used his ancestral merit to bring to Bratzlav; Reb Yekusiel of Tirhovitza, who was *maggid* to over eighty towns and villages; and Reb Yitzhak of Tirhovitza, who kept awesome devotions for the the Rebbe.

So why should Reb Nosson and Reb Naftali be so singled-out? Because it was the particular characteristic of Reb Nosson—and Reb Naftali to a lesser degree—to be reflective about the intentions and ultimate import of all the Rebbe's words, whether given to themselves or to others, and to appreciate the unique gifts of the other Hasidim as they had been honed and developed by the Rebbe.

THAT EVENING, REBBE NAHMAN gave a teaching on the importance of clapping one's hands in prayer, speaking of how this practice helps to purify all of creation.[919] Reb Nosson became so inspired by this teaching that he ran out into the fields after the tish and began to yell, "A fire is burning in Bratzlav... A fire is burning in Bratzlav... Light this fire in my heart!"[920]

By his own inspiration and fervor, Reb Nosson knew that he had found his spiritual home. When the Shabbat was over, he immediately wrote down the Rebbe's teaching from memory.

Reb Nahman of Tulchin (1813-1884), Reb Nosson's closest disciple used to say: "The reason Reb Nosson received more from Rebbe Nahman than the other disciples was because of the long winter nights in the Ukraine. When Rebbe Nahman would reveal his profound Torah on *erev Shabbat*, everyone was inspired. But long after the others went to bed, Reb Nosson used to take his inspiration out for a walk along the Bug River, where he would pray through the night that the Rebbe's Torah should light a fire in his heart!"[921]

Old and New Paths

When Reb Nosson first came to Bratzlav, he was awed by the prayer of elder Hasidim like Reb Shmuel Yitzhak of Dashev and thought only of how much trouble he had in his own prayer. No matter how much he tried, he just couldn't seem to focus. Rebbe Nahman confided to Reb Yitzhak of Tirhovitza that Reb Nosson was a *ba'al mahshoveh,* 'a deep thinker,' which is one of the twenty-four characteristics that make it difficult to bring a person into intimacy with God; for the thoughts get between one and God, and between one and one's own heart.[922] So the Rebbe's solution was to put Reb Nosson's discursive mind into the service of God through *hitbodedut* (extemporaneous prayer). He put an arm around his shoulder, took him aside and said, "It's very good to pour your heart out to God just as you would to a true friend."[923]

This was just the breakthrough he needed. One of the drawbacks in learning to interpret texts as Reb Nosson had is that it is hard to stop interpreting. So it's no wonder that he found it difficult to pray out of the *siddur* (prayer book). He probably couldn't stop himself from looking at it as just text in need of interpretation, instead of a vehicle through which he might address God. Thus, Rebbe Nahman gave him a different prayer-option without a text.

I have heard in Rebbe Nahman's name regarding hitbodedut, *that the forces of opposition already know how to obstruct all the prayers, supplications, and petitions that have come down to us in the* siddur, *and lie in wait to assail us at every turn. Like thieves and bandits lying in wait along a well-traveled road, the forces of opposition have learned to attack us where we are weakest and most vulnerable. But if one takes a new path, traveling a road as yet unknown, one is safe from the bandits waiting in the usual places. For* hitbodedut *with God is always new, spontaneously welling up in the heart and exploring uncharted territory. So there is no way for the intercepting forces to trap you! Still, Rebbe Nahman urged us to pray from the siddur as well.*[924]

Martin Buber used to speak of *Der auss atz der Gewohnheit,* "the leprosy of habit."⁹²⁵ This is at least one of the 'thieves and bandits' that attacks us during the time of prayer. But when one takes "a new path, traveling a road as yet unknown," the habitual mind has nothing to grasp hold of, and one can go on unimpeded.

Nevertheless, the Ḥiddushei ha-RIM, Reb Yitzhak Meir of Ger (1789-1866) makes an interesting point with regard to the 'new paths.' He says: "When the highway was blocked by bandits, the Ba'al Shem Tov found a sideroad to avoid them. But later, the bandits got smart and blocked that road too. So let's go back to the highway, for there at least we can see the road."⁹²⁶ That is to say, the traditional path is reliable, well-trodden, and shouldn't be abandoned for the 'sideroads' we must occasionally take to avoid the 'bandits.'

But as Reb Nosson notes above, Rebbe Nahman isn't suggesting that *hitbodedut* replace the daily prayers of the *siddur.* He only wants to give his Hasidim another option for entering into God's presence. And the wonderful thing about *hitbodedut* is that it actually breathes new life into the daily prayers. For where do we get many of the phrases that we use in *hitbodedut?* When you look at Reb Nosson's book of prayers, *Likkutei Tefillot,* you see that it is filled with stock phrases from the *siddur.* However, once that phrase is used in *hitbodedut* in a significant way, it brings that significance *back* to the daily prayers, allowing the phrase to take on an entirely new meaning the next time you say it!

Elsewhere Reb Nosson repeats Rebbe Nahman's gentle advice to those who have difficulties staying connected to the entire prayer service in the *siddur.*

IN THE REBBE'S TALKS, *he makes it clear that most people cannot recite the entire prayer service with focus and feeling, but only a small part of it.*⁹²⁷ *This is because everyone prays best that part of the service that harmonizes with their own spiritual station. As it says in the Zohar, "There are hand people and there are feet people."*⁹²⁸ *So one should not be surprised to find themselves concentrating better on one portion than another, or discouraged when their attention falters after moving on from this portion, suddenly realizing that the connection to* kavanah *(intention) has been cut. Sometimes, this is just how it has to be. Just pray the rest of the service very simply. In this way, you may merit be roused once again through God's mercy, to feel fervor in the heart as you pray.*

What if you do not become aroused again? What can you do? Maybe you will be allowed to say a psalm or a prayer of petition properly, and with true kavanah.⁹²⁹

Here is another example of Rebbe Nahman 'never insisting,' but always finding a way to create an opening for a little holiness to enter into one's service, even if takes leniency. In the same way, Reb Nosson once asked a man who had trouble feeling devotion in the daily prayers, "Are the prayer services the only form of devotion you have?" Then he went on to say: "There are plenty of devotions. If you don't feel one word, there are many other words. If you don't feel the prayers during the service, you can always recite Psalms or other prayers."⁹³⁰ You see, it is not the way of Bratzlav to force a situation, trying to create a spark where there is none. Instead, the Bratzlaver Hasid blows on the spark that exists, however small, hoping to create a flame that will spread to other areas!

---

*I HAVE HEARD that Rebbe Nahman would say, sometimes a person experiences a rush of teshuvah and a yearning for God in a particular place. Right then, right there, in that very place, one needs to harness the energy of that rush of teshuvah, taking hold of the longing and investing more energy into it with prayer. Even if it is only a few words, one should not move from the spot until they have been uttered. Do this even if it seems an inappropriate place, a place that is not dedicated to Torah and prayer, for it may be that once you move from there, the mood will be broken. We saw Rebbe Nahman do this himself on a number of occasions.*⁹³¹

My Rebbe, Reb Yosef Yitzhak Schneersohn, once said that when one finds oneself taking a detour through another town or road unexpectedly, one should pray in that place to raise the sparks that need to be released there. Furthermore, Rebbe Nahman seems to be suggesting that there are actually 'axial moments' in time and space upon which certain spiritual events may turn. Thus, by praying in that very place, in that very moment, a person may bring about the redemption of that place in time!

It is clear that Reb Nosson took this suggestion of Rebbe Nahman's to heart, and in his later life, he even became famous for praying spontaneously whenever and wherever he was moved to do so, or wherever he was when it was time for the daily prayers—no matter how strange the location. Often, this had unintended results, sometimes moving the people around him to *teshuvah*...

---

*WHEN REB NOSSON BEGAN TRAVELING throughout the region spreading Bratzlav Hasidut, he became accustomed to praying in the carriage. On one of these occasions, after he had gotten out and gone into the inn, his driver said to some Hasidim, "Today I drove a Jew who prayed so beautifully that I cried . . . and so did my horses!"*⁹³²

So even though Reb Nosson continued to be 'a deep thinker'—well-known for the breadth and depth of his knowledge—he was even more celebrated among Bratzlaver Hasidim for the fervor of his prayers. Indeed, he believed that his prayers were the secret of his profound understanding of Rebbe Nahman and his Torah. Once, when discussing Rebbe Nahman's teaching on the *or ha-ganuz*, the 'hidden light'—i.e., that a person who wishes to taste the 'hidden light' of Torah must examine themselves thoroughly in *hitbodedut*[933]—Reb Nosson said, "And whoever would taste the 'hidden light' which is Rebbe Nahman must likewise practice *hitbodedut!*"[934]

The Rebbe's Collaborator

Shortly after he met Rebbe Nahman in 1802, Reb Nosson began writing down all of the Rebbe's major teachings from memory, and even some of his conversations. This was partly done out of sheer enthusiasm, and partly because Rebbe Nahman had been explicit about his desire to have his teachings recorded. As Reb Nosson later wrote:

> WHEN I FIRST BEGAN *to draw near the Rebbe, he said to some people in my absence, "I thank God for sending me this young man who will ensure that not a single word of mine will ever be lost again." His desire was that I should record every word that came out of his mouth, his teachings and discourses, and even his casual conversations, which were also Torah. In this way, not a single word would ever be lost again.*[935]

Clearly, Rebbe Nahman knew that he had found something special in Reb Nosson, and I suspect, it was something more than a mere 'scribe.' After all, there were others who had recorded the Rebbe's teachings before him; and if all that he needed was someone who could memorize and write the teachings down, Rebbe Nahman could surely have found someone else who was willing to do the work. What he really needed was someone who combined great intellectual abilities and a refined literary skill with the devotional temperament of a Hasid, and the spiritual grit to become a *tzaddik*. In effect, he needed someone who would be both an apprentice and a collaborator in the development of Bratzlav Ḥasidut.

> ONCE, THE REBBE CAME INTO HIS HOUSE *and asked for me (Nosson), and was disappointed that I was not there at that moment; for he had no one to whom he could reveal what had come to him.* "I can hold a tremendous amount within me," *he said,*

"and I never speak until the water is about to overflow, but at this moment, I don't even have someone to tell!"⁹³⁶

When I first became his disciple, he said to me: "If you will stay pure and maintain your sincerity, you'll hear a great deal from me, for I need someone with whom I can speak. Often, I am charged with revealing particular things, and I need someone to hear them."

On a number of occasions, he revealed Torah to whoever happened to be with him at the time. Once, he told me about a time when he had given a teaching to a man who didn't understand a word he had said, saying, "I simply had to reveal that teaching in that moment, so when I saw this man coming along, I said it to him!" But this wasn't what he wanted; he wanted his words to be heard by someone who could understand them, even if it was only a little.⁹³⁷

Reb Nosson was the one disciple who could truly follow Rebbe Nahman's incredibly sophisticated teaching, somehow grasping its basic content as it was being spoken, and later making his own map of the salient features contained in it. Though he was much more linear in his own thinking, he was nevertheless able to make the many intuitive leaps between the seemingly disparate ideas in Rebbe Nahman's Torah. Because of this, he was the ideal container for catching the waters overflowing from the Rebbe and a perfect conduit for directing the flow to others in a manner they could handle.

In his biography of Rebbe Nahman, Arthur Green points out (while commenting on the composition of the *Likkutei MaHaRaN*) that Reb Nosson was far more than a mere memorizer and recorder of teachings, but also a skilled translator and one of the best Hebrew stylists of his day:

Like most of the theoretical works of Hasidism, these were abbreviated transcriptions of informal talks, originally delivered to the assembled Hasidim around the Sabbath or festival table. While such talks were always delivered in Yiddish, it seemed fitting that the master's words be preserved in Hebrew, the proper tongue for sacred writings if not for oral use. Nahman's teachings in their written form were often the combined product of the master's thought and homiletical genius and the disciple's fine sense of Hebrew literary style, a rare virtue among Hasidic authors.⁹³⁸

You see, Reb Nosson would memorize the Rebbe's teaching in Yiddish, prepare a translation of it into Hebrew, and then show it to the Rebbe in order to get his feedback on the translation. In this process, there were likely many gaps that needed to be filled in by Reb Nosson himself—partly because he was translating from a richly populated Yiddish vocabulary to a relatively sparse Hebrew, and partly in order to make the connections for the Rebbe's Hasidim who might have difficulty following the Rebbe's thought. Reb Nosson discusses this in his 1821 introduction to the *Likkutei MaHaRaN*:

> I therefore saw fit and made it my business . . . to expand and explain the material further. I did this in accordance with what I knew and understood to be the intent of the teaching, in line with what I heard from his holy lips. As for the lessons which had been written in the Rebbe's own holy language, I've neither subtracted from nor added to them, not even so much as a single letter.[939]

As these 'expansions' and 'explanations' were usually checked and approved by the Rebbe himself (and since Reb Nosson understood them best) there was no reason for anyone to doubt that these were indeed the Rebbe's teachings. Nevertheless, Rebbe Nahman wanted to give Reb Nosson the maximum amount of credit:

ONCE, THE REBBE SAID TO ME (NOSSON), *"Seeing that you have such a great share in this book, you should really feel encouraged!"* This was the Likkutei MaHaRaN, which was being printed at the time. He went on to say that the whole book was really mine, because without my efforts, it would never have come into existence. Then he added: *"You know something of this book's true greatness and its holiness, and you should have faith in its greatness. They've printed a thousand copies, each one of which will pass through the hands of several people!"* He said this to encourage me, seeing as I had had a part in something that would do so much good in the world. . . .[940]

On another occasion, he said: *"Every one of you has a share in my Torah, but Nosson has the greatest share. If it had not been for him, you wouldn't have a single page of my book!"*[941]

In 1805, Rebbe Nahman asked Reb Nosson to begin copying-out all the major teachings he had recorded so far, so that they could be bound together in one volume. Reb Naftali and Reb Nosson worked diligently to accomplish this task for the next three months, Reb Naftali reading the transcripts aloud while Reb Nosson copied them.[942] This manuscript (supplemented by a number of later transcripts) became the basis for the first printing of the *Likkutei MaHaRaN*, the 'collected teachings of our teacher, *rabbeinu* Nahman,' first published in 1808 while the Rebbe was still alive. The 286 teachings of this volume comprise what is now considered part I of the *Likkutei MaHaRaN*. Part II, known as *Likkutei MaHaRaN Tinyana*, contains 125 new teachings, and was published three years later in 1811, a year after the Rebbe's passing.[943]

In addition to the teachings of the *Likkutei MaHaRaN*, Reb Nosson also edited and translated the Rebbe's amazing collection of stories and parables, *Sippurei Ma'asiot*, which we have already discussed in Chapter 9. But perhaps equally significant to Bratzlav Hasidim are the many first-hand accounts, biographical details, conversations, smaller teachings, and casual comments of Rebbe Nahman that Reb Nosson recorded in *Shivhei ha-RaN, Sihot ha-Ran*, and *Hayyei MaHaRaN*. These form the basis of a Bratzlaver Hasid's understanding of Rebbe Nahman and provide clues to his views on almost every aspect of life.

Yehoshua's Torah Novellae

Early in 1803, only about eight months after they had met, Rebbe Nahman began to call Reb Nosson his "Yehoshua" (Joshua, the heir and chief disciple of Moses), and to speak to him about developing his own Torah *novellae*, or novel interpretations of Torah.

It was Purim, *and the Rebbe had left Bratzlav to be with some of his Hasidim in Medvedevka. Reb Nosson, not wanting to be parted from the Rebbe, decided that he would make the long journey to Medvedevka to spend Purim there as well. Though he had not informed the Rebbe of his decision, somehow he seemed to know that Reb Nosson would be coming. For in the middle of the Purim celebration, he said: "My student, Yehoshua, whose name is Nosson, also wants to be here with you. Nevertheless, he will complete the Purim holiday on Shushan Purim."[944] So when Reb Nosson finally arrived in Medvedevka sometime after midnight and knocked on the door of the* beit midrash, *the* shammes *(caretaker) who answered the door, asked him, "Are you Yehoshua Nosson?"*

A day later, Rebbe Nahman spoke to Reb Nosson alone, saying: "Do you remember my teaching about Moshe and Yehoshua, the master and the disciple?[945] Know that you are that disciple, even though there are others who are older than you, and who are also very pious. Nevertheless, it is so because 'Yehoshua was a young man,' and therefore, he 'would not leave the tent.' "[946]

Shortly thereafter, Rebbe Nahman began to talk to Reb Nosson about developing novel Torah interpretations. The Rebbe spoke of how the three commandments given to the people before they entered the land of Yisra'el were related to a teaching he had recently given, and that these three were also of the category of repentance. Reb Nosson asked "How?" And Rebbe Nahman answered, "This is for you to say."[947]

> IMMEDIATELY, I BEGAN TO THINK about this and, as I was leaving his house for my own lodgings, I was inspired with some very beautiful new ideas. As soon as I reached my lodgings, I found something to write with and wrote down the thoughts that had come to me. This was the beginning of my training in developing novellae from his teachings; and he had helped me to do this with such kindness, and such subtlety! The next day, I brought him what I had written, and he was pleased. He smiled and said, "If you stick with it, you can really learn to do this." Even so, I ceased to pursue it any further until I had covered more ground in my study of halakhah and kabbalah.[948]

For a while, Rebbe Nahman asked Reb Nosson to refrain from writing these ideas down. Presumably, the process was not yet ripe. Nevertheless, he continued to train him and made it clear to his other disciples that this was something he encouraged: "I have already given you good, pure powers of imagination, and you are entitled to develop original Torah ideas. What I myself grasp through wisdom, you can now grasp with your powers of imagination." It was at this time (in the Fall of 1804), that he taught *Likkutei MaHaRaN I*, 54, which discusses the pure use of the imagination, and the errors into which many fall regarding it. After this, he took Reb Nosson aside and gave him personal instructions.[949]

Just before Rosh Hashanah, 1807, Rebbe Nahman contracted tuberculosis, which appears to have had a major impact on what he taught the Hasidim that New Year. For the teaching he gave at that time—*Likkutei MaHaRaN I*, 61—is now looked upon as his last will and testament by Bratzlaver Hasidim, seeing as it spells out the ways in which he wanted his followers to conduct themselves when he was no longer among the living.[950] But even more interesting from our point of view is the fact that Rebbe Nahman seems to be giving Reb Nosson a kind of *smikhah*, or 'ordination' in this teaching.

Quoting the final passage of Deuteronomy dealing with Moses' death— "Now Joshua son of Nun was filled with the spirit of wisdom because

Moses had laid his hands upon him" (34:9)—the Rebbe who had so often compared Reb Nosson to Joshua in the presence of others, now connects the ordination of the disciple by the 'hand' of the master and the idea of the 'hand that writes.' This was a clear reference to Reb Nosson and his literary activity.[951] Apparently, through his own writing and the propagation of the Rebbe's teachings that he had himself recorded, he would be the Rebbe's successor, the carrier of his Torah into the world. As Reb Nahman Goldstein of Tcherin (d. 1894), who devoted himself to Reb Nosson's work, writes in his commentary on the *Likkutei MaHaRaN:* "And the truth is that all the power of Reb Nosson's pen—'the hand that wrote'—came from the spirit of wisdom which the Rebbe radiated to him through the 'hand of ordainment' that he laid upon him."[952]

Teachings to Arouse the Soul

Reb Nosson's most original teachings are found in his mammoth, eight volume *Likkutei Halakhot*, in which he explains the inner dimension of Jewish law and each *mitzvah* in the light of Rebbe Nahman's teaching. Fortunately for us, Reb Alter of Teplik (d. 1919), who culled Rebbe Nahman's pithy teachings for arousing the soul in *Meshivat Nefesh*, also gathered similar teachings from Reb Nosson's *Likkutei Halakhot* for the second half of that work. What follows are a small collection of Reb Nosson's gems from *Meshivat Nefesh*.

THOSE WHO ARE READY TO HAVE COMPASSION ON THEMSELVES—*considering their eternal end, and wanting to mend all that they have damaged—should pay no attention to negative thoughts, but should see themselves as being created anew everyday. This is why we recite all of the blessings of thanksgiving (given in the prayer book) each morning, as it is explained in the* Shulḥan Arukh. *For one's service has to be completely new everyday.*[953]

Every child of Yisra'el has numerous mitzvot to perform each day, and each of those should be performed as if it were a new mitzvah that had never been performed before. But to do this, you have to recognize and remember that this day and its experiences have never happened before, nor will they ever exist again. Consequently, your service to the holy One must be new as well. You have to know that the duties and obligations of this day are completely unique in this generation, designed for you alone! It is not for angels to do them, nor for the tzaddikim in paradise. Only you can do them; only those who are living can praise God today—this day![954] *It doesn't matter what level you are on, only you can give thanks and praise God as you must do it.*[955]

When Reb Nosson says that we "should pay no attention to negative thoughts" he is asking us to let go of those thoughts that have to do with regret over things in the past. He says this in much the same spirit as Reb Yitzhak Meir of Ger interprets the verse, "Turn away from evil and do good." (Ps. 34:15)[956] For the Gerer says: "No matter how much you turn it—this way and that—mud remains mud. In the time that you are wasting doing that, you could be making pearls for the crown of God. Therefore, leave the evil behind, and turn to the good."[957]

WHEN SOMEONE WANTS TO COME CLOSER TO GOD, *they have to know that obstacles will rise up before them, especially after they have begun to make a little progress. Even when they begin to purify themselves after years, they fall again, unexpectedly, as the old desires and sinful impulses rise up with even greater force. This is because they have not yet fully cleansed themselves of their 'soiled garments' from which these desires and impulses arise. It is necessary to expend a great effort to divest oneself of these "soiled garments."*[958]

There is a phenomenon in which piles of old rags and clothing have been known to spontaneously combust. In the same way, the "soiled garments" that have not been cleaned and washed out can, from time to time, lead to 'spontaneous combustion' in terms of old desires and sinful impulses.

OFTEN, THOSE WHO STRUGGLE IN THEIR SERVICE TO GOD *make a good start but fall suddenly; then they may start again, only to find themselves falling again, perhaps even falling back completely, God forbid. Nevertheless, even the smallest good that they have succeeded in doing leaves an imprint. Even these little bits of good are awesome, and essential for the work of redemption.*[959]

This teaching goes along with Rebbe Nahman's saying, "You have to find a *good-point* (n'kuddah tovah), even in yourself."[960] Because, once you've found a good-point in the midst of all the guilt and accusations, you can hold on to it and keep yourself from slipping into depression and discouragement. For all the 'shoulds' and 'shouldn'ts' you have in your life, find something that you have done in God's service that will allow you to say, "I've done some good; I'm not altogether bad."

THE SAGES TELL US *that there is nothing that can withstand the power of* teshuvah, *'repentance,' and it is held in readiness for one, even up to the hour of one's death.*⁹⁶¹ *Even if you have sinned a thousand times, every little stirring to 'return' to God in* teshuvah *is counted in the balance. As it says the Zohar, "No good stirring is ever lost."*⁹⁶² *For it is through* teshuvah *that one's transgressions are actually turned into merit,*⁹⁶³ *and what has been damaged may be mended as the divine light is drawn into the lower regions where the damage occurred.*⁹⁶⁴

Once, Reb Shmuel of Lubavitch (1834-1882) said, "When a person sighs in regret, that too is a *teshuvah*."⁹⁶⁵ Likewise, Reb Nosson says that "every little stirring to 'return' to God in *teshuvah*" makes a difference. Nothing good is lost, it all counts in the balance of merit for both the world and the individual. There no good act, however small, that is not counted, no contrition that doesn't make a difference. For when we sincerely repent of the damage we have caused, we draw a little of the divine light into those dark places which are so seldom illuminated.

ALL THE WARS IN THE WORLD *are really only reflections of the one war against the* yetzer ha-ra, *the 'negative impulse.' Even the conflicts one has with enemies in the material world are nothing but the war against one's own negative impulse. Thus, the real war to be fought is the war against the* yetzer ha-ra. *This is why the priests would speak to the people of Yisra'el before they went out to war against their enemies, because these really represented their own obstacles to a life of holiness. For our Sages have said, "Corresponding to a person's enemies in the 'lower world are also enemies in the worlds above."*⁹⁶⁶ *And when a person begins to battle the 'enemies above,' 'enemies below' rise up to assail them and prevent them from serving God. But this is precisely when one must stand firm and hold the line against the enemy, fighting with all one's strength in the service of God!*⁹⁶⁷

Today, many people are familiar with the Arabic word, *jihad*, which is usually translated as 'holy war.' But Sufis have long been at pains to point out that the word itself only means, 'struggle.' There is no such thing as a 'holy' war, at least not as extremists speak about it. There is only the 'struggle' to create peace. Nevertheless, like Reb Nosson, most Sufis tend to think of the references to "war" and "struggle" in the *Qur'an* as allusions to the struggle with the *nafs*, the tyrannical 'ego' within. This is often called the "greater *jihad*," as the following story shows:

> **When Muhammad and the early Muslims were returning from a major battle, he turned to his companions and said, "Now we are leaving the lesser *jihad* and going to the greater *jihad*." The warriors were stunned at his words. They were exhausted, their arrows were gone, their swords and lances were blunted or broken. The Prophet went on, "The greater *jihad* is the battle with what is in your breasts."**[968]

But Reb Nosson, anticipating the psychologist Carl Jung, also wants to say that the external conflicts that we have in our lives, and in our society, really reflect the conflct with the *yetzer ha-ra*, the 'negative impulse' within. "Thus, the real war to be fought is the war against the *yetzer ha-ra*." If this battle were to be fought and won, there might be less need for external conflicts in our lives. Nevertheless, when the "enemies below" do rise up to assail you, remember that they are only reflections of your inner conflict, and fight the "enemies above" instead.

On the other hand, we also have to know when *not* to fight. When I was a teenager working in the furrier's shop, some of the workers had pornographic pictures hanging on the walls; and being a *yeshiva bokher*, this caused me a lot of trouble with my *yetzer ha-ra*. My desire to look was constantly fighting with my desire not to look. So I talked to Rabbi Hodakov (later the Rebbe's chief-of-staff) about it. He said to me: "When you go to work, take the *yetzer ha-ra* and the *yetzer ha-tov* and lock 'em up in the closet. You can take 'em out later on." That is to say, the battle doesn't have to be continuous; there are times when you can steer your mind away from the battle and say: "Right now, I have to work and serve my God and my employer; I can't afford to do battle!"

IT IS SIMPLY A PART OF OUR EXISTENCE that we must endure time and change—treacherous seas, rivers, and the oceans' deeps, serpent and scorpion infested deserts and wildernesses. For it is only through such trials that we become worthy of entering the gates of holiness. This requires a strength almost beyond measure. Thus, there are some who think that their trials are so extreme that they cannot be endured. But this is not true; it is only that they have become ensnared in the trap of despair and ceased to hope for help from God. This is why the Rebbe cried out continually, Gevalt, zeit eikh nisht m'ya'esh! *"No! You must not despair!" And the word,* gevalt, *he extended, as if in extreme objection.*[969]

The first time I really took notice of Rebbe Nahman was in 1945, as all of Europe was on fire, and the crematoria of the concentration camps were sending up blue smoke. It was a very difficult time. But there was a Yiddish play in New York at the time based on this phrase of Rebbe Nahman—*Gevalt! Yidden zeit eikh nisht ma'ya'esh!* "Jews, you must not despair!" And it showed a scene of a little *shtibl* (prayer-house) in Warsaw where this teaching of Rebbe Nahman was being repeated. That made a strong impression on me.

The Yiddish, *m'ya'esh*, is difficult to translate while keeping the full sense of the word intact. The Hebrew on which it is based, *yi'ush*, is basically to 'give up hope,' or 'despair.' But it also has a sense of 'collapsing in on yourself' and 'not holding out any more.' Imagine someone swimming for the shore, struggling with exhaustion and in danger of drowning. There is a point at which it is very hard to keep on swimming; and if, at that point, they give up and say, "I can't do anymore," that's *mi'ya'esh*. It's like surrendering to the inevitable when it isn't yet inevitable! Reb Nosson and Rebbe Nahman are constantly imploring us to not to give up hope. For them, despair is an arrogant presumption. Who knows what will be? Who knows what God will do? Our job is to keep trying!

I Am Not Leaving You!

After Rebbe Nahman had passed on, perhaps no one mourned him more deeply than Reb Nosson. As he later wrote upon returning to Nemirov, "I arrived home heartbroken, an orphan with no father, a lost soul with no-one to seek after him."[970] And yet, he also wondered what the Rebbe had meant by his final gesture, which said, "I am not leaving you—God forbid!"[971]

Though the Rebbe had not left any explicit will regarding the future of his Hasidim, Reb Nosson knew, instinctively, that he had already given them everything they needed. It was communicated in everything he had said and done for the last eight years. And this, it turned out, was the immediate answer to Reb Nosson's question—*The Rebbe lived on in his teachings!* Thus, even as he was making his way home after the funeral in Uman, he and Reb Naftali stopped off in Dashev to raise funds for the printing of the Rebbe's teachings that had been collected since the first publication of the *Likkutei MaHaRaN*.

But that is not where it would end, for Reb Nosson soon found that the Hasidim also needed someone to rouse them from their slumber. As executor of the Rebbe's estate, he was required to travel to Bratzlav again to settle the Rebbe's affairs—collecting on his investments, selling his property, and seeing to the needs of his daughters, who now looked upon him as surrogate father. On one of his first visits there, he was astonished to find that the Bratzlaver Hasidim were already beginning to "drift away" from the Rebbe's teachings. This was most noticeable in their prayers, which had become somewhat tepid. This was partly due to the fact that they no longer had their own *beit midrash* in which to pray. For the Bratzlaver *beit midrash* had been attached to the Rebbe's home which had burned earlier in the year. So now the Rebbe's followers were forced to pray in the main synagogue, where the fervor of their prayers was less appreciated.

After only a few days, Reb Nosson had motivated the Hasidim of Bratzlav to pray as they used to and to begin raising funds for the building of their own *shtibl*, or prayer-house. He gave the first donation himself, and within a few weeks, the Hasidim were praying together again in a small, makeshift *shtibl* of their own. Immediately, people began to sense something new in this. For in the past, when the Rebbe of a town like Bratzlav had died, the Hasidim were sad, but soon passed into some other Hasidic fold in a nearby town. And indeed, this was precisely what had begun to happen before Reb Nosson arrived. So when the residents of Bratzlav noticed that the Rebbe's Hasidim were again becoming active and started to ask why, the answer came back, "Because Reb Nosson has returned to Bratzlav."[972]

But Reb Nosson knew that the Rebbe lived on in more than just his teachings. He also lived on in his Hasidim; and somehow, he was still working for them. In his last months, he had hinted at this often enough. Even the day before his passing, he had said: "None of you have anything to worry about, seeing as I am going before you. Those who have already passed on might have had some ground for concern, but you, you don't have to worry at all. If the souls which have not known me are awaiting this *tikkun* from me, then you can certainly be confident." Thus, Reb Nosson was convinced that the Rebbe was actively making a way for them in the next world. *He was still their Rebbe!*

Now he knew that the Hasidim must return to Uman, to pray at the Rebbe's *tziun* (grave-site)![973] And because the Rebbe had always spoken of the importance of being with him on Rosh Hashanah, the Jewish New Year, Reb Nosson began planning a pilgrimage to the Rebbe's grave at that time. But if it was going to work, he would need the support of the other senior disciples. So, on January 26th, 1811, just four months after the Rebbe's passing, he organized a smaller pilgrimage for the senior disciples on Rosh Ḥodesh Shevat, which is also considered a new year's date. In that first group were Reb Yoske, the Rebbe's son-in-law, Ahron the Rav of Bratzlav, his son Reb Tzvi Aryeh, and a few others. Reb Shmuel Yitzhak of Dashev had to travel separately and arrived a little later than the others. Thus, Reb Shmuel Yitzhak went straight to the grave and prayed there in the frigid weather until well after midnight. Meanwhile, the other Bratzlav Hasidim were in the *beit midrash* with Reb Nosson, who spoke of the Rebbe all night long! Later, when Reb Shmuel Yitzhak heard about the joyous atmosphere of the group, he said, "I was at the Rebbe's grave, but Reb Nosson had already drawn the Rebbe to himself!"[974]

This was the first pilgrimage Bratzlaver Hasidim ever made to Uman, and it was the true beginning of all the work that followed.[975]

In Search of the Tzaddik

Now Reb Nosson understood his task; he must continue to rouse the Hasidim to faith in the Rebbe's teachings. But first, they had to know that the Rebbe was still there for them. They had to see for themselves how he had spoken of this in his discourses, just as he had spoken about nearly every aspect of life. So even as he continued to print the *Likkutei MaHaRaN*—sometimes illegally on a printing press in his own home—he also began to think of printing the other works Rebbe Nahman had suggested he write back in 1805. The first was the *Kitzur Likkutei MaHaRaN* in which he had distilled the major themes and action-directives from the *Likkutei MaHaRaN*. For as Reb Nosson points out in the introduction to that work, the Rebbe's purpose was always to bring people to practical action, "for the main thing is not the learning but the doing." (Avot 1:17)[976] Later, he took this one step further, separating the Rebbe's counsels (*etzot*) according to subject in a work called *Likkutei Etzot*, from which the following passages on the *tzaddik* are drawn.

ONE MUST BE DISCERNING AND SEARCH diligently *for the true tzaddik, for the true tzaddik has access to ruah ha-kodesh, the 'spirit of holiness.' The root of perfect faith is the belief in the divine creation of the world, and this belief is imparted to one by the true tzaddik. As this belief requires that one overcome and penetrate the power of illusion, no one but the true tzaddik—who has access to ruah ha-kodesh—can accomplish it. By destroying illusion, the true tzaddik strengthens one's faith in the creation and renewal of the world.*

Every one on Earth, from the smallest to the greatest, must take care in searching for a true tzaddik all their life. For the Torah does not address itself to the 'dead,' meaning those who don't really wish to find 'life,' those who do not take heed for their soul and actively seek its redemption. The Torah only addresses itself to those who actually want to be saved from the pervasive sense of emptiness and purposelessness in this life....

But even if you are fortunate enough to find a Rebbe, or a friend who has received guidance from a true tzaddik, who can helpfully speak to the condition of your soul with living words of truth, you must nevertheless continue 'seeking.' Even if you succeed in correcting something in yourself, the search must continue because the human being does not stand still. Many actions do not have the effect you intend them to have, especially in our day and age, as you well know, so you must continue to seek for the true tzaddik who accesses ruaḥ ha-kodesh, the 'spirit of holiness.' Nevertheless, it is not the search for the bodily appearance of the tzaddik that is so important; one must search for the tzaddik's 'spirit of holiness.' For only the ruaḥ ha-kodesh is able to penetrate and dispel the illusion.

Indeed, the illusion was created to be penetrated and dispelled by the ruaḥ ha-kodesh of the true tzaddik. So one who has not yet found such a being, must surely seek them out. One must seek them out with all their strength, going all over the world—on one's hands and knees, if necessary—all one's days, hoping to find the true tzaddik, and through them, the 'life of one's soul,' if only for one day, or even one hour before one's death!

Even if you find the tzaddik, you must continue to be a seeker, for one's soul is still dark, and does not yet feel delight in the truth of the tzaddik's holy counsel, and so is still far from its tikkun, or 'repair.' Again, finding of the 'spirit of holiness' of the tzaddik is the most important objective. One who sincerely seeks the tzaddik will surely find them, for "God does not require the impossible of God's children, and one who says that she or he has sought and found is to be believed."

Even the true teacher must search and seek in order to re-discover the holiness of their own teacher's ruaḥ ha-kodesh (which they have received) until it is again found within them. Thus, one is truly able to guide, counsel, and speak to the conditions of the people who call on him or her. For, it is extremely difficult to counsel and help anyone possessing 'free will.'[977] Only by the amazing graces of God, which the tzaddik draws down from the upper worlds, and true merit from below, is it possible to counsel in truth. Thus, in working with people to bring them to themselves, one must work at great depth, a depth scarcely imaginable. Therefore, one must seek and search and plead with one's teacher, a friend or disciple, and then only can one find the 'spirit of holiness.'[978]

So here in Reb Nosson's distillation of Rebbe Nahman's teachings are numerous clues to how the Bratzlaver Hasid conceives of the *tzaddik*. First—although the *tzaddik* appears to be the object of one's search, it is really the *tzaddik*'s open connection to the *ruah ha-kodesh*, or the 'spirit of holiness' that is to be desired. However, it is not enough to find a *tzaddik* with such a connection; one must also put their teachings into practice.[979] This allows one to discover the "life of one's soul." Likewise, there are some who, with the aid of the *tzaddik*, may also discover a connection to *ruah ha-kodesh* within themselves, and thus have the power to "guide, counsel, and speak to the conditions of the people." Nevertheless, one must never become complacent in this, but seek to renew the connection in every moment.

The "true *tzaddik*" of greatest consequence to Bratzlaver Hasidim, of course, is Rebbe Nahman himself, whose connection to *ruah ha-kodesh* is crystallized in his profound teachings. Through these and the living connection to *ruah ha-kodesh* that was awakened in his disciples, particulary Reb Nosson, the flow from the divine source remains open, allowing everyone to reach the same heights as Reb Noson and Rebbe Nahman (as the ideal and accessible models)—at least in potential. For Rebbe Nahman tells us: "Any person can attain my levels and become just like me. It all depends on how hard you try." You see, even though Rebbe Nahman is seen as a *tzaddik* of destiny, he made it absolutely clear that he had earned all the levels he had attained:

> This is the trouble. You think that *tzaddikim* attain greatness merely because they have a great soul. This is absolutely wrong! I worked very hard for all this. I put much effort into attaining what I did. But you think because I have a great soul, because I am a descendant of the Ba'al Shem Tov (his great-grandson), that this is why I attained these levels. You are mistaken. It is because of the devotions and efforts I put in.[980]

It is precisely because he did it through his own efforts, and not through ancestral merit or any special status, that he can assure us that we can do it too. This was at the heart of his teachings, and distinguished him from Rebbes like his uncle Barukh of Mezhbizh and Reb Avraham of Kalisk. He believed in the potential of his Hasidim to do what he had done.

You see, the real paradox of Rebbe Nahman's teaching is that while he seems to set himself at the top, it is only for the purpose of raising everyone else up to his level. For he was not content with making 'decent Hasidim' out his people, he wanted to make them all *tzaddikim!*

In 1819, the Rebbe's grandson Reb Yisra'el married the great-granddaughter of Reb Mordecai of Chernobyl. During the wedding in Chernobyl, there were many Bratzlaver Hasidim present, including Reb Nosson. Watching them dance, Reb Mordecai said aloud, "These are not just Hasidim dancing, these are *tzaddikim!*"[981]

By The Consent of Our Master, Rebbe Nahman

Even though Rebbe Nahman is understood to be an *epochal* Rebbe, opening an era that will last until the coming of the Messiah, that doesn't mean that Bratzlav Hasidism doesn't continue to have Rebbes as some have supposed—*it does*. It's just that they do their work under the auspices of Rebbe Nahman, keeping an open connection to his *ruah ha-kodesh*, and continuing his teachings in the tradition of Reb Nosson. Though the title 'Rebbe' is usually reserved for Rebbe Nahman alone, the Rebbe-function in Bratzlav continues unabated through leaders *(manhigim)* who sometimes attain the status of *tzaddikim*, most of whom trace their lineage directly back to Reb Nosson himself. Thus it is said in relation to him: "Fortunate are the eyes that saw Rebbe Nahman's eyes; and fortunate are the eyes that saw the eyes that saw the Rebbe's eyes. And so on from generation to generation."[982]

Interestingly enough, this issue actually came up in Reb Nosson's lifetime, and his reaction did much to shape the future of how Bratzlav leaders looked at themselves.

The night before Shavuot in 1834, *almost 24 years after the Rebbe's passing, eighty Bratzlaver Hasidim—old and new—gathered together in Bratzlav with Reb Nosson. Among them was Reb Shimon, Rebbe Nahman's first disciple, who was visiting from* Eretz Yisra'el.

As Reb Nosson taught before all the Hasidim on yontif (the holiday), Reb Shimon appeared surprised and said: "I always thought of Reb Nosson as a follower of the Rebbe. Now I see that he is the Rebbe himself! I know about gutte Yiddin (tzaddikim). *I abandoned all thought of other tzaddikim and attached myself to a young man (Rebbe Nahman), even though I was older than him. So I know a gutten Yid when I see one, and I tell you, Reb Nosson is the tzaddik of the generation!"*

Soon after, many others began to echo his words, saying—"Reb Nosson is the Rebbe." But Reb Nosson would not hear it. Unable to stand being compared to his beloved Rebbe, he yelled, "I know I'm not the Rebbe!" and became irritable, fearing that pride might somehow take hold of him. Then, as the guests were departing, he said, "Now that you have received the Torah, be careful not to make a golden calf."[983]

Reb Nosson never dressed in a silk *bekeshe* or wore a fur *shtreimel* as Rebbes wore at that time, but continued to dress as he had always done, in a simple suit and a simple hat. In this way, he made his point.[984] He was still the 'Rebbe's man,' and did his work in his name.

In this same spirit, Reb Nosson wrote the following letter "by the consent of our master, Rebbe Nahman, the well-spring of wisdom." As you will see, his intention was that the Bratzlaver novice should read it as if it were personally addressed to him or her. He left it up to the reader to supply the effective expression, reading the letter out loud, visualizing themselves as being in the presence of Reb Nosson, the Rebbe's steward.

DEAR (ENUNCIATE YOUR OWN NAME CLEARLY) *the son/daughter of (your parent's name), my friend and disciple, it is you I am calling; therefore, I beg you to take a minute and listen to what I have to say.*

I want you to realize how much effort it has taken to draw you closer; indeed, it has taken miracles! But one of the conditions on which I insist before taking a disciple is that they do not allow themselves to be deceived by anyone—even themselves.

Now, you have often heard my counsel regarding hitbodedut, *spontaneous and solitary prayer: you can receive everything that you need, realize all that you need to realize, and make all the* tikkunim *or 'repairs' you need to make through* hitbodedut. *For* hitbodedut *is a conversation in the presence of the holy One, asking for everything that you need—both materially and spiritually—confessing all that you have done wrong—whether intentionally or not—and expressing gratitude to God for all the material and spiritual gifts you have received.*

God has granted this to me: anyone who attends to this practice—simply and honestly standing for an hour before God each day—will receive great merit from it and be free from heavenly prosecution. Even if you don't experience any awakening in hitbodedut, *even if you are blocked in the effort, as long as it is done with the yearning to express yourself to God, you will certainly benefit from it. For in this work, everything can be made whole again: one's* nefesh, ruaḥ, *and* neshamah *(animative, emotive, and intellectual souls), all the* olamot *(worlds) that depend on God, the first* adam *(human being) to the last, and even* our Mashiaḥ (Messiah)! All this is true, established, prepared, and effective. I promise you this, and take the responsibility for everything that I have said.

Nevertheless, I must also tell you that such a simple and powerful tikkun as this arouses opposition on all fronts. The Sitra Aḥra, the 'Other Side,' will raise questions and objections in you, urging you to skepticism, impatience, and making excuses for delaying your hitbodedut, to take you away from this tikkun.

Brother/sister, beloved of my heart, have some compassion for yourself! Open your eyes and understand how unhappy the Sitra Aḥra intends to make you, how it schemes to keep you in spiritual poverty and nakedness, unable to receive the benefit of these powerful tikkunim available through hitbodedut, which touch infinity itself!

I know how much you are prepared to offer God, and yet, in simple things you allow yourself to be deceived. Cast aside the short term benefits of daily life, the business matters, and your little schemes! Run and save yourself! For, in time, you will certainly thank God for this counsel—Amen.

By the consent of our master, Rebbe Nahman, the well-spring of wisdom,

Nosson of Nemirov.[985]

This is a wonderful example of Reb Nosson's spiritual guidance, encouraging his disciples to keep up the practice of *hitbodedut*, and to fortify themselves against "self-deception" and the "questions and objections" of the Other Side.

Though we have not been able to explore it here, these were especially difficult years for the Bratzlaver Hasidim. Reb Nosson was arrested and imprisoned. People routinely threw stones at his home, and once an attempt was even made on his life. Things were just as bad for his disciples, and sometimes worse. All of them paid the price for being different, and for living up to their ideals. And because of this, so much of Reb Nosson's spiritual guidance was simple encouragement sent in letters to his Hasidim:

The suffering is bad enough while you are going through it, God save us! No matter what, though, do not dwell at all on your difficulties! Be extremely careful to heed my advice, and do not let your mind be troubled in the least over this. Just study Torah, pray and go about your business. Relax your mind with things that cheer you and bring yourself to joy, even, if need be, with silliness. You have no idea what is really going on in the world![986]

These letters were later collected and published as *Alim li-Terufah*, 'leaves of healing,' and have since been published in English in their entirety as *Eternally Yours*, and in a small book of gems called, *Healing Leaves: Prescriptions for Inner Strength, Meaning, and Hope*.

Straight to the Rebbe!

Once, Rebbe Nahman was speaking to someone about his illness and saying that he felt good that at least he had been able to help a few people to improve themselves. The person he was speaking to answered, "That is true; for I know that Reb Nosson will certainly be a *tzaddik*." But the Rebbe corrected him, and said, "No, I tell you he is already a *tzaddik!*"[987]

From the time Reb Nosson first came to Bratzlav on September 18th, 1802, to the day of his passing there on December 20th, 1844 (10 Tevet, 5605), he had undergone a profound transformation. Gone was the young man who was tortured by a sense of futility and meaninglessness, the young man of whom the Rebbe said: "What can I tell you? With his brilliance, he only has to glance at a synagogue to tell you the details of its grandeur; but when he looks at himself, he sees only mud." In his place was a man who was forged of steel, who found meaning and hope in the smallest details of life, and who was bold in every action. He had found his purpose, and pursued it with dogged persistence for over forty years until he had successfully established Bratzlav Ḥasidut.

WHEN REB NOSSON PASSED AWAY, *it was just before* Shabbat *in Bratzlav. Thus, the news of his death did not begin to reach his friends and disciples outside of Bratzlav until days afterward. Nevertheless, that evening, Reb Nosson's oldest and closest friend, Reb Naftali, dreamt that he saw Reb Nosson running. So he called out to him, "Nosson, my brother! Where are you running to?" Without breaking stride, Reb Nosson called back, "Straight to the Rebbe!"*

When Reb Naftali awoke, he knew that Reb Nosson had passed on. Later, he told his own disciples, "I knew it would not be long; I could tell by the way he danced on Rosh Hashanah."[988]

Those who would know more about Reb Nosson should read Chaim Kramer's amazing biography, *Through Fire and Water*. For it is impossible to do justice to such a rich and courageous life in the space of one short chapter; but neither could we bear to keep silent about him as so many others have done. It is ironic that the Herculean task he took on to preserve Rebbe Nahman's legacy has made him all but invisible to many admirers of the Rebbe. For today, Rebbe Nahman is recognized as one of the most original and significant masters in the whole history of the Hasidic movement, and even as one of the more significant personages in the history of Judaism. Thus, the shadow he casts over Reb Nosson is also a testimony of Nosson's own success. Nevertheless, we wanted to take this opportunity to show you something of how he is viewed among Bratzlav Hasidim who know his worth better than any one else. In their eyes, he is a genius who is revered only slightly less than the Rebbe himself, and who is honored as a model of Hasidic leadership.

The old Jewish cemetery in Bratzlav overlooking the Bug River
Photo by Ayla Grafstein

Appendix:
Moshe Shneuri, Defender of the Faith

ACCORDING TO MOST SOURCES, Reb Moshe Shneuri, the youngest son of Reb Shneur Zalman of Liadi, was a lively and profoundly gifted child with strong charisma.[1436] However, much more is to be gleaned from the eyewitness account that we quoted earlier with regard to his elder brother, Reb Dov Baer (Chapter 4, "Twin Guardians of the Community"). Now, the same eyewitness goes on to describe the other two sons of the Alter Rebbe:

> *THE MIDDLE SON, HAYYIM AVRAHAM, tended to isolate himself, becoming immersed in his studies with deep and silent concentration, and was more inclined to contemplation than talking. Very different was Moshe, the youngest son of the Rebbe, who was a lively boy of about fourteen or fifteen. His eyes sparkled with intelligence and great confidence, and he loved to talk and debate with others. I was told that he was a genius with an extraordinary memory and mental acuity, already thoroughly proficient in the entire Talmud and well-schooled in the philosophy of religion (ḥakira), having such great works as the* Moreh Nevukim, Sefer al-Kuzari, *and the* Ikkarim *at his finger-tips!*[1437]

The same source tells us that at sixteen years old, Reb Moshe was instructed in both Russian and French by Reb Moshe Meisels, at the Alter Rebbe's suggestion, and quickly became fluent in both.[1438] This knowledge of

European languages turned out to be important to several stories regarding him. For when his father was first arrested in 1798, when he was 18 years old, he was very upset and begged to be allowed to go to St. Petersburg to defend him with his fluent Russian and French, both of which were official languages of the elite in the Empire. And though he was prevented from going (by his father's own injunction against any family member coming to St. Petersburg), he was confident in his ability to gain his father's release, saying "I would gain an audience with the Czar himself, if necessary, and with no trouble at all I would triumph over the prosecution."[1439]

However, when next the Alter Rebbe was arrested two years later, he did indeed take Reb Moshe along as a companion and translator. My Rebbe has written: "Reb Moshe's handsome appearance, his polite demeanor, and his methodical way of speaking made a favorable impression on the officials. But most of all, they were impressed by his fluent and idiomatic use of the Russian language, and they were even more amazed by his beautiful and lucid French."[1440] However, his supreme confidence and love of debate also drew him into dangerous territory.

The Rebbe goes on to tell how Reb Moshe was invited to the homes of various Christian officials and allowed to read in their libraries. Already familiar with Christian beliefs, he became even more fluent in Christian theology and was only too ready to debate the priests who had tried to draw he and his father into traps in court. Thus, he began to debate with them outside of the courtroom in the homes of his Christian acquaintances, winning debate after debate, and making many enemies. Finally, he was warned about the possible consequences of his actions, but he was undeterred. When the Alter Rebbe learned about this, he was very worried for his son and remembered the curse of Reb Shlomo Karliner (Chapter 4, "The Curse") who had said, "You are afraid of a ḥillul ha-Shem; you will suffer a ḥillul ha-Shem caused by this boy (Reb Moshe, who was present)." Fortunately, little came of it at the time and they left St. Petersburg in peace.[1441]

Later, Reb Moshe became his father's most efficient administrator, especially in his dealings with the Russian government, often traveling on the Rebbe's behalf to St. Petersburg. Then, as Napoleon approached shortly before his father's death, Reb Moshe helped in the war effort, moving from his home in Ulla to Droia, where the French intelligence service had its headquarters. He soon became an able assistant in the headquarters, and thus an effective spy for the Russians![1442]

However, shortly after his father's passing, traditions and certainties about Reb Moshe seem to scatter on the winds. In 1813, when the final redaction of the *Tanya* was published, Reb Moshe gives his own approbation to the work along with his brothers, Reb Dov Baer and Reb Hayyim Avraham. But in 1814, when their father's *Shulḥan Arukh* is finally published, approbations are given by both Reb Dov Baer and Reb Hayyim Avraham, but Reb Moshe is conspicuously absent.

When I was young, I heard various strange and conflicting 'rumors' about Reb Moshe—e.g., that he had converted to Christianity, or that he had gone crazy. Later, I encountered sources that described Reb Dov Baer as a devious ignoramus who slandered his brother, Reb Moshe and forced him to relinquish his claim on the leadership of HaBaD. Others said that he left the community and converted to Christianity, or simply went mad, as I had heard, ending his days a wandering pauper, or emigrating to the Holy Land.[1443] What these defamatory rumors say to me is that Reb Moshe was likely considered a potential successor of his father for the leadership of HaBaD, and that supporters of both Reb Dov Baer and Reb Moshe are likely responsible for these negative representations of each. Like the other two candidates (Reb Dov Baer and Reb Ahron HaLevi), Reb Moshe was also allowed to give discourses to the Hasidim and was one of the few authoritative memorizers of the Rebbe's discourses.[1444] Whether there was actually any bad blood between Reb Dov Baer and Reb Moshe is unknown. HaBaD-Lubavitch sources, as far as I know, have little to say about the matter. However, once in 1935, my Rebbe was asked whether Reb Moshe had ever done *teshuvah* for his transgressions, and the Rebbe reportedly said: "God forbid! He hadn't done anything he needed to do *teshuvah* for! He was a complete *tzaddik*." He then went on to talk about eleven manuscripts of Reb Moshe's that he had in his possession that he relies upon for proper understanding of *Ḥasidut*.[1445]

Recently, I heard a story from a young HaBaD Hasid who appears to be a descendant of Reb Moshe that would seem to clear up most of the rumors:

AFTER THE PASSING OF REB SHNEUR ZALMAN *and the defeat of Napoleon, Czar Alexander of Russia wished to confer a special honor on the descendants of Reb Shneur Zalman who had acted so devotedly in the service of the empire during the French invasion. His descendants were to be "Honored Citizens in Perpetuity," which was a close as a Jew could come to a peerage in Russia. Thus, the three* sons of Reb Shneur Zalman—Reb Dov Baer, Reb Hayyim Avraham, and Reb Moshe—were granted an audience with Czar Alexander, with a group of many others being given similar honors for service to their country. Nevertheless, the priest who had been designated 'master of ceremonies' was reluctant to see this honor conferred upon them. Thus, he tried to make them uncomfortable and continually pushed back their audience. Reb Moshe, speaking flawless Russian and French, and already familiar with the customs of the Russian nobility, saw exactly what was happening, and when they were finally brought before the Czar, gave the priest a piece of his mind.

The Czar, enjoying the discomfiture of the priest, showed great deference to the children of the Alter Rebbe, and suggested, "Maybe the two of you (Reb Moshe and the priest) have more to discuss about the differences in your religions?" Of course, Reb Moshe said he would be glad to discuss these things. So Reb Moshe debated the priest and easily defeated him. Then, more and more senior opponents were brought before him, all of which were defeated by his scintillating intellect.

Unfortunately, this eventually brought on the trouble his father had feared all those years before. Fearing he would win a final debate with the emissaries of the Russian Orthodox Church, thugs were hired to abduct Reb Moshe and to imprison him until he was forced to convert, thus saving face for the Church. He was then secretly imprisoned in Vladimir. However, after four days, a miracle occurred—his guards fell into a deep sleep and he walked out of the prison unnoticed, and disappeared.

Fearing to bring further trouble to himself and his family, he settled into a quiet exile.[1446]

Notes

CHAPTER 1

1   Zalman Schachter-Shalomi and Joel Segel, *Jewish with Feeling: A Guide to Meaningful Jewish Practice*, New York: Riverhead Books. 2005; David Cooper, *God Is a Verb: Kabbalah and the Practice of Mystical Judaism*, New York: Riverhead Books. 1998.
2   Noson Gurary, *Chasidism: Its Development, Theology, and Practice*, Lanham, Maryland: Jason Aronson, 2006; Chaim Kramer, *Crossing the Narrow Bridge*, Jerusalem: Breslov Research Institute, 1989; Nissan Mindel, *Rabbi Schneur Zalman of Liadi*, New York: Kehot Publication Society, 1969; and Aryeh Kaplan, *Until the Mashiach: The Life of Rabbi Nachman*, Jerusalem: Breslov Research Institute, 1985.
3   This work is available in English in a lovely two-volume translation by Nissan Mindel, though with the somewhat misleading title, *Lubavitcher Rabbi's Memoirs*. A more literal and correct rendering would be *The Book of Remembrances*, as these are not things remembered from Rabbi Yosef Yitzhak Schneersohn's own life, but stories about the *tzaddikim nistarim* that he had learned from elder Hasidim and the members of his own family.
4   During the period the Rebbe covers, the mission of the *tzaddikim nistarim* was to relieve the suffering of Jews in Eastern Europe after the terrible massacres of 1648-49.
5   "Only to do justice and to love goodness, and to walk modestly with your God" (Mic. 6:8), *JPS Hebrew-English* TANAKH: *The Traditional Hebrew Text and the New JPS Translation*. All translations in the notes, except where otherwise indicated, are from the new JPS translation.
6   Joseph I. Schneersohn, trans. Nissan Mindel, *Lubavitcher Rabbi's Memoirs: Volume One*, 31.
7   Zalman Schachter-Shalomi and Netanel Miles-Yepez, *A Heart Afire: Stories and Teachings of the Early Hasidic Masters*, 21.

8 The word "herself" is used here because the soul is considered feminine.
9 Presumably, this refers to the ascended master, Ahiyah ha-Shiloni.
10 Ibid., 23-24.
11 Ibid., 3-8.
12 Schneersohn, *Lubavitcher Rabbi's Memoirs: Volume One*, 31.
13 Ibid., 44.
14 Ibid., 31.
15 This surname for Barukh appears in Yosef Yitzchak Schneersohn, trans. Uri Kaploun, *Likkutei Dibburim: Volume 5*, 299. *Weis kval* means, 'white spring,' probably referring to the name of his estate upon which his son, Shneur Zalman, is reported to have discovered a spring. See Nissan Mindel, *Rabbi Schneur Zalman: Volume I: Biography*, 29.
16 In Joseph I. Schneersohn, trans. Nissan Mindel, *Lubavitcher Rabbi's Memoirs: Volume Two: Revised Edition*, 208, the genealogy is given as follows: Rabbi Yehudah Loew of Prague to his son Betzalel, to his son Shmuel, to his son Yehudah Leib, to his son Moshe, to his son Shneur Zalman, to his son Barukh, who was the father of Shneur Zalman of Liadi.
17 Ibid., 196, 251. This refers to Rabbi Yoel ben Yitzchak Aizik Halpern, Ba'al Shem of Zamoshtch I (d. ca. 1713), not Rabbi Yoel ben Uri, Ba'al Shem of Zamoshtch II (d. ca. 1755). See Immanuel Etkes, trans. Saadya Sternberg, *Besht: Magician, Mystic, and Leader*, 11-12, 25-26, 33-42.
18 Schneersohn, *Lubavitcher Rabbi's Memoirs: Volume One*, 46-71.
19 Ibid., 160-65.
20 Ibid., 162.
21 Ibid., 86 and 115.
22 Shaul Shimon Deutsch, "The Last Years of Reb Boruch – The Alter Rebbe's Father," *The Chasidic Historical Review*, 4-7, cites a source that suggests that Reb Barukh was actually an enemy of the Hasidic movement, but Deutsch writes that this does not seem to be based on any known evidence. According to this article, Reb Barukh died in Hungary, in a place called Serentch, or Selish, while apparently continuing the life of a *tzaddik nistar*. As he lay dying, he is reported to have said: "Two of my children need to be notified. To one you need only hint of my demise, and one you won't have to notify, since he will know by himself."
23 Schneersohn, *Lubavitcher Rabbi's Memoirs: Volume One*, 94-96, and Yosef Yitzchak Schneersohn, trans. Uri Kaploun, *Likkutei Dibburim: Volume 4*, 129.
24 "God made the two great lights, the greater light to dominate the day and the lesser light to dominate the night, and the stars. And God set them in the expanse of the sky to shine upon the earth" (Gen. 1:16-17).
25 "Arise, shine, for your light has dawned" (Isa. 60:1).
26 It is also sometimes said that Reb Shneur Zalman's soul was that of the RaShBA, Rabbi Shlomo ben Aderet (1235-1310), who defended Maimonides.
27 Some have speculated that Shneur comes from the Spanish, *señor*, a title of courtesy used before a surname, ultimately deriving from the Latin, *senior*, 'lord' or 'elder.'
28 "And he named him Noaḥ, saying, 'This one will provide us relief from our work and the toil of our hands' " (Gen. 5:29).
29 According to the Midrash, Rosh Hashanah is celebrated on the 6th day of creation, when Adam was created. So, counting backward, the first day of creation, is actually the 25th of Elul.
30 Lev. 12:3.
31 "I greatly rejoice in the Lord" (Isa. 61:10).
32 Learned at a ḤaBaD-Lubavitch *farbrengen*. —Z.M.S-S. See Yosef Yitzchak Schneersohn,

trans. Uri Kaploun, *Likkutei Dibburim: Volume 3*, 242-46, and Mindel, *Rabbi Schneur Zalman*, 24-25 for parallel accounts of the circumstances surrounding Reb Shneur Zalman's birth.
33   The Rabbis say that when Abraham was sitting at the entrance to his tent and was visited by the angels, this also occurred on the crucial third day after his circumcision (mentioned at the end of Parshat Lekh Lekha).
34   Learned at a ḤaBaD-Lubavitch *farbrengen*. —Z.M.S-S. This last advice was given a year later. See Schneersohn, *Likkutei Dibburim: Volume 3*, 246, and Mindel, *Rabbi Schneur Zalman*, 25-26 for another account of these meetings.
35   See "*Mitzvot* and *Berakhot*" in Chapter 6, where Rebbe Nahman's mother takes similar precautions. A very nice teaching on the evil eye was also given by Rabbi Efraim Kenig, the son of Rabbi Gedaliah Kenig, and brother of Rabbi Elazar Kenig of S'fat. In it, he writes: "It might seem as though there is no way to be saved from this type of power. However, on a deeper level, we see that Yosef possessed the special quality against the evil eye because he never 'fed' his eye on something that didn't belong to him." Efraim Kenig, "The Power of Vision," *Tzaddik*, 7.
36   Mindel, *Rabbi Schneur Zalman*, 26.
37   "The Lord bless you and protect you! The Lord deal kindly and graciously with you! The Lord bestow His favor upon you and grant you peace!" (Num. 6:24-26).
38   Learned at a ḤaBaD-Lubavitch *farbrengen*. —Z.M.S-S. See Schneersohn, *Likkutei Dibburim: Volume 3*, 246-47, and Mindel, *Rabbi Schneur Zalman*, 26-27 for another English version of this story.
39   See Harry M. Rabinowicz, *Hasidism: The Movement and Its Masters*, 83.
40   Mindel, *Rabbi Schneur Zalman*, 28.
41   Learned at a ḤaBaD-Lubavitch *farbrengen*. —Z.M.S-S. See Schneersohn, *Likkutei Dibburim: Volume 4*, 129.
42   Learned at a ḤaBaD-Lubavitch *farbrengen*. —Z.M.S-S. See Mindel, *Rabbi Schneur Zalman*, 30-31 for another English version of this tradition.
43   Learned at a ḤaBaD-Lubavitch *farbrengen*. —Z.M.S-S.
44   Mindel, *Rabbi Schneur Zalman*, 31.
45   This is basically a condensed paraphrase of a teaching reported by my Rebbe, Yosef Yitzhak Schneersohn in 1949. —Z.M.S-S. See Schneersohn, *Likkutei Dibburim: Volume 4*, 7-8.
46   The book-length introduction to the *Sh'nei Luḥot ha-B'rit*, "*Toldot Adam*" was translated into English by Miles Krassen as *The Generations of Adam*.
47   When I was a young Hasid, I studied the entire SheLoH because I had read that the Alter Rebbe had studied it with his young companions in Vitebsk. —Z.M.S-S.
48   Talmud, Yevamot 109b.
49   Learned at a ḤaBaD-Lubavitch *farbrengen*. —Z.M.S-S. See Schneersohn, *Likkutei Dibburim: Volume 4*, 224-225.
50   Mindel, *Rabbi Schneur Zalman*, 35-36. See Martin Buber, trans. Olga Marx, *Tales of the Hasidim: The Early Masters*, 265 ("No Returning"), 265-66 ("Permission"), and Rabinowicz, *Hasidism*, 84.
51   The *ḥayyot ha-kodesh* of the *Merkavah* are described Ezekiel 1, and again in Ezekiel 10.
52   "Dashing to and fro [among] the creatures was something that looked like flares" (Ezek. 1:14)
53   "Each of them had a human face [at the front]; each of the four had the face of a lion on the right; each of the four had the face of an ox on the left; and each of the four had the face of an eagle [at the back]" (Ezek. 1:10).
54   This is a reference to the stilling of the wings of the *ḥayyot ha-kodesh* and the hands

that could be seen beneath their wings as described in Ezekiel: "When they moved, I could hear the sound of their wings like the sounds of mighty waters, like the sounds of *Shaddai*, a tumult like the din of an army. When they stood still, they would let their wings droop" (1:24) and "They had the figures of human beings" (1:5) and "They had human hands below their wings" (1:8).

55   Yosef Yitchak Schneersohn, trans. Nissan Mindel and Zalman Posner, *On the Study of Chasidus: A Trilogy of Chasidic Essays*, 51 says, "No doubt," continued my brother, "had the Maggid not entered the hall at that moment, some of the men would have simply expired as a result of their tremendous yearning and desire to unite with the Almighty."

56   "It was I who made the earth and created man upon it" (Isa. 45:12).

57   Learned at a ḤaBaD-Lubavitch *farbrengen*. However, a version of this is also found in my Rebbe's *Kuntres Torat ha-Ḥasidut*, later translated into English as "On the Teachings of Chasidus" by my former colleague Zalman I. Posner in Schneersohn, *On the Study of Chasidus*, 50–53. — Z.M.S-S. See Mindel, *Rabbi Schneur Zalman*, 36–38 for another English version of this story.

58   Schneersohn, *On the Study of Chasidus*, 51.

59   Schneersohn, *Likkutei Dibburim: Volume 5*, 32.

60   There also seems to be more than a little synchronicity in this moment; for the situation seems like the perfect lure with which to hook the soul which the Ba'al Shem Tov had said would "illuminate the world with two kinds of light—the light of *nigleh*, the manifest Torah, and the light of *nistar*, the hidden Torah." But perhaps we should not be surprised, for this was very much as it had been when the holy Ba'al Shem had hooked the Maggid with precisely the revelation *he* needed, and using the same text from Ezekiel!

61   Learned at a ḤaBaD-Lubavitch *farbrengen*. —Z.M.S-S. For alternate English versions, see Buber, *Tales of the Hasidim: The Early Masters*, 266 ("The Gaze of the Master"), and Rabinowicz, *Hasidism*, 85. A story is also told in the Sufi tradition of the first time Muhyiddin Ibn 'Arabi saw Jalaluddin Rumi as a child following behind his father, who was also a great mystic: "As Baha'uddin and young Jalaluddin took their leave, Ibn 'Arabi said, 'Amazing, that an ocean is following a small lake!'" Muhyiddin Ibn 'Arabi, trans. Tosun Bayrak, *Ibn 'Arabi: Divine Governance of the Human Kingdom*, xiv.

62   Only the first part of this scenario is imagination; the Maggid telling his son Avraham about Reb Shneur Zalman is actually a ḤaBaD tradition. See Mindel, *Rabbi Schneur Zalman*, 25.

63   See Schachter-Shalomi and Miles-Yepez, *A Heart Afire*, 239–40 for an account of Avraham the Malakh's name, and all of Chapter 8, "The Heavens of the Angel: The Lonely Path of Avraham the Malakh" for details of his life and teachings.

64   Learned at a ḤaBaD-Lubavitch *farbrengen*. —Z.M.S-S. Also in Schachter-Shalomi and Miles-Yepez, *A Heart Afire*, 240.

65   Learned at a ḤaBaD-Lubavitch *farbrengen*. —Z.M.S-S. Also see Rabinowicz, *Hasidism*, 85–86.

66   Learned at a ḤaBaD-Lubavitch *farbrengen*. —Z.M.S-S.

67   Learned at a ḤaBaD-Lubavitch *farbrengen*. —Z.M.S-S. This story is also given in Schachter-Shalomi and Miles-Yepez, *A Heart Afire*, 242, and a different English version is found in Chaim Dalfin, *Farbrengen: Inspirational Stories and Anecdotes*, 24–25 ("A Simple Bagel").

68   According to Reb Hayyim Shmuel of Kreslava, a disciple of the Maggid, Reb Avraham the Malakh used to speak of Reb Shneur Zalman "in the most laudatory terms." Schneersohn, *Likkutei Dibburim: Volume 4*, 50.

69   Learned at a ḤaBaD-Lubavitch *farbrengen*. —Z.M.S-S. For other versions of this part of the story, see Yosef Yitzchak Schneersohn, trans. Uri Kaploun, *Likkutei Dibburim: Volume 1*, 68–69, Mindel, *Rabbi Schneur Zalman*, 133–34, and Buber, *Tales of the Hasidim: The*

Early Masters, 267 ("Concerning Ardent Zeal"). This teaching was also given in Schachter-Shalomi and Miles-Yepez, *A Heart Afire*, 240–41.

70   See Zalman Schachter-Shalomi and Netanel Miles-Yepez, *A Merciful God: Stories and Teachings of the Holy Rebbe, Levi Yitzhak of Berditchev* and Samuel H. Dresner, *Levi Yitzhak of Berditchev: Portrait of a Hasidic Master* for further details of Reb Levi Yitzhak's life and teachings.

71   My dear friend, Reb Shlomo Carlebach, also tells a wonderful, little-known story involving both Reb Shneur Zalman and Reb Levi Yitzhak from their early days in Mezritch called "The Alter Rebbe and the 10,000 Rubles."

72   Learned at a ḤaBaD-Lubavitch *farbrengen*. —Z.M.S-S. Interestingly, Reb Nosson of Nemirov, who was once a disciple of Reb Levi Yitzhak of Berditchev teaches: "If you pray quickly, you might go through the entire service caught up in a single foreign thought! But if you pray more slowly, you might still be able to arrest your foreign thoughts a few times" Chaim Kramer, ed. Avraham Greenbaum, *Through Fire and Water: The Life of Reb Noson of Breslov*, 562.

73   See Schachter-Shalomi and Miles-Yepez, *A Heart Afire*, 252.

74   Idries Shah, *The Sufis*, 388.

75   Aftab-Ud-Din Ahmad, Introduction to Muhyuddin Abdul Qadir Gilani, trans. Aftab-Ud-Din Ahmad, *Futuh al-Ghaib: The Revelations of the Unseen*, xvi. Two of the best examples of this concept are to be found in two different novels: in Ian Dallas, *The Book of Strangers*, 40–51, is a wonderful account of Shaykh Sidi Abu'l-Hasan ash-Shadhili's journey to the *qutub* of his time, Sidi Moulay Abd as-Salam ibn Mashish; and in Z'ev ben Shimon Halevi, *The Anointed: A Kabbalistic Novel*, 227, Don Immanuel Cordovero becomes for a critical moment the *tzaddik ha-dor* and *qutub*, acting "as the sacrificial oil that allowed the wheels of human history to turn and not jam."

76   Learned at a ḤaBaD-Lubavitch *farbrengen* from my *mashpiyya*, Rabbi Yisra'el Jacobson. —Z.M.S-S. Also in Schachter-Shalomi and Miles-Yepez, *A Heart Afire*, 227. See Buber, *Tales of the Hasidim: The Early Masters*, 112 ("The Left Foot"). The problem with the Aliker Rebbe is that he, Rabbi Tzvi Aryeh Landau, lived from 1759–1811, and he would have been less than 12-years-old at this time. However, he was a disciple of Rabbi Yehiel Mikeleh of Zlotchov who might have been a candidate.

77   Miles Krassen in his *Uniter of Heaven and Earth: Rabbi Meshullam Feibush Heller of Zbarazh and the Rise of Hasidism in Galicia*, 232 notes 182 and 183, writes: "Heschel's view that R. Pinhas's opposition to 'the Maggid' was addressed to Dov Ber of Mezeritch has now been corrected. Altshuler has shown that 'the Maggid' in question was most likely Yehiel Mikhel [of Zlotchov]." . . . "Altshuler has suggested that R. Pinhas may have been bitter about the loss of some of his disciples to the Maggid of Zlotchov."

78   Learned at a ḤaBaD-Lubavitch *farbrengen*. —Z.M.S-S. This story was also told in *Kovetz ha-Tamim*, vol. 2, 49, no. 143. Another English version is found in Jacob Immanuel Schochet, *The Great Maggid: The Life and Teachings of Rabbi Dov Ber of Mezhirech: Volume One: Rabbi Dov Ber of Mezhirech and His Leadership of Chassidism: A Biography*, 115–19. Dalfin, *Farbrengen*, 25–26 ("Going for Broke") translates another version in which Reb Shneur Zalman says this to Reb Ahron of Karlin.

79   See Abraham J. Heschel, ed. Samuel Dresner, *The Circle of the Baal Shem Tov: Studies in Hasidism*, 19–29 ("The Way of R. Pinhas and the Way of the Maggid") on the relationship between the Reb Pinhas and the Maggid.

80   Ibid., 21: "R. Pinhas welcomed him warmly and urged him to remain with him so that he might instruct him in the language of the birds and other lofty matters. R. Shneur Zalman apparently remained in Korzec for a period, but would not forsake the way of

the Maggid." In note 111, Heschel also reports that he said, "I have received the qualities of truth and humility from R. Pinhas of Korzec," and that apparently, one of his own discourses was based on a conversation he overheard Reb Pinhas having with his wife. Buber, *Tales of the Hasidim: The Early Masters*, 266–67 ("The Language of Birds") suggests that he actually learned the language of the birds from Reb Pinhas.

81 Jacob Immanuel Schochet, *Rabbi Israel Baal Shem Tov: A Monograph on the Life and Teachings of the Founder of Chassidism*, 88–90, and Schochet, *The Great Maggid*, 85.
82 Schochet, *The Great Maggid*, 209.
83 Ibid., 180–81.
84 Ibid., 182–83.
85 *Kovetz ha-Tamim*, vol. 2, 62, no. 156. Also Schochet, *The Great Maggid*, 183–84.
86 Schochet, *The Great Maggid*, 184.
87 Learned at a ḤaBaD-Lubavitch *farbrengen*. —Z.M.S-S. A much longer and more complete version in English is given in Yosef Yitzchak Schneersohn, trans. Uri Kaploun, *Likkutei Dibburim: Volume 2*, 149–60.
88 See Schneersohn, *Likkutei Dibburim: Volume 1*, 209–10.
89 Among Hasidic lineages of Poland, he is still known simply as the *Rav*, or the Rav of Liadi.
90 Mindel, *Rabbi Schneur Zalman*, 40.
91 Reb Hayyim Shmuel of Kreslava, a disciple of the Maggid, reports that the Maggid once deferred to Reb Shneur Zalman's judgment on a question of *kashrut*, regarding a blemish in the lung of a cow. Schneersohn, *Likkutei Dibburim: Volume 4*, 50.
92 The other judge was Reb Menachem Mendel of Vitebsk. Ibid., 50.
93 Yosef Karo conceived the *Shulḥan Arukh* as being for the common person, and thus presented only the laws, giving no sources or explanation. The Alter Rebbe also saw it as being for the common person, but felt it best to explain how the decision was arrived at in a clear and simple way.
94 Rabbi Dov Baer Shneuri and Rabbi Hayyim Avraham Shneuri.
95 "Moses undertook to expound this Teaching" (Deut. 1:5).
96 By this fact, we can date the completion of these sections around Tishrei, 1771.
97 There is a famous anecdote that surrounds this visit: Once, Reb Shmelke and Reb Pinhas, who were both great talmudic scholars, came to Rovno seeking advice. They had each been offered the position of chief-rabbi in two different cities in Germany—Nikolsburg and Frankfurt—but they did not know which of them should accept which invitation. So they waited outside of the Maggid's study in order to discuss it with him. Then, from behind the door they heard the Maggid call out, "Let Reb Shmelke *of Nikolsburg* come in first."
98 Translated from the facing Hebrew text of the new English-Hebrew Edition of Shneur Zalman of Liadi, ed. and trans. Eliyahu Touger and Uri Kaploun, *The Shulchan Aruch of Rabbi Shneur Zalman of Liadi: Bilingual Edition: Volume 1*, 31, 33.
99 See "Phases of Composition and Publication" in ibid., 14–17, and "Conflict and Division" in Chapter 3 for an account of the origin of the fire.
100 Ibid., 16–17, 20–21.
101 See "Defining the *Halachah* as Practiced" in ibid., 17–19, where it is described how ḤaBaD Hasidim follow the principle of abrogation, always following the later ruling, often not found in the *Shulḥan Arukh ha-Rav*, but in the Rav's *siddur*. Also, regarding the *Shulḥan Arukh ha-Rav* being incomplete, it is worth mentioning that the Hasid and great halakhist, Rabbi Nehemia of Dubrovna wrote additional material in another work to make up for what was burned in the fire.

102 The *Mishnah Berurah* does not replace the *Shulḥan Arukh ha-Rav*; it is basically the *Shulḥan Arukh* of Yosef Karo and Moshe Isserles brought up to date for the Hofetz Hayyim's day. Serious students will review the *Shulḥan Arukh ha-Rav* because it is seen almost as an extension of the RaMBaM's *Mishneh Torah*—giving you the halakhah with explanations and minority opinions. See "The Alter Rebbe's Shulchan Aruch: A Halakhic Milestone" in ibid., 12–14 for an overview of the universal praise won by the work.

Many non-Hasidic scholars have even praised the work: Once, Rabbi David of Karlin, who usually frowned on the work of the later authorities, was seen studying the Rav's *Shulḥan Arukh*. Amazed, his colleague asked him, "I thought you only studied the work of the *Rishonim* (the greater, early authorities), and that the work of the *Aharonim* (the lesser, later authorities) was unworthy of study?" Rabbi David replied, "The Rav is a *Rishon*, not an *Aharon*."

This sentiment was to be echoed many times by his contemporaries. Reb Hayyim of Tzanz asked, "Is there any one among the scholars of the later generations who compares to him?" And his friend, Reb Levi Yitzhak of Berditchev is reported to have said, "If he had lived in the era of the RIF (Rabbi Yitzhak al-Fasi) or the RaMBaM (Rabbi Moshe ben Maimon) he would have been one of them." His grandson, Reb Menachem Mendel I of Lubavitch, himself a very great halakhic authority, went further than them all, saying: "If my grandfather would have lived in the time of the *tannaim* he would have been a great *tanna*; if he had lived in the time of the prophets he would have been a great prophet. My grandfather was a *tanna* and a prophet, but because the generation was unworthy this was hidden except for those who were worthy." Schneersohn, *Likkutei Dibburim: Volume 4*, 224.

103 It is reported that Reb Mordecai of Chernobyl said, "My father (R. [Nahum] Chernobyl) once told me that the Rebbe (the Maggid of Mezritch) regarded the Rav (the Alter Rebbe) as a child." Schneersohn, *Likkutei Dibburim: Volume 1*, 209. When I was in yeshiva, I heard the following anecdote: There was once a disciple of the Maggid from a town called Wolpe, who in ḤaBaD sources is called the Wolper. The story is that he had fallen away from the path and become an alcoholic. Well, one day he showed up in Liozhna where Reb Shneur Zalman was Rebbe and stood at the door to listen as Reb Shneur Zalman was teaching. Afterward, he was heard to say, "We all drank the milk of the Maggid, but he got the cream." Then he went out for a moment to go to the outhouse. Seeing that he was gone, an overzealous Hasid of Reb Shneur Zalman quickly went through his bag to see if there were any writings in it from the Maggid. Well, the Wolper came back and found the Hasid going through his bag and said, "What are you doing with my bag?" The young Hasid says, "I was looking to see if you had any writings ... Anything from the Maggid." He says, "You fools ... For us, the Rebbe, his soul, and his words were all one ... We didn't need any writings." Then he disappeared, and no one knows what happened to him. —Z.M.S-S. See Buber, *Tales of the Hasidim: The Early Masters*, 269–70 ("Out of One Bowl").

104 So he, Reb Menachem Mendel, and Reb Zushya, approached the Maggid and told him about the Rav's illness. Schneersohn, *Likkutei Dibburim: Volume 1*, 210.

105 Learned at a ḤaBaD-Lubavitch *farbrengen*. —Z.M.S-S. See Schneersohn, *Likkutei Dibburim: Volume 1*, 210.

106 Schneersohn, *Likkutei Dibburim: Volume 1*, 210.

107 Schochet, *The Great Maggid*, 184–85.

108 This is *not* a quote from a contemporary document, but from Schochet, *The Great Maggid*, 185.

109 Around the same time the report was sent to the Ga'on, an epidemic broke out in Vilna claiming the lives of many children. Thus, the Hasidim became a convenient

scapegoat for this epidemic—apparently a 'heavenly judgment' for allowing the Hasidic heresy to continue. See Schochet, *The Great Maggid*, 184-97, and Mindel, *Rabbi Schneur Zalman*, 47-48 for more details on these events.

110   "Thus Israel attached itself to Baal-peor, and the Lord was incensed with Israel" (Num. 25:3). In the Talmud, there is a description of two forms of idolatry: one is the *Markules*, for which one had to throw a stone at the idol, and the harder you threw it, and the more stones you threw, the better was your worship; the idolatry of Ba'al Pe'or involved defacation on the idol itself. So, the Vilna Ga'on likened somersaults and turning one's backside up to the idolatrous practice of Ba'al Pe'or. It was like exposing oneself in idolatrous worship, or defacating in public. A funny story is told in the Talmud: there was a Jew who wanted to insult *Markules*, so he threw stones at it with such anger and vigor that the priest came out and says, "No one has worshipped *Markules* as well as you have in years!" Likewise, a similar story was told how he *accidentally* worshipped Ba'al Pe'or.

111   The *Zemer Aritzim v'Horvot Tzurim* was a booklet reproducing the text of the ban and other letters of condemnation, as well as an attack on the Hasidim by the author. See Schochet, *The Great Maggid*, 192, 160-66.

112   David Tzvi Hillman, ed., *Iggrot Ba'al ha-Tanya*, 175.

113   Learned at a ḤaBaD-Lubavitch *farbrengen*. —Z.M.S-S. See Schochet, *The Great Maggid*, 209-10, Buber, *Tales of the Hasidim: The Early Masters*, 111 ("Conjuring") for other versions of this story.

114   Learned at a ḤaBaD-Lubavitch *farbrengen*. —Z.M.S-S.

115   Learned at a ḤaBaD-Lubavitch *farbrengen*. —Z.M.S-S. See Schneersohn, *Likkutei Dibburim: Volume 1*, 68-69, Buber, *Tales of the Hasidim: The Early Masters*, 267 ("Concerning Ardent Zeal"), Mindel, *Rabbi Schneur Zalman*, 133-34 for other versions of this story. In Abraham J. Heschel, *The Circle of the Baal Shem Tov: Studies in Hasidism*, 21, the Malakh says, *"Fohr, fohr, kuk nit oif die ferd"* (Ride, ride, pay no attention to the horses)—that is to say, ignore the animal body and outrun it instead of trying to discipline it.

116   *Kovetz ha-Tamim*, vol. 7, 29, no. 665.

117   See Schachter-Shalomi and Miles-Yepez, *A Heart Afire*, 288-89, 305, 335-36.

118   See Wolf Zeev Rabinowitsch, *Lithuanian Hasidism*, 25 for a discussion of Reb Menachem Mendel's time in Minsk.

119   This was his age at the time of the Maggid's passing.

120   See Buber, *Tales of the Hasidim: The Early Masters*, 267 ("At the Lower End").

121   Ibid., 175-76 ("His Childhood"). At that time, the holy Ba'al Shem told him a parable of oxen and a plow that foretold his future.

122   Learned at a ḤaBaD-Lubavitch *farbrengen*. —Z.M.S-S. Compare with Buber, *Tales of the Hasidim: The Early Masters*, 178 and Louis I. Newman with Samuel Spitz, *The Hasidic Anthology: Tales and Teachings of the Hasidim*, 294, where this is spoken by Ya'akov Yosef of Polonoyye.

123   Schneersohn, *Likkutei Dibburim: Volume 4*, 225-26 and Schneersohn, *Likkutei Dibburim: Volume 5*, 320.

124   Learned at a ḤaBaD-Lubavitch *farbrengen*. —Z.M.S-S. Schneersohn, *Likkutei Dibburim: Volume 5*, 320-21 may be an alternate version. Once, a woman came to Reb Levi Yitzhak of Berditchev and said, "Please pray that I should be fertile." And he replied, "It will cost you 300 rubles." "300 rubles," she says, "For 300 rubles, I can pray myself!" So he says, "That's my point; your prayer will be fulfilled."

125   Mindel, *Rabbi Schneur Zalman*, 51.

126   Reb Shneur Zalman was always respectful of the Ga'on of Vilna. Ibid., 51.

127   Hillman, *Iggrot Ba'al ha-Tanya*, 95. I have also heard a version where it was the mother

of the Ga'on who forbade him to speak to them, and in that version he escapes out the window to avoid them. —Z.M.S-S.

128   Ibid., 95, which continues: "Then we traveled to Shklov to debate there, but it didn't happen. It was not arranged. We saw that they had nothing to answer us with and had 'hung themselves on the greater tree' [meaning, they would only follow the lead of the Vilna Ga'on]. I'm sure he [the Ga'on] must have heard what we had to say from someone he considered reliable; but coming from that well-known agent, it is likely that everything we had said was probably explained in such a way that we would come out wrong. [...] I found that there is no one in Lithuania who would dare to stand up against the Ga'on; but in the far away countries like Turkey, Italy, most of Germany, greater Poland, and lesser Poland [Galitzia] it is different.

129   These events were remembered and reported by his brother, Reb Yehudah Leib of Yanovitch.

130   Learned at a ḤaBaD-Lubavitch *farbrengen*. —Z.M.S-S. See Schneersohn, *Likkutei Dibburim: Volume 2*, 213-19 and Schneersohn, *Likkutei Dibburim: Volume 4*, 225-26 for a more complete and detailed account.

131   See Mindel, *Rabbi Schneur Zalman*, 57-61.

Chapter 2

132   Reb Shneur Zalman's brothers: Reb Yehudah Leib, Reb Mordecai, and Reb Moshe were very great scholars—but understandably overshadowed by their older brother—and were later responsible for guiding the Torah studies of ḤaBaD Hasidim. Reb Yehudah Leib was the Rosh Yeshiva of all three *ḥadarim*. A nice description of the brothers' abilities is given in Nissan Mindel, *Rabbi Schneur Zalman: Volume I: Biography*, 103-04.

133   Ibid., 84.

134   Yosef Yitzchak Schneersohn, trans. Uri Kaploun, *Likkutei Dibburim: Volume 4*, 226. However, in Yosef Yitzchak Schneersohn, trans. Uri Kaploun, *Likkutei Dibburim: Volume 1*, 67, it says that *Ḥeder Alef* was founded in 1778, but Yosef Yitzchak Schneersohn, trans. Uri Kaploun, *Likkutei Dibburim: Volume 2*, 219, suggests that 1776 is the correct date. Moreover, it seems likely that a version existed long before for those like Reb Yosef *Kol-Bo* and Reb Pinhas Reizes, who seem to have come to him sometime between 1771 and 1773.

135   The students of *Ḥeder Alef* were already gifted scholars, and anywhere else would have been considered *rabbanim* of great distinction.

136   Schneersohn, *Likkutei Dibburim: Volume 1*, 67.

137   Learned at a ḤaBaD-Lubavitch *farbrengen*. —Z.M.S-S. See Schneersohn, *Likkutei Dibburim: Volume 1*, 308-313 and Yosef Yitzhak Schneersohn, trans. Shimon Neubort, *Branches of the Chassidic Menorah: Volume I*, 148-49 for more background on this story by the Rebbe.

138   Schneersohn, *Likkutei Dibburim: Volume 4*, 226.

139   Schneersohn, *Likkutei Dibburim: Volume 1*, 67 and Mindel, *Rabbi Schneur Zalman*, 68, 79-80.

140   Reb Shneur Zalman once chided one of his grandchildren, saying: "Why don't you listen to me? You know who knows how to listen? The *pashute Yidden* (simple Jews) know how to listen. Once, I was staying at the inn of an old Jew who lived far outside of town. He knew that I was a disciple of the Maggid and thus he treated me with great respect. I noticed that there were not many Jews in the area with whom he could make a *minyan*, so I mentioned to him that, at this point in his life, it might be better if he lived nearer to town. I went to sleep that night, and when I awoke in the morning, the old couple were packing a wagon. I asked them where they were going, and they said, 'We're moving

nearer to town!' You see, they knew how to listen!" Another story of Reb Shneur Zalman's appreciation of *pashute Yidden* is found in Zalman Schachter-Shalomi and Netanel Miles-Yepez, *A Heart Afire: Stories and Teachings of the Early Hasidic Masters*, 162.
141   See Ibid., 44-54, 161-67 on the love of simple Jews.
142   See Schneersohn, *Likkutei Dibburim: Volume 2*, 106, Yosef Yitzchak Schneersohn, trans. Uri Kaploun, *Likkutei Dibburim: Volume 5*, 32, and Schachter-Shalomi and Miles-Yepez, *A Heart Afire*, 230.
143   It is said that those simple Jews often couldn't understand the talks of the Rebbe; but since they knew the verses he quoted from the Ḥumash, they would remember these in order and report: "And the Rebbe said this *passuk*... and this *passuk*... and this *passuk*," reporting them in sequence so that some connection might be made between them.
144   Ibid., 107, and on 108 he writes: "This teaching inspired thousands of ordinary Jews" [...] "Some of these quite simple people became so refined thereby that not only was their actual appearance ennobled: they also developed a certain refinement of understanding in the profoundest concepts of [Ḥasidut]."
145   Schneersohn, *Likkutei Dibburim: Volume 5*, 32 "This was the policy of the [Alter] Rebbe—to *create* receptors, regardless of whether the minds and sensibilities of the individuals concerned were marvelous, mediocre or modest."
146   Learned at a ḤaBaD-Lubavitch *farbrengen*. —Z.M.S-S. See Schneersohn, *Likkutei Dibburim: Volume 5*, 164, and Sholom DovBer Avtzon, *Reb Shmuel Munkis*, 19-20 for other versions of this anecdote in English.
147   Schneersohn, *Likkutei Dibburim: Volume 1*, 88: The Rebbe, Reb Shmuel of Lubavitch was reported to have said of the Alter Rebbe: "And he was the Rebbe—and where there is a Rebbe there are [Hasidim]" [...] "That is, [Hasidim] who are active in *avodah*. But if one is a [Hasid] who is not a [Hasid], this causes the Rebbe to cease to be a Rebbe. The Alter Rebbe was a Rebbe, so he made [Hasidim]."
148   Schneersohn, *Likkutei Dibburim: Volume 4*, 53.
149   Rabbi Zelmele of Slutzk's life and participation in these matters, as well as other aspects of the debate in Minsk, are extensively detailed in Schneersohn, *Branches of the Chassidic Menorah*, 63-66, 79-92, and 99-136.
150   "An angel of the Lord appeared to him in a blazing fire out of a bush. He gazed, and there was a bush all aflame, yet the bush was not consumed. Moses said, 'I must turn aside to look at this marvelous sight; why doesn't the bush burn up?' " (Exod. 3:2-3).
151   "Are trees of the field human to withdraw before you into the besieged city?" (Deut. 20:19).
152   Talmud, Ta'anit 7a.
153   Talmud, Ta'anit 7a; Mekhilta to Exod. 19:18.
154   Abridgement of the teaching found in Yosef Yitzchak Schneersohn, *Kuntres Bikkur Chicago*, 22. The complete teaching with commentary is given in Schachter-Shalomi and Miles-Yepez, *A Heart Afire*, 44-54 ("The Heart Afire").
155   See Chapter 1, "You Have Lost Your Head."
156   See Mindel, *Rabbi Schneur Zalman*, 68-74 for a more detailed account of the debate.
157   This is simplified version of a very subtle argument based on distinctly Hindu values and philosophical premises. See His Holiness Jagadguru Sri Shankaracharaya of Kanchi Kamakoti Peetham, Candrasekharendra Sarasvati, trans. T.M.P. Mahadevan, *Adi Sankara: His Life & Times*, 144-63 for a more complete version of this story and its arguments.
158   Heschel's remarks to the 28th World Zionist Congress in Edward K. Kaplan, *Spiritual Radical: Abraham Joshua Heschel in America, 1940-1972*, 361. Back in the Lubavitch *yeshiva* we used to joke about *mitnagdim* who would wrap themselves up in exegetic knots without

ever having touched the source of inspiration. We saw them as kind of dense or clueless when it came to the real point. I remember one of the jokes we used to tell went like this: A *mitnaged* comes to Lubavitch from a *mitnaged yeshiva* and begins talking to the Hasidim. He immediately starts to brag, saying, "You know, when I pray, I am totally out of my body." Why is he saying this? Because, for a long time he has been hearing how the Hasidim always say, "When the Rebbe is *davenen*, he is—*b'hitpashtut ha-gashmiut*—totally out of his body." So like a good *mitnaged*, he says, "What's so special about that; I can do that too!" Before long, they start *davenen Minḥah* in Lubavitch, and one of the Hasidim takes a pin and waits for the *mitnaged* to bow down for *modim*, to give it to him in the *tush*, thinking, "We'll see if he's out of his body." When it comes time for thanksgiving, the *mitnaged* bows and the Hasid sticks him in the *tush* with the pin. Amazingly, he doesn't react at all, he doesn't even move! The Hasid can't believe it. Later, when the *mitnaged* bows down for the last time, the Hasid does it again, and he winced. After they had all finished *davenen*, the Hasidim all gather around him and say, "Yeah, sure you were out of your body." And the *mitnaged* responds, "Ah! . . . But the first time?" —Z.M.S-S.

159   This is a simplified paraphrase. See Yeshayahu Leibowitz, ed. Eliezer Goldman, trans. Eliezer Goldman, Yoram Navon, Zvi Jacobson, Gershon Levi, and Raphael Levy, *Judaism, Human Values, and the Jewish State*, 30-36 ("On Prayer").

160   Schneersohn, *Likkutei Dibburim: Volume 1*, 95, 283-84; Schneersohn, *Likkutei Dibburim: Volume 4*, 226-27; and Yosef Yitchak Schneersohn, trans. Nissan Mindel and Zalman Posner, *On the Study of Chasidus: A Trilogy of Chasidic Essays*, 20.

161   See Chapter 4, "The Curse" for the full account of this debate.

162   See Chapter 1, "The Opponents" and "You Have Lost Your Head."

163   See Tzvi M. Rabinowicz, "Nahum of Chernobyl," The Encyclopedia of Hasidism, 339-40. Arthur Green has translated significant portions of his teachings in *Menahem Nahum of Chernobyl: Upright Practices, The Light of the Eyes*, New York: Paulist Press, 1982.

164   Ibid., 339.

165   Joseph I. Schneersohn, trans. Nissan Mindel, *Lubavitcher Rabbi's Memoirs: Volume Two: Revised Edition*, 194. By the time she was 10 years old, "Her generosity was a byword."

166   Ibid., 195-96, 209-10, 254, 250-51, 257-58, and 283. In time, the elder Devorah Leah would write down all of the oral traditions of her ancestors, especially those of the *tzaddikim nistarim*, which are preserved in these volumes of the Lubavitcher Rebbe.

167   Reb Shneur Zalman also had another gifted daughter named Freida, about whom it says in Hayyim Meir Hielman, *Beit Rebbe*, 114: "She was very beloved of our Rebbe, and he would even say Ḥasidut for her. When her brother, the Mittler Rebbe [Reb Dov Baer] wanted to hear a teaching on a particular subject, he would ask her to inquire with their father about this subject, and he would eavesdrop while the Rebbe taught her."

168   Schneersohn, *Likkutei Dibburim: Volume 4*, 232.

169   Talmud, Kiddushin 30a. This is a metaphor for a defiant challenge.

170   Remember, both his father and grandfather made their living from the yield of their orchards.

171   Just as Reb Shneur Zalman always spoke of the Ba'al Shem Tov as his *zeide*, or 'grandfather,' so too his children spoke of him as their "great-grandfather," and of the Maggid of Mezritch as their "grandfather."

172   Learned at a ḤaBaD-Lubavitch *farbrengen*. —Z.M.S-S. See Schneersohn, *Likkutei Dibburim: Volume 4*, 232-36, and Schneersohn, *Likkutei Dibburim: Volume 1*, 96-97, 102 for more details.

173   Schneersohn, *Likkutei Dibburim: Volume 4*, 236.

174   See Harry M. Rabinowicz, *Hasidism: The Movement and Its Masters*, 341-50 ("Lady Rabbis and

Rabbinic Daughters") and Tzvi M. Rabinowicz, "Women," *The Encyclopedia of Hasidism*, 539-41.

175   Mindel, *Rabbi Schneur Zalman*, 107, and David Tzvi Hillman, ed., *Iggrot Ba'al ha-Tanya*, on 58, which begins the first set of *takkanot,* where Reb Shneur Zalman writes: "When you all come here with your problems, I despise my life and I think of leaving" [. . .] "Where did you find that one should ask a Rebbe about all these material things?" This is difficult because Saul comes to Samuel about his missing donkeys. In any event, he finishes the letter by saying, "I beg you not to drive me away from this country."

176   Ibid., 149. When Reb Levi Yitzhak of Berditchev first read the *Tanya,* he is reported to have said, "Such a great God in such a small book!"

177   "No, the thing is very close to you, in your mouth and in your heart, to observe it." (Deut. 30:14).

178   *Talmud,* Niddah 30b.

179   *Mishnah,* Avot 2:13.

180   Talmud, Berakhot 7b, 66a.

181   Zohar II:117b.

182   Talmud, Berakhot 61b.

183   Talmud, Bava Metzia 86a.

184   *Sefer Shel Beinonim,* Chapter 1, translated from the facing Hebrew text of Schneur Zalman of Liadi, trans. Nissan Mindel, Nisen Mangel, Zalman I. Posner, Jacob I. Schochet, *Likutei Amarim: Tanya: Bi-Lingual Edition,* 2.

185   "For I am poor and needy, and my heart is pierced within me." (Ps. 109:22).

186   *Sefer Shel Beinonim,* Chapter 1, translated from the facing Hebrew text of Schneur Zalman of Liadi, *Likutei Amarim: Tanya: Bi-Lingual Edition,* 4.

187   As Reb Shneur Zalman presents it, it sometimes looks as if the *nefesh ha-elohit* (which might be thought of as the divine *nature*) represents all that is 'good,' while the *nefesh ha-behamit* (the animal *nature*) represents all that is 'evil.' But this is not accurate. Evil is what is energized by the three defiling *kelippot.* Reb Shneur Zalman only makes the animal nature the 'face' of evil, because he sees no reason to look further into the nature of evil, to look beyond the animal nature into realms of experience that should not be delved into. For he asks, Why would one acquaint oneself thoroughly with the nature of evil? Of course, animals, the animating principle, and the animal nature are not evil; it is merely a question of place. For a lion to behave as a lion in the Savannah of Africa is not evil; but for a human being to behave as a lion in Brooklyn is out of place, and thus evil in Reb Shneur Zalman's system. While the human being certainly incorporates an animal nature and has animal needs, it is not to live from that place and its scale of values. It must live by a human nature and a human scale of values. If a scrap of meat falls on the floor, it is unacceptable for us to tear into one another tooth and nail as two dogs might.

188   Yosef Wineberg, ed. Uri Kaploun, trans. Levy Wineberg and Sholom B. Wineberg, *Lessons in Tanya: Volume I,* 171. Also Adin Steinsaltz, trans. Yehuda Hanegbi, *The Long Shorter Way: Discourses on Chasidic Thought,* 85, and Adin Steinsaltz, ed. Meir Hanegbi, trans. Yaacov Tauber, *Opening the Tanya: Discovering the Moral and Mystical Teachings of a Classic Work of Kabbalah,* 288.

189   This presentation of the five categories as momentary states of consciousness was evolved while I was trying to work out a coherent description of Sufi and Hasidic terms around the same subject, as is seen in the brief discussion of *aḥwal* and *maqamat* in the following paragraphs. —N.M-Y.

190   *Sefer Shel Beinonim,* Chapter 12, translated from the facing Hebrew text of Schneur Zalman of Liadi, *Likutei Amarim: Tanya: Bi-Lingual Edition,* 48.

191   In *assiyah,* if your only concern is to please the physical body, you are in the mind-

space of the *rasha gamur*. If you are in the energy of the body, that is the *ruḥniut d'assiyah*, and you are a *rasha sh'eino gamur*. In *yetzirah*, it is *mahtzeh al-mahtzeh*, 'half-and-half.' This is the *beinoni*. In *b'riyah* is the *tzaddik sh'eino gamur*. In *atzilut* is the *tzaddik gamur*. On this level, they say that there are certain *neshamot* that come in with almost 'pre-set' levels making the person more at home in one world than another.

192   "Shun evil and do good" (Ps. 34:15). In some translations, this is numbered Ps. 34:14.
193   "But your iniquities have been a barrier between you and your God" (Isa. 59:2).
194   Learned at a ḤaBaD-Lubavitch *farbrengen*. —Z.M.S-S. See Schneersohn, *Likkutei Dibburim: Volume 1*, 61-62; also unnamed in Schneersohn, *Likkutei Dibburim: Volume 5*, 148-49.
195   "[L]et those who love Your name exult in You." (Ps. 5:12)
196   *Sefer Shel Beinonim*, Chapter 14, translated from the facing Hebrew text of Schneur Zalman of Liadi, *Likutei Amarim: Tanya: Bi-Lingual Edition*, 60.
197   When asked what he was, Reb Shneur Zalman also answered, "I am a *beinoni*."
198   Learned at a ḤaBaD-Lubavitch *farbrengen*. —Z.M.S-S. See Chaim Dalfin, *Chasidim Farbreng*, 104, and Sholom DovBer Avtzon, *Reb Hillel Paritcher*, 4.
199   See Schneersohn, *Likkutei Dibburim: Volume 5*, 31-32 which says that the sole concern of the *tzaddik* is to function as a *mashpiyya*, a mentor who channels light to a *mekabel*, who receives that light.
200   One of the activities banned by Rabbeinu Gershom (known as the 'Light of the Exile') was the reading of other people's mail. In order impress the seriousness of this breach of trust upon the bearer, the writer of the letter would thus mark the envelope B"ḤaDRa'G (B'Ḥerem D'Rabbeinu Gershom). So, by marking his manuscript with B"ḤaDRa'G, and adding that the ban would not even be removed in the next world, Reb Shneur Zalman wanted to ensure that no one would read the book.
201   Learned at a ḤaBaD-Lubavitch *farbrengen*. —Z.M.S-S.
202   See Schachter-Shalomi and Miles-Yepez, *A Heart Afire*, 329 for an anecdote of Reb Shneur Zalman regarding Reb Elimelekh of Lizhensk and his *No'am Elimelekh*.
203   Ibid., 294 ("The Tzaddik").
204   Dalfin, *Chasidim Farbreng*, 80 says: "Reb Shmuel [Levitin] was told by the Freirdiker Rebbe [Reb Yosef Yitzhak of Lubavitch] if the Alter Rebbe would not have gone to Mezritch he would have written a *[Sefer Shel Tzaddikim]*. In order to write a *[Sefer Shel Beinonim]* he had to go to the [Maggid]."
205   Hasidim used to say that an ordinary day in Reb Itche *der Masmid*'s life would begin at about seven in the morning, when he would get up from a hard wooden bench in the *beit midrash* and proceed straight to the *mikveh*. After returning to the *beit midrash*, he would sit down to study *Ḥasidut* for several hours. Then, around noon, he would begin to *daven* his morning prayers, which took most of the afternoon because of his great *deveikut*, and thus led naturally into the afternoon and evening prayers, which only ended late in the evening! Around midnight, Reb Itche quickly ate a little meal before beginning the midnight lament. Around three o'clock in the morning, he would resume his study for two more hours, sitting with his feet in a bucket of cold water to prevent him from falling asleep. Then, around five o'clock in the morning, he would say to himself, "Nu! I should get ready for the day ahead!" Then he would stretch-out on a bench of the *beit midrash* to sleep for about two hours before starting the whole cycle over again! Of course, our reaction today (based on the values of our culture) might be somewhere between an admiring awe and an understandable revulsion; nevertheless, Reb Itche's prodigious commitment to a life of holiness was undeniable. And, according to the values of that time and that environment, Reb Itche was truly a *beinoni shel ha-Tanya*.
206   *Sefer Yetzirah* 1:2.

207   See Part IV: *Iggeret ha-Kodesh*, Chapter 15, in Schneur Zalman of Liadi, *Likutei Amarim: Tanya: Bi-Lingual Edition*, 465-77 for the most thorough presentation of the *sefirot* in the *Tanya*. I have always wanted to gather a group of students to study this chapter along with the presentation of the *sefirot* in Reb Avraham ha-Malakh's *Ḥesed L'Avraham*. —Z.M.S-S. See Schachter-Shalomi and Miles-Yepez, *A Heart Afire*, 254-71 ("The Fiftieth Gate") for a translation of the latter text.

208   See Schachter-Shalomi and Miles-Yepez, *A Heart Afire*, 260 for more on the *sefirot* as "multiples."

209   Midrash Rabbah, B'reishit 3:4. In the Psalms it says: "Bless the LORD, O my soul; O LORD, my God, You are very great; You are clothed in glory and majesty, wrapped in a robe of light; You spread the heavens like a tent cloth." (Ps. 104:1-2)

210   "[...] Let us make man in our image, after our likeness." (Gen. 1:26)

211   Infrared is close to black and receives all the colors.

212   I kept one of these for myself, and gave the others as gifts to Rabbi Abraham Joshua Heschel, Rabbi Everett Gendler, Rabbi Arthur Green, and my brother-in-law, Tuvia Scharfman. —Z.M.S-S.

213   See Chaim Dalfin, *Who's Who in Lubavitch*, 192-99 ("Reb Chenoch Hendel Lieberman") for a short biography of Reb Hendel.

214   Kabbalists have long noted that the letters of the word *ḥokhmah*, 'wisdom,' may be rearranged to spell *koaḥ mah*, alluding to another level meaning within the *sefirah*, and disclosing its essence as the 'potentiality of what-is.' See Zohar III:28a, 34a, and Schachter-Shalomi and Miles-Yepez, *A Heart Afire*, 246-47 for more on this subject.

215   See the discussion in Zalman Schachter-Shalomi, ed. N. Miles-Yepez, *Wrapped in a Holy Flame: Teachings and Tales of the Hasidic Masters*, 130-32. In Sholom DovBer Schneersohn, trans. Y. Eliezer Danziger, *Tract on Prayer*, 27, it says, "*[Da'at]*, as is known, is what enables a person to bind himself to an idea or concept."

216   "Now the man knew his wife Eve, and she conceived and bore Cain" (Gen. 4:1).

217   *Sefer Shel Beinonim*, Chapter 3, translated from the facing Hebrew text of Schneur Zalman of Liadi, *Likutei Amarim: Tanya: Bi-Lingual Edition*, 10, 12.

218   Schneersohn, *Tract on Prayer*, 27.

219   See Part IV: *Iggeret ha-Kodesh*, Chapter 15, in Schneur Zalman of Liadi, *Likutei Amarim: Tanya: Bi-Lingual Edition*, 477.

220   We're grateful to Rabbi Miles (Moshe Ahron) Krassen for bringing this *ma'amar* to our attention.

221   Moreinu (our teacher) Ha-Rav (the rabbi) Shmuel Eidels (1555–1631), Moreinu (our teacher) Ha-Rav (the rabbi) Meir Shif (1608–1644), and Asher ben Yehiel (ca. 1250-1327).

222   See Schneersohn, *On the Study of Chasidus*, 42, and Martin Buber, trans. Olga Marx, *Tales of the Hasidim: The Early Masters*, 269 ("What He Prayed With") for other versions of this story in English.

223   The "old way" refers to the contemplative technique of Mezhbizh and possibly Mezritch. But the weaknesses he attributes to general contemplation are not those of the "old way," but of a version of the "old way" without proper preparation and understanding that may lead some to fall into the potential errors of general contemplation. Thus, he offers his Hasidim the safer route of detailed contemplation. See Schachter-Shalomi and Miles-Yepez, *A Heart Afire*, 223 for other 'safety innovations' of Reb Shneur Zalman.

224   Prov. 18:2.

225   Shneur Zalman of Liadi, *Ma'amarei Admur ha-Zaken: Inyanim*, 159-161 ("*Hitbonenut Klalit u'Fratit*").

226 Rabbi Avraham Hein, the son of the RaDaTz (Rabbi David Tzvi Hein), as quoted in Herbert Weiner, *9 ½ Mystics: The Kabbala Today*, 264. This saying is also attributed to Rav Avraham Yitzhak Kook.
227 See Schachter-Shalomi and Miles-Yepez, *A Heart Afire*, 180-92 for an example of the Maggid of Mezritch's *tish* and teaching.
228 "Know therefore this day and keep in mind that the Lord alone is God in heaven above and on earth below; there is none other." (Deut. 4:39)
229 There are 613 commandments in the Torah. If you were to talk to an observant Jew and say, "That's a *mitzvah*," it is understood that you are talking about something that is the highest priority; it is what God asks you to do. Therefore, every once in a while you hear someone make a demand of somebody else, saying, "For God's sake, do this for me!" This is another way of saying, "I'm not asking this for my sake, but for the sake of the one who says, 'Thou shalt love thy neighbor as thyself.'" At one time, that was powerful enough. So when Reb Shneur Zalman says that they are two distinct commandments: one commandment dealing with knowledge and another dealing with faith, he means you cannot fulfill them properly if you mix them up. You really have to know the distinction between knowledge and faith.
230 "And you, my son Solomon, know the God of your father, and serve Him with single mind and fervent heart" (1 Chron. 28:9). Notice how more of the verse than was quoted is relevant to what Reb Shneur Zalman says in this passage.
231 "[T]hey had faith in the Lord and His servant Moses (Ex. 14:31). When Reb Shneur Zalman says, "Know the God of your parents" and "And they believed, having faith in Yah," he is setting-up 'proof-texts' for his listeners; but in terms of his own *hitbonenut*, you can also imagine him assembling all the relevant scriptural quotes in his mind so that he can construct a coherent picture of reality from them. So one of them speaks about knowledge and the other about faith. And it is important to note that we are not talking 'having faith,' as noun, but of 'faith-ing,' as a verb; for faith is not a something that I can acquire, but something I can do. So he says afterward, "believing that the blessed and holy One is giving life to everything . . . does *not* deserve to be called 'faith.' "
232 "For I am the Lord—I have not changed" (Mal. 3:6).
233 "But I would behold God while still in my flesh" (Job 19:26).
234 My beloved uncle, Frederick Barrymore Miles, of blessed memory. —N.M-Y.
235 Duncan MacDougall in "The Soul: Hypothesis Concerning Soul Substance Together with Experimental Evidence of The Existence of Such Substance," *American Medicine*, long ago wrote of his experiment concerning the 'weight' of the soul: "At the end of three hours and forty minutes he expired and suddenly coincident with death the beam end dropped with an audible stroke hitting against the lower limiting bar and remaining there with no rebound. The loss was ascertained to be three-fourths of an ounce." For more on the existence of the 'soul,' see Edward W. Bastian and Tina L. Staley, ed. Netanel Miles-Yepez, *Living Fully, Dying Well: Reflecting on Death to Find Your Life's Meaning*, 89-102 ("Life After Life?"), and 103-10 ("Afterlife and Reincarnation Reconsidered").
236 "Lift high you eyes and see: Who created these?" (Isa. 40:26).
237 Notice the word, "recognition," used here with regard to *da'at*, 'knowledge.' It is something that I *recognize*. To *cognize* means that 'I know it,' and to *re-cognize* means that 'I know it again.' So the use of this word here takes us back to the opening *passuk*, "And you shall *know today, and put it back into your heart* . . ." This in turn opens us up to "feeling." So both "recognition" and "feeling" are key words in this passage.
238 Shneur Zalman of Liadi, ed. Menachem Mendel Schneersohn, *Likkutei Torah* ("Ve-Yada'ata").
239 Paul Tillich, *Dynamics of Faith*, 31.

240 Carl Jung's interview with John Freeman on "Face to Face: Professor Jung" in 1959.
241 From another perspective, though, we might also relate this to the Gaian Hypothesis, which sees the earth as alive and dependant for that life on numerous inter-related ecosystems. In that case, what is the one factor, that once removed, would send a cascading life-failure through the entire system?
242 "You keep them all alive" (Neh. 9:6).

Chapter 3

243 *Kovetz ha-Tamim*, vol. 7, 27, no. 663.
244 Apparently, this was the holy rabbi Pinhas of Frankfut, but I do not know any traditions regarding these "objections."
245 A version of this list is found in Yosef Yitzchak Schneersohn, trans. Uri Kaploun, *Likkutei Dibburim: Volume 5*, 34. There it says that Reb Shlomo of Karlin was the colleague with whom he disagreed regarding Napoleon, but as Reb Shlomo had passed on in 1792, it was either an early argument, or may have involved another Rebbe.
246 Tzvi M. Rabinowicz, "Abraham HaKohen of Kalisk," *The Encyclopedia of Hasidism*, 6.
247 This was seen as the most malicious act in the whole history of enmity between the Hasidim and *mitnagdim*, because a Jew had put thousands of other Jews in terrible jeopardy. His accuser was a man who called himself "Hirsh Davidovitch" of Vilna, but later investigators could find no trace of any such person, and some believe this to have been a false name used by one of the *mitnagdim*, instigated or perhaps even arranged by Rabbi Avigdor Hayyimovitch, a disgruntled *mitnaged* who later accused Reb Shneur Zalman openly of disloyalty to the Czarist government in 1800.
248 Learned from Rabbi Meir Schwartzman, ob"m, a Gerer Hasid who wrote books on Hasidism. He lived in Winnipeg and would often come when I had a *farbrengen* for *yud-tet-kislev*. —Z.M.S-S. For alternate English versions, see Sholom DovBer Avtzon, *Reb Shmuel Munkis*, 32-35 ("The Moment of Truth") and Chaim Dalfin, *Farbrengen: Inspirational Stories and Anecdotes*, 57-58 ("Fearless Rebbe"). There is also a reference to this incident in Schneersohn, *Likkutei Dibburim: Volume 5*, 134.
249 Learned at a HaBaD-Lubavitch *farbrengen*. —Z.M.S-S. See the alternate versions of this story in Schneersohn, *Likkutei Dibburim: Volume 5*, 121, and Avtzon, *Reb Shmuel Munkis*, 7-14 ("Whose Desire Is It?").
250 "And all the peoples of the earth shall see that the Lord's name is proclaimed over you, and they shall stand in fear of you." (Deut. 28:10)
251 Learned from Rabbi Meir Schwartzman. —Z.M.S-S. I believe this anecdote is also told in Mikhael Levi Rodkinson's *Sefer Shivhei ha-Rav*.
252 Yosef Yitzchak Schneersohn, trans. Uri Kaploun, *Likkutei Dibburim: Volume 1*, 28 note ** and Nissan Mindel, *Rabbi Schneur Zalman*, 164.
253 "The Lord God called out to the man and said to him, "Where are you?" (Gen.3:9)
254 Learned at a HaBaD-Lubavitch *farbrengen*. —Z.M.S-S. This story is also found in Hayyim Meir Hielman, *Beit Rebbe*, 57. Other English versions may be found in Mindel, *Rabbi Schneur Zalman*, 169-70, Martin Buber, *The Way of Man: According to the Teachings of Hasidism*, 9-14 ("Heart-Searching") which gives some commentary, and Martin Buber, trans. Olga Marx, *Tales of the Hasidim: The Early Masters*, 268-69 ("Where Are You?").
255 Thomas Keating, *The Human Condition: Contemplation and Transformation*, 7.
256 The Maggid of Mezritch and the Ba'al Shem Tov had both come to him in a vision

and assured him that he would be freed. See Mindel, *Rabbi Schneur Zalman*, 176-77.

257 Mordecai Teitelbaum, *Ha-Rav mi'Liadi*, 123-24. This story was originally given as a first hand account by Nahum Schneersohn, the son of Reb Dov Baer Shneuri, who was known as a very reliable reporter of events. In the same place, it is also written: "Other officers and princes of the country were impressed with the way in which the Alter Rebbe spoke about divine matters; for all over the country they heard about how he had defended himself, and how he explained his point of view. Mr. Shmuel Schneersohn, one of the descendents of the Rebbe, heard from his father that once, one of the great ministers and nobles of the empire was traveling on the highway to Mohilev when he stopped at a postal station to exchange horses and to rest for awhile. He then went and got a room at a small hotel, and while on his way to his room, he happened to see an older man wrapped in a *tallit* and *tefillin* with his face turned to the wall, praying in the corner of a large room with great fervor and awe. The minister stood there, rooted to his place until the old man completed his prayers, for he did not wish to disturb him from the service of God. When he had completed his prayers, the minister smiled kindly at him and put out his hand to greet the man, saying: "Sir, from your prayer I recognize that you belong to that sect of Rabbi Barukhovitch." When the man asked him how he knew about the Rebbe and his manner of prayer, he answered: "How could I not know him? It was he who explained to us what is meant by the phrase, 'the effulgence the Infinite.'"

258 Rabbi Meir, one of the great *tannaim* of the *Mishnah*, called, *Ba'al ha-Neis*, 'master of miracles,' said that he would intercede for whoever would give *tzedakah* (charity) for his soul, and the money should be distributed to the poor of *Eretz Yisra'el*. Rabbi Meir's grave is in Tiberias where most of the Hasidic community was located.

259 A full account of the arrest, imprisonment, and release can be found in Mindel, *Rabbi Schneur Zalman*, 156-88.

260 Both the passing of the Maggid and the release of Reb Shneur Zalman took place on the Tuesday (the day on which God said "It is good" twice) of Parshat Va-yeshev, 26 years apart! Schneersohn, *Likkutei Dibburim: Volume 1*, 211.

261 David Tzvi Hillman, ed., *Iggrot Ba'al ha-Tanya*, 114. See Mindel, *Rabbi Schneur Zalman*, 184-85 for a fuller English translation.

262 Schneersohn, *Likkutei Dibburim: Volume 1*, 210.

263 This was the topic of my doctoral dissertaion at Hebrew Union College, later published as *Spiritual Intimacy: A Study of Counseling in Hasidism*. —Z.M.S-S.

264 The sources of these definitions are: Mishnah, Shekalim 6:2; Talmud, Yevamot 62a; and Midrash Rabbah, B'reishit 20.

265 "Shun evil and do good" (Ps. 34:15).

266 Translated from the facing Hebrew text of Yosef Yitzchak Schneersohn, trans. Zalman I. Posner, Yitschak Meir Kagan, and Sholom B. Wineberg, ed. Menachem Mendel Schneerson, *HaYom Yom... "From Day to Day,"* 86.

267 Zalman Meshullam Schachter-Shalomi, *Spiritual Intimacy: A Study of Counseling in Hasidism*, 116-20.

268 Schneersohn, *Likkutei Dibburim: Volume 5*, 122.

269 Mindel, *Rabbi Schneur Zalman*, 103-105.

270 Ibid., 138.

271 Ibid., 104.

272 Learned at a ḤaBaD-Lubavitch *farbrengen*. —Z.M.S-S.

273 Hearing this anecdote, it's hard to ignore its similarity to the two strong counsels Reb Shneur Zalman was given by Reb Avraham the Malakh in Chapter 1, "Of Horses and Men" and "Let the Horses Run."

274 Learned at a ḤaBaD-Lubavitch *farbrengen*. —Z.M.S-S.

275 Learned at a ḤaBaD-Lubavitch *farbrengen*. —Z.M.S-S.
276 Learned at a ḤaBaD-Lubavitch *farbrengen*. —Z.M.S-S.
277 Mindel, *Rabbi Schneur Zalman*, 196-204.
278 Learned at a ḤaBaD-Lubavitch *farbrengen*. —Z.M.S-S. This story is also found in Hielman, *Beit Rebbe*, 58. Another English version may be found in Mindel, *Rabbi Schneur Zalman*, 171-72, and a long literary version is given in Zalman Shneour, trans. Moshe Spiegel, "Czar Paul and Rabbi Shneour Zalman," *Restless Spirit: Selected Writings of Zalman Shneour*, 207-18. Mindel places this story in the time of Reb Shneur Zalman's first arrest, but I am inclined to go with Zalman Shneour who places it during the second arrest.
279 Mindel, *Rabbi Schneur Zalman*, 204-11, 216-17.
280 Learned at a ḤaBaD-Lubavitch *farbrengen*. —Z.M.S-S. A version of this is also found in Avtzon, *Reb Shmuel Munkis*, 41-44 ("My Mechutan!").
281 Samuel H. Dresner, *Levi Yitzhak of Berditchev: Portrait of a Hasidic Master*, 92-93. See Chaim Dalfin, *Chasidim Farbreng*, 121 ("Special Yetzer Hara") for another anecdote of Reb Levi Yitzhak from the wedding in Zhlobin, reported by my old friend, Avraham Weingarten. Also Chapter 1, "Davenen Fast, and Davenen Slow."
282 Hielman, *Beit Rebbe*, 31 note 2. Also Buber, *Tales of the Hasidim: The Early Masters*, 267 ("To God").
283 Schneersohn, *Likkutei Dibburim: Volume 5*, 32.
284 In this context, "exiles" refers to penitential pilrimages.
285 Buber, *Tales of the Hasidim: The Early Masters*, 52 ("Against Mortification of the Flesh").
286 Louis I. Newman and Samuel Spitz, *The Hasidic Anthology: Tales and Teachings of the Hasidim*, 203 ("The Besht on 'Joy'").
287 "Let Israel rejoice in its maker" (Ps. 149:2).
288 "O maidens of Zion, go forth and gaze upon King Solomon" (Songs 3:11).
289 Chapter 46 in Schneur Zalman of Liadi, *Likutei Amarim: Tanya: Bi-Lingual Edition*, 241-47.
290 Hillman, *Iggrot Ba'al ha-Tanya*, 212. Naftali Loewenthal, *Communicating the Infinite: The Emergence of the ḤaBaD School*, 261 note 53 writes: "Hillman identifies the recipient as R. Yitzhak of Ula, the brother-in-law of R. Moshe, the youngest son of R. Shneur Zalman. The same R. Yitzhak is termed a 'major *hasid*' by Hielman, who likewise seems to identify him as the recipient of this letter" [. . .] "However, Levine, on the basis of manuscript evidence identifies him as R. Yitzhak Yafeh of Kopys, possibly the father of R. Yisrael Yaffe, the printer."
291 See the larger discussion Schneersohn, *Likkutei Dibburim: Volume 1*, 128.
292 "But the righteous man is rewarded with life for his fidelity." (Hab. 2:4)
293 Midrash Rabbah, B'reishit 95.
294 Hillman, *Iggrot Ba'al ha-Tanya*, 108, and Avraham of Kalisk, *Hibbat ha-Aretz*, 70a-b. More of this correspondence is translated in Mindel, *Rabbi Schneur Zalman*, 223-24, and Rivka Schatz Uffenheimer, trans. Jonathan Chipman, *Hasidism as Mysticism: Quietistic Elements in Eighteenth Century Thought*, 257-58.
295 Likewise, Rebbe Nahman of Bratzlav saw no barriers impeding the ascent of souls: "Do not say that I arrived where I did because of an exalted soul: it was work that raised me, and can raise you also." *Naḥal Nove'a*, 42.
296 Hillman, *Iggrot Ba'al ha-Tanya*, 108. More of this correspondence is translated in Mindel, *Rabbi Schneur Zalman*, 225-26.
297 Ibid., 169.
298 Ibid., 171.
299 See Chapter 7, "The Great Pilgrimage to Eretz Yisra'el." Reb Avraham of Kalisker was a *kohen*, and a *kohen* is supposed to be a kind person. But in Yiddish culture, we also speak

of the *kohen* who is angry, a *baizer kohen*; whenever something doesn't quite fit in with what they want, they get angry. Reb Shneur Zalman, on the other hand, is more accepting of diverse opinions and more expansive in his vision. The Rabbis say, "Who is wise? One who sees what the results will be." Reb Shneur Zalman always saw the results in the long-term. For instance, the people who saw the immediate results of Napoleon were able to say, "Let Napoleon win." But Reb Shneur Zalman saw further and sided with the Czar. Likewise, it was clear that his *Tanya* would become more and more necessary for Hasidim in the long-term.

300   "But the king shall rejoice in God; all who swear by Him shall exult, when the mouth of liars is stopped." (Ps. 63:12)
301   Hillman, *Iggrot Ba'al ha-Tanya*, 171. More of Reb Avraham of Kalisk's epistolary comments on this matter are translated in Mindel, *Rabbi Schneur Zalman*, 228-30, and Schatz Uffenheimer, *Hasidism as Mysticism*, 258-59.
302   And the life of Rebbe Nahman of Bratzlav as well, as may be seen in Chapter 7, "The Great Pilgrimage to Eretz Yisra'el."
303   Talmud, Hagigah 15b.
304   "The LORD is king, He is robed in grandeur" (Ps. 93:1).
305   Zalman Schachter-Shalomi and Netanel Miles-Yepez, *A Heart Afire: Stories and Teachings of the Early Hasidic Masters*, 175.
306   This may have been Tulchin, as it is unclear to me when Reb Barukh moved to Mezhbizh.
307   "Who may ascend to the mountain of the LORD? Who may stand in His holy place?" (Ps. 24:3)
308   Ps. 24:4.
309   "The earth is the LORD's and all that it holds" (Ps. 24:1).
310   Rebbe Nahman had visited Reb Shneur Zalman years before (see Chapter 8).
311   According to Aryeh Kaplan, ed. Dovid Shapiro, *Until the Mashiach: Rabbi Nachman's Biography: An Annotated Chronology*, 178-79, this was January 27th, 1810.
312   Shmuel Horowitz, ed., *Avane'ha Barzel*, 46, and A. H. Glitzenstein, *Sefer ha-Toldot: Admur ha-Zaken*. For another English version, see Moshe Mykoff, *Once Upon a Tzaddik: Tales of Rebbe Nachman of Breslov*, 102-03 ("The Lord of Thousands and 'Feter Boruch'").
313   Goethe said, "That which you inherit from your ancestors, if you would claim it, you must earn it."
314   Reb Barukh of Mezhbizh made the parental merit of his grandfather, the Ba'al Shem Tov, the issue of much of his ministry. In Poland and Galicia, the term *einikl*, 'grandson,' came to denote a 'derivative Rebbe.' The Rebbe's grandson did not need to claim heroic virtue for himself. He could, however, act as his ancestor's proxy and by his merit. Rebbes who had a unique contribution to make would value their pedigree less than their own achievement and merit. Rebbe Nahman of Bratzlav saw himself as being a *hiddush*, independent of his great-grandfather, the Ba'al Shem Tov. Not many children and grandchildren dared to make real innovations. Instead, they saw themselves as their parents' deputies, zealously guarding the rules of the ancestral heritage.

Reb Barukh saw himself as a kind of 'king of kings,' and he believed that the other *tzaddikim* should acknowledge his status as such. Later it was a similar situation with Reb Yisra'el of Rhyzhin, the great-grandson of the Maggid of Mezritch. It was as if he was the King of Israel in exile. Thus, Reb Barukh thought of himself as the leader of the generation and wanted everyone to stand in his presence, as they might in a court of royalty; for he read the phrase in the *Zohar*, "That I might be counted among the righteous," as "I should be counted as the leader, the first among the *tzaddikim*." Thus, when Reb Hirsh Leib of Alik

came to visit Reb Barukh of Mezhbizh, Reb Barukh told his *gabbai* to remove all the chairs from the room except his own, which he would sit upon as a throne. But Reb Hirsh Leib anticipating such a move, asked his own *gabbai* to bring a chair along. So Reb Hirsh Leib comes before Reb Barukh and sits down in the chair his *gabbai* has set down for him. Then Reb Barukh says: "How dare you sit in my presence? I am a ḥad b'dore, the unique one of the generation!" But Reb Hirsh Leib said, "I'm *also* the unique one of the generation!" "How can there be two ḥad b'dores?" asked Reb Barukh. Reb Hirsh Leib answered, "Because there are two ḥad gadyas in the *haggadah!*" This refers to the song sung on Pesaḥ where the line, ḥad gadya, 'one little lamb' is repeated twice! He knew just how to get at Reb Barukh.
315   Learned at a ḤaBaD-Lubavitch *farbrengen*. —Z.M.S-S. Also found in Rodkinson, *Shivḥei ha-Rav*, 17a.
316   For a thorough discussion of the historical development of *Ayin*, and by extension, *Ain Sof*, see Daniel C. Matt, "Ayin: The Concept of Nothingness in Jewish Mysticism" in ed. Lawrence Fine's *Essential Papers on Kabbalah*, 67-108.
317   "For I am the Lord—I have not changed" (Mal. 3:6).
318   For more on the metaphor of 'Light' in the Kabbalah, see J. Immanuel Schochet, "Anthropomorphism and Metaphors" in Benzion Rader, ed., *To Touch the Divine: A Jewish Mysticism Primer*, 123-25.
319   Nevertheless, these were completely homogenous, having no distinguishable separation that would imply a limitation in the absolutely simple essence. Aryeh Kaplan, ed. Abraham Sutton, *Innerspace: Introduction to Kabbalah, Meditation and Prophecy*, 121.
320   In Dalfin, *Chasidim Farbreng*, 53, my *mashpiyya*, Reb Shmuel Levitin reported in the name of Reb Hillel of Paritch, who reported in the name of the Reb Shneur Zalman of Liadi, that the Maggid of Mezritch had said that "Do not desecrate my holy name," refers to *tzimtzum* not being *kepshuto*, 'literal.' One should not think that there was a ḥalal, a 'void' in God's holy name, for God was present even in the midst of the *tzimtzum* which made a space for the universe.
321   Moshe Cordovero, *Pardes Rimonim*, Sha'ar 3, chapter 1. See the discussion in Noson Gurary, *Chasidism: Its Development, Theology, and Practice*, 67-68. I highly recommend this excellent little book as a guide to all the issues regarding Reb Shneur Zalman's approach to *tzimtzum* and its implications.
322   Hayyim Vital, *Etz Ḥayyim*, 1:1:2. A complete translation may be found in Donald Wilder Menzi and Zwe Padeh, trans., *The Tree of Life: Chayyim Vital's Introduction to the Kabbalah of Isaac Luria: The Palace of Adam Kadmon*, 11-15.
323   Hillman, *Iggrot Ba'al ha-Tanya*, beginning on 95, Reb Shneur Zalman writes: "[. . .] we heard from his disciples, that the great Ga'on and Hasid, considered what I had written in the *Likkutei Amarim*—in which I explained *m'malleh kol almin, le'it attar panui minei* ('there's no place empty of him') in a simple way—a great heresy, to say that God is found even in lower things. It is for this reason that they burned that book. [*Tzava'at ha-RiBaSh* according to *Beit Rebbe*.] [. . .] And that which I said in the *Tanya* about 'raising the sparks,' this is only found in the *kabbalah* of the Ari ha-Kodesh, but I know that the Ga'on and Hasid does not accept the *kabbalah* of the Ari in its entirety, which comes from the mouth of Eliyahu. He says that only a portion came from Eliyahu, and the rest is from his great wisdom. Thus, we don't have to believe it. Also, he argues that there are many [editor's] errors in the Ari's writings." The note continues: "Concerning this, Reb Hayyim of Volozhin, the chief disciple of the Ga'on, says: 'How could people suggest that the Ari ha-Kodesh was not accepted by him [the Ga'on]? [He explains] The Ga'on looked many times into this matter, and found that he had to fix some of the mistakes that had crept in to the writings of Reb Hayyim Vital [who published the Ari's teachings].' But even Hayyim of Volozhin didn't

accept everything of the Ari ha-Kodesh."
324 *Sifra d'Tzeniuta*, Likkutim.
325 Gurary, *Chasidism*, 104.
326 Gurary, *Chasidism*, 106; Maimonides, trans. Shlomo Pines, *The Guide of the Perplexed*, 119. Another possible conclusion about the paradox of *tzimtzum* was reached by Rabbi Shaul Baumann who made attempts to bridge the gap between the interpretation of the literalist Vilna Ga'on and metaphorical Shneur Zalman of Liadi. Baumann writes in his *Miftahay Hokhmat ha-Emet* that both can be right. For him, the God-ness that is not removed is the God-ness of *malkhut sheb' malkhut sheb'Ain Sof*, 'the receptive of the receptive of the *Ain Sof*.' What is left of God is the divine openness, the divine receptivity. Therefore, the Alter Rebbe is satisfied because God is still present, and the Vilna Ga'on is likewise appeased because the 'fullness' of God is removed.
327 "For I fill both heaven and earth—declares the Lord." (Jer. 23:24)
328 The philosopher Shankara says, "If the universe is real, the infinitude of the Self will be affected; the scriptures will no longer be authoritative." Sankaracarya Bhagavatpada, ed. & trans. John Grimes, *The Vivekacudamani of Sankaracarya Bhagavatpada: An Introduction and Translation*, 162.
329 Gurary, *Chasidism*, p.107-10.
330 See Zalman Schachter-Shalomi and Netanel Miles-Yepez, "God Hidden, Whereabouts Unknown," *Spectrum: A Journal of Renewal Spirituality*, where we have discussed many of the same issues around the concept of *tzimtzum*.
331 Isa. 44:6.
332 Kaplan, *Innerspace*, 121.
333 Zalman Schachter-Shalomi, ed. N. Miles-Yepez, *Wrapped in a Holy Flame: Teachings and Tales of the Hasidic Masters*, 190-91.
334 Daniel C. Matt, trans., *The Zohar: Pritzker Edition*, 107-08, from *Parshat B'reshit*, "In the Beginning" (Genesis 1:1-6:8) "At the head of potency of the King, He engraved engravings in luster on high. A spark of impenetrable darkness flashed within the concealed of the concealed, from the head of Infinity—a cluster of vapor forming in formlessness, thrust in a ring, not white, not black, not red, not green, no color at all." According to Kaplan, *Innerspace*, 121, this lamp "blocks out everything that could possibly exist but does not" because the *kav* penetrated it afterword. The *kav* is the 'ray' of light that penetrates the empty space after the initial 'withdrawal' of *tzimtzum*. So, even after the 'concept of lack' was created, a controlled ray of light re-entered the sphere to create creation, to fill that 'conceptual lack.' *Tzimtzum* allows for creation, but still requires some of that light in the form of the *kav* to effect that creation. This is the basic paradox: the *Or Ain Sof* had to vacate the space, leaving it empty of light, but also had to re-enter the space so that it is again full of light. So, truly, there is "no place empty" of God.
335 "You are clothed in glory and majesty, wrapped in a robe of light" (Ps. 104:2) and "He made darkness His screen" (Ps. 18:12).
336 Dr. John Allen Grimes, then professor at Michigan State University, a scholar of Advaita Vedanta, and a true philosopher-devotee. — N.M-Y. See John Grimes, *A Concise Dictionary of Indian Philosophy: Sanskrit Terms Defined in English: New and Revised Edition*, 189. In Dalfin, *Chasidim Farbreng*, 40, Reb Shalom Dov Baer of Lubavitch is also reported by my *mashpiyya*, Reb Yisra'el Jacobson to have said: "In the beginning of creation G-d's Infinite light was taken for granted, meaning the norm was G-dliness. Now, after creation, the world, which obscures G-dliness, is taken for granted." — Z.M.S-S.
337 In Tom Stoppard's *Rosencrantz and Guildenstern are Dead*, 61, it says: "We cross our bridges when we come to them and burn them behind us, with nothing to show for our

progress except a memory of the smell of smoke, and a presumption that once our eyes watered." This story of *Maya* is told in many versions. See Heinrich Zimmer, ed. Joseph Campbell, *Myths and Symbols in Indian Art and Civilization*, 27-35. Another version of this motif is found in Hermann Hesse, trans. Richard and Clara Winston, *The Glass Bead Game (Magister Ludi)*, 520-58 ("The Indian Life").

338   "It is the power of the supreme Lord [. . .] It is this which gives birth to the entire world. It is neither real nor unreal [. . .] It is supremely wonderful and of an inexpressible form." Sankaracarya, *The Vivekacudamani of Sankaracarya Bhagavatpada*, 109-10. "It is what is called illusory. *Maya* is of that nature. It is indeterminable (*anirvacaniya*). It is not real nor unreal. What it is one cannot say. [. . .] It is neither real or unreal; it is of a third category. If we say it is not, then how does it appear? If we say it is real, then how does it get negated? [. . .] If we say it is different from the supreme Self that would be impossible. It is not also correct to say that it *is* the supreme Self." Candrasekharendra Sarasvati, trans. T.M.P. Mahadevan, *Adi Sankara: His Life & Times*, 58.

339   "None but the Lord shall be exhalted in that day." (Isa. 2:11,17)

340   *Sefer Shel Beinonim*, Chapter 36, translated from the facing Hebrew text of Schneur Zalman of Liadi, *Likutei Amarim*, 164.

341   Maimonides' introduction to the *Mishneh Torah*. See Isadore Twersky, ed., *A Maimonides Reader*, 46. This idea is also mirrored in the *Vivekacudamani*, the 'crest jewel of discrimination,' of the Hindu philosopher, Shankara, when he says: "Therefore, this supreme Absolute is Real, non-dual, utterly pure, the essence of knowledge [. . .] The wise realize the supreme Truth, which is void of the distinctions of knower, the object known, and the act of knowledge; which is infinite, indeterminate, totally unbroken pure consciousness. Sankaracarya, *The Vivekacudamani of Sankaracarya Bhagavatpada*, 164-65.

342   "For My plans are not your plans, nor are My ways your ways—declares the Lord. But as the heavens are high above the earth, so are My ways high above your ways and My plans above your plans." (Isa. 55:8-9)

343   "Would you discover the mystery of God? Would you discover the limit of the Almighty?" (Job 11:7)

344   "Do You have the eyes of flesh? Is Your vision that of mere men?" (Job 10:4)

345   See Twersky, *A Maimonides Reader*, 46. Similarly, Shankara writes in the *Vivekacudamani* (from the standpoint of the absolute God as the one, authentic Self): "That which, in itself, perceives everything but which nothing can perceive; that which illumines the mind and so on, but which itself cannot be illumined. That is the Self. That by which the universe is pervaded, but which nothing pervades; which shining, all this, which is not of the nature of effulgence, shines. That is the Self." Sankaracarya, *The Vivekacudamani of Sankaracarya Bhagavatpada*, 119-20.

346   "For the commandment is a lamp, the teaching is a light" (Prov. 6:23).

347   Shneur Zalman of Liadi, *Torah Or*, MiKetz 39a.

348   See Schachter-Shalomi and Netanel Miles-Yepez, *A Heart Afire*, 202.

349   See Chapter 1, "A Little Higher Than the Angels."

350   "Know therefore this day and keep in mind that the Lord alone is God in heaven above and on earth below; there is none other." (Deut. 4:39)

351   Shneur Zalman of Liadi, *Likkutei Torah*, Vol. 3, 37d.

352   *Sefer Shel Beinonim*, Chapter 5, Schneur Zalman of Liadi, *Likutei Amarim*, 17-21, and Shneur Zalman of Liadi, *Likkutei Torah*, Vol. 3, 48d.

353   See *Sefer Shel Beinonim*, Chapter 47, Schneur Zalman of Liadi, *Likutei Amarim*, 249.

354   In the same way, the observances of Hinduism are not undermined. Still, some might ask, "Why all these elaborate rituals? Will not silent prayer do?" "The answer is to be

found, if we rightly understand the significance of these ritualistic offerings, namely, that a true devotee acknowledges the ultimate source and the inner substance of these objects of his enjoyment and uses them only after tendering them to that source in humble gratitude." Candrasekharendra Sarasvati, "Temple Worship," *Kamakoti Vani*, 23-24.

355 In Shneur Zalman of Liadi, ed. Menachem Mendel Schneersohn, *Likkutei Torah* ("Ve-Yada'ata"), it says: "The Torah and *mitzvot* are the 248 channels through which the category of the transcendent is drawn down to us. Generally, the 248 *mitzvot* are divided into three facets—right, left and the middle—which represent the *Torah*—teaching, *avodah*—worship, and *gemilut ḥasadim*—acts of loving-kindness."

356 See David Zeller, *The Soul of the Story: Meetings with Remarkable People*, 138-44 ("Nakasono Sensei: Meeting the Shinto Priest") for more on the Jew's relationship to *mitzvot*.

357 Napoleon is reported to have said, "I will never accept any proposals that will obligate the Jewish people to leave France, because to me the Jews are the same as any other citizen in our country. It takes weakness to chase them out of the country, but it takes strength to assimilate them." Simon Schwarzfuchs, *Napoleon, the Jews and the Sanhedrin*, 50.

358 See Tzvi M. Rabinowicz, "Napoleon Bonaparte" *The Encyclopedia of Hasidism*, 340, Harry M. Rabinowicz, *Hasidism: The Movement and Its Masters*, 88-89, 118-19, and Martin Buber's Hasidic novel, *For the Sake of Heaven*, which is set against the backdrop of Napoleon's invasion.

359 Hillman, *Iggrot Ba'al ha-Tanya*, 238.

360 According to some sources, it was 2 viorsts. A viorst is .662 miles.

361 Learned at a ḤaBaD-Lubavitch *farbrengen*. —Z.M.S-S. See Schneersohn, *Likkutei Dibburim: Volume 1*, 33-34 for the definitive account.

362 Rabinowicz, *Hasidism*, 89.

363 Timothy Wilson-Smith, *Napoleon: Man of War, Man of Peace*, 125.

364 Midrash Rabbah, B'reishit 8.

365 "Nefesh ha-Sh'feila" in *Boneh Yerushalayim*.

366 Chapter 9, "The Turkey Prince."

367 Learned at a ḤaBaD-Lubavitch *farbrengen*. —Z.M.S-S. See Buber, *Tales of the Hasidim*, 271 ("Seeing").

368 In the Kabbalah, there is a notion that everything of is made up of the word of God. For God says in Genesis, "Be, light!" and there was light, so it is extrapolated that it is God's word that makes-up creation, and God's speaking that sustains creation in every moment. See Schachter-Shalomi, *Wrapped in a Holy Flame*, 185-95, and David Sheinkin, ed. Edward Hoffman, *Path of the Kabbalah*, 50-51, 57-59.

369 See Chapter 1, "The New Soul."

Chapter 4

370 In Yosef Yitzchak Schneersohn, trans. Zalman I. Posner, Yitschak Meir Kagan, and Sholom B. Wineberg, ed. Menachem Mendel Schneerson, *HaYom Yom... "From Day to Day,"* 43, it says, "The Mittler Rebbe's family name was [Shneuri]." Louis Jacobs, in his *Seeker of Unity: The Life and Works of Aaron of Starosselje*, 12, says of Reb Ahron HaLevi, "he is, indeed, generally considered to be the favorite and most distinguished pupil of the master." This is a generally accepted statement.

371 The main source for information about Reb Ahron HaLevi's life is found in Hayyim Meir Hielman's classic chronicle of ḤaBaD Hasidism, *Beit Rebbe*, and most of the translations about Reb Ahron in this chapter come from this source. However, we have done our best to supplement with material from Tzvi Hirsh of Tchashnik's *haskamah* (approbation) to Reb Ahron's *Avodat ha-Levi*, Mikhael Levi Rodkinson's *Sefer Shivḥei ha-Rav*, as well as ḤaBaD oral traditions that I learned in my youth, and a few which were preserved by my Rebbe. —Z.M.S-S.

372 The most thorough side-by-side presentations of the lives and thought of Reb Dov Baer and Reb Ahron HaLevi in English are found in Avrum M. Ehrlich's *Leadership in the ḤaBaD Movement: A Critical Evaluation of ḤaBaD Leadership, History, and Succession*, Rachel Elior's *The Paradoxical Ascent to God: The Kabbalistic Theosophy of ḤaBaD Hasidism*, Louis Jacobs' *On Ecstasy: A Tract by Dobh Baer* and *Seeker of Unity: The Life and Works of Aaron of Starosselje*, and Naftali Loewenthal's *Communicating the Infinite: The Emergence of the ḤaBaD School*.

373 Learned at a ḤaBaD-Lubavitch *farbrengen*. —Z.M.S-S. However, it appears that this is also found in Yosef Yitzhak Schneersohn, *Kuntres Ḥai Elul*. See Nissan Mindel, *Rabbi Schneur Zalman*, 49 for the same basic account.

374 Yosef Yitzchak Schneersohn, trans. Uri Kaploun, *Likkutei Dibburim: Volume 2*, 42. Often a Rebbe would call upon a young man and ask him to teach his own children. So it happened that Reb Shneur Zalman summoned a younger disciple of the Maggid to be a tutor for Reb Dov Baer, and said to him: "Let us assist each other in the *mitzvot* we must fulfill. You must fulfill the *mitzvah* to feed your wife and children. I must fulfill the *mitzvah* to teach my children diligently. (Deut. 11:19) You take on my task and I shall take on yours." Then he explained to the *melammed* what he must teach him—"First he must learn the *alef bet*. But what is an *alef*? An upper *yud* and a lower *yud* with a slash between them. The *yud* above is the soul, the *yid* below is the body of a Jew, and the line that joins them is faith. Eliezer Steinman, *Sefer Be'er ha-Ḥasidut: Mishnat ḤaBaD*: Volume II, 174. (Also found in Schneersohn, *HaYom Yom . . . "From Day to Day,"* 26.) Obviously, he is telling him that the child must be taught more than the letters and the basics.

375 See Epictetus in ed. Whitney J. Oates, *The Stoic and Epicurean Philosophers: The Complete Extant Writings of Epicurus, Epictetus, Lucretius, Marcus Aurelius*, 224-26, and trans. Sharon Lebell, *The Art of Living: The Classic Manual on Virtue, Happiness, and Effectiveness*, 3, "Happiness and freedom begin with a clear understanding of one principle: Some things are within our control, and some things are not."

376 Learned at a ḤaBaD-Lubavitch *farbrengen*. —Z.M.S-S. Compare with Schneersohn, *Likkutei Dibburim: Volume 2*, 44-45. This teaching is all based on Psalms 135:16-18: "They have mouths, but cannot speak; they have eyes, but cannot see; they have ears, but cannot hear, nor is their breath in their mouths. Those who fashion them, all who trust in them, shall become like them." It should be noted that this very topic was a major theme in Reb Dov Baer's letter often added as an introduction to his *Kuntres ha-Hitpa'alut*. A translation of it can be found in Louis Jacobs, trans., *On Ecstasy: A Tract by Dobh Baer*, 177-87.

377 Hielman, *Beit Rebbe*, 134.

378 See Chapter 1, "Halakhah and a Little Hasidism."

379 Jacobs, *Seeker of Unity*, 12, and Ehrlich, *Leadership in the ḤaBaD Movement*, 167-68.

380 This age is in accord with what is written on frontispiece of Reb Ahron HaLevi's *Sha'arei ha-Yiḥud ve-ha-Emunah*, which states that he had been a disciple of the Alter Rebbe for thirty years.

381 This is how the archangel Michael is described.

382 "The lifebreath of man is the lamp of the Lord" (Prov. 20:27).

383 "In that day, Israel shall be a third partner with Egypt and Assyria as a blessing on earth" (Isa. 19:24).

384 "Blessed is the LORD, God of Israel, from eternity to eternity" (Ps. 41:14).
385 "O LORD, I set my hope on You" (Ps. 25:1).
386 I recently came across this wonderful story in Yosef Yitzhak Schneersohn, trans. Shimon Neubort, *Branches of the Chassidic Menorah: Volume I*, 121-25, which has a translation of this story from notes the Rebbe had made and which were once circulated among the Hasidim. The version given here is basically a condensed retelling from the Rebbe's notes.
387 See "A Hidden Light" in Chapter 3. In Ahron HaLevi of Staroshelye, *Sha'arei ha-Yihud ve-ha-Emunah*, Gate 2, Chapter 15, it says: "The chief aim is that the glory of God be revealed in the world as it exists from our perspective [. . .] and that there be no divisions in our understanding of reality. This is achieved by means of Torah study, and through our prayer and worship; for when the separate being (*yesh*) of things is made transparent (*bittul*) to the source, all the walls are broken through and the veils are rent asunder—even from our perspective. That is to say, through the work of prayer, the unity of God is revealed in the lower worlds, and these worlds are made transparent to the blessed and unifying essence of God, so that the worlds no longer appear to have a separate existence, God forbid. The infinite nature of God, who is blessed, is also revealed through the Torah and its *mitzvot*."
388 In Reb Pinhas Reizes' original account, Reb Ahron was called 'Arkeh Orshayer,' which was an affectionate way of saying, 'Ahron from Orsha.'
389 See "The Maggid of Liozhna's Wisdom, Understanding, and Knowledge" and "The Great Sacrifice" in Chapter 2.
390 See Zalman Schachter-Shalomi and Netanel Miles-Yepez, *A Heart Afire: Stories and Teachings of the Early Hasidic Masters*, 176-80 ("A New Holy Fellowship"), and Tzvi M. Rabinowicz, "Aaron the Great of Karlin," *The Encyclopedia of Hasidism*, 4, for more on Reb Ahron of Karlin. On Reb Shlomo of Karlin, see Tzvi M. Rabinowicz, "Shlomoh of Karlin," *The Encyclopedia of Hasidism*, 456. It is likely that the differences on contemplation are those outlined by Reb Shneur Zalman in Chapter 2 on "Two Kinds of Contemplation."
391 Once, when the Alter Rebbe (who usually read the Torah for the congregation) was away for Parshat Ki Tavo', when the curses are read in the section of admonition, Reb Dov Baer, who was not yet *bar mitzvah*, heard another read the curses. He was so anguished afterward that his father was not certain that he would be able to fast on Yom Kippur. When the Hasidim asked him why—after all, he heard that section every year—he replied, "When my father reads it, no one curses." A version of this story can be found in Schneersohn, *HaYom Yom . . . "From Day to Day,"* 88. Another HaBaD tradition says that the 'curse' Reb Shlomo Karliner uttered had to do with Reb Shneur Zalman's youngest son, Moshe, who was also present at the time the second curse was uttered.
392 We have added some details to the account given here from Yosef Yitzhak Schneersohn, trans. Uri Kaploun, *Likkutei Dibburim: Volume 1*, 309, which tells the story of Reb Shlomo of Karlin and Reb Binyomin Kletzker. See Chapter 2, "The Maggid of Liozhna's Wisdom, Understanding, and Knowledge."
393 Learned at a HaBaD-Lubavitch *farbrengen*. —Z.M.S-S. Here we have retold the story based on the eyewitness account of Reb Pinhas Reizes, originally told in the first person. See Schneersohn, *Likkutei Dibburim: Volume 2*, 181-86, and Mindel, *Rabbi Schneur Zalman*, 75-79 for other versions in English.
394 Rabinowicz, "Shlomoh of Karlin," *The Encyclopedia of Hasidism*, 456-57.
395 Tzvi M. Rabinowicz, "Zeev Wolf of Zhitomir," *The Encyclopedia of Hasidism*, 556-57, and Schneersohn, *Likkutei Dibburim: Volume 1*, 309. His *Or ha-Meir* is considered a classic of Hasidic wisdom.
396 Arthur Green and Barry W. Holtz, eds. and trans., *Your Word is Fire: The Hasidic Masters*

on Contemplative Prayer, 96.

397 *Zohar* II: 204b, III: 80-82, and the *Zohar Ḥadash,* B'reishit 11.

398 *Sefer Shel Beinonim,* Chapter 2, translated from the facing Hebrew text of Schneur Zalman of Liadi, *Likutei Amarim: Tanya: Bi-Lingual Edition,* 10.

399 Learned at a ḤaBaD-Lubavitch *farbrengen.* —Z.M.S-S.

400 Learned at a ḤaBaD-Lubavitch *farbrengen.* —Z.M.S-S.

401 Learned at a ḤaBaD-Lubavitch *farbrengen.* —Z.M.S-S.

402 Puran Bair and Susanna Bair, ed. Asatar Bair, *Living from the Heart: Heart Rhythm Meditation for Energy, Clarity, Vision, and Inner Peace,* 54. Puran and Susanna are both senior disciples of Pir Vilayat Inayat-Khan.

403 Slightly adapted with the permission of the author, Zia Inayat-Khan, *The Chishti Silsila of Pir-o-Murshid Inayat Khan,* 32-33 ("Hazrat Khwaja Qutb al-Din Bakhtiyar Kaki"). Also Zia Inayat-Khan, "The 'Silsila-I Sufian': From Khwaja Mu'in al-Din Chishti to Sayyid Abu Hashim Madani," *A Pearl in Wine: Essays on the Life, Music and Sufism of Hazrat Inayat Khan,* 277-78, and Carl W. Ernst and Bruce B. Lawrence, *Sufi Martyrs of Love: The Chishti Order in South Asia and Beyond,* 153-54 on Khwaja Qutb ad-Din.

404 A final story of rebuke is found in Chaim Dalfin, *Chasidim Farbreng,* 98, and concerns *mesirat nefesh.*

405 Schneersohn, *HaYom Yom . . . "From Day to Day,"* A10, 68.

406 The Maskil's full account is found in A. H. Glitzenstein, *Sefer ha-Toldot: Admur ha-Zaken,* 173-77. A complete English translation can be found in Mindel, *Rabbi Schneur Zalman,* 132-41.

407 Mindel, *Rabbi Schneur Zalman,* 107, 110, and Loewenthal, *Communicating the Infinite,* 102. See also David Tzvi Hillman, ed., *Iggrot Ba'al ha-Tanya,* 58: "Once the prayer leader begins *Hodu,* let no one walk back and forth in front of those who are praying. This is definitely forbidden according to the *Gemara,* and you should remove anyone who transgresses this. Do not let that person come to my son [Reb Dov Baer], may he live, until witnesses declare that person careful in these matters." In another passage, he writes, "Those who are traveling to me for Rosh Ḥodesh, and need to ask me something concerning Torah, should write out their question, and I will answer them in writing, or orally through my son [Reb Dov Baer]."

408 Jacobs, *Seeker of Unity,* 25 note 8. In Hielman, *Beit Rebbe,* 134, it says: "It is known that he (Reb Ahron HaLevi) wrote letters to the Hasidim on behalf of the Rebbe, strengthening them in their service and urging them to do their duty. Always he did whatever was necessary for our master, the Alter Rebbe."

409 Hielman, *Beit Rebbe,* 134, says: "When our master, the Alter Rebbe, was arrested and taken to Petersburg, Reb Ahron showed great self-sacrifice for the Rebbe, and did everything he possibly could to help."

410 Ibid., 56.

411 Learned at a ḤaBaD-Lubavitch *farbrengen.* —Z.M.S-S.

412 Loewenthal, *Communicating the Infinite,* 256 note 12. See Hillman, *Iggrot Ba'al ha-Tanya,* 217-21.

413 Yiddish for 'middle.' He is called the Mittler Rebbe because he comes between his father, Reb Shneur Zalman, the Alter Rebbe, and his son-in-law, Reb Menachem Mendel I, the Tzemah Tzedek.

414 Hielman, *Beit Rebbe,* 134.

415 In Dalfin, *Chasidim Farbreng,* 56, it says: "Reb Shmuel [Levitin, my *mashpiyya*] had two letters from Reb [Ahron] where he addresses him [Reb Dov Baer] with loving terms as a best friend. It was noticeable from the letters that he was not fully aware of the holiness

of the Mittler Rebbe. This is because the Mittler Rebbe was so modest that he hid his holiness to the point that even his best friend was fooled. Reb [Ahron] encouraged him to despise material indulgences and other ideas in *[avodat ha-Shem]*. He thought the Mittler Rebbe needed to hear this from him because he wasn't doing so." Obviously, this shows the prejudice of a loyal ḤaBaD-Lubavitcher in this matter, but it also speaks to the level of relationship that once existed between them. There is more on this correspondence in Loewenthal, *Communicating the Infinite*, 266-68 note 142.

416 Learned at a ḤaBaD-Lubavitch *farbrengen*. —Z.M.S-S. We believe this anecdote is also found in Hielman's *Beit Rebbe*, but we have not been able to find it. The elder Hasid's remark is a play on what is commonly said of *ḥokhmah* and *binah*, "the two lovers who are not separated."

417 Learned at a ḤaBaD-Lubavitch *farbrengen* as a teaching of my Rebbe, Reb Yosef Yitzhak Schneerson. Later I found that he was actually quoting a teaching of Reb Dov Baer. —Z.M.S-S. Compare this with Yosef Yitzchak Schneersohn, trans. Uri Kaploun, *Likkutei Dibburim: Volume 3*, 32, where the Rebbe gives a slightly different version handed down from his father and grandfather.

418 Loewenthal, *Communicating the Infinite*, 110.

419 Learned at a ḤaBaD-Lubavitch *farbrengen*. —Z.M.S-S. The first sentence is found in Hielman, *Beit Rebbe*, 184. We believe the latter part is also in *Beit Rebbe*, but we have not been able to find it. Reb Dov Baer's Hasid, Reb Ya'akov Kaidener, *Sippurim Nora'im*, 33 also wrote: "On Rosh Hashanah he prayed for a very long time, standing in the *Amidah* for about three hours, and I saw not the slightest movement from him. He was just like a pillar of iron stuck in the ground."

420 Schachter-Shalomi and Miles-Yepez, *A Heart Afire*, 271 ("Reaching Too High").

421 *Likkutei Yekarim*, 15d, as translated in Green and Holtz, *Your Word is Fire*, 84. An alternate translation, based on *Or Torah*, 160b, is given in Rivka Schatz Uffenheimer, trans. Jonathan Chipman, *Hasidism as Mysticism: Quietistic Elements in Eighteenth Century Hasidic Thought*, 185: ". . . thus in prayer he is able to engage in the service of prayer to God, so that his service is not visible to people at all. He makes no motion whatever of his limbs, but only within his inward soul it is burning in his heart, and he will cry out in silence because of his excitement in this matter, so that his inner service shall be greater than the service apparent from his limbs."

422 Kaidener, *Sippurim Nora'im*, 32.

423 Jacobs, *Seeker of Unity*, 13.

424 Hielman, *Beit Rebbe*, 134. Loewenthal, *Communicating the Infinite*, 112, says: "There is little doubt that in the lifetime of R. Shneur Zalman, his leading disciple, R. [Ahron HaLevi] was a member of a small elite who prayed with overtly extravagant enthusiasm."

425 Martin Buber, trans. Olga Marx, *Tales of the Hasidim: The Early Masters*, 49-50 ("Trembling").

426 *Tzava'at ha-RiBaSh*, 58, as translated in Or Rose and Ebn D. Leader, eds. and trans., *God in All Moments: Mystical and Practical Spiritual Wisdom from Hasidic Masters*, 29 ("The Word: Body and Soul").

427 Hielman, *Beit Rebbe*, 31 note 2.

428 Ibid., 31 note 2.

429 As quoted in Jacobs, *On Ecstasy*, 49 note 34.

430 Learned from Hasidim. —Z.M.S-S.

431 Hielman, *Beit Rebbe*, 134.

432 Reb Yehudah Leib of Yanovitch, the Alter Rebbe's brother and chief aide, in spite of denying Reb Ahron's claims to leadership, calls him the "leading disciple" of the Alter

Rebbe. Ibid., 184.

433   These are things that come out later in the letters that Reb Yehudah Leib of Yanovitch and Reb Pinhas Reizes write is support of Reb Dov Baer.

434   The only known comment on the matter from Reb Shneur Zalman is that reported by his brother, Reb Yehudah Leib, which said, "Suffering is only considered such when it is contrary to one's desire." Ibid., 189. Loewenthal, *Communicating the Infinite*, 257 note 13, says: "[. . .] which seems to imply he expected [Reb Ahron] to have a philosophical attitude about his problems." This is the most likely explanation of the cryptic comment, though Reb Yehudah Leib was not a disinterested reporter.

435   See Zalman Alpert, "The Rogue Chasid: Michael Levi Rodkinson," *The Chasidic Historical Review*, 28-30.

436   According to *Beit Rebbe*, it was four years.

437   Mikhael Levi Rodkinson, *Sefer Shivḥei ha-Rav*, 18a. We are grateful to Elliot Ginsburg at the University of Michigan who managed to obtain this rare book for us and sent us the text from which to translate.

438   See Ernst and Lawrence, *Sufi Martyrs of Love*, 154. These actions are repeated in countless tales through the generations of Sufism.

439   Schachter-Shalomi and Miles-Yepez, *A Heart Afire*, 173-74 ("A Bear in the Forest").

440   This is a clear reference to the Messiah's answer to the Ba'al Shem Tov, who asked, "When will the Messiah come?" Ibid., 62.

441   See Chapter 2, "The Great Sacrifice."

442   See Chapter 5, "Counseling Hasidim." It is very likely that Reb Ahron HaLevi may have gotten similar instructions when the Rebbe blessed him in that intimate moment three years earlier.

443   Hillman, *Iggrot Ba'al ha-Tanya*, 203-04. Reb Pinhas Reizes' open letter to the ḤaBaD community continues: "However, when the Rebbe and his son were out of the country, many decided to follow their own wishes, for there was no one holding them back. Then, 'certain people,' whose hearts were turning away from the household of the Rebbe, whose soul is in Eden, and from his progeny after him, with bitterness and gall followed the promptings of their own hearts and tied crowns to those who do not in truth deserve them. They despised our Rebbe, Reb Dov Baer, as a shepherd, and turned their ears away from his Torah in favor of a 'stranger' who is not of the Rebbe's seed. Therefore, I can no longer be silent and hold back what I know of the Rebbe's intentions, who wished his son—and no one else—to be our shepherd. Greater wisdom has he given over to him to hear, to learn, and to teach the words of the living God with intellectual clarity, like a spring that is overflowing, a source of wisdom and holy Torah. He is like a cistern that is completely full, for he has absorbed the teachings of our Rebbe like a sponge, missing not a single drop. His speech is extremely clear and his words are orderly, everything in its right place with him. Knowing all this, who would dare to transgress the holy command of our Rebbe? Therefore, my brothers, be careful with your souls and show kindness to the memory of our Rebbe, shielding and protecting the Rebbe, his son. Let us serve before his son, the Rebbe, as we served before his holy father in order that his great holiness should not be forgotten. He planted in our souls the splendor of his holy light, and each of us was able to draw it forth according to our capacity. His holy words still exist and are available to those who seek them through his son. This Torah is our delight and our protector for all eternity, never forsaking us. Let the spirit pour upon us from above and be a help to us. And when we return to Zion, let us see this with our own eyes. The words of the one who speaks these things in faithfulness, Pinhas ben Henokh Schick."

444   Learned from Hasidim. —Z.M.S-S.

445 Hielman, *Beit Rebbe*, 184.
446 Ibid., 46 note 2.
447 Ibid., 187.
448 Loewenthal, *Communicating the Infinite*, 135-36, 270 note 158.
449 Ibid., 135, 270 notes 158, 159, and 160.
450 Hielman, *Beit Rebbe*, 134.
451 Ibid., 134 note 3.

Chapter 5

452 Yosef Yitzchak Schneersohn, trans. Zalman I. Posner, Yitschak Meir Kagan, and Sholom B. Wineberg, ed. Menachem Mendel Schneerson, *HaYom Yom… "From Day to Day,"* 34.
453 See Zalman Schachter-Shalomi, ed. N. Miles-Yepez, *Wrapped in a Holy Flame: Teachings and Tales of the Hasidic Masters*, 185-95 on the *Sha'ar ha-Yihud ve-ha-Emunah* of Reb Shneur Zalman.
454 "It has been clearly demonstrated to you that the Lord alone is God; *(ain od milvado)* there is none beside Him." (Deut. 4:35)
455 Learned at a HaBaD-Lubavitch *farbrengen*. —Z.M.S-S.
456 The *Ana b'Koah* prayer attributed to Rabbi Nehunia ben HaKanah.
457 This anecdote is also found in Chaim Dalfin, *Chasidim Farbreng*, 56.
458 The *haskamah* of Rabbi Tzvi Hirsh of Tchashnik in Reb Ahron HaLevi's *Avodat ha-Levi*.
459 Avraham Abele of Herson, *Beit Avraham*, 37.
460 My *mashpiyya*, Reb Shmuel Levitin, once told us: "On Yom Kippur between *Musaf* and *Minhah*, the Alter Rebbe and his son would go into the Rebbe's study and learn together. Once, the door remained ajar, and young Menachem Mendel, the Rebbe's grandson, listened outside the door. From outside, he heard the Rebbe say, 'The accusing angels have brought about a heavenly decree against me for revealing too much *Hasidut*.' The room was silent for a moment, then Reb Dov Baer said, 'Please say *Hasidut* for me.' — Z.M.S-S. This anecdote is also found in Dalfin, *Chasidim Farbreng*, 55-56.
461 Hayyim Meir Hielman, *Beit Rebbe*, 184.
462 David Tzvi Hillman, *Iggrot Ba'al ha-Tanya*, 204.
463 Reb Yitzhak Moshe of Yass was known as a great memorizer and repeater of Reb Dov Baer's discourses *(ma'amarim)*. Once while he was in the town of Reb Avraham Yehoshua Heschel of Apt, he repeated one of the discourses of Reb Dov Baer to the Hasidim there; but when the Apter Rebbe heard it, he said—"Do you mean to conquer the 'queen' in my 'home'?" The rest of this anecdote, reported by Reb Leibel Kramer, concerns Reb Yitzhak Moshe's fears that this breach of etiquette may have shortened his life. Thus he went to see Reb Dov Baer and told him what had happened. Reb Dov Baer blessed him for a long life (he lived to be 102), but told him never to do such a thing again. Dalfin, *Chasidim Farbreng*, 46.
464 Learned at a HaBaD-Lubavitch *farbrengen*. —Z.M.S-S.
465 See Chapter 4, "The Commander of God's Armies."
466 One of Reb Dov Baer's special festivals was Lag b'Omer, upon which he and his Hasidim would go out into the fields together. Even though he did not wash and break bread, he would partake of *mashkeh* (alcohol) with the Hasidim, though he was not supposed to because of his health. Many wonders were seen at that time, most involving childless couples who were blessed with children. So the Hasidim waited all year to spend

Lag b'Omer with the Rebbe. Schneersohn, *HaYom Yom*, 55.
467 The Rebbe, Reb Yosef Yitzhak Schneersohn's preface to Dov Baer Shneuri's *Poke'ah Ivrim*.
468 See Zalman Schachter-Shalomi and Netanel Miles-Yepez, *A Heart Afire: Stories and Teachings of the Early Hasidic Masters*, 142.
469 Learned at a ḤaBaD-Lubavitch *farbrengen*. —Z.M.S-S. A version of this is also found in Chaim Dalfin, *Farbrengen: Inspirational Stories and Anecdotes*, 54-56 ("Finding His Own 'Sins'").
470 The other authoritative interpreters are: Dov Baer Shneuri of Lubavitch (1773-1827), Menachem Mendel Schneersohn I of Lubavitch (1789-1866), Yitzhak Eisik HaLevi Epstein of Homil (1780-1857), and Hillel ben Meir HaLevi of Paritch (1795-1864).
471 Louis Jacobs, *Seeker of Unity: The Life and Works of Aaron of Starosselje*, 157. Recently, a colleague told me that a group of non-ḤaBaD Hasidim approached a famous Israeli scholar, an acknowledged expert on Reb Ahron HaLevi, to have his works explained to them. Because the scholar was a woman, they first wanted to make sure that her husband was not the real author of her studies. But after they were made aware of her unmistakable erudition, they sat down to learn about Reb Ahron's radical non-dualism! —Z.M.S-S.
472 Hielman, *Beit Rebbe*, 134.
473 See Jacobs, *Seeker of Unity*, 72.
474 Ahron HaLevi of Staroshelye, *Sha'arei ha-Yiḥud ve-ha-Emunah*, Gate 2, Chapter 26.
475 Sankaracarya Bhagavatpada, ed. & trans. John Grimes, *The Vivekacudamani of Sankaracarya Bhagavatpada: An Introduction and Translation*, 32.
476 Ibid., 32.
477 The word, *Brahman* comes from the root *brh*, meaning, "to expand."
478 T.M.P. Mahadevan, *Invitation to Indian Philosophy*, 388-89. In R. Balasubramanian, "Advaita: An Overview," *Perspectives of Theism and Absolutism in Indian Philosophy*, 60-61, it says: "It is Brahman that is God or *Ishvara* in relation to the world. He is not only source and support of the world, but also its moral governor. He is the wielder of *maya (mayin)* and is not affected by it. It means that He is both omnipotent and omniscient. It is He who reveals the *Veda* at the beginning of every cycle for the benefit of jivas. He is the object of worship and meditation. So long as there is jiva as well as the world, there is *Ishvara*."
479 See Shalom DovBer Schneersohn, trans. Eliyahu Touger, *To Know G-d: VeYadaata*, 12.
480 Admittedly, we would never have come across this note in Reb Ahron's dense work if it were not for the fact the Louis Jacobs had already made a presentation of it in his *Seeker of Unity*, 105-08. Nevertheless, we felt it was important enough to repeat it in this work for an altogether different audience.
481 Midrash Rabbah, Devarim 2:27; Yalkut 269.
482 "Now I know that the Lord is greater than all gods" (Ex. 18:11).
483 Here, the letter *ayin* stands for its numerical equivalent, 70.
484 "Now I know that there is no God in the whole world except in Israel!" (2 Kings 5:15)
485 "[. . .] for the Lord your God is the only God in heaven above and on earth below." (Josh. 2:11)
486 Ahron HaLevi of Staroshelye, *Sha'arei ha-Yiḥud ve-ha-Emunah*, Gate 1, Chapter 22, says: "I saw that some people erroneously described *tzimtzum*, the 'contraction' as taking place within Divinity, prior to emanation [. . .] understanding the words of the *kabbalah* and the concept of *tzimtzum* literally, believing that God actually contracted and withdrew the light of Divinity in order to create the world. That is to say, there was actually a withdrawal of the blessed substance of Divinity, God forbid! No, the *tzimtzum* did not occur in God at all, nor could any darkness obscure God's light; this view of *tzimtzum* weakens

the foundations of faith in God's unity, limiting God's power [...] God forbid that there should be any lack in Divinity, withdrawal of God's substance, or limitation in God's power; an actual *tzimtzum* implies change, which should not be imputed to *Ain Sof*, the 'Infinite One.'" Here, Reb Ahron HaLevi is obviously returning to the disagreement with the literal interpreters of *tzimtzum*. Nevertheless, he adds a simple but significant objection to the literalist interpretation, saying—"this view of *tzimtzum* weakens the foundations of faith in God's unity, limiting God's power." How does it weaken the foundations of faith to believe that God actually withdrew the divine substance to make a place for creation? If God is all powerful, then nothing can limit that power, there can be nothing separate or other than God!

487 "Know therefore this day and keep in mind that the Lord alone is God in heaven above and on earth below; there is none other." (Deut. 4:39)

488 Ahron HaLevi of Staroshelye, *Sha'arei ha-Yiḥud ve-ha-Emunah*, Gate 4, note on 22-44. Another précis of this interesting teaching is also presented in Jacobs, *Seeker of Unity*, 105-09.

489 The four views presented by Gurary are: *tzimtzum* is meant literally, and takes place in the essence of God (the view of Rabbi Immanuel Hai Riki and the Rabbi Eliyahu ben Shlomo, the Ga'on of Vilna); *tzimtzum* is meant literally, but takes place in the *Or Ain Sof*, not in God's essence (the view of Rabbi Yonatan Eibeshutz); *tzimtzum* is not meant literally, but takes place in the essence of God (the view of Rabbi Hayyim of Volozhin); and finally, *tzimtzum* is not meant literally, and takes place only in the *Or Ain Sof*, and not in the essence of God (the view of Reb Shneur Zalman) Noson Gurary, *Chasidism: Its Development, Theology, and Practice*, 102-10.

490 This text is also known as *Sha'ar ha-Yiḥud*, but we have stayed with *Kuntres ha-Hitbonenut* to avoid confusion with other works. The quote from the Rebbe is translated from the Hebrew of Schneersohn, *HaYom Yom*, 37.

491 Talmud, Sukkah 28b.

492 Once Reb Shneur Zalman of Liadi told a Hasid, "One ought to be a *bar da'at*—a 'child of knowing.' Later, that Hasid asked Reb Dov Baer what the Alter Rebbe had meant. "A *bar da'at*," he said, "is one who prepares properly before tackling a concept they want to master." See Yosef Yitzchak Schneersohn, trans. Uri Kaploun, *Likkutei Dibburim: Volume 3*, 15-16. See Yosef Yitzchak Schneersohn, trans. Uri Kaploun, *Likkutei Dibburim: Volume 5*, 228-30 for another description of *hitbonenut* where study is prescribed beforehand.

493 In his own teachings touching upon *hitbonenut*, Reb Shneur Zalman is always stressing, *ba umka d'liba*, "In the depths of the heart." So this isn't only in the mind; he wants it in the depths of the heart. He uses "depths," plural; for there is a "depth of height," and there is a "depth of deep." And to connect the depth of height and the depth of deep, is very important.

494 "All the fountains of the great deep burst apart" (Gen. 7:11).

495 This is a play on "But where can wisdom be found" (Job 28:12).

496 Catherine Shainberg, *Kabbalah and the Power of Dreaming*, 3-4, and Jill Bolte Taylor, *My Stroke of Insight: A Brain Scientist's Personal Journey*.

497 Moses Maimonides, trans. Shlomo Pines, *The Guide of the Perplexed*, 7: "We are like someone in a very dark night over whom lightning flashes time and time again."

498 *Sefer Yetzirah* 1:4.

499 Selections from Chapter 1 of *Sha'ar ha-Yiḥud* in Dov Baer of Lubavitch, *Ner Mitzvah ve-Torah Or*.

500 Abraham Joshua Heschel, *God in Search of Man: A Philosophy of Judaism*, 5.

501 In Schneersohn, *Likkutei Dibburim: Volume 5*, 19-20, it says: "In former generations

young men were not admitted to hear [ma'amarim] being delivered by the Rebbe of their generation. They first had to be familiar with the *Seder [Histlshelut]*, at least know all of its stations. This is what the Mittler Rebbe's *[Sha'ar ha-Yihud]* is all about—it explains the nature of *[hitbonenut]* and also the themes upon which one should meditate, and this entails knowing the *[hasidishe]* stations." Yosef Yitzchak Schneersohn, trans. Uri Kaploun, *Likkutei Dibburim: Volume 2*, 96 discusses the refinement and elimination of undesirable traits through contemplation in prayer.

502   This was on 46th Street, between 15th and 16th Avenue. —Z.M.S-S.

503   Part of this presentation on *hitbonenut* has been adapted from Zalman M. Schachter-Shalomi, ed. Robert Michael Esformes, *Gate to the Heart: An Evolving Process*, 12-15.

504   See Schachter-Shalomi and Miles-Yepez, *A Heart Afire*, 143.

505   The first edition of *A First Step: A Primer of a Jew's Spiritual Life*, which contained material on *hitbonenut*, was published privately around 1958, and was later updated as *Gate to the Heart: An Evolving Process* in 1993.

506   *Vipassana*, the Pali for 'insight,' is the word that is used for meditation practice by many western Buddhists of the Theravadin school. *Shamatha-Vipashyana* is the more complete Sanskrit name for Buddhist meditation practice, meaning 'tranquility and insight.'

507   Schachter-Shalomi, *Gate to the Heart*, 28, and Jeff Roth, *Jewish Meditation Practices for Everyday Life*, 26-30.

508   In the Arabic original, the word used is *fikr* (qualified by *ilm*, 'philosophical,' or 'scientific'), which means 'contemplation' or 'reflection.' See Javad Nurbakhsh, *In the Paradise of the Sufis*, 51-66.

509   Translated from the facing Hebrew of Avraham ben HaRambam, trans. Yaakov Wincelberg, *The Guide to Serving G-d*, 12, and checked against facing Arabic of Samuel Rosenblatt, ed. and trans., *The High Ways to Perfection of Abraham Maimonides*, 142.

510   As our friend and colleague Father Thomas Keating is so fond of pointing-out.

511   See Louis Jacobs, trans., *On Ecstasy: A Tract by Dobh Baer*. The original edition was published as *Tract on Ecstasy*.

512   See Zalman M. Schachter, "A Letter on a Tract on Ecstasy," in *Conservative Judaism*, Spring, 1964.

513   This refers to a pastoral letter written to his Hasidim, part of which touches on this subject and which is usually printed with the *Kuntres ha-Hitpa'alut*. Part of it is translated in this chapter, and a full translation may be found in Jacobs, trans., *On Ecstasy*, 177-87.

514   Letter of Reb Dov Baer printed with the *Kuntres ha-Hitpa'alut* in Dov Baer of Lubavitch and Hillel ben Meir of Paritch, *Likkutei Bi'urim*.

515   See Chapter 4, "The Training of Rebbes."

516   Exod. 23:25.

517   "For there is not one good man on earth who does what is best and doesn't err." (Eccles. 7:20)

518   See Schachter-Shalomi and Miles-Yepez, *A Heart Afire*, 265-269.

519   Ahron HaLevi of Staroshelye, *Sha'arei ha-Avodah*, Introduction.

520   See Chogyam Trungpa, ed. John Baker and Marvin Casper, *Cutting Through Spiritual Materialism*, Boston: Shambhala Publications, 1987.

521   This is in agreement with Reb Ahron, who says: "Now, I have spent a lot of time on this matter because there are many who have turned away from reason, and who have somehow derived from this teaching the idea that one must practice *hitbonenut* without creating any awakening in the heart. Thus, they hang empty vessels on our teacher, whose soul is in Eden, attributing vain and useless teachings to him which are opposed to Torah. In truth, the heart is of supreme importance in Torah, and the purpose of knowledge, it

can be demonstrated, is only to purify the heart. For, wherever you find a reference to knowledge in scripture you will also find a reference to the awakening of the heart in the same context." Ahron HaLevi of Staroshelye, *Sha'arei ha-Avodah*, Introduction.
522 Jer. 12:8.
523 "Their heart cried out to the Lord" (Lam. 2:18)
524 "In their adversity they cried to the Lord" (Ps. 107:6).
525 Letter of Reb Dov Baer printed with the *Kuntres ha-Hitpa'alut* in Dov Baer of Lubavitch and Hillel ben Meir of Paritch, *Likkutei Bi'urim*. Interestingly, 'inauthentic' expressions of ecstasy were also a concern in Sufism, and a portion of Sheikh Shahab ad-Din Suhrwardi's great manual of Sufism was devoted to a criticism of this. See Shahab ad-Din Suhrawardi, trans. H. Wilberforce Clarke, *The 'Awarif-u'l-Ma'arif*, 58-59.
526 This seems to have been the ideal of the so called "old way" as well, for many teachings of the Ba'al Shem Tov and the Maggid of Mezritch also speak to the purification of self-awareness in contemplation. See Arthur Green and Barry W. Holtz, eds. and trans., *Your Word is Fire: The Hasidic Masters on Contemplative Prayer*, 54-65 ("Beyond the Walls of Self").
527 Deut. 30:14. Quoted on the title page of the *Tanya*.
528 "Only one is my dove, my perfect one" (Songs 6:9).
529 Mishnah, Avot, 2:16.
530 Ahron HaLevi of Staroshelye, *Sha'arei ha-Avodah*, Introduction.
531 As we have already seen, Reb Dov Baer was used to this level of absorption in his own *hitbonenut*. Once, while Reb Shneur Zalman was on his way to the *mikveh*, he happened to look into the window of Reb Dov Baer's house as he was passing. He stopped, noticing that Reb Dov Baer who was smoking a pipe appeared to be lost in his *hitbonenut*. Concerned that perhaps he should not be smoking while so unaware of the outside world, he went inside and removed the pipe from his son's mouth. Later, when he was returning from the *mikveh*, he again looked in the window and saw that Reb Dov Baer still appeared to puffing on one side of his mouth as if he were still smoking the pipe! This anecdote, reported by my *mashpiyya*, Reb Shmuel Levitin, may be found in Dalfin, *Chasidim Farbreng*, 55. — Z.M.S-S.
532 *Kuntres ha-Hitpa'alut*, Chapter 1, in Dov Baer of Lubavitch and Hillel ben Meir of Paritch, *Likkutei Bi'urim*.
533 Ibid.
534 See Martin Buber, trans. Olga Marx, *Tales of the Hasidim: The Early Masters*, 256-57 ("The Impure Fire").
535 Hielman, *Beit Rebbe*, 134 note 3. This comment was followed by the story of Reb Ahron at the *ohel* of the Alter Rebbe, found at the end of Chapter 4. In Dalfin, *Chasidim Farbreng*, 56, Reb Shalom Dov Baer of Lubavitch is also reported to have said, "Reb Ahron had a Godly ecstasy [...]."
536 This was also the birthday of his father, Reb Shneur Zalman, as well as that of the Ba'al Shem Tov.
537 Ibid., 191.
538 Ibid., 198 note 2, 199 notes 2 and 3. It is unclear whether Reb Ahron was released ten days before on the 1st of Kislev, or on the 10th with Reb Dov Baer. Louis Jacobs, "Aaron of Starosselje," *The Encyclopedia of Hasidism*, 3.
539 Presumably disciples who were still living at the time of the writing of the *Beit Rebbe*.
540 When the Tzemah Tzedek was chosen to succeed the Mittler Rebbe, Reb Dov Baer in Lubavitch, Reb Ahron HaLevi said: "Thank God, a descendant of the Rebbe's children is following in his footsteps." Ibid., 134 note 3.

541   Ibid., 134. He does not tell us what works these stories are found in, nor do we know of any such works that are still extant.

Chapter 6

542   See Eliezer Steinmann, trans. Haim Shachter, *The Garden of Hassidism*, 95-96 where he says, Reb Nahman Horodenker "was senior in years and in noble descent, and perhaps also in learning, to Reb [Yisra'el Ba'al] Shem Tov."
543   Aryeh Kaplan, ed. Dovid Shapiro, *Until the Mashiach: Rabbi Nachman's Biography: An Annotated Chronology*, 226.
544   See Immanuel Etkes, trans. Saadya Sternberg, *The Besht: Magician, Mystic, and Leader*, 158-159 on the men of the Brod *kloiz*.
545   See Abraham J. Heschel, ed. Samuel Dresner, *The Circle of the Baal Shem Tov: Studies in Hasidism*, 63, 92, 93 on the dates of Nahman of Horodenka's trips to *Eretz Yisra'el* before the Fall of 1740, in 1741, and in 1763/1764.
546   *Shivḥei ha-Besht*, 239. See Dan Ben-Amos and Jerome R. Mintz, eds. and trans., *In Praise of the Baal Shem Tov [Shivḥei ha-Besht]: The Earliest Collection of Legends about the Founder of Hasidism*, 185, for another translation of this anecdote.
547   Tzvi M. Rabinowicz, "Nahman of Horodenka," *The Encyclopedia of Hasidism*, 338.
548   Kaplan, *Until the Mashiach*, 226.
549   See Zalman Schachter-Shalomi and Netanel Miles-Yepez, *A Heart Afire: Stories and Teachings of the Early Hasidic Masters*, 26-44 ("Divine Providence") on the 'conversion' of a *mitnaged*, 155-61 ("Words and Reality") on the 'conversion' of Rabbi Dov Baer, the Maggid of Mezritch.
550   *Shivḥei ha-Besht*, 112. See Ben-Amos and Mintz, *In Praise of the Baal Shem Tov*, 156, for a translation of this anecdote.
551   Steinmann, *The Garden of Hassidism*, 95-96. In Louis I. Newman and Samuel Spitz, eds. and trans., *The Hasidic Anthology: Tales and Teachings of the Hasidim*, 312, a similar tradition is quoted: Rabbi [Nahman] Horodenker said: "There are two ways of curing offenders. Some claim a cure by inflicting privations, but these usually result in the transgressor becoming embittered against society, and cruel henceforth. Others effect a cure through persuasions which oftentimes transform the sinner into a man of kindness and helpfulness."
552   See Schachter-Shalomi and Miles-Yepez, *A Heart Afire*, 139 on the "new way" of the Ba'al Shem Tov.
553   See Heschel, *The Circle of the Baal Shem Tov*, 149-150, for a discussion of this title as applied to Reb Nahman of Horodenka.
554   See Jacob Immanuel Schochet, *The Great Maggid: The Life and Teachings of Rabbi Dov Ber of Mezhirech*, 43, 81, where, more than once, Reb Nahman of Horodenka was sent bearing letters and messages to the Maggid of Mezritch, inviting him for a visit and later urging him to take care of his health.
555   See Etkes, *The Besht*, 187 where the relationship between the Ba'al Shem Tov and Nahman of Horodenka is discussed; see Buxbaum, *The Light and Fire of the Baal Shem Tov*, 295-96 ("Witness to a Debate"), where Nahman of Horodenka is witness to a debate between the Ba'al Shem Tov and the Ari.
556   Kaplan, *Until the Mashiach*, 323 mentions the relationship to Rabbi Yitzhak of Drohobitch, a great kabbalist and colleague of the Ba'al Shem Tov, and the father of Mikhele of Zlotchov. See Heschel, *The Circle of the Baal Shem Tov*, 152-81 ("Rabbi Isaac of Drohobycz").

557 Ibid., "Chart II" diagrams the ancestry of Rebbe Nahman of Bratzlav, and shows the name of the first father-in-law of Nahman of Horodenka, Yitzhak II of Zholkiev.
558 Ibid., 226 mentions the death of his first wife.
559 Mark Zborowski and Elizabeth Herzog, *Life Is With People: The Culture of the Shtetl*, 289-90.
560 Ibid., 290.
561 It seems that Reb Nahman of Horodenka was being sensitive to the burdens that this marriage might put on his bride, being so young and married to a man of his age. But it is also possible that there was another unspoken consideration in the story. The sister of Yitzhak of Drohobitch may have been divorced or widowed as well, and before having had a child. Thus, to marry her would be a *mitzvah* that Reb Nahman could not ignore. Nevertheless, it seems to me, the greatest objection was probably that Reb Nahman Horodenker desired to return to *Eretz Yisra'el*, and was continually discouraged by the Ba'al Shem Tov. Thus, he may have seen this marriage as an impediment to his return.
562 See Newman and Spitz, *The Hasidic Anthology*, 472-73, for another version of this story.
563 I first learned the major part of this story from Rabbi Leah Novick in Boulder, Colorado in 2002, and later reconciled it with other Hasidic traditions. — N.M-Y. See Kaplan, *Until the Mashiach*, 323 on "Rabbi Simcha."
564 Kaplan, *Until the Mashiach*, 1, which mentions Reb Nahman Horodenker's living in the house of the Ba'al Shem Tov, and how Simhah was brought up in the house; 322-323, which tells of the disappearance of Reb Nahman Horodenker, the move into house of the Ba'al Shem Tov, and care of Simhah by Adel; Arthur Green, *Tormented Master: A Life of Rabbi Nahman of Bratslav*, 54 note 10: "Sometime before the death of the Ba'al Shem Tov in 1760 Nahman of Horodenka took up residence in [Mezhbizh], where his brother Aryeh Leib served as town rabbi during the [BeShT's] lifetime."
565 Zborowski and Herzog, *Life Is With People*, 271-77 on the rules of making proper marriage alliances.
566 There are also Hasidic *ma'asiot* that are dismissive of these rules: Once, a grandchild of Yisra'el of Rhyzhin was about to be engaged to a grandchild of Tzvi Hirsh of Rymanov; and while they were writing the *tenaim*, the engagement, the Rhyziner says, "I am the son of Shalom Shakhna of Prohobitch, who is the son of Avraham the Malakh, who is the son of Dov Baer, the Maggid of Mezritch . . ." and he goes on for a while, and when he stops, he says, "And how about you?" The Rymanover answered, "I was orphaned of my father, Yehudah Leib, of blessed memory, when I was just ten years old, and I was raised by my uncle, a humble tailor—new things he never spoiled, and old things he always fixed." The Rhyzhiner nodded his head and said, "Good. Enough with the *yiḥus*."
567 See Schachter-Shalomi and Miles-Yepez, *A Heart Afire*, 10-12 on the inn of Eliezer, father of the Ba'al Shem Tov.
568 Green, *Tormented Master*, 54 note 13: "The family of the Ba'al Shem Tov also claimed Davidic lineage, via the descendants of R. Moshe Isserles."
569 I first learned a part of this story from Rabbi Leah Novick in Boulder, Colorado in 2002, and later reconciled it with other Hasidic traditions. — N.M-Y.
570 In the traditional *siddur*.
571 This was not a problem in the first match arranged by the Ba'al Shem Tov, as the sister of Yitzhak of Drohobitch had a similarly distinguished ancestry.
572 See Buxbaum, *The Light and Fire of the Baal Shem Tov*, 296-97 ("The Ark of the Covenant"); Kaplan, *Until the Mashiach*, 227.
573 *Shivḥei ha-Besht*, 201. See Ben-Amos and Mintz, *In Praise of the Baal Shem Tov*, 152, and Etkes, *The Besht*, 188 for other translations of this anecdote.
574 Heschel, *The Circle of the Baal Shem Tov*, 40-41 gives the full anecdote reported by

Rafael of Bershad (the leading disciple of Pinhas of Koretz), and on 40 note 198, Heschel gives the Yiddish, *"Ikh hob nit gefilt azoine pleitzes."* Lit: "I did not feel shoulders broad enough in anyone."

575   Ibid., 64 note 84, which says that the party included Rabbi Menachem Mendel of Premyshlan, Rabbi Leib of Linitz, Rabbi Friedel of Brod, Rabbi David ben Mendel of Premyshlan, Rabbi Wolf, Rabbi Yisra'el, and Rabbi Yosef.

576   Rabinowicz, "Nahman of Horodenka," *The Encyclopedia of Hasidism*, 338; Heschel, *The Circle of the Baal Shem Tov*, 64.

577   Green, *Tormented Master*, 25.

578   Rabinowicz, "Nahman of Horodenka," *The Encyclopedia of Hasidism*, 338.

579   Nathan of Breslov, trans. Avraham Greenbaum, ed. Moshe Mykoff, *Tzaddik: A Portrait of Rabbi Nachman*, 33 note 53.

580   Steinmann, *The Garden of Hassidism*, 95-96.

581   Feiga and Simhah were married in 1763. If she was about 13 at the time, this would put her birth at around 1750. According to Bratzlav sources, she died on the 19th of Adar, 5561 (March 3/4, 1801).

582   Rabbi Yisra'el ben Shabbetai, the Maggid of Kozhnitz (1733-1815) was a special case, being named after Yisra'el Ba'al Shem Tov within his own lifetime, and at the specific direction of the Ba'al Shem Tov.

583   See Schachter-Shalomi and Miles-Yepez, *A Heart Afire*, 123, where the child Yisra'el died three days after the *brit*. Nevertheless, Kaplan, *Until the Mashiach*, 326-27 ("Rabbi Yisroel"), mentions other traditions that say, two years, and even the possibility that he lived to young adulthood.

584   We have already told a version of this tale in Schachter-Shalomi and Miles-Yepez, *A Heart Afire*, 122-125 ("Adel and Feiga and the Light of the Ba'al Shem Tov") with special reference to Rebbe Nahman's grandmother, Adel. I first learned this story from Rabbi Leah Novick in Boulder, Colorado in 2002, and later reconciled it with other Bratzlav traditions. —N.M-Y. See Kaplan, *Until the Mashiach*, 2, which mentions Rebbe Nahman's brother Yisra'el and discusses which brother was born first; and 326-327, which tells variations of the story of Yisra'el *Met*, 'the dead.'

585   I even went so far as to search for his grave when I was in Czechoslovakia. —Z.M.S-S.

586   "This is the story of Isaac, son of Abraham. Abraham begot Isaac." (Gen. 25:19) Why the redundancy? Abraham, who was *ḥesed*, begot Isaac, who was *gevurah*, intentionally. The sense is, you don't need two of the same thing; you need the two sides for balance.

587   There are some sources that say that Nahman of Horodenka died in 1780, but this seems unlikely, as Rebbe Nahman's parents almost certainly would not have named their child Nahman if he were still living. Thus, Reb Nahman Horodenker probably died somewhere between 1765 and 1772.

588   See Kaplan, *Until the Mashiach*, 324-26 ("Feiga") for another version of this story.

589   Rebbe Nahman was born on the first day of Nissan, 5532 (April 4th, 1772).

590   See Moshe Mykoff, *Once Upon a Tzaddik: Tales of Rebbe Nachman of Breslov*, 9.

591   Why do we wash the hands when we arise from sleep? Because it is thought that during sleep an evil spirit comes and rests on the body. That is to say, because the soul ascends to higher regions during sleep, evil spirits may take the opportunity to come in and make a nice warm bed in your body, like a cat coming in to warm itself in the morning. Therefore, one washes it off when one awakes.

592   Raymond J. DeMaille, ed., *The Sixth Grandfather: Black Elk's Teachings Given to John G. Neihardt*, 379.

593   Inayat Khan, *The Art of Personality: The Sufi Message: Volume III*, 13.

594 Once, when Rabbi Nahum of Chernobyl, who had been a disciple of the Ba'al Shem Tov and the Maggid of Mezritch both, was passing through Mezhbizh, he stopped to pay his respects to the family of the holy Ba'al Shem and to *daven* with the Hasidim there. Hearing that Feiga had given birth to a son, he asked to see the little heir to both the venerable Nahman of Horodenka and the Ba'al Shem Tov. When Feiga brought the child to the Chernobyler Rebbe, Reb Nahum looked closely at the eyes of Nahman and then exclaimed, "This boy has 'beautiful eyes.' " This was the expression the initiated used to describe someone of great spiritual potential. On another occasion, the Chernobyler Rebbe said of little Nahman, "The Torah says that 'the awe of God should be on your faces'; this awe is clearly seen on this child's face." Mykoff, *Once Upon a Tzaddik*, 8-9.
595 See Mykoff, *Once Upon a Tzaddik*, 9.
596 Green, *Tormented Master*, 24, points out that 1772 "was a crucial turning point in the history of Hasidism. It was early in that year that the first bans against the [Hasidim] were proclaimed by the communal leaders of Vilna and Brody." He also notes that it was the year of the partition of Poland between the Russian and Austrian empires, as well as the year of the death of the Maggid of Mezritch. Kaplan, *Until the Mashiach*, 3 mentions the ḥerem specifically as occurring on this date.
597 See Mykoff, *Once Upon a Tzaddik*, 97-98 ("Opposition Help's the Soul"). A similar story is told about why Reb Barukh ridiculed Reb Levi Yitzhak of Berditchev. For when someone else also ridiculed Reb Levi Yitzhak in his presence, Reb Barukh chided him and said: "Fool, when I ridicule him, it is to prolong his life. You don't realize how holy a person he really is!"
598 See Green, *Tormented Master*, 94-134 "Conflict and Growth" on Rebbe Nahman's disputes with other Rebbes.
599 Reb Hayyim of Krasnoye was a close disciple of the Ba'al Shem Tov and a good friend of Pinhas of Koretz. See Tzvi M. Rabinowicz, "Hayyim of Krasnoye," *The Encyclopedia of Hasidism*, 195; also Kaplan, *Until the Mashiach*, 241-42 ("Rabbi Chaim of Krassnoy"). For more on Reb Ya'akov Yosef of Polonoye, see Tzvi M. Rabinowicz, "Jacob Joseph HaKohen of Polonnoye," *The Encyclopedia of Hasidism*, 239-40, or Samuel H. Dresner, *The Zaddik: The Doctrine of the Zaddik According to the Writings of Rabbi Yaakov Yosef of Polnoy*, ca. 1960.
600 See Mykoff, *Once Upon a Tzaddik*, 10-11 ("A Journey to the 'Toldos' ") for another version of the story; also Kaplan, *Until the Mashiach*, 3.
601 The Harry Potter novels of British author, J.K. Rowling, tell the story of a orphaned boy in the ordinary world who suddenly learns that he is actually descended from a family of wizards, and that he has been personally 'marked' for an extraordinary destiny. The first novel, *Harry Potter and the Sorcerer's Stone*, is written more for children, but the six sequels grow in sophistication as the characters age.
602 See Heschel, *The Circle of the Baal Shem Tov*, 18.
603 Ibid., 18.
604 See Green, *Tormented Master*, 26, where Simhah: "is described in late [Bratzlav] sources as a saintly but retiring figure. Unfortunately, we know nothing more of Nahman's father." On 28, he says, "We know from a casual reference that he was still alive as late as 1807, and it may well be that he outlived his famous son."
605 Ibid., 25.
606 Ps. 2:7. Compare this statement with 2 Samuel 7:14.
607 Nosson of Nemirov, *Shivḥei ha-RaN*, 3. See Nathan of Nemirov, trans. Aryeh Kaplan, ed. Zvi Aryeh Rosenfeld, *Rabbi Nachman's Wisdom: Shevachey HaRan & Sichos HaRan*, 6.
608 Nathan of Nemirov, *Rabbi Nachman's Wisdom*, 6 note 4.
609 Green, *Tormented Master*, 33.

610 Nosson of Nemirov, *Shivḥei ha-RaN*, 3. See Nathan of Nemirov, *Rabbi Nachman's Wisdom*, 6.
611 See Green, *Tormented Master*, 25, and 53 notes 8 and 9.
612 Nosson of Nemirov, *Shivḥei ha-RaN*, 19. See Nathan of Nemirov, *Rabbi Nachman's Wisdom*, 21.
613 *Sha'arei Tzion* is a book of devotional prayers first published in 1662 by the kabbalist, Rabbi Natan Neta of Spira.
614 See Nosson of Nemirov, *Shivḥei ha-RaN*, 10 for the original version of this anecdote and the context around it. Also Nathan of Nemirov, *Rabbi Nachman's Wisdom*, 10-11. Though the presentation of this anecdote is somewhat altered here, all of the elements may be found in the original.
615 Alter of Teplik, ed., *Hishtap'khut ha-Nefesh*, 1 (*Likkutei MaHaRaN Tinyana*, 73). see Aryeh Kaplan, ed. and trans., *Outpouring of the Soul: Rabbi Nachman's Path in Meditation*, 18.
616 Ibid., 23 (*Siḥot ha-RaN* 67). See Kaplan, *Outpouring of the Soul*, 38. Judaism has largely been preservation minded, asking, How can we ensure a basic level of observance? How can we see that even the ignorant will pray properly? But as the RaMBaM points out, the only biblical commandment in Torah regarding prayer is that you should pray when you have a need! Also Nathan of Nemirov, *Rabbi Nachman's Wisdom*, 364-65 on this topic.
617 Nosson of Nemirov, *Shivḥei ha-RaN*, 5. See Nathan of Nemirov, *Rabbi Nachman's Wisdom*, 7-10.
618 See Schachter-Shalomi and Miles-Yepez, *A Heart Afire*, 3-24 on the Ba'al Shem Tov and the *tzaddikim nistarim*.
619 See Green, *Tormented Master*, 29-30 on speculation about Rebbe Nahman in his childhood.
620 Ibid., 34 says: "Little is recorded of the personality of Nahman's wife," and 55 note 36 says, "*[Neveh Tzaddikim]* is the source for Nahman's wife's name, which is not mentioned by [Nosson]."
621 Ibid., 33 says: "somewhat wealthy tax-farmer who lived in the small village of Usyatin, near the town of Smela, on the western shores of the Dnieper some two hundred miles to the east of [Mezhbizh]," and 55 note 36 says, "Nahman's father-in-law came from a well-known family in Zaslav."
622 Ibid., 56 note 40 says: "When Nahman and [Shimon] were together in Istanbul on their way to the Holy Land, [Shimon] spoke to others as though he were Nahman's older chaperone [. . .] This could only be said by one who appeared significantly older."
623 Ibid., 35 explores the possible psychological import of this conversation for Rebbe Nahman.
624 Nosson of Nemirov, *Ḥayyei MaHaRaN*, 4:2-3, Nosson of Nemirov, *Shivḥei ha-RaN*, 3, and Shmuel Horowitz, ed., *Avane'ha Barzel*, 51. See Nathan of Breslov, *Tzaddik*, 13-15, and Nathan of Nemirov, *Rabbi Nachman's Wisdom*, 6.
625 Nathan of Breslov, *Tzaddik*, 14.
626 See Zalman M. Schachter-Shalomi with Donald Gropman, *First Steps to a New Jewish Spirit*, 21-23, and Zalman M. Schachter-Shalomi, ed. N. Miles-Yepez, *Wrapped in a Holy Flame: Teachings and Tales of the Hasidic Masters*, 195-196.
627 Alter of Teplik, *Hishtap'khut ha-Nefesh*, 43. See Kaplan, *Outpouring of the Soul*, 50, and Nathan of Breslov, *Tzaddik*, 15-16.
628 Ibid., 28. See Nathan of Nemirov, *Rabbi Nachman's Wisdom*, 364 and 306.
629 Walt Whitman, *Leaves of Grass*, 573 ("The Mystic Trumpeter"). The question, "What is the grass?" is on 58 ("Song of Myself").
630 Green, *Tormented Master*, 36.

631 Nosson of Nemirov, Siḥot ha-RaN, 117. See Nathan of Nemirov, *Rabbi Nachman's Wisdom*, 245.
632 Nathan of Nemirov, *Rabbi Nachman's Wisdom*, 5-6.
633 Ibid., 7, 13, and 13 note 24; also Green, *Tormented Master*, 27, 31.
634 Green, *Tormented Master*, 26.
635 Nathan of Breslov, *Tzaddik*, 13-14.
636 Mishnah, Bava Kama 2:3.
637 See Mykoff, *Once Upon a Tzaddik*, 20-23 ("The Dog and the Goat").
638 Avraham Hazan, *Kokhavei Or*, 66. See Mykoff, *Once Upon a Tzaddik*, 23-24 ("The Secret is Revealed").

Chapter 7

639 Nathan of Breslov, trans. Avraham Greenbaum, ed. Moshe Mykoff, *Tzaddik: A Portrait of Rabbi Nachman*, 14, and Arthur Green, *Tormented Master: A Life of Rabbi Nahman of Bratslav*, 41.
640 Ibid., 17, and Green, *Tormented Master*, 42, and 58 note 68.
641 Ibid., 17-18, and Green, *Tormented Master*, 39, 43.
642 Green, *Tormented Master*, 43-44, quotes: "The day on which our late and sainted master arrived in [Bratzlav] was a Tuesday, which was the market day. People spoke about him, telling how he despised the ways of the famous ones who proclaimed the center of worship to be gatherings where people eat and drink. (Once our master said: 'I can no longer stand their festivities!') Our master would only speak of Torah and prayer and order people to confess to him [. . .]"
643 Ibid., 44-46 for a discussion of Rebbe Nahman's disciples from Dashev, and Aryeh Kaplan, ed. Dovid Shapiro, *Until the Mashiach: The Life of Rabbi Nachman*, 299-301, and 312-314 for short biographies of Reb Yudel and Reb Yekusiel.
644 Ibid., 6.
645 Nathan of Nemirov, trans. Aryeh Kaplan, ed. Zvi Aryeh Rosenfeld, *Rabbi Nachman's Wisdom: Shevachey HaRan & Sichos HaRan*, 2.
646 We do not know the identity of the second attendant who accompanied Rebbe Nahman to Kamenitz.
647 Nosson of Nemirov, *Ḥayyei MaHaRaN*, 129. See Nathan of Breslov, *Tzaddik*, 45, and Nathan of Nemirov, *Rabbi Nachman's Wisdom*, 33, for another English translation and further details.
648 Martin Buber, trans. Maurice Friedman, *The Tales of Rabbi Nachman*, 185.
649 Nosson of Nemirov, *Shivḥei ha-RaN*, 2:2. See Nathan of Nemirov, *Rabbi Nachman's Wisdom*, 33-35, and Nathan of Breslov, *Tzaddik*, 45-46.
650 See Green, *Tormented Master*, 66 on the connection between Kamenitz and the Frankists, and 88 note 16 on the bans on Jewish settlement there.
651 See Yitzhak Buxbaum, *The Light and Fire of the Baal Shem Tov*, 334-35 ("The Debates with the Frankists"). For greater historical context and more specific information, see Gershom Scholem, *Kabbalah*, 287-309 ("Jacob Frank and the Frankists").
652 See ibid., 335-36 ("Fighting Fire with Fire"), and Scholem, *Kabbalah*, 295-300.
653 See ibid., 336-37 ("The Wailing of the Shechinah") and ("Renewed Hostility").
654 Green, *Tormented Master*, 66 mentions Hillel Zeitlin's contention that perhaps Rebbe Nahman was attempting to "win back" the souls of the Frankists for Judaism, but says: "This theory, however, misses the mark in one crucial way: we know of no community of

Frankists surviving in [Kamenitz] as late as 1798, and it seems highly unlikely that there was one." Nevertheless, we cannot discount the possibility that there remained Frankist converts or their descendants there, and the possibility, consistent with Rebbe Nahman's later teachings, that he was working for the souls of the Frankists who had already passed on in that place.

655 Schnapps is a drink that can be received from gentiles.
656 See Buxbaum, *The Light and Fire of the Baal Shem Tov*, 36-39 ("The Secret Manuscript of Rabbi Adam Ba'al Shem") for more on the writings in the rock.
657 Nosson of Nemirov, *Shivḥei ha-RaN*, 2:3,4. See Nathan of Nemirov, *Rabbi Nachman's Wisdom*, 35, and a similar statement in Nathan of Breslov, *Tzaddik*, 46.
658 "My soul is attached to You; Your right hand supports me." (Ps. 63:9)
659 Nosson of Nemirov, *Ḥayyei MaHaRaN*, 130. See Nathan of Breslov, *Tzaddik*, 46.
660 Green, *Tormented Master*, 6 says: "As [Nosson] himself had not appeared on the scene in [Bratzlav] until 1802, none of this knowledge was firsthand; it was rather a combination of what the master had told regarding himself and the recollections of disciples of longer standing and members of Nahman's family."
661 Nathan of Nemirov, *Rabbi Nachman's Wisdom*, 1.
662 Kaplan, *Until the Mashiach*, 28 note 7, and see Nathan of Breslov, *Tzaddik*, 50 for indirect indications of this belief, as well as Green, *Tormented Master*, 65 and 88 note 22.
663 Avraham Hazan, *Kokhavei Or*, 18. See Moshe Mykoff, *Once Upon a Tzaddik: Tales of Rebbe Nachman of Breslov*, 68-69 ("Not Using the Crown of Torah") for another translation of the story.
664 Talmud, Megillah, 15a.
665 This last phrase is worth giving over in the Yiddish: *Vorim di greste helft is shoin dort.*
666 Nosson of Nemirov, *Shivḥei ha-RaN*, 2:5,6. See Nathan of Nemirov, *Rabbi Nachman's Wisdom*, 35-37. This last quote by Rebbe Nahman can also be rendered, "He is the Lord; He will do what He deems right." (1 Sam. 3:18)
667 Nathan of Nemirov, *Rabbi Nachman's Wisdom*, 37.
668 See Zalman Schachter-Shalomi and Netanel Miles-Yepez, *A Heart Afire: Stories and Teachings of the Early Hasidic Masters*, 111-113 ("A Worthy Companion") for the story of the Ba'al Shem Tov's attempted journey to the Holy Land.
669 Inayat Khan, *Gathekas for Candidates*, 38 ("Gatheka 14: The Doctrine of Karma"). This quote is taken from the gender inclusive version.
670 According to Nathan of Breslov, *Tzaddik*, 47, the Rebbe spent Shavuot in Herson, where he gave a teaching on "He reduced the storm to a whisper" (Ps. 107:29). In Herson, there were a number of disciples of Reb Shneur Zalman of Liozhna, who showed him teachings from their Rebbe. But Rebbe Nahman took issue with the teachings and showed them how they could not be correct. This may have been a genuine disagreement, or merely a problem caused by an incorrectly recorded teaching. It is well-known that the *mitnagdim* had printed intentionally altered versions of Reb Shneur Zalman's *Tanya* and distributed them to poison his reputation. See Nissan Mindel, *Rabbi Schneur Zalman: Volume I: Biography*, 146-48.
671 Rebbe Nahman was twenty-six at the time. This also tells us that Reb Shimon may have been significantly older than Rebbe Nahman. See Green, *Tormented Master*, 56 note 40.
672 Nosson of Nemirov, *Shivḥei ha-RaN*, 2:9, and Nosson of Nemirov, *Ḥayyei MaHaRaN*, 139. See Nathan of Nemirov, *Rabbi Nachman's Wisdom*, 37-40, and Nathan of Breslov, *Tzaddik*, 51-52.
673 See Chapter 3, "The First Arrest and Liberation—Yud-Tet-Kislev."
674 Green, *Tormented Master*, 89 says: "It is not clear whether they took him to be a [mitnaged] or a [Hasid] of [Shneur] Zalman of Liadi, whose controversy with [Avraham] Kalisker of Tiberias had broken out a year earlier."

675 Nosson of Nemirov, *Shivḥei ha-RaN*, 2:9. See Nathan of Nemirov, *Rabbi Nachman's Wisdom*, 40.
676 Inayat Khan, *Sufi Mysticism: The Sufi Message Volume X*, 66.
677 *Tikkunei Zohar*, 30.
678 "How good and how pleasant it is that brothers dwell together." (Ps. 133:1)
679 Nosson of Nemirov, *Shivḥei ha-RaN*, 2:10. See Nathan of Nemirov, *Rabbi Nachman's Wisdom*, 40-45.
680 Green, *Tormented Master*, 67.
681 For an overview of the Sabbatean movement and its transgressive practices, see Scholem, *Kabbalah*, 244-309.
682 See Zalman Schachter-Shalomi, ed. N. Miles-Yepez, *Wrapped in a Holy Flame: Teachings and Tales of the Hasidic Masters*, 177.
683 Thanks to Eve Ilsen for giving me a first-hand account. —N.M-Y.
684 This is especially problematic when the idea of 'good,' often coming from an outside system of values, is not in accord with the truth of our being. For instance, if an artist accepts in some way that painting is 'wrong,' or if a person naturally inclined to mathematics and accounting feels compelled to enter the rabbinate.
685 A nice description is found in Robert A. Johnson, *Owning Your Own Shadow: Understanding the Dark Side of the Psyche*, 4-5: "We are all born whole and, let us hope, will die whole. But somewhere early on our way, we eat one of the wonderful fruits of the tree of knowledge, things separate into good and evil, and we begin the shadow-making process; we divide our lives. In the cultural process we sort out our God-given characteristics into those that are acceptable to our society and those that have to be put away. This is wonderful and necessary, and there would be no civilized behavior without this sorting out of good and evil. But the refused and unacceptable characteristics do not go away; they only collect in the dark corners of our personality. When they have been hidden long enough, they take on a life of their own—the shadow life. The shadow is that which has not entered adequately into consciousness. It is the despised quarter of our being. It often has an energy potential nearly as great as that of our ego. If it accumulates more energy than our ego, it erupts as an overpowering rage or some indiscretion that slips past us; or we have a depression or an accident that seems to have its own purpose. The shadow gone autonomous is a terrible monster in our psychic house."
686 Though I have only alluded to this notion here, shadow is intimately bound up with projection of our own shadow (unacceptable) qualities onto an *other*, either something or someone in our environment.
687 This is somewhat a combination of the Kabbalistic worldview with that of Jungian psychology. C. G. Jung, ed. Joseph Campbell, trans. R.F.C. Hull, *The Portable Jung*, 145-46, says: "The shadow is a moral problem that challenges the whole ego personality, for no one can become conscious of the shadow without considerable moral effort. To become conscious of it involves recognizing the dark aspects of the personality as present and real. [. . .] Closer examination of the dark characteristics—that is, the inferiorities constituting the shadow—reveals that they have an *emotional* nature, a kind of autonomy, and accordingly an obsessive or, better, possessive quality. [. . .] Let us suppose that a certain individual shows no inclination whatever to recognize his projections. The projection-making factor then has a free hand and can realize its object—if it has one—or bring about some other situation characteristic of its power."
688 Nathan of Nemirov, *Rabbi Nachman's Wisdom*, 90.
689 The great Sufi master, Khwaja Baha' ad-Din, founder of the very refined Naqshbandi school is famous for saying (while being roughed up), "This humiliation is a means with

which to serve and satisfy the All-Powerful." John G. Bennett, *Masters of Wisdom*, 175.
690 Johnson, *Owning Your Own Shadow*, 23: "Does that mean that I have to be as destructive as I am creative, as dark as I am light? Yes, but I have some control over how or where I will pay the dark price. I can make a ceremony or ritual soon after doing some creative work and restore my balance in that way."
691 See Schachter-Shalomi and Miles-Yepez, *A Heart Afire*, 308-09 where Elimelekh of Lizhensk deals with this same subject, except through creative visualizations.
692 Nathan of Nemirov, *Rabbi Nachman's Wisdom*, 91.
693 Johnson, *Owning Your Own Shadow*, 19-20.
694 Nathan of Nemirov, *Rabbi Nachman's Wisdom*, 90-92, tells a wonderful parable about this kind of sacrifice.
695 J. G. Bennett, *Gurdjieff: Making a New World*, 204-13 ("The Law of Reciprocal Maintenance").
696 "Human beings have the unique property of being potentially able to make the special conscious efforts necessary to help God." E. J. Gold, *The Joy of Sacrifice: Secrets of the Sufi Way*, 4. This interesting work is a good presentation of Gurdjieff's teaching around sacrifice.
697 Bennett, *Gurdjieff*, 212: "the unique feature of Gurdjieff's teaching consists in the connection he makes between self-perfecting and fulfillment of a cosmic obligation. Conscious labour and intentional suffering can be very simply expressed as 'Service and Sacrifice'. These two are the instruments whereby man is transformed. By them he liberates the energies needed for the *Trogoautoegocratic* Process, he acquires his own imperishable being and he prepares a better future for his descendants. Those who repudiate the obligation incurred by our existence in human form, lose their human nature and 'perish like dogs'."
698 Notice how close this notion is to the *Shema*, Deut. 11:13-21.
699 If we were to find out the shadow-cost of peace, it might just be that 5,000 people being executed is the shadow-cost of peace! And if this were the case, there would be volunteers. I would volunteer too. — Z.M.S-S.
700 Johnson, *Owning Your Own Shadow*, 27: "Any repair of our fractured world must start with individuals who have the insight and courage to own their own shadow." Also Green, *Tormented Master*, 52.
701 Nosson of Nemirov, *Shivḥei ha-RaN*, 2:11. See Nathan of Nemirov, *Rabbi Nachman's Wisdom*, 42-47.
702 Nathan of Nemirov, *Rabbi Nachman's Wisdom*, 38.
703 It is possible that these little 'war games' he played with the children were actually reflecting the larger conflict that was going on between the French and the Turks. For Napoleon had invaded the Sultan's territory in Egypt and Palestine at this time, and everything Rebbe Nahman did on this journey was under the shadow of this international conflict.
704 Nosson of Nemirov, *Shivḥei ha-RaN*, 2:12. See Nathan of Nemirov, *Rabbi Nachman's Wisdom*, 47-48.
705 See Nathan of Nemirov, *Rabbi Nachman's Wisdom*, 92, where Rebbe Nahman says: "A man might insult a [tzaddik], and without realizing it, be doing him a great service. The [tzaddik] may have been condemned to death for some misdeed. The shame he experienced might then take the place of his death sentence."
706 Kabir Helminski, *The Knowing Heart: A Sufi Path of Transformation*, excerpts from 243, 244, 245.
707 After he reached *Eretz Yisra'el*, he settled for a short time in Haifa, and then later moved to Tiberias, where he became close to Avraham of Kalisk, a fellow disciple of

the Maggid. He died there in 1823, and is buried in the cemetery in Tiberias. See Tzvi M. Rabinowicz, "Zeev Wolf of Stary Ostrog," *The Encyclopedia of Hasidism*, 556; Kaplan, *Until the Mashiach*, 235-36 ("Rabbi Zev Wolf of Charni-Ostrov"); and Miles Krassen, *Uniter of Heaven and Earth: Rabbi Meshullam Feibush Heller of Zbarazh and the Rise of Hasidism in Eastern Galicia*, 37-38.

708 Nathan of Nemirov, *Rabbi Nachman's Wisdom*, 49 note 38: "Rabbi Naftali ben [Yitzhak] Katz of Posen, who started out to the Holy Land, but passed away in Istanbul on 26 [Tevet], 5479 (1719). He was an ancestor of Rabbi [Nahman], lived in [Bratzlav] for a while, and his journey paralleled that of Rabbi [Nahman] in many ways. His grave was considered a shrine for pilgrims to the Holy Land, and there is a record that it was also visited by Rabbi Menachem Mendel of Vitebsk on his journey there." Rabbi Naftali Katz was considered to be sort of a Ba'al Shem Tov-type character as well. KaTz stands for *kohen tzedek*.

709 The quote at the end is "For wherever you go, I will go; wherever you lodge, I will lodge; your people shall be my people, and your God my God. Where you die, I will die, and there I will be buried." (Ruth 1:16-17)

710 "By His word He raised a storm wind that made the waves surge. Mounting up to the heaven, plunging down to the depths, disgorging in their misery." (Psalms 107:25-26)

711 "He reduced the storm to a whisper; the waves were stilled. They rejoiced when all was quiet." (Psalms 107:29-30)

712 Nosson of Nemirov, *Shivḥei ha-RaN*, 2:14. See Nathan of Nemirov, *Rabbi Nachman's Wisdom*, 49-53.

713 See Nathan of Breslov, *Tzaddik*, 49-50, for a description of help for the sea voyage that Rebbe Nahman received in a vision from Rabbi Menachem Mendel of Vitebsk.

714 Nosson of Nemirov, *Shivḥei ha-RaN*, 2:16. See Nathan of Nemirov, *Rabbi Nachman's Wisdom*, 53-55.

715 Ibid., 2:17. See Nathan of Nemirov, *Rabbi Nachman's Wisdom*, 56-57. Reb Nosson goes on to speculate that some thought the Rebbe had suggested that this was the Evil One incarnate, but he is not sure of this and does not commit to this interpretation.

716 For example, there was a profound meeting between the kabbalist, Rabbi Moshe Galanti and a dervish of Damascus, and earlier than that, Rabbi Yosef ibn Aknin, the disciple of Maimonides, actually learned with the Muslim philosopher Averroes (Ibn Rushd), before meeting the RaMBaM.

717 Buber, *The Tales of Rabbi Nachman*, 198.

718 See Samuel Rosenblatt, ed. and trans., *The High Ways to Perfection of Abraham Maimonides: Volume II*, 321 where he speaks of Sufis taking on the ways of the prophets of Yisra'el. A much more developed discussion of Avraham Maimonides relationship to Sufism, as well as that of his children, may be found in the introductions to Samuel Rosenblatt, ed. and trans., *The High Ways to Perfection of Abraham Maimonides*, 48-53, and Paul Fenton, ed. and trans., *The Treatise of the Pool: Al-Maqala al-Ḥawdiyya by 'Obadyah Maimonides*, 1-46.

719 Green, *Tormented Master*, 71-72 offers other explanations.

720 Zvi Mark is the author of *Mysticism and Madness: The Religious Thought of Rabbi Nachman of Bratslav*, Continuum, 2009.

721 Kaplan, *Rabbi Nachman's Wisdom*, 113, 114, says: "My grandfather, Rabbi [Nahman] Horodenker, of blessed memory, told the following story: I was once travelling on a ship. We ran out of provisions and were without food for several days. Finally we reached an Arab city, where there were no Jews. An Arab took me in and offered me food. I had not eaten for several days, and quickly washed my hands and said the blessing for bread. I was just about to take a bite, when a thought entered my mind: 'Do not eat the bread of

one with a mean eye.' A random thought is not without meaning, and I did not know what to do. I had already said the blessing, but I realized the significance of this thought, and was determined not to eat anything of this Arab. Just then another thought entered my mind. 'I have commanded the Arabs to feed you.'" Rebbe Nahman added, "A confusing thought may enter your mind, but if you stand firm, G-d will send you another thought to encourage you."

722 Nosson of Nemirov, *Shivḥei ha-RaN*, 2:18. See Nathan of Nemirov, *Rabbi Nachman's Wisdom*, 57.

723 Nathan of Nemirov, *Rabbi Nachman's Wisdom*, 57.

724 Chapters 26-29 in the *Tanya* take you to the same place, telling us what to do with the broken-heartedness before we go to the place of awe before God in the 40s.

725 Nosson of Nemirov, *Shivḥei ha-RaN*, 2:18. See Nathan of Nemirov, *Rabbi Nachman's Wisdom*, 57-58.

726 In *Naḥal Nove'a*, 38, Rebbe Nahman says, "He who counsels must not insist that his advice be followed. Nothing on earth is complete, and evil is included in everything. I am very firm—on not insisting." Also, "Only the soft and gentle way in teaching, coughing, and counseling."

727 Green, *Tormented Master*, 70, suggests other possibilities, including the possibility that these statements were ruses to fool the "demonic powers."

728 Rabbi Tzvi Hirsh ben Avraham Segel of Harki (Gorki) (1760-1828) was a disciple of Menachem Mendel of Vitebsk and one of the leaders of the Hasidic community in *Eretz Yisra'el*. See Kaplan, *Until the Mashiach*, 234-35 "Rabbi Zvi Segel Harker."

729 Nosson of Nemirov, *Shivḥei ha-RaN*, 2:19. See Nathan of Nemirov, *Rabbi Nachman's Wisdom*, 58-60.

730 See Chapter 1, "The Opponents," "You Have Lost Your Head," and Chapter 3, "Conflict and Division."

731 It is unfortunate that many Hasidic groups have not sunk their roots into the land of Israel and connected themselves to the chthonic attunement that the land demands of them. The fur hats and black coats are an import of the exilic conditions; and while appropriate there, they do not suit the climate of Israel. With the exception of the Hasidim of Reb Ahrele Roth, who wear striped abbayes, most others continue to dress in the way of their Eastern European ancestors. It was different for the people in the circle of the Ari who dressed like Oriental Jews.

732 Nosson of Nemirov, *Shivḥei ha-RaN*, 2:19. See Nathan of Nemirov, *Rabbi Nachman's Wisdom*, 62-64.

733 See Nathan of Breslov, *Tzaddik*, 48, where visiting the grave of his grandfather, Rabbi Nahman Horodenker is given as a reason for his journey, as he was no longer able to send messages through the grave of Rabbi Yeshaya of Yanov, who was buried in Smela. In Nathan of Nemirov, *Rabbi Nachman's Wisdom*, 22, we learn that he would also send messages to the Ba'al Shem Tov through the same. Who was this Yeshaya of Yanov? Green, *Tormented Master*, 56 note 44, says that "[Abraham Joshua] Heschel has shown him to be none other than [Yesha'ayahu of Dynavitz], the editor of the *[Tzava'at ha-RiBaSh]*."

734 Contemporary scholarship believes that the *Zohar* was primarily authored by Rabbi Moshe de Leon in the 13th-century, with others authoring smaller layers of the text at other times. Moshe de Leon himself claimed that he had only edited it from an ancient manuscript in his possession, whose true author was Rabbi Shimon bar Yohai. This is the accepted traditional view. Some who would make a marriage between both views have suggested that Moshe de Leon may have channeled Shimon bar Yohai to create the *Zohar*. See Arthur Green, *A Guide to the Zohar*, 162-68 ("The Question of Authorship.").

735 Green, *Tormented Master*, 11-14, and 73 on Shimon bar Yohai in the Bratzlav tradition.

736 Eccles. 10:17.
737 Hos. 11:10. Translated from the Zohar III: 79a-b.
738 Nosson of Nemirov, *Shivḥei ha-RaN*, 2:31. See Nathan of Nemirov, *Rabbi Nachman's Wisdom*, 93-95.
739 Nathan of Nemirov, *Rabbi Nachman's Wisdom*, 38.
740 Ps. 107:27.
741 It is significant that he includes Adel in this group. It is a real testimony to her spiritual power. Also, all three survived disasters at sea. See Schachter-Shalomi and Miles-Yepez, *A Heart Afire*, 111-113 ("A Worthy Companion") and Chapter 6, on Nahman of Horodenka's own seas passage.
742 Nosson of Nemirov, *Shivḥei ha-RaN*, 2:21. See Nathan of Nemirov, *Rabbi Nachman's Wisdom*, 75-79.
743 In the Introduction to *Rabbi Nachman's Wisdom*, 2, Reb Nosson writes: "We have no desire to retell any of the Rebbe's miracles and wonders. Our only concern is to present ideas that can bring others closer to G-d." Green, *Tormented Master*, 7, says: "In contrast to all other Hasidic chroniclers of his day, he explicitly excludes all miracle tales from his writings, with the exception of certain tales of supernatural rescue on the seas in his account of Nahman's journey to the Holy Land. It is certain that such tales already abounded in [Nosson's] lifetime; many of them were later collected and published by subsequent disciples. [Nosson], however, would have no truck with such fantasies."
744 Green, *Tormented Master*, 15.
745 Nosson of Nemirov, *Shivḥei ha-RaN*, 2:26. See Nathan of Nemirov, *Rabbi Nachman's Wisdom*, 89-90.
746 Talmud, Hagiga 14b.
747 Green, *Tormented Master*, 3, and 4: "To express it differently, one might say that here the entirety of Jewish tradition is being used in a wholly personal way, to a degree unknown previously. The psychological complexities of the individual and the theological mysteries of the universe are intertwined to an extent that makes any attempt at separating them seem foolhardy."

Chapter 8

748 The substance of Rebbe Nahman's meetings with Mordecai of Neshkiz, Tzvi Aryeh of Alik, and to a much lesser extent, Shneur Zalman of Liadi, are detailed in Nathan of Breslov, trans. Avraham Greenbaum, ed. Moshe Mykoff, *Tzaddik: A Portrait of Rabbi Nachman*, 21-24.
749 The results of this mission are unclear. See Arthur Green, *Tormented Master: A Life of Rabbi Nahman of Bratslav*, 99; and Aryeh Kaplan, *Until the Mashiach: The Life of Rabbi Nahman*, 53.
750 See Kaplan, *Until the Mashiach*, 53, 178-79; and Moshe Mykoff, *Once Upon a Tzaddik: Tales of Rebbe Nachman of Breslov*, 100-103 ("The 'Baal HaTanya'").
751 Shmuel Horowitz, ed., *Avane'ha Barzel*, 46.
752 Nathan of Nemirov, trans. Aryeh Kaplan, ed. Zvi Aryeh Rosenfeld, *Rabbi Nachman's Wisdom: Shevachey HaRan & Sichos HaRan*, 436. See Green, *Tormented Master*, 94-134 ('Conflict and Growth') for a historical analysis of Rebbe Nahman's conflict with the Shpola Zeide and his uncle Barukh, and his defense by Reb Levi Yitzhak of Berditchev.
753 See Mykoff, *Once Upon a Tzaddik*, 73-74 ("The Terhovitza Magid").
754 "If I ascend to heaven, You are there; if I descend to Sheol, You are there too." (Ps. 139:8)
755 Zohar III: 292a.

756 Alter of Teplik, ed., *Meshivat Nefesh*, 1, (*Likkutei MaHaRaN I*, 6:4,11,12); See Nahman of Breslov, trans. Avraham Greenbaum, *Restore My Soul*, 13-15, for an alternate translation.
757 "Dashing to and fro [among] the creatures was something that looked like flares." (Ezek. 1:14)
758 "Seven times the righteous man falls and gets up" (Prov. 24:16).
759 "Though he stumbles, he does not fall down" (Ps. 37:24). *Sha'ar ha-Yiḥud ve-ha-Emunah*, Introduction, translated from the facing Hebrew text of Schneur Zalman of Liadi, *Likutei Amarim: Tanya: Bi-Lingual Edition*, 286.
760 Learned at a ḤaBaD-Lubavitch *farbrengen*. —Z.M.S-S.
761 "When you pass through water, I will be with you; through streams, they shall not overwhelm you. When you walk through fire, you shall not be scorched; through flame, it shall not burn you." (Isa. 43:2)
762 Alter of Teplik *Meshivat Nefesh*, 5 (*Likkutei MaHaRaN I*, 22:11). See Nahman of Breslov, *Restore My Soul*, 16-17, and Nathan of Nemirov, *Rabbi Nachman's Wisdom*, 7-8 for more on this topic.
763 Nathan of Nemirov, *Rabbi Nachman's Wisdom*, 14, 29.
764 Alter of Teplik, *Meshivat Nefesh*, 6 (*Likkutei MaHaRaN I*, 25:2,3,7). See Nahman of Breslov, *Restore My Soul*, 17-18, and "The Great Pilgrimage to Eretz Yisra'el" in the previous chapter for more on this topic.
765 The gravitational force is often assumed to act directly towards the centre of the Earth, but the direction varies slightly because the Earth is not a perfectly uniform sphere.
766 "Surely this Instruction which I enjoin upon you this day is not too baffling for you, nor is it beyond reach." (Deut. 30:11) Alter of Teplik, *Meshivat Nefesh*, 11 (*Likkutei MaHaRaN I*, 33). See Nahman of Breslov, *Restore My Soul*, 20.
767 Alter of Teplik, *Meshivat Nefesh*, 13 (*Likkutei MaHaRaN I*, 33). See Nahman of Breslov, *Restore My Soul*, 21.
768 "Know therefore this day and keep in mind that the Lord alone is God in heaven above and on earth below; there is none other." (Deut. 4:39)
769 Alter of Teplik, *Meshivat Nefesh*, 16 (*Likkutei MaHaRaN I*, 72). See Nahman of Breslov, *Restore My Soul*, 22.
770 "So the Lord said to him, 'Go down, and come back together with Aaron; but let not the priests or the people break through to come up to the Lord, lest He break out against them.' " (Exod. 19:24)
771 Alter of Teplik, *Meshivat Nefesh*, 17 (*Likkutei MaHaRaN I*, 72). See Nahman of Breslov, *Restore My Soul*, 22.
772 I have changed his name to protect his identity. —Z.M.S-S.
773 *Arbeit* is German for 'work.'
774 Ibid., 18 (*Likkutei MaHaRaN I*, 72). See Nahman of Breslov, *Restore My Soul*, 22-23.
775 "Do not be sad, for your rejoicing in the Lord is the source of your strength." (Neh. 8:10) Alter of Teplik, *Meshivat Nefesh*, 19 (*Likkutei MaHaRaN I*: 72). See Nahman of Breslov, *Restore My Soul*, 23.
776 Alter of Teplik, *Meshivat Nefesh*, 20 (*Likkutei MaHaRaN I*, 72). See Nahman of Breslov, *Restore My Soul*, 23.
777 Chapter 6, "The Words Yet Unsaid" and "Praying in Nature."
778 "You are children of the Lord your God." (Deut. 14:1)
779 The Yiddish is, *Ikh kh'rikh nisht mit di stievel in himmel her'ein.*
780 Learned from Bratzlaver Hasidim. —Z.M.S-S. See Nathan of Breslov, *Tzaddik*, 369, and Aryeh Kaplan, *Outpouring of the Soul*, 51 for alternate versions of this story.

781   See Nathan of Nemirov, *Rabbi Nachman's Wisdom*, 299.
782   Talmud, Kiddushin 36a.
783   Alter of Teplik, ed., *Hishtap'khut ha-Nefesh*, 17 (*Siḥot ha-RaN* 7). See Aryeh Kaplan, ed. and trans., *Outpouring of the Soul: Rabbi Nachman's Path in Meditation*, 35, and Nathan of Nemirov, *Rabbi Nachman's Wisdom*, 112 for alternate translations.
784   Translated from the German.
785   Alter of Teplik, *Hishtap'khut ha-Nefesh*, 2 (*Likkutei MaHaRaN Tinyana* 25). See Aryeh Kaplan, *Outpouring of the Soul*, 20-21.
786   There is actually a precedent for *hitbodedut* in the grandfather of Rebbe Nahman, Nahman of Horodenka, who was known to say that Exodus 34:3, "No one shall come up with you" refers to the way in which one should pray, for "You should imagine that you are praying before God in solitude, with no one else there before whom you might want to make a display." This is wholly in the spirit of *hitbodedut* as Rebbe Nahman later taught it. For Rebbe Nahman's *hitbodedut* refers to unaffected prayer, prayed in 'solitude,' or if with others, as if 'alone' without worrying what others might think of your pure expression before God.
787   Howard Thurman, *Disciplines of the Spirit*, 97-98.
788   Ibid., 100. "Thy will be done" comes from Matthew 6:10.
789   Alter of Teplik, *Hishtap'khut ha-Nefesh*, 4 (*Likkutei MaHaRaN Tinyana* 96). See Aryeh Kaplan, *Outpouring of the Soul*, 24.
790   Ibid., 48. See Aryeh Kaplan, *Outpouring of the Soul*, 54-55, and Nathan of Breslov, *Tzaddik*, 371-372.
791   "[. . .] and not to ignore your own kin." (Isa. 58:7)
792   See Aryeh Yaakov Leib's *Mivsari Eḥzeh: Sodot ha-Guf al Pi ha-Kabbalah*, 'From My Flesh I see God: The Secrets of the Body According to the Kabbalah.'
793   The practice is called "Sulam Chi: Prayer in Motion." Michael Kagan is a scientist, a teacher of Jewish spirituality, and the author of *The Holistic Haggadah: How Will You Be Different This Passover Night?* Levi Ben-Shmuel is a teacher of Tai Chi Chuan, a singer-songwriter, and co-host of Transitions Radio Magazine in Santa Fe, New Mexico.
794   "But I would behold God while still in my flesh" (Job 19:26).
795   *Etzem*, 'bone,' the 'essence,' the 'soul.' A Rebbe is also the 'bone' and the Hasidim are the 'flesh.' If they will refine themselves, the Rebbe will be able to teach them of his or her realizations.
796   Talmud, Ketubot 62a.
797   Nahman of Bratzlav, ed. Nosson of Nemirov, *Likkutei MaHaRaN I*, 22:5.
798   Much of this is treated in my books, Zalman M. Schachter-Shalomi, ed. Robert Michael Esformes, *Gate to the Heart: An Evolving Process*, 46-47, and Zalman M. Schachter-Shalomi with Donald Gropman, *First Steps to a New Jewish Spirit: Reb Zalman's Guide to Recapturing the Intimacy & Ecstasy in Your Relationship with God*, 39-46.
799   Initially, we hoped to format it to surround the teaching in the way *gemara* would surround a portion of *mishnah* in the Talmud, not interrupting it, but enfolding it like a treasure.
800   *Ha-olam*, 'the world,' can also be read *he'elem*, 'hidden.' Thus, "God, for Mercy's sake, created hiddenness to reveal Mercy"
801   In my original translation, this was rendered, "Without His giving life / Nothing is is-ing." However, English is not felicitous to this kind of usage. In Hebrew you could use the word, *havayah*, 'beingness,' or 'is-ness' to make this point that God is constantly keeping the world in existence in every moment.
802   Talmud, Pesahim 102a.

803 Interestingly, the singer Matisyahu has a song in which he puts this idea into his own words: In the beginning of time / Before the mountains were made / Before the sky split / ha-Shem sits / In peace and harmony / Creates the space for a new baby / We stay empty in the vision of the King / For His dream to manifest in we / Princes and priests will come / Run and emerge / As the surge flows like rain / To see, to see the day it come / When the King will look into His kingdom / Into my being / And see His-self happy / Believe in me / I believe in We. Matisyahu, "7 Beggars," *Light: Bonus Track Version*, Sony Music Entertainment, 2009.
804 See the discussion about the Lamp of Darkness in Chapter 3, "A Hidden Light."
805 Here it actually says, *Da'a*, "Know!"
806 Mishnah, Avot 2:14.
807 Rebbe Nahman didn't give much credit to technology; but there is a difference between the offal used to twist the world for the sake of power, and that used for the sake of healing and improving the lives of people.
808 This is a condensed version of version of what Rebbe Nahman says here. In Nachman of Breslov, trans. Moshe Mykoff, *Likutey Moharan: Volume 7 (Lessons 58-64)*, 393, it says: "For example, this is comparable to when someone postulates an untrue argument in Talmud and its commentaries. Since there is no learned individual to answer the question that arises from this argument, it therefore seems that he has postulated a superior argument and insight, even though in truth it is not at all [a valid] argument."
809 "All who go to her cannot return and find again the paths of life." (Prov. 2:19)
810 Zohar III: 225a.
811 Exod. 3:18.
812 Martin Buber, trans. Ronald Gregor Smith, *I and Thou*, 3.
813 This is an interpretation I evolved while dialoguing with my good friend, Gen-la Chokyi Dakpa (Michael Gregory), a teacher of Tibetan Buddhism. —N.M-Y.
814 Martin Buber, *Israel and the World: Essays in a Time of Crisis*, 21-24.
815 Whitney J. Oates, ed., *The Stoic and Epicurean Philosophers*, xvii, and Dagobert D. Runes, ed., *Dictionary of Philosophy*, 93.
816 Mishnah, Sanhedrin 10:1.
817 Mishnah, Avot 3:15.
818 "By the word of the Lord the heavens were made, by the breath of His mouth, all their host." (Ps. 33:6)
819 These are the five modifiers of speech.
820 Length, width, depth, time and substance.
821 "You have made them all with wisdom" (Ps. 104:24).
822 Talmud, Menakhot 29b.
823 See Green, *Tormented Master*, 32-33, on Rebbe Nahman's identification with Akiva's martyrdom.
824 "Now Moses was a very humble man, more so than any other man on earth." (Num. 12:2)
825 Nathan of Nemirov, *Rabbi Nachman's Wisdom*, 25.
826 Learned from Hasidim. —Z.M.S-S.
827 Green, *Tormented Master*, vix.
828 Mishnah, Avot 1:17.
829 Talmud, Hagigah 15b.
830 If we rise high enough, to *atzilut*, everything can be reconciled.
831 In J.R.R. Tolkien, ed. Christopher Tolkien, *The Silmarillion*, 15-17, is a passage that might almost have been snatched from the *kabbalah* of the Ari and Rebbe Nahman on the

unfolding of the divine plan in creation through music. Also J.R.R. Tolkien, ed. Christopher Tolkien, *The Book of Lost Tales: Part One*, 52-55.

832 "The song of silence" stands in contrast to his emphasis on talking to God in *hitbodedut*. But remember, *hitbodedut* means, 'aloneness,' 'seclusion,' which is to say, without the silence of the place of aloneness, the words of *hitbodedut* could not arise; they need to gestate in that matrix of stillness.

833 It doesn't say, "Moshe sang," but he "will sing," because his song hasn't been sung yet. It is not finished. "Then Moses and the Israelites sang this song to the Lord." (Exod. 15:1)

834 "Out of the depths I call You, O Lord. O Lord, listen to my cry" (Ps. 130:1).

835 "The death of His faithful ones is grievous in the Lord's sight." (Ps. 116:15)

836 Prov. 25:16.

837 Talmud, Hagiga 14b. Reb Hayyim of Chernovitz said: Of the four who entered the Pardes, only Rabbi Akiva left in peace. This was because he was in love with his wife, and they were very close. Ben Azzai looked and died because he never married. Ben Zoma was a widower, and seeing his wife there, but not being able to stay, lost his mind. Elisha ben Abuya was divorced and he went to "evil culture."

838 Talmud, Hagiga 15a.

839 Moshe Shamir, trans. Zalman Schachter, "The Other One: A Translation of M. Shamir's 'Al Suso B'Shabbat,'" *Jewish Heritage*, Spring 1965.

840 Talmud, Hagiga 15b.

841 For a different more sympathetic view of Elisha ben Abuya, read Milton Steinberg's wonderful novel, *As A Driven Leaf*.

842 See the chapter, "The Descent of the Gods" in C.S. Lewis's *That Hideous Strength: A Modern Fairy-Tale for Grown-Ups*.

843 "For I have hardened his heart" (Exod. 10:1).

844 "[. . .] in order that I may display these My signs among them" (Exod. 10:1).

845 "[. . .] how I made a mockery of the Egyptians" (Exod. 10:2).

846 "[. . .] in order that you may know that I am the Lord." (Exod. 10:2)

847 "So Moses and Aaron went to Pharoah" (Exod. 10:3).

848 "For if you refuse to let My people go, tomorrow I will bring the locusts on your territory." (Exod. 10:4)

849 Nahman of Bratzlav, *Likkutei MaHaRaN I*, 64.

850 "Come to Pharoah" is like, "Come and See" as it says in the Zohar.

851 "Now the man knew his wife Eve" (Gen. 4:1).

CHAPTER 9

852 In Yiddish, *Ikh vell shoin an-heiben ma'asios der-tzeilen*. Nahman of Bratzlav, ed. Nosson of Nemirov, *Sippurei Ma'asiot*, Introduction. See Nachman of Breslov, trans. Aryeh Kaplan, *Rabbi Nachman's Stories*, 8.

853 Ibid., Introduction. See Nachman of Breslov, *Rabbi Nachman's Stories*, 9.

854 As well as the wisdom that came from their own prayers.

855 Helen Kazantzakis, trans. Amy Mims, *Nikos Kazantzakis: A Biography*, 84-89, and Elie Wiesel, trans. Marion Wiesel, *All Rivers Run to the Sea: Memoirs*, 111, 201-202. He may also have learned them from Elie Weisel, who knew both of them.

856 Nikos Kazantzakis, trans. P.A. Bien, *Report to Greco*, 474. Kazantzakis thought of Rebbe

Nahman as the *prostak*, "a simple, cheerful, sainted man who used to advise his disciples how they too could become simple, cheerful, and sainted."

857   In the original story, the Hasidim say, "Rabbi Zadig." Obviously, Kazantzakis didn't get it quite right. It was probably, "a certain *tzaddik*."

858   In this, you can hear a translation of *bubbe maises*.

859   This is the story as it has remained in my memory, and also how I have told it through the years. However, it differs in detail from the original. —Z.M.S-S. See ibid., 474-75.

860   "Every single day Mordecai would walk about in front of the court of the harem, to learn how Esther was faring and what was happening to her." (Esther 2:11)

861   Nahman of Bratzlav, ed. Nosson of Nemirov, *Likkutei MaHaRaN I, 203*.

862   Ibid., 234.

863   "God saw that the light was good, and God separated the light from the darkness." (Gen. 1:4)

864   Midrash Rabbah, B'reishit 20.

865   Nachman of Breslov, *Rabbi Nachman's Stories*, 28.

866   In 1972, I made a studio recording of myself reading my own translation (then printed in booklet form) of "The Tale of the Seven Beggars," with musical accompaniment by Joseph and Nathan Segel. This has now been re-released as Zalman Schachter-Shalomi, *Rabbi Nahman of Bratzlav's Tale of the Seven Beggars*, Boulder, Colorado: Albion-Andalus Inc., 2010. The full translation is now available as Nahman of Bratzlav, trans. Zalman Schachter-Shalomi, ed. Netanel Miles-Yepez, *Tale of the Seven Beggars*, Boulder, Colorado: Albion-Andalus Inc., 2010. The Introduction and first three stories are reproduced here with permission. —Z.M.S-S.

867   There are several excellent translations of the "Tale of the Seven Beggars," some of which have extensive and helpful commentaries. These may be found in Martin Buber's *The Tales of Rabbi Nachman*, Aryeh Kaplan's *Rabbi Nachman's Stories*, Miles Krassen's audio recording, *Invoking the Seven Beggars*, our own *The Tale of the Seven Beggars*, and Adin Steinsaltz' *Beggars and Prayers*.

868   Nahman of Bratzlav, *Sippurei Ma'asiot*, 405-87.

869   Learned from Bratzlaver Hasidim. —Z.M.S-S. See See Nachman of Breslov, *Rabbi Nachman's Stories*, 479-80.

870   Once, an American woman came to see Reb Avraham Yehoshua Heschel, the Kopitchinitzer Rebbe of New York, with a problem requiring prayer. The Rebbe then helped her understand and to motivate her by comparing prayer to an audience with the President of the United States. By temporarily entering into the woman's own symbol system, the Rebbe was able to bring her to an understanding of her problem and its solution.

871   Nosson of Nemirov, *Siḥot ha-RaN* in *Shivḥei ha-RaN*, 149.

872   Zalman Schachter-Shalomi and Netanel Miles-Yepez, *A Heart Afire: Stories and Teachings of the Early Hasidic Masters*, 18 ("The Hidden History of the Ba'al Shem Tov").

873   Inayat Khan, *Spiritual Liberty: The Sufi Message: Volume V*, 233.

874   Nosson of Nemirov, *Ḥayyei MaHaRaN*, 85. See Nathan of Breslov, trans. Avraham Greenbaum, ed. Moshe Mykoff, *Tzaddik: A Portrait of Rebbe Nachman*, 212-15 for another translation.

875   Schachter-Shalomi and Miles-Yepez, *A Heart Afire*, 112 ("A Worthy Companion").

876   Nosson of Nemirov, *Ḥayyei MaHaRaN*, 91. See Nathan of Breslov, *Tzaddik*, 219-21.

877   Kalonymus Kalman Shapira, trans. and ed., Yehoshua Starrett, *To Heal the Soul: The Spiritual Journal of a Chasidic Rebbe*, 41-42.

878   Nosson of Nemirov, *Ḥayyei MaHaRaN*, 85. See Nathan of Breslov, *Tzaddik*, 212. Versions of all three of these dreams were previously published in Zalman Schachter, ed. Philip

Mandelkorn and Stephen Gerstman, *Fragments of a Future Scroll*, 95-100. —Z.M.S-S.
879   Harry M. Rabinowicz, *Hasidism: The Movement and Its Masters*, 100.
880   See Martin Buber, trans. Olga Marx, *Tales of the Hasidim: The Early Masters*, 233 ("A Period Extended"). In Buber, the words about sacrifice are from the same year in a story of Rosh Hashanah ("The Last Blowing of the Ram's Horn"). See Samuel Dresner, *Levi Yitzhak of Berditchev: Portrait of a Hasidic Master*, 197-200 ("Death of the Rebbe") for a more detailed account. We have also published a similar version of these events in Zalman Schachter-Shalomi and Netanel Miles-Yepez, *A Merciful God: Stories and Teachings of the Holy Rebbe, Levi Yitzhak of Berditchev*, 96-99 ("Sweetening One Last Judgement").
881   Dresner, *Levi Yitzhak of Berditchev*, 200-01, 218, note 1 translation of *Siḥot ha-RaN*, 196-197 in *Shivḥei ha-RaN*. Reb Nahman's discourse is in *Likkutei MaHaRaN Tinyana* 67, 68.
882   Nathan of Breslov, *Tzaddik*, 87; Aryeh Kaplan, ed. Dovid Shapiro, *Until the Mashiach: Rabbi Nachman's Biography: An Annotated Chronology*, 167, 183, 185-187, 279.
883   The Gonta Massacre of 1768, named after the Cossack commander Ivan Gonta, resulted in the death of approximately 20,000 Jews. See Arthur Green, *Tormented Master: A Life of Rabbi Nahman of Bratslav*, 272, note 57 and Kaplan, *Until the Mashiach*, 188, 277-284.
884   Nosson of Nemirov, *Ḥayyei MaHaRaN*, 190. See Nathan of Breslov, *Tzaddik*, 90.
885   See Moshe Mykoff, ed. and trans., *Once Upon a Tzaddik: Tales of Rebbe Nahman of Breslov*, 19.
886   See Yakov Travis, "Adorning the Souls of the Dead: Rabbi Nahman of Bratslav and Tikkun Ha-Neshamot," in Shaul Magid, ed., *God's Voice from the Void: Old and New Studies in Bratslav Hasidism*, 155–92.
887   Nosson of Nemirov, *Ḥayyei MaHaRaN*, 197. See Nathan of Breslov, *Tzaddik*, 98.
888   Nathan of Breslov, *Tzaddik*, 61. 68-70.
889   Nosson of Nemirov, *Ḥayyei MaHaRaN*, 191. See Nathan of Breslov, *Tzaddik*, 91.
890   Nosson of Nemirov, *Yemei MoHaRNaT I*, 62-64.
891   Nathan of Breslov, *Tzaddik*, 70, 123. See Chaim Kramer, ed. Moshe Mykoff, *Crossing the Narrow Bridge: A Practical Guide to Rebbe Nachman's Teachings*, 309-311.

CHAPTER 10

892   A Bratzlaver proverb. See Chaim Kramer, ed. Avraham Greenbaum, *Through Fire and Water: The Life of Reb Noson of Breslov*, xi.
893   Kramer, *Through Fire and Water*, 12.
894   The name "Hayyim" has been added to the story.
895   See Kramer, *Through Fire and Water*, 11-12, and Moshe Mykoff, ed. and trans., *Once Upon a Tzaddik: Tales of Rebbe Nachman of Breslov*, 48-49 ("What's the Meaning of Life?").
896   This is interesting, as Nosson didn't have the reputation for Torah genius that was usually looked for in prospective sons-in-law. It is likely that the discerning Rabbi David Tzvi saw more deeply. When asked about his choice, he responded: "Among the young men offered for my daughter were some who were more learned than Reb [Nosson]. But I took Reb [Nosson] because he had nice [broad] shoulders." Ibid., 12.
897   Nosson was in awe of his father-in-law's great learning, and even more so of his great saintliness. During those years, Reb Nosson later remembered, he could hardly imagine how Moses could have been any greater than Rabbi David Tzvi! Ibid., 14.
898   Ibid., 15, 29. As Kramer put it, 6, Reb Nosson suffered from a "most modern problem—a problem that cast everything else in shadow: he was haunted by a sense of futility."

899   Ibid., 13-14, 22-24. Rabbi David Tzvi had actually been attracted to Hasidism and was impressed by the piety of Reb Pinhas of Koretz and Reb Mikeleh of Zlotchov, but despised the fighting between their disciples. This soured him on the Hasidic movement and also influenced Reb Nosson's early views.
900   See ibid., 24-25.
901   Mykoff, *Once Upon a Tzaddik*, 49 ("Chossid and Misnaged").
902   Kramer, *Through Fire and Water*, 25. He also visited Gedaliah of Linitz, Avraham Dov of Khmelnik, and Mordecai of Kremenitz. Reb Nosson was a much beloved disciple of Reb Levi Yitzhak of Berditchev and was even responsible for recording some of his teachings. Even after Reb Nosson became the Hasid of Rebbe Nahman, he continued to serve Reb Levi Yitzhak, often at Rebbe Nahman's request. Reb Levi Yitzhak appears to shown no jealousy in this situation.
903   Later, in Bratzlav Reb Nosson performs the same task without the slightest discontent. Mykoff, *Once Upon a Tzaddik*, 52 ("Great Humility").
904   Shmuel Horowitz, ed., *Avane'ha Barzel*, 3. See Kramer, *Through Fire and Water*, 7-8, 25-27, for another version of this story.
905   Kramer, *Through Fire and Water*, 14, 27-29.
906   Nosson of Nemirov, *Ḥayyei MaHaRaN*, 115. See Nathan of Breslov, trans. Avraham Greenbaum, ed. Moshe Mykoff, *Tzaddik: A Portrait of Rebbe Nachman*, 29.
907   Horowitz, *Avane'ha Barzel*, 5.
908   Mykoff, *Once Upon a Tzaddik*, 49, 77-79, for more on Reb Lippa.
909   Nosson of Nemirov, *Ḥayyei MaHaRaN (Shivḥei MaHaRaN)* 333. See Nathan of Breslov, *Tzaddik*, 296.
910   Nathan of Breslov, *Tzaddik*, 296 note 46 suggests that this may have been referring to Reb Nosson's dream of Rebbe Nahman.
911   See Mykoff, *Once Upon a Tzaddik*, 52, where Reb Nosson borrows s copy of *Shivḥei ha-Ari* from Rebbe Nahman and notes the story of how the Ari praised Hayyim Vital highly when he first came to him.
912   Levi Yitzhak Bender, *Siaḥ Sarfei Kodesh I*, 631. Also in Kramer, *Through Fire and Water*, 575.
913   See Mykoff, *Once Upon a Tzaddik*, 50-51, and Kramer, *Through Fire and Water*, 37-39.
914   Talmud, Sanhedrin 52b.
915   Avraham Hazan, *Kokhavei Or*, 3.
916   Learned from Bratzlaver Hasidim. —Z.M.S-S. Bender, *Siaḥ Sarfei Kodesh I*, 102.
917   Talmud, Pesahim 102a.
918   Nahman of Bratzlav, ed. Nosson of Nemirov, *Likkutei MaHaRaN I*, 140. See Nachman of Breslov, trans. Moshe Mykoff, ed. Moshe Mykoff, Ozer Bergman, and Chaim Kramer, *Likutey Moharan: Volume 10 (Lessons 109-194)*, 163-165.
919   Nahman of Bratzlav, *Likkutei MaHaRaN I*, 44. See Nachman of Breslov, trans. Moshe Mykoff, ed. Moshe Mykoff, Ozer Bergman, and Chaim Kramer, *Likutey Moharan: Volume 5 (Lessons 33-48)*, 349-69.
920   Bender, *Siaḥ Sarfei Kodesh I*, 689.
921   Kramer, *Through Fire and Water*, 64.
922   Ibid., 42, 50.
923   Learned from Bratzlaver Hasidim. —Z.M.S-S. Also in Kramer, *Through Fire and Water*, 46, and Ozer Bergman, *Where Earth and Heaven Kiss*, 27. See Kramer, *Through Fire and Water*, 82-83, for more of Rebbe Nahman's advice to Reb Nosson on *hitbodedut*.
924   Alter of Teplik, ed., *Hishtap'khut ha-Nefesh*, 5 (*Likkutei MaHaRaN Tinyana* 97). See Aryeh Kaplan, ed. and trans., *Outpouring of the Soul: Rabbi Nachman's Path in Meditation*, 24-25, for an alternate translation.
925   Reb Nosson called this the "quagmire of routine." Kramer, *Through Fire and Water*, 498.

926 Learned from Hasidim. —Z.M.S-S. Also told of Reb Naftali of Ropshitz.
927 Nathan of Nemirov, trans. Aryeh Kaplan, ed. Zvi Aryeh Rosenfeld, *Rabbi Nachman's Wisdom: Shevachay HaRan & Sichos HaRan*, 180: "The Rebbe also said that it may be impossible to go through the entire service with proper devotion. Still, each person can say a small portion with true feeling."
928 *Tikkunei Zohar* 18.
929 Alter of Teplik, *Hishtap'khut ha-Nefesh*, 14. See Aryeh Kaplan, *Outpouring of the Soul*, 32.
930 Kramer, *Through Fire and Water*, 562.
931 Alter of Teplik, *Hishtap'khut ha-Nefesh*, 15 (*Likkutei MaHaRaN Tinyana* 124). See Aryeh Kaplan, *Outpouring of the Soul*, 34.
932 Bender, *Siaḥ Sarfei Kodesh I*, 593. Also Kramer, *Through Fire and Water*, 559.
933 *Likkutei MaHaRaN I*, 15. In Noson of Breslov, trans. Yaakov Gabel, ed. Moshe Schorr, and Y. Hall, *Abridged Likutey Moharan*, 107, it says: A person who wishes to experience a taste of the "hidden light"—that is, the secrets of the Torah to be revealed in the future—must elevate the attribute of fear to its source. This elevation is accomplished through "judgment"—namely, through *hitbodedut* and conversing with one's Creator, whereby a person expresses his heart before God and evaluates and judges himself on his activities.
934 Horowitz, *Avane'ha Barzel*, 47.
935 Nosson of Nemirov, *Ḥayyei MaHaRaN*, 367. See Nathan of Breslov, *Tzaddik*, 315.
936 Various sources speak of how important it is for the Rebbe to be 'milked.' For if it doesn't happen, the nex ideas don't come in.
937 Nosson of Nemirov, *Ḥayyei MaHaRaN*, 368. See Nathan of Breslov, *Tzaddik*, 315-16.
938 Green, *Tormented Master*, 5. Many Hasidic writings are criticized for their poor style and grammar.
939 Nachman of Breslov, trans. Moshe Mykoff and Simcha Bergman, ed. Moshe Mykoff, Ozer Bergman, and Chaim Kramer, *Likutey Moharan: Volume 1 (Lessons 1-6)*, 16 (second pagination set from the back of the book).
940 Nosson of Nemirov, *Ḥayyei MaHaRaN*, 369. See Nathan of Breslov, *Tzaddik*, 316.
941 Ibid., 370. See Nathan of Breslov, *Tzaddik*, 316-17.
942 Kramer, *Through Fire and Water*, 100.
943 The majority of the teachings in both volumes were recorded by Reb Nosson, though some labeled *leshon Rabbeinu*, 'in the tongue of our master,' were recorded by Rebbe Nahman, and a few others labeled *leshon ḥaverim*, 'in the tongue of our fellows,' were written down by Reb Avraham Peterburger, a Hasid of Rebbe Nahman who recorded several teachings before Reb Nosson's time. The majority of Rebbe Nahman's teachings date from 1801-1810, but a few may date as early as 1789-1790. In 1821, Reb Nosson re-edited both parts and printed new editions on his own printing press in Bratzlav, calling it the "Mohilev Press," because he did not have a permit from the censor, as there was a prohibition against printing Hasidic books at the time. Aryeh Kaplan, ed. Dovid Shapiro, *Until the Mashiach: Rabbi Nachman's Biography: An Annotated Chronology*, 287.
944 See Kramer, *Through Fire and Water*, 72.
945 *Likkutei MaHaRaN I*, 6.
946 "And he would then return to the camp; but his attendant, Joshua son of Nun, a youth, would not stir out of the Tent." (Exod. 33:11) See Kramer, *Through Fire and Water*, 70-73.
947 See Kramer, *Through Fire and Water*, 74-75, and Nathan of Breslov, *Tzaddik*, 128.
948 Nosson of Nemirov, *Ḥayyei MaHaRaN*, 2. See Nathan of Breslov, *Tzaddik*, 128-29.
949 Kramer, *Through Fire and Water*, 98-99, and Nathan of Breslov, *Tzaddik*, 417.
950 Nachman of Breslov, trans. Moshe Mykoff, ed. Moshe Mykoff, Ozer Bergman, and Chaim Kramer, *Likutey Moharan: Volume 7 (Lessons 58-64)*, 193 note 1.

951 Ahron the Rav says, "We knew clearly that the Rebbe was referring to Reb [Nosson]. Kramer, *Through Fire and Water*, 548.
952 See ibid., 141, and Nachman of Breslov, *Likutey Moharan: Volume 7*, 210-13 notes 41-45.
953 See Avraham Greenbaum, ed. and trans., *Restore My Soul! Meshivat Nefesh*, 40.
954 This has to do with the issue "And these words which I command you—*today*." Stick to today, and not to the past.
955 Alter of Teplik, ed., *Meshivat Nefesh*, Pt. II (*Likkutei Halakhot*) 14. See Greenbaum, *Restore My Soul*, 47-48, for an alternate translation.
956 "Shun evil and do good" (Ps. 34:15). In some translations, this is numbered Psalms 34:14.
957 See Martin Buber, trans. Olga Marx, *Tales of the Hasidim: The Later Masters*, 306-07 ("The Sermon") for another version.
958 "Take the filthy gaments off him!" (Zech. 3:4). Alter of Teplik, *Meshivat Nefesh*, Pt. II (*Likkutei Halakhot*) 19. See Greenbaum, *Restore My Soul*, 51.
959 Alter of Teplik, *Meshivat Nefesh*, Pt. II (*Likkutei Halakhot*) 33. See Greenbaum, *Restore My Soul*, 61-62.
960 See Chaim Kramer, ed. Moshe Mykoff, *Crossing the Narrow Bridge: A Practical Guide to Rebbe Nachman's Teachings*, 39.
961 Midrash Rabbah, Devarim 2:15.
962 Zohar II: 150b.
963 Talmud, Yoma 86b.
964 Alter of Teplik, *Meshivat Nefesh*, Pt. II (*Likkutei Halakhot*) 30. See Greenbaum, *Restore My Soul*, 58.
965 Learned at a ḤaBaD-Lubavitch *farbrengen*. —Z.M.S-S.
966 Talmud, Sanhedrin 44b, 103b.
967 Alter of Teplik, *Meshivat Nefesh*, Pt. II (*Likkutei Halakhot*) 69. See Greenbaum, *Restore My Soul*, 85-86.
968 Robert Frager, *Heart, Self, & Soul: The Sufi Psychology of Growth, Balance, and Harmony*, 129-30. The war at that time was a war against extreme persecution. Muslims were being killed for being Muslims.
969 Alter of Teplik, *Meshivat Nefesh*, Pt. II (*Likkutei Halakhot*) 100. See Greenbaum, *Restore My Soul*, 106.
970 Kramer, *Through Fire and Water*, 213.
971 See Chapter 9, "Uman—City of Lost Souls."
972 Ibid., 218-21.
973 Ibid., 217-18.
974 In ibid., 141, Reb Nahman of Tcherin is quoted as saying: One of the ideas in the Rebbe's lesson that Rosh [Hashanah] is that there is an overall leader and individual leaders. Those of the Rebbe's followers who were older than Reb [Nosson] would find it difficult to place themselves under Reb [Nosson's] tutelage. They were worthy leaders in their own right but, nevertheless, they were individual leaders. It was Reb [Nosson] who merited the mantle of the "overall" leader, for it was he who brought forth his master's teachings in a way that made them available for all of Jewry. Unquestionably Reb [Nosson] would also have felt uncomfortable had he been forced to accept the mantle of leadership over them too. But when it came to leading the new generation and directing them in their devotions, Reb [Nosson] had no equal.
975 Ibid., 222-27.
976 Ibid., 100.
977 See Chapter 9, "Uman—City of Lost Souls."
978 Nosson of Nemirov, *Likkutei Etzot*, "Tzaddik."

979 Reb Nosson attached importance to attaching oneself to a *tzaddik*, but never did he advocate giving up personal responsibility. See Kramer, *Through Fire and Water*, 365.
980 *Siḥot ha-RaN* 165 and 166, as quoted in Kramer, *Crossing the Narrow Bridge*, 315-16.
981 Levi Yitzhak Bender, *Siaḥ Sarfei Kodesh III*, 242. See Kramer, *Through Fire and Water*, 257 for more information.
982 Horowitz, *Avane'ha Barzel*, 91. The first statement is attributed to Reb Nosson, while "And so on from generation to generation" is attributed to the great Bratzlaver Hasid, Reb Avraham Hazan.
983 See Kramer, *Through Fire and Water*, 366-67.
984 Once a well-known rabbinic leader asked some Bratzlaver Hasidim, "Why do you make so much of Reb Nosson? Even the hat he wears is simple!" Ibid., 251.
985 This was translated many years ago from an old edition of *Hishtap'khut ha-Nefesh* which I can no longer locate.
986 Noson of Breslov, ed. Yitzchok Leib Bell, trans. Yaakov Gabel, *Healing Leaves: Prescriptions for Inner Strength, Meaning, and Hope*, 95.
987 Nosson of Nemirov, *Ḥayyei MaHaRaN*, 333 and 579. See Nathan of Breslov, *Tzaddik*, 296, 442.
988 Bender, *Siaḥ Sarfei Kodesh I*, 655, 656. See Mykoff, *Once Upon a Tzaddik*, 56 ("Straight to the Rebbe").
989 See Yosef Yitzchak Schneersohn, ed. Menachem Mendel Schneerson, trans. Zalman I. Posner *et al*, *HaYom Yom . . . "From Day to Day,"* 90 on Reb Moshe's childhood study habits.
990 A. H. Glitzenstein, *Sefer ha-Toldot: Admur ha-Zaken*, 173-77. Another English translation of this account can be found in Nissan Mindel, *Rabbi Schneur Zalman*, 132-41.
991 Mindel, *Rabbi Schneur Zalman*, 297 note 35, summarizing Glitzenstein, *Sefer ha-Toldot*, 209.
992 Yosef Yitzchak Schneersohn, trans. Shimon Neubort, *Branches of the Chassidic Menorah: Volume I*, 170-71, and Mindel, *Rabbi Schneur Zalman*, 180.
993 Schneersohn, *Branches of the Chassidic Menorah*, 173.
994 Ibid., 173-81.
995 Ibid., 182-85.
996 All of this is found in Avrum M. Ehrlich, *Leadership in the ḤaBaD Movement: A Critical Evaluation of ḤaBaD Leadership, History, and Succession*, 162-63, 189-190 notes 2 and 3, quoting Rachel Elior's Hebrew article on the succession and a primary work by A. B. Gottlober.
997 Naftali Loewenthal, *Communicating the Infinite: The Emergence of the ḤaBaD School*, 67, 102.
998 Chaim Dalfin, *Chasidim Farbreng*, 35 note 6.
999 Conflation of this Hasid's account with another reported by Rabbi Yitzhak Hendel in Dalfin, *Chasidim Farbreng*, 35.

Glossary

adam kadmon (**primeval human**) The human being in God's conception; also the pre-atzilic level of divine emanations.
Adonai (**my lords**) A name of God in the plural connected with the attribute of sovereignty (*malkhut*).
aggadah (**Aram., lore; pl. *aggadot***) Non-legal material in the rabbinic literature.
ahavah (**love**) Love, often paired with fear/awe (*yirah*).
Ain Sof (**without end**) The Infinite Nothing; the kabbalistic designation for the absolute, transcendent Godhead.
aliyat ha-neshamah (**ascent of the soul**) A journey of the consciousness to elevated worlds of Divinity.
am ha-aretz (**a person of the land**) Before the coming of the Ba'al Shem Tov, someone who was judged a peasant and, therefore, an ignoramus or a boor.
Amidah (**standing**) The prayer of *atzilut* in Jewish liturgy, the eighteen benedictions recited three times daily; on *Shabbat* and *Yamim Tovim*, the *Amidah* has only seven benedictions.
assiyah (**deed**) The world of doing or action according to kabbalistic teachings; the lowest world, just below *yetzirah*.
atzilut (**emanation, nearness**) The world of being according to kabbalistic teachings; the highest of the four worlds. In the kabbalistic cosmogony, it is the archetypal world.
atzmiut (**bone-ness**) The absolute essence.
avodah (**service**) Often used as a synonym for prayer, as in *avodah sh'b'lev* (service of the heart), or as in *shlemut ha-avodah* (true and complete service) to God.
avodat ha-Shem (**service of God**) Often synonymous with prayer.

ayin (**nothingness**) The quality of divine transcendence, no-thing-ness.

ba'al mofet (**miracle worker**) A Hasidic Rebbe known for working wonders or producing miracles.

ba'al teshuvah (**master of the turning; pl.** *ba'alei teshuvah*) One who has turned back to God, a penitent or repentant person, a person who has undergone a conversion experience.

ba'alei shem (**masters of the name; sing.** *ba'al shem*) Typically itinerant folk healers of one sort or another thought to use the names of angels and demons as well as the names of God to create miraculous outcomes; also the title of proto-Hasidic leaders, such as Eliyahu Ba'al Shem, Yoel Ba'al Shem, and Adam Ba'al Shem.

Barukh ha-Shem (**blessed is the name**) A statement of gratitude to God.

bar mitzvah (**son of the commandment**) A boy of thirteen years old, who is now obligated to keep the *mitzvot*.

batlan (**idler; pl.** *batlanim*) Though called an 'idler' or a 'loafer,' the *batlan* is actually one who is supported by the community as a professional religious.

beit din (**house of judgment**) A Jewish court of law made up of three *dayyanim* (judges).

beit midrash (**house of study or investigation; also** *beit ha-midrash*) Place for religious services and study.

bekeshe (**Yid./Turkish**) A long-sleeved gown or kaftan fastened by a sash (*gartel*) worn by Hasidim on *Shabbat* and festivals.

berakhah (**pl.** *berakhot*) Blessing.

beri'ah (**creation**) The world of knowing according to the kabbalistic teachings; the world above *yetzirah* and produced from *atzilut*.

binah (**understanding**) The second/third of the *sefirot* (divine emanations).

bittul ha-yesh (**annihilation of existence**) Self-annihilation, effacing or making the ego transparent.

bokher (**unmarried youth**) A poor student or an unmarried youth.

brit milah (**covenant of circumcision**)

da'at (**knowledge**) Intimate knowledge; an intermediary *sefirah* very important in the HaBaD system of thought.

daven (**pray**), *davenen* (**prayer, praying**) More colloquial way to speak of *tefillah* (prayer), and yet *davenen* is also more than merely formal prayer, or prayer as a formality; it is living the liturgical life in truth. The word itself is possibly derived from the Latin *divinum*, 'the divine,' as in doing divine work.

dayyan (**judge**) A judge of Jewish communal affairs.

derashot (**interpretations**) Torah interpretations.

devar Torah (**a word of Torah**) A teaching.

deveikut (**adhering, clinging**) Intimate absorption in God, adhering, sticking, or clinging to God in deep devotion and love.

epikores (**idolator, heretic**)

etzah (**counsel, advice pl.** *etzot*) Spiritual counsel or advice; direction to be followed, solution to a problem, those points of advice with which you can make for a change and a difference.

farbrengen (**Yid., time spent together**) A session of Hasidic fellowship, at times presided over by a *mashpiyya* or, occasionally, the Rebbe, during which Hasidim gather for the purpose of telling stories, singing, drinking, and learning the teachings of the Rebbes.
gabbai (**attendant**) Attendant of the Rebbe.
galut (**exile**) Referring to the exile of the *Shekhinah* or Divine Presence from the world.
Gan Eden (**garden of delight**) The Garden of Eden, Paradise.
ga'on (pride, splendor; pl. ge'onim) Genius; a title given to an exceptionally brilliant talmudist.
gevurah (**strength, severity**) One of the ten *sefirot*, also called *din* (judgment).
goyim (**nations; sing. goy**) Non-Jews.
ḤaBaD (**wisdom, understanding, knowledge**) An acronym for three *sefirot*—*ḥokhmah, binah, da'at;* the name of a Hasidic school of thought and practice, as well as a lineage founded by Shneur Zalman of Liadi (1745–1813).
ḥakirah (**philosophy of religion**) Probing with the mind, or philosophy of religion with reference to Judaism.
halakhah (**way to walk**) The process; Jewish law.
ha-Shem (**the name**) A term used in place of the unpronounceable name of God, Y-H-V-H.
hashgaḥah pratit (**specific providence**) Divine providence as it relates to the most specific and minute details of our lives.
Hasid (**one who is pious**) A member of the Hasidic movement; a person who has a Hasidic Rebbe.
Hasidim (**pious ones**) Followers of the third religious movement by that name, founded by Yisra'el, Ba'al Shem Tov in the seventeenth century. The earlier Hasidim were the desert Hasidim mentioned in the Talmud, the *Hasidim ha-Rishonim*, and the Hasidim of medieval Germany, followers of Yehudah HeHasid, the Hasidei Ashkenaz, and the Sufi-influenced Egyptian Hasidism of Avraham Maimonides in the thirteenth century.
Ḥasidut (**piety**) Hasidism, the teachings of the Hasidim.
Havdalah (**separation**) Ritual separating the *Shabbat* from the week.
ḥeder (**room; pl. ḥadarim**) A traditional school of elementary Jewish education.
ḥerem (**ban**) Excommunication.
ḥesed (**lovingkindness**) One of the ten *sefirot*. Also known as *gedulah* (largesse).
ḥevra (**sing. ḥaver**) Fellowship.
ḥevra kaddisha (**holy fellowship**) Burial society.
ḥevraya kaddisha (**holy fellowship**) The inner circle of a Rebbe's disciples.
ḥevruta (**study partnership**)
hitbodedut (**self-seclusion, aloneness**) A general term for meditation in the Jewish tradition, and a technical term in Bratzlav Hasidism for the daily practice of secluding oneself for extemporaneous prayer.
hitbonenut (**self-inspection, self-building**) A general term for meditation in the Jewish tradition, and a technical term in ḤaBaD Hasidism for contemplation,

discursive meditation, looking deeply into oneself or into a sublime idea.
hitkashrut (**self-binding**) Commitment to a Rebbe.
hod (**glory**) One of the ten *sefirot*.
ḥokhmah (**wisdom**) The first/second of the *sefirot* (divine emanations) or *maskilim*.
Ḥumash (**fifth**) A book-bound edition of the Torah, as opposed to a scroll.
ḥuppah (**wedding canopy**)
hush ha-tziyur (**imaginative faculty**) The use of the imaginative ability or faculty of the mind.
kabbalah (**tradition**) The Jewish mystical tradition.
Kaddish (**Aram., holy**) The mourner's prayer after the death of a close relative, usually after the death of a parent; the child who recites the prayers after the death of his parent.
kadmut ha-sekhel (**beginning of awareness**) The causative source in Divinity analogous to preverbal awareness for us, which is before we are able to think in words.
kappote (**Yid./Latin**) A long-frock coat worn by Hasidim, or a long-sleeved gown or kaftan fastened by a sash (*gartel*) worn by Hasidim on *Shabbat* and festivals.
kashrut (**fitness**) Laws that define what is ritually fit and prepared, as opposed to *treif* (unfit).
kavanah (**intention, aiming; pl.** *kavanot*) Divine intentionality, the spiritual concentration invested in the service of God.
kelippah (**shell, husk; pl.** *kelippot*) A metaphysical husk or shell formed around and obscuring a spark (*nitzotz*) of Divinity; a synonym for the energy system of evil.
Kiddush (**sanctification**) The prayer of sanctification recited over wine on the *Shabbat* and festivals.
kiddush ha-Shem (**sanctification for the name**) Sanctification or sacrifice for God, often refers to martyrdom.
kitrug (**accusation**) A complaint lodged against Yisra'el by Satan.
kloiz (**conventicle; pl.** *kloizen*) Prayer house.
kohen (**priest**) Of the priestly caste of Judaism.
kvittel (**Yid. short note**) A brief but formal communication or request from a Hasid to a Rebbe written on a slip of paper.
leben (**heart**) An affectionate appellation.
lekakh (Yid.) From the German *lebkuchen*, a honey and spice cake.
levush (**garment**) A covering; a technical term for the cloak one becomes invested (thought, word, or deed) in the HaBaD philosophy.
ma'amar (**oral discourse; pl.** *ma'amarim*) Oral discourses of the Hasidic Rebbes.
Ma'ariv (**evening prayer**) The evening prayer service.
ma'aseh (**deed, work, story; pl.** *ma'asiot*) A story of deeds in the Hasidic tradition; the outermost garment of the soul.
maggid (**speaks**) An endowed or itinerant preacher of sermons; also a familiar spirit.
maḥshavah (**thought; pl.** *maḥshavot*) The innermost garment of the soul.
maḥshavot zarot (**strange thoughts**) Disturbing thoughts during prayer.
majordomo (**Latin, maior domus, highest person of the house**) The person who is in charge of all the Rebbe's affairs.

makom (**space**) A synonym for God.
malkhut (**kingdom, sovereignty, majesty**) One of the ten *sefirot*, specifically representing the feminine, the *Shekhinah*.
mashal (**parable; pl.** *mashalim*) An analog or parable used in teaching.
Mashiaḥ (**anointed**) The Messiah.
mashpiyya (**influencer; pl.** *mashpiyyim*) A guide, spiritual director, or mentor in Hasidism.
maskil (**that which causes success; pl.** *maskilim*) In the Jewish Haskalah (enlightenment) movement, a follower of the Haskalah.
melammed (**teacher**) A Hebrew-school teacher.
melavah malkhah (**escorting the queen**) The meal which follows *Shabbat*.
mensch (**Yiddish, human being; pl.** *menschen*) An exemplary human being.
middot (**attribute; sing.** *middah*) Emotional attributes of Divinity; the modes of being, investment, attitude, and affect. Generally correspond to the lower seven *sefirot*; in ḤaBaD thought, each *middah* is a consequence of a *sekhel* (an intelligence, a thought sequence or idea syndrome), consisting of *ḥokhmah*, *binah*, and *da'at*.
midrash (**interpretation; pl.** *midrashim*) Method of interpreting Torah, or a collection of such interpretations.
mikveh (**gathering of water; pl.** *mikvaot*) Ritual immersion pool for purification; ritual bath.
Minḥah (**gift**) The afternoon prayer service.
minyan (**number**) Quorum of ten; the minimum number of ten Jews required for communal prayer.
mitnaged (**opponent; pl.** *mitnagdim*) An opponent of the Hasidim, anti-Hasid.
mitzvah (**connection; pl.** *mitzvot*) A commandment or God-connection in the Jewish tradition, popularly equated with a good deed.
m'malleh kol almin (**Aram., fills all worlds**) The immanent light of God in creation.
Moḥin d'gadlut (**expansive mind**) The mind of enlightenment, inclusion, or expanded awareness.
Moḥin d'katnut (**constricted mind**) The limiting mind, or narrow awareness.
naḥat (also *naḥas*) A feeling of deep satisfaction.
nebukh (**Yiddish, alas!**) Poor, pitiful; an expression of sympathy or alarm.
nefesh (**anima**) The lowest soul level; the animative function of the soul.
Ne'ilah (**closing**) Special prayer in Jewish liturgy recited at the conclusion of the Day of Atonement, Yom Kippur.
neshamah (**soul; pl.** *neshamot*) The level of the soul coming between *ruaḥ* and *ḥayyah*; the intellectual or communicating manifestation of the soul.
neshamah klalit (**general soul**) A collective soul, a soul connected in its root to many other souls; a Rebbe.
netzaḥ (**victory**) One of the ten *sefirot;* denotes effectiveness.
nigleh (**revealed**) As in manifest or revealed Torah, or a revealed master.
niggun (**melody; pl.** *niggunim*) A Hasidic melody, often wordless, which Abraham Joshua Heschel once described as "a tune in search of its own unattainable end."

nistar (**hidden**) Hidden, concealed, or secret, as in hidden Torah, or a hidden *tzaddik* (*tzaddik nistar*).
nitzotz (**spark; pl.** *nitzotzot*) Sparks of Divinity buried in the dense and subtle substances of creation, sparks captive in *kelippot*.
nokhah p'nai ha-Shem (**facing the name**) Being in the presence of God, done as if in the presence of God.
olam (**pl.** *olamot*) The world, universe.
olam ha-ba (**world-to-come**) Heaven, Paradise.
olam ha-mashal (**world of the imagination**) Imaginative world of metaphysical possibility.
PaRDeS (**orchard, paradise**) An acrostic denoting a fourfold approach to Torah interpretation, including: *peshat*, the "simple" reading of the text; *remez*, the "hint," leading to a search for meaning by which our daily life is enhanced; *derash*, the allegorical "interpretation" that turns us away from the superficial and helps us live a more spiritually meaningful life; and *sod*, the "secret" hidden deep and undisclosed.
parsha (**portion; pl.** *parshiot*) Torah portion of the week.
pashute Yidden (**Yid., uncomplicated Jews**) Simple Jews of uncomplicated faith.
penimi (**inward**) An inner-directed person.
peshat (**simple**) Simple meaning of the Torah.
pidyon nefesh (**soul ransom; pl.** *pidyonot*) The monetary donation given to a Rebbe.
pilpul (**sharp analysis**) Sharp intellectual discernment; casuistic argument, hair splitting.
rav A city's chief rabbi and authority on legal matters.
reb A term of respect and friendly admiration.
Rebbe The spiritual leader of a Hasidic community.
Rebbetzin (**rabbi's wife**) A Rebbe's wife or daughter.
Ribbono shel Olam (**master of the universe**) An appellation for the Divine.
ruah (**spirit, breath**) In Kabbalistic terminology, the spirit in human beings; the emotive function of the soul.
ruah ha-kodesh (**spirit of holiness**) The holy spirit, also the *Shekhinah*.
sedra (**section**) Torah section of the week; same as *parsha*.
sefer (**pl.** *sefarim*) Book.
sefirot (**expressions; sing.** *sefirah*) The ten divine emanations or attributes that manifest themselves in the four worlds; the lower seven *sefirot* are the same as *middot*.
seudah (**pl.** *seudot*) Meal.
Shaharit (**dawn**) The morning prayer service.
shaliah (**emissary**) An emissary of a Rebbe.
Shalom aleikhem (**peace be unto you**) A greeting.
shalosh seudot (**third meal**) The third meal of *Shabbat*.
shirayim (**Yid.**) Food favors from the Rebbe to the Hasid; leftovers from the Rebbe's meal distributed to or taken by his followers.

Shekhinah (**dwelling, presence**) The divine in-dwelling, the Presence of God in creation.
shema (**hear**) The statement that says, "Hear O Yisra'el, *Y-H-V-H* is our God, *Y-H-V-H* is One."
shidduk (**match**) A maritial match.
shofar (**horn**) Ram's horn blown on Rosh Hashanah as part of the ritual.
shuckelen (**swaying in prayer**) A swaying movement associated with Hasidic prayer.
shtetl (**Yid.**) Small town or village.
shtibl (**Yid. little room**) A Hasidic conventicle. Same as *kloiz*.
shtreimel (**probably old High German**) Festive fur hat worn on *Shabbat* by most Rebbes and some Hasidim.
shul (**Yid.**) House of worship, synagogue.
siddur (**order**) A Jewish prayer book.
simḥah (**joy**) Joy; a joyous occasion.
Sitra Aḥra (**the side of the otherness**) The negative or evil aspect of the universe.
smikhah (**ordination**) A rabbinic ordination.
sovev kol almin (**Aramaic, surrounds all worlds**) The light of God that transcendently encompasses the world.
sukkah (**booth**) Temporary hut constructed for Sukkot.
tallit Prayer shawl.
talmidim (disciples; sing., talmid) In this context, disciples of the Rebbe.
Tefillah Prayer.
tefillin Small leather boxes attached to the head and arm for prayer containing scrolls with Exod. 13:1–10, 13:11–16, Deut. 6:4–9, 11:13–21.
Tehillim Psalms.
teshuvah (**turning**) Repentance, penitence.
tiferet (**beauty**) One of the ten *sefirot*.
tikkun (**ordering, repairing**) Divine attunement and the act of making spiritual reparations.
Tikkun Ḥatzot (**midnight repair**) A midnight service of lamentation over the destruction of the Temple.
tish (**Yiddish table**) The public table of the Rebbe; ritual meal with the Rebbe.
Torah (**instruction**) Specifically the five books of Moses, but generally any Jewish teaching.
tzaddeket (**feminine righteous one**) A righteous woman.
tzaddik (**the righteous one; pl.** *tzaddikim*) A term for a saintly, righteous person, a charismatic leader, and particularly for a Hasidic leader or teacher, a Rebbe.
tzaddik gamur (**complete** *tzaddik*) A perfect *tzaddik* in the system of ḤaBaD who no longer even feels an urge to sin.
tzaddik ha-dor (**the righteous person of the generation**) The leader of the generation.
tzaddikim nistarim (**sing.** *tzaddik nistar*) Hidden righteous ones.
tzedakah (**righteousness**) Charity.

tzimtzum (**contraction; pl.** *tzimtzumim*) The self-concealment of God.
tzitzit (*fringes*) The ritual threads hanging from the tallit to signify the 613 *mitzvot* and to remind one to observe them.
yahrzeit (**Yiddish, time of year**) A death anniversary, usually celebrated in memory of saints or special persons.
yeḥidut (**one-ing**) A Hasid's private encounter with the Rebbe.
yesh (**being**) Manifestation.
yeshiva (**pl.** *yeshivot*) An advanced academy for studying Torah, especially for the training of rabbis.
yesh mi'ain (**something from nothing**) An expression of how God created the universe; the same as *creatio ex nihilo*.
yesod (**foundation**) One of the ten *sefirot*.
yetzer ha-ra (**evil inclination**) Negative impulse; the opposite of the *yetzer ha-tov* (positive impulse).
yetzirah (**formation**) The world of feeling according to kabbalistic teachings; the world of angels, formed from *beri'ah*.
yirah (**awe**) Awe/fear, often paired with love (*ahavah*).
Yisra'el (**God-wrestler**) The community of Jews and the mythic landscape of Judaism.
yontif (**Yiddish holiday**) Hebrew *yom tov*, 'good day.'
zeide Grandfather.

Bibliography

Hebrew Works

Ahron ben Moshe HaLevi (Horowitz) of Staroshelye. *Avodat ha-Levi.* Lemberg: [no publisher], 1866.
———. *Sha'arei ha-Avodah.* Shklov: [no publisher], 1821.
———. *Sha'arei ha-Yiḥud ve-ha-Emunah.* Shklov: [no publisher], 1820.
Alter (Moshe Yehoshua Bezhilianski) of Teplik, ed.. *Hishtap'khut ha-Nefesh.* Jerusalem: Torat ha-Netzaḥ, [no year].
——— ed.. *Meshivat Nefesh.* Jerusalem: *Torat ha-Netzaḥ*, [no year].
Avraham Abele of Herson, *Beit Avraham.* Zhilkov: [no publisher], 1837.
Avraham ben Alexander HaKohen of Kalisk. *Ḥibbat ha-Aretz.* Jerusalem: [no publisher], 1897.
Avraham ben Dov Baer of Fastov and Avraham of Kalisk. *Ḥesed L'Avraham.* Jerusalem: Siftei Tzaddikim, 1995.
Behovsky, Hayyim Eliezer Cohen, ed. *Boneh Yerushalayim.* Jerusalem: [no publisher], 1926.
Bender, Levi Yitzhak. *Siaḥ Sarfei Kodesh.* (Vol. I) Jerusalem: Agudat Meshekh ha-Naḥal, 1988.
———. *Siaḥ Sarfei Kodesh.* (Vol. III) Jerusalem: Agudat Meshekh ha-Naḥal, 1991.
Dov Baer ben Avraham of Mezritch. *Likkutei Yekarim.* Lemberg: [no publisher], 1865.

———. *Or Torah*. Jerusalem: [no publisher], 1956.
Dov Baer (Shneuri) of Lubavitch and Hillel ben Meir of Paritch. *Likkutei Bi'urim*. Warsaw: [no publisher], 1868.
———. *Ner Mitzvah ve-Torah Or*. New York: [no publisher], 1958.
———. *Poke'aḥ Ivrim*. New York: Agudat Ḥasidei ḤaBaD, 1940.
Elimelekh ben Eliezer of Lizhensk. *No'am Elimelekh*. 2 vols. Critical ed. Gedaliah Nigal. Jerusalem: Mossad Harav Kook, 1978.
Glitzenstein, A. H. *Sefer ha-Toldot: Admur ha-Zaken*. Brooklyn, New York: Kehot Publication Society, 1967.
Hazan, Avraham. *Kokhavei Or*. Jerusalem: [no publisher], [no year].
Hielman, Hayyim Meir. *Beit Rebbe*. Berditchev: [no publisher], 1903.
Hillman, David Tzvi, ed. *Iggrot Ba'al ha-Tanya*. Jerusalem: Mesorah, 1953.
Horowitz, Shmuel, ed., *Avane'ha Barzel* (printed with *Kokhavei Or*). Jerusalem: [no publisher], 1972.
Kaidener, Ya'akov. *Sippurim Nora'im*. Jerusalem: [no publisher], 1957.
Kovetz ha-Tamim. 8 vols. Otwock-Warsaw: Yeshivot Tomhej Temimim, 1938.
Levi Yitzhak ben Meir of Berditchev. *Kedushat Levi*. Jerusalem: Torat ha-Netzaḥ, 1993.
Moshe Hayyim Efraim of Sudilkov. *Degel Maḥanei Efraim*. Jerusalem: [no publisher], 1963.
Naḥal Nove'a. Jerusalem: Yitzhak Zilberman, 1961.
Nahman ben Simhah of Bratzlav. *Likkutei MaHaRaN*. Ed. Nosson of Nemirov. Jerusalem: [no publisher], 1969.
———. *Sippurei Ma'asiot*. Ed. Nosson of Nemirov. Jerusalem: [no publisher], 1990.
Nosson (Sternhartz) of Nemirov. *Ḥayyei MaHaRaN*. Jerusalem: Torat ha-Netzaḥ, 1991.
———. *Likkutei Etzot*. Jerusalem: Ha-Meshulash, 1970.
———. *Shivḥei ha-RaN*. Jerusalem: Torat ha-Netzaḥ, 1991.
———. *Yemei MoHaRNaT*. Jerusalem: Agudat Meshekh ha-Naḥal, 1982.
Rodkinsohn, Mikhael Levi. *Sefer Shivḥei ha-Rav*. Munkacs: Druck von Blayer & Kohn, 1895.
Schneersohn, Yosef Yitzhak. *Kuntres Bikkur Chicago*. Brooklyn, New York: Kehot Publications, 1944.
———. *Kuntres Ḥai Elul*. Brooklyn, New York: Kehot Publication Society, 1943.
———. *Sefer ha-Zikhronot*. 2 vols. Kehot Publication Society, [no date].
Shivḥei ha-BeShT. Ed. Israel Jaffe. Kopusht: [no publisher], 1814.
Shneur Zalman ben Barukh of Liadi. *Likkutei Torah*. Ed. Menachem Mendel Schneersohn. Vilna: [no publisher], 1904.
———. *Ma'amarei Admur ha-Zaken: Inyanim*. Brooklyn, New York: Kehot Publication Society, 2008.
———. *Torah Or*. Ed. Menachem Mendel Schneersohn. Brooklyn, New York: Kehot Publication Society, 2001.
Steinman, Eliezer, ed.. *Sefer Be'er ha-Ḥasidut: Mishnat ḤaBaD* (Vol. II). Tel Aviv: Knesset, [no year].

Teitelbaum, Mordecai. *Ha-Rav mi'Liadi.* Warsaw: Tuschija, 1913.
Ya'akov Yosef of Polonoye. *Toldot Ya'akov Yosef.* Jerusalem: [no publisher], 1973.
Yisra'el ben Eliezer of Mezhbizh. *Tzava'at ha-RiBaSh.* Jerusalem: [no publisher], 1948.
Zev Wolf of Zhitomir. *Or ha-Meir.* New York: Ziv Publishing Co., 1954.

Works on HaBaD Hasidism in English

Alpert, Zalman. "The Rogue Chasid: Michael Levi Rodkinson." *The Chasidic Historical Review 1*, no. 3 (April/May 1996): 28-30.
Avtzon, Sholom DovBer. *Reb Hillel Paritcher.* Brooklyn, New York: Rabbi Sholom D. Avtzon, 2007.
———. *Reb Shmuel Munkis.* Brooklyn, New York: Rabbi Sholom D. Avtzon, 2000.
Dalfin, Chaim. *Chasidim Farbreng.* New York: Jewish Enrichment Press, 2002.
———. *Farbrengen: Inspirational Stories and Anecdotes.* Ed. Chaya Sara Cantor. New York: Otsar Sifrei Lubavitch, 1999.
———. *Who's Who in Lubavitch.* Brooklyn, New York: Jewish Enrichment Press, 2003.
Deutsch, Shaul Shimon. "The Last Years of Reb Boruch – The Alter Rebbe's Father." *The Chasidic Historical Review 1*, no. 2 (January/February 1996): 4-7.
Dobh Baer of Lubavitch. *On Ecstasy: A Tract by Dobh Baer.* Trans. Louis Jacobs. Chappaqua, New York: Rossell Books, 1982.
Ehrlich, Avrum M.. *Leadership in the HaBaD Movement: A Critical Evaluation of HaBaD Leadership, History, and Succession.* Northvale, New Jersey: Jason Aronson Inc., 2000.
Elior, Rachel. *The Paradoxical Ascent to God: The Kabbalistic Theosophy of HaBaD Hasidism.* Trans. Jeffrey M. Green. Albany, New York: State University of New York Press, 1993.
Gurary, Noson. *Chasidism: Its Development, Theology, and Practice.* Northvale, New Jersey: Jason Aronson Inc., 1997.
Jacobs, Louis. *Seeker of Unity: The Life and Works of Aaron of Starosselje.* New York: Basic Books, 1966.
Loewenthal, Naftali. *Communicating the Infinite: The Emergence of the HaBaD School.* Chicago: University of Chicago, 1990.
Mindel, Nissan. *Rabbi Schneur Zalman: Volume I: Biography.* Brooklyn, New York: Kehot Publication Society, 1969.
Rader, Benzion, ed.. *To Touch the Divine: A Jewish Mysticism Primer.* Brooklyn, New York: Merkos L'Inyonei Chinuch, 1989.
Schachter, Zalman M.. "A Letter on a Tract on Ecstasy." *Conservative Judaism.* (spring 1964).
Schneersohn, Joseph I.. *Lubavitcher Rabbi's Memoirs: Volume One.* Trans. Nissan Mindel. Brooklyn, New York: Kehot Publication Society, 1993.
———. *Lubavitcher Rabbi's Memoirs: Volume Two: Revised Edition.* Trans. Nissan Mindel. Brooklyn, New York: Kehot Publication Society, 2004.

Schneersohn, Shalom DovBer. *To Know G-d: VeYadaata*. Trans. Eliyahu Touger. Brooklyn, New York: Kehot Publication Society, 1993.

Schneersohn, Sholom DovBer. *Tract on Prayer.* Trans. Y. Eliezer Danziger. Brooklyn, New York: Kehot Publication Society, 1992.

Schneersohn, Yosef Yitzchak. *Branches of the Chassidic Menorah: Volume I.* Trans. Shimon Neubort. Brooklyn, New York: Sichos in English, 1998.

———. *HaYom Yom... "From Day to Day"*. Ed. Menachem Mendel Schneerson. Trans. Zalman I. Posner *et al.* Brooklyn, New York: Kehot Publication Society, 2000.

———. *Likkutei Dibburim: Volume 1*. Trans. Uri Kaploun. Brooklyn, New York: Kehot Publication Society, 1987.

———. *Likkutei Dibburim: Volume 2*. Trans. Uri Kaploun. Brooklyn, New York: Kehot Publication Society, 1988.

———. *Likkutei Dibburim: Volume 3*. Trans. Uri Kaploun. Brooklyn, New York: Kehot Publication Society, 1990.

———. *Likkutei Dibburim: Volume 4*. Trans. Uri Kaploun. Brooklyn, New York: Kehot Publication Society, 1997.

———. *Likkutei Dibburim: Volume 5*. Trans. Uri Kaploun. Brooklyn, New York: Kehot Publication Society, 2000.

———. *On the Study of Chasidus: A Trilogy of Chasidic Essays*. Trans. Nissan Mindel and Zalman Posner. Brooklyn, New York: Kehot Publication Society, 1997.

———. *Saying Tehillim*. Trans. Zalman I. Posner. Brooklyn, New York: Kehot Publication Society, 1988.

Shneur Zalman ben Barukh of Liadi. *Likutei Amarim: Tanya: Bi-Lingual Edition*. Trans. Nissan Mindel, Nisen Mangel, Zalman I. Posner, Jacob I. Schochet. Brooklyn, New York: Kehot Publication Society, 1993.

———. *The Shulchan Aruch of Rabbi Shneur Zalman of Liadi: Bilingual Edition: Volume 1: Orach Chayim, Sec. 1-24*. Ed. and Trans. Eliyahu Touger and Uri Kaploun. Brooklyn, New York: Kehot Publication Society, 2004.

Steinsaltz, Adin. *The Long Shorter Way: Discourses on Chasidic Thought*. Ed. and Trans. Yehuda Hanegbi. Northvale, New Jersey: Jason Aronson Inc., 1988.

———. *Opening the Tanya: Discovering the Moral and Mystical Teachings of a Classic Work of Kabbalah*. Ed. Meir Hanegbi. Trans. Yaacov Tauber. San Francisco, California: Jossey-Bass, 2003.

Wineberg, Yosef. *Lessons in Tanya: Volume I*. Trans. Levy Wineberg and Sholom B. Wineberg. Ed. Uri Kaploun. Brooklyn, New York: Kehot Publication Society, 1982.

Works on Bratzlav Hasidism in English

Bergman, Ozer. *Where Earth and Heaven Kiss: A Guide to Rebbe Nachman's Path of Meditation*. Monsey, New York: Breslov Research Institute, 2006.

Buber, Martin. *The Tales of Rabbi Nachman*. Trans, Maurice Friedman. New York: Horizon Press, 1956.

Green, Arthur. *Tormented Master: A Life of Rabbi Nahman of Bratslav*. University,

Alabama: The University of Alabama Press, 1979.
Greenbaum, Avraham, ed. and trans.. *Restore My Soul! Meshivat Nefesh*. Monsey, New York: Breslov Research Institute, 1980.
Kaplan, Aryeh, ed. and trans.. *Outpouring of the Soul: Rabbi Nachman's Path in Meditation*. Monsey, New York: Breslov Research Institute, 1980.
———. *Until the Mashiach: Rabbi Nachman's Biography: An Annotated Chronology*. Ed. Dovid Shapiro. Far Rockaway, New York: Breslov Research Institute, 1985.
Kenig, Efraim. "The Power of Vision," *Tzaddik: In the Name of Rebbe Nachman of Breslev*. (Chanukah Issue 5760): 6-7.
Kramer, Chaim. *Crossing the Narrow Bridge: A Practical Guide to Rebbe Nachman's Teachings*. Ed. Moshe Mykoff. Monsey, New York: Breslov Research Institute, 1989.
———. *Through Fire and Water: The Life of Reb Noson of Breslov*. Ed. Avraham Greenbaum. Monsey, New York: Breslov Research Institute, 1992.
Kramer, Chaim, with Avraham Sutton, eds.. *Anatomy of the Soul*. Monsey, New York: Breslov Research Institute, 1998.
Mark, Zvi. *Mysticism and Madness: The Religious Thought of Rabbi Nachman of Bratslav*. New York: Continuum, 2009.
Mykoff, Moshe, ed. and trans.. *Once Upon a Tzaddik: Tales of Rebbe Nachman of Breslov*. Jerusalem: Jewish Treasures Publishing, 1989.
Nachman of Breslov. *Likutey Moharan: Volume 1 (Lessons 1-6)*. Trans. Moshe Mykoff and Simcha Bergman. Ed. Moshe Mykoff, Ozer Bergman, and Chaim Kramer. Monsey, New York: Breslov Research Institute, 1995.
———. *Likutey Moharan: Volume 5 (Lessons 33-48)*. Trans. Moshe Mykoff. Ed. Moshe Mykoff, Ozer Bergman, and Chaim Kramer. Monsey, New York: Breslov Research Institute, 1997.
———. *Likutey Moharan: Volume 7 (Lessons 58-64)*. Trans. Moshe Mykoff. Ed. Moshe Mykoff, Ozer Bergman, and Chaim Kramer. Monsey, New York: Breslov Research Institute, 2003.
———. *Likutey Moharan: Volume 10 (Lessons 109-194)*. Trans. Moshe Mykoff. Ed. Moshe Mykoff, Ozer Bergman, and Chaim Kramer. Monsey, New York: Breslov Research Institute, 1999.
———. *Rabbi Nachman's Stories*. Trans. Aryeh Kaplan. Ed. Moshe Mykoff. Monsey, New York: Breslov Research Institute, 1983.
Nahman of Bratzlav. *The Tale of the Seven Beggars*. Trans. Zalman Schachter-Shalomi. Ed. Netanel Miles-Yepez. Boulder, Colorado: Albion-Andalus Inc., 2010.
Nathan of Breslov. *Tzaddik: A Portrait of Rabbi Nachman*. Trans. Avraham Greenbaum. Ed. Moshe Mykoff. Monsey, New York: Breslov Research Institute, 1987.
Nathan of Nemirov. *Rabbi Nachman's Wisdom: Shevachey HaRan & Sichos HaRan*. Trans. Aryeh Kaplan. Ed. Zvi Aryeh Rosenfeld. Monsey, New York: Breslov Research Institute, 1973.
Nosson of Breslov. *Healing Leaves: Prescriptions for Inner Strength, Meaning, and Hope*. Ed. Yitzchok Leib Bell. Trans. Yaakov Gabel. Monsey, New York: Breslov Research Institute, 2006.
Steinsaltz, Adin. *Beggars and Prayers*. Ed. Jonathan Omer-Man. Trans. Yehuda

Hanegbi, Herzlia Dobkin, Deborah French, and Freema Gottlieb. New York: Basic Books, 1979.

Travis, Yakov. "Adorning the Souls of the Dead: Rabbi Nahman of Bratslav and Tikkun Ha-Neshamot." In *God's Voice from the Void: Old and New Studies in Bratslav Hasidism*. Ed. Shaul Magid. Albany, New York: State University of New York Press, 2001.

Hasidic and Kabbalistic Works in English

Ben-Amos, Dan, and Jerome R. Mintz, eds. & trans. *In Praise of the Baal Shem Tov [Shivḥei ha-Besht]: The Earliest Collection of Legends about the Founder of Hasidism*. Bloomington, Indiana: Indiana University Press, 1970.

Martin Buber. *For the Sake of Heaven*. Trans. Ludwig Lewisohn. Philadelphia, Pennsylvania: The Jewish Publication Society of America, 1945.

———. *Tales of the Hasidim: The Early Masters*. Trans. Olga Marx. New York: Schocken Books, 1947.

———. *Tales of the Hasidim: The Later Masters*. Trans. Olga Marx. New York: Schocken Books, 1948.

———. *The Way of Man: According to the Teachings of Hasidism*. New York: Citadel Press, 1967.

Buxbaum, Yitzhak. *The Light and Fire of the Baal Shem Tov*. New York: Continuum, 2005.

Carlebach, Shlomo. "The Alter Rebbe and the 10,000 Rubles." *Agada* 1, no. 1 (Summer, 1981).

Cooper, David A.. *God Is a Verb: Kabbalah and the Practice of Mystical Judaism*. New York: Riverhead Books, 1997.

Dresner, Samuel H.. *Levi Yitzhak of Berditchev: Portrait of a Hasidic Master*. New York: Hartmore House, 1974.

———. *The Zaddik: The Doctrine of the Zaddik According to the Writings of Rabbi Yaakov Yosef of Polnoy*. New York: Abelard-Schuman, [no year].

Etkes, Immanuel. *Besht: Magician, Mystic, and Leader*. Trans. Saadya Sternberg. Waltham, Massachusetts: Brandeis University Press, 2005.

Green, Arthur. *A Guide to the Zohar*. Stanford, California: Stanford University Press, 2004.

Green, Arthur, and Barry W. Holtz, eds. & trans.. *Your Word is Fire: The Hasidic Masters on Contemplative Prayer*. Woodstock, Vermont: Jewish Lights Publishing, 1993.

Heschel, Abraham J.. *The Circle of the Baal Shem Tov: Studies in Hasidism*. Ed. Samuel H. Dresner. Chicago: The University of Chicago Press, 1985.

Horowitz, Isaiah. *The Generations of Adam*. Ed. and Trans. Miles Krassen. New York: Paulist Press, 1996.

Kaplan, Aryeh. *Chasidic Masters: History, Biography and Thought: Revised 2nd Edition*. New York: Moznaim Publishing Corporation, 1984.

———. *Innerspace: Introduction to Kabbalah, Meditation and Prophecy*. Ed. Avraham Sutton. Jerusalem: Moznaim Publishing Corporation, 1991.

Krassen, Miles. *Uniter of Heaven and Earth: Rabbi Meshullam Feibush Heller of Zbarazh and the Rise of Hasidism in Galicia*. Albany, New York: State University of New York Press, 1998.

Matt, Daniel C.. "Ayin: The Concept of Nothingness in Jewish Mysticism." In *Essential Papers on Kabbalah*. Ed. Lawrence Fine. New York: New York University Press, 1995.

——— ed. and trans.. *The Zohar: Pritzker Edition*. Stanford, California: Stanford University Press, 2004.

Menahem Nahum of Chernobyl. *Menahem Nahum of Chernobyl: Upright Practices, The Light of the Eyes*. Trans. Arthur Green. New York: Paulist Press, 1982.

Newman, Louis I., and Samuel Spitz, eds. and trans.. *The Hasidic Anthology: Tales and Teachings of the Hasidim*. New York: Schocken Books, 1968.

Rabinowicz, Harry M.. *Hasidism: The Movement and Its Masters*. Northvale, New Jersey: Jason Aronson Inc., 1988.

Rabinowicz, Tzvi M., ed.. *The Encyclopedia of Hasidism*. Northvale, New Jersey: Jason Aronson Inc., 1996.

Rabinowitsch, Wolf Zeev. *Lithuanian Hasidism*. New York: Schocken Books, 1971.

Rose, Or, and Ebn D. Leader, eds. and trans.. *God in All Moments: Mystical & Practical Spiritual Wisdom from Hasidic Masters*. Woodstock, Vermont: Jewish Lights Publishing, 2004.

Roth, Jeff. *Jewish Meditation Practices for Everyday Life: Awakening Your Heart, Connecting with God*. Woodstock, Vermont: Jewish Lights Publishing, 2009.

Schachter, Meshullam Zalman. *The First Step: A Primer of a Jew's Spiritual Life*. Winnipeg, Manitoba: David Jackson, ca. 1958.

Schachter, Zalman. *Fragments of a Future Scroll: Hassidism for the Aquarian Age*. Ed. Philip Mandelkorn and Stephen Gerstman. Germantown, Pennsylvania: Leaves of Grass Press, 1975.

Schachter-Shalomi, Zalman, and Netanel Miles-Yepez, *A Heart Afire: Stories and Teachings of the Early Hasidic Masters*. Philadelphia, Pennsylvania: Jewish Publication Society, 2009.

———. "God Hidden, Whereabouts Unknown." *Spectrum: A Journal of Renewal Spirituality* 2, nos. 1 and 2 (Winter/Spring/Summer/Fall, 2006).

———. *A Merciful God: Stories and Teachings of the Holy Rebbe, Levi Yitzhak of Berditchev*. Boulder, Colorado: Albion-Andalus Inc., 2010.

Schachter-Shalomi, Zalman M. *Wrapped in a Holy Flame: Teachings and Tales of the Hasidic Masters*. Ed. N. Miles-Yepez. San Francisco: Jossey-Bass, 2003.

Schachter-Shalomi, Zalman Meshullam. *Spiritual Intimacy: A Study of Counseling in Hasidism*. Northvale, New Jersey: Jason Aronson Inc., 1991.

Schatz Uffenheimer, Rivka. *Hasidism as Mysticism: Quietistic Elements in Eighteenth Century Hasidic Thought*. Trans. Jonathan Chipman. Princeton, NJ: Princeton University Press, 1993.

Schochet, Jacob Immanuel. *The Great Maggid: The Life and Teachings of Rabbi Dov Ber of Mezhirech*. New York: Kehot Publication Society, 1990.

———. *Rabbi Israel Baal Shem Tov: A Monograph on the Life and Teachings of the Founder*

of Chassidism. Toronto: Lieberman's Publishing House, 1961.
Scholem, Gershom. *Kabbalah.* New York: Quadrangle, 1974.
Shainberg, Catherine. *Kabbalah and the Power of Dreaming: Awakening the Visionary Life.* Rochester, Vermont: Inner Traditions, 2005.
Shapira, Kalonymus Kalman. *To Heal the Soul: The Spiritual Journal of a Chasidic Rebbe.* Trans. and Ed. Yehoshua Starrett. Lanham, Maryland: Rowman & Litlefield Publishers, 2004.
Sheinkin, David. *Path of the Kabbalah.* Ed. Edward Hoffman. New York: Paragon House, 1986.
Steinmann, Eliezer. *The Garden of Hassidism.* Trans. Haim Shachter. The World Zionist Organization, 1961.
Vital, Chayyim. *The Tree of Life: Chayyim Vital s Introduction to the Kabbalah of Isaac Luria: The Palace of Adam Kadmon.* Trans. Donald Wilder Menzi and Zwe Padeh. Northvale, New Jersey: Jason Aronson Inc., 1999.
Weiner, Herbert. *9 ½ Mystics: The Kabbala Today.* Collier Books, 1992.

Non-Hasidic or Kabbalistic Works

Avraham ben HaRambam. *The Guide to Serving God.* Trans. Yaakov Wincelberg. New York: Feldheim Publishers, 2008.
Bair, Puran, and Susanna Bair. *Living from the Heart: Heart Rhythm Meditation for Energy, Clarity, Vision, and Inner Peace.* Ed. Asatar Bair. Tucson, Arizona: Living Heart Media, 2010.
Bastian, Edward W., and Tina L. Staley. *Living Fully, Dying Well: Reflecting on Death to Find Your Life's Meaning.* Ed. Netanel Miles-Yepez. Boulder, Colorado: Sounds True Inc., 2009.
Bennett, J.G.. *Gurdjieff: Making a New World.* San Francisco: Harper & Row Publishers, 1973.
Bennett, John G.. *Masters of Wisdom.* London: Turnstone Books, 1977.
Buber, Martin. *I and Thou: Second Edition.* Trans. Ronald Gregor Smith. New York: Charles Scribner's Sons, 1958.
———. *Israel and the World: Essays in a Time of Crisis.* New York: Schocken Books, 1948.
Candrasekharendra Sarasvati. *Adi Sankara: His Life & Times.* Trans. T.M.P. Mahadevan. Bombay: Bharatiya Vidya Bhavan, 1988.
———. "Temple Worship." *Kamakoti Vani* 4, no. 10 (October, 1972): 23-24.
Dallas, Ian. *The Book of Strangers.* Albany, New York: State University of New York Press, 1988.
DeMaille, Raymond J., ed., *The Sixth Grandfather: Black Elk's Teachings Given to John G. Neihardt.* Lincoln, Nebraska: University of Nebraska Press, 1985.
Epictetus. *The Art of Living: The Classic Manual on Virtue, Happiness, and Effectiveness.* Trans. Sharon Lebell. San Francisco, California: Harper-Collins, 1995.
Ernst, Carl W., and Bruce B. Lawrence. *Sufi Martyrs of Love: The Chishti Order in South Asia and Beyond.* New York: Palgrave MacMillan, 2002.

Frager, Robert. *Heart, Self, & Soul: The Sufi Psychology of Growth, Balance, and Harmony.* Wheaton, Illinois: Quest Books, 1999.

Gilani, Muhyuddin Abdul Qadir. *Futuh al-Ghaib: The Revelations of the Unseen.* Trans. Aftab-Ud-Din Ahmad. Delhi: Kitab Bhavan, 1990.

Gold, E. J.. *The Joy of Sacrifice: Secrets of the Sufi Way.* [no city]: IDHHB, Inc. and HOHM Press, 1978.

Grimes, John, ed.. *A Concise Dictionary of Indian Philosophy: Sanskrit Terms Defined in English: New and Revised Edition.* Albany, New York: State University of New York Press, 1996.

Halevi, Z'ev ben Shimon. *The Anointed: A Kabbalistic Novel.* Bath: Gateway Books, 1992.

Helminski, Kabir. *The Knowing Heart: A Sufi Path of Transformation.* Boston, Massachusetts: Shambhala Publications, 1999.

Heschel, Abraham Joshua. *God in Search of Man: A Philosophy of Judaism.* New York: Farrar, Straus and Giroux, 1955.

Hesse, Hermann. *The Glass Bead Game (Magister Ludi).* Trans. Richard and Clara Winston. New York: Holt, Rinehart and Winston, 1969.

Ibn 'Arabi, Muhyiddin. *Ibn 'Arabi: Divine Governance of the Human Kingdom.* Trans. Tosun Bayrak. Louisville, Kentucky: Fons Vitae, 1997.

Johnson, Robert A.. *Owning Your Own Shadow: Understanding the Dark Side of the Psyche.* San Francisco, California: HarperSanFrancisco, 1991.

JPS Hebrew-English TANAKH: The Traditional Hebrew Text and the New JPS Translation - Second Edition. Philadelphia: The Jewish Publication Society, 1999.

Jung, C. G.. *The Portable Jung.* Ed. Joseph Campbell. Trans. R.F.C. Hull. New York: Viking Press, 1974.

Kagan, Michael. *The Holistic Haggadah: How Will You Be Different This Passover Night?* New York: Urim Publications, 2004.

Kaplan, Edward K.. *Spiritual Radical: Abraham Joshua Heschel in America, 1940-1972.* New Haven, CT: Yale University Press, 2007.

Kazantzakis, Helen. *Nikos Kazantzakis: A Biography.* Trans. Amy Mims. New York: Simon and Schuster, 1968.

Kazantzakis, Nikos. *Report to Greco.* Trans. P.A. Bien. New York: Simon and Schuster, 1965.

Keating, Thomas. *The Human Condition: Contemplation and Transformation.* New York: Paulist Press, 1999:

Khan, Inayat. *The Art of Personality: The Sufi Message: Volume III.* Delhi: Motilal Banarsidass, 1994.

———. *Gathekas for Candidates.* Private Publication. (Gender Inclusive Version).

———. *Spiritual Liberty: The Sufi Message: Volume V.* Delhi: Motilal Banarsidass, 1995.

———. *Sufi Mysticism: The Sufi Message Volume X.* Delhi: Motilal Banarsidass, 1995.

Khan, Zia Inayat. *The Chishti Silsila of Pir-o-Murshid Inayat Khan.* [no city]: Sufi Order International North American Secretariat, 2001.

——— ed.. *A Pearl in Wine: Essays on the Life, Music and Sufism of Hazrat Inayat Khan.* New Lebanon, New York: Omega Publications, 2001.

Leibowitz, Yeshayahu. *Judaism, Human Values, and the Jewish State.* Ed. Eliezer Goldman. Trans. Eliezer Goldman, Yoram Navon, Zvi Jacobson, Gershon Levi, and Raphael Levy. Cambridge, Massachussetts: Harvard University Press, 1992.

Lewis, C.S.. *That Hideous Strength: A Modern Fairy-Tale for Grown-Ups.* London: Pan, 1983.

Mahadevan, T.M.P.. *Invitation to Indian Philosophy.* New Delhi: Arnold-Heinemann Publishers, 1974.

MacDougall, Duncan. "The Soul: Hypothesis Concerning Soul Substance Together with Experimental Evidence of The Existence of Such Substance." *American Medicine* (April, 1907).

Maimonides. *The Guide of the Perplexed.* Trans. Shlomo Pines. Chicago: University of Chicago Press, 1963.

Maimonides, 'Obadyah. *The Treatise of the Pool: Al-Maqala al-Ḥawdiyya.* Trans. and Ed. Paul Fenton. London: Octagon Press, 1981.

Narasimhachari, M., V. A. Devasenapathi, R. Balasubramanian, eds.. *Perspectives of Theism and Absolutism in Indian Philosophy.* Madras: Ramakrishna Mission, 1978.

Nurbakhsh, Javad. *In the Paradise of the Sufis.* New York: Khaniqahi-Nimatullahi Publications, 1979.

Oates, Whitney J., ed.. *The Stoic and Epicurean Philosophers: The Complete Extant Writings of Epicurus, Epictetus, Lucretius, Marcus Aurelius.* New York: Random House, 1940.

Rosenblatt, Samuel, ed. and trans.. *The High Ways to Perfection of Abraham Maimonides.* New York: Columbia University Press, 1927.

——— ed. and trans.. *The High Ways to Perfection of Abraham Maimonides.* Baltimore, Maryland: The Johns Hopkins Press, 1938.

Rowling, J.K.. *Harry Potter and the Sorcerer's Stone.* New York: Scholastic Press, 1997.

Runes, Dagobert D., ed., *Dictionary of Philosophy.* Totowa, New Jersey: Littlefield, Adams & Co., 1972.

Sankaracarya Bhagavatpada. *The Vivekacudamani of Sankaracarya Bhagavatpada: An Introduction and Translation.* Ed. and Trans. John Grimes. Delhi: Motilal Banarsidass Publishers, 2004.

Schachter-Shalomi, Zalman M. *Gate to the Heart: An Evolving Process.* Ed. Robert Michael Esformes. Philadelphia, Pennsylvania: [no publisher], 1993.

Schachter-Shalomi, Zalman M., with Donald Gropman. *First Steps to a New Jewish Spirit: Reb Zalman's Guide to Recapturing the Intimacy & Ecstasy in Your Relationship with God.* Woodstock, Vermont: Jewish Lights Publishing, 2003.

Schachter-Shalomi, Zalman, with Joel Segel. *Jewish with Feeling: A Guide to Meaningful Jewish Practice.* New York: Riverhead Books, 2005.

Schwarzfuchs, Simon. *Napoleon, the Jews and the Sanhedrin.* London: Routledge & Keegan Paul, 1979.

Shah, Idries. *The Sufis.* Garden City, New York: Doubleday & Company, 1964.

Shamir, Moshe, trans. Zalman Schachter. "The Other One: A Translation of M. Shamir's 'Al Suso B'Shabbat,'" *Jewish Heritage* (Spring 1965).

Shneour, Zalman. *Restless Spirit: Selected Writings of Zalman Shneour.* Trans. Moshe

Spiegel. New York: Thomas Yoseloff, 1963.
Steinberg, Milton. *As a Driven Leaf.* New York: Behrman House, 1966.
Stoppard, Tom. *Rosencrantz and Guildenstern are Dead.* New York, Grove Press, 1967.
Suhrawardi, Shahab ad-Din. *The 'Awarif-u'l-Ma'arif.* Trans. H. Wilberforce Clarke. Lajore: Sh. Muhammad Ashraf, 1973.
Taylor, Jill Bolte. *My Stroke of Insight: A Brain Scientist's Personal Journey.* New York: Viking, 2008.
Thurman, Howard. *Disciplines of the Spirit.* New York: Harper & Row Publishers, 1963.
Tillich, Paul. *Dynamics of Faith.* New York: Harper & Row Publishers, 1957.
Tolkien, J.R.R.. *The Book of Lost Tales: Part One.* Ed. Christopher Tolkien. Boston: Houghton Mifflin Company, 1984.
———. *The Silmarillion.* Ed. Christopher Tolkien. Boston: Houghton Mifflin Company, 1977.
Trungpa, Chogyam. *Cutting Through Spiritual Materialism.* Ed. John Baker and Marvin Casper. Boston: Shambhala Publications, 1987.
Twersky, Isadore, ed.. *A Maimonides Reader.* New York: Behrman House Publishers, 1972.
Whitman, Walt. *Leaves of Grass.* New York: Barnes & Noble Books, 2004.
Wiesel, Elie. *All Rivers Run to the Sea: Memoirs.* Trans. Marion Wiesel. New York: Alfred A. Knopf, 1995.
Wilson-Smith, Timothy. *Napoleon: Man of War, Man of Peace.* New York: Carroll & Graf Publishers, 2002.
Zborowski, Mark, and Elizabeth Herzog. *Life Is With People: The Culture of the Shtetl.* New York: Schocken Books, 1952.
Zeller, David. *The Soul of the Story: Meetings with Remarkable People.* Woodstock, Vermont: Jewish Lights Publishing, 2006.
Zimmer, Heinrich. *Myths and Symbols in Indian Art and Civilization.* Ed. Joseph Campbell. New York: Bollingen Foundation/Pantheon Books, 1946.

Video Recordings

Matter of Heart: The Extraordinary Journey of C.G. Jung into the Soul of Man. DVD. Directed by Mark Whitney. Los Angeles, California: King Video, 1985. (DVD Extra: "Face to Face: Professor Jung" with John Freeman. BBC Worldwide Ltd., 1959.)
Uzhpizin. DVD. Directed by Gidi Dar. Israel: New Line Home Entertainment, 2005.

Sound Recordings

Krassen, Miles, and Richard Kaplan. *Invoking the Seven Beggars: A Neo-Hasidic Method for Inner Transformation.* Miles Krassen, perf., Richard Kaplan, piano and vocals. Rain of Blessings compact disc. 2004.
Matisyahu, perf.. "7 Beggars." *Light: Bonus Track Edition.* M4a File 2009 iTunes, www.iTunes.com (downloaded April 7, 2010).

Schachter-Shalomi, Zalman, Joseph Segel, and Nathan Segel. *Rabbi Nahman of Bratzlav's Tale of the Seven Beggars.* Zalman Schachter-Shalomi, perf., Joseph and Nathan Segel, guitar and vocals. Albion-Andalus Inc. compact disc. 2010.

About the Authors

ZALMAN SCHACHTER-SHALOMI, better known as 'Reb Zalman,' was born in Zholkiew, Poland, in 1924. His family fled the Nazi oppression in 1938 and finally landed in New York City in 1941. Descended from a distinguished family of Belzer Hasidim, he became a ḤaBaD Hasid as a teenager while still living in Antwerp, Belgium. He was later ordained by ḤaBaD-Lubavitch in 1947 and became one of the Lubavitcher Rebbe's first generation of outreach workers. He later earned his M.A. in psychology from Boston University in 1956 and a D.H.L. from Hebrew Union College in 1968. He is professor emeritus of Psychology of Religion and Jewish Mysticism at Temple University and is World Wisdom Chair holder emeritus at Naropa University. Today he is primarily known as the Rebbe and father of the neo-Hasidic Jewish Renewal movement and is widely considered one of the world's foremost authorities on Hasidism and Kabbalah. He is the author of *Spiritual Intimacy: A Study of Counseling in Hasidism* (1991), *Jewish with Feeling: Guide to a Meaningful Jewish Practice* (2005), co-author of *A Heart Afire: Stories and Teachings of the Early Hasidic Masters* (2009). Reb Zalman currently lives in Boulder, Colorado.

NETANEL MILES-YEPEZ was born in Battle Creek, Michigan, in 1972, and is descended from a Sefardi family of crypto-Jews (*anusim*, "forced converts"), who trace their ancestry from Mexico back to medieval

Portugal and Spain. He studied History of Religions at Michigan State University and Contemplative Religion at Naropa University, specializing in comparative religion and non-dual philosophies. He has been a personal student of Rabbi Zalman Schachter-Shalomi since 1998, and co-founded the Sufi-Hasidic, Inayati-Maimuni Order with him in 2004, fusing the Sufi and Hasidic principles of spirituality and practice espoused by Rabbi Avraham Maimuni in thirteenth century Egypt with the teachings of the Ba'al Shem Tov and Hazrat Inayat Khan. He is the editor of *The Common Heart: An Experience of Interreligious Dialogue* (2006), and co-author or *A Heart Afire: Stories and Teachings of the Early Hasidic Masters* (2009) and *A Merciful God: Stories and Teachings of the Holy Rebbe, Levi Yitzhak of Berditchev* (2010). He lives in Boulder, Colorado, where he is a spiritual counselor, writer, and painter.

Index

A

Abba of Tchashnik, 148-49, 179.
Abbaye (ca. 280-340), 75, 78.
Adam (Ba'al Shem) of Ropshitz, 24, 25, 436, 454.
Advaita Vedanta, 63-65, 134-35, 184, 417, 426.
Ahron ben Moshe HaLevi (Horowitz) of Staroshelye (1766-1828): 58, 63, 143-73, 175-208, 395, 419, 420, 421, 426; on awakening the heart, 177, 198-99, 201-02, 204, 428-29; and the court of the Alter Rebbe, 158-59, 164-66, 422, 423; on *da'at*, 199; descendent of Yeshaya Horowitz, 147; early life of, 147; first encounter with Shneur Zalman of Liadi, 63, 147-149; friendship with Dov Baer of Lubavitch, 150-53, 159-60, 171, 172, 173, 208, 422-23; and fundraising for the release of Shneur Zalman from prison, 159, 422; gossip against, 164-66, 424; at the grave of Shneur Zalman in Haditch, 173; and HaBaD-Staroshelye, 143-44, 160-67, 170-73, 176-77, 182-88, 196-206, 206-08; on *hitbonenut*, 196-206, 428-29; on *hitpa'alut*, 196-206, 428-29; imprisonment and release of, 207; manner of prayer, 160-64, 423; on prayer, 176, 196-206, 421; on mysticism wedded to Torah and mitzvot, 148-49, 176-77, 188, 428-29; on non-dualism, 177, 182-88, 421, 426; ordination of, 164-67, 424; on "perspectival" language, 183-85, 421; subjects of written works, 176; on *tzimtzum*, 185-88, 426-27; responsibilities in Shneur Zalman's court, 156, 158-59, 422; similarities to Shneur Zalman, 163; teaching younger Hasidim, 156, 158-59, 165, 172, 422, 423; use of power tested by Shneur Zalman, 156.

Ahron (the Rav) ben Moshe of Bratzlav, 368, 382, 450.
Ahron Ya'akov of Slutzk, 61.
Ahron of Zhitomir, 118.
Ain Sof (Or Ain Sof), 81, 89, 90, 130, 131, 133, 135, 141, 149, 299, 300, 301, 304, 307, 316, 317, 416, 417, 427, 453.
Alexander I, Czar of Russia (1777-1825), 116, 138, 395, 396.
Alter (Moshe Yehoshua Bezhilianski) of Teplik (d. 1919), 294, 377.
Aryeh Leib ben Barukh Gerundi (the Shpola Zeide, 1725-1811), 280, 353, 441.
assiyah, 18, 301, 408, 409, 453.
atzilut, 18, 37, 156, 299, 301, 316, 409, 444, 453, 454.
Averroes (ibn Rushd), 439.
Avraham (the Malakh) ben Dov Baer of Fastov (1741-1776): 36-38, 39, 46, 51, 52, 53, 150, 156, 157, 161, 400, 404, 410, 413, 431; on the discipline of the body, 38; relationship with Shneur Zalman of Liadi, 36-38, 52; on transcending the body, 52.
Avraham ibn Ezra (1089-1164), 320.
Avraham HaKohen of Kalisk (1741-1810): 34, 35, 42-44, 49-50, 51, 55-56, 66, 72, 95, 103, 104, 122-25, 126, 253, 255, 270-72, 385, 415, 438; and Ba'al Shem Tov as spiritual ideal, 42, 271; and Barukh of Mezhbizh, 271; behavior of disciples, 42-44, 49, 123-25, 252-55, 259-60; in *Eretz Yisra'el*, 104, 253, 270-72; incident in Shklov, 42-44, 49; Nahman of Bratzlav on, 270-72; prayer and service of, 55, 270-72; rebuked by Levi Yitzhak of Berdichev, 123-25; rebuked by the Maggid of Mezritch, 43, 49-50; rebuked by Shneur Zalman of Liadi, 49-50; on tzaddikism, 122-23, 126, 385.
Avraham ben Moshe Maimuni (Avraham Maimonides, 1186-1237), 195-96, 267, 439, 455.
Avraham Yehoshua Heschel of Apt (the Apter Rav, Ohev Yisra'el, d. 1825), 12, 73, 90, 425.
Avigdor ben Hayyim, 115-16, 412.
ayin, 91, 93, 98, 179, 416, 454.

B

Ba'al Shem Tov (Yisra'el ben Eliezer, 1698-1760): 15, 23-34, 36, 37, 39, 40, 42, 45, 49, 53, 56, 57, 59, 61, 62-63, 66, 67, 69, 70, 71, 72, 73, 83, 109, 119, 127, 128, 129, 141, 143, 155, 165, 167, 171, 183, 213-25, 227-30, 232, 234, 235, 238, 239, 240, 241, 243, 244, 245-49, 251, 257, 260, 263, 264, 270, 271, 272, 276, 280, 295, 298, 346-49, 350-51, 354-56, 365, 370, 385, 400, 404, 407, 412, 415, 424, 429, 430, 431, 432, 433, 434, 436, 439, 440, 453, 455; attitude toward the body, 37, 119, 215-16, 295, 298; birthday of, 27, 221; and the birth of Nahman of Bratzlav, 213, 216-20, 221-24; and Barukh of Liozhna, 26-29; on the cultivation of

Rebbes, 25, 42, 45; early life and travels of, 23-24, 232; on the evil eye, 29-30; and the Frankists, 246-49; as "fertilized ovum" of Hasidut, 18; and hidden *tzaddikim*, 23-28, 240; instructions to Shneur Zalman's parents, 27-30; intensity of prayer of, 162; journey to *Eretz Yisra'el*, 251, 264, 350-51, 436; main doctrines and teachings of, 25, 26-27, 32, 37, 62-63, 119, 216, 298; and Nahman of Horodenka, 213-21, 431; on prayer, 155, 162, 230, 370, 429; and Shneur Zalman's birth and destiny, 27-34, 56, 59, 66, 71-72, 73, 141, 400; and teacher Ahiyah ha-Shiloni, 24, 346-48; on the third day after circumcision, 28-29.

Baha' ad-Din Naqshbandi, 437.

Bair, Puran and Susanna, 157, 422.

Barukh (Portugaler) the Batlan, 26, 68.

Barukh ben Shneur Zalman (Weiskvaliker) of Liozhna, 26-32, 67, 121, 398.

Barukh ben Yehiel (of Tulchin) of Mezhbizh (1753-1811), 123, 127-30, 169, 225-27, 228-29, 230, 232, 255, 271, 280, 353, 362, 385, 415-16, 433, 441.

beinoni, 74-85, 123, 409.

Ben-Shmuel, Levi, 297.

Bergman, Ozer, 294.

binah, 18, 40, 52, 81, 85, 86, 87, 88, 89, 90, 148, 188, 189, 191, 192, 197, 423, 454, 455, 457.

Binyomin of Kletsk (Kletsker): 58, 153, 177, 421; and Shlomo of Karlin, 58, 153, 421; on work, 177.

B'nai Or tallit, 186-87.

Bonaparte, Napoleon (1769-1821), 103, 138-40, 207, 276, 394, 395, 412, 415, 419, 438.

Boteach, Shmuley, 16.

Brahman: 184, 426.

b'riyah, 409.

Buber, Martin (1878-1965): 245-46, 266-67, 306, 325, 370, 402, 419, 447; on faith ("holy insecurity"), 306; on the I-Thou relationship, 306; on the "leprosy of habit", 370.

C

Carlebach, Shlomo (1925-1994), 16, 401.

Candrasekharendra Sarasvati, 406, 418, 419.

Chogyam Trungpa, 200.

Cooper, David, 20.

Cordovero, Moshe ben Ya'akov (1522-1570), 366.

D

da'at, 18-19, 52, 81, 85, 86, 87, 88, 90, 98-99, 100, 102, 192, 193, 199, 410, 411, 427, 454, 455.

Dalai Lama, 320.
David of Karlin, 403.
David ha-Melekh, 214, 218, 220, 231.
David ben Mendel of Premyshlan, 432.
David Tzvi Orbach (d.1808), 360, 363, 447, 448.
Dembowski, (Bishop) Nicholas, 244.
descent for the sake of ascent: 12, 255-59, 260, 261, 269, 284, 288.
Devorah Leah bat Shneur Zalman (aunt of the Alter Rebbe): 30, 67-69, 407; and desire to study; 67-69; husband Yosef Yitzhak of Vitebsk, 31, 32, 69; and taking Shneur Zalman to the Ba'al Shem Tov, 30.

Devorah Leah bat Shneur Zalman (daughter of the Alter Rebbe): 66-73; great sacrifice of, 66-73; husband Shalom Shakhna, 73; mother of Menachem Mendel, third Lubavitcher Rebbe, 73; as *Rebbetzin*, 71, 72, 73.

Dov Baer ben Shneur Zalman of Lubavitch (Mittler Rebbe, 1773-1827): 33, 84, 92, 95, 143-73, 175-208, 280, 393, 395, 396, 402, 407, 413, 421, 423, 424, 425, 427; and Akiva Eiger, 207; anger over treatment of Ahron HaLevi at the Alter Rebbe's grave, 173; on *bar da'at*, 427; on *binah*, 188, 189, 191, 192, 197; birth predicted by the Maggid of Mezritch, 144-45; care for his Hasidim, 175, 425; criticizes a Hasid's *davenen*, 154-55; on *da'at*, 192-93; and the dispute between the Alter Rebbe and Shlomo of Karlin over *mitnagdim*, 150-54; education of, 145, 420; endorsement by Alter Rebbe to lead HaBaD Hasidism, 167-69; on finding his own sins; friendship with Ahron HaLevi of Staroshelye, 150-53, 159-60, 171, 172, 173, 208, 422-23; on *girsa*, 188-89; health of, 180, 207, 425; on *hitbonenut*, 92, 95, 188-94; on *hitpa'alut*, 196-206; on *hokhmah*, 191-92; on the idols of commerce, 145-47; on importance of friendship amongst Hasidim, 160; imprisonment and release of, 207; on *iyyun*, 188-89, 190, 192; and *Lag b'Omer*, 425; last words of, 208; and Levi Yitzhak of Berditchev, 117, 161-62, 179; on looking at the soul's root in *yehidut*, 180-81; marriage to Sheina, 154; prayer of, 154-55, 160-64, 423; public teaching of, 158, 178-79, 425; responsibilities in Shneur Zalman's court, 157-60, 422; similarities to Avraham the Malakh, 150, 156, 157, 161; smoking a pipe during *hitbonenut*, 429; subjects of written works, 175.

E
Elazar of Disna, 124-25.
Eliezer Rokeah of Amsterdam, 215.
Elimelekh ben Eliezer Lippa of Lizhensk (the Rebbe Reb Melekh, 1717-1786): 52, 84, 205, 409, 438; on prayer in *nogah*, 205; on *tzaddikim*, 84.

Elior, Rachel, 208, 451.
Elisha ben Abuya (Aher, "the other one"): 126, 318-19, 445; in Milton Steinberg's novel, 445; in Moshe Shamir's story, 319; in the *Pardes*, 318-19, 445; Rabbi Meir on, 126, 319.
Eliyahu (Ba'al Shem) of Zamostch, 25, 68-69, 454.
Eliyahu ben Shlomo Zalman (Ga'on of Vilna, 1720-1797): 33-34, 42, 44, 49, 50, 54, 132, 187, 188, 226, 403, 404, 405, 417, 427.
emunah, 98-99.
epikoros, 301, 303, 307-08, 323.
Epicurus, 308.

F
Fleer, Gedaliah, 16.
Fourth turning of Hasidism, 20.
Frank, Jacob (1726-1791), 247-48, 435-36.
Freida bat Shneur Zalman (daughter of the Alter Rebbe), 407.

G
Gendler, Everett, 410.
gevurah, 18, 40, 85, 86, 87, 90, 272, 346, 432, 455.
Goethe, Johann Wolfgang, 415.
Gomez, Little Joe, 116.
Green, Arthur, 237, 269, 273, 277, 278, 373, 407, 410, 431, 433, 435, 436, 439, 440, 441, 444, 449.
Greenglass, Menachem Ze'ev (ca. 1917-2011), 280.
Grimes, John Allen, 184, 417.
Gurary, Noson, 20, 188, 416, 427.
Gurdjieff, G.I., 259, 438.

H
HaGaT, 18, 87.
hal (ahwal), 81-82, 408.
halakhah, 11, 30-31, 36, 37, 46, 48, 58, 103, 109, 118, 214, 215, 282-83, 376, 403, 455.
Hannah, Barbara, 258.
Hanukkah, 319.
Hayyim Avraham ben Shneur Zalman (son of the Alter Rebbe), 47-48, 207, 393, 395, 396.
Hayyim of Chernovitz, 445.
Hayyim (Halberstam) of Tzanz (1797-1876), 403.

Hayyim ibn Attar (1696-1743), 215.
Hayyim of Krasnoye, 227, 229, 433.
Hayyim Rafael ben Ahron HaLevi (Horowitz) of Staroshelye (son of Ahron HaLevi),
Hayyim Rappaport, 248.
Hayyim Shmuel of Kreslava, 400, 402.
Hayyim Vital (1542-1620), 364-67, 416.
Hayyim of Volozhin (1749-1821), 188, 416, 427.
Hazan, Avraham, 451.
Hielman, Hayyim Meir, 208, 407, 420, 422.
Hein, Avraham, 411.
Hein, David Tzvi (RaDaTz), 411.
Heine, Heinrich, 11.
Heschel, Abraham Joshua (1907-1972): 65, 193, 401, 402, 404, 410, 431-32, 440, 457; on "religious behaviorism", 65; on "situational thinking", 193.
Heschel, Avraham Yehoshua of Kopitchinitz (1888-1967), 446.
hesed, 18, 40, 85, 86, 87, 90, 272, 346, 432, 455.
Hesse, Herman, 418.
Hillel: representing *hesed.*
Hillel ben Meir HaLevi of Paritch (1795-1864), 83, 84, 207, 416.
hitbodedut, 231-32, 235, 239-40, 278, 289-94, 369, 370, 372, 387, 388, 443, 445, 448, 449, 455.
hitbonenut, 85-97, 102, 130, 149, 156, 175, 176, 188-96, 196-206, 410, 411, 421, 427, 428-29, 455.
hitpa'alut, 90-96, 175, 196-206, 428-29.
hod, 40, 85, 86, 87, 319, 456.
hokhmah, 18, 40, 52, 81, 85, 86, 87, 88, 90, 121, 148, 191, 192, 410, 423, 455, 456, 457.

I
Ibn 'Arabi, Muhyiddin, 400.
Ignatian Method, 93.
Immanuel Hai Riki, 427.
Inayat-Khan, Vilayat, 422.
Inayat-Khan, Zia, 157, 422.

J
Jacobs, Louis, 182, 196, 208, 419, 422, 426, 427.
Jacobson, Yisra'el (1895-1975), 16, 195, 401, 417.
Jalaluddin Rumi, 400.
Jung, C.G., 72, 100-01, 198, 256-59, 380, 437.

K

Kagan, Michael, 297, 443.
KaHaB, 18-19.
Kamenitz, 244-49, 251, 328, 435.
Kaplan, Aryeh (1934-1983), 17, 20, 133, 244, 294, 417, 431, 432.
Karma, 77, 251-52.
Keating, Thomas, 108, 428.
kelippah (kelippot), 77, 284, 285, 286, 307, 408, 456, 458.
Kenig, Gedaliah Ahron (1921-1980), 16, 18-19, 399.
keter, 18-19, 191.
Khan, Hazrat Inayat: 225, 251-52, 253-54, 347-48; on the education of infants, 225; on *karma*, 251-52; and the soul, 347-48; on testing disciples, 253-54.
Kramer, Chaim, 16, 20, 294, 298, 389, 448.

L

Leibowitz, Yeshayahu (1903-1994), 65.
Levi Yitzhak ben Meir of Berditchev (1740-1809): 11, 18, 39, 43, 49, 50-51, 110, 112-13, 115, 117-18, 123-25, 161-62, 179, 280, 352-53, 357, 362, 363, 401, 403, 404, 408, 414, 433, 441, 448; and Avraham of Kalisk, 43, 123-25; Barukh of Mezhbizh on, 433; and Dov Baer of Lubavitch, 161-62, 179; family attacked by *mitnagdim*, 50-51; and HaGaT, 18; "heart cell" of Hasidism, 18; and Nahman of Bratzlav, 280, 352-53, 357, 441, 448; and Nosson of Nemirov, 362, 363, 401, 448; prayer of, 39, 117-18, 401; and Shneur Zalman of Liadi, 39, 49, 110, 112-13, 117-18, 161-62, 179, 403, 408, 414; spiritual guidance of, 112-13, 404.
Levitin, Shmuel (1882-1974), 177, 409, 416, 422, 425, 429.
Lieberman, Hendel (1900-1976), 87, 410.
Loewenthal, Naftali, 208, 414, 423, 424.

M

madhyamika, 323.
Maggid of Mezritch (Dov Baer ben Avraham, 1704-1772): 15, 18, 29, 31, 33-37, 39-53, 55, 56, 57, 59, 61, 62, 63, 66, 67, 71, 73, 103, 110, 117, 123, 124, 126, 143, 144-45, 150, 152, 161, 162, 165, 167, 169, 171, 183, 221, 238, 239, 240, 241, 242, 244, 262, 361, 400, 401, 402, 403, 404, 405, 407, 409, 411, 412-13, 415, 416, 420, 429, 430, 431, 433, 439; and angels, 34-36, 400; Dov Baer of Lubavitch, 144-45; investiture of, 167; on the last three days of life, 144-45; and new *Shulhan Arukh*, 46-48; passing of, 51-52, 144-45; and Pinhas of Koretz, 40-41, 401, 402; and prayer, 161, 162; on pride, 126; remembered by the Wolper, 403; and Shnuer Zalman of Liadi, 29, 31, 33-37, 39-53, 55, 56, 57,

59, 71, 73, 103, 110, 123-24, 400, 402, 403, 404, 405, 409, 412-13, 429; "stem cell" of *Hasidut* 18; as the *tzaddik ha-dor* 39-40; and *tzimtzum,* 416; *yahrzeit* of, 51, 55, 110, 413.

Mahadevan, T.M.P., 184.

malkhut, 85, 86, 87, 109, 116, 148, 417, 453, 457.

Mandana Mishra (Sureshvara), 64-65.

maqam (maqamat), 81-82, 408.

Matisyahu (singer), 16, 444.

maya, 134-35, 140, 335, 418, 426.

Meir Margoliot (1700-1790), 248.

Menachem Mendel ben Moshe of Vitebsk (of Horodok, 1730-1788): 43, 46, 49, 50, 51, 52-56, 67, 103-04, 109, 122, 124, 271, 402, 403, 404, 439, 440; and Avraham of Kalisk, 43, 50, 55-56, 103-04, 124, 122, 271; childhood of, 53; and *Eretz Yisra'el,* 56, 103-04, 109, 271; and the Ga'on of Vilna, 49, 54; and the Maggid of Mezritch, 50, 51, 52-53, 55, 124, 402, 403; and Shneur Zalman of Liadi, 43, 46, 50, 51, 52-56, 103-04, 122, 124, 403.

Menachem Mendel of Rymonov (1745-1815), 138.

Menachem Mendel ben Shalom Shakhna Schneersohn of Lubavitch I (Tzemah Tzedek, 1789-1866): 32, 73, 114-15, 118-19, 122, 141, 144, 149, 163, 173, 206, 207, 403, 422, 425, 426.

Merton, Thomas, 108.

Meshullam Feibush (Heller) of Zbarazh (d. ca.1795), 262.

Mikhael David ben Ahron HaLevi (Horowitz) of Vitebsk (son of Ahron HaLevi of Staroshelye), 208.

m'malleh kol almin, 89, 100, 101, 185, 194, 309, 416, 457.

Mordecai ben Barukh (brother of Shneur Zalman of Liadi), 57, 111, 405.

Mordecai ben Nahum of Chernobyl, 169, 386, 403.

Mordecai of Lekhovitch, 164.

Mordecai of Neshkhiz (1752-1800), 279, 365, 441.

Morgenstern, Yitzhak Meir, 17.

Moses (Moshe *rabbeinu*), 62, 63, 185, 187, 199, 312-13, 364, 375, 376, 377, 402, 406, 411, 444, 445, 447.

Moshe ben Barukh (brother of Shneur Zalman of Liadi), 57, 111, 405.

Moshe ben Maimon (RaMBaM; Maimonides, ca.1135-1204), 19, 61, 131, 136, 158, 267, 398, 403, 427, 434, 439.

Moshe ben Nahman (RaMBaN; Nahmanides, 1194-1270), 158.

Moshe ben Shneur Zalman (Shneuri, son of the Alter Rebbe, b. 1780): 150-54, 172, 393-96, 421; and Shlomo of Karlin's curse, 150-54, 394, 421; debates with Christians, 394, 395-96; language abilities of, 393-94; brilliance of, 393; and succession, 172, 395.

Moshe de Leon (ca. 1250-1305), 440.
Moshe Galanti, 439.
Moshe Hayyim Efraim ben Yehiel of Sudlikov (1746-1790), 216, 229-30.
Moshe Isserles (1520-1572), 47, 218, 403, 431.
Moshe Khinkes, 128.
Moshe Meisels, 58, 70-72, 73, 138, 393.
Moshe Vilenker, 58, 70-72, 73, 111, 172.
Mu'in ad-Din Chishti of Ajmer, 167, 422.

N

Naftali ben Isaac Katz of Posen (d.1719), 263, 264, 439.
Naftali Hertz ben Yehudah (Weinberg) of Nemirov (of Uman, 1780-1860): 363-65, 367-68, 374, 381, 389.
Nahman ben Simhah of Bratzlav (1772-1810): 11-13, 15-20, 72, 102, 123, 127-28, 140, 213-42, 243-78, 279-323, 325-57, 359-90, 399, 414, 415, 431, 433, 434, 435-36, 439, 440-41, 443, 444, 446, 448, 449, 450; and Aryeh Leib, the Shpola Zeide, 227, 280, 353, 441; on astrology, 320; and Avraham of Kalisk, 270-72; on "axial moments", 371; and the Ba'al Shem Tov, 213, 216-20, 221-24, 230, 232, 234, 235, 238-40, 244, 245-46, 248, 249, 251, 260, 263, 264, 270, 271, 276, 280, 346, 348, 349, 350, 355-56, 365, 385, 415; and Barukh of Mezhbizh, 127-28, 225-26, 227, 228, 229, 230, 232, 255, 280, 353, 385, 441; on the body, 294-98; *brit* of, 225; at cave of Hillel, 272; at cave of Shimon bar Yohai, 272; childhood struggles of, 236-42, 434; and depression, 265, 269, 280, 288, 330, 354, 378; and "descent for the sake of ascent", 255-59, 260, 261, 269, 284, 288; on despair, 282, 287-88, 380-81; dreams of, 344-53; as an "epochal" Rebbe, 386; and grandfather, Nahman of Horodenka, 221-24, 440, 443; and grandson, Yisra'el, 289; at grave of Shammai, 272; on *halakhah*, 282-83; on Hasidim as *tzaddikim*, 244, 385-86; on heresy, 305-06; as a *hiddush*, 213, 415; on *hitbodedut*, 231-32, 235, 239-40, 278, 289-94, 369, 370, 372, 387, 388, 443, 445, 448, 449, 455; and hostile Hasidim in Istanbul, 252-55, 259-61; journey to Kamenitz of, 244-49, 436; and KaHaB, 18; on *kavanah*, 370; on *kelippot*, 284-85; and Levi Yitzhak of Berditchev, 280, 352-53, 357, 441, 448; on *m'malleh kol almin*, 309; and mother Feiga, 221-27, 245; and Naftali of Nemirov, 363-65, 367-68, 374, 381, 389; Nahum of Chernobyl on, 433; and Nosson of Nemirov, 359-90, 441, 448, 450; on not insisting, 269, 371, 440; and obstacles, 226, 251, 255-59, 284, 288; pilgrimage to *Eretz Yira'el* of, 249-78; on the *Psalms*, 231; on the "outer sciences", 301-02, 305, 309; relocation to Bratzlav of, 363; and Shimon of Krementchug, 233-35, 236, 242, 243, 245-46, 249-277, 325, 356, 368, 386, 434, 436; and Shneur Zalman of Liadi, 127-28, 237, 279-80, 436, 441; on the *siddur*, 369-70; and *sovev kol almin*, 309; on *teshuvah*, 282, 285,

371; and the Turk (Ishmaelite), 265-68; on the *tzaddik*, 383-86; on *tzimtzum*, 299-301; on "unholy desire", 286-87; on the Void, 298-323; wedding day of, 232-34; work with the souls of the dead, 355.

Nahman of Horodenka (1680-1766): 213-21, 222-23, 228, 240, 260, 270, 272, 276, 349, 364, 430, 431, 432, 433, 441, 443; and Eliezer Rokeah of Amsterdam, 215; and *Eretz Yisra'el*, 214-15, 217, 220-21, 430; lineage of, 214, 218-19; marriage of, 216-18; Nahman of Bratzlav on, 221; Pinhas of Koretz on, 221; prayer of, 216, 443; scholarship of, 214-16; son, Shimson Hayyim, 214-15, 270; son, Simhah, 218-20, 433.

Nahman ben Tzvi Aryeh (Goldstein) of Tcherin (d. 1894), 377, 450.

Nahman (Hazan) of Tulchin (1813-1884), 368-69.

Nahum ben Tzvi Hirsch of Chernobyl (1730-1798), 12-13, 67, 169, 403, 433.

Naqshbandi Sufis, 437.

Narada, 134-35.

Natan Neta Shapira of Krakow (1585-1633), 219, 434.

nefesh, 67, 77, 78, 83, 88, 89, 93, 111, 155, 169, 198, 334, 347, 387, 408, 422, 457, 458.

Nehemia of Dubrovna, 402.

neshamah, 83, 155, 334, 347, 387, 453, 457.

netzah, 40, 85, 86, 457.

nitzotzot, 302, 307, 458.

Noah of Lekhovitch, 164, 208.

Nosson ben Naftali (Sternhartz) of Nemirov (of Bratzlav, 1780-1844): 102, 230, 235, 244, 245, 249, 250, 258, 269, 272, 276-77, 280, 281-82, 284, 290-91, 298, 299, 312, 313, 325, 328, 342, 345, 352, 353, 354, 356, 359-90, 401, 436, 439, 441, 447, 448, 449, 450, 451; on being new everyday, 377; childhood of, 359-62, 448; creates "fire on paper", 281-82, 298; and creation of Bratzlav ideal, 359, 385, 386, 388; on creation of *Likkutei MaHaRaN* and other works, 374-75, 383; declared a *tzaddik* by Nahman of Bratzlav, 389; de-emphasis of miracles, 276-77; and dream of the ladder, 362-63; on expanding and explaining teachings, 374, 450; and futility, 362, 389, 447; first meeting with Rebbe Nahman, 363-64; and *hitbodedut*, 290-91, 369-72, 387-88; on hope amidst trials, 380; on the importance of *ru'ah ha-kodesh*, 383-85; on importance of the *tzaddik,* 383-85, 451; letter to Bratzlaver novices, 387-88; and Levi Yitzhak of Berditchev, 362, 363, 401, 448; literary style of, 244, 299, 372-73; marriage to Esther Sheindel, 360; on Moses as a human being, 313; and Naftali of Nemirov, 363-65, 367-68, 374, 381, 389; Nahman of Tcherin on, 377, 450; Nahman of Tulchin on, 368-69; persecution of, 388; pilgrimage to Uman, 382-83; on prayer, 290-91, 369-72, 387-88, 401; previous incarnations of, 364-67; recognition of Nahman of Bratzlav as his Rebbe, 365; on the *Sitra Ahra*, 388; on the "good-point", 378;

on "soiled garments", 378; spontaneous prayer of, 371; as successor to Rebbe Nahman, 377, 450; on *teshuvah*, 371, 379; on *tikkun*, 387-88; and Torah *novellae,* 375-76; as a *tzaddik* and Rebbe, 386-390, 450, 451; as "Yehoshua", 364, 375; on the *yetzer ha-ra*, 379-80.

O
Odesser, Yisra'el Baer (1888-1994), 16.
Oglala Sioux, 224.
olam ha-tikkun, 19.
olam ha-tohu, 19.

P
Paul I, Czar of Russia (1754-1801), 115-16, 414.
Peterburger, Avraham, 449.
Pinhas ben Avraham Abba Shapira of Koretz (1726-1791), 41, 195, 220-21, 225, 228-29, 243, 244, 262, 401-02, 432, 433, 448.
Pinhas Reizes: 45, 58, 70-72, 150-54, 167-69, 178, 405, 424; on Dov Baer of Lubavitch, 167-69, 178, 421, 424; witnesses to the incident with Shlomo of Karlin, 150-54, 421; witness to Devorah Leah's resolve, 70-72; witness to Shneur Zalman's teaching in Shklov, 45.
Pinhas ben Tzvi Hirsh Horowitz of Frankfurt (1730-1805), 46, 48, 412.
Purva-Mimamsa, 64-65.

Q
Qutb ad-Din Bakhtiyar Kaki of Delhi, 157, 167, 422.
qutub, 40, 401.

R
Rabbah bar Nahmani (ca. 270-330), 75-76, 83.
Rabban Gamliel (1st-century C.E.), 219.
Rabbi Akiva ben Yosef (ca. 50-ca.135), 273, 277, 286, 309, 312, 318, 444, 445.
Rabbi Meir (Ba'al ha-Neis; 2nd-century C.E.), 109, 126, 319, 413.
Rabbi Shimon ben Azzai (2nd-century C.E.), 286, 318, 445.
Rabbi Shimon ben Zoma (2nd-century C.E.), 318, 445.
Rafael of Bershad (d. ca. 1825), 432.
Rand, Shuli, 16.
Rashi (Shlomo Yitzhaki, 1040-1105), 61, 62, 63, 92, 107, 219.
Rodkinson, Mikhael Levi (1845-1904), 166.
Rosenfeld, Zvi Aryeh (1922-1978), 16, 19.
Rowling, J.K., 433.

S

Sabbatean movement, 437.

Salesian Method, 93.

Schneersohn, Nahum ben Dov Baer (of Niezhin), 108-09, 413.

Schneersohn, Shalom Dov Baer ben Shmuel of Lubavitch (1860-1920), 185, 410, 417, 429.

Schneersohn, Shmuel ben Menachem Mendel of Lubavitch (1834-1882), 379, 413.

Schneersohn, Yosef Yitzhak ben Shalom Dov Baer of Lubavitch (1880-1950), 15-16, 58, 59-60, 84-85, 157-58, 193, 371, 397, 398, 399, 405, 406, 409, 421, 423, 426.

Schneerson, Menachem Mendel ben Levi Yitzhak of Lubavitch II (1902-1994), 16, 19, 79, 182.

Scholem, Gershom (1897-1982), 320.

Sefer Shel Beinonim, 74-85, 436.

Shabbatai Tzvi (1626-1676), 25.

shadow, 198, 255-59, 261, 437, 438.

Shahab ad-Din Suhrawardi, 429.

shahada, 186, 306.

Shainberg, Catherine, 191.

Shalom Shakna ben Avraham of Prohobitch (1771-1803), 255, 362, 431.

Shamir, Moshe (1921-2004), 319.

Shammai, 272.

Shankara (Adi Shankaracharya), 63-65, 417, 418.

Shaul Baumann, 417.

Sheldrake, Rupert, 72.

Shimon bar Yohai, 35, 272-73, 364-65, 440.

Shimon ben Baer of Krementchug: 233-35, 236, 242, 243, 245-46, 249-277, 325, 356, 368, 386, 434, 436; first meeting with Nahman of Bratzlav, 233-35; humility of, 249-50; and journey to *Eretz Yisra'el*, 249-277; on Nosson of Nemirov as the *tzaddik* of the generation, 386.

Shimshon Hayyim (cousin of Nahman of Bratzlav), 214-15, 270.

Shlomo ben Meir of Karlin (1738-1792), 35, 58, 66, 72, 95, 103, 123, 150-54, 394, 412, 421.

Shlomo Rafaels, 145-47.

Shmuel ("Shmelke") ben Tzvi Hirsh Horowitz of Nikolsburg (1726-1778), 39, 48, 402.

Shmuel Munkes, 58, 60, 105-06, 117-18, 145-47, 150.

Shmuel Yitzhak of Dashev, 294-95, 368, 369, 383.

Shneour, Zalman (1887-1959), 414.

Shneur Zalman ben Barukh of Liadi (Barukhovitch, Liozhna Maggid, the Alter Rebbe, 1745-1812): 15, 18, 20, 23-56, 57-102, 103-141, 143-73, 183, 237, 253, 271, 279-80, 283, 365, 393, 395, 396, 398, 399, 400, 401, 403, 404, 405, 406, 408, 409, 411, 412, 413, 414, 415, 416, 417, 419, 420, 421, 422, 423, 427, 436, 441, 455; arrest and imprisonment, 103-10, 114-16, 412, 413, 414; and Avraham of Kalisk, 49-50, 55, 103, 104, 122-26, 271, 414-15; and Avraham the Malakh, 36-38, 52, 400; and Ba'al Shem Tov, 27-34, 56, 59, 66, 71-72, 73, 141, 400, 407; and Barukh of Mezhbizh, 127-30; and the *beinoni*, 74-85, 408, 409; birth of, 27-29, 399; "brain cell" of *Hasidut*, 18; on broken-heartedness in prayer, 119-22; called "our Ga'on", 46-47, 49; counseling of, 110-14, 140, 344, 408; and Czar Alexander of Russia, 116, 138, 395, 396; and Czar Paul I of Russia, 115-16, 414; and daughter Freida, 407; and daughter Devorah Leah, 66-73; debates with *mitnagdim*, 49-50, 61-65, 83, 147-48, 405, 406; early life of, 237, 398; final letter of, 140; final *yehidut* with Ahron HaLevi of Staroshelye, 166; finding a master, 33-36; fundraising for the Hasidim in the Holy Land, 103-10, 114-16, 253, 279; fundraising for Jews forced into cities, 127-28; and the Ga'on of Vilna, 33-34, 44, 49, 50, 54, 132, 404, 417; and his *hadarim*, 57-60, 74, 150, 405; on *hitbonenut*, 85-97, 421, 427, 429; on joy in prayer, 119-22; last words of, 141; and Levi Yitzhak of Berditchev, 39, 49, 110, 112-13, 117-18, 161-62, 179, 401, 403, 408, 414; and the Maggid of Mezritch, 29, 31, 33-37, 39-53, 55, 56, 57, 59, 71, 73, 103, 110, 123-24, 400, 402, 403, 404, 405, 409, 412-13, 416, 429; marriage to Shterna, 32, 34, 113; and Menachem Mendel of Vitebsk, 43, 46, 50, 51, 52-56, 103-04, 122, 124, 403; mission to Shklov, 44-45; and Nahman of Bratzlav, 127-28, 237, 279-80, 436, 441; and Napoleon Bonaparte, 395, 415; and new *Shulhan Arukh*, 46-48; and *nigleh* and *nistar*, 28, 36, 141, 400; parable of the King's majesty, 200; and *pashute Yidden*, 405, 406; and Pinhas of Koretz, 41, 401; prayer of, 117-19, 162-63; *Sefer Shel Beinonim* of, 74-85, 436; and *Sefer Shel Tzaddikim*, 83-84, 129, 130, 409; and Shlomo of Karlin, 35, 58, 66, 72, 95, 103, 123, 150-54, 394, 412, 421; and Shmuel Munkes, 58, 60, 105-06, 117-18, 150; and son Hayyim Avraham, 393, 395, 396; and son Moshe, 15-54, 393-96, 421; studies with Yosef Yitzhak of Vitebsk, 31-32, 67; and superintendant of the Peter and Paul Fortress, 107-09; teaching style of, 20, 118; ten kinds of suffering for Hasidim, 103; on toiling for the Torah, 32; on Torah and *mitzvot*, 65, 81, 83, 136-37, 148-49, 419; on the *tzaddik*, 74-85, 283; on *tzimtzum*, 130-37, 141, 417, 427; visited by "the Wolper", 403; and the wedding in Zhlobin, 117-19, 179, 414; and *yehidut*, 110-14, 140, 180, 344, 408.

Shulhan Arukh, 46-48, 65, 83, 103, 118, 129, 130, 224, 377, 395, 402, 403.

Simhah ben Nahman, 218-20, 433.

sovev kol almin, 89, 131, 185, 309, 459.

Sufism, 12, 40, 81-82, 156-57, 167, 195, 225, 251-52, 253-54, 262, 265-68, 293, 306, 347, 379-80, 400, 408, 424, 428, 429, 439, 450, 455.

Steinberg, Milton (1903-1950), 445.
Steinsaltz, Adin, 17, 446.
Sternhartz, Avraham (1862-1955), 16.
Stoppard, Tom, 417.
Sutton, Abraham, 298.

T
Theophan the Recluse (1815-1894), 290.
Thurman, Howard (1899-1981), 292-94.
tiferet, 18, 85, 86, 87, 459.
tikkun, 19-20, 32, 180, 181, 248, 354, 355, 356, 357, 368, 382, 384, 387, 388, 459.
Tillich, Paul, 100.
tohu, 19, 32.
Tolkien, J.R.R., 444-45.
tzaddik ha-dor, 39-40, 401, 459.
tzaddikim nistarim, 23-29, 232, 397, 407, 459.
tzimtzum, 130-38, 141, 182-88, 300-01, 416-17, 426-27, 460.
Tzvi Aryeh (Landau) of Alik (1759-1811): 39-40, 279, 401, 415-16, 441; and Barukh of Mezhbizh, 415-16; as *tzaddik ha-dor*, 39-40, 401.
Tzvi Hirsch ben Avraham Segel of Harki (Gorki) (1760-1828), 270, 440.
Tzvi Hirsh of Rymanov, 431.
Tzvi Hirsh of Tchashnik, 176-77, 420, 425.

V
Vedas, 64-65.
von Franz, Marie-Louise, 258.

W
Whitman, Walt, 235-36.
Wolper, the, 403.

Y
Ya'akov Yitzhak (Horowitz, Hozeh) of Lublin, 52, 205, 313.
Ya'akov Yosef haKohen ben Tzvi Katz (Maggid) of Polonoye (Ba'al ha-Toldot, d. 1782), 115, 216, 221, 227-29, 404.
Yagid, Meshullam Zalman, 222.
Yagid, Moshe, 219.
Yehiel Mikhele ben Yitzhak of Zlotchov (ca. 1731-1786), 50, 214, 365, 401, 430, 448.

Yehudah Leib ben Barukh of Yanovitch (brother of the Alter Rebbe), 34-35, 55, 57, 405, 423, 424.
Yehudah Lieb Segal of Vitebsk, 32.
Yehudah Loew of Prague (ca. 1520-1609), 26, 219, 398.
Yekusiel of Lieple, 58, 82.
Yekusiel (Maggid) of Tirhovitza, 244, 281, 368.
Yeshaya Horowitz (SheLoH ha-Kodesh, ca. 1570-1626), 33, 147, 399.
Yesha'ayahu (Yeshaya) of Yanov (of Dynavitz), 440.
yesod, 85, 86, 87, 460.
yetzirah, 18, 409, 453, 454, 460.
Yisra'el Meir Kagan (the Hofetz Hayyim, 1838-1933), 48, 403.
Yisra'el ben Shabbetai Hofstein (Maggid) of Kozhnitz (1733-1815), 52, 138, 432.
Yisra'el ben Shalom Shakhna of Rhyzhin (1797-1851), 415, 431.
Yissakhar Dov Kabilniker of Lubavitch, 31, 55.
Yissakhar Dov Baer (d. ca. 1795), 243.
Yitzhak ben Yosef of Drohobitch (1700-1768), 216-17, 430, 431.
Yitzhak Eisik ben Mordecai HaLevi (Epstein) of Homil (ca. 1780-1857), 58, 69, 71, 84, 207, 426.
Yitzhak al-Fasi (RIF, 1013-1103), 403.
Yitzhak HaLevi Horowitz (Reb Itche *der Masmid*, ca. 1885-1941), 84-85, 409.
Yitzhak ben Shlomo Luria (Ari ha-Kodesh, 1534-1572), 33, 131, 301, 348, 364-65, 366-67.
Yitzhak Meir ben Yisra'el (Alter) of Ger (Hiddushei ha-RIM, 1789-1866), 370, 378.
Yitzhak of Tirhovitza, 281, 368-69.
Yohanan ha-Sandlar (200-300), 219.
Yonatan Eibeshutz (ca. 1680-1764), 38, 188, 427.
Yosef ibn Aknin (ca. 1150-ca-1220), 439.
Yosef ibn Gikatilla (1238-ca.1305), 195.
Yosef ben Efraim Karo (1488-1575), 47, 402, 403.
Yosef "Kol-Bo" of Shklov, 44-45, 145-47, 405.
Yosef Yitzhak of Vitebsk, 31-33, 67, 69.
Yudel of Dashev, 244, 368, 435.

Z
Zalman Henyes, 150, 152.
Zeitlin, Hillel (1871-1942), 17, 435.
Zelmele of Slutzk, 61, 406.
Ze'ev Wolf ben Naftali Tzvi of Charni-Ostrog (d. 1823), 260-63, 266, 268, 439.
Ze'ev Wolf of Zhitomir (d. 1798), 66, 150, 153-54, 421.
Zushya ben Eliezer Lippa of Anipol (d. 1800), 43, 46, 49, 262, 361-62, 403.

misled P1
stripped P2

973-610-4766
David Malcho